CW00456081

# GENERAL & MRS. EARLE WHEELER

Their Rise to Chairman of the Joint Chiefs of
Staff Amid America's Descent into Vietnam

## COLONEL MARK A. VINEY
### U.S. ARMY, RETIRED

Copyright © 2022 by Mark A. Viney

All rights reserved. No part of this publication may be reproduced, distributed, or transmitted in any form or by any means, including photocopying, recording, or other electronic or mechanical methods, without the prior written permission of the publisher, except in the case of brief quotations embodied in critical reviews and certain other non-commercial uses permitted by copyright law. For permission requests, write to the author, addressed "Attention: Permissions" at mviney503@gmail. com.

Viney Development Solutions, LLC
101 Wando Reach Rd.
Charleston, SC 29492

Ordering Information:
For details, contact mviney503@gmail. com

Print ISBN: 978-1-66780-902-1
eBook ISBN: 978-1-66780-903-8

Printed in the United States of America on SFI Certified paper.

First Edition

# CONTENTS

Foreward by Brigadier General (Retired) John S. Brown ...............................1

Introduction .................................................................................................3

1. Formative Years (January 1908 – June 1941) ......................................8

    Early Life ................................................................................................8

    Initial Military Service ........................................................................11

    West Point ............................................................................................13

    Betty .....................................................................................................19

    Fort Benning ........................................................................................21

    War Clouds Form ................................................................................23

    China ....................................................................................................25

    West Point ............................................................................................27

2. World War II (June 1941 - September 1945) ......................................29

    Stateside ...............................................................................................29

    1942 .....................................................................................................32

    Joint Chiefs Of Staff ...........................................................................33

    Florida-Mississippi-Florida-Mississippi ..........................................34

    Mobilization ........................................................................................35

    Road Trips ...........................................................................................36

    1943 .....................................................................................................37

    Training Divisions ...............................................................................40

    War Hits Home ...................................................................................40

    Replacements .......................................................................................42

    1944 .....................................................................................................42

    France ...................................................................................................42

    1945 .....................................................................................................43

    Alsace ...................................................................................................45

    Central Germany .................................................................................58

    Change Of Mission .............................................................................60

    Victory In Europe! ..............................................................................63

    Post-Hostilities ....................................................................................65

3. Post-War Years (October 1945 – November 1952) ...........................95

    Demobilization ....................................................................................95

Fort Sill ..................................................................................95

1946 .....................................................................................95

Paris .....................................................................................96

1947 .....................................................................................98

National Security Act .......................................................98

U.s. Constabulary .............................................................99

Bamberg-Heidelberg-Stuttgart .......................................102

Iron Curtain .......................................................................107

1948 .....................................................................................108

Threat Of War ...................................................................108

1949 .....................................................................................113

National War College ........................................................114

NATO ..................................................................................115

1949 Amendment To The National Security Act ............116

Indochina ............................................................................117

1950 .....................................................................................119

War In Korea ......................................................................120

First Joint Staff Tour ..........................................................121

Fairfax .................................................................................121

Indochina ............................................................................122

1951 .....................................................................................123

Trieste ..................................................................................124

It Must Be Done .................................................................130

1952 .....................................................................................136

Manpower Crisis ................................................................141

Indochina ............................................................................142

Pomp And Circumstance ..................................................143

**4. Herr General (November 1952 – September 1958)** ................153

Indochina ............................................................................153

Naples ..................................................................................155

1953 .....................................................................................156

Korea ...................................................................................157

Indochina ............................................................................159

Eisenhower's Nsc ...............................................................160

Naples ..................................................................................161

Defense Reorganization ....................................................166

The New Look .................................................................167

Berchtesgaden .............................................................169

1954 ...............................................................................170

Naples ...........................................................................170

Indochina......................................................................171

NATO.............................................................................174

Naples............................................................................174

Ravello...........................................................................181

Drudgery........................................................................184

Fall ................................................................................185

1955 ...............................................................................187

Massive Retaliation........................................................187

Bim ...............................................................................189

Second Dc Tour .............................................................191

1956 ...............................................................................193

Vietnam ........................................................................193

1957 ...............................................................................194

Cold War........................................................................194

Little Rock......................................................................195

1958 ...............................................................................198

Bim Graduates...............................................................198

Brushfires.......................................................................199

Defense Budgets.............................................................200

Defense Reorganization .................................................201

Army Reorganization.....................................................204

Army Rearmament.........................................................205

Army Manpower............................................................206

**5. Rising Star (September 1958 - September 1962)** ...................**208**

Fort Hood ......................................................................208

1959 ...............................................................................212

Southeast Asia................................................................212

Mexico...........................................................................213

1960 ...............................................................................215

Bim ...............................................................................215

Third DC Tour ...............................................................216

1961 ...............................................................................217

New Frontiersmen ..............................................................217

Cold War ..........................................................................220

Bay of Pigs .......................................................................221

Laos ................................................................................222

Taylor ..............................................................................223

Quantitative Analysis .......................................................227

Whiz Kids ........................................................................230

Sidelined ..........................................................................231

Flexible Response .............................................................233

Army Build-Up .................................................................234

Vietnam ...........................................................................235

DOD Consolidation ..........................................................237

Quarters 16-A ...................................................................238

1962 ................................................................................240

Fourth European Tour .......................................................240

Paris ................................................................................241

Margie .............................................................................244

Vietnam ...........................................................................245

Army Reorganization ........................................................247

ROAD ..............................................................................248

Civil Rights ......................................................................249

You Don't Say No to the President .....................................249

**6. Chief of Staff of the Army (October 1962 – November 1963)** ...............253

Mississippi .......................................................................253

Quarters 1 ........................................................................255

Taylor ..............................................................................257

Southeast Asia ..................................................................258

Cuban Missile Crisis ..........................................................259

Front Office ......................................................................264

Thanksgiving ....................................................................266

Army-Navy Game .............................................................267

Army Reserves ..................................................................267

1963 ................................................................................268

Vietnam is the Place ..........................................................268

Air Mobility .....................................................................276

Early Spring ......................................................................277

Puerto Rico ........................................................................279

Back to Work .....................................................................282

Alabama ............................................................................283

Washington ........................................................................284

Summer ..............................................................................288

Finland ..............................................................................294

Cold War ...........................................................................297

Turning Point ....................................................................298

Kennedy's Assassination ....................................................300

**7. New Administration (November 1963 – July 1964) ...............306**

Disharmony in the Tank .....................................................307

New Old Team ...................................................................309

Johnson .............................................................................310

Taylor ................................................................................313

1964 ..................................................................................313

Official Functions ..............................................................313

Frustrated and Misled ........................................................315

Quarters 1 .........................................................................316

Army Matters .....................................................................319

Tuesday Luncheons ............................................................320

Far East .............................................................................321

Germany ............................................................................323

Entertaining .......................................................................323

Fort Monroe ......................................................................325

Aides .................................................................................327

England ..............................................................................327

New Country Team .............................................................330

Wheeler's Selection ............................................................331

Wheeler's Replacement .......................................................339

Taylor's Legacy ..................................................................341

Farewell .............................................................................342

**8. Chairman of the Joint Chiefs of Staff (July 1964 – December 1966) ......344**

Swearing-In .......................................................................344

Straight to Work ................................................................347

Room 2E878 ......................................................................349

Quarters 6 .......................................................................................351
Harkins Retires ..............................................................................352
Tiger by the Jowls .........................................................................354
Math Tutor......................................................................................354
1965 .................................................................................................355
McConnell .......................................................................................356
Honolulu..........................................................................................360
After Hours ....................................................................................361
Europe.............................................................................................364
Off Duty..........................................................................................365
Ailes Departs .................................................................................365
Saigon Trip.....................................................................................366
Washington.....................................................................................366
November .......................................................................................369
Far East Trip ..................................................................................372
1966 .................................................................................................374
Social Functions............................................................................374
Honolulu..........................................................................................376
Armchair Generals ........................................................................376
Weekends........................................................................................377
Reappointment...............................................................................379
Man of Martinsburg.......................................................................381
NATO ..............................................................................................382
Eye Surgery....................................................................................383
Ugly Duckling Manor .....................................................................384
Town and Country .........................................................................386
Frequent Flyer ...............................................................................387
Worldwide Commitments...............................................................389
Christmas........................................................................................391

**9. Pinnacle (January 1967 – July 1970)** .......................................**393**

1967 .................................................................................................393
Martinsburg.....................................................................................393
Growing Unpopularity....................................................................394
Quarters 6 ......................................................................................395
Guam & Home.................................................................................396
NATO Departs France ...................................................................398

London .................................................................................400

Westmoreland Returns to Washington.............................401

Other Matters .......................................................................402

Social Functions ..................................................................405

Saigon Trip...........................................................................407

Moorer ...................................................................................407

Heart Attack .........................................................................408

Antiwar Sentiment ..............................................................413

Reorganizing the Reserves.................................................413

Westmoreland Returns to DC.............................................414

1968 .......................................................................................417

Turmoil at Home .................................................................419

Good for the Soul ................................................................421

MACV Changes Command .................................................422

Storms in Washington.........................................................423

Military Leader Transitions................................................423

NATO ....................................................................................424

Force Restructuring ............................................................426

Transition..............................................................................427

1969 .......................................................................................428

Resignation ..........................................................................429

Laird, Nixon, and the Chiefs .............................................431

All-Volunteer Force.............................................................432

Eisenhower Passes ..............................................................433

SACEUR ................................................................................434

SALT.......................................................................................436

1970 .......................................................................................437

At Long Last .........................................................................437

USS Billfish ...........................................................................438

Turkey ...................................................................................441

Last Month in Uniform.......................................................442

Paris .......................................................................................442

May It Be Said, "Well Done" ..............................................443

**10. The Least Pompous Great Man (July 1970 – December 1975) ..............450**

1970 .......................................................................................450

Taking Stock.........................................................................450

Appalling State ...................................................................452

Modern Volunteer Army ...................................................452

USS Billfish .....................................................................453

1971 ...............................................................................454

Groton ............................................................................454

Martinsburg.....................................................................454

FBI Investigation.............................................................456

1972 ...............................................................................459

Declining Health..............................................................459

1973 ...............................................................................460

Cambodia Bombing Hearings ...........................................461

1974 ...............................................................................463

1975 ...............................................................................463

Wheeler Passes ................................................................463

Funeral ...........................................................................465

Public Accolades..............................................................468

Personal Condolences.......................................................470

Epilogue ..........................................................................474

Conclusion.......................................................................476

**Appendix** ...........................................................................**478**

**Chapter Notes** ...................................................................**480**

**Bibliography** .....................................................................**547**

**Index** ................................................................................**573**

# FOREWARD

To understand history, we should understand the men who made it. For far too long General Earle G. "Bus" Wheeler has lacked an actual and accessible biography. This is despite the critical role he played as Chief of Staff of the Army and then Chairman of the Joint Chiefs of Staff from 1962 through 1970, the years most central to our Vietnam experience. Over time, a diminished understanding of Wheeler has contributed to a diminished understanding of much else. Now Colonel Mark A. Viney has remedied the deficiency with this remarkable portrait. Drawing on untapped sources, largely from within the Wheeler family, as well as on sources previously exploited, he has drawn into focus the man, his career, the Army in which he served, and his role in the history of his time.

Mark Viney's companion book, *Determined to Persist: General Earle Wheeler, the Joint Chiefs of Staff, and the Military's Foiled Pursuit of Victory in Vietnam*, addresses Wheeler's and the Joint Chiefs of Staff's role in the contentious formulation of Vietnam policy during the Johnson and Nixon Administrations. Far from passive, Wheeler and the Joint Chiefs pressed for their approach to winning the war with energy and conviction. Rebuffed within the Johnson Administration, they considered resigning *en masse* and "going public". Imbued with a sense of duty and deference to civil authority, they did not. They thought the nation would be better served if they stayed. As it was, most believed the United States "won the war and then pissed it away ..." even with its flawed policies.

*General & Mrs. Earle Wheeler* presents the back story of Wheeler's time at the peak of his profession. Here we also find his formative World War II experiences, his climb through positions of increasing rank and responsibility, and his maturation as a leader and staff officer. Wheeler plays a significant but little-known role at Little Rock, accumulates a healthy mix of assignments, and bears witness to some of the most important institutional debates of the late 1950s and early 1960s. Viney's discussion of Wheeler's career tells us a lot about the Army of his times as well as about his experiences in it. This in itself is useful history.

The previously untapped sources Viney draws upon include troves of personal letters provided by the family, perhaps most notably those of Wheeler's wife Betty. These, reinforced by reminisces from Wheeler's son Dr. Gilmore S. Wheeler, amount to a social history of our Army from the 1930s through the 1970s. Even the greatest soldiers have families, loved ones, and lives out of uniform. Social activities matter in any institution and can either consolidate or corrupt it.

Colonel Mark A. Viney is uniquely qualified to write this book. He is a fourth-generation officer imbued with a sense of the Army's history, and himself the veteran of five overseas deployments. He has served as Director of the U.S. Army Heritage and Education Center, one of our most significant historical and archival facilities. Thus, Viney possesses a unique appreciation of the issues at hand. I recommend that the reader sit back, relax, and find out who General Earle G. Wheeler was and why he matters.

- Brigadier General (Retired) John S. Brown, United States Army

# INTRODUCTION

Since the position of Chairman of the Joint Chiefs of Staff was established in 1949, only 20 general and flag officers have attained this pinnacle of the U.S. military profession. Each of their stories is remarkable, yet the story of perhaps the most distinguished member of this small, elite fraternity has never been told—until now.

General Earle Gilmore "Bus" Wheeler, U.S. Army, became the senior military advisor to President Lyndon B. Johnson in 1964 and continued in this role under President Richard M. Nixon. As the longest serving Chairman, Wheeler shaped civilian-military relations during an extraordinary, six-year period marked by America's growing involvement in the Vietnam War, its zenith, and the beginning of U.S. disengagement.

In my companion volume to this book, *Determined to Persist: General Earle Wheeler, the Joint Chiefs of Staff, and the Military's Foiled Pursuit of Victory in Vietnam*, I correct longstanding misperceptions about Wheeler and his fellow Chiefs in the contentious formulation of Vietnam policy.

For over two decades, the authoritative work on the machinations of Johnson's Vietnam policy was H. R. McMaster's national bestseller, *Dereliction of Duty: Johnson, McNamara, the Joint Chiefs of Staff, and the Lies That Led to Vietnam*.

As former Chief of Staff of the Army, General (Retired) George W. Casey, Jr., observed, "Some of (McMaster's book) doesn't ring true. There has to have been more to the story." [1] Indeed, there was. *Determined to Persist* conclusively disproves McMaster's mischaracterization of Wheeler and the Chiefs as derelict, passive accomplices to civilian mismanagement of the Vietnam War.

*Determined to Persist* takes readers inside the White House, the Pentagon, and the U.S. military headquarters in Hawaii and South Vietnam. Based on contemporaneous correspondence, recently declassified top-secret documents, interviews with participants, and their memoirs, the book traces the internal debates, tensions, and critical inflection points in the Vietnam War during the Kennedy, Johnson, and Nixon Administrations.

In disgust with the unfolding Vietnam debacle that he endeavored forcefully but unsuccessfully to prevent, Wheeler shredded his memoirs upon which he had labored in retirement for two years. He died three years later. Thus, *Determined to Persist* is a story the protagonist never wanted written.

With the backing of the Wheeler family, *Determined to Persist* restores voice to a key foreign policy advisor to three U.S. Presidents who had remained an enigma for over 45 years. In so doing, it casts civilian-military relations during the Vietnam era in a whole new light.

In researching *Determined to Persist*, I realized the back story of Wheeler's tenure as Chairman and his exceptional, 32-year ascendancy were equally compelling stories worth being told. Hence, the genesis of *General & Mrs. Earle Wheeler*.

As a fourth generation U.S. Army officer, I grew up listening to my forefathers' war stories from World War II, Korea, Vietnam, the Dominican Republic, and Grenada. I also listened to my grandmothers' stories of what military family life was like during the 1920s to 1970s. As an Army brat, I experienced challenges and sacrifices like those endured by earlier Army families.

Much of what I read in the Wheeler family collection of personal correspondence resonated deeply with me. I'm sure the excerpts of these letters presented herein will resonate with other service members and their families, as well. Some of the passages are quoted at length, and many contain grammatical errors. Intent upon readers discovering Bus Wheeler and his wife Betty in their own words, I have resisted the temptation to overly paraphrase, summarize, or edit them.

When Wheeler became Chairman of the Joint Chiefs of Staff, he was already haggard. He had served nearly eight of the past fourteen years in the Pentagon in demanding, key positions on the Army and Joint Staffs, including most recently a two-year tour as Chief of Staff of the Army. He had always put in long hours on the job, even on weekends and holidays. He had found practically no time for relaxation or exercise. His six foot two, broad shouldered figure was slightly stooped and somewhat overweight. A 56-year old, long-time smoker, Wheeler suffered from associated medical conditions that warranted his retirement instead of his elevation to Chairman. His evening hours were often spent hosting or attending official social functions with his beautiful and devoted wife of 34 years, the former Frances "Betty" Rogers Howell. Wheeler would ultimately serve a grueling six-year term as Chairman. Quite literally, he worked himself to death.

In tracing the progression of Wheeler's career, I highlight the formative experiences in his professional development. Significantly, Wheeler was often on the frontline of conflict, first against Imperial Japan, then against Nazi Germany, and then against the Soviet Union, but also on the domestic frontlines of the desegregation and civil rights movements and, of course, the civilian-military disharmony of the Vietnam era.

Wheeler's service in World War II merits considerable treatment for two reasons. First, because critics of his appointments to serve as Chief of Staff of the Army and Chairman of the Joint Chiefs of Staff decried his lack of combat experience relative to those combat-decorated officers who held those positions before him. An infantry officer, Wheeler served during the war in several division-level staff officer capacities. While he did not earn any valor awards for gallantly leading infantry assaults, Wheeler did master operational-level administration and logistics, two skills directly underpinning his rise through the general officer ranks. "Having served as a division Chief of Staff," General Casey says, "I can tell you that job does indeed prepare you to be a general officer." [2] Secondly, Wheeler's numerous wartime letters are the only known extant examples of his substantive, candid, most personal thoughts. Thus, they provide insights into his character, demeanor, and personal philosophies available nowhere else.

In appearance, Bus Wheeler was tall, dark, and handsome. He wore his hair short and slicked back in the usual style of his generation. His dress green or khaki uniform was simply adorned with a pair of U.S. collar insignia, seven ribbons, the Army Staff Identification Badge, and four silver stars on each epaulet. He wore dark-framed glasses and spoke in a deep, assertive, yet approachable voice.[3] Betty Wheeler was petite, tanned, immaculately coifed and attired, and always *tres chic*. The Wheelers were a very attractive couple.

Bus Wheeler's character is illuminated by the new primary source materials underpinning this book. Among his many fine attributes, he was eminently decent, hard-working, self-sacrificing, diplomatic, articulate, suave, no-nonsense yet personable, congenial, gregarious, and humorous. He was a devoted family man, a patriotic American, and an exceptional officer. It is no wonder that he rose to the pinnacle of the military profession.

Betty Wheeler enjoyed the adventurous aspects of the military lifestyle and the many opportunities for volunteer work—on her own her terms. She enjoyed the dinner parties and receptions, but not the obligatory coffees and luncheons with other officers' wives with whom she felt very little in common. A daughter of considerable wealth, Betty was a *grande dame* in a poor man's Army. Her hard work, social skills, and hospitality played an essential and substantial role in the success of her husband's military career. Nurtured by mutual respect, support, and love, Bus and Betty Wheeler made a great team.[4]

Against a backdrop of America's increasing role in containing Communism in Indochina, this book presents a social history of U.S. Army officer families during the Interwar, World War II, and Cold War periods. Officers' typically long work hours severely limited the time they spent with their children. Frequent moves between duty stations commonly meant that children attended multiple schools during a single school year. Officers' wives were obligated to support a packed, invasive calendar of social and volunteer obligations. Meager pay, substandard housing, and long separations were the norm, but so too were opportunities for Army families to experience camaraderie, build lifelong friendships, to travel and experience other cultures.

The views contained herein are my own and do not represent the policies or positions of the U.S. Army or the U.S. Government. As this book was written while I was still serving on active duty as a U.S. Army officer, it required clearance from the Defense Office of Pre-publication and Security Review. For that, I am grateful to Mr. Paul J. Jacobsmeyer.

I am particularly grateful for the encouragement and material support provided by Dr. Gilmore S. "Bim" Wheeler, the Wheeler's only child, and his gracious wife Judy.

I also wish to thank the following individuals for their reviews and constructive inputs on the draft of this book: General (Retired) George W. Casey, Jr.; Brigadier General (Retired) John S. Brown; Dr. Nick Phelan; and Dr. William T. Allison.

This book is dedicated to my recently deceased grandfather, Colonel (Retired) George C. Viney, and to his devoted wife of more than 75 years, my grandmother, Margaret "Peg" Viney. I am very proud of their service to our country.

More so, this book also dedicated to the Lord, from whom all my blessings have flowed.

- Colonel (Retired) Mark A. Viney, United States Army

# CHAPTER 1

## Formative Years
## (January 1908 – June 1941)

### *Early Life*

Earl Gilmore Stone was born in Washington, DC on 13 January 1908. As a young child growing up near Dupont Circle, Earl was called "Buster" or "Bus" by his family. Friends and colleagues throughout his adult life would also call him Bus.[1]

*Earl G. "Bus" Stone circa 1912, about age 4, Washington, DC.*
*(Wheeler Family Records).*

His father, Dock Samuel Stone, was originally from Columbia, South Carolina. His mother, Ida "Mums" or "Mumsie" Gilmore, was the daughter of Amos I. *Gillmore* from Richland County, South Carolina. Bus was raised a Baptist in an unhappy home.

*Bus circa 1918, about age 10, Washington, DC. (Wheeler Family Records).*

Despite his mother's faith, "Mums" was an alcoholic, a self-centered, and often spiteful woman, who out of sheer mean-spiritedness forbade her two children from seeing their father after she left him. Stone had contracted tuberculosis and died in 1922 before their divorce was finalized. Bus loved his mother, but was greatly disappointed in her, often referring to her in his adulthood as "that stupid little woman." [2]

Bus's personality and manner of speaking may have been influenced by his mother's alcoholism. Some teens who live with alcoholic parents become afraid to speak out or show any normal anger or emotion because they worry it may trigger a parent's drinking. Bus would grow into a man of few words who always kept his emotions in check. Yet, he was no shrinking violet, either. [3]

After leaving her dying husband, Bus's mother soon began dating an Army Major. Bus liked him and hoped he would marry his mother. He was then an impressionable fourteen-year-old and was likely influenced by this officer to become a soldier two years later. The Major's relationship with Bus's mother did not last long, however.

Seemingly out of the blue, Mums married a local dentist from Virginia, Clifton F. Wheeler. Their union came as a complete surprise to Bus and his younger sister, Helen Friedrich "Dottie" Stone, who went to school one morning as Stones and came home to discover they were now Wheelers. On 14

September 1923, they were adopted by their stepfather, himself an alcoholic and only eight years older than Bus. Eventually, they established a cordial relationship. Bus steadfastly refused to call him *father* as Mums wished but called him by his name instead.

Mums eventually gave him and Dottie a stepsister, Betty Jean Wheeler. Bus's maternal uncle, Athol "Nunky" Gilmore, lived nearby and was a surrogate father during Bus's turbulent early teen years.[4]

As a young man, Bus developed lifelong passions for fishing and reading. He was also active in the Boy Scouts. At around age twelve, Bus began smoking cigarettes, a practice not uncommon at that time. He and his best friend, George Deuhring, often took the streetcar to the end of the line and camped in Anacostia, which was then a forest.[5]

Growing up in bustling Washington, DC, Bus loved to escape each summer to his maternal aunt and uncle's farm near rural Jenkinsville, North Carolina. Some of his fondest memories were of hunting and fishing there with his cousins. His aunt Sallie "Siddie" Douglass, wife of Charles B. "CB" Douglass, had always thought very highly of Bus's dad, Dock Stone. She was appalled that her sister had left him and could not believe that Ida would not let her children see their dying father. Secretly, she invited her sick, estranged brother-in-law to their farm so that he could visit with Bus and Dottie. After CB and Siddie moved to Washington, their daughter Inez "Sis" Douglass dated and eventually married Deuhring.[6]

*Bus Wheeler circa 1924, about age 16 while attending Eastern High School, Washington, DC. (Wheeler Family Records).*

Attending Eastern High School, Bus was a decent, but somewhat indifferent student. His yearbook noted, "So keen was he for the military life that he participated for three years" in his school's prestigious cadet corps with Deuhring. Bus also belonged to the Phi Alpha Epsilon fraternity. He loved baseball and was a good pitcher until a career-ending line drive struck his throwing shoulder. Bus starred in the leading role of a school play that was favorably reviewed in a Washington newspaper. A dapper dresser and ladies' man, he was lauded in his yearbook for his skill at "flirting with more than one girl at a time." He graduated on 21 June 1925. [7]

Bus did not hold any jobs while in high school, but afterwards performed clerical work for the Southern Railroad Company from September 1925 to June 1926. [8]

## *Initial Military Service*

*Best friends Private George Deuhring (left) and Sergeant Earl Wheeler, Washington, DC National Guard, circa 1927. (Wheeler Family Records).*

On 4 August 1924, sixteen year-old Bus enlisted in the Washington, DC National Guard, as cadets at his school commonly did. He joined Deuhring, who was a year older, in E Company, 121st Engineers. Bus would later boast that he "got a Private's stripe before I got a high school diploma." During his four-year enlistment, Wheeler would compete on the company marksmanship team, attain the rank of Sergeant, and ultimately serve as a Platoon Sergeant.

Wheeler's enlistment, which ended on 2 July 1928, instilled in him an enduring empathy for common Soldiers, as well as a commonsensical approach toward discipline.[9]

*Sergeant Earl Wheeler, E Company, 121st Engineers, Washington, DC National Guard, circa 1927. (Wheeler Family Records).*

In September 1927, Wheeler followed Deuhring to Colonel Millard's Preparatory School, which was at that time the only school of its kind modeled on the United States Military Academy's system of instruction by sections and the Cadet Honor Code.[10]

As a youth, Bus contracted "the usual childhood illnesses," including measles, mumps, chickenpox, and whooping cough. He had grown up tall and lanky. Having recently lost considerable weight during a nasty bout with the flu, Bus feared he was too skinny to meet West Point's physical requirements. He gorged himself on peanuts and bananas in order to gain weight as rapidly possible. He passed the requisite physical exam, but many years would pass before he ate peanuts again. He never did eat another banana, and the smell alone made him nauseous. (Years later, whenever his son teased him by sticking a banana under his nose, Bus would give him "a sharply-worded rebuke.") [11]

## *West Point*

*Bus Wheeler, Dupont Circle, Washington, DC, 20 February 1928, five days before he accepted an appointment to West Point. (Wheeler Family Records).*

On 25 February 1928, Wheeler accepted an appointment to the United States Military Academy. Soon after, he informed Colonel Millard that he would have to drop out of prep school for the remaining few months because he was out of money and could no longer afford the tuition. Millard told him flatly, "Bus, you are going to West Point. Pay me when you have the money." [12]

*George D Deuhring (left), Ida "Mums" Wheeler, and Earl Wheeler, Washington, DC, circa 1928. (Wheeler Family Records).*

Wheeler entered the academy that summer and was assigned to M Company as a member of the Class of 1932. Deuhring was already there in K Company with the Class of 1930. Wheeler would excel as a cadet, particularly in the academic and military aspects of cadet life.[13]

In the early fall of Wheeler's Plebe (freshman) year, Deuhring reported, "Bus ... is doing very well – in fact, he is doing very, very well. If he keeps it up he will probably wear stars [on his collar denoting academic merit]." [14]

By mid-October, Bus "was moved out of his house [room], so he could live with a couple of men who are 'D' [deficient] and help them get out of the hole. ... He [is] pretty peeved about it." Deuhring added, "That is the first time I ever heard of anything like that being done." [15]

*Ida "Mums" Wheeler (left), Betty Jean Wheeler, Cadet Earl "Bus" Wheeler, Helen Friedrich "Dottie" Wheeler, West Point, New York, circa 1929. (Wheeler Family Records).*

Wheeler was highly proficient in math and the sciences. He was an excellent writer, too, but awful in Spanish. Throughout his four years at the academy, he devoted considerable time to tutoring deficient cadets. [16]

Wheeler's prior enlisted service served him well in the military realm of cadet development. Over summer training between his Cow (junior) and Firstie (senior) years, he was rated above average as a Squad Leader during Cavalry Camp at Lake Popolopen. Despite nursing a two-inch laceration on his lower right leg from having been kicked by a horse during a cavalry hike on 10 July 1931, Wheeler still earned an above-average rating for "firing two good problems" during the Conduct of Fire exercise that day.[17]

Bus hated horses. As a city boy, he had not had much exposure to them growing up. He also hated being reprimanded. Once, during an indoor equitation class in Thayer Hall, he was assigned a particularly ornery horse who refused to stand still and repeatedly disrupted the instructor's presentation. When the officer shouted, "Mr. Wheeler, get control of that goddamn horse!", Bus seethed.[18]

Having already served four years as an enlisted man, Wheeler took a relatively compassionate, more "relaxed" approach to discipline and the hazing of Plebes than did most other upperclassmen. [19]

He himself conformed well to the demanding requirements of the cadet disciplinary system. Wheeler received 64 demerits during his Plebe year and another 49 during his Yearling (sophomore) year. As a Cow, he received just 31 demerits and only 30 more during his Firstie year. His infractions were typical, innocuous, and ranged from having spots on his dress coat at supper, to fingerprints on his visor, a dirty wash basin, an improperly cleaned trash bin, an improperly folded hand towel, and gloves that were not neatly folded during inspection. He occasionally received demerits for being late to formation or class. His most egregious violation was appearing once in an incomplete uniform on "the stoops" (front porch) of his barracks.

Wheeler was a decent cadet athlete. A member of the academy's lacrosse team during his Yearling year, he also participated in compulsory boxing, swimming, dancing, and equitation. He played intramural baseball, basketball, football, as well as tennis, polo, and golf. He particularly enjoyed and showed great skill at rifle and pistol marksmanship. [20]

*In his second summer as a West Point cadet, Wheeler stood almost 75 inches tall, weighed 146 pounds, and had a mere 28-inch waistline. (Wheeler Family Records).*

An annual physical exam during his second summer at the academy rated the tall, gangly cadet in excellent health. Wheeler stood 6 feet, 2 3/4 inches tall, weighed 146 pounds, and had a mere 28-inch waistline. He would only gain eight more pounds by graduation.[21]

Wheeler's maturity and exceptional performance as a Plebe were rewarded by his selection as an Acting Company Commander when the upper three classes departed for Christmas break. Subsequently, he would attain the usual promotions in cadet rank: to Acting Corporal at the end of his Plebe year; to Corporal the following summer; and, as a new Firstie, to Lieutenant on 11 June 1931.[22]

All cadets, regardless of faith, were required to attend compulsory weekly church services. Bus was a believer but kept his faith private. As a cadet, he self-identified as a Baptist. (He would later regard himself as a general Protestant, probably in consequence of attending the general Protestant services typically offered in Army chapels.) [23]

*Wheeler's West Point yearbook portrait, circa 1932. (Wheeler Family Records).*

In what limited spare time he had as a cadet, Wheeler contributed to his class's historical narrative and to *The Howitzer* yearbook. According to the edition from his Firstie year, Bus's idea of heaven was "lying in the grass near Trophy Point with a good mystery novel and a tin of Lucky Strikes". He would always be a voracious reader, mysteries and American Civil War history among his favorite subjects. After lights out, Bus also enjoyed "galloping dominoes", cadet slang for throwing dice.[24]

*Cadets Earl Wheeler (far right), Jim Woolnough (far left), Jim Churchill, and an unidentified cadet, West Point, circa 1932. (Wheeler Family Records).*

For three years, Bus kept the same two "wives" (roommates), Jim Woolnough and Jim Churchill. (The trio would remain close throughout their long Army careers. In 1967, Woolnough would figure into Wheeler's plan for achieving military victory in Vietnam and would retire as a four-star general. Churchill would retire as a Colonel and pass away on the Wheelers' farm in Martinsburg, West Virginia.) [25]

In the 1930s, West Point cadets were considered quite the catch for daughters of American society. For a time, Bus dated a Dupont heiress. At a society party in the fall of 1930, he earned a reputation as a "snake" for charming Frances "Betty" Rogers Howell away from her cadet date. Pretty, petite, and precocious, Betty was a sixteen-year old "vamp" with large, pale blue eyes and wavy light brown hair, the daughter of a wealthy manufacturing executive.[26]

*Sixteen-year old "vamp" Betty Howell, Old Greenwich, Connecticut, circa 1930. (Wheeler Family Records)*

Betty and Bus dated for a while, broke up, and reunited during his Firstie year when she accepted his invitation to attend a costume hop in Cullum Hall. Her mother, Rebecca "Becca" Howell, a very proper Christian Scientist, selected her costume—a Turkish belly dancer. Betty's top covered her to the neck, but her pants were diaphanous pantaloons with toreador pants underneath.

The following day, Bus's Tactical Officer cautioned him. "Mr. Wheeler, you have to understand that who you pick to consort with, let alone marry, will influence how you will advance in the Army. Based on the woman I saw you with last night, you need to be very careful." [27] (As it turned out, Betty would lovingly support Bus throughout his 38-year career and substantially contribute to his rise to the pinnacle of the military profession. With unmatched style, grace, and devotion, she would be his co-partner in military service.)

On 10 June 1932, Wheeler graduated from the academy ranked number 62 among 262 graduates in his class. Henceforth, he would finish at the top of his class in every professional military school he attended, from the Infantry School's Basic Course through the National War College.[28]

## *Betty*

On the same Friday as Bus's graduation and commissioning as an Infantry Second Lieutenant, he and Betty were married at her family's home in Old Greenwich, Connecticut. Woolnough and Churchill were his best men. [29]

*Frances "Betty" Rogers Howell during her tomboy and riding stage circa 1925, about age 10, Old Greenwich, Connecticut. (Wheeler Family Records).*

Betty was a child of privilege born on Flatbush Avenue in Brooklyn, where her family lived until her tenth year. The Howells then moved into a grand home on Sound Beach Avenue in Old Greenwich. Her father, Walter

Robinson Howell, was an executive of the Bradford Corporation, a British textile company with mills in Massachusetts. Also head of the National Dyeing Association, Howell was considerably wealthy, but not "rich." Served by maids and a Polish cook, the Howell family lived comfortably throughout the Great Depression. Walter had given Betty a brand new, yellow 1929 Ford Roadster for her sixteenth birthday. She graduated from high school at the Southern Seminary, a "young ladies' finishing school" in Buena Vista, Virginia. In 1942, the Howells would move into an even grander waterfront home in Old Greenwich. [30]

*Wheeler's tactical officer cautioned him to be "very careful" about Betty, lest his career suffer, Old Greenwich, Connecticut, circa 1930. (Wheeler Family Records).*

The Howells often vacationed on Nantucket and knew everyone of consequence on the island. Betty's father rented the "Heart's Ease" cottage for the newlyweds to enjoy a two-month honeymoon before Bus reported to the Infantry School at Fort Benning, Georgia.

That summer, Bus taught Betty to cook, something she had never had any reason to learn. She began dying her hair platinum, which made her a dead ringer for Marlene Dietrich. She also loved to tan and would always maintain her color whenever possible. (This exposure would eventually lead to skin cancer in her later years.) [31]

The attractive couple would forge an enduring partnership based on mutual love, support, and respect. "She was absolutely the love of my father's life and his partner – equal," recalls Gilmore "Bim" Wheeler, the couple's only son.[32]

Preferring the company of men and often finding women's groups tedious and boring, Betty considered herself "a man's lady."

Betty would always go to great lengths to make a proper "family home" in whatever quarters the family inhabited, for no matter how short a time. [33]

Betty was a professionally skilled seamstress. Not only did she sew all her own clothing, but made drapes and slip covers for the furniture. With her father in the textile industry, she always obtained cloth at no cost. (Until Bus's promotion to Brigadier General, her sewing skills would come in handy since his meager Army salary was always stretched very thin. Even as "First Lady of the United States Armed Forces," Betty sewed all her clothing, including formal gowns. She would continue sewing until late in life when arthritis caught up with her.) [34]

Throughout Bus's career, Betty ran their household. Like Bus, she was no shrinking violet. She would always maintain good relations with the "help," whom they employed from the beginning. (Even after he earned his fourth star, she would continue to involve herself in every aspect of official functions, which they frequently hosted. This included planning and testing all menus.) [35]

## *Fort Benning*

During Wheeler's formative years at Fort Benning, he distinguished himself academically, militarily, and socially as a bright young officer whose star was clearly on the rise. Wheeler graduated from the Infantry School at the top of his class on 18 August 1932. He remained at Fort Benning, where he and Woolnough would serve in the same battalion of the 29th Infantry Regiment until 31 August 1936. [36]

*Second Lieutenant Earl Wheeler, 29th Infantry Regiment, Fort Benning, Georgia, circa 1933. (Wheeler Family Records).*

Woolnough's father was the Assistant Chief of Staff of the Infantry School. During the Commandant's extended illness, Colonel Woolnough ran the post, and as such, exerted considerable influence over his son's career. "Bus always felt Jim had preference, which he did!" Betty recalled.[37]

Jim's parents had attended the Wheelers' wedding, and at his mother's insistence, the young couple stayed in the Woolnough's large quarters until quarters became available for them.[38]

As a wedding gift, Betty's father had given the couple $10,000 - an enormous sum in those days. One of Bus's first checks went to Colonel Millard to repay his prep school tuition. This substantial reserve would sustain the couple through his lean company grade officer years. It would also enable the Wheelers to entertain his superiors, a break from Army tradition.

Their house parties would engender lasting personal relationships and pay handsome rewards for Bus's career progression, although the young couple never intended it that way. "Bus was no bootlicker," said Betty. "And it made him mad as hell when he heard that some of the other officers had him called that." Betty explained that they hosted his superiors simply because she had been raised "that if someone gave you an invitation, you were obliged to reciprocate." Bus thought the idea made perfect sense. "Maybe I was the bootlicker," Betty laughed.[39]

Three years after his commissioning, Wheeler was examined by a promotion board of five officers from various Fort Benning units. On 9 August 1935, he was promoted to First Lieutenant. [40]

His first name was spelled "Earl" on his birth certificate. Growing up, he preferred to spell it "Earle," which is how it appeared in his high school yearbook. He used both spellings at West Point. To prevent further confusion, on 1 May 1936, the Army approved his request to officially change his first name from "Earl" to "Earle" in the Official Army Register.[41]

During the 1930s, U.S. Army officers were frequently detailed to other organizations, such as the Civilian Conservation Corps or the Reserve Officers Training Corps. On 7 June 1935, Wheeler was detailed on detached duty to the Georgia Military College in Milledgeville, Georgia for a one-year tour as an instructor. During this assignment, the Wheelers befriended local artist Frank Herring and his wife, Frances. Interestingly, Frank, a white man, was acclaimed for the authenticity of his paintings of "colored people." (Twenty-eight years later, the Wheelers would return to Milledgeville where Bus, as Chief of Staff of the Army, would deliver the college's commencement address.) [42]

## *War Clouds Form*

Meanwhile, U.S. national security policy since 1921 had accepted the premise that future wars with other major powers, except possibly Japan, could be avoided. National decision-makers had pursued that goal by maintaining a minimum of defensive military strength, avoiding entangling commitments with Old World nations, and by using U.S. good offices to promote international peace and the limitations of armaments. [43]

War clouds had begun forming in 1931, when the Japanese seized Manchuria and defied the diplomatic efforts of the League of Nations and the U.S. to end the occupation. Japan left the League in 1933 and a year later announced that it would not be bound by the postwar system of arms control treaties that had begun with the Washington Naval Conference after the last of its obligations under that system expired in 1936.

In Europe, Hitler had come to power in Germany in 1933, denounced the Treaty of Versailles, embarked on rearmament, and occupied the demilitarized

Rhineland by 1936. Italy's Benito Mussolini launched his own war of aggression by attacking Ethiopia in 1935. Spain's 1936 revolution produced a third dictatorship and an extended civil war that would become a proving ground for weapons and tactics later used in World War II.[44]

In response to these developments, the U.S. Congress would pass a series of neutrality acts between 1935 and 1937, hoping to avoid entanglement in another European conflict. The U.S. tried to strengthen its international position in other ways by opening diplomatic relations with the Soviet Union in 1933, by promising eventual independence to the Philippines in 1934, by liquidating its protectorates in the Caribbean area, and by generally pursuing a good neighbor policy toward Latin America.

No quick changes in U.S. military policy would follow, but beginning in 1935, the U.S. Armed Forces began receiving larger appropriations to allow them to improve their readiness for action. Changes in the Army over the next three years would reflect the increasingly critical international situation and the careful planning of the War Department during General Douglas MacArthur's tour as Chief of Staff of the Army in 1930-1935. His recommendations led to a reorganization of combat forces and a modest increase in their size, accompanied by more realistic planning for using U.S. manpower and industrial might for war should it become necessary.

The German annexation of Austria in March 1938 and the Czech crisis that September would awaken the U.S. and the other democratic nations to the imminence of another great world conflict, which began with Japan's 1937 invasion of China. [45]

Meanwhile at Fort Benning, Bus passed his off-duty time reading and writing fictional short stories. One of them, "Pachy Dermo," was published in the popular *Blue Book* magazine and concerned a man who consumed a secret potion and gained the strength of an elephant. In an obvious theft of his creative property a few years later, a film starring the famous actor Joe E. Brown appeared with the same story but a different title. Amused, Bus never pursued the matter of royalties.[46]

On 1 September 1936, Wheeler reported to the Infantry School's ten-month Regular Course. As a student, he sustained a concussion in a truck accident, suffered double vision, and felt "woozy" for about ten days. He graduated at the top of his class on 13 July 1937.[47]

## China

Wheeler's academic prowess led to his follow-on assignment to one of the U.S. Army's premier overseas outfits, the 15th Infantry Regiment, stationed in Tientsin, China. The outstanding reputation he would further burnish for himself there and the professional connections he would make in this elite regiment would directly influence the trajectory of his career during World War II.

Only the best officers received the plum assignments to China and the Philippines, which were on the frontline of rising tensions with the expansionist Japanese Empire. Wheeler determined to perform his duties to the utmost of his abilities. Arriving in Tientsin on 21 November 1937, he eventually commanded "I" Company in the regiment's 3rd Battalion. [48]

*First Lieutenant Wheeler, his name now spelled "Earle", commanded Company I, 3rd Battalion, 15th Infantry Regiment in Tientsin, China, circa Fall 1937. Wheeler is in the first row, tenth from left in lighter color overcoat. (Wheeler Family Records).*

Bus was proud of the 15th Infantry and enjoyed a great reputation among its troops. "We always put a little extra into it when Lt. Wheeler was Officer of the Guard," wrote one of his soldiers. "Frankly, we never thought he would get anywhere. He was too kind to the enlisted men." [49]

This assignment was an accompanied tour, meaning Betty was authorized to accompany Bus. He had requested passports for them back in April while still attending the Infantry School. Both were excited as neither had ever travelled abroad before. In July, their household goods were crated for shipment, but the Japanese invasion that month compelled the U.S. War Department to restrict dependent travel to China. Consequently, Betty returned to her parents' house in Old Greenwich.[50]

It was just as well. Although Japan had overrun China, it was not at war with the U.S. and would not be for another four years. Still, the Japanese occupiers of Tientsin made no secret of their disdain for the Americans, whose presence they found intolerable. Tensions flared, and serious incidents between Japanese and American soldiers occurred before the 15th Infantry was withdrawn on 2 March 1938.[51]

Wheeler's experiences in China shaped his outlook for the remainder of his life. He never forgot, he once told an interviewer, the Japanese campaign against the relatively helpless Chinese.[52]

Bus and Betty were happily reunited when the 15th Infantry Regiment arrived at Fort Lewis, Washington in late March. They would remain there with the regiment another two years.[53]

*Officers of the prestigious 15th Infantry Regiment, Fort Lewis, Washington, circa 1939. Wheeler is in the second row, fifth from right. An excellent marksmen and avid hunter, Wheeler curiously does not wear an Expert Marksman Badge as do many of his peers. (Wheeler Family Records).*

Among the list of 15th Infantry alumni from the Interwar Period were many fine officers who would rise to fame during World War II, including

George C. Marshall, Matthew B. Ridgway, Joseph Stilwell, and Walton H. Walker.[54]

Dwight D. Eisenhower and his wife Mamie joined the regiment just before the Wheelers departed. "Initially, Bus could not stand Eisenhower in the slightest," Betty recalled. "He had absolutely no use for him whatsoever."

What soured him on Eisenhower was an incident in which the new regimental commander dressed down some junior officers in front of their peers and their enlisted men. It should have been handled in private, Wheeler felt.

However, "there was no way that Bus would not be loyal to the commander, whomever he was," Betty said. (Bus would eventually grow to admire Eisenhower. Their paths would converge again in the 1950s, and a close friendship would develop between them and their wives in the 1960s.) [55]

## *West Point*

When the time came for Bus to consider his next assignment in early 1940, Betty was several months pregnant. Woolnough had encouraged Bus to join him as a mathematics instructor at West Point. Bus wasn't so sure. Betty encouraged him to do whatever he wanted, but insisted in no uncertain terms that she did not want to deliver their baby with just her mother's help. She wanted him to be there for the birth. [56]

Bus got the message, so he applied for and was accepted to teach in the Mathematics Department. That spring, he and Betty drove from Fort Lewis to West Point. On 20 July, she gave birth to son Gilmore "Bim" Stone Wheeler, who would be the couple's only child.[57]

The Wheelers had been married almost eight years when Betty finally got pregnant. They had had fertility issues and wondered whether they would ever have children. Their friends began having babies shortly after marriage.

As the gender of unborn babies could not be foretold in those days, expectant mothers referred to them as "the baby" or "it". This irritated Betty to no end, so when she became pregnant, she determined that her child would go by "Bim", whether it was a boy or a girl. Alluding to his first name "Earle", Bus once joked that if they ever had a daughter, they should name her "Gearle." [58]

Eight years after his commissioning, on 9 September 1940, Wheeler was promoted to temporary Captain. The next morning, he asked his sleepy cadets if any of them noticed anything different in the classroom. After a few moments, one of them observed that Wheeler was now wearing Captain's bars. This cadet happened to be the class "goat", meaning he had the lowest academic marks among all his classmates. Feeling generous, Wheeler rewarded him with a perfect 3.0 grade for that day's class. "It was probably the highest grade he ever received," Wheeler's son later suggested. (Betty recalled that many years later Bus was stopped in the Pentagon by an officer. "Sir, I know you don't remember me, but …". It was the class goat who wanted to thank Wheeler for having had such a profound impact on his career.) [59]

A couple weeks before Wheeler's promotion, Congress approved the induction of the National Guard into federal service and activation of the organized reserves to fill the ranks of the Army. During the last six months of 1940, the active Army would more than double in strength, and by mid-1941, it would achieve its planned strength of 1.5 million officers and men.[60]

Wheeler enjoyed teaching math to cadets and was quite good at it. But with war looming, he and many of his faculty colleagues longed for active service in the field army. This included Bus's close friend, Captain James "Jimmy" Gavin in the Tactics Department. Gavin once jokingly propositioned Betty to escape to New York City with him for a weekend tryst. He wasn't serious, though, and the Wheelers just laughed it off. (Wheeler and Gavin would remain friends over the years, even through the contentious Vietnam War period when Gavin delivered testimony before Congress that was highly critical of U.S. military strategy and, by extension, Wheeler.) [61]

# CHAPTER 2

## WORLD WAR II
## (JUNE 1941 - SEPTEMBER 1945)

### *Stateside*

Wheeler's exceptional record, professional reputation, and personal connections with senior officers facilitated his release from West Point, but not to combat as soon as he would have liked. Much of his wartime service would occur stateside and would equip him well with resource management and other senior staff officer skills that would later distinguish him as a general officer.

While serving with the 15th Infantry in Tientsin and Fort Lewis, Wheeler had impressed his Regimental Commander, Colonel Fred L. Walker. By early 1941, Walker was a Brigadier General serving as the Assistant Division Commander of the 2nd Infantry Division. Later that year, after his promotion to Major General and selection as Commanding General of the 36th Infantry Division of the Texas National Guard, Walker succeeded in pulling Wheeler from the academy to serve as his Aide-de-Camp.[1]

Bus wasn't keen on becoming an Aide, but it was a ticket out of West Point. "Goddamn it, Bus!" exclaimed Gavin when he heard the news. "If you can escape this place within a year, I'll escape, too." Gavin succeeded in April by volunteering for the new paratrooper force. Rapid promotions would follow, and Gavin would serve with distinction as the Commanding General of the 82nd Airborne Division during the war.[2]

In June, Bus, Betty, and eleven-month old Bim moved to Fort Sam Houston in San Antonio. When the division relocated in early October to Camp Bowie, near Brownwood, Texas, for extended training, the Wheelers vacated their new quarters in anticipation of following the division. Without orders, though, Betty and Bim were stuck at Fort Sam Houston for the time being.

Walker made frequent business trips to San Antonio, usually over the weekends. Bus always accompanied him and so was able to spend some brief time with his family who had moved in with their old friends from Fort Benning, Captain Paul and Helen Paschal, in their quarters at 209 Artillery Post.

On 7 October, Betty wrote:

> I had such a nice weekend with Bus, but it was awfully hard to see him take off again. … You should have seen Bim waving to Bus when he left yesterday. … [Bus] still hasn't any orders, so it's a case of he's there but we're here. After waiting two months for him to come home, the letdown is terrific. … I'm beginning to feel that I'm having a marriage by correspondence! [3]

As it became increasingly apparent that the U.S. would eventually be drawn into the war, Walker was "terribly busy" training his division for combat. Still, administrative matters required his time and attention, including the unique politics associated with commanding a National Guard division. In early October, Walker took Wheeler with him to the Dallas fair.

"It's a gathering of all the Texas bigwigs," Betty explained. "The National Guard is definitely politics. I think it will be quite an experience for both of us before we're through." [4]

Walker later wrote of Wheeler:

> [He] is blessed with a high IQ and has unusually good judgment. To me he is more than an Aide, and I do not hesitate to discuss my problems with him. … I have given Wheeler the job of going to each regiment and separate battalion to inspect its paper work and property accounts and to instruct the responsible enlisted men in how to keep their records. [5]

Walker also delegated some of his administrative duties to Wheeler, who gained valuable experience interacting with elected and civic group officials. He dealt with the National Association for the Advancement of Colored People (NAACP) over an incident involving the arrest of several black soldiers for disorderliness in Brownwood. (Almost sixteen years later, he would hearken back to this experience when tasked to help diffuse the desegregation crisis in Little Rock, Arkansas.) [6]

On 13 October, Betty reported, "Well, the news I'd hoped to hear [about receiving orders to move to Brownwood] hasn't come through, and things are certainly mixed up." She admitted that she had little to complain about, though:

> Bus will probably get down nearly every weekend. ... There is
> nothing like being nine years married and a mother, and find
> yourself being courted weekends! ... Well, there's no reason
> for making plans. I should know now it can't be done. ... I
> might better count my blessings. After all, here I am. [The
> Pascals] love Bim. Helen runs the house with two servants.
> I have a nursemaid, and I can see Bus every week. Certainly,
> I'm well taken care of. ... Aside from missing Bus, I'm very
> comfortable!!! [7]

"Bus got down for the weekend," she wrote a week later. "General Walker has been very good about having some official business for Bus to attend to, because in that way he can have a car and a driver. I just feel like I don't see him at all. The time just flies by, and of course here we have very little time to ourselves." [8]

In mid-October, Walker nominated Wheeler to attend the Command and General Staff College's Special G-1/G-4 Course with the intention that Wheeler would rejoin the division afterward. "Bus may go to [Fort] Leavenworth in December," Betty wrote. "It's a two month course now. If he goes, I want to go, even though Helen says I can just stay here." [9]

Betty was growing anxious about the looming war:

> [We] will put the furniture in storage the end of this month.
> You don't know how I hate to do it. I don't know why I should,
> as we can get it out anytime, but it does seem so final, like
> shutting the door and wondering if you're ever going to open
> it again. ... The war seems to be moving close, awfully fast. ...
> [We] will just have to enjoy every day as much as possible. If
> [Bus] can just get to Leavenworth, I guess those two months
> are assured us! [10]

On 9 December - two days after the Japanese attack on Pearl Harbor that brought the U.S. into the war - the Wheelers arrived at Fort Leavenworth.

Betty set to work establishing their household in an unfurnished, two-room apartment over a garage at 1330 South Broadway in Leavenworth.

With Bus's departure for combat an eventual certainty now that the U.S. was at war, he and Betty realized that this Christmas could be their last together, at least for the foreseeable future. "I brought the tree lights and a few small balls," Betty wrote. "[We] picked out a small tree. We are definitely going to have as much Christmas as possible, turkey and all." [11]

Betty informed her parents:

> From the little news we've had from [the 36th Infantry Division at] Brownwood, I feel sure I'll be home in February [to live with them in Old Greenwich for the duration of the war]. According to a letter Bus had ... the [division] is moving. Still in the U.S., of course. But from the little I can glean, after this step, it may be today, tomorrow, or next year but overseas is the next step. [12]

As the new year approached with uncertain tidings, the Wheelers enjoyed a pleasant Christmas. The day after, Betty recorded:

> Bim is in bed, supper is over, and the dishes done. Bus is studying. ... The lights are lit. ... We have had a good Christmas. It rained, but we were so glad to be together. It was a close shave, and we've counted our blessings. ... Bus wanted a field jacket, which he got himself. ... We did have such a nice day. It will be a Christmas to remember. [13]

## 1942

Having served almost ten years as an officer, Wheeler was promoted to temporary Major on 1 February 1942. Later that month, he graduated from the Special G-1/G-4 Course at the top of his class. [14]

*While serving as Aide-de-Camp to the Commanding General, 36th Infantry Division, Texas National Guard, Wheeler (front row, third from left) earned top marks at the Command and General Staff College's Special G-1/G-4 Course, Fort Leavenworth, Kansas, October - December 1941. (Wheeler Family Records).*

During the dramatic growth of the Army in 1942, Wheeler would receive a series of rapid promotions. He became a permanent Captain on 10 June and a temporary Lieutenant Colonel on 11 November.[15]

## *Joint Chiefs of Staff*

Meanwhile at the national level, a new organization, the Joint Chiefs of Staff (JCS), was formed and reflected tension between the need to integrate military advice into the national security process and the desire to retain civilian control over the defense establishment. In January, President Franklin D. Roosevelt established the JCS to satisfy the exigencies of America's newly formed military alliance with Great Britain. During World War II, the JCS would plan and direct U.S. military strategy, manage matériel and manpower, and coordinate among the nation's military allies. [16]

## *Florida-Mississippi-Florida-Mississippi*

In early March, Wheeler rejoined the 36th Infantry Division, which had relocated in his absence to Camp Blanding, Florida. In April, he assumed command of the 2nd Battalion, 141st Infantry Regiment. Simultaneously, he applied his recent schooling to "straighten out an unsatisfactory property condition" in the Regimental Supply Office. Colonel Nat S. Perrine, the Regimental Commander, praised Wheeler's "untiring efforts and ... the excellent results that you have accomplished. Your spirit of cheerful cooperation in these additional duties, as well as the regular duties of Battalion Commander, has contributed greatly in making this an outstanding regiment." [17]

After just six months, Wheeler was forced to relinquish command, much to his great disappointment. His stellar performance at Fort Leavenworth had caught the attention of the War Department, who as Walker put it, "would not rest until they have him on the General Staff." Eager to command his battalion in combat, Wheeler begged Walker to intercede. Walker would have liked to retain him but appreciated that the Army had much bigger needs for an officer of Wheeler's exceptional talent. Accordingly, he did not oppose Wheeler's reassignment to the 99th Infantry Division, then being formed at Camp Blanding. [18]

Walker wrote:

> When [Wheeler] finished the course at The General Staff School ... I received the report of his work. He stood number one in the G-4 course, and either number one or two in the other courses. I knew the moment I saw the report that the War Department would mark him for General Staff duty. Sure enough, I received a telegram assigning him to General 'Tommy' Lawrence's new 99th Division. Bus came to see me. He does not want to leave the 36th nor do I want to lose him, but nothing would be gained by my doing so. He is marked for better and higher assignments and he should comply with orders. I am sorry to lose him, but he paved the way to the General Staff by standing high at Leavenworth. He was disappointed at my action, said I did not understand his problem, and was not happy. I suspect he thinks I am trying

to get rid of him, and he does not realize that I am doing    ·
what I believe to be in his best interest. [19]

Wheeler later recalled:

> I was unhappy. During the preceding year, I had become
> deeply involved in the life and future of the division. I was
> closely associated with General Walker. I knew the problems
> of personnel, organization, training, standards of perfor-
> mance and discipline with which he had to cope. I did my
> best to help and, in doing so, my duties went considerably
> beyond those usually assigned to an aide. In the course of my
> work I came to know, like and respect a large number of offi-
> cers and enlisted men. In short, I was at home in the division,
> and I hated to leave it. [20]

Wheeler's fate instead was to become the Assistant Chief of Staff for
Operations (G-3) of the 99th Infantry Division. Serving in that critical capacity between October 1942 and March 1943, he would oversee the division's
formation and movement some 650 miles from Camp Blanding to the newly
constructed Camp Van Dorn near Natchez, Mississippi. (As it turned out, the
officer who replaced Wheeler in battalion command would be killed in action
thirteen months later during the division's assault landing at Salerno, Italy.) [21]

## *Mobilization*

Wheeler's reassignment occurred against the backdrop of the continuing explosive growth of the Army. By the end of 1942, it would grow to a
strength of 5. 4 million officers and men. Although this was still well under the
8. 2 million authorization that President Franklin D. Roosevelt had established
in November, the mobilization of ground combat elements was already near-
ing completion. Seventy-three divisions had been formed, and no more than
100 were expected to be activated.

The division was the basic fighting team of arms and services combined
into portions designed for continuous offensive action under normal battle
conditions. A triangular organization, the infantry division was comprised of
three infantry regiments, four artillery battalions, a reconnaissance troop, and
engineer, ordnance, signal, quartermaster, medical, and military police units.

Each regiment could readily be teamed with an artillery battalion. Reinforced with other elements of the division or with elements assigned by corps or army headquarters, it formed the regimental combat team. The total strength of an infantry division was 14,253 men.

The strength of Army ground combat units would hardly increase at all after 1942, even though 16 divisions and some 350 separate artillery and engineer battalions were later added. These additional units would be formed by means of redistribution and economies within the existing personnel allotments in the same categories. [22]

### *Road Trips*

"The trip [from Camp Blanding to Camp Van Dorn] was hectic," Betty reported on 8 September.

> Bus, I'm sure, wished the better part of the trip that he'd left us behind. However, I know he's glad we're here. … Bus seems to like [the Commanding General, Major General Thompson] Lawrence very much. … I think he is pleased that he is G-3. It's a rather important job. [23]

Wheeler would serve two tours of duty at Camp Van Dorn, the only Army officer to serve there with both the 99th and 63rd Infantry Divisions. Both times, Betty and young Bim lived about ninety minutes away in Natchez.

"As long as I can, I want to be as near Bus as possible," she explained. "Even if we only see him a couple of times a month. The camp is in the process of being built, and we have hopes that when the workers leave we can [live somewhere] closer than 50 miles away." [24]

Obtaining housing in rural Mississippi was a huge challenge for the influx of military families since very little was available to begin with. Fortunately for the Wheelers, the Beltzhoover family had converted the former slave quarters of their 1838 mansion "Green Leaves" into an apartment and had agreed to rent it to Betty. [25]

*Bim Wheeler plays outside "Green Leaves", the antebellum home in Natchez, Mississippi, where he and Betty lived for three years during World War II. (Wheeler Family Records).*

For Christmas that year, Santa Claus brought Bim a pedal car repainted in Army olive drab with a white star on each side, a replica .45-caliber cap pistol, and a hand-cranked toy machine gun that fired wooden bullets. [26]

## 1943

Over the winter of 1942-43, Wheeler briefly returned to Fort Leavenworth by himself to attend the Command and General Staff College's New Division Course. Yet again, he received top honors. [27]

On 12 January 1943, Betty wrote:

> We almost had [another] change of station. … They telephoned from Washington, Army Ground Forces G-3, that if [Bus] was available he was to be sent to Washington immediately! Thank God General Lawrence said that he wasn't available. I dread Washington in peacetime without taking on an overcrowded city. Once again, it doesn't hurt to be asked for, and as Bus says, it gives him an inkling of General Lawrence's opinion of him. The only thing I hate about it is that every time he's asked to go someplace, very shortly something else turns up. I'm almost superstitious about it. I do love it here, and I'm not ready to leave yet! [28]

Three days later she added, "Let's hope wherever we could [go], it's not Washington! I don't want to cope with Bus's [alcoholic] mother either. It would be terrible to live with. … I have no faith that I could cope with it, and I don't want to try." (Ironically, they would later be reassigned to Washington—four times in fact—and spend 14 total years there. As Betty feared, they would indeed find it a challenge dealing with and caring for "Mums".) [29]

Major General Louis E. Hibbs would profoundly influence the trajectory of Wheeler's career for the remainder of the war. Back in early 1942, while Wheeler was in battalion command, Hibbs commanded the 36th Infantry Division's Division Artillery. Following Hibbs's selection to organize and command the new 63rd Infantry Division in March 1943, Walker "asked him if he had decided upon a Chief of Staff". When Hibbs replied he had not, Walker recommended Wheeler. Hibbs "said he had not previously thought of him, but Bus was just the person he would like to have." [30]

*Colonel Wheeler as Chief of Staff, 63rd Infantry Division, Camp Van Dorn, Mississippi, circa Fall 1943. (Wheeler Family Records).*

Wheeler's selection that May meant moving his family back to Camp Blanding since the 63rd would be activated there. He had only been with the 99th at Camp Van Dorn about eight months. Eleven days after the 63rd "Blood and Fire" Infantry Division's activation ceremony on 15 June, Wheeler was promoted to temporary Colonel. [31]

"Bus probably won't get [home more often] than weekends," Betty had written on 7 May. "There is of course a terrific amount of work to do getting the division started, but on top of all that, he's very much on the spot. His junior years are causing a furor, if you know what I mean!" [32]

The cadre manning the new division had come from the 98th Infantry Division at Camp Breckenridge, Kentucky. After three months of initial cadre training, the division relocated to Camp Van Dorn once the 99th Infantry Division shipped out for Europe. The Wheelers' second tour at Camp Blanding ended late that August when they repacked their car and trekked right back to Mississippi. [33]

Their multiple trips across the Deep South occurred before the advent of highways, motels, and fast food restaurants. Betty packed sandwiches, usually chicken, in a tin sandwich box. She also filled a thermos with coffee and another with milk. To relieve the boredom, Betty played the "sign game" with Bim. They also sang songs, "Marsey Doats" and "Pistol Packing Mama" among their favorites.

Bus, who always enjoyed a good joke, helped pass the time by telling jokes, some of which were pretty awful. Bim recalled one: "A mother hen built her nest under an orange tree. One day, as she and her chicks were out walking, an orange fell out the tree and into the nest. When the hen and offspring returned, the chicks saw the orange and danced around the nest singing, 'Look at the orange mamalade!'" [34]

Years later, whenever Bus told a particularly awful joke, the family would all groan. With a serene look on his face, he would say, "I've got a million of them." To which Betty and Bim would reply in unison, "Yeah, and all of them are sooo bad!" [35]

During one of the Wheelers' trips between Florida and Mississippi, they stopped at a very nice but overcrowded hotel. Per wartime regulation, Bus always travelled in uniform. Expecting prompt service and perturbed at having to wait for the desk clerk's attention, Bus finally interrupted him to inquire about a room. The clerk snipped back, "Don't you know there's a war going on?" His impudence infuriated Bus, but he bit his tongue.

The following morning, Bus led the family dog Gus on a leash through the hotel lobby as Betty and Bim followed behind. When the housebroken dog proceeded to lift his leg to relieve himself on the leg of a large table, Bus made no attempt to stop him. Proceeding out the door, Bus quipped, "That's exactly the way I feel, Gus." [36]

Exhausted travelers often had to take whatever lodging they could find. Once, the Wheelers spent the night in a brothel, but didn't realize it until the next morning. They'd been given a room "decorated like a fifteen-year old girl's bedroom", all pink, frilly, and very clean. The proprietors were friendly and polite enough, and even opened up the kitchen to feed the tired couple and their toddler. [37]

## *Training Divisions*

Wheeler's reassignments between the 36th, 99th, and 63rd Infantry Divisions were incidental to Marshall's plan for the organization and training of 100 combat divisions. Recalling the untrained divisions that the U.S. sent overseas in World War I, Marshall determined from the start to provide thorough and realistic training for large units in the continental United States, culminating in large-scale maneuvers by corps and armies. Since all divisions had been activated by August and the mass deployment of the Army overseas would not begin until late in that year, most divisions were thoroughly trained. The major threat to an orderly training program would occur in 1944, when many trained divisions had to be skeletonized to meet the demand for trained replacements. Equipment shortages were a serious obstacle to effective training in early 1943, as in 1942, as was the shortage of trained commissioned and noncommissioned officers to provide cadres. [38]

## *War Hits Home*

The 36th Infantry Division, which had briefly served in North Africa, became the first U.S. division to invade the continent of Europe on 9 September during its assault landings near Salerno, 25 miles southeast of Naples. Reacting in strength against the landings, the Germans mounted a vigorous counterattack that threatened to split the beachhead and force the Allies to abandon part of it. For four days, the issue was in doubt. Quick reinforcement of the ground troops (including a regiment of paratroopers jumping into the beachhead), gallant fighting, liberal air support, and naval gunfire at last repulsed the German attack. Not until 17 November would the Germans begin to withdraw. [39]

Reflecting upon Roosevelt's address to the nation in the wake of the landings, Betty wrote:

> This is a very memorable night. … Somehow, the invasion has been talked of for so long, that tonight it hasn't really registered. All day, it has been one of those things, that [it] had at last come. … I listened to Mr. Roosevelt, and suddenly this ceased to be another [ordinary] day. For what this day must mean to so many people. I'm not thinking of the conquered and what hopes it must bring to them, but the plain ordinary fathers and mothers of this country. … I know how blessed Bim and I have been. It's something you can't say in words, now or ever. … I told you we had heard 50% of the 36th [Division] was wiped out. That wasn't true. Officially, a mere 35%. And of Bus's battalion, they made the initial landing at Salerno, [and] there is practically no one left [including his replacement in command.] I know what I have to thank God for.
>
> My heart goes out to those who know their men are in there, and the heart ache it will mean to so many.
>
> I talked to Bus earlier tonight. … It was silly, but I felt I had to talk to him, just to share my gratitude for being able to pick up the telephone and in seconds hear his voice. [40]

Betty added that Hibbs had planned to send Bus to the Mediterranean on 1 June as an observer:

> Things came up that Louis felt he needed him here. Bus would have arrived just in time [for the Salerno landings], and while his personal danger compared to the men in combat would have been slight, the element would have been there nevertheless. … Don't think I'm not thankful for my peace of mind concerning my own this night. [41]

## *Replacements*

In September, soldiers collected from reception centers all over the country rapidly brought the 63rd Infantry Division up to strength. By November, they had completed basic and small unit training and anticipated advanced and larger maneuvers. That did not occur because in December all of the division's Privates, Privates First Class, and some noncommissioned officers and junior officers were reassigned to other divisions that had been alerted for deployment. The process of receiving replacements and training them up only to have them reassigned as fillers for other deploying divisions would be repeated twice again before the division was itself finally alerted for movement overseas.

## 1944

During March-April 1944, the 63rd was brought up to full strength with replacements from training centers, as well as soldiers reassigned from the Army Specialist Training Program and the Army Air Corps Cadet Program. These programs had been cut back and their participants released for assignment to the infantry. [42]

As the division reached full strength yet again, training started anew. By November, the 63rd would be ready for deployment. As if Wheeler didn't have enough on his plate during the incredibly busy month of October, he suffered an appendicitis, which may have prevented him from accompanying the division's advance party when it departed for Camp Shanks, New York on 6 November. [43]

When the division departed for Europe, Betty and Bim remained in Natchez with the Beltzhoovers - whose company she greatly enjoyed - rather than returning to her parents' home in Old Greenwich. The Wheelers expected the 63rd to return to Camp Van Dorn after the war to demobilize. [44]

## *France*

The 63rd's advance party arrived in Marseille, France on 8 December. Under the designation Task Force Harris, it trained at Haguenau and protected the east flank of Lieutenant General Alexander M. Patch's 7th Army along the

Rhine River. The task force fought defensively from 22 December and trained and patrolled in the Vosges and the Maginot Line area.

# 1945

Task Force Harris halted a German offensive south of Bitche on 1-19 January 1945. The 63rd Division's 254th Infantry Regiment participated in bitter fighting to liberate Colmar. The Division Artillery and other units landed in southern France on 14 January, and on 8 February, the division commenced operations as a unit. [45]

As this was Wheeler's first trip abroad, certain aspects of French culture fascinated him, including the "b-day" in his bathroom. "I can't help but think it has a use other than emptying dirty water," Bus pondered in his first letter to Betty. "Perhaps a foot bath?" [46]

"I lost $45 in a poker game on the way over," he confessed. "I will take care to see that this doesn't happen again." [47]

Evidencing his talent as a writer, Bus painted vivid pictures of war-torn Europe for Betty:

> I have been impressed by the sober look of the [French] people. The only persons we've seen laughing and apparently carefree are the children. ... The populace has a sort of depressed, expectant look—as if they were all wondering what the hell was going to happen next.
>
> It is cold as hell. ... [Many French women] go barelegged [as] stockings are apparently at a premium. ... This is unfortunate for the constant cold weather and exposure turns their legs a peculiar color -- a reddish hue sort of like the legs on a cold storage turkey. [48]

He would often vent about the broad scope and relentless pace of his duties as a wartime division Chief of Staff. "I have been working quite hard," he wrote. "There is so damn much to do and time passes us. I feel the responsibility more than ever before." [49]

"The first side to run out of paper is going to lose!" Bus exclaimed a few days later when he also lamented, "[It] seems to take twice as much energy to get half as much done here." [50]

"I have a bit of a cold," Bus reported on 17 January. "That is SOP over here. Everyone has a cold. [I] did have an upset stomach for a few days -- probably the change in water, food, and climate as well as a few bugs." [51]

Fortunately for Wheeler, a Brigadier General who was going home sick, "presented me with a fine, warm jacket -- lined with pile -- to go under my field jacket. [It] is just enough too big for me so that I can put on another suit of woolen underwear, a sweater, and two shirts, and my field jacket over that, then my field overcoat. If I can still walk I shall heat a couple of rocks to carry around in my pockets." Wheeler also affected an infantry blue scarf. [52]

*Wheeler affected an Infantry blue scarf while serving as Chief of Staff, 63rd Infantry Division, Germany, Spring 1945. (Wheeler Family Records).*

Wheeler wrote:

> The destruction of this war is terrific, sweetheart. And everywhere, I must add. Wrecked trucks, burned vehicles, wrecked buildings—flattened by artillery and by bombs. And, of course, the cemeteries—and hospitals—make one realize the price that some Americans are paying. It is sobering, I can tell you that. ... Oddly enough, these things make

me think of you and Bim, and I thank God that neither of you is exposed to this. Jesus! [53]

## *Alsace*

"We are in Alsace now as part of the 7th Army," Bus reported on 1 February.

> The whole place—including the population—is a mixture of French and German. As a matter of fact, most of the populace looks German rather than French. Most of the signs are in German and, I've been told, there are many Nazi sympathizers in the region. Naturally, these gentlemen are not very active at present. [54]

> Every village shows signs of war—buildings destroyed, no electricity, no water except pumps, bridges blown to hell, most factories destroyed, railroads and power lines wrecked. It will be many years before this country can come back. [55]

The 63rd Infantry Division moved to Willerwald the next day. The advance elements under Task Force Harris rejoined it there four days later. On the seventh, the division conducted local raids and patrols, then pushed forward. [56]

Bus wrote:

> I must admit that, after being a professional soldier these several years, warfare leaves me with a sense of unreality. I am somewhat surprised at myself, sweetness. Even when I hear a plane overhead, the ack-ack banging away and the tracers flowing up into the darkness, it still doesn't seem to be real. The artillery booms away for hours on end; Kraut prisoners come down the road; I visit the forward areas—and still I expect to wake up and find that I am back at [Camp] Van Dorn. Heigh-ho! [57]

"The senior staff members eat in what we call the Commanding General's Mess," Bus explained. "We have 12 or 13 regular members. ... The food is delicious, no less. ... We have a Frenchman (civilian) for our principal cook. ... [He] really knows his business. ... [The French] can make a palatable dish out of nothing; give them a can of C-Rations and I swear they can turn out a banquet." [58]

The novelty of the general's mess soon wore off, however. Three weeks later, he wrote, "There is nothing to look forward to except mail and meals. Since the meals are monotonous too, that leaves mail our only recreation. Of course, I am far better off than the poor lads in the foxholes whose life (believe it or not) is monotony to the Nth degree." [59]

Work on the division staff was no joy either, as Bus explained:

What a damned monotonous life this is! The work isn't monotonous, however; it is mountainous. Most of us—the G's [division primary staff officers] anyway—are putting in 16 hours a day. I expect the burden to lighten in the future. ... I think it just as well that we are busy; otherwise, the whole business would get us down. [60]

In these circumstances of long periods of monotony punctuated by episodes of intense excitement, Bus's thoughts would always turn to his family. "Oh, darling, I've missed you and Bim so damned much this last month. I am very thankful that you all are where you are—safely away from this mess." [61]

Betty was pregnant when Bus departed the States in December but lost the baby girl not long thereafter. "May I ask," Bus wrote in early February, "what in the world gave Bim the idea that his little sister had eaten rat poison? Or did he just think it up himself? Somehow I'm a bit sorry about little sister; but I reckon (with your approval and cooperation) that can be rectified at a future date!" [62]

Regarding Betty's brother, Lieutenant Walter "Bob" R. Howell, Jr., Bus wrote, "I am sorry to hear that Bob is in Italy. If he were in this theater, I could undoubtedly get him [transferred to the 63rd]. As it is, I will try, but no promises!" [63]

I'm not going to write much about how terribly I miss you and Bim. There is no use in making us unhappy by dwelling on that. You know that I am thinking of you constantly and wishing that I were with you again. Well, perhaps it won't be so very long, darling. We can hope that, at least. [64]

Wheeler often visited the division's frontline infantrymen and empathized about the harsh winter conditions they endured. As a senior member of the division staff, his living conditions were "pretty good," a fact he fully appreciated.

> I have a room right next to the office, where I sleep. [My enlisted orderly, Sergeant Richard] Belmore has made me very comfortable -- a canvas cot, a little iron stove, and electric light which runs off the headquarters generator (I can use my electric razor), a wash basin lacking running water but which will drain, and a French pot to heat water in. [65]

On 11 February, Bus reported on the "queer weather lately" :

> When I got here, there was a good foot of snow on the ground and the cold ... was something to write home about! ... Since then, we have had a thaw followed by warm rain which, together, literally turned this section of Europe into a lake. Since then, the weather cannot make up its mind. For half an hour, there is a beautiful blue sky, warm sun, and a flock of our bombers bellowing overhead as they depart for the Reich. This is followed with no notice by a driving cold rain, sleet, hail, and high winds. ... Probably tomorrow there will be a dusting of snow on the ground as there was this morning. [66]

Conditions were much different three days later:

> Today the weather has been beautiful; blue sky, warm sun, Spring itself. Just how long this will last is doubtful. After the lousy weather we've suffered through, it's about time we got a break. However, I think it very chancy to even hope—in this part of the world—that Spring is here to stay. [67]

Escaping the division command post to visit the troops, Wheeler observed:

> I have been interested in watching the reaction of our people to this relatively new environment. Most of them react by working harder than ever before in their lives. ... Some of the troops and junior officers seem to go a bit native at first.

I mean by that that they have seen too many of Mauldin's cartoons depicting the combat soldier with a three day beard, covered with mud, and generally unkempt. That lasts until you snap them out of it and make them realize we don't act like that. Then they settle down and start to soldiering.

We have had only one or two crack ups—meaning people who lose all sense of responsibility just because they are no longer in the States. On the whole, the behavior is remarkably good. As a matter of fact, our people are very well disciplined. [68]

"Today was Sunday," Bus recounted on 11 February. "I really didn't know it, being as we are on a seven-day, 16-hour-a-day schedule. ... [Some officers and men of the division headquarters] went to [the local village] church and no doubt returned feeling spiritually refreshed. I shall try it myself one of these Sundays. This morning, I was harassed by a number of details, and my temper was not Christian-like a bit." [69]

The daily rat race continues. The massive detail, not to mention the mounds of paper, continues also. I am barely keeping my head above water. I suppose that one of these mornings I'll come into my office and find no papers stacked on my desk, but by that time I'll probably be too mimeograph-drunk to appreciate it. If we'd only push the paper to one side and get on with the war, I believe we'd settle the Krauts in short order. Perhaps that is why the Russians do so well: I've heard that their standards of literacy are not very high. [70]

He continued to vent two days later:

The work doesn't let up much. Of course, there are many reasons why the good old paper war goes on at this terrific rate at present. I hope to calm folks down and get that squared away before much longer.

There is an advantage to the long hours we put in here; that is, we don't have time to think very much about other things than our duties. I get up at 6:30, eat, get to my desk by 7:30. Usually stop at 12:30 for lunch and return at 1:30. At 5:30 we have a drink (sometimes not)·then eat supper. After supper at 7:00 we have a staff meeting lasting about an hour. Then I work until about 11:00 and go to bed. It's 11:30 now—my usual time to be finishing a letter to you and starting to hit my sleeping bag. [71]

The following day, Bus exploded:

Damn this paperwork! I've never seen so much wood pulp marked up with ink. If I never read anything again, it'll be too soon. And damn these people—particularly the ones of ours who got here a month before us—who have acquired all the airs and graces of veterans of nine campaigns. By Jesus, I'm going to lock a few heels around this asylum and get the lead out of their butts! [72]

"I am very well taken care of as far as being warm, fed, and reasonably clean," Bus later reported more calmly. "I could use an honest-to-God bath, however. We have a shower unit not too far away which I intend to patronize—perhaps tomorrow if I'm not too busy." [73]

By mid-February, Bus was really feeling the strain:

I am trying to get to bed early tonight. I've been staying up too damn late. … This has been a hectic day, piled on top of other hectic days. Sometimes I feel as if we are making bricks with no straw and damn little mud. Don't take that last literally; there's plenty of mud, darling, up over your boot tops in places. [74]

The division forced a crossing of the Saar River on 17 February, leading the re-entrance of the 7th Army onto German soil. It then mopped up the enemy in Muhlen Woods. [75]

On 22 February, Bus described for Betty more frontline fighting that he had observed:

I saw a very interesting thing the other day. Some ten or twelve Krauts with a couple of machine guns were holed up in a house which had been turned into a pillbox. They were so located that they blocked the road and, in general, were a confounded nuisance. We hauled up an armored car, some infantry, and a 3" gun and went to work on it. The armored car could do them no harm, and the infantry couldn't get close enough to do business. So we started in on them with the 3". Literally, the damned house was shot to pieces. After six rounds the plaster dust and smoke was so thick that the house was invisible. Three more rounds and out came the Krauts—those that could walk. That's the only way to handle these people: knock the everlasting hell out of them! [76]

"I haven't been sleeping much lately," Bus continued. Nor had he had any time to write home since the 15th.

On the night of the 16th I didn't get to bed until nearly 1:00 AM; I was up at 3:30 and on the go. Events developed in such a way that we—the General and I—did not get to bed at all the following night. In fact I laid down about four in the afternoon of the 18th and slept for an hour only. Then I was awakened, and we went to work again. That night wasn't so bad. I got the General down about 12:30 in the morning and I slept until 3:30, then to work again. He slept until 6:00 AM. The 19th was normal and we have been able to get to bed with reasonable frequency, although until today we have been very rushed. [77]

"The improvement in the weather has helped everyone," Bus reported the following day, "particularly the men in the foxholes. The nights are still quite cold, but most of the days, except when it rains, have been quite pleasant—springlike, in fact." [78]

Bus reminded Betty:

You recall, that I wrote you of the sense of unreality I have concerning this whole business here. That still persists. I imagine it is because the days melt into the other with no particular break to mark one from the other. The routine is work from 7:30 AM to 11:00 PM (unless I work longer as I did the past week); then a drink before bed, and then sleep—but not enough of it! [79]

Betty had expressed concern for his safety. "Darling, you mustn't worry about me. My job doesn't require me to be leading attacks. I'm still a desk soldier." [80]

*As a wartime division chief of staff, Wheeler gained senior staff officer expertise that directly underpinned his success as a general officer. Somewhere in southwestern Germany, circa March 1945. (Wheeler Family Records).*

Usually monitoring combat operations from the division command post, Bus recounted a particular joint operation:

> This afternoon I listened in while the air people attacked a target for us on our front. It was quite fascinating to hear the flight leader giving orders to his pilots, and then hear him report six direct hits on target; the target in this case being a large factory which has been a thorn in our side. They flattened it too; a swell job. Only hope there were 500 Krauts in it! [81]

"By the way," he added, "our outfit has made a great name for itself over here. We have been complemented by the Corps Commander for the 'fine planning, and the professional touch displayed' in our work. Nice, eh?" [82]

On 1 March, Bus replied to Betty's query:

> You asked … if the front is different from what I had expected. Honestly, Betty, it isn't. As you know, I am not overburdened with boyish illusions as to the glamour of warfare, etc. It's a

goddamn dirty business—killing people. I find myself, however, developing a steady rage against the Germans. [83]

He added:

Yesterday I got out and did a bit of looking around. I took the CG's armored car and rode up through some of Germany that we have taken; the Krauts don't like it either! I talked to some of our people who have without exception been doing a bang-up job. Must admit that as a desk soldier ... I was impressed by the calmness of our people. The Krauts were busting a few mortar shells about—and, Darling, I could hear them all full well! I kept thinking (but don't admit this, please) 'the next round the bastards shoot will be in here.' But it wasn't. I got back to my poop sheets with little incident. [84]

Continuing, he provided a glimpse of his very strong sense of duty and selfless service:

I have probably been a mite dilatory in my correspondence lately. However, I will offer no excuses because I know that you know that I write to you whenever I possibly can. That is not as often as I'd like, dearest. But I have duties to perform that take precedence over my own desires! Don't think that I am perturbed over my hours or any piddling thing like that. The hours are those which are dictated by our position. The goddamn Krauts have something to do with it. [85]

This "has been a long day with lots of piddling details to be handled," Bus later confided. "Just the type of day in fact that I despise. People talking at me all the time and, seemingly, damn little getting done."

Four days later, he added: "Oh God, I get tired of listening to people talk at me about every subject known to man. People are awful long-winded." [86]

The following week, Wheeler's enlisted orderly said to him, "Colonel, you must be working awful hard. ... You look tired all the time." [87]

"The weather here of late hasn't been too bad," Bus reported on 3 March. "In fact, the days have, on the whole, been spring-like. The nights have been cold, usually with frost. Yesterday and today the weather has been queer: bright sun for an hour followed by snow squalls." [88]

*Wheeler yearned to command an infantry regiment and visited the front as often as his command post duties allowed. Here, a Lieutenant holds a small potted plant to conceal Wheeler's colonel insignia as he surveys German positions near Gudingen, Germany, 3 March 1945. (Wheeler Family Records).*

On 7 March, Bus brought Betty up to date after the division's bitter fighting at Gudingen. "You'll gather that we have been busy again. We have, but we have not gone in for anything as strenuous as the first [major operation] I wrote you about. We have managed to get to sleep reasonably early and otherwise conduct ourselves in a more normal manner." [89]

"There is nothing, I believe, as downright boresome as warfare," Bus continued. "Of course, now and then there is some excitement. But not too often. Anyway, having the everlasting hell scared out of you isn't much fun either." [90]

When Colonel Edward P. Lukert relinquished command of the division's 253rd Infantry Regiment, "[I] tried to get the General to give Lukert's job to me," Bus reported. "But he wouldn't hear of it. Actually, I'm not too disappointed. What I'm doing is important." [91]

This passage is insightful about Wheeler's obedience as a subordinate. He argued his positions cogently and with conviction, but with the good sense of knowing when to accept a contrary decision rendered. (Throughout his career, Wheeler would consistently offer and defend sound recommendations to his superiors. Sometimes they were rejected, as would often occur during his tenure as Chairman of the Joint Chiefs of Staff. When that happened, he dutifully carried out the higher authority's decision.)

"The weather has been a bit better lately," Bus reported on 8 March. "In fact, we've had a couple of days that were like early spring. Quite a bit of rain, however, to keep us in the mud and not too happy. I myself have had the sniffles for a couple of days." [92]

Meanwhile back in Natchez, Betty was doing her part for the war effort as a volunteer nurse. (She would continue to volunteer with the American Red Cross and in servicemen's clubs throughout Bus's career.) Bus "received a letter tonight dated 28 February. It said mainly that you had survived your first tour in the hospital. I never thought for a moment that you would not, sweetness. Still, it's good to get word that things are going well among the bedpans." [93]

"This is a dreary existence," Bus lamented. "The sooner it is over with, the better for all of us. Of course, if we feel it is dreary, just think of the Krauts' emotions! Sometimes I wonder though." [94]

> I went with the General the other night to listen in on the questioning of two German officer prisoners. ... One cannot help having conflicting emotions under these circumstances. When I think of our people—our men—not to mention the people of Europe, I want to swear. On the other hand, human suffering goes beyond borders. [95]

With the 63rd continuously pressing forward in the offense, the division command post displaced frequently:

> We have been at this long enough now to have established practices in setting up for living and operating. For instance, when they set up my office (next to the General's) with the help just across the hall or next door, they also establish my living quarters on the same floor. For example, we are now in a hotel building. Our offices and my sleeping apartment are on the same floor. Of course, the room I sleep in has the window knocked out, but that is unimportant since I'm never there except to sleep, and Belmore has installed a pretty fair blackout curtain. [96]

He added:

> The three general officers have living quarters built into trucks (we call them 'vans') and these are parked nearby. The vans are really high class quarters. They have built-in closets, seats, one bunk, a sink with running water, and a gasoline heating stove. I have seen a smaller model built from a 1-ton trailer for the staffs of higher headquarters. I intend to make one of those for myself. They are nice because they provide a place to keep clothes.
>
> Of course, I am tied day and night to the telephone, so in some respects my present arrangement is better for me, particularly at night. [97]

The Siegfried Line now blocked the Americans' advance. On 14 March, Hibbs sent a message of encouragement to his soldiers:

> Before tomorrow, the 7th Army attacks along its entire front. In the coming attack you will again strike first, into and through the Siegfried Line—blasting a hole in the enemy's vaunted West Wall, last barrier to the Rhine. Beyond the Siegfried Line lies crumbling Germany, the Rhine and final victory. Your immediate task is to open the gate for our armored divisions. Only the best of the infantry is equal to that task. Yours is the honor and glory—take it away! Pay dirt lies ahead. Blood and Fire drives in for the kill. The world will be watching you. Strike hard, fast and viciously—victory comes by outfighting and outlasting the enemy! [98]

The following day, the 63rd achieved the 7th Army's first penetration of the Siegfried Line at Ormeshiem. It fought its way through the "German pillboxes and Dragon's teeth of the vaunted German defenses" at St. Ingbert and Hassel by 22 March, having previously taken Spiesen, Nuenkirchen, and Erbach. The division's successful breach "paved the way for armor to roll north and make the 7th Army's historic link up with the 3rd Army." [99]

"My congratulations, hot shots!" Hibbs wrote on 21 March. "This is a day you can remember. This day you made history!" [100]

Responding to a letter from Betty two days later, Bus corrected her misperception that all had been quiet on the 7th Army front:

> These past few days have been most active. … Darling, when the newspapers mention inactivity on an Army front, it is relative. If you aren't attacking, the activity decreases rapidly from front to rear. Meaning that the soldier sitting in a foxhole is active all the time because at any moment some Kraut may zero in on him with a mortar or a machine gun. In a regimental headquarters things are quiet unless they are putting on a raid or two. At the division headquarters, all is quiet unless we are operating in the attack. Of course, when one rises to the Army stratosphere anything less than a full-scale Army offensive is a quiet period. I can assure you that even though we have made no 7th Army headlines in the States, we in the 63rd are going to beat hell. We have put on four operations prior to this last big effort. As a matter of fact, the first was the toughest and most nerve-racking. Actually, today we are resting; the first time in months that we have been out of contact with the enemy. No doubt we'll be going again soon. [101]

Wheeler continued:

> Last night was queer. After all the tension and excitement of the last week—15 March, 22 March inclusive—it was odd as hell to find suddenly that everything around us was quiet and peaceful. We set up the CP in one end of a fair-sized city which is located in beautiful country, rolling hills and well-kept fields dotted with nice forests of pine and fir. The weather was beautiful too: a warm, sunny day. I had a hot shower and changed clothes. Then we had a couple of drinks, a swell dinner with champagne, and then to bed. Honestly, Betty, I've never enjoyed sleeping more. My God, I was tired. Belmore had spread my bedding roll on a good bed in the house where my office is located – box springs with a really good hair mattress on top. I slept for eight hours without moving, the first night in ten that I've had more than five broken-up hours. [102]

"We have made a name for ourselves in the 7th Army," Wheeler boasted on 23 March. "General Patch told [General] Hibbs today that we have done a swell job. Two different corps have been fighting over who is to have us. And if I say so myself, we deserve all the praise we have gotten, and more. Our people fight!" [103]

"I am being awarded the Bronze Star," he informed. "Not for bravery, sweetheart; staff officers aren't required to be; we get them for not falling down dead when things are tighter than a new pair of shoes." [104]

Betty noticed from the pictures Bus sent home that he had lost weight. He responded:

> Yes, darling, I have lost weight. It is more from nervous tension than anything else. The responsibility during operations is terrific; there is always the feeling that something may go wrong. Of course, you can't like the feeling of being shelled either. When you stand and listen to the damned things come in, whistling, it sort of tenses you up a bit. However, sweetheart, you mustn't worry about me for, actually, there is no reason to do so. My job doesn't call for me to lead assaults on pillboxes. I just help to figure out how it can be done. And usually I'm in a nice, safe cellar. [105]

He also updated her on his efforts to reassign her brother Bob to the 63rd:

> As soon as I knew where he was located I called the [7th] Army and asked if it could be arranged. They assured me that if the General would sign the request it was in the bag more or less. I wrote the letter today and he signed it. In fact, he was damn nice about it: he insisted on adding a paragraph saying that he was personally aware of Second Lieutenant Howell's abilities and he particularly desired him in this division. [106]

Wheeler's award ceremony occurred on 26 March. "The General said when he pinned the [Bronze Star] on me that I had performed so many meritorious acts [from 15 February to 22 March] that he didn't know which to choose to cite me for. Modesty is not my failing, sweetheart, as you can tell from the way I have blown my own horn by telling you that!" [107]

## *Central Germany*

The 63rd Infantry Division crossed the Rhine at Neuschloss on 28 March, moved to Viernheim, and captured Heidelberg on the 30th. During its final month of grueling combat, the division would break the back of German resistance while fighting over an exceptionally broad front of several hundred miles of hilly, wooded country with frequent steep ascents, the whole interlaced with rivers and streams running across the division's path. [108]

In early April, Bus described parts of Germany that had yet to experience the ravages of war, through which the division was advancing rapidly.

> This country is very pretty. It is intensively cultivated, very clean and very neat. It is more rugged than I had expected and more wooded in certain areas. ... The houses here are quite nice, even in the smaller towns.

> The small and medium-sized towns are not badly shot up. The contrast between here and Alsace is notable in that respect. Also, I find the people looking healthy and well-fed and (which I suppose I should have expected, but didn't) and much better dressed. As a rule the children are clean, warmly dressed, and pert.

> The populace as a whole is trying to be friendly, at least on the surface. Many of them, no doubt, hate our guts and hide their feelings waiting for the chance to get even. Of course, we have most strict orders regarding fraternization with Germans. However, I foresee a hell of a time enforcing those orders. There are many pretty girls and I have seen them smiling at our GIs and giving every indication of being willing to cooperate. Moreover, there are the small children who, like all kids, are around goggle-eyed to see the soldiers and equipment. In many towns I have seen women and kids waving at our men riding by.

> We continue to progress, rather fluidly since we broke through the Siegfried Line. ... The outfit is red hot, no doubt of that, darling. We have made a real name for ourselves. The [7th] Army staff says very frankly that ours is the best new

division they have ever seen; and far better than they had ever in their wildest dreams hope to see.

One Army staff officer told me yesterday that the two best divisions in 7th Army were the 63rd and an old outfit that has been in every action beginning with the landing in Africa. As a matter of fact that division has had more combat experience than any other division in the entire U.S. Army; it's one I used to serve with a long time ago [the 3rd Infantry Division]. He told me that the general consensus of opinion was that when we had had half the combat experience of the veteran outfit, we'd be twice as good! [109]

Continuing to advance, the 63rd crossed the Neckar River near Mosbach and the Jagst River. Heavy resistance slowed its attack on Adelsheim, Mockmuhl, and Bad Wimpfen. The division then switched front to the southeast, capturing Lampoldshausen and clearing the Hardthauser Woods on 7 April. [110]

After "the spring unwound suddenly in the enemy machine," the division launched "an almost incredible 'pursuit march' through Württemberg and Bavaria," Bus wrote. "[It] harried the broken Germans, who, though definitely withdrawing, turned at bay more than once and even managed savage armored counterattacks." [111]

The general presented ... one of our Lieutenants ... the Silver Star for a very brave and gallant act. A couple of days later he was riding along in his Jeep 5 miles behind our front lines while we were bombing a town just in front of us that was causing us trouble. One of the planes had a bomb jam in the bomb rack, unknown to the pilot. As he came out of his dive, he headed over our lines. A few seconds later the jammed a bomb fell free and struck near the Lieutenant's Jeep. He was killed; his driver wasn't even scratched. I don't know, sweetness, what the score is. I reckon you just die when your time comes in one way or another. [112]

The division secured a bridgehead over the Kocher River near Weissbach, and it took Schwabisch Hall on the seventeenth. [113]

"I'm tired and sleepy as hell tonight," Bus wrote in a letter he started on 8 April. "We have been traveling fast and far (see your newspapers) and the mail hasn't caught up. ... There is literally no news to impart. We're fighting a bit, moving quite a lot, and it is all damned boring, I assure you." [114]

"This portion of Germany is beautiful," Bus continued four days later. "Nothing I saw in France can compare to it. It is far more rugged than I had imagined. In fact it can be characterized as 'big country.' The hills are tremendous, the forests frequent and large." [115]

> The population in this section we have been fighting over it gives me the impression that they are secretly glad that we are here at last. We came in here the day after this town was taken. It was not much harmed; we bombed it a little to loosen up the Krauts, thereby destroying a house or two. Seemingly there is no resentment toward us, at least none that is apparent. Of course, I cannot say how people react in other parts of Germany; I understand that they are a different breed of cat. [116]

## Change of Mission

Advance elements of the 63rd crossed the Rems River and rushed to the Danube, which the division crossed on 25 April. It then took Leipheim and pushed on to Landsberg in the Sauer Valley. Now within sight of the Bavarian Alps, the division was withdrawn from the line on 28 April for security duty and "a much needed rest" in northern Württemberg from the Rhine to Darmstadt and Wurzburg on the line to Stuttgart and Speyer. [117]

When the division's relief was completed at noon on 29 April, it had been in contact with the enemy for 125 days. Having fought across the German frontier, through the Siegfried Line and across the Palatinate, from the Rhine to within sight of the Alps, it had been in the line continuously since 22 December, except for three days between the Siegfried Line breakthrough and the Rhine crossing.

Major General F. W. Milburn, Commanding General, XXI Corps, sent a congratulatory message to Hibbs:

During its operational attachment to this command from 19 to 27 April 1945, the 63rd Infantry Division again, and characteristically, distinguished itself by relentless pursuit of the enemy, by aggressive exploitation of opportunities, and excellent command and staff procedure.

In the numerous towns taken, the rapid advance over difficult terrain, in the capturing of several bridges intact, the officers and enlisted men of the division demonstrated the same initiative, fighting spirit and leadership that were evident in their past performances under this headquarters.

I wish to commend you and all the personnel under your command on a superior performance and on the success of every mission undertaken. [118]

In turn, Hibbs sent a congratulatory message of his own to the division on 1 May:

Blood and Fire, you're getting a break, and a well-earned one, from combat. ... It's been tough going, but a glorious record lies behind you on which you will build more glory for yourselves in the future. ... As the left division of the VI Corps, you fought east from the Rhine over a period of three weeks of continuous day and night combat contact with the enemy[;] during which you seized from the enemy over four-fifths of all ground gained by the VI Corps[;] during which you forced the withdrawal of the 17th SS Panzer Division from the field of battle[;] during which you fought for, seized and held the key bridgehead to terrain which forced the enemy to abandon Heilbronn and the position to its east[;] and during which you, at the end, opened the way for the subsequent rapid drive of the VI Corps to the south. Then, as the right division of the XXI Corps, you continued for a week to fight your way to the south across the Danube. This was a period of combat over wide fronts, rugged terrain, long distances, deep river valleys, great fatigue through sleepless days and nights. ... You have just turned over to the 36th Infantry Division the ground to which you drove, during that last week, 60 miles beyond the Danube River. You have been withdrawn to a noncombat area, there to guard installations while you refit, repair and retrain. ... It marks the beginning of preparations for the next period of combat. These must be done well and promptly. [119]

The future action Hibbs referred to was the anticipated final assault against the Germans' rumored National Redoubt in the Bavarian and Austrian Alps. He intended to give Wheeler command of an infantry regiment for this last operation. [120]

Nazi propaganda had touted the redoubt as a fortified mountain area garrisoned by fanatical SS troops who would fight to the last man. "Rumors of the wildest sort are prevalent everywhere," Wheeler recorded. "It is rather hard to discern what to believe and what to laugh at. Even the wildest tales prove true now and then." [121]

The National Redoubt would prove a phantom, an effective deception that had influenced Eisenhower's decision to restrain American forces from seizing Berlin before the Russians could reach it. [122]

While the division rested, Bus caught Betty up on events. "While the Krauts are very busy trying to save their skins, we have been even busier putting the wood on them. The past two weeks have been a mad house—one of the better rat races!" [123]

"Sweetheart, actually I am very proud of my Bronze Star Medal," he confided. "Didn't mean to low rate myself. Incidentally, the General has put me for the Legion of Merit, too." [124]

Our CP (is) a castle of usable proportions and in very good shape. The place was filled with very beautiful furniture, a number of good paintings, and a most interesting and valuable collection of hunting prints and pictures (engravings) of horses.

So you see, darling, sometimes we do all right for ourselves. Of course, on other occasions we aren't so fortunate. However, since the cellar I lived in just before we broke through the Siegfried Line, things have in general been rather pleasant. And I must admit that I didn't mind the cellar at the time since the Krauts were throwing stuff into our village. The cellar was safer.

I meant to tell you about my trailer. I feel as the General did when he got his van: I'm overwhelmed that the U.S. Army should ever provide anything so nice for a Colonel! This is it—I have a 1-ton trailer which has been built into living quarters. A factory made job from the equivalent of the French Pullman Works. It has a built-in bunk, a wash-stand with running water, mirror, closets, drawers and stor-age compartments by the dozen, an oil stove, a small desk, a bench, electric lights, etc. It is, literally, a hell of a swell job. ... All that I possess in Europe is safely installed, including my radio. So soon as I have a telephone installed, I'm all set. So now, darling, you don't have to worry about the conditions under which I exist. Whether the CP is in a cellar or a castle, I am all set. [125]

## *Victory in Europe!*

By 5 May, it was readily apparent that the Nazis were collapsing rapidly. The 63rd would conduct no more offensive operations, and Wheeler would no longer require his beloved van. He observed:

This war is on its last legs, staggering to a close. It has been obvious that such was the case for the last week. The resis-tance has been spotty and half-hearted and prisoners have been numerous. The bulk of the civilian populace of this area are heartily sick of war; there is actually very little resentment towards the American forces. Part of the attitude is doubtless put on; but numbers of these people—particularly the farm-ers and the petty shopkeepers are happy to have survived the bombings and the battles with a bit of property left them. Some of the strong Nazis we know are still lurking in the background awaiting a chance to knife us in the back.

It makes one angry, though, to think of the band we have had killed and maimed during these last few hopeless (from the military point of view) weeks of fighting. A man killed during the pursuit of a hopelessly beaten enemy is still there, as dead as if he were killed on D-Day on the Normandy beaches.

Of course, there have been lots of Krauts knocked off the past couple of weeks. But, somehow, it doesn't make us feel any kindlier toward the goddamned Nazis who have prolonged the war for their own protection.

Oh, well –CBI [China-Burma-India Theater], here we come! [126]

The following day, after the division command post had relocated once more, Bus wrote:

The weather lately has been terrible; cold, raw, rainy sleet and snow. Today it is still raining but rather warmer. I am getting tired, this time of year, of wearing a heavy jacket and my field overcoat and still freezing to death.

Our CP and billets just now are most comfortable. We have a large hotel in rather a nice town—a health bath in peace times on the order of Hot Springs (only the springs are not hot!) My office is large and light and cold. The officers' quarters are in another, rather smaller place. However, I have a large room with adjoining bath. In the room I have a large double bed of the type the Krauts like. Actually it is two large single beds hooked together. Altogether I'm very comfortable. In fact, the peace and quiet is almost too much for me. [127]

"It seems odd to wake up at five in the morning in a pitch black room (blacked out, of course) and hear absolutely no noise except perhaps the guards on the veranda outside," Bus wrote the following day. "After living with the sound of artillery day and night you seem to expect it. However, I'll probably get used to it. [128]

Bus's thoughts turned to the future. His letters reflect the general assumption that the division would soon redeploy from Europe, transit and reconstitute in the continental United States, and then deploy to the Pacific. The 63rd would not, as Bus later pointed out to Betty, be part of the Army of Occupation in Germany, although the headquarters of both the 3rd and 7th Armies were. [129]

The sands of this war are running out, I think. ... Just what the future holds, I do not know. The CBI, I reckon. Although, even conjecture is fruitless at present. I would like to come home, even if but for a short time, before taking off for China again. Of course, we haven't been gone so very long, but it seems long because I miss you and Bim so very much. And I have the feeling that service in the East may be for a considerable period. The distances there are vast; and while events, from all reports, are leaning in our favor, it may take many months to make our weight felt sufficiently to bring things to a close. [130]

Following the announcement of victory in Europe, Bus wrote:

Well, the goddamned war is over, I reckon—at least in the ETO. There still remains the CBI for us. And, of course, we are very valuable, being fresh too and robust and (if I do say so!) good! ... I was most interested in the attitude of the men. Actually, darling, they were completely apathetic. I was, also; but I expected that there would be a spontaneous outburst of something or other that I would remember to my dying day. There wasn't. Literally, no one was excited, perturbed, upset or—to tell the truth—anything more than interested. I am still examining people to find out why. Of course, we had been in the line so goddamned long that I think anything less than a salvo of 88's left everyone cool and collected (no pun intended). When those babies came in, we all took to the ditches and cellars in complete unison. [131]

"With the war over, I am safe and you don't have to worry about me," he promised. "Not that you ever did—I am a very careful guy!" [132]

## Post-Hostilities

Besides an end to combat operations, victory also brought new perks for the victors, including Wheeler:

I now have a sedan, a brand-new Mercedes-Benz sedan. It is a swell piece of machinery, complete with jump seats, shades and beautiful grey upholstery. We captured it from the Krauts;

I imagine that some German division commander owned it at one time—very recently for it has less than 1,000 kilometers on it when I acquired it. The damn thing approaches a limousine—it has a glass (window) that slides across the rear of the front seat that separates the passenger from the driver. What swank! [133]

An automobile aficionado, Bus was happy to substitute the tactical vehicles he had been getting around in for his new Mercedes.

"This section of Germany is simply lovely," Wheeler wrote. "Today I ran up to a town to inspect and I must say that I was impressed by the cleanliness, the order, and the determination of the Krauts to keep their country as it always has been, a model of order." [134]

He also observed the tremendous post-war repatriation issue:

Every time I travel the roads these days I am impressed (appalled, in fact) at the damage the Germans have done to Europe. One problem alone, displaced persons, is enough to indict them. You must have read of these people, for I know that the situation has been the subject of radio comment and many articles in newspapers and magazines. 'Displaced persons' is the general title given to Russians, Poles, French, Lithuanians, Greeks, Italians, Dutch, Armenians, Czechs, Belgians and God only knows what other nationalities who were imported into Germany for labor. They were the 'slaves' who tilled the fields and worked in the factories while German manpower conquered Europe. Now they are on the loose and we have a real job in corralling them and, eventually, repatriating them.

Some of them—and I am not speaking of released PWs [prisoners of war] or inmates of concentration camps—are in a deplorable state. They try to hurry along the roads to the frontiers—just moving, I think, without any particular reason just because for four or five years they have been forced to remain static. We cannot, of course, have them wandering around. They are a health and security hazard. Hence, a tremendous task of freezing them and thereafter caring for them.

I tell you, darling, the military government lads have taken unto themselves a task that I want no part of. [135] (Wheeler did not know then that two years later he would, in fact, deal with repatriation and other occupation issues as a member of the U.S. Constabulary.)

Commenting upon the Allies' political situation, Bus's letter to Betty on 10 May is the only known self-expression of his conservative political views extant. Army officers were supposed to be apolitical, and smart ones kept their beliefs to themselves. This letter also illustrates his self-effacing nature:

I have not mentioned the death of Mr. Roosevelt as yet in any of my letters. Personally, I regret him; and, I believe, so do many others who are not Democrats—or of any other political belief except American! The problems facing our country are tremendous; in fact, Betty, I find that these people (the Krauts etc.) expect us to straighten out their affairs for them.

Mr. Churchill is a very old man; Mr. Truman—I sincerely hope—has stature to cope with the very heavy problems falling upon him. Europe today is a powder keg with 49 different fuses laid to it. Oh, hell, who am I to worry about these matters. A damn Colonel, GSC [General Staff Corps], who is by nature a 'worrier' and a pseudo-intellectual. Nuts, my sweet! [136]

"It was after midnight (last night) before I got rid of everyone," Wheeler added. "Strangely enough, one would expect business (my affairs) to slack off after hostilities ceased. Actually I am busier than ever although on different matters." [137]

A couple days later, he wrote. "Somehow or other there seems to be very little to write about these days; and yet there should be. I suppose I am suffering a bit of a letdown after the excitement of the past few months." [138]

*Wheeler and two staff officers visit Rohrbach, Germany, 18 May 1945. (Wheeler Family Records).*

Restless, Wheeler enjoyed occasional opportunities to flee the division headquarters:

> I made another inspection trip yesterday afternoon through some of the country we fought over in the last couple of weeks of the war. As I've written you so many times that you are probably bored hearing it, this is as beautiful country as I have ever seen. A golf course with orchards, you might say. The country is hilly and cut by streams through every valley; the hills are big, rounded hogbacks for the most part and are cultivated extensively: vineyards particularly. This section is most fertile and the industry of the population adds to the production and charm. Actually, there are no salvage yards and no dumps. The forests are largely reforestation projects and, being planted, provide a rather pleasing impression of regularity and order. The smaller, country towns are more picturesque when viewed from the top of a ridge; the roofs are all of reddish tile which has weathered in several shades. The houses themselves are large and substantial. But, just as

in France, the peasantry live in the same buildings as their stock and measure their wealth by the size of their manure pile. However, the peasants themselves are clean looking and manage to keep their kids clean also—amazingly so when you see the houses. Speaking of kids, I've never in my born days seen so many. In Germany anyone who has only three or four must be regarded as practically childless.

They are nice-looking brats, too; a high percentage of them are blond and blue-eyed with very fair skins. The women are attractive, too. The young ones are robustly built – ahem! Rather sturdy in the legs, broad in the hips, and well-developed breasts. But no fraternizing! [139]

Bus had big news for Betty about her brother. "I just got word that one Lieutenant Walter R. Howell, Jr., is being transferred to the division. He hasn't arrived as yet—and probably won't for some time." Bus had heard from Betty's father that Bob had been wounded and "that he is having a case of nerves. … I imagine … that the difficulties of travel these days explain the delay, for surely he is out of the hospital by now." [140]

Bus also had big news about his career:

The General gave a small party to the G's, the regimental commanders, the battalion commanders etc., at which he presented some decorations. He very unexpectedly (since I had prepared the list, I knew who was on it) pinned on me the Oak Leaf Cluster to the Bronze Star. … [He also made] very flattering remarks … to the assembled multitude regarding my abilities, performance of duty, etc. [141]

"I have also been recommended for the Legion of Merit," Bus added. "That award is made, however, by [the Theater Commander] so whether I get it or not remains to be seen." [142]

*Wheeler (second from left), Hibbs (center), and Hibbs's personal staff officers, Bad Murgentheim, Germany, Summer 1945. (Wheeler Family Records).]*

Most significantly, Hibbs had also recommended Wheeler for promotion to Brigadier General—for the second time. His memorandum is quoted in its entirety for the tremendous insight it provides into Wheeler's professional qualifications and personal attributes:

> Brilliant officer of maturity well beyond his years, having well-balanced and unusually sound judgment in military matters, administrative and tactical. He has a fine and forceful personality. He has demonstrated superior leadership qualities. He is deft in handling personnel and personal affairs. Deft in handling staff. He is calm, quick and accurate in decision and execution, even in times of stress. Superior qualities of initiative and self-reliance. Professionally highly qualified infantryman who has commanded all units to include the battalion. Physically active, courageous and energetic. Emotionally stable and dependable, and hits in the pinches with promptness and accuracy. He inspires confidence in subordinates and superiors alike. Thoroughly schooled and experienced in all things that concern the infantry division. Strict, effective disciplinarian.

Specialties—the infantry division in all its operations. The operation of staffs. Infantry combat, and the infantry—artillery team. Notable qualities—mature good judgment. Effectiveness under stress. Effectiveness as a disciplinarian. Sound tactical conceptions. High initiative and self-reliance. Inspires confidence. Superior leadership. Achievements—most notable and compelling his performance in a superior manner as Chief of Staff of this division for over two years.

On the list of my subordinate officers arranged in the order which I recommend their promotion, this officer is number one and the list contains two names.

Col. Wheeler's two-years' superior performance as my Chief of Staff covers the whole gamut of division activities and operations, from activation through four months of combat, and his knowledge of the infantry division is therefore detailed and complete in all things that touch it. His professional qualification for superior performance of duty as an Assistant Division Commander is unquestioned. If necessity arose, I could turn over to him command of the division, in combat or out, with full confidence in his successful handling of it for an indefinite period. His record of experience lacks combat command, but this I consider immaterial in view of the fact of the greater weight which attaches to his combat experience as Chief of Staff, which duty has been performed in a superior manner. (I had a definite plan set up to give him command of an infantry regiment so as to place this combat command duty on his record, but the European war collapsed in our faces before the plan could be carried out!)

I have once before recommended Colonel Wheeler's promotion to the grade of Brigadier General at the cost of a Chief of Staff whom I have small hopes of replacing by one of capacity approaching his. I again recommend his promotion. In spite of Colonel Wheeler's youth (which, in fact, I consider an asset rather than otherwise) or any other consideration, I know of no present Assistant Division Commander better qualified for that duty or better able to perform it. It goes without saying that I would be tremendously pleased to have him in my command. Signed, Louis E. Hibbs, Maj. Gen., U.S. Army, Commanding [143]

Bus's candid response to Betty about Hibb's glowing recommendation is equally revealing of his self-image:

The situation being what it is, I don't expect to get [the promotion], at least not this side of the CBI. I got a copy of [it] this morning and, honestly, sweetheart, I felt as if I had better get out and get going. You know that General Hibbs never does anything half-heartedly. He certainly went whole hog on this. As you know, I have a moderately high appreciation of my abilities but he left me sort of breathless—you know, 'high intelligence, profound military knowledge, calmness under stress, leadership, courage, respected by subordinates and juniors alike'—and ended up by saying, 'If needed, I could even turn over command of the division to Colonel Wheeler either in combat or out with perfect confidence that he would handle successfully any situation, however complex, which might arise.'

The letter of recommendation made me feel rather humble, for I ain't that good, honey, much as I'd like to think so. I'm going to get a copy of the letter typed and carry it with me. Then, the next time I get the everlasting hell scared out of me or I'm somewhat up in the air and don't know what to do, I'll pull it out and read it and tell myself, 'Bus you've got to do better than this. See what the General thinks of you!'

When the Division Commander writes the Theater Commander that he thinks you are irreplaceable as a Chief of Staff because no one he knows possesses the same combination of abilities, but advocates your promotion anyway as a benefit to the Army as a whole—well, that's something to live up to. And I will sure as hell try! [144]

On the same day he recommended Wheeler for promotion, Hibbs reminded the soldiers of his division that the war wasn't over:

Victory throughout the rest of the world lies across the Pacific. There next you take your Blood and Fire to settle the account with the Jap. Time's a-wastin' to relearn lost skills, to mold new teammates to the Blood and Fire pattern, to build upon your battle wisdom and to set your eyes on the pay dirt that lies on the other side of the world, where the Jap 'ain't seen nothing yet,' but where you're going to show him and the world the greatest team that ever went into battle! [145]

Hibbs was fighting an uphill battle to keep his soldiers focused against the many distractors of peacetime. "This beautiful spring weather has made me lazy as all get out," Bus admitted. "I hardly have the ambition to move. Spring plus the end of the war has hit the whole damn outfit, in fact." [146]

In mid-May, Wheeler took a three-day pass to Paris for some much needed rest and relaxation:

I drove my Mercedes; Belmore accompanied me, of course. … It was a perfect day and the countryside was lovely with the apple blossoms out, the flowers all over the hillsides and the Krauts pursuing bucolic efforts rather than shooting burp guns and panzerfausts. We stayed the night in Nancy and reached Paris the next afternoon.

They allow you three nights in town. We were put up at the Hotel Louvre, a fairly decent one run by the Red Cross. It is not quite as grand as The Ritz, which is nearby, where I had stayed with the General [in] January.

It was too late by the time we got there to get theater tickets so we went to a dance at the hotel intending to go out later to see the sights of Montmartre. So we did about 11:30 PM and discovered that the MPs closed the hot spots as of 11:00. Nevertheless, it was most interesting. The Place Pigalle … was a madhouse. 'Pig Alley' as the savage Americans call it. The French are completely uninhibited and public lovemaking means nothing to them apparently. Our people adopt the continental custom most readily; our guys and their gals were oblivious to the world in carriages, autos, 'rollos'—a sort of bicycle which pulls a bathtub holding two people—and just standing on street corners or sitting on ledges or leaning against a wall.

After strolling around a while we climbed the mountain which gives the place its name to the Church of the Sacred Heart (I believe that's the name). From the square in front of the church you can get the most marvelous view of Paris. The lights seemed to float in the air below you. The moon was just at quarter but bright; the clouds were thin and scattering, just enough to set off the moon and stars. It was a perfect evening. [147]

"Betty, I don't think I've ever before missed you so much," Bus pined. "I don't like for you not to be with me when I am doing the things that you and I get so much pleasure out of doing together." [148] (Neither of them realized that they would be stationed in Paris the following year.)

After regarding the scene from the terrace we stopped at a little café and had a couple of drinks of something that only a Frenchman can consume. … I was much interested in the people in the place. The four of us were the only Americans present. The rest were very evidently the neighborhood trade and were types straight out of a movie—flowing ties, funny clothes, exotic hairdos and colors running to lavender and greens, open work shoes with no socks, shorts, slacks on one big gal that she must have grown into. In short, Betty just too artsy and Left Bank-ish for words. But most amusing, my sweet.

Next morning we went shopping. … I sent you a pair of silk stockings, darling. You've got to wear them even if they don't fit or if they have a run in them. They cost me 700 francs. They're supposed to be Italian silk and the real thing. Sure wish I could be with you to admire them on you. [149]

Our second evening in Paris we took in the Folies. … The dancing was good, the chorus good-looking, with several very spectacular numbers … complete with naked girls hanging from the chandeliers.

[On the] last evening we went to the Casino. ... The show at the Casino was better than the Folies. I must say that the little pantomimist at the Folies was hard to beat, but the one at the Casino was at least as good. I haven't laughed so hard in years. Of course, it was pretty dirty but it was clever dirt. [150]

To illustrate, Bus retold a joke he had heard:

"Did you hear the story of the 12-year-old lad who was flying to visit his grandparents? He wanted to take his puppy with him so he slipped the little dog down inside his pants. After they had been in the air an hour or so, the stewardess noticed the kid squirming around in his seat in very evident distress. She went to him and asked what was the matter. The kid explained that he had brought his puppy along by hiding him in his pants.

"Oh," the stewardess laughed; "that explains it; your puppy isn't house-broken, is he?"

"He sure isn't, lady," the kid answered; "he isn't even weaned yet!" [151]

Bus summarized his impressions of the Parisian revues: "1) acres and acres of bare bosoms, 2) clever and funny pantomime of the bedroom variety. Knowing me, you realize that I thoroughly enjoyed the shows!"

The second afternoon we took a rubberneck tour around Paris. It was quite enjoyable. Some of the places such as the tomb of Napoleon, etc. I had seen [in] January. However, I got a good view of the church of Notre Dame de Paris and had the wherefores of the Louvre explained to me. We were quartered near there in the Hotel Louvre so I went back next morning and walk through the gardens. The museum is open.

[The] next morning I spent walking. It was marvelous, no less. A most beautiful day in a most interesting city.

That afternoon we drove out to Versailles. It was most interesting although the bulk of the paintings, furnishings, and statuary which were removed by the French in 1940 had not yet been replaced. Nevertheless, I enjoyed the drive and the gardens. They are simply tremendous. ... Remarkable place.

Must have been hell to live in though—like living in Grand Central Station. [152]

Bus had requested the transfer of Betty's brother to the 63rd Infantry Division two-and-a-half months earlier. When he finally reported in, wounded and possibly suffering from post-traumatic stress disorder, Bus reported:

> [Bob] looks pretty good; he is quite sad and seems to be more nervous than before, if biting his fingernails is any criterion. He has a scar that runs above his left temple back into his hair. He tells me that the wound in his back was very slight; however, he became infected, which I think is the reason he got out of the convalescent hospital only on the 16th day. He spent last night here with me and I sent him down to [Colonel] Bose's regiment [in Tauberbischofsheim] after lunch today. [153]

"No news to speak of," Bus wrote three days later. "Just the same old grind—mounds of papers, much talk of points for discharge, or talk of return to the States. I have 97 points myself—or will if I am awarded the Legion of Merit. Of course, that is a matter purely of academic interest insofar as I am concerned. I still have 17 years to do before I can retire [with 30 years of service]." [154]

A change in weather the following day lifted his spirits. "This is a beautiful day. I appreciated it all the more because it is the first after several days of gloomy, miserable weather. This is the sort of day that makes you feel glad that you're alive; the sun and the air seemed to go." [155]

Bus was, as previously stated, a voracious reader. He now found some time to indulge his interest:

> I have started in to read *Lee's Lieutenants*; and beginning with volume 1 because I never really sat down at leisure and read it with my mind devoted fully to the task. In reading the forward, I was somewhat startled to find how much I agree with some of Dr. Freeman's comments on the qualifications for high command. I realize that my opinions have been crystallized by what I have seen and done here in the ETO, for I always leaned to the opinion that proper administration and

appreciation of logistics are the bedrock upon which tactics must be based. Now I know that from experience as well as from logic and textbooks. [156]

The headquarters of the 63rd Infantry Division had relocated to the "nice little town" of Bad Murgentheim on the Tauber River.

> It is a resort town; 'bad' means 'bath', I believe. This place is noted for its sulfur baths and springs. Kaiser Wilhelm used to frequent the place. As a result the town is lousy with doctors (now departed with the Wehrmacht mostly), sanatoriums (private) and several nice hotels, two of which we use as a CP and officers' quarters. [157]

*Wheeler on balcony of commanding general's quarters, Bad Murgentheim, Germany, Summer 1945. (Wheeler Family Records).*

Wheeler shared a large house with Hibbs on the side of one of the high hills overlooking the town and the Tauber Valley:

> It [is] a really lovely place [and] has a marvelous garden built on terraces cut into the hillside; the living room, music room, dining room, and a small drawing room are very nice indeed:

large rooms with tremendous windows. From the dining room the establishment opens onto a paved portico, thence into the gardens. Upstairs we have only one nice suite which the general occupies. However, my room is nice enough, though small, as are those of the two aides. The third floor has three or four bedrooms, and the basement as many more for servants. We have the mess personnel for General Hibbs's mess living there. Also, we have rounded up three Latvian housemaids and two gardeners. In fact, we have an establishment—or should it be called a ménage? [158]

"We are more than comfortable. The wine is good, plentiful, and cheap. The food ain't bad at all," he continued. "But despite all that, I miss you, sweetness, more than I care to write; and much, much more than I care to think about. So I won't!" [159]

Three days later, he wrote, "I am busy, very busy; but the stuff is piddling and inconsequential compared to the rather stark realities of combat. I think perhaps I'm suffering the let down now, a sort of delayed reaction. ... I am feeling in the dumps today." [160]

Bus's spirits rose again the following week. "The weather continues to be good and the countryside is correspondingly beautiful. I would like to be lying up on our sun deck sopping up some rays instead of being holed up in this office, but I am expecting a high powered gent from Army to heave in and heckle me." [161]

I have been feeling very well these days. My few hours in the sun have browned me up a bit—not nearly as black as (your letter) says you and Bim have become, but not bad. As time permits, I intend to get more, particularly on my legs and middle. The latter, by the way, is a bit slimmer than when you last saw me. My trousers have several pleats on them, and my contour is correspondingly less than of a field officer. I don't regret the pounds, but I believe my hair is a little thinner, too; and I discovered a gray hair the other day in my sideburns. Guess I'm collapsing slowly—or should I say 'relapsing'— into middle age. [162]

He also reported:

> We are getting ready to celebrate (the 63rd Infantry Division's) Activation Day. I suppose we'll be able to have our usual field meet. Now, of course, it is more than ever important to provide some good entertainment for our people. So far, our Special Services Officer has done well in obtaining a number of live shows as well as movies. But we could use even more. The one great drawback to providing the works is a lack of females. And as long as we are in Germany, I suppose the article will remain in 'critical short supply' as the quartermasters say. [163]

His letter to Betty written a week before their 13th anniversary is the most intimate of all his wartime letters and is worth quoting at length, for it well-illustrates the depth of devotion and mutual high regard that underpinned their marriage:

> You seem to be worried about whether I would prefer my leave (when I get home!) in New York or Natchez. I honestly think we should leave that in the laps of the gods, sweetness. As long as I'm away, I want you to be where you are happiest. If it is Natchez, swell; if it is Connecticut, that's swell, too. Or perhaps you're going to want to change about from time to time. I know one thing, Betty, when I get home (and I won't even make a wild guess as to that) I'll be happy and satisfied and have a good time wherever you are. I don't need excitement, or plays, or anything else. I've had quite a bit of the first! What I need is domesticity in large doses. In the years that we've been married, you haven't made a model husband of me by a long shot, darling, but you have certainly succeeded in making a happy and convinced one (meaning convinced that I am not happy when I'm away from you.)
>
> It's all your fault, too, because I am not sure that, if I had been so unfortunate as to marry someone else, I would have been happy, contented or even very nice about it. That is why I love you more all the time. I've heard you laugh because I told you that you are nice to me. Well, by God, you always have

been nice to me; and I do appreciate it. You don't nag me; you listen to me even when I'm talking about myself; you have perfectly beautiful children (one anyway!); you remain the beautiful Ms. Howell even after these years (and you know how I love pretty women); you are smart and intelligent—in fact, darling, if I were not madly in love with you already, I'd fall in love with you at first sight. It would be nice if that sight were not too long delayed!

I've tried not to write you letters telling you how much I miss you because I was afraid that I'd depress you and make you unhappy. But, Betty, I don't mind what you write me. When you want to blow off a bit of steam about your ma', or say that you miss me, go ahead; I love it. If anything, it makes me feel closer to you because I feel that you are telling me what you really think and feel, rather than just writing a letter to amuse me. As you know, I am interested, as always, about everything that concerns you—house, clothes, friends, and incidents. In fact, gal, the more I think of it, I honestly must be in love with you! [164]

On the day of their anniversary, he gushed:

Thirteen years is a long time when you sit down and count them one by one. In retrospect, thirteen years isn't long at all. At least, the years that we have been married have gone very quickly. When you're happy, of course, time slips away; and that is what has happened to us. (Can I say 'us' rather than 'we'?) [165]

"I have been working hard all day," he continued. "The paper is certainly flying around Germany since V-E Day. For once, I honestly didn't mind putting in ten hours at my desk, for I have been a bit depressed all day and I did not want my mind to wander off to the United States and you." [166]

I've been thinking of you—and Bim— so damned much today that I'm all bound up inside and my thoughts are bouncing around like the keys on a mechanical piano. Dearest, I love you so very much indeed; and I miss you so very much. I wish that I could count the days until I see you again; but, unfortunately, that is impossible. Tonight I think I shall go down to our officers club, get myself slightly high, and spend the evening crying in my beer.

Well, we are getting into the sixth month now. That my sweet, has been a long, long time. Now that we have stopped (fighting), it gets longer every day—meaning that the days themselves dragged by. Nothing like a bit of shooting to make you unperceptive of time, space, and place! [167]

The 63rd Infantry Division celebrated the second anniversary of its activation on 15 June:

We moved about one-third of the outfit here to Bad Murgentheim and had a field day—track events, military events, baseball games, etc. That night we threw a buffet supper and dance at our club. It was most successful – 60! count 'em 60! beautiful nurses attended. I had sent scouts out all over southern Germany to all the hospitals we could find and so, with a little effort, we arranged a swell evening. A group of 10 coming from one outfit actually appeared in evening dresses. Officers swooned at the sight. Women who spoke English and wore dresses, not uniforms! Boy, oh, boy! [168]

Bus ran into his brother-in-law at the club. "Bob is in good spirits and is looking better already. ... He is palling around with a couple of Lieutenants from his company. He tells me that he is getting along in fine shape. I think that he is, too; he looks much better than when he came to us." [169]

Meanwhile, Bus was still shouldering a heavy load:

I have been stuck at this damn desk lately. Efficiency reports, decorations and awards, and other poop sheets have come in in a perfect flood. I can put in 14 hours a day with no perceptible lowering of the stack. I have been checking all decorations and awards myself in an effort to get some citations written which cover the man's deeds and please the General. Seemingly, no one in this damned division can write a grammatical sentence. You should see some of them! [170]

Realizing that Wheeler needed a break as much as he did, Hibbs directed him to accompany him to the French Riviera for a week of R&R leave. Bus was conflicted about going, but did not protest strongly:

> It sounds swell to me even though I feel a bit selfish, having already been to Paris. A bit of sunshine while lying on the beach will be highly enjoyable. ... I have been after [the General] for a month to take a break. The other day he agreed to go but said that I have to go also. It's hard to take! Actually, I don't give a damn. My trip to Paris fixed me up -- financially, too. Still they tell me that Cannes is the best deal in all Europe, so I reckon we will have a good time. ... Actually, I don't suppose that I should go; there is a hell of a lot of work to do here. But I suppose somehow or other things will get along just as well. If I broke a leg, they'd have to do their own work anyway. [171]

A few sun-drenched days after flying down to Cannes, Bus enthused:

> No fooling, darling, this place has Paris skinned a mile. I feel better than I have in months. Literally, I have nothing to think about—just eat, drink, and sleep. It's swell. [172]

> The pace around here is terrific. ... We get up in the morning about 8:00, have a leisurely breakfast, and leave in time to drive to Eden Roc by 10:00. Eden Roc is an appendage of the Hotel Du Cap, the one that we were slated to stay at on arrival. It has a beach—without any sand whatsoever. However, they have a pool, floats, ... a snack bar (and bar), dressing rooms, etc. The water is a beautifully clear, clear green. I've been lying on a mat in the sun, then taking a plunge, then the sun, etc. until I am tanning nicely. We get back to the Villa by 12:30, have a couple of drinks, then eat. The food has been marvelous, by the way. In the afternoon we read, nap, or just sit. Cocktails are served promptly at 6:30; dinner at 7:30. The General and I have been taking one car out at night and have gone cruising along La Croissettte, which is the boulevard that skirts the harbor. We drop in at one or another of the

nightclubs for a drink and then home by 12:00 or 1:00. The aides, of course, take off. [173]

On 3 July, Hibbs's entourage began the long drive back to Bad Murgentheim. "We have had ourselves a really swell vacation," Bus wrote. "So swell, in fact, that I am tired out. It'll take me a week to recover. The General is in fine fettle -- so am I. ... I must say that this has been a marvelous vacation. As the General says, 'this happens only once a war'!" [174]

Bus wrote from Genoa, Italy:

> We are traveling through a very beautiful country. Yesterday afternoon we came along the Italian Riviera. Very barren, steep mountains that come up out of the sea, with the road winding back and forth around the headlands. Monte Carlo is most attractive. Seemingly, it was untouched by the war. The hotels and villas are extremely lovely. [175]

From Verona, he described:

> If I were to give a thumbnail sketch of Italy it would be: scenery, dirt, priests, and Italians. The scenery is truly superb. In fact, I cannot recall ever seeing a grander country. It is, however, bleak and largely uncultivated. Having seen it, it is easy to understand why Italy is relatively a poor country. [176]

"Maybe someday, sweetheart, we can do some of this [vacation] together and really have ourselves a time," Bus suggested. "It would be great fun to take you from Marseille to Munich and then down to Cannes. Heigh-ho! I can dream, can't I?" [177] (His wish would come true six years later when they were stationed in Italy.)

Crossing the Brenner Pass from Italy into Austria, he noted:

> Our drive today was most interesting. Of course, mountains covered with snow, mountain meadows covered with wildflowers, mountain brooks are the same all over the world. One new feature though were the vineyards which covered every square inch of usable soil. Much of the ground is no good. And the mountains are so precipitous that most of them can be used only to put castles and monasteries on. They have done that. [178]

The area had been heavily damaged during the war:

I was interested to see how thoroughly many of the towns had been liberated. ... The towns in Italy and Austria were well flattened, particularly near railroad lines, terminals, and freight yards. The same was true of the highway itself—which, incidentally, is very good. One freight yard we passed was as nice a (bombing) job as I've seen in Europe. Very evidently the bombers caught an ammunition train in the yards. Everything for several miles was literally standing on end. At one point the bombs had actually changed the course of the river which runs south into Italy. It must've been tough bombing too. The mountains are very high and the pass is quite narrow and winding.

What we saw explains most graphically what happened to the Krauts toward the end of the war. They couldn't move supplies south nor could they move their Italian armies north to face us when we jumped into the Siegfried Line in March. I'm damn glad they couldn't. It was tough enough as it was.

The party toasted the Allies' victory. "We lunched today in the Brenner Pass on K-rations, champagne, with vermouth aperitifs. Mussolini and Hitler probably turned over in their graves." [179]

"After a most exhausting day's run," they arrived back at division headquarters late the following night:

In a way, after the splendor in which we lived at Cannes, it is rather nice to be back home on the Tauber River. The hills at sunset are as beautiful as ever; the grain is getting ripe so that the fields have long strips of gold cutting through them: a new feature that was nonexistent when we left for France. [180]

*Major General Louis Hibbs presents Wheeler the Legion of Merit, Bad Murgentheim, Germany, 13 May 1945. (Wheeler Family Records).*

On 13 July, Wheeler was awarded the Legion of Merit. The citation read:

> For exceptionally meritorious conduct in the performance of outstanding services as Chief of Staff, 63rd Infantry Division for the period of 2 January -14 February 1945 and from 23 March - 28 April 1945. Colonel Wheeler coordinated the efforts of the division staff with vigor, imagination and outstanding professional skill. His unflagging efforts and military abilities contributed directly to the success of the combat operations of the division during this period when the 63rd Infantry Division invaded Germany, pierced the Siegfried Line and thereafter in a series of fast-moving actions smashed every enemy force opposing them. [181]

"It is quite a gaudy medal," Bus confessed. "I feel like a Russian field marshal every time I look at it." [182]

The following day, he laid out for Betty the several possibilities for his future:

> Any one of several things can happen to me: (a) I can stay with the division; (b) I can be sent direct to the CBI; (c) I can be sent to another outfit which will (1) go back through the States to the Pacific, or (2) stay here in the Occupation Forces.

As long as the General stays (a) is the probability, for it is most unusual take the Chief of Staff of an outfit without the CG's consent. General Hibbs has told me that he will oppose any attempt to take me unless it is obviously to my advantage, i. e., Chief of Staff of a Corps or something of the sort. If (a) holds, I will see you sometime in the foreseeable future. Of course, if the General goes elsewhere, I will go with him if it is humanly possible. Let's not think about (b). If (c) (1) occurs I'll be seeing you; if (c) (2)—well, I don't know when I'll rejoin you sweetness. Not too long, I hope—either here or there. [183]

Wheeler's future was very much still up in the air in the middle of July:

Things here are a hell of a mess. I am much afraid that I will be redeployed clear out of the division. It would be a terrible blow to me to leave General Hibbs. I am hanging on in the hope that we will get a bite on one of several lines we have out. Of course, if he can get another assignment it will be perfect, then I'll go right along with him. [184]

"The paperwork is stacking up higher and higher, day by day," Bus reported. "It is most discouraging. Just when I think that I have cleaned my desk Sgt. Pollard wheels in another stack." [185]

Betty was envious of his trip to Cannes:

Darling, I don't blame you. ... In fact, I regretted the whole time that you could not be there with me because we would have had FUN! High-ho! Our next vacation will be in the States somewhere. And, Mrs. Wheeler, I expect that that will be FUN!! In fact, dear, I feel that just being with you again is about the nicest thing I can ever hope for. [186]

Upon the six-month anniversary of the division's deployment overseas, Belmore sewed a gold service stripe on Wheeler's combat jacket. "Only six months have gone by ... but it seems much, much longer," Bus reflected. [187]

He was still working through the backlog of paperwork two weeks after his trip to Cannes. "Yesterday was one hell of a day. I sat at this desk up to my ears all day. Nothing that I would call too important, just an awful lot of it. The war is over, so everyone is writing poop." [188]

Having made a name for himself with the 7th Army headquarters, Wheeler was a sought-after officer:

> The General saved me today from a job which would have kept me in Germany for a least another year, probably longer. A narrow escape! He happened to fly down to Army Headquarters this morning to see General Haislip and in the course of conversation mentioned that he intended to keep me with him. Whereupon General Haislip said that he himself had a job for me and had intended of grabbing me off. But that he would refrain in view of General Hibbs's desires. [189]

> Of course, what [General Hibbs and I] both want is to go to the CBI. I've almost got to do so if I am to get anywhere. The General said last night that he had hoped that I would be promoted. Personally, I don't believe there is a chance of that in this theater now that the war has folded. Had the recommendation gone in a month earlier I might have got it—but not now. [190]

When Hibbs was selected to serve as the Commandant of the U.S. Army Field Artillery School at Fort Sill, Oklahoma, Bus informed Betty:

> The General is coming home, and shortly thereafter, unless something most dire happens, I will too. He insists that he will get a spot for me with him, and I am sure that he will do so. How will you like having a nice set of quarters on a permanent post again? [191]

On 22 July, Wheeler escorted Hibbs to the division airstrip and saw him off on the first leg of his journey home. Earlier that morning, a farewell formation was held for the General in front of the division C. P. with a company from each subordinate unit. "It was very affecting—and effective," Bus reported. The previous evening, "the senior commanders and staff officers of the old guard" held a dinner party for him. Wheeler reflected:

> I feel as if a chapter in my life is at last finished. And, I must admit, that I feel quite depressed about it. The associations

here in the division have been most pleasant -- in fact, more than that. 'Inspiring' is a better word. We have gone through some mighty tough places together; I have seen more courage, loyalty, devotion to duty, and hard, and intelligent work than I thought the human race capable of. Of course, without the things I name we would never have been as successful and never have achieved a combat record that we did. [192]

With Hibbs gone and the division's two other general officers away, Wheeler served as "Division Commander, pro tem" on 23-29 July:

Since there is a provision of regulations that officers of the General Staff cannot command troops, we issued an order relieving me from the G. S. C. and returning me to the infantry. I then signed a general order assuming command of the division. My first experience doing that! Maybe I'll do it again someday. [193] (He would, thirteen years later.)

Despite the additional responsibilities of commanding the division, "days here are very much the same," he wrote. "By which I mean they sort of merge over into the other. The only change is an occasional storm. I must admit that this life gets damn monotonous. I should hate like sin to become an Army of Occupation hero. The CBI is more better yet!" [194]

Now that I am in command, I find that I am just as bad off as before. Of course, I'm acting as my own Chief of Staff, hence I am just doing two jobs. The papers are piled up mountain high. I've been at this damned desk all day, talking to people and in the interims between callers frantically throwing paper in every direction. [195]

*Jack Benny (far right), Ingrid Bergman (second from left), Martha Tilton (center front), Larry Adler, Dave Le Winter, and other USO performers with Wheeler (center rear), 63rd Infantry Division headquarters, Bad Murgentheim, Germany, late July 1945. (Wheeler Family Records).*

A diversion in late July, musician and funny man Jack Benny and his troupe of travelling performers arrived in Bad Murgentheim "on rather short notice" to put on a USO show for the troops. [196] Accompanying Benny was the beautiful Swedish actress Ingrid Bergman, star of the 1942 movie *Casablanca*. Martha Tilton, Larry Adler, and pianist Dave Le Winter were the other performers. Wheeler invited the group to stay with him in the Commanding General's quarters.

> Benny and the other men had dinner in one of the E. M. [enlisted men] messes; the gals were pooped out: they had given one show that day and had driven 125 miles. We didn't return from the show [for the 63rd] until nearly 10 o'clock. I served drinks and a buffet supper. All went off very nicely. Adler and Le Winter played the piano and sang. Bergman sang (not very well). Benny played his violin (extremely well!).

Bergman, by the way, is an extremely handsome, big girl (about 5'8", I'd say). She is a personality type and better looking in the flesh than on the screen. [197]

Bus also mentioned that "Bob … enjoyed himself immensely." He had recently moved his brother-in-law to the division headquarters to serve as an assistant athletic officer. [198]

What Bus did not share with Betty is that when Bob stopped by Bus's room to say goodnight, he found Bus and Bergman, both in their pajamas and bathrobes, enjoying a nightcap. Although Bus certainly appreciated Bergman's beauty and charm, it is unlikely that he engaged in any improprieties with her. This assumes, of course, that she found his looks and charm equally attractive, as most women did. [199] On the contrary, he was very self-disciplined and completely devoted and loyal to Betty, to whom he'd recently written:

> I agree with your choice of phrases. I, too, need a 'congenial companion' -- and who could that be? No one but you, sweetheart, as we both well know. The trouble is you have made these thirteen years too pleasant. I can't forget how much fun we have had together. I also think of how much fun we're going to have together when I come home. [200]

Bus was also deeply concerned about her health. Betty was then dealing with a potentially life-threatening medical issue, and he did not want to give her any reason for concern.

As previously mentioned, the couple had long had fertility issues. Betty recently suffered a miscarriage, perhaps not her first. As a Christian Scientist, she had always been loath to visit the doctor, but her lingering "feminine" issues could no longer be ignored. She saw an OB/GYN doctor in New Orleans and underwent surgery around 18 July. She convalesced there over a week. The couple had wanted to try again for a girl after the war. Without Bus there, Betty was now facing the reality that they would have no more children. He tried to console her:

> I understand perfectly that you are feeling horribly depressed and entirely out of sorts with the world at having this happen to you. On the other hand, darling, I think it most fortunate that you have gone to good doctors and have ascertained

what it is, and has been, causing you so much misery. Had you suffered along with it much longer, no doubt it would have gone into a chronic stage. That would be bad. [201]

He gently admonished her, too:

From what you write, I gather that you must be very careful of yourself from some time to come. Okay! Be careful. You have always had a tendency to disregard your aches and pains and to carry on regardless of discomfort. You must stop that practice. As I look at it, the next few months are going to influence profoundly your physical well-being for the rest of your life. Therefore, you must—simply must, Betty—do exactly as Dr. Altenberger instructed you down to the last iota—corset and all!

I don't think I need a new model; the old model just needs a bit of first echelon maintenance. And you're the only one who can do that maintaining, sweetheart. Take care of yourself for me. After all, despite the time that we have been separated, you still belong to me. I won't permit you to mistreat and run down my property!

Darling, I'm so damn sorry that you have been miserable. The hell of it is that I can do nothing about it whatsoever—except offer good advice. Which, I may add, Mrs. Wheeler, I expect you to follow.

Your news today makes me even more impatient to come home and see you and learn for myself how you are getting along. … Darling, I close with the admonition to be careful—and patient—and to follow exactly what the medicos have told you to do—even if it irks you. All this will work out in the long run if you will do that. [202]

In a separate letter, Bus charged his five-year old son to look after his mother:

Dear Bim, the doctors have told Betty that she must not carry things or stoop down. Since I am not there to remind her to be careful, I expect you to tell her for me. Otherwise, she is likely to get sick, and that would be terrible, wouldn't it? ... Remind Betty that I will be angry if she picks up things or carries things around. [203]

Bus sent letters and occasional presents to his son. One package Bim received contained a toy German bomber made of plaster of paris. It had broken during shipment, so Betty helped him glue it back together. Bus also sent him a German child's gas mask. In one letter he included a picture of his jeep, on whose windshield frame Belmore had stenciled "BIM" in big, white letters. [204]

After a week of pulling double duty while in command of the 63rd, Bus confided, "I am so damned tired tonight -- tired of sitting at that desk and working on papers. ... This has been a week indeed. I've been extremely busy; with the CG gone ... I have been doing a hell of a lot of work. Nothing important, you understand; but it all takes time." [205]

Bus had never had time or interest for golf, tennis, or other sports. He loved to hunt and fish, however. Having frequently mentioned to Betty what terrific game lands this part of Germany featured, he went out as often as he could. (A frequent hunting companion during his later tour with the U.S. Constabulary would be Artillery officer Lieutenant Colonel Berton "Bert" E. Spivy, Jr. Twenty years later, Wheeler, as Chairman of the Joint Chiefs of Staff, would appoint Spivy as the Director for Plans and Policy (J-5) on the Joint Staff. In April 1967, Wheeler would promote Spivy to Director of the Joint Staff.) [206]

Wheeler may have expected his workload to lighten after the division's two Brigadier Generals returned, but it didn't. "I am tired as hell in consequence of a full day at my desk poring over papers," he wrote several days later. "In fact, I've acquired a headache from too much reading. Nothing, however, that a good night's sleep won't cure." [207]

The generals' return brought new challenges. "[The Acting Division Commander, Brigadier] General [Frederick M.] Harris is driving me nuts. He seems to confuse me with his aides, among other things. Suppose I should not criticize; instead, I should be thankful that I have been so fortunate in the past in my commanders." [208]

With Hibbs departed for the States, Wheeler's plan to rejoin his benefactor seemed in doubt. "[7th] Army is making passes at me; and something else is in the wind which I don't like the sound of," he wrote at the beginning of August. "I am waiting most impatiently for some information from General Hibbs." [209]

Bus was homesick for his family and ready to get home:

> Darling, I do hope your armor plate [corset] is helping you. Although you did not say so explicitly, I gather that you are miserable on your return from New Orleans. Please get some rest and otherwise take care of yourself. I cannot express how it affects me to learn that you are ill -- if not actively -- at least suffering the inconvenience and pain despite being able to move around. ... A kiss and a hug for Bim. And for you, sweetness, all the love there is in the world.– Buster [210]

The 63rd Infantry Division's preparations for redeployment to the Asia-Pacific Theater and the invasion of Japan were obviated by the Japanese capitulation on 15 August. The division would be inactivated on 27 September at Camp Myles Standish, Massachusetts. [211]

Credited with participation in the Ardennes-Alsace, Rhineland, and Central Europe campaigns, the division had rendered an enviable combat record during the war. Subordinate units earned three Distinguished Unit Citations, and one member of the division was awarded the Medal of Honor. [212]

As the division's Chief of Staff, Wheeler had helped direct and support its combat operations that halted the German drive in Alsace-Lorraine, breached the Siegfried Line, seized Heidelberg, and crossed the Danube River. Over the two years encompassing the division's pre-deployment, combat, and post-hostility periods, he had developed invaluable experience with issues of higher command, including especially strategy, administration, and logistics management. [213]

A staff officer who had served under Wheeler in the 63rd, Brigadier General (Retired) Arch Hamblen, recalled in 1975:

> He embodied all the good virtues we each individually seek. We ... knew ... he was *the real guiding light* to each of our

destinies. All of us knew that Bus was the one behind all the success our division achieved.

I was more fortunate than many for I not only worked directly for him for awhile at Camp Van Dorn, Mississippi, but I was near him on several of my assignments. He was always so kind, so supportive, so cheerful with me. If anyone has ever truly embodied the West Point motto 'Duty, Honor, Country', he did.

It has been said that a good beginning is half the battle won. So in my case, it was the great beginning that Bus gave me in the 63rd Division that did so much to motivate me in my Army career, resulting in my promotion to Brigadier General. [214]

*For the second time in late August 1945, Wheeler assumed temporary command of the 63rd Infantry Division. On 1-12 September, he served as Acting Assistant Division Commander, Bad Murgentheim, Germany. (Wheeler Family Records).*

While the division's subordinate units began redeploying to the States in late August, Wheeler again assumed temporary command of it for two, three-day periods. On 1-12 September, he served as Acting Assistant Division Commander. He had been waiting for orders to rejoin Hibbs at Fort Sill. They eventually came through, but he would not depart Europe until October. [215]

# CHAPTER 3

## POST-WAR YEARS
## (OCTOBER 1945 – NOVEMBER 1952)

### *Demobilization*

After Japan's surrender, the public, Congress, and the troops upset War and Navy Department plans for an orderly demobilization process. The Army felt the greatest pressure and released half of its 8 million troops by the end of 1945. However, in early 1946, the Army slowed the return of troops from abroad to meet its overseas responsibilities.

Throughout the demobilization, about half of the Army's diminishing strength remained overseas, the bulk of which with the occupation of Germany and Japan. The Army also maintained a significant force in the southern portion of the former Japanese colony of Korea and smaller forces in Austria and the Italian province of Trieste.

The Army would become a volunteer body of 684,000 ground troops and 306,000 airmen by 30 June 1947. It would still be large for a peacetime army, but the loss of capable maintenance specialists would result in a widespread deterioration of equipment. Active Army units, understrength and infused with barely trained replacements, represented only shadows of the efficient organizations that they had been at the end of the war. [1]

### *Fort Sill*

Wheeler returned to the States in October 1945. After several weeks of leave, he reported to Fort Sill, Oklahoma on 5 December. There, he rejoined his wartime benefactor Hibbs and served as an instructor at the Field Artillery School's Department of Combined Arms. [2]

### 1946

Hibbs had already awarded Wheeler the Legion of Merit and two Bronze Star Medals for separate periods of his two-year tour as the Chief of

Staff of the 63rd Infantry Division. Now, he retroactively awarded him an Army Commendation Ribbon "for his superior performance of duty and exceptional achievement as Chief of Staff … from 15 June 1943 to 30 November 1944," a period not covered by his previous awards. [3]

Betty was intrigued by Bus's tales of Europe. He had loved almost everything about it, except for being without his family. Europe had become the new frontline as tensions rose between the Western Allies and the Soviet Union. Bus determined to seek an accompanied tour there. As a well-connected "team man" with a stellar reputation as a staff administrator, he soon got his wish. [4]

Upon the conclusion of Wheeler's tour with the Field Artillery School, Hibbs awarded him a second Army Commendation Ribbon on 13 May 1946. [5]

### *Paris*

Just eight months after departing Europe, Wheeler returned. Assigned to the European Command's Western Base Section in Paris, he served as its Assistant Chief of Staff, G-4 for six weeks, Acting Chief of Staff for ten more, and then its Deputy Chief of Staff, Operations until 31 December. [6]

Shipping to move U.S. military dependents to Europe was severely restricted, so when Bus departed in May, Betty and Bim moved in with her parents in Old Greenwich to await travel orders. [7]

Finally receiving them in November, they embarked on the ship *General Ballou*. It was a perilous crossing. In the ship's wild pitching and rolling, passengers going down the hall walked up on the wall and back down on the deck. They held onto their plates so that they wouldn't slide off the table. Betty had to secure six-year old Bim to his bunk with several leather waist belts. Bus was informed of the possibility that his dependents could be lost at sea. [8]

Happy to be safe on dry land again, the weary Wheelers were met by an Army Lieutenant, who escorted them to Paris. The family's new quarters were in a castle-like chateau in Vaucresson, a suburb of Paris. Wheeler's aide, Captain Junior LaPointe, had obtained the huge house for them to share with the family of Brigadier General Charles "Charlie" Rich, his overbearing wife (also named Betty), and their two young daughters.

This proved to be a "marriage made in hell," as Betty Rich was most unpleasant and domineering. During the war, Charlie kept a French mistress, who may either have been the cause or effect of his wife's ill humor. Betty Rich ruled the roost and forbid any of the children downstairs after dinner. She also had the only privately-owned automobile, which she never let Betty Wheeler borrow, nor did she ever give her a ride anywhere.

"It was the hardest thing I had ever been through in my entire life," Betty Wheeler recalled. (Seventeen years later, a warm and most gracious Betty Rich would escort Betty Wheeler around Fort Benning while Bus attended to business there as the Chief of Staff of the Army.) [9]

The winter of 1946-47 was one of the coldest in recent history. The Europeans suffered greatly from shortages of coal and food. Even U.S. military dependents were subject to rationing. No antifreeze was available, except for use in military vehicles. For those fortunate to own automobiles, the answer was vodka, which was available in copious quantities at U.S. military "Class Six" stores.

During a Christmas party in the chateau, the alcohol ran out sometime in the wee hours of the morning. LaPointe simply went outside to his jeep, which had been "civilianized" with the addition of an aluminum cab, drained the radiator of its vodka, and the party continued. [10]

The U.S. Army had a long tradition of hard drinking that continued through the Postwar Period. Bus drank frequently like most of his contemporaries but was always controlled. He preferred scotch, while Betty liked wine. Both enjoyed very dry martinis before dinner, even while dining alone. They drank beer during warmer months. [11]

At the racetrack, Bus once made a friendly bet with six-year old Bim on whose horse would win. With his horse in the lead, he mocked Bim's pick. The track had a small bridge for the horses to cross, and Bim predicted that his dad's horse would stumble on the bridge and that his horse would win. To his delight and Bus's chagrin, that's exactly what happened. [12]

## 1947

As tensions rose with the Soviet Union over the occupation of Germany, Wheeler longed to get closer to the action. He received orders to join Major General Ernest Harmon's staff of the prestigious U.S. Constabulary shortly after the new year. Recognizing Wheeler's seven months of service with the European Command, the French government awarded him the Legion of Honor in the grade of Chevalier on 8 January 1947. It was the first of many foreign decorations he would eventually receive. [13]

*A French general awards Wheeler the Legion of Honor for his service with the European Command's Western Base Section, Paris, France, 8 January 1947. (Wheeler Family Records).*

## *National Security Act*

Wheeler's return to Europe had occurred against the backdrop of efforts by senior civilian and military officials in Washington to reorganize the nation's national security system to cope with a changed world. The three-year debate culminated with the passage of the National Security Act of 1947.

This act created a National Security Council (NSC) and a loosely federated National Military Establishment. The latter was not an executive department of the federal government, although a civilian Secretary of Defense with cabinet rank headed the organization. Only a minimal number of civilians assisted him in coordinating the Armed Services. The Air Force became a separate Service equal to the Army and Navy, and the law designated all three as executive departments. They were led by civilian secretaries who lacked cabinet rank but enjoyed direct access to the President.

Members of the National Security Council included the Secretary of State, the Secretary of Defense, the three Service Secretaries, and heads of other governmental agencies as appointed by the President.

The National Military Establishment included the Departments of the Army, Navy, and Air Force and the Office of the Secretary of Defense. The Secretary of Defense exercised general direction over the three departments.

The Joint Chiefs of Staff, composed of the uniformed "Chiefs" of the three Services, became a statutory body in the Office of the Secretary of Defense. Concluding that the most senior professional officers from each of the Services could offer the best military advice to the "national command authority," Congress designated the Chiefs as the "principal military advisors" to the President, the National Security Council, and the Secretary of Defense, but left their obligations toward the Legislative Branch undefined. Meeting together, each Service Chief would have to "justify his case before a group of intelligent partners." Congress believed that the Chiefs, meeting together as a corporate body, comprised the best forum from which to obtain military advice. The Chiefs would also formulate joint military plans, establish unified (multiservice) commands in various parts of the world, as well as single Service (subsequently called specified) commands, and give strategic direction to those commands. [14]

## U.S. Constabulary

Wheeler's assignment to the U.S. Constabulary in January occurred during an evolutionary period of the Allied occupation of Germany.

Under a common occupation policy developed primarily at the Yalta and Potsdam conferences in 1945, the Allied Powers had assumed joint authority over Germany. American, British, Soviet, and French forces occupied separate zones. National matters came before an Allied Control Council composed of the commanders of the four occupation armies. The Allies had similarly divided and governed the German capital, Berlin, which lay deep in the Soviet zone.

In the American zone, U.S. Army occupation troops had proceeded rapidly with disarmament, demilitarization, and the eradication of Nazi influence from German life. American officials participated as members of the International Military Tribunal that tried 22 major leaders of the Nazi party for war crimes. The Office of Military Government supervised German civil affairs within the American zone, working increasingly through German local, state, and zonal agencies, which military government officials staffed with politically reliable men. A special U.S. Constabulary, which the Army organized as demobilization cut away the strength of tactical units in Germany, operated as a mobile police force.

Each of the other occupying powers organized itself along similar lines, but the Allied Control Council could act only by unanimous agreement. It failed to achieve unanimity on such nationwide matters as central economic administrative agencies, political parties, labor organizations, foreign and internal trade, currency, and land reform. Soviet demands and dissents accounted for most of the failures. Each zone inevitably became a self-contained administrative and economic unit.

Two years after the German surrender, the wartime Allies had made very little progress toward restoring German national life. In January 1947, the British and the Americans began coordinating their zonal economic policies. The eventual result, which would emerge in September 1949, was a Germany divided between the Federal Republic of Germany in the areas of the American, British, and French zones and a Communist government in the Soviet zone in the East. [15]

At the beginning of the occupation of Germany, American tactical units conducted military government administration in addition to their normal missions. Within a few months, special organizations were created to handle military government affairs exclusively, and tactical units were freed from this responsibility.

Shortly before the German surrender, Harmon's 4th Armored Division was notified that it would become the permanent occupation division. During the summer of 1945, Harmon's headquarters coordinated efforts to reestablish the borders, establish law and order, and generally assist German communities in recovering from the war.

The American Zone of Occupation encompassed more than 40,000 square miles and included nearly 1,400 miles of international and regional boundaries, extending from Austria in the south to the British zone in the north, and from Czechoslovakia and the Soviet zone in the east to the Rhine River and the French zone in the West. Roughly the size of Pennsylvania, it was inhabited by more than 16 million German citizens, as well as more than half a million displaced persons. It included many major cities, Frankfurt and Munich among the largest.

After implementing its occupation zones in southern Germany, U.S. forces also took responsibility for a section of Berlin and the city of Bremerhaven, which served as the main port and supply hub for U.S. forces in Germany. The U.S. also occupied a zone in Austria. [16]

In October 1945, Eisenhower announced the formation of a special constabulary of 38,000 men to control the U.S. Zone of Occupation. An elite force, it was composed of the highest caliber personnel available under the voluntary reenlistment program, equipped with an efficient communications network and sufficient vehicles and liaison airplanes to make it highly mobile.

The mission of the U.S. Constabulary was to maintain general military and civil security, assist in accomplishing the U.S. government's objectives, and to control the borders of the U.S. Zone of Occupation. Cooperating with the growing German police forces, the constabulary hunted for black marketers and former Nazi leaders and conducted general law enforcement and traffic control.

The seven remaining U.S. cavalry groups in Europe were absorbed into the U.S. Constabulary, and like the 4th Armored Division's armored infantry, field artillery, tank, tank destroyer, and anti-aircraft battalions, were converted into constabulary squadrons and regiments. [17]

Few soldiers in these tactical units were trained in their new principal role of police duties, and there were no field manuals or precedents from which to teach them urban, rural, and border security operations. The need for a U.S. Constabulary School to teach guidelines and doctrine was evident, and a Constabulary training program was developed in January 1946. [18]

The U.S. Constabulary's initial unit training had focused on occupation and police duties at the expense of combat readiness, but that situation began to change within a few months of their activation as German authorities assumed greater responsibility for maintaining law and order. Additionally, tensions increased between the Soviets and Western Allies, making the threat of war very real. [19]

In May 1947, Major General Withers A. "Pinkie" Burress assumed command of the U.S. Constabulary from Harmon and oversaw a gradual shift from police missions to tactical training. Assisting him in this endeavor was Wheeler, who, with a great reputation as a wartime unit trainer, had assumed duties as Assistant Chief of Staff, G-3 on 9 January. Wheeler would serve in this capacity for the next two-and-a-half, dramatic years. [20]

### *Bamberg-Heidelberg-Stuttgart*

Wheeler's assignment to the U.S. Constabulary headquarters meant relocating his family to Bamberg in Bavaria. Late in the war, Bamberg municipal officials had wisely surrendered their charming medieval city to advancing U.S. forces rather than have it reduced to rubble in urban fighting. After only a few weeks there, and before their furniture had even arrived from Paris, the Wheelers moved again when the Constabulary headquarters relocated to Heidelberg.

Situated on mountains astride the Neckar River, Heidelberg was a beautiful, medieval university town. Like Bamberg, the city had escaped the war largely unscathed since Wheeler's 63rd Infantry Division demanded the city's surrender in lieu of its destruction.

The Wheelers would occupy two houses in Heidelberg, the first on the mountainside across the river from the old city center. Numerous wooden packing crates filled the backyard during their move-in. Bim enjoyed several afternoons building forts out of them and was very unhappy when a detail of soldiers finally hauled them away. [21]

The Wheelers soon adopted a German Shorthaired Pointer that had been abandoned in a fenced-in yard of an empty house in their neighborhood, German civilians were severely economically depressed, and every commodity was rationed. The dog's tail had been cropped, and he appeared to be in good health. Apparently, he had belonged to a good family that was unable to keep him and so left him in a neighborhood full of American families. Bim was present when a U.S. military policeman let the dog out of the yard. Since it didn't have a collar, Bim dragged the dog home with his arms around his neck. Bus agreed to let him keep it, and they named him Heidle. [22]

Proving himself a great hunting companion, Heidle hunted anything and instinctively seemed to know what game he was expected to go after at any given time. An upland game bird hunter, Heidle also retrieved waterfowl over the side of a boat. He also accompanied Bus on numerous hunts for wild boar and deer.

On one trip, young Bim also tagged along, following behind Bus with a little cork gun. A rabbit popped up. Bus fired two shots at it but missed. The rabbit took off across a field headed for some woods. Without command, Heidle took off after the rabbit, killed and retrieved it. He sat down in front of Bus and proudly dropped the rabbit at his feet. [23]

Wartime experiences had led the Joint Chiefs of Staff to establish the Armed Forces Staff College (AFSC) to educate officers from all Services in planning and conducting joint military operations. During 1947, Wheeler completed the AFSC's five-month Regular Equivalent Course—another military school from which he received top marks. [24]

*Wheeler (top left), Lieutenant Colonel Bert Spivy (top right), and two unidentified staff Colonels, U.S. Constabulary headquarters, Heidelberg, Germany, before Wheeler was demoted to Lieutenant Colonel on 1 July 1947. (Wheeler Family Records).*

Betty employed a pair of German servants, a cook named Greta and a maid named Lisle. When Bus came home on the evening of 1 July with different rank insignia than his Colonel's eagles, Greta assumed that he had been promoted and addressed him as "Herr General." Unfortunately, he hadn't been promoted, but rather demoted to temporary Lieutenant Colonel. As part of the Army's postwar drawdown, Regular Army officers were reduced in temporary rank, while Reserve officers retained theirs. [25]

Furious and disillusioned, Bus asked Betty's father to find him a lawyer and purchase some land for them on Casey Key, Florida. The Howells kept a modest property there called "SunSandSea," a cinder block house facing the Gulf of Mexico that the Wheelers had visited during Bus's stateside wartime tours. Having decided to resign his commission and live as a writer in the Keys *a la* Ernest Hemingway, Bus hired an architect to design a house for them.

The only reason he did not resign was because the Army had recently announced that it would implement a new twenty-year retirement program. He only had six years to go, and it seemed prudent to get over the insult and soldier on. Bus was impatient by nature, but logic kept his temper in check. [26]

Meanwhile, the Wheelers moved into a second house directly on the river nearby a bridge to the old town. The U.S. Officers Club was directly across from it, below and to the left of the prominent *Heidelberger Schloss* castle.

Bus and Betty frequently left seven-year old Bim at home with their servants while they ate dinner at the club. On one such evening, unbeknownst to the adults, Bim and a friend had gotten hold of some fireworks that were like fat, paper-wrapped pencils that shot sparks like a sparkler. His playroom was on the second floor of the house and had a large window that provided access to the roof. After dusk, the boys climbed out and lit their fireworks. A phone in the playroom soon rang. It was Bus, who asked Bim whether he was out on the roof playing with matches. Bim asked how he knew.

"I am your father, and I know everything," Bus replied. "Now get back inside and stop playing with matches." [27]

Growing fears of a Soviet invasion of Western Europe prompted several precautions to be taken in the likelihood of sudden armed conflict. American military dependents were issued dog tags to facilitate their rapid evacuation back to the States. Off-duty U.S. Army officers carried their personal weapons with them in case they had to report for duty immediately.

Whenever the Wheelers hosted a party in their house, their walk-in closet in the front hall looked like an arms room with . 45 caliber pistols, M1 carbines, M1 rifles, and Thompson submachine guns.

One evening, Bus hosted an all-male "smoker" attended by Burress, a veteran of both World Wars. Bim snuck downstairs to eavesdrop on the officers enjoying cognac and cigars after dinner. The conversation turned to the French.

"Ah yes, the French," exclaimed Burress. "Drink their wine, take their medals, and f___ their women!"

At some point, Bus realized that little ears were listening. He later asked Bim whether he had understood what the General had said. Having spent a great deal of time around enlisted men, Bim replied, "Sure, pop." [28]

Later that year, the U.S. Constabulary headquarters relocated yet again, this time to Stuttgart. This move meant that Bim would attend four differ- ent schools in First Grade. (Recurring moves of rapid frequency would be the norm until his Sophomore year of high school. In fact, during Bim's first nine years of school, he would attend at least two schools per grade.) [29]

Unlike Bamberg or Heidelberg, Stuttgart had taken a real pounding during the war. The city sat in a bowl at the base of a mountain. When the Wheelers arrived, there were only two buildings left somewhat intact downtown. Both were occupied by the U.S. Army, one as an office building, the other as a Post Exchange (PX). The bomb-damaged PX building was eventually condemned. Rubble from destroyed buildings had been removed, leaving only their outlines along the empty streets.

The Wheelers found a magnificent house on the mountainside overlooking the city at 56 *Feuerbacher Heide*, Stuttgart West. The house had a central foyer of marble with pillars supporting a second-floor balcony and twin marble staircases rising on either side to the second floor.

"I loved that house," Betty recalled. A fine property, the only reason why the Wheelers got it was because it was filthy and damaged from having served as a children's hospital at the end of the war. Betty led the paint and bucket brigade to get the house back into livable shape. [30]

Bim discovered a treasure trove of abandoned German army equipment, helmets, belts, and other items in the basement. When the family later rotated back to the States, he was greatly disappointed that Bus wouldn't pay the shipping for him to keep his collection. [31]

When the Wheelers moved in, someone stole Betty's suitcases. It didn't take long for the *polizei* to determine that the gardener had taken them.

Lisle, their maid, had accompanied them from Heidelberg. They hired a new cook, a very nice young woman named Berta, whose husband had been killed in the war. Berta had a daughter named Helgie who was about Bim's age. (Betty and Berta would remain in touch for many years.) [32]

Somehow, Bus became acquainted with the author John Steinbeck. A fellow car aficionado, Steinbeck had recently acquired a very rare T87 Tatra while visiting Czechoslovakia. While driving it back to France for shipment to the States, he burned up the engine. Requiring factory repair, Steinbeck was unable to take it with him when he departed Europe. Through a mutual friend, Bus took possession of the Tatra, got it fixed, and drove the car for several weeks until orders for its shipment arrived. The chocolate brown Tatra featured an air-cooled engine in back, three headlights vice the usual two, plus a significant "dorsal fin" down the back. [33]

Bus drove the Tatra to Garmisch-Partenkirchen for a family vacation during the winter of 1947-48. They stayed at the General Patton Hotel, which, along with numerous facilities across Germany and Austria, had been designated as Armed Forces Recreation Centers. The Wheelers loved vacationing in Garmisch and would return many times throughout Bus's career. A highlight of this trip was the "ice follies" show they watched while dining at tiered tables around the 1936 Olympic ice rink. [34]

## Iron Curtain

Soviet intransigence, as demonstrated in Germany, Korea, and elsewhere, had dashed U.S. hopes for Great Power unity. The Soviet Union, warned former British Prime Minister Winston S. Churchill back in early 1946, had lowered an "Iron Curtain" across the European continent. The Soviets quickly drew eastern Germany, Poland, Hungary, Romania, Bulgaria, Yugoslavia, and Albania behind that curtain. In Greece, where political and economic disorder led to civil war, the rebels received support from Albania, Bulgaria, and Yugoslavia. In the Near East, the Soviets kept a grip on Iran by leaving troops there beyond the time specified in the wartime arrangement. They also tried to intimidate Turkey into giving them special privileges in connection with the strategic Dardanelles. In Asia, besides insisting on full control in northern Korea, the Soviet Union had turned Manchuria over to the Chinese Communists under Mao Tse-tung and was encouraging him in a renewed effort to wrest power from Chiang Kai-shek and the Kuomintang government. [35]

France aligned with the West, and the Truman Administration's Cold War policies increased American commitments to the French. The Truman Doctrine, formulated in early 1947, specifically applied to Greece and Turkey, but enunciated the principle that the U.S. would assist countries resisting aggression. The Marshall Plan, announced in June 1947, was intended to provide U.S. economic assistance to European countries, including France, in their postwar recovery programs. [36]

The Truman Administration foresaw no inherent limits to the Soviets' outward push. Each Communist gain, it seemed, would serve as a springboard from which to attempt another. With a large part of the world still suffering from the ravages of war, the possibilities appeared limitless. Truman responded by blocking any extension of Communist influence—a policy known as containment. Viewing the industrialized European continent as the decisive area, the Administration at first limited its containment policy to Western Europe, the Mediterranean, and the Middle East and sought other solutions in East Asia.

The U.S. constructed its containment strategy around its economic strength, an approach based on the judgment that the U.S. monopoly on atomic weapons would deter the Soviet Union from direct military aggression in favor of exploiting civil strife in countries prostrated by the war. This strategy focused on providing economic assistance to friends and former enemies alike to alleviate the social conditions conducive to Communist expansion.

## 1948

In March 1948, Truman declared before Congress his confidence "that the determination of the free countries of Europe to protect themselves will be matched by an equal determination on our part to help them." [37]

Out of all this activity grew the basis of postwar international relations: West versus East, anti-Communists against Communists, and those nations aligned with the U.S. confronting those assembled under the leadership of the Soviet Union, a Cold War between power blocs. Leadership of the Western bloc fell to the United States, because it was the only Western power with sufficient resources to take the lead in containing Soviet expansion. [38]

### *Threat of War*

With the recovery of German society and its economy, the U.S. Constabulary's original mission was greatly diminished. In 1948, its mission and organization evolved to meet emerging requirements, and its transition to preparation for combat began. [39]

In June, in protest to Western attempts to establish a national government and against efforts to institute currency reforms in Berlin, the Soviet Union moved to force the Americans, British, and French out of Berlin by blockading the road and rail lines through the Soviet occupation zone over which troops and supplies from the West reached the Allied sectors of the city.

General Lucius D. Clay, the U.S. Military Governor, requested authorization to run armored columns down the roads to test Soviet resolve by crashing through these barricades. Senior British and American leaders feared such an action would precipitate a war with the Soviets. Instead, U.S. and British aircraft commenced the "Berlin Airlift" to fly food, fuel, and other necessities to keep the Allied sectors of Berlin supplied. [40]

Betty's parents happened to be in Germany visiting the Wheelers. Due to the real possibility of war breaking out, Bus decided that Bim would return to the States with his grandparents. Betty would remain with him as long as the situation allowed.

On 23 June, the Wheelers accompanied their eight-year old son to the Howells' stateroom aboard the Dutch ocean liner *New Amsterdam* in Rotterdam.

"When you and Bus closed the door, Bim really broke down and sobbed like his heart was really breaking," Betty's mother 'Becca' later wrote. "I just held him tight and let him cry for a bit. Then dad spied you at the port hole, and (Bim) pulled himself together to look out and wave again."

"I never went away and left my mother before," Bim said. Embarrassed, he explained, "You get to cry when you leave your own mother. I hope I never have to do it again."

Becca replied, "Well, Bus has had to go away and leave Betty so many times, and this time she is going to stay with him, and you're going away."

"Do you s'pose Bus cried?" Bim asked.

"I told him I thought, 'Maybe so, when nobody looked.'" [41]

Soon recovering from the initial trauma of separation, Bim enjoyed exploring the ship. After months on a plain, rationed diet, he devoured steaks for both lunches and dinners throughout the voyage. [42]

Wheeler—promoted to permanent Lieutenant Colonel on 1 July—planned and executed the last major reorganization of the U.S. Constabulary in anticipation of a Soviet invasion of western Germany in response to the Berlin Airlift. Its personnel and equipment were cross-leveled and balanced with the 1st Infantry Division, making them both about normal division strength. Three of its nine Constabulary regiments were quickly refitted as armored cavalry regiments and equipped with additional M-8 armored cars and more infantry heavy weapons. These were given a combat mission but remained organic to the U.S. Constabulary. The remainder of its forces continued their "traditional" security missions, but increasingly even these forces were shifted from police functions to training for war and were redeployed to the border areas. Under Wheeler's oversight, forces were continually and gradually cut from the U.S. Constabulary to cross-level into existing tactical formations. [43]

Tensions between the Western Allies and Soviets remained high over the fall and winter, but the likelihood of war was uncertain. According to the *New York Herald Tribune* on 14 September, "General Lucius D. Clay, American Military Governor of Germany, predicted today a long siege of Berlin, accompanied by a sharp winter expansion of the number of aircraft supplying the blockaded city, but no war over Berlin in the immediate future." [44]

"I certainly don't believe war is around the corner," the General said. [45]

The Howells were not mollified. In fact, they were worried sick over whether Betty would make it out of Europe if the Soviets invaded.

> The news is bad, bad, and our concern for you very deep. How I wish you would come back home, and return [to Germany] later, if times more serene roll around. I know Bus will act with all the foresight and wisdom humanly possible, and would wish to save you as much as we would. Bim is, and will be loved and cared for, that's true, but dad and I are getting older, … so for our sake, and Bim's, as well as yours don't jeopardize your safety too long. It's pretty important to Bim not to have both parents held as hostages somewhere in Russia. That is a concern here, that our people will be held in many places so that we do not use our [atomic] bomb. I do

realize the value of Buster's home, and your time together, and you know, and we don't your plans and chance for getting out in time. I do frankly believe [the United States is] meant to be scared and weakened because we dare not do other than put our energies to work for war. I do not think [the Soviets] want the war. They want Germany as a toe hold in that part of Europe. Oh well. Bus knows better than we do. I presume the wives would be sent home were it not for the fear of the morale of our own men, naturally not men like Bus. Our love and prayers are certainly pouring out, and our present concern may be unwarranted. [46]

A devout Christian Scientist, Becca always looked for opportunities to spread the Good News. The following passage reveals the depth of religious conviction in the Howell family and attests to Betty's faith. Becca wrote:

I am going to send a lot of tiny pamphlets. You might want to give some away. The strong people who survive ordeals are those who know how to think their way through. Like wealth in the bank, I know you have reserves of understanding from which to draw and give to others, safely stored through the good times for full use in the bad ones. [47]

The following day's news was not encouraging:

Secretary of State George C. Marshall tacitly recognized today that relations between the Soviet Union and the Western powers have worsened during the last week or ten days. His statements … remarkable for unrelieved pessimism, lent support to reports from abroad that there was little chance for concrete results from the Moscow negotiations on Berlin, and that the whole issue would be turned over to the United Nations General Assembly which meets in Paris next week. [48]

"Dad feels I must be careful not to say anything that sounds frightening, and I know that, too," Becca wrote. … "Anyway, the papers this morning say that Gen. Clay says 'war is not imminent. Headlines [the] night before last were a foot high that the Russians had fixed an X date for the invasion of Germany, rumor being somewhere near our elections. Even Bim can read that, and he hears the radio, too. He understands now perfectly why he is here and you are there, and I think he should." [49]

Bim told his grandmother, "Well, Bus is strong and he's got guns, and I know he can take care of himself, but if the Russians go into Germany, they'll be stronger than the Americans in Germany. I know that much, and it's no place for Betty." [50]

Becca assured him that she "would get to safety in the unlikely event that the Russians would get to Stuttgart." [51]

A couple days later, she advised Betty, "Dad says … the outlook [for potential war with the Soviets] is far darker than ever before, and to be careful." [52]

A month later, Becca still fretted:

> You may be gone by the time this reaches Germany. I still keep hoping from day to day Bus will not think it so necessary. It's not right, really, for us to say what we think so strongly and then keep hoping Bus doesn't agree. It puts an awful load of responsibility on him, and makes him feel he shouldn't take any risk. Truth is, we read every word that's printed on the 'crisis', which has been so termed for a long time now, and with you on the spot, we are just scared stiff. God only knows how hard I've tried to keep it all off my mind, and to keep occupied (not) to worry. [53]

*As the threat of a possible Soviet invasion of Western Europe loomed in 1948, the Wheelers evacuated their eight-year old son Bim to live with his grandparents Walter & Becca Howell in Old Greenwich, Connecticut. (Wheeler Family Records).*

Becca also reassured Betty that Bim had adjusted well to life with his grandparents.

"Bim told me how Bus would beat the reveille on his drum to wake him up," Becca wrote.

She asked, "Oh Bim, you must miss them. Don't you?"

"No," said Bim. "I don't very much. You see they're always with me, and I'm always with them."

Becca looked surprised.

Bim added, "You know – in spirit."

"Oh, I guess Betty told you that," his grandmother replied.

"I've always known that," Bim continued. "I've known that ever since Bus went to war, that Bus was always with me, and I was with Bus, wherever we were."

Becca replied, "Well, that's wonderful you know it."

To Betty, she added, "It has been really wonderful that he does seem to be at home here." [54]

## 1949

In preparation for the anticipated Soviet invasion, the European Command conducted Exercise Snowdrop, a winter training exercise, on 14-23 January 1949.

Following its successful conclusion, Major General Isaac D. White, Commanding General of the U.S. Constabulary, commended Wheeler for his leading role in the success of the exercise. White's letter of commendation evidences how well Wheeler's wartime experiences had prepared him for senior leadership positions:

> During the planning period, preceding the maneuver, the responsibility for designing an exercise which would illustrate the tactical role of all units participating, afford maximum training value, and provide a test of equipment and operational plans and procedures was largely yours. The completed planning at the start of the exercise and its subsequent

success give evidence of your keen grasp of the situation and your talents for organization and planning.

As Assistant Chief of Staff, G-3 of the Constabulary Corps during the play of exercise, your performance was marked by a sound knowledge of logistics, tactics, and techniques. Your initiative and your ability to estimate rapidly a situation and arrive at a sound, practical decision were noteworthy. At all times you displayed a cheerful willingness to cooperate with and assist all persons with whom you came in contact. Your selfless and untiring devotion to duty set an example worthy of emulation by all. [55]

The success of the Berlin Airlift and an effective counter-blockade, which shut off shipments of goods to the Soviet sector from West Germany, finally compelled the Soviets to lift their blockade in May 1949. [56]

With tensions subsiding in Europe, it was a good time for Wheeler to depart the U.S. Constabulary, which he did on 26 June, bound for Washington, D. C. to attend the prestigious National War College. [57]

## *National War College*

A few months earlier, Betty had preceded Bus back to the States and rejoined Bim at her parents' magnificent, new house on Long Island Sound. It had a spectacular view and a 100-foot steel pier with a gazebo at the end. The large home contained a separate apartment occupied by Betty's brother Bob and his family. [58]

Betty and Bim would remain there and occupy an apartment above the Howells' huge, multi-car garage while Bus focused on his intensive studies in Washington, D. C. This suit Betty just fine. While excited and supportive of Bus's career progression, she dreaded moving to Washington and having to deal with his alcoholic, self-centered, and mean-spirited mother. [59]

When Bus finally returned from Germany and first entered his in-laws' house, he called out to his dog Gus, who had remained with them for the past three years. Gus was fat, old, and nearly blind by then, but upon hearing his master's familiar voice, "fell into a quivering ball of delight". [60]

Bim was overjoyed to be with both his parents for the first time in almost eighteen months. He had also missed Heidle whom Bus had brought home with him. Betty's father had a "stupid" pedigree boxer named Eric. Somehow, Eric made it upstairs to the Wheeler's apartment above the garage and attacked Heidle in the living room. [61]

Attempting to break up the dogfight, Bus was bitten numerous times on both arms. He later sought treatment at Walter Reed Army Hospital for the bites, which had become infected. Prescribed penicillin, he had an allergic reaction manifested by an abdominal rash. (The scars would remain visible. Eric would later die from consuming poisoned rat bait set by an exterminator.) [62]

Despite his discomfort, Bus enjoyed several weeks of leave with Betty's family before reporting to the National War College at Fort McNair on 21 July. [63]

During the postwar unification of the Armed Services, the Joint Chiefs of Staff founded the National War College as the military's highest institution of professional military education to develop senior officers and civilians for duties connected with the execution of national policy at the highest levels. [64]

Wheeler could not have spent a more important year studying national security strategy. Academic discussions were spurred by myriad, important Cold War developments, including the establishment of NATO, passage of the 1949 Amendment to the National Security Act, the Soviets' surprise acquisition of the atomic bomb, and outbreak of war in Korea. Other topics debated by Wheeler's class included Truman's executive order to desegregate the Armed Services and the continuing struggle of France to maintain its colonial possessions in Indochina.

## *NATO*

In April, the U.S. had joined Canada and ten Western European nations in the North Atlantic Treaty Organization (NATO) so that "an armed attack against one or more of them" would "be considered an attack against them all." This provision was intended to discourage a Soviet march on Europe. In joining NATO, the U.S. pledged that it would fight to protect common Allied interests in Europe and thus explicitly enlarged the U.S. policy of containment beyond the economic realm. [65]

The Western Allies had appreciated that war with the Soviet Union would pose immense dangers. Joint war plans had anticipated the possibility of a Soviet sweep deep into Western Europe. Initial post-war iterations of these plans envisioned that the Western occupation forces would simply withdraw from the continent as quickly as possible. Subsequent versions envisioned a fighting retreat and possible maintenance of an enclave from which to launch a counteroffensive once the United States had mobilized. Only with the advent of NATO would joint planners seriously consider the defense of Western Europe in depth. [66]

## *1949 Amendment to the National Security Act*

The primary weakness of the National Security Act of 1947 was not that it left the Armed Services more federated than unified, but that the Secretary of Defense, empowered to exercise only general supervision, could do little more than encourage cooperation among the departments. Furthermore, giving the three Service Secretaries direct access to the President tended to confuse lines of authority. An amendment to the act was passed in 1949 that partially corrected these deficiencies. It converted the National Military Establishment into an executive department, renamed the Department of Defense. [67]

This legislation also reduced the Departments of the Army, Navy, and Air Force to military departments within the Department of Defense and added a Chairman to preside over the Joint Chiefs of Staff without any further substantive powers. The Secretary of Defense received at least some of the appropriate responsibility and authority to make him truly the central figure in coordinating the activities of the three Services. The three Service Secretaries retained their authority to administer affairs within their respective departments, while the departments remained the principal agencies for administering, training, and supporting their respective forces. The Service Chiefs, in their capacity as members of the Joint Chiefs of Staff, retained primary responsibility for military operations. [68]

## *Indochina*  ·

Between 1945 and 1950, the Communist threat to Indochina developed into a major national security issue for the United States.

After the Japanese surrender, U.S. forces in the Asian-Pacific Theater focused on demobilization and the occupation of former enemy territory. The emerging challenge of a Cold War between the free nations and the Communist Bloc did not seem to entail any involvement in the embattled French possessions of Southeast Asia. Although Ho Chi Minh was undoubtedly a Communist, the Viet Minh appeared to disinterested Americans as a nationalist coalition fighting French colonialism. [69]

Post-war foreign policy aimed to disassociate the U.S. from Indochina as much as possible. While recognizing French sovereignty, the U.S. did not consider itself obliged to help France regain control and did not want to appear to be helping. Nevertheless, in September 1945, U.S. ships transported two French divisions previously promised for the war effort to Indochina. [70]

The subsequent seven-year war between the Communist-led forces of North Vietnam, or the Democratic Republic of Vietnam (DRV), and the forces of the French Union would eventually lead to the creation of two states, each claiming to embody this Vietnamese national identity. [71]

In late 1946, war broke out between the French and Viet Minh. Attempts at conciliation failed. A succession of governments in Paris and the French authorities in Indochina tried both political and military solutions to no avail. A major offensive against the Viet Minh by seemingly overwhelming French Union Forces in late 1947 ended without decisive results. The proposed political solution, rallying non-Communist Vietnamese around the former Emperor Bao Dai, was undermined by suspicions that the French had no intention of granting real independence. [72]

The Berlin Crisis had drawn France into the creation of a democratic West Germany, and on 12 April, France joined in the creation of NATO. The fact that over 100,000 of its best troops and substantial sums of money that the Republic could hardly spare were tied down in Indochina limited the contribution that the French could make toward European defense. A settlement of the war along the lines of the Bao Dai solution began to seem the preferable alternative to the United States. It allowed the U.S. to oppose Communism, to favor independence for colonized Asian peoples, and to get its French ally out of a debilitating mess. [73]

In September—two to three years ahead of Western intelligence estimates—an explosion over Siberia announced that the Soviets had obtained an atomic weapon. This surprise fostered the impression that the Communist Bloc was on the move and prompted a broad review of the entire political and strategic situation at the highest levels within the National Security Council, Department of State, and Department of Defense. [74]

The Indochinese situation during the latter half of 1949 offered little hope for improvement. Most discouraging was evidence of closer ties between Ho Chi Minh and Mao Tse-tung. Ho Chi Minh had previously posed as a genuine anti-colonial patriot fighting for a democratic, independent Vietnam. Now, he publicly identified himself more closely with international Communism. [75]

On the heels of the Soviets' atomic achievement, the civil war in China ended in favor of the Chinese Communists. The defeated Nationalists withdrew to the island of Taiwan in December. [76]

An NSC study in December warned of the threat of Communist expansion in the Far East to U.S. security. It reaffirmed that the loss of Asia to Communism would secure for the Soviet Union and deny to the U.S. a power potential of the first magnitude, a major source of raw materials, and control of coastal and overseas lines of communication. It would also seriously threaten America's defensive island chain.

To counter this danger, U.S. objectives in Asia should include the reduction and eventual elimination of Soviet influence and the prevention of any power relationships that might threaten "the peace, national independence, or stability of the Asiatic nations." Specifically, the study proposed that the U.S. provide military assistance and advice to Asian nations threatened by external aggression and internal subversion and use its influence to resolve the nationalist-colonialist conflict to satisfy nationalist demands with minimum strain on the colonial powers. [77]

The Joint Chiefs of Staff recommended an integrated policy toward Asia, embodying concrete courses of action. "The time has come," they declared, "for determination, development, and implementation of definite United States steps in Asia; otherwise, this nation will risk an even greater and more disastrous defeat in the ideological conflict in that area." [78]

According to the Secretaries of State and Defense:

> The choice of confronting the United States is [either] to support the French in Indochina or to face the extension of Communism over the remainder of the continental area of Southeast Asia and possibly farther westward. We would then be obligated [either] to make staggering investments in that part of Southeast Asia remaining outside of Communist domination or to withdraw to a much-contracted Pacific line of defense. [79]

France's defeat could mean the end of its empire and status as a great power, and it would be a blow to U.S. prestige. The Chiefs supported this assessment and favored establishing a U.S. military aid group in Indochina and machinery for interdepartmental coordination of aid to Indochina. The military aid program would give the JCS a critical role in policy concerning Indochina. [80]

Alarmed by the Communist victory in China, the U.S. Department of State looked for ways to avert a Communist Vietnam. French officials had suggested in 1948 that U.S. economic assistance to the Bao Dai regime would help stabilize Vietnam. Likewise, the weaknesses of French Union Forces in Indochina were attributed to a lack of adequate equipment. By the time the French government formally requested assistance in February 1950, the Departments of State and Defense had already begun planning for such an aid program. [81]

## 1950

Approving NSC 64 on 24 April 1950, Truman directed "that all practicable measures be taken to prevent further Communist expansion in Southeast Asia." The most direct means of attaining the overall objective lay in concentrating U.S. efforts on the battle for Indochina. [82]

That spring, the U.S. initiated a program of military assistance to French and Associated States forces fighting in Indochina, as well as a program of economic aid designed to stabilize the economies of Vietnam, Laos, and Cambodia. [83]

## *War in Korea*

On 30 June, Wheeler graduated from the National War College at the top of his class. The ceremony was abuzz over the North Korean invasion of South Korea five days earlier. [84]

In a narrow sense, the invasion was merely an escalation of a continuing civil war among Koreans that began with Japan's defeat in 1945. More broadly, it marked an eruption of the Cold War between the U.S. and the Soviet Union into open hostilities because each of the Great Powers backed one of the competing governments. [85]

The U.S. had responded to the emergence of a bipolar world with a policy of containing the political ambitions of the Communist Bloc while at the same time deterring general war. [86]

The Chiefs had come to share Ambassador George Kennan's view of the ensuing Cold War as being "a state of international tension, wherein political, economic, technological, sociological, psychological, paramilitary, and military measures short of overt armed conflict involving regular military forces are employed to achieve national objectives." [87]

While the beginning of the war in Korea came as a surprise to U.S. leaders, the National Security Council had already noted a new aggressiveness on the part of the Communist Bloc. [88]

Since the Communist victory in China, the U.S. had applied its policy of containment in Asia. In January, Secretary of State Dean G. Acheson had publicly defined the U.S. "defense line" in Asia as running south from the Aleutian Islands to Japan, to the Ryukyu Islands, and then to the Philippines. This delineation raised a question about Taiwan and Korea, which lay outside the line. Acheson stated that if they were attacked, "the initial reliance must be on the people attacked to resist it and then upon the commitments of the entire world under the Charter of the United Nations." The question remained whether the Communist Bloc would construe Acheson's statement as a definite U.S. commitment to defend Taiwan and Korea if they came under attack. [89]

When war erupted in Korea, the U.S. had not yet backed its containment policy with a matching military establishment. However, the subsequent three-year Korean War would catalyze a major shift in U.S. military policy by providing a crisis atmosphere that allowed the nation to mobilize for one war in Asia and rearm to deter another war in Europe. [90]

The war would devastate Korea, lead to a large expansion of the U.S. Armed Services and U.S. military presence around the world, and it would frustrate many on both sides by ending in an armistice that left the peninsula still divided. [91]

## First Joint Staff Tour

Now educated on the major national security issues confronting the U.S. at this pivotal Cold War moment, Wheeler was assigned to the Joint Staff where he would assist implementation of the recently reformulated national security strategy for containing Communist expansion.

On 1 July, he was assigned to the Intelligence and Security Section, Joint Intelligence Group, Office of the Joint Chiefs of Staff. This assignment, which dealt with highly classified material, occurred during the "Red Scare" when fears of Communist infiltration of the federal government and the military were high. The FBI conducted "an immediate, thorough, [and] discreet investigation" and found no issues with Wheeler's character, associations, and loyalty. [92]

Wheeler was promoted to temporary Colonel on 7 September 1950. Upon completing six months of Joint Staff duty on 1 January 1951, he would be authorized to wear the Department of Defense Identification Badge, which members of the Joint Staff wore prior to the establishment of the Joint Chiefs of Staff Identification Badge in early 1963. [93]

## Fairfax

In January, Betty and Bim had rejoined Bus in Northern Virginia. They had driven down from Connecticut in her new Crosley Hotshot, a tiny, two-seat convertible with flimsy, removable sheet metal doors that could be replaced with a canvas strap across the open-door frame. Their trip in the low-slung Crosley was both frigid and hair-raising, as Betty's head reached only about halfway up the tires of passing semi-trailers. [94]

After eighteen years of marriage, the Wheelers purchased their first home in Fairfax with some help from her parents— a small, newly constructed house on Fairfax Station Road.

At that time, the town of Fairfax was separated from Arlington by 45 minutes of open highway driving along Route 50. The only traffic light along this undeveloped route was at Fort Myer.

Bim rode his bicycle about a mile between home and Fairfax Elementary School, where he would attend Fourth Grade and half of the following school year. [95]

"The house is a love," Betty wrote soon before they moved in in August. "It didn't look nearly as big as I remembered. I guess we were so thrilled with it, it grew and grew in our minds! However, it has a sense of space, and there are no little rooms, may be not big, but not little, if you can understand that. Anyway, I can't wait to get my hands on it." [96]

As Bus rewarded himself for completing the National War College with a new Austin sedan, Betty counted their blessings to her parents:

> Bus is so pleased with his new car. We just feel as though we're overflowing with material and spiritual riches. Two cars and a house! I have certainly had a great many material riches bestowed on me in the last couple of years. All of which has been very wonderful and greatly appreciated. The house, though, is something so very special and unbelievable, that it does seem as though there should be some way Bus, Bim, and I could express ourselves, and really say 'thank you' for making the house possible. So, even though we don't express ourselves, please know how very deeply we feel, and how very happy and thrilled we are. [97]

## *Indochina*

Meanwhile, the first shipments of U.S. equipment for Indochina were being prepared for loading when North Korea invaded the South. The war in Indochina was viewed as part of a broader struggle in the Far East. When

Truman decided to send ground troops to South Korea, he also ordered an acceleration of the aid program for the French in Indochina. The challenge was to find the means to fight in Korea and at the same time provide ever-increasing quantities of material to the French Union Forces in Southeast Asia. The possibility of direct intervention by the Chinese Communists against the French also loomed until they appeared in North Korea in November. [98]

Although the Chinese intervention in Korea lowered the chance of China coming directly to the aid of the Viet Minh, the situation was grim in Europe and the Far East that fall. [99]

There was widespread fear that the Korean "feint" was a preliminary to full-scale war in Europe. According to historian Lawrence S. Kaplan, "Rather than retreat from Europe, American policymakers envisioned the North Korean invasion of South Korea as part of the global Communist assault against the West. ... The United States embraced the [NATO] alliance and intended to fortify it and reshape it as a military organization." [100]

Acheson succeeded in galvanizing the NATO Allies to agree to a unified military command, to which Truman appointed Eisenhower as the Supreme Allied Commander, Europe (SACEUR) in December. Eisenhower's appointment gave tangible evidence that the U.S. was firmly committed to resist what was perceived at the time as a "clear and present danger" from the Soviet-dominated East. American troops would reinforce Europe, but the Allies had to do their part. The diversion of many of France's best officers and noncommissioned officers to Indochina became even more serious. [101]

# 1951

At the beginning of 1951, the situation in Indochina was dire, but Truman was reluctant to increase aid to the French. Meanwhile, stabilization of the front in Korea and the beginning of the buildup of U.S. military force in Europe provided some breathing space to U.S. and its Allies. Negotiations between the United Nations Command and the Communist forces in Korea commenced in July, but soon deadlocked. In Indochina, the French gained some local successes. [102]

United States policy regarding Indochina changed little that year, although pressures for change increased. The Chiefs regarded the Chinese intervention in Korea as having so changed the general strategic situation in the Far East that new basic decisions at the political level were required. [103]

On 14 September, the Chiefs recommended to the new Secretary of Defense, Robert A. Lovett—who had recently succeeded Marshall—that the National Security Council conduct a review. [104]

Many military officers did not share the alarmist views of the "domino" theorists. Some questioned whether Laos, Indonesia, and India would all fall if South Vietnam crumbled under Communist pressure. The Joint Chiefs of Staff Strategic Plans Committee argued as early as 1951 that "even limited involvement in Vietnam 'could only lead to a dilemma similar to that in Korea, which is insoluble by military action." Fear of appearing ineffectual against the global Communist threat overwhelmed such warnings, however. [105]

The Chiefs contended that "it would be in the United States security interest to take military action short of the actual employment of ground forces in Indochina to prevent the fall of that country to Communism." This statement modified existing policy that no U.S. Armed Forces would be committed in Indochina other than air and naval forces required to aid in a French evacuation of Tonkin. The opening of armistice negotiations in Korea in July had shaped the Chiefs' calculations, since conclusion of an armistice would release strong Communist forces that could be directed against Indochina. [106]

## *Trieste*

Once again, another benefactor whom Wheeler had impressed in a previous assignment provided a huge boost to his career. Major General Edmond B. Sebree had commanded the U.S. Constabulary's 2nd Brigade while Wheeler served as its Assistant Chief of Staff, G-3. Sebree was now commanding the Trieste United States Troops (TRUST), an elite, 5,000-man, combined arms organization occupying the Free Territory of Trieste. Defending the frontline against the Communist menace in the Balkans, TRUST consisted of the 351st Infantry Regiment with supporting artillery, armor, and support units.

On 30 August, Sebree offered Wheeler command of the 351st. "I would like very much to see you get this regiment if you are interested and we can swing it. … Let me know at once if you are available and want the job." Naturally, Wheeler jumped at this golden opportunity to command one of the most prestigious outfits in the U.S. Army. [107]

Located about an hour from Venice, Trieste was a seaport between Italy and Yugoslavia at the northern end of the Adriatic Sea. The terrain around the city was mountainous and beautiful. As a Free Territory, Trieste was divided into two zones, the northern being the British-United States Zone and the southern the Yugoslav Zone. The Allied Military Government would administer the zone until the appointment of a governor by the United Nations. [108]

In a welcome letter to Wheeler dated 7 September, Sebree wrote:

> I think you'll find this a pleasant station and probably the best regimental command in the Army. … The regiment is in fine shape and can get along on its own power for a month or two so you don't have to break your neck in getting over here. … I am very happy over the prospect of serving with you again and hope that nothing happens to interfere with your assignment. [109]

A week later, Wheeler's sponsor and the Acting Regimental Commander, Lieutenant Colonel James I. Muir, sent him an informative and insightful letter of introduction:

> The regiment has a very fine reputation, and is one that is well deserved. As you have probably already gathered from G-3, we like to think that we are the best in Europe. Though I am probably badly prejudiced, I think this is really so. The regiment is right now a reflection of its former Commanding Officer, Colonel [Paul] Caraway, who left yesterday for SHAPE, but the standards are very high; discipline is good, training is above average, morale and pride in unit are excellent. The V. D. [venereal disease] rate has increased recently, but I believe it is about Army average. The court-martial rate has gone up also, but we are taking advantage of the 'two or more previous convictions' clause, and getting rid of all the bums. The officers are generally above average, and we're

getting rid of the few bums we have there, too. All in all, I think you have a regiment you'll be proud to command. There is a substantial turnover in personnel due about the time you arrive, but we are supposed to have replacements for those shipping out, and the situation should not be too grim.

There is a goodly sprinkling of West Point graduates among the officers, including me (your [Regimental] Executive [Officer]), one Battalion Commander, one Company Commander, and 15 Lieutenants. There are quite a few reserve officers called to active duty from NCO status in the regiment, also, generally doing quite well. I have nevertheless found that the biggest problem in the regiment is the personnel problem. It seems to be never ending.

Our next biggest problem is engendered by the troop housing situation. The three battalions are quartered in three different *casermas*, separated by some miles, and this increases the administration problem, and tends to build up battalion esprit at the expense of regimental esprit. The latter of these problems is not unduly serious; the problem of administration by separate *casermas* occasionally is. We additionally have one separate company, fourteen miles from everyone else, and this doesn't help matters. However, none of these problems are world shakers, and are vexatious and annoying rather than truly serious.

Dependent housing is rough also, but is being very slowly solved. You have a fine big set of quarters waiting for you which we will maintain until your arrival.

We have a good variety of soldier athletics, including baseball, football, basketball and boxing. Swimming is available during the summer but not as an organized competition. There are tennis courts, but no golf course. The latter is available at Venice, two hours by car, or at Velden in Austria, some four hours by car. Each battalion has an indoor small bore range, each company has a small bore rifle team, each battalion has a small bore pistol team, and regimental rifle and pistol small bore teams are involved in competitions with outside organizations. We are planning a small arms invitational meet in November, and interest in all this is moderately high. There is also a newly opened skeet range. Deep-sea fishing is available, but there is only one river in Trieste, and it is nearly entirely underground. Hunting and fishing are excellent in Austria and Germany, one day by car.

We are looking forward to your arrival, and hope that you will enjoy Trieste and the regiment as much as we have. You'll find a good regiment, a vigorous training schedule, an interesting group of people, and a shattering social whirl, but it's a good station and an interesting one. [110]

Having received confirmation of Wheeler's assignment a few days later, Sebree wrote him again:

I am delighted with your assignment and believe that you will like it as well. ... Comparing service here with service in Germany I believe that I prefer Trieste largely because I have an independent command and something I can sink my teeth into. For the same reason I believe that a regimental command here is a better job than one in Germany, although the location here is more confining and there is an element of claustrophobia. Anyway, I don't know of anyone I would rather have with me than you and I hope you will like this setup. [111]

Wheeler concluded his tour with the Joint Staff on 1 October. The family enjoyed a pleasant voyage to Trieste aboard the *U.S. S. Goethels*. The "boat" made several ports of call en route, including Casablanca and Athens. Bim met up with several young enlisted men aboard ship who were also bound for Trieste. One of them wore a bullet that had wounded him in Korea on a chain around his neck. Another Soldier was originally from Trieste and had immigrated to America. He was happy to be returning home and would later introduce Bim to his mother. [112]

Betty recorded their arrival in Trieste:

> We docked a little after nine [on 7 November]. Photographers came aboard. We were quite in the limelight. ... A Sergeant took our bags and Heidle to the house. The day was overcast [and] quite foggy, so we missed the beautiful view of the harbor as we came in. It's the first bad weather. Every port was so glorious and for sightseeing, better we had it that way. ... The band was playing. The Muirs took us to Miramare Castle to see General & Mrs. Sebree. ... We had coffee and stayed about an hour. Then to [the village of] Opicina [to inspect our new] home.
>
> Bus [then] went off ... to meet his Battalion Commanders and lunch. ... General & Mrs. Sebree had a cocktail party that evening. It seems that they have one [whenever] the boat comes in for those arriving and those taking off. [113]

Betty described Bus's assumption of command ceremony the following morning:

> The parade was at 11:00. ... It was very impressive, naturally, because to us there was so much significance. The weather was overcast, and it rained for a minute and then stopped, so we weren't soaked. ... The parade was followed by a reception at the club. ... It was a lovely party. Shook hands with mobs of people – regiment, TRUST, British, etc. I know I shall never know the names of all the people. Talk about a sea of faces. [114]

*Wheeler assumed command of the prestigious 351st Infantry Regiment on 8 November 1951. (Wheeler Family Records).*

The 351st Infantry Regiment was garrisoned in a former Italian Army *caserme*, or barracks, near Opicina well up the mountainside from Trieste. American military families were also quartered there, but the dependents' school was located down in the city. This would mean hairy bus rides back and forth for Bim, now a fifth grader.

The TRUST headquarters, officers club, and the Commanding General's quarters were in Miramare Castle, which had been built around 1860 by Prince Ferdinand Maximillian, who later became the French Emperor of Mexico. The castle was spectacularly situated on the water and featured a beautiful park. Bim and his friends would spend a fair amount of time there swimming at the TRUST officers club pool. [115]

"The regimental [officers] club [in Opicina] is quite nice," wrote Betty. "There are (free) movies for the children every Friday night, and we are practically on the club's doorstep. Saturday nights are known as 'ankle-biter nights' for all the children there for the supper buffet and more movies." [116]

"There are two commissaries, one down in Trieste and the other for the 351st in Opicina," she continued. "Naturally, the commissary that is mainly for the 351st isn't going to do anything but their poor best by me." [117]

The Wheelers' official duties commenced immediately. "A new [enlisted men's] club was opening that … Bus was asked to attend and open it officially.

… It was quite an occasion. A few speeches, a ribbon was cut and dancing started. We stayed long enough to have a drink and dance a dance, and then on to our own [officers] club." [118]

## *It Must Be Done*

Betty had always enjoyed the ceremonial and social aspects of life as an Army officer's wife. She had also enjoyed her various volunteer roles providing motherly support to young, mostly single, and sometimes wounded, soldiers. She had not, however, found any joy or satisfaction in her responsibilities for dealing with other officers' wives. In fact, she considered it sheer drudgery. Betty found women tedious and was often quite catty toward them. Nevertheless, she had and always would meet expectations of her and performed her roles with the same sense of self-sacrificing devotion to duty with which Bus always performed his.

Betty was made the Honorary President of the Regimental Ladies Club, and much to her ire, was obliged to attend every board meeting. After her first club function, she vented to her mother, "Geez-be-beez, the luncheon was lengthy, the speaker a bore." [119]

Betty had a talent for learning foreign languages. She soon began taking Italian lessons three times a week while Bim was at school. Bus took them as often as his busy schedule allowed. Despite his struggle with Spanish at the academy, Bus would eventually communicate fairly well in Italian, French, and German. The attractive couple's language skills and affinity for European culture complemented their natural friendliness, enabling them to bond with many Europeans of all classes during their many tours there. [120]

In late November, Betty reported:

> We really enjoyed our Sunday afternoon tea engagement. [Major] General Sir John Winterton, [commander of the British zone of Trieste, is] a most handsome older man. Lady Winterton a dear, very British, but naturally very homely. They live in a castle in Tristiana about 25 minutes from Opicina. The castle rises right up out of the sea, like a picture in a story book. It's quite an establishment, very beautiful.

Tremendous, of course, but with all its grandness, room after livable room. We had a lovely time. [121]

A week later, Betty reported:

Sunday we went to church. … Came home and had our first callers. We have had a hard time trying to decide when to receive. Also, everyone is so stiff. We hope to break them down socially. We finally decided that we'd hold open house on Sunday after church until 1:30 or 2:00. Come, bring the children, have a drink or beer. Bim said he'd take over on the children. We're going to try it, for it looks like the only time we can be sure of being here without constantly making a change. [122]

Three months later, the Wheelers would change their receiving hours to 4:30 to 6:00 PM on Sunday afternoons. [123]

It didn't take long for Betty to feel overwhelmed by expectations of her as the Regimental Commander's wife:

I now have the Alter Guild hanging over my head, for there are too few women, trying to do too much, and resenting it. So, now I've got to have a session with [Father O'Conor, the Chief of Chaplains] and find out just what the functions of an Altar Guild are. I thought it strictly a church affair, and the minister's province - certainly not the regimental C. O.' s wife I should add. [124]

Two days later, she added:

Father O'Conor … feels too that the Altar Guild, as it stands, has served its purpose, and should be incorporated into the Women's Clubs. At least we see eye to eye that the same ten people can't carry cake to the hospital every week and entertain the soldiers without collapsing, and at the moment that is the outstanding contribution. Also, as there is no Red Cross here. Much needed. [125]

Many spouses in today's Army can relate to Betty's frustration that she vented to her mother:

At two o'clock, the Women's Club board meets. I don't know whether I can take it or not. For me, it's hard, hard work, particularly due to complete lack of interest. I have deep sympathy for the poor souls that I'm about to force to take part in several activities. However, the regiment is behind these things, and if we each do our part, we can spare too few [wives] being too burdened. I haven't done anything yet, and I'm [already] weighted down!" [126]

The demanding social requirements incumbent upon Army officer families were underpinned by the fact that most families kept several live-in servants. The Wheelers employed three domestics in Trieste. Lena was a hardworking maid/cook, a devoutly Catholic, fifty-something year old "little gnome of a person with yellow, buck teeth" who spoke no English. Sophie was a displaced Sudeten German, whom the family later replaced as maid with Pina, a tall, beautiful Italian. Pino, a married Italian man, was their gardener. [127]

"I finally, after all these weeks got around to showing Lena how to fry eggs the way Bus likes them," wrote Betty. "Otherwise, she is a good cook, although as yet I haven't found her exceptional. But, oh such a willing worker." [128]

Betty struggled to adjust to the couple's heavy load of new responsibilities. "There are so damn many things to do! Bus feels that we should put in an appearance at the club if possible (and church, too)." [129]

"I got up and got Bim off to school, had my coffee with Bus, then I went back to bed and stayed there until noon. I wish I could go back now, but I have to be at the 1st Battalion PX to sell raffle tickets. More [to support the displaced persons] Christmas fund. I would just as soon die as go. I just hate to ask people for money." [130]

Two days later, she lamented. "How I hate ladies luncheon clubs. I know I'll hate it more before I'm through [with this tour]." [131]

Bus appreciated everything Betty did to support his career, and he sang her praises to her parents. "We are busy as all get out and I am working very hard. So is Betty in her way! However, we like it and are extremely pleased that all has turned out as it has." [132]

Six weeks after arriving in Trieste, the Wheeler's car still had not arrived. Betty wrote:

> I will be so glad when we have the car [delivered on the boat]. I hate to go with other people, especially to a party. That's been one good thing about being near the club. We can come and go without being dependent on anyone. The car should be in on Friday. I think driving around here will be difficult. The Italians drive with their souls, plus *vino*!" [133]

Bim had a class project to develop a radio commercial for dog washing soap. He struggled to come up with a suitable name for the product. Bus suggested "Canine Clean" and the slogan, "And when you reach for your hair; you will find it isn't there! Use Canine Clean!" [134]

For the holidays, "[Bim's school] had the Christmas play at the theater," wrote Betty. "From the first grade *thru* high school took part. It was very sweet, and the children loved it. Bus went with me." (From then on, Bus's official duties as a general officer—not a lack of desire—would prevent him from attending any more of Bim's academic, sports, or scouting events until Bim's high school graduation in 1958.) [135]

Bim saw quite a lot of his father in Trieste. He visited Bus's office at the end of each workday and rode home with him. One day, the enlisted clerk told him to wait before entering because the commander was occupied. Eventually, the door opened, and two soldiers walked out.

Bim asked his dad what was going on. They had volunteered to go to Korea, he replied. Bus said he understood why veterans of World War II didn't want to volunteer to fight in Korea, but he felt that volunteers should receive special recognition. Bim later recalled his father often remarked how hard it had been during the war to see dead American soldiers in their foxholes. [136]

Bus's soldiers adopted his son as a sort of unit mascot. Bim often ate in their mess halls and umpired their baseball games. Bus also allowed him to hang out at the officers club, which had a great library on military history. The club's Officer-in-Charge was First Lieutenant Jack C. Montgomery, who had earned the Medal of Honor during World War II. At the end of his tour, Montgomery gave Bim a German P-38 pistol and shoulder holster as a farewell gift. Bim also befriended the Regimental Chaplain, a paratrooper who had served at Bastogne with the 101st Airborne Division. [137]

Besides Wheeler and Montgomery, another of TRUST's most famous alumni was Private (ultimately Colonel) David Hackworth, one of the most decorated officers in U.S. Army history. Hackworth attributed his enviable record of combat successes to the high standards of discipline and training instilled in him during his formative years in TRUST. [138]

The 351st Infantry's training area at Valbruna was located on a plateau in a mountainous area near Trieste. Bus often allowed eleven-year old Bim to tag along to observe training exercises. Getting to Valbruna required a very hairy jeep ride up the mountain along a winding dirt road with very sharp turns. So sharp, in fact, that the driver had to stop and back up at almost every turn. Bim bounced along in the back seat. Every time the jeep backed up, the end hung over the steep precipice, much to Bim's horror.

At the training area, which was littered with unexploded ordnance, Bus and Bim camped in a command trailer like the one Bus enjoyed during the war. At a small arms range, Bus took the opportunity to shoot his souvenir German Lugar. While observing a mock attack on a village, Bim noticed two soldiers randomly blazing away with their weapons for no apparent reason. He pointed out their lack of fire discipline to his father, who in turn instructed the Officer-in-Charge of the exercise to correct the deficiency. [139]

*General officer's field mess, Valbruna Training Area, near Trieste, May 1952. Major General Edmond B. Sebree (second from left, next to Wheeler) commanded the Trieste United States*

*Troops (TRUST), an elite, 5,000-man command that included Wheeler's 351st Infantry Regiment. (Wheeler Family Records).*

Betty's letter to her mother on 27 December illustrates the crush of social activities that typified regimental life during the Postwar Period, especially during the holidays.

> Saturday was the regimental Christmas formal dance. ... We went to the club for dinner (beforehand) with the officers & wives of the 3rd Battalion. They had invited the officers & wives of the 3rd British Battalion. They were an extremely pleasant group, and we had a good time. The dance itself seemed highly successful.
>
> Sunday, Bus and I went to church at 3rd Battalion. Stella & Billy Salter brought us home [since the boat carrying the Wheelers' car still had not arrived]. They stopped in for a beer, and along came the usual Sunday callers. We all went to the buffet [dinner at the club], and Bim & I stayed on for the movie. [140]

On Christmas Eve, the Wheelers enjoyed "a very lovely Christmas dinner" with a turkey cooked by the club. According to Betty, they attended a mass at 11:30 PM, "a joint affair with British & American catholic chaplains officiating. There were mobs & mobs & mobs of people, but there were reserved seats for us. The church itself is very beautiful, and the music was a treat. The ceremony [was] a rather heathenish show. ... It was a high mass, and there was communion. It took forever. We finally got home after two. ... Bus opened the champagne, and we opened the packages." [141]

> Bus & I got up at nine and went to 1st Battalion to church. They had a very short, sweet Christmas service. ... We had a good dinner at Hdqs. Co., and afterwards brought about ten back to the house for a brandy. We had been invited to several egg nog parties later in the day, but gave that up – enough is enough. ... I had let the help go. When Bim came in about ten, we gathered in the kitchen for turkey sandwiches and milk, and so to bed. A truly satisfactory Christmas day all the way around.

[The day after Christmas], we went to a wedding at 2<sup>nd</sup> Battalion chapel. A catholic wedding, lasting almost an hour. The actual service, until the bride & groom take communion is very lovely, but from there on it's drawn out & paganish. I felt as though I'd been living in church.

The reception wasn't until one, so Bus and I went to the commissary, came home and had a bowl of soup, and then off again. … We skipped a cocktail party … and all of us went to bed early. [142]

## 1952

Two weeks into the New Year, the commander of the regiment's supporting tank company invited the Wheelers to lunch at his mess:

It seems each week they have a special birthday table for all the boys with birthdays that week. There was a most beautiful cake and an awfully good lunch. Each birthday boy can draw and the winner gets a three day pass. Seems to be a nice custom. At the same time, Bus was made an honorary member of Tank Co.. Given a scroll, and his name had been engraved on a large silver cup bearing the names of other honorary members. It was most pleasant and we really got a kick out of it. [143]

*Wheeler (second from right) observes mortar crew training, Valbruna Training Area, near Trieste, Fall 1952. (Wheeler Family Records).*

As the Regimental Commander, Wheeler often worked extended hours on many evenings. "Poor Bus has been out every night this week," Betty wrote on 17 January 1952. "Monday & Wednesday night in the field. Tuesday the bachelor dinner." As if existing requirements weren't already enough, "Bus wants to start entertaining people as they leave." Later that week, he and Betty "were at the castle by 6:45 [PM for the] boat party. Got home around 11:30 ready to drop." [144]

The blistering pace wasn't just wearing on Betty, but on Bus, too. Nevertheless, illness did not prevent him from performing his duties. "Bus felt miserably Sunday so he stayed in bed until time to receive [callers]." The following morning, he departed work early. "He had a miserable cold, running nose and weeping eyes." By Tuesday, he felt better and "went off to the office, although he did say he might come home early." [145]

A month later, social requirements still had not abated. "Lena was off tonight," wrote Betty, "so when I came in fixed a dinner of sorts. We have gone out so much. … Amazing how quickly one can forget how to [prepare] three meals a day!" This statement also reveals the extent to which the Wheelers, like most Army officer families, relied upon on their hired help for cooking, cleaning, and babysitting. [146]

On 15 February, the Wheelers attended a memorial service for recently deceased King George VI of Great Britain. Betty recounted the stirring, solemn event held in Trieste's *Politeama Rossetti* theater:

"It was quite a thing to attend. I had never heard the funeral march in its entirety. It's not all so gloomy – solemn – but magnificent." [147]

The Wheelers were seated in the first balcony of the theater, which was horseshoe shaped like an opera house. In the first section below them were British officers and families, plus other important guests. Seated behind them were the troops and less important guests. The top gallery of the theater was also filled with British troops.

> The hymns were beautiful, the voices being mainly male, and so very many. They followed the band leader so well. Also, they seem to have a custom where just before the last verse is sung, there is a ruffle on the drums and then the voices raise to full volume.

> The stage was hung with black curtains, and at the center was King George's crest. In front of the band was an altar with flowers and candles, and on either side of the front of the stage two very beautiful wreaths.

> It was interesting the way the prayers were said: 'Let us pray for King George ... for the mourners ... for Lady Queen Elizabeth ... for the Commonwealth of Great Britain ... for peace'

> The lament was played on bagpipes. It was very mournful and very eerie. ... This was followed by almost a minute of silence, and then from the top of the house the buglers played 'The Last Post' (similar to our 'Taps'). Then another full minute of silence, and then 'Reveille'. I don't have the words to express the impressiveness of the ceremony. When they sang 'God Save the Queen', you felt something well up inside of you. Here was a tremendous theater, filled except for very few [seats] with British subjects, and all of them lifting their

voices to their Queen - for the first time. I'm so glad that we were fortunate enough to be able to attend. [148]

In late March, demonstrations erupted in Trieste over which countries should control the city and the surrounding areas of the Free Territory.

Betty apprised her parents of the situation:

> I'm sure Trieste has been in the news. It was pretty serious business around here on Saturday. The formal dinner and dance were cancelled on Saturday night. Too many people would have had to come through town. They say that this is the worst demonstration that they have ever had. Started, they say, by a group of men, that it is unbelievable don't have more sense. Supposedly the trouble was not the Communists. There is a very definite feeling that the tempo was well set up in advance. [149]

Bus's personal assessment of the situation in a letter to Betty's father is one of the few examples extant of his candid, unofficial thoughts on national security matters.

> Your recent letters enclosing the clippings relative to our troubles here in Trieste are most interesting for we have little information (other than what comes to me officially) as to what the world thinks goes on. That is, except for the fact that all troops were restricted to barracks and I warned Betty & Bim not to go down the hill into town, we really had no contact with the disturbance. I enclose an editorial from a local newspaper. It was printed the day before in Italian. I believe it gives the true picture as the average, moderate man sees it. Of course, the average, moderate man exists here in small numbers. Everyone is either a rich-bitch (few) or aching poor (myriad).
>
> Don't take what I have written as a wash-out of these troubles. They are real – and dangerous. Essentially it comes down to this:

a) The Italians want us (U.S. & U. K.) to give back both Zone A & Zone B (the Yugoslav area of Trieste) to them & to fight a war with Yugoslavia, if necessary, to do this.

b) The Jugs [Yugoslavians] will probably settle for a division of the area, i. e., Zone A (Trieste & adjacent territory) to Italy; Zone B to them.

c) The whole problem is complicated by the mixture of population. The city of Trieste is predominantly Italian. The countryside is, on the whole, Jug. The two races hate each other's guts.

d) The troubles here were caused by a group of irresponsible Italian nationalist politicians. The Italian government was behind it *sub rosa*. (This is a personal opinion. Please don't quote [me], unless it has been set forth in American newspapers.)

e) There will never be any real relaxation of tension here as long as the two races and the Italian & Jug governments are in power. There can be a temporary adjudication only. … A melancholy situation, I think.

f) I am sick & tired of the whole god-damn crew here in Europe. Every Italian & every German will tell you that he hated and opposed Mussolini and Hitler. Except for the characters who filled the concentration camps every one of them is lying in his teeth. Sometimes I even suspect the concentration camp heroes!

Now as to your [upcoming] trip – I cannot see how that will be affected by these troubles. No American was molested in any way nor will we be. Of course, 1 May is the Communist day. We may, and possibly will, have trouble. Commies versus the Fascist-Italian Irredentist-Nationalist groups. Also, May is election month in Italy. The only possible difficulty that I can foresee is that I may not be able to get away from Trieste. Other than that (and you will probably not even see

what goes on) there will be no bar to you all having a perfectly marvelous time.

When I was at the [National] War College a classmate of
mine, John Armstrong, now dead, described Trieste as 'a car-
buncle on the crotch of Europe.' How right he was! [150]

"Very interested in the clippings," Betty added in a separate note to her
mother. "The 'Stars & Stripes' is such a poor paper. Mario Angel [her Italian
language instructor] said the Trieste [paper] spoke of 'blood flowing in the
streets'. Our telephone rang constantly and Bus was given a blow by blow
description. Up here [in Opicina], we ourselves were completely out of it." [151]

Betty's official duties continued to frustrate her:

The Sergeants' wives have raised so much hell over the cake
[that the Ladies' Club baked for troops in the hospital every
week], and given the girl running the roster such fits that we
are closing them out. The few girls that have been working
are very upset, but it's a mess. Oh me, I was never cut out for
this. [152]

## Manpower Crisis

Meanwhile, as the static phase of the Korean War continued, the U.S.
Army became an institution in crisis. The opening of armistice negotiations
had erased the crisis atmosphere of 1950 and early 1951, and traditional fears
about the dangers to the U.S. economy from high military spending reasserted
themselves. Truman and the Congress cut military spending and allocated a
greater share of the defense budget to the Air Force to expand the nuclear
deterrent force. These cuts, along with the decisions to institute an individual
rotation policy in Korea and not to hold draftees and mobilized guardsmen
and reservists for the duration of the war, left the Army unable to support all
its commitments.

The Army gave first priority in personnel to supporting the 8th Army
in Korea and second priority to supporting the 7th Army in Germany, but
commanders in both armies complained of serious declines in their units'
proficiency. In the continental United States, the manpower crisis crippled

the Army's contribution to building an air defense system, nearly destroyed the Army training system, and by the end of 1952 would once again ruin the General Reserve (of its seven divisions, only the 82nd Airborne Division was ready for deployment). [153]

While the manpower crisis had negative effects on unit readiness, it did force the Army to finally comply with Truman's 1948 executive order to eliminate all segregation of troops by race. The Navy and Air Force abolished all their African American units by June 1950. The Army, with more African American members than the other Services, would take almost four years longer to fully desegregate.

With only a partial mobilization for war and high casualties in Korea, racial segregation began to break down in the 8th Army during 1950 as some commanders accepted any replacements they could obtain. In 1951, the Army had begun a racial integration program for units in Korea and would later extend it to the rest of the Service. [154]

News of the Army's expanding desegregation caused a stir. "What do I do if a Negro officer asks me to dance?" Betty asked Bus.

"You dance with him," he replied. [155]

Betty's concern was premature. TRUST would be the last major Army command to integrate and would not receive its first black soldiers until April 1953, five months after the Wheelers departed. [156]

(Wheeler would contend with the race issue throughout his career. He would help diffuse the Little Rock Crisis of 1957, and later still, as Chief of Staff of the Army, he would oversee the Army's participation in the crisis surrounding James Meredith's enrollment at the University of Mississippi in 1962.) [157]

## *Indochina*

Meanwhile, by the end of 1951, other agencies of the U.S. government had joined the Chiefs in calling for a review of U.S. policy toward Indochina. Almost six months would pass, however, before the President and the National Security Council formally approved a new policy. [158]

The NSC postulated that "the loss of any of the countries of Southeast Asia to Communist aggression would have critical psychological, political and economic consequences." The objective of U.S. policy in the region would be to prevent countries "from passing into the Communist orbit, and to assist them to develop will and ability to resist Communism from within and without." This was the first clear articulation of the Domino Theory, the enduring rationale for fighting Communism in Southeast Asia. [159]

Still, the U.S. remained reluctant to use its forces in defending the ground anywhere in Southeast Asia. The Chiefs could not foresee that truce talks in Korea would not produce a cease-fire for another year and a half, and they were concerned that the fighting might move to Indochina. A NATO meeting in Lisbon, Portugal in February 1952 committed the Allies to the build-up in Europe, to include arming the West Germans. Neither the French nor the Americans could envision sending more men to fight in Indochina.

American policy turned to deterring the Chinese from intervening in the Indochina war. If deterrence failed, the Chiefs favored direct action against Communist China. NSC 124/2, adopted in June, authorized planning for such operations. The British and French feared provoking the Communists, and consensus proved impossible. Even without overt Chinese intervention, the prospects for French success in Indochina seemed slim. Neither the military nor the political situation was much improved, and the French public was showing signs of losing faith in the war. However, U.S. aid had eased the burden on France's economy. [160]

## *Pomp and Circumstance*

On 17 June, Sebree signed a memorandum recommending Wheeler for promotion to Brigadier General.

> I wish to commend you and make record of my commendation for your superior performance of duty as Commanding Officer of the 351st Infantry. Your performance of duty has been characterized by dependability, intelligence, professional superiority and the capacity for impressing your will on others by a degree of leadership found in few officers. The 351st Infantry Regiment, under your command, has consistently improved in discipline, administration and performance. You have displayed, in many ways and at all times,

every qualification expected in a general officer. I have recommended you for promotion to the next higher grade. [161]

June was a busy month for U.S. forces in Trieste. On 27 June, Sebree was replaced by Major General William B. Bradford, and Brigadier General John L. Whitelaw assumed duties as Deputy Commanding General, TRUST. [162]

Betty recounted the considerable pomp, circumstance, and socializing that marked these transitions:

> I'm having a reception for 50 people for General & Mrs. Whitelaw. The regiment is having a review – the Wheelers [hosting and paying for] the reception. Bus doesn't feel that he can make or rather ask the club to pay for it – and it must be done. [163]

> Tuesday … the troops gave (General Whitelaw) a beautiful review. Wednesday was General Sebree's day – and another beautiful review. … The review was followed by a reception in the [Miramare] castle garden. … [Another senior couple] picked that night of all nights to have a tremendous cocktail party. We didn't feel that we could stay away. We got back to the club around 8:30 and had dinner there.

> Thursday – thank God was a free day. We had a quiet dinner … and as soon as we had coffee made a beeline for the bed. It was a little after eight. Bus just got settled and the phone rang. Bless his heart – he had to go to Valbruna, so out of bed he got – dressed and packed and off he went.

> The boat got in about 11:30 [AM] on Friday. Bus made it back in time to get to the honor guard. … The boat party was from six-thirty to eight-thirty and dinner at the little castle after that.

> Saturday morning was General Bradford's review. … Saturday evening [there was] a cocktail party for General Whitelaw. We felt that we must attend. I could have cried I was so tired, and looked it! However, we made it – and afterwards stopped by the club for a sandwich – and final goodbye

to the departing staff. They had to be back on the boat at midnight – so we got home at a reasonable hour – and slept like logs.

Sunday at eleven the boat sailed. There was an honor guard for General Sebree in the Plaza Unitas. ... Never have I seen anything more impressive – out of the castle grounds to the gang plank – the troops were lining the side of the road. Then in the square itself was the honor guard, a whole battalion. When the band played the 'Star Spangled Banner', I thought that I would burst.

The new 2nd Battalion Commander arrived – with his wife – so we had them in for cocktails Sunday afternoon. [164]

A British fleet arrived in Trieste as part of the TRUST change of command activities. Leading it was Admiral of the Fleet Lord Louis Mountbatten, 1st Earl Mountbatten of Burma, second cousin once removed from the recently crowned Queen Elizabeth II. [165] Betty reported:

[That morning] there was an honor guard at the castle. Bus took Bim and me along – and we went up on the balcony over the *portechere* to watch. The band was out, and a company. The band played 'God Save the Queen' and the 'Star Spangled Banner'. This has been a week of honor guards and parades, and at each ceremony, you felt you had never seen the troops look better.

The Admiral (Mountbatten) is fine looking, quite divine in fact, and in his white uniform with all his medals, and the gold sword, a sight to see. ... We got to meet him and Lady [Edwina] Mountbatten at close quarters. I have to admit I got a tremendous kick out of it. [166]

The Wheelers chatted with the Mountbattens at a dance that evening aboard the HMS *Glasgow*. The couples hit it off immediately. (Through many subsequent encounters over the years, a close friendship would develop. Mountbatten would later give Bus a framed portrait signed with his nickname "Dickie" that he insisted Bus address him by rather than any of his official titles.) [167]

At the busy week's conclusion, Betty mused that field training at "Valbruna will seem restful to Bus after the commotion here." [168]

*Major General William B. Bradford (in passenger seat) replaced Sebree in command of TRUST on 27 June 1952. Here, he inspects a 351st Infantry Regiment field problem with Wheeler (in back seat), Valbruna Training Area, near Trieste, 9 September 1952. (Wheeler Family Records).*

The 351st Infantry Regiment celebrated its Organization Day on 6 August. "We had ceremonies in the 2nd Battalion (area) at 9:30," wrote Betty. "Bus gave short talk, followed by General Bradford. It didn't last more than 45 minutes. It was a holiday after that." [169]

The following week, the Wheelers and a few other American couples availed themselves of the rare opportunity to visit *Jugoslavia* with Dr. Zemjac, head of the *Jugoslav* delegation, and his wife whom Betty found "quite attractive." [170]

> We took our car (the Austin) and Dr. Zemjac his. … Very shortly after we crossed the border, we cut off on a country road, and from there on all day. The roads twisted and turned. With horn honking, we took the inside of every curve anywhere from forty to fifty miles an hour. The cattle unfortunately couldn't honk back, and some of the oxen are almost as big as the car. We met a hay wagon on one turn,

and we were scraping the hay and the bushes. Thrilling to say the least!

As the area around Trieste is barren and rocky, so was the first area in *Jugoslavia*. The scenery became pretty in the first valley, and in the second river valley it was beautiful. We were being taken to see a partisan hospital.

We drove until close to eleven and stopped at the side of a beautiful stream. … for a half hour or more. The Zemjacs had an ice box. We all got out and had sandwiches and fruit, ice cold beer and *slivovitz*.

From 8:30 until almost five, we passed nothing and met one truck and one bus. That doesn't count the hay wagon we almost took [out], or the countless oxen, or bicyclists, or ourselves that almost got killed!

We finally came to a little village way out in the country. We debarked, and the climb began. We walked for almost a mile, straight up! … The trail was beside a rushing stream. … During the war, the Germans had been living in the little village. … The little hospital was built right under the Germans' nose. It was the only partisan hospital that wasn't eventually discovered. All the wood for the buildings, and all the equipment was man carried at night, the men walking in the stream, so that there was no possibility of being tracked by dogs. … The wounded were carried on litters. … Only the guides were not blindfolded.

The hospital is absolutely primitive. What is most interesting to me is the fact that the minute the war was over a trail was blazed and the little hospital became a museum for all to see. They too must have had a faith and trust that peace had really come and they would never need it again. Please God they never do.

We ate in the little village. The food was simple but good. We all enjoyed it. We had more *slivovitz*, and beer and wine, but we were anything but swanky. Then on to Posthumia to see a cave ... that is about 50 kms from Opicina. Will go back there with Bim in the fall.

[Inside the cave, we] boarded a little train and rode for ten minutes. ... The first big area was called the ball room. From the ceiling hung the most massive beautiful crystal chandelier, and the wall fixtures matched. I learned later that the Germans had used the area as ... a storeroom. The partisans had entered from the rear and burned it. The black stalactites and stalagmites were discolored by smoke.

We were in the cave for two hours. When we got on the train for the ride out we were freezing. Had hot tea and a drink, and on home. It was a wonderful day, and will be long remembered. [171]

The busy pace of commanding an infantry regiment continued through the fall. "Unfortunately, while it seemed so simple last May to think we'd get away again in September, we can't," wrote Betty on 17 August. "Bus has three new Lt. Col.' s coming in, and after the 10th [the regiment] will be in Germany on maneuvers [from mid-September] until Oct. 1st." [172]

*Betty clowns over Bus's shoulder during one of their countless official social engagements, Trieste, Summer 1952. (Wheeler Family Records).*

Holiday weekends offered no respite. "[On 29 August], Bus was guest speaker at a reserve officers' dinner. … Last night was the regimental stag dinner. … Bus worked all Labor Day." [173]

Due to a last-minute scheduling change, the Wheelers had to leave a party they were hosting in their quarters to attend a party for visiting Chief of Staff of the Army, General J. Lawton Collins, and his wife. [174] Betty reported:

> The guests arrived [at our house] at 6:30. We left the house at 7:10! There were about six couples waiting for us when we got back. General & Mrs. Collins arrived a day late, and therefore the Bradford's party was postponed. Naturally for something like that, we would not have been very smart to stay away. Also we wanted to go! Had there only been the newcomers, I could have postponed mine, but I did have turkeys bought! Anyway, it was for the people leaving, and naturally with the boat leaving (in two more days), the time was full. Also, there is nothing worse than thinking you're eating out, and to discover you have to plan for (an alternative).
>
> [Our guests] ate their way through over twenty-five pounds of potato salad. That's a ½ lb. a person. I couldn't believe it. Out of three turkeys, I have legs and wings and slices for a couple sandwiches, and the better part of a canned ham of 13 lbs. Lena deviled 60 eggs, and there are two left. They must have been hungry. It was such a silly feeling to come

downstairs this morning and find the house a shambles and not know how everything went. Lena got Bus's breakfast at six, and she was so cheery when I came at seven. Everybody had a wonderful time – ate, ate, and ate – she was so pleased. But next time I must buy less bread! Certainly I have never entertained like this before (and hope when or if I do again there is an expense account to go with it!). So it is wonderful that even though Lena can't go on her own, at least she loves to cook, and enjoys the party. She and Maria were singing away this morning. The task ahead seemed tremendous (to me!).

The Bradford's dinner party was lovely – turkey too! … Mrs. [Gladys] Collins is lovely. He, much younger looking than his pictures would lead you to believe. [175]

In late September, the Wheelers anticipated a visit from Bus's mother "Mums" who was touring Europe and had sent postcards ahead of her from London and Brussels. Betty dreaded hosting her "very domineering and controlling" mother-in-law but intended to take her to Naples and Venice. "Bus will try to arrange business so that maybe he can fly to Naples and we can come home via Rome for a couple of days, and San Marino." [176]

Betty took Mums on day trips to Nove, Sistiana, and Chivedale. The Wheelers took her along to the regimental formal following a buffet dinner at another officer's house. Betty wrote:

We got to the club at 9:30. We have been having a receiving line. All the people going out are on it, and all the newest arrivals. I know [Mums] got a tremendous kick out of standing next to Bus. All the men were very sweet to her, and each one of our party danced with her. If you want to know the truth, it gave me a lump in my throat. [177]

Betty added that she hadn't been sleeping well lately:

Probably a bit of not being able to sleep is that … we will be leaving here next month! So, it's hang on to your hats and here we go again. This time I feel like we're one step ahead of the sheriff, or about to enter the poor house! General

Bradford called Bus on Saturday. He had gotten a personal letter from Gen. [Anthony C.] McAuliffe telling him that Bus would get orders to go to Naples, reporting next month, and it would probably mean a promotion. Well to be a tenant in Miramare [Castle] it takes two stars and to get two stars you have to get one. So, as we step upstairs, which it must mean (Bus doesn't know yet what the job is) eventually, we start apartment hunting. Dear God. We haven't told Bim, and I feel saddest for him because the [toy] trains are just now working and taking shape, and I doubt if we can afford a "train room" if we could find it. Housing is difficult, and the Italians are taking full advantage of it, so rents are sky high. We're naturally keeping mum about it until the orders are in. … At the present time, don't talk about it.

As bright as the star is, I think Bus is a little sick that it couldn't have come [in conjunction] with our departure from here. It will undoubtedly be in March or April before he gets it. However, I'm all set to love Naples, and everything will work itself out. Also, the orders aren't here yet! … Actually, this should be joyous news, so it's utterly ridiculous that we should have long faces. It's the goal Bus has been working toward, and the second star usually isn't too many years after the first! [178]

*Bradford promotes Wheeler to Brigadier General in Miramare Castle, Trieste, 8 November 1952. (Wheeler Family Records).*

A day after relinquishing command of the 351st, Wheeler was, in fact, promoted to temporary Brigadier General on 8 November in a ceremony in Miramare Castle officiated by Bradford. Prior to departing for Naples twelve days later, he served temporarily as the Deputy Commanding General, TRUST. [179]

# CHAPTER 4

## HERR GENERAL
## (NOVEMBER 1952 – SEPTEMBER 1958)

### *Indochina*

By the end of 1952, the military outlook in Indochina was dreary, and the political scene no brighter. The Bao Dai government had little more popular support than it had enjoyed in January and had few prospects for gaining support.

The situation did not seem hopeless to the U.S. government, but the word "stalemate" appeared more frequently in reports from Saigon, in intelligence estimates, and in conversations among U.S. officials. American planners sought to prevent the entry of Communist China, and to strengthen friendly forces so that the stalemate could be broken.

Four important trends emerged during this period regarding U.S. policy toward the Indochinese War. First, Washington, together with Paris and Saigon, became a center of political and military strategic planning for the war. The vital military aid program was determined in the U.S. capital, and numerous consultations between American, British, and French officials were held there. Second, the U.S. was drawn into closer cooperation with the British and French on the problems of the region. Fearing that this might lead to a combined command or to increased U.S. responsibility for the Indochinese conflict, the Joint Chiefs of Staff protested with little success. Third, the threat of Communist Chinese intervention began to dwarf other factors in the Southeast Asian picture, and the French seemed obsessed with this danger. Finally, French resolve began to crack under the triple burden of the Indochinese War, European rearmament, and the chronic instability of its government. By no means ignored in U.S. planning, rapid progress of this trend was not generally foreseen.

The promulgation of NSC 124/2 was the most important development in U.S. policy toward Indochina in 1952. Pursuantly, the U.S. government would become more involved in the Southeast Asian struggle against Communism.

However, the U.S. kept responsibility for the war in the hands of the French. It refused to be drawn into a combined military command in Southeast Asia, and sidestepped participation in a purely local defense of Indochina. American representatives backed the French position on Indochina in the United Nations and in international conferences, and they assured the French government of continued U.S. support for France's war efforts. Furthermore, the Truman Administration expanded the military aid program for Indochina and publicized its contribution to the war.

One provision of NSC 124/2, the obligation to educate the American people concerning the importance of Southeast Asia to U.S. security in order to prepare them for the courses of action contemplated by the National Security Council, was neglected during 1952. A progress report the following summer would find no indication that public opinion would support a contribution to the Indochinese War other than the current aid program. American military participation would not be acceptable to the public. [1]

' With presidential approval of NSC 124/2, the Chiefs had a firm policy for planning, which included consideration of unilateral action against Chinese Communist aggression in Southeast Asia. On 29 August, they directed the Commander-in-Chief, Pacific Command (CINCPAC) to make unilateral plans, which, in addition to preparing for unilateral action, would develop a U.S. position in the event of an agreement for Allied combined planning. CINCPAC was instructed to plan for a naval blockade of Communist China, for supporting participation of Chinese Nationalist forces in hostilities, for assisting in evacuation of the Tonkin Delta, and for military action against selected targets held by Communist China.

On 6 October, the military representatives of the United Kingdom, France, Australia, and New Zealand met with a U.S. delegation in Washington. The conference report generally conformed to long-standing JCS positions, including the assertion that:

> A combination of all coercive measures including the defense of the areas of aggression, interdiction of the lines of communication, a full sea blockade and air attacks on all suitable targets of military significance in China, insofar as they are within the allied capabilities, plus reinforcements in time

and scale as may be practicable in the immediate area, offers the best prospect of causing Communist China to cease an aggression. [2]

## *Naples*

Meanwhile, the Wheelers had driven to Naples, where Bus assumed duties as the Readiness Officer for Headquarters, Allied Forces Southern Europe (HAFSE) on 24 November. [3]

*As a Brigadier General, Wheeler served in the Allied Forces Southern Europe headquarters in Naples, Italy from 1952 to 1955. (Wheeler Family Records).*

The Wheelers stayed in the Grand Hotel Europa before finding a tiny apartment on the *Via Caracciola*, the main boulevard running along the Bay of Naples. Space-wise, it was a huge step down from their massive quarters in Trieste, but with Mount Vesuvius off to the south and Capri several miles away across the wide bay, the Wheelers immediately understood the saying, "See Naples and die." [4]

Upon closer inspection, the magnificent view was far from perfect. Naples and the Neapolitans were still recovering from the war. Ships that had been sunk to block the harbor still had not been salvaged. Docks that had been damaged were under repair. The Neapolitans were still very poor, and some families even lived in caves. [5]

## 1953

The Wheelers had heard of the Italian custom of throwing out all the broken furniture and crockery into the street on New Year's Eve, but they were shocked the next morning by the sheer amount of debris lining the boulevard.

Their apartment was next to the U.S. Embassy, which was located on the square at the northern end of the big, downtown park. During summers, a sizable amusement park named Luna Park operated there. [6]

Twelve-year old Bim and his friends enjoyed the park, but more often they made mischief. One time, they targeted some *Carabinieri* horses with darts blown from homemade blowguns that they had fashioned out pieces of pipe. Another time, the boys grew bored dropping water balloons from the fourth floor of their apartment building onto passersby below and switched to bombing them with paper shopping bags filled with water instead. The building's concierge kept the boys out of trouble with irate pedestrians, but he did tell their parents.

The Wheelers gave Bim a lot of freedom relative to his age. They enforced a simple rule of behavior: they expected him to use good judgment. Whenever he didn't, he faced Bus's wrath.

Bus never actually yelled, and he didn't curse much when he was angry. Rather, while casting a "baleful eye," he calmly explained to Bim or whomever had disappointed him how they had let him down, let the country down, and let themselves down. According to Bim, by the time he had finished, "You were psychologically destroyed. You wished he'd just have yelled or pulled out the belt." Bim always dreaded what followed whenever he heard his father say, "Come over here and sit down. I want to talk to you, son." [7]

(Years later, an Army Colonel who had worked for Wheeler told Bim that his father was the greatest ass chewer ever. Bim interrupted him with a recital of what his ass chewings sounded like. Astounded, the Colonel asked him how he knew. Bim replied, "You only got it when you worked for him. I've had a whole lifetime of them!" ) [8]

The Wheelers had begun allowing Bim to drink an occasional beer at around eleven years old, which was not uncommon in those days, especially in Europe. From when Bim was a youngster, they had encouraged him to address them as "Bus and Betty". By the time they moved to Trieste, he began calling them "Mom and Pop." Whenever he was in trouble, it was "Mother and Bus." Whenever he was in real trouble with his father, it was "Sir." [9]

Bim recalls his father as kind and loving. Once, when Bim accidently jammed an *Xacto* knife into his thigh while building a model airplane, Bus took him the dispensary. As a Navy corpsman sewed up the wound without any painkiller, Bus held his son's hand the whole time. [10]

When Bim decided to write a book "reminiscent of 'The Hardy Boys' [mystery series]", Bus encouraged him. Betty recounted:

> ... The plot seems to be his own, and he told [Betty] all of it. It has kept him busy, and if it never goes beyond the three chapters already written, it is good practice. ... Bus said Bim's book was too much like the Hardy Boys. After much conversation, Bim has taken up short stories and [is] attempting to follow a pattern that Bus laid out for him. [11]

Soon after arriving in Naples, Betty, who for twenty years had dyed her naturally light brown hair platinum blonde, began varying her hair color. She may have felt she stood out too much and didn't appreciate being cat-called. Or, she may have believed that a general's wife needed a more understated look. For whatever reason, and much to Bus's dissatisfaction and Bim's horror, she came home one day with dark hair in lieu of her platinum tresses. Their pleas failed to dissuade her. From then on, she would mostly just highlight her natural color. [12]

## *Korea*

An armistice was signed on 27 July, suspending the war in Korea. The war's impact reached far beyond the peninsula. Despite criticism of the armistice by those who agreed with MacArthur that there is no substitute for victory, the U. N. Command had upheld the principle of suppressing armed aggression.

For China, the war had brought several benefits. It had maintained North Korea as a buffer state on its sensitive northern border. Soviet assistance, especially in improving the Chinese Army and Air Force, gave China a more powerful military posture at war's end than when it had intervened. Its performance in Korea, despite vast losses, had won China respect as a nation to be reckoned with, not only in Asia, but also in world affairs. [13]

For the United States, the war brought a major change in its containment strategy against the Soviet Union. Instead of relying principally on economic and political tools backed by a small nuclear deterrent force, containment's emphasis shifted during the war to military means. [14]

The war had provided the political context for rearmament and the development of NATO. Since 1950, the U.S. had tripled the size of its Armed Forces and quadrupled its defense budget. It also redefined the Communist threat to a challenge of global proportions. The war had drawn the U.S. into a more active role in Asia, which now joined Europe as part of the Free World system of collective, forward defense. During the war or shortly after its conclusion, the U.S. entered mutual security agreements with Japan (which began its own rearmament), the Republic of Korea, Taiwan, the Philippines, Australia, and New Zealand. More ominously, the Truman Administration increased its support to the French war in Indochina, but it also demanded that the French develop Laos, Cambodia, and Vietnam as autonomous states. [15]

While President Eisenhower would reduce military spending after the war, the U.S. Armed Forces would remain much larger than they had been in 1950, possess many more and increasingly powerful nuclear weapons, and would be ensured a steady supply of manpower by the retention of conscription. The U.S. military, after the humiliating and bloody defeats of the Korean War's first six months, would shift its focus from preparing for a World War II-type mobilization to maintaining forces ready for immediate use. This larger military, eager to put the frustrations of the war behind it, would now be widely dispersed around the world, including Indochina, where U.S. advisors would assist the new Republic of Vietnam.

Although the Korean War ended in a stalemate, it had clearly shown that the U.S. was the only nation strong enough to offer determined resistance to Communist expansion. In the past, the nation had turned to its military only when threatened. From 1953 onward, however, it would have little choice but to use its armed forces as an open and indispensable element in its conduct of foreign affairs. Confronting opponents who regarded war as a logical and necessary extension of politics, the U.S. would turn their own tactics against them by backing its diplomats with the threat of force. The American people accepted the new approach with remarkable composure. In so doing, they revealed a willingness to shoulder not only the huge costs, but also the heavy moral obligations that leadership of the West necessarily entailed. [16]

## *Indochina*

The new Eisenhower Administration changed little in U.S. policy toward Indochina. The end of the war in Korea removed the main competitor for increased aid funds for that area.

At the same time, the Administration brought in new faces. Secretary of State John Foster Dulles advocated exploiting U.S. atomic power as a deterrent to Communist aggression. Secretary of Defense Charles E. Wilson reassessed the defense budget. The President also had the opportunity to make made new appointments to the Joint Chiefs of Staff. Completed by the end of the summer, this organization brought in Admiral Arthur W. Radford became Chairman; General Matthew B. Ridgway became Chief of Staff of the Army; Admiral Robert P. Carney became Chief of Naval Operations; and General Nathan F. Twining became Chief of Staff of the Air Force.

For the United States, the struggle for Southeast Asia appeared in 1953 as a continuation of the fight against Communist Chinese aggression waged in Korea. Dulles conveyed veiled warnings to the Chinese during the truce talks. With the armistice at the end of July, American leaders feared that the enemy might shift efforts to Southeast Asia. Accordingly, the government intended to give major financial support to the French, sought to deter outside intervention, and considered what to do should deterrence fail. [17]

The Chiefs were closely involved in the months-long U.S. endeavor to gain French commitment to an Indochina plan that held reasonable promise of success. Besides making numerous detailed decisions regarding the aid program, the Chiefs' responsibility included planning for contingencies other than the successful conclusion to the war.

A Joint Staff study conducted in early 1953 had concluded that if Communist Chinese aggression drove the French out of Indochina, there was no feasible course of military action that the U.S. could take in Indochina to prevent Communist forces from overrunning the country. Furthermore, extension of full U.S. and Allied counteraction to the portion of China contiguous to the Tonkin border would not halt the aggression. To succeed, the U.S. must apply all available coercive measures against the Chinese mainland, including a naval blockade and air attacks on all targets of military significance. Preventing the Far Eastern situation from reaching such a state was a prime objective of U.S. policy. [18]

Ridgway, while serving as Commander of United Nations forces in Korea, advised that "civilian authorities ... need to work closely with military authorities in setting attainable goals and in selecting the means to attain them." Further presaging the difficulties of strategic decision-making in Vietnam, Ridgway said, "A war without goals would be most dangerous of all, and nearly as dangerous would be a war with only some vaguely stated aim, such as 'victory' or 'freedom from aggression' or 'the right of the people to choose their own government.'" [19]

## Eisenhower's NSC

According to Bobby Cutler, Eisenhower's first National Security Assistant:

President Eisenhower used the National Security Council as a vital mechanism to assure that all sides of an issue could be known by him before coming to his decision. He wanted a skilled planning arm to gather from informed sources that material relevant to each issue, to winnow and to test that material in the crucible of argument, and to bring the integrated, exactly phrased result before the Council for debate in his presence.

The National Security Council has emerged as a mechanism of the Executive Branch ... equal in importance to the Cabinet. ... Out of the grinding of these minds comes a refinement of the raw material into valuable metal, out of the frank assertion of different views, backed up by preparation that searches every nook and cranny, merges a resolution that reasonable men can support. [20]

## *Naples*

Meanwhile in Naples, Betty resumed her volunteer work in late summer 1953. She reported:

> Saturday night, I did my first stint at the U.S.O. The place itself is quite beautiful for a center of its kind. There are still no junior hostesses, and the jukebox has not arrived, so it's still quite quiet. As Bus will be away, most of the time until at least Christmas, I can give quite a few evenings. ... I'll try to take on a morning a week. [21]

Weeks later, Betty wrote:

> Sitting on a stool behind the counter at the U.S. O. I am so tired! I worked down here [two nights ago]. Baked two cakes. It's unbelievable, the joy with which they're received. I can't take on steady baking, though. One cake every Saturday is enough. However, when I work nights I'll bring a couple. This is proving a most interesting experience. In the hospital [in Trieste], I was on a steady move so [I] never really had time to talk to the boys. Here, I listen and listen. Girls, love, marriage, babies, and money! This is proving the best thing that could have been done for [the U.S. servicemen] in Naples. [22]

In mid-August, Lena, the Wheelers' maid and cook from Trieste, moved to Naples and resumed working for them while sharing their tiny apartment. She adored the family and was very kind to Bim who was entering his difficult teenage years. Besides her household duties, Lena also did the shopping. Although she was authorized to make purchases for the family from the U.S. commissary with a note from Betty, she often made many purchases on the Italian economy, something uncommon for most American families. (When the Wheelers' tour in Naples ended, they would ask to Lena to return to the States with them. Although she had become part of the family, she declined, claiming that she was afraid of boats and of flying. She and Betty would correspond in Italian for many years.) [23]

For some time, the Wheelers also employed a young Italian man named Vicenzo. He had gotten his girlfriend pregnant, and being Catholic, he married her. He and Betty visited Vicenzo and his wife when she had the baby. They were living in an apartment, or rather a compartment constructed out of unpainted cinder blocks inside and out. The floor was dirt and the latrine was a hole in the floor. Since he was in dire need of income, Bus helped get him a job at the U.S. Officers Club in Bagnoli. [24]

When Bus departed Naples on a two-week business trip to Washington, DC on 14 August, Betty advised her parents:

> I really don't think that there is any likelihood of our [moving back] to the U.S.. We can't be at all sure that when Bus finishes here, we won't stay in Europe. Doesn't it seem strange to think that Bim will have had five out of eight years in school in Europe? Bus sort of hopes that while he is in Washington he can find out how long this tour of duty will be. I hope we stay for another year, or at least until spring. But I suppose I'd leap if we got wind of a move. [25]

While Bus was in the States, Betty and Bim drove up to Garmisch. On the way up, they visited Trieste.

"It has been quite an experience to return [after ten months in Naples]," Betty wrote. "There is only a small group [from the Wheelers' yearlong tour there], but such warmth. And over and over again, 'If you and the General were only here.' Makes you feel good anyway." [26]

During their five days in Trieste, Betty attended two luncheons, two dinner parties, two cocktail parties, two dinners at the club, a tea, and a coffee. She wrote:

> I was entertained too much! Mrs. McFadden, the new [Major] General's wife [is] a very friendly older person, very different from Polly [Sebree] and Lois Bradford. ... Even though there were few people left that we knew, the warmth and affection from [those] remaining did your heart good. I gather Bus is sorely missed. I got enough to know that Bus will be wise not to go back. There is too much the men would like to tell him. I think it would be better not to hear. [27]

In Garmisch, the Wheelers stayed at Haus Tannenberg, a formerly private large home now a VIP guest house on the Riesersee.

"It's so quiet," Betty wrote. "It's lovely. Bim is playing pool. His new love, and when he's rich he's going to buy a pool table! ... We have a lovely suite. Can hardly complain!"

On 1 September, Bus returned from the States and joined them "bearing gifts and mail." [28]

After enjoying six days of leave, Wheeler signed-in to the NATO school in Garmisch. While he attended classes, Bim swam in the Riesersee while Betty "sunned and rested" in a chaise lounge in the garden. They also rowed around the lake in a rowboat. Betty reported:

> There were other people in the house, but I was there alone all day (some days Bim had lunch with me). The maid brought sandwiches to my side, and for the four days Bus was at school I did not stir. ... Wednesday night we went to an ice show. A regular night club. We had dinner there, danced, saw the show, danced, and on home. ... We really had a lot of fun. ... Friday night we took a British Brigadier and a Greek Major General to dinner. Bim played pool while we had drinks. There was a floor show of Bavarian dances. Really very good. We had a lot of fun. Our Greek general spoke no English. He understood it fortunately, and Bus did a good job with his French. I could remember a few words. Anyway, it was a successful evening. [29]

One afternoon during their stay in Garmisch, the Wheelers drove up to the Armed Forces Recreation Center at Chiemsee. On an island in the lake was an unfinished palace built by King Ludwig II of Bavaria that they were eager to visit.

> Four thousand candles are lit and there is a concert. ... It was almost three-thirty when we arrived. The concert started at 8:15 and the boat left at 7:30. We decided to have a drink and dinner. The inn had a pool table, so after we ate the boys played a little pool and I went to the library and read. When we arrived Bus put in his reservation for the boat trip. While we were at lunch, the Lieutenant who runs the inn told Bus that he could have a boat for us and if we left at 7:15 we could beat the crowd. It was perfect. At seven fifteen the Lieutenant

escorted us to what looked like an overgrown Cris Craft, and off we went. It's about a half hour ride. The sun was just setting. … The sky and water were pink. It was beautiful. By the time we arrived it was dark. Our "chauffer" spoke English and he took us to the (palace). It is about a ten minute walk. There was electricity inside the palace. The lower halls that are unfinished were lit with enough candles to see by. And then we stepped into the hall where the grand staircase is, and from there on every crystal chandelier was lit. I don't think you can imagine the sight. We walked through everything but Ludwig's private apartment. The hall of mirrors was lit with 2,000 candles. It was breathtakingly beautiful. There was string ensemble, but it was not a concert in the true sense. That made it perfect for us, as we were able to see it all and leave, thanks to our boat. As it was, it was going on ten before we got back to the inn. We stopped for sandwiches and coffee and back to Garmisch. It was a long ride, but oh so worth it. Another unforgettably beautiful evening. [30]

The family had "a bit of misfortune" on their return to Naples.

We were so glad it wasn't worse. It didn't mar our trip. In Verona, Bus stopped to ask a policeman the way to the hotel and a car ran into the door. Fortunately, Bus's leg was inside. It delayed us getting out of Verona, but that gave us a delightful stop in Pisa. Bim was so pleased with 'the tower' [from a previous trip with Betty] that he was most anxious for Bus to see it. After dinner, we took a carriage and drove out. We went a roundabout way, so I got to see a bit more of the city than formerly. I could have stayed in Verona several days. [31]

The Wheelers received saddening news upon their return to Naples.

"Merritt, one of the boys who drives for Bus, was killed in a motorcycle accident on Sunday. We feel awful. He was such a sweet youngster." [32]

Naples, meanwhile, was amid a weeklong *festa*. Betty reported:

You should see our fair city. The grand finale is Monday night, and they tell me it gets gayer and gayer. … It is beautiful along the waterfront. At intervals, electric signs, bowls of fruit, flowers, some figures in costume. It is unbelievable. Our back street is nothing but lights. There is a sign, practically in our living room, a silvery cascading waterfall. … The lights are fairyland. Their "Coney Island" is on other streets with all sorts of amusements. They said that there was a parade (four nights ago) that started at 9 P. M. and lasted until 4 A. M., but it's nothing (they say) compared to what is yet to come! Wouldn't you know, Bus has to go to Turkey tonight for a week. I was so in hopes that we could go out tonight and walk through the park and see the sights. [33]

Wheeler took frequent business trips to Germany, France, Greece, Turkey, and the States.

"Bus got in around three-thirty on Friday," Betty wrote. "He takes off tomorrow (Wednesday) morning to be gone until next Monday. What a bore. It's so maddening when it includes a weekend." [34]

Nine days later, she wrote. "Bus got in from Germany at one, Sunday morning [28 September. While there] on Friday, he woke up with a fever of a hundred and three. By Saturday, the fever was gone so he came on home. He felt miserable Sunday, small wonder, as it is a terrific drive. He worked half a day on Monday. I think it's about over now." [35]

A few days before Wheeler was promoted to permanent Colonel on 6 October, his mother visited the family in Naples.

"Isn't it a shame that she wouldn't let me call her Ida?" Betty mused to her own mother. "[After 21 years of marriage], I still choke over the 'Mumsie.'" It's so silly. I can say it, and write to her, but I find it very difficult to use. And I should stop *Mrs. W'ing* her in my letters. Bless her heart, the 'Mumsie' suits her now." [36]

"Somehow, this seems a very exciting birthday," Betty gushed on 28 October. "If my life to now is just a sample, how wonderful!" [37]

She and Bus had truly enjoyed their many years in Europe. They travelled extensively whenever Bus's scheduled allowed. They toured all the major cities and, of course, visited the historical sites of Pompei and Herculaneum not far from Naples. In Pompei, Bus viewed a Roman brothel decorated with erotic frescoes. As only adult male tourists were permitted to enter, Betty and Bim waited outside for him.

Many U.S. military families complained about the Italians and living in Italy. Not so the Wheelers, who made numerous Italian friends. One was Joe Quattrone, a Vice President with the Bank of Italy. His wife Rose was an American who had lived in Italy so long that she spoke English with an Italian accent. Joe's nickname for Bus was "Roman Emperor," and Betty was "Wide Eyed American Princess." (The Quattrones would remain lifelong friends of the Wheelers. After Bus's death in 1975, Rose would move to Martinsburg, West Virginia to be near Betty.) [38]

The Wheelers also befriended their Italian tailor. They enjoyed dinners at his family's house and dined out together every so often. [39]

Some of the Wheelers' other Italian friends owned a restaurant in the Posilipo district on the northern side of Naples. On a high cliff overlooking the bay, the restaurant had a spectacular view. The Wheelers dined there often. On their first visit, the owner's grandson, a toddler, was outside on the terrace wearing nothing but an undershirt. "My god," Betty remarked, "I think he would be embarrassed." Bus replied, "He is, 'im bare assed." [40]

Another time, Bus and Bim both drank *Birra Peroni*. After Bus inadvertently ordered a second round of inferior *Birra Perioni* and tasted it, he opined that it "should be poured back into the horse." [41]

## *Defense Reorganization*

On 1 July 1953, Eisenhower reorganized the Department of Defense and the Joint Chiefs of Staff at the expense of the separate Services. He enhanced the authority of the Secretary of Defense by increasing the number of Assistant Secretaries from three to nine. In a bow to the military, the Chairman of the Joint Chiefs of Staff became the principal military advisor to the Secretary of Defense and to the President. He was also given the authority to manage the Joint Staff and approve the selection of officers to serve on it. Eisenhower expected the Chairman to recruit officers who would focus not just on the interests of their own Service, but on "national planning for the overall common defense." [42]

Historian Robert Jordan points out that there have been occasional criticisms that the Chairman of the Joint Chiefs of Staff either had too much authority to speak out or too little. "Critics of the system seem to have forgotten that one of the complaints about the Joint Chiefs in the mid-1950s ... was that Admiral Arthur Radford had too much influence with President Eisenhower, not too little." In fact, Ridgway and then General Maxwell D. Taylor claimed that Eisenhower's massive retaliation strategy and his reduction of the Army's size represented an excessive dependency on Radford's military advice. [43]

## The New Look

With the end of hostilities in Korea, the Eisenhower Administration had to provide for the nation's defense by determining a strategy for the future and by configuring the Armed Forces to carry it out. Torn between pressures from worldwide commitments and a desire to cut back on defense spending, Eisenhower approved NSC-162/2, his "New Look" strategy on 29 October. Dubbed the "New Look" by Radford, this policy placed major emphasis upon airpower and America's nuclear superiority. Its name did not imply an abrupt change from the Truman Administration's containment policy, but sought, rather, to reduce the military budget by minimizing conventional forces and maximizing nuclear forces. Accompanying this shift was increased reliance on covert operations against unfriendly regimes.

"The basic decision," observed Dulles, "was to depend primarily upon a great capacity to retaliate, instantly, by means and at places of our choosing." This would allow the Department of Defense to mold the Armed Forces into a shape that best suited official policy without having to prepare for every threat the Communists might pose. [44]

"The logical thing," according to Radford, "was to emphasize America's nuclear striking power and to rely on indigenous ground forces as a first line of defense against local aggression. American forces should be redeployed to the United States where they would be reorganized to form a small, highly mobile strategic reserve that could come to the aid of our allies in the event of a war." [45]

With the new emphasis on massive retaliation, the Air Force would increase the size of its strategic bombing forces, spending huge sums on new bombers and missiles. The Navy would concentrate on developing a new submarine-launched nuclear missile (the Polaris), and the Army would seek to perfect tactical nuclear weapons to support the soldier on the battlefield. Since the military budget divided along Service rather than functional lines, the annual allocation of funds almost inevitably provoked bitter infighting. [46]

With continual bickering among the Services over their respective budgetary justifications, any hope of an orderly system of war planning fell by the wayside because of the situation, which had taken on a dimension that was more than just a "roles and missions" dispute. To make matters even more confusing, the Chiefs would air their complaints before Congress, much to Eisenhower's intense displeasure.

Eisenhower contemplated ways to control the Chiefs' testimony. In a meeting on 25 January 1960, Twining, then Chairman, would admit that he was troubled by [the Senate] Preparedness Committee's practice of requiring the Chiefs to testify under oath. ... The President had a simple solution for such situations: "Any military man who appears before the group and is required to take an oath," he said, "should refuse to give any opinion and judgment and limit his testimony strictly to facts." [47]

Over time, the Air Force's share of the budget would become so large that it diminished the U.S. capacity to wage a conventional war. As it did, opposition to massive retaliation mounted. Ridgway was particularly pointed in his criticism. He would note in June 1955 that as Soviet nuclear capabilities grew, nuclear parity between the two sides would ensure that neither had an advantage. When that parity occurred, the Soviets could gain the edge by provoking confrontations so limited in size that they could never justly resort to nuclear weapons. Armed with "leftovers" from the budget process, conventional U.S. forces would lack the means to respond. A balanced force was necessary, Ridgway implied, one that could cope with either a general or a limited war.

Taylor, Ridgway's successor as Chief of Staff of the Army, would support his plea, as would many prominent academics. Change, however, would not come until the end of the decade, when the Soviet Union's parity with the U.S. was no longer in dispute. At that point, supporters of the nuclear option had little choice but to concede that a general war would result in mutual self-destruction and that massive retaliation should only be a *last* resort. [48]

## *Berchtesgaden*

On 12 December, Betty's parents visited them in Europe for the third time. There was no room in the family's small apartment, so the Howells stayed in the Grand Hotel Europa. During their stay, Betty's father taught Bim how to play gin rummy. (On quiet, stay-at-home evenings, the Wheelers often enjoyed playing games of chance, dominoes and cribbage among their favorites.) After seeing Naples, Capri, and Rome with Betty's parents, the Wheelers drove up to the Armed Forces Recreation Center in Berchtesgaden for the holidays. [49]

Driving their Austin, they entered Germany through the Brenner Pass. The weather was miserable with a great amount of snowfall. At one point, Bus stopped to purchase some chains and had them fitted to the wheels. It was extremely cold, and the Austin's heater was inadequate. Bim sat in the backseat wrapped in a blanket. The snow was piled along the shoulder much higher than the cars. This made traversing the pass tricky because only one lane of traffic was open to both directions. There were "pullovers" every so often to allow cars to pass each other. The Wheelers proceeded with caution. Whenever they encountered another car coming toward them, one of them had to back up to the nearest "pullover". It was a hairy trip, but they made it without incident.

When they arrived at the customs post on the border with Germany, they were queried by a border policeman in a military-style uniform. From the back seat, Bim leaned forward to his father and commented on the German's "Hitler hat". Bus whispered, "Keep your mouth shut!" He also gave him his "baleful eyeball," later described by Bim as an incredulous, "Am I really hearing this?" look that Bus gave whenever he was exasperated or deeply disappointed. [50]

During the Nazi era, Berchtesgaden was the party elite's playground. Adolf Hitler had three residences there, the Berghof and the Eagles Nest being the most famous. Other top Nazi leaders like Goering, Goebbels, and Bormann also had villas there. An SS *kaserne* and numerous other military installations were located nearby. Apropos of Wheeler, Berchtesgaden was the center of the rumored National Redoubt against which he was supposed to lead the assault regiment. The town was heavily damaged in one of the final Allied bombing raids in April 1945.

The Wheelers stayed in the former Nazi Party hotel, the Platterhof, which was rebuilt in 1952 and renamed the Hotel General Walker for use by the U.S. Armed Forces. The hotel had a game room where Bus challenged his son to a game of pool. Bim was confident in his own skills, so he accepted "the old man's" challenge. Bus ran the table on him.

"Where did that come from?" Bim exclaimed.

"Son," Bus replied, "that's just a sign of a misspent youth!" [51]

## 1954

### *Naples*

In early January 1954, the Wheelers began looking for a new place to rent on the mountainside above Naples. One reason for their search was that in their apartment, Heidle could not be let out on his own. They had to walk him on the street, and it had become tiresome. Not only that, he had been attacked by several dogs and seriously injured.

"We have taken him to the vet every other day," wrote Betty. "His head is still tied up, and now we're redoing the bandage every half day." Heidle was an active dog, which didn't help his healing process. "[He] tore his stitches again. We are very worried. We never leave him alone a minute and Bus is sleeping in the double bed with him." [52]

After looking at four other apartments, the Wheelers found a new, single story garden house high on the mountain on *Via Aniello Falcone* near the Vomero on 25 January. Bus and Bim liked it, but Betty wasn't so keen. [53]

> The decision is still up in the air. ... There is a beautiful view ... [but] it leaves me cold. However, ... I'm worn out with [walking] Heidle [several times daily], and God knows Bus must be, and to be able to stick him [outside] would be something. So, with everybody else satisfied, if they will hold it until March 1st [I] imagine that we'll take it. ... Actually,

we've had a more than perfect year, and to be able to put Heidle out of mind, might make the rest of the time here equally perfect! The terrace is quite lovely, and once the warm weather comes we probably will be out all of the time. There are three bedrooms, larger than here, and we will have a storeroom plus a large garage. The view is lovely … way up, [and we can see] straight across to Sorrento and Capri. No Vesuvio, but I've certainly had a beautiful year of looking. [54]

Another reason the Wheelers needed a new house was because the housing allowance for U.S. military families had been cut. "The fact that the rent will be considerably less than here, and makes it about comparable to the cut in the station allowance, we feel very encouraged," Betty explained. "At least, we feel the price goes along with what we're getting." [55]

Bus signed the contract on 25 January, Betty reported.

Our landlord … told Bus that this was the first apartment he had ever rented and he feels that as it is to a military man he is lucky. We learned a new one – Italians deem it good luck to pass a soldier on the street, but to have one in your house is too good to be true! I would say the good fortune is coming our way too. They assure us the terrace will be finished by March 1st and that everything will be in good order. [56]

## *Indochina*

As France's situation in Vietnam deteriorated during 1953 and 1954, the Eisenhower Administration was forced to consider direct military intervention to save the beleaguered garrison at Dien Bien Phu and to possibly take a larger general role in the fighting. Ultimately, Eisenhower rejected military intervention and decided to try to deal with the consequences of the now certain French defeat through diplomacy.

Dien Bien Phu fell on 7 May, and the U.S. reconciled itself to a partition of Vietnam under the Geneva Agreements. Following Geneva, the U.S. turned to building a collective defense organization for Southeast Asia. It also took a direct hand in training and equipping armed forces of the new anti-Communist state of South Vietnam, gradually supplanting France as South Vietnam's principle foreign sponsor. [57]

The Chiefs subscribed to the view that a Communist takeover of Vietnam would undermine the U.S. strategic position in the Far East. They regularly endorsed military aid to the French and sought to assist in the training and equipping of indigenous armed forces. Yet, they presciently approached with caution direct U.S. military engagement in the Indochina conflict. Any such engagement, especially of ground troops, would divert scarce resources from higher priority tasks, such as the war in Korea and the NATO buildup in Europe, to a costly and likely indecisive campaign. In the context of planning for a general war with the Communist Bloc, the Chiefs considered Indochina devoid of significant strategic interest and urged that the U.S. avoid any commitment to fight there. In their view, the defense of Indochina, whether in a limited or general war, should be the responsibility of U.S. Allies and indigenous forces.

The Chiefs clearly preferred to counter Communist aggression in Indochina with U.S. sea and air power. Besides strikes and direct support of Allied troops in combat, they advocated air attacks on enemy bases and lines of communication in the People's Republic of China, the ultimate source of Communist strength. Their contingency plans for defeating an overt Chinese attack on Southeast Asia—a possibility always in their minds—called for an extensive air atomic assault on Chinese targets combined with a naval blockade of the mainland and perhaps a Chinese Nationalist invasion from Taiwan. As the Vietnam situation unfolded after 1954, discussion of nuclear weapons, Nationalists, and attacking China would fade away; but the Chiefs' preference for decisive air and naval pressure on the source of aggression over indecisive local ground operations would remain constant during the policy debate. [58]

Ridgway, the Chief of Staff of the Army, commented on his view of the relationship between the military leadership and the civilian decision-makers:

> The statesman, the senior civilian authority, says to the soldier (and by 'soldier' I mean the professional military man -- the Army, the Navy, and Air Force as represented in the persons of the [Joint] Chiefs of Staff): 'This is our national policy. This is what we wish to accomplish, or would like to

do. What military means are required to support it?' The soldier studies this problem in detail. 'Very well,' he says to the statesman. 'Here is what your policy will require in men and guns, and ships and planes.' If civilian authority finds the cost to be greater than the country can bear, then either the objectives themselves should be modified, or the responsibility for the risks involved should be forthrightly accepted. Under no circumstances, regardless of pressures from whatever source or motive, should the professional military man yield, or compromise his judgment for other than convincing military reasons. To do otherwise would be to destroy his usefulness. [59]

The Chiefs, like other U.S. officials, believed they understood the reasons for France's defeat in Indochina. French military strategy had been overly defensive, lacking the dash and determination required to press home perceived advantages of numbers, mobility, and firepower, thus violating the Principles of War. On the political side, the French had refused until too late to take actions that would have given Bao Dai's regime credibility as a rallying point for non-Communist Vietnamese nationalists. Without a strong indigenous government, the French had failed to develop effective local armed forces to control and pacify the country. If these errors could be rectified and a workable collective Southeast Asia defense organization established, U.S. officials were confident that they could preserve South Vietnam, Cambodia, and Laos for the Free World.

They would have their chance to try. On 8 September at Manila, the U.S., Great Britain, France, Australia, New Zealand, the Philippines, Thailand, and Pakistan signed a treaty creating the Southeast Asia Treaty Organization (SEATO). The three states of former French Indochina—South Vietnam, Cambodia, and Laos—were barred from joining by the Geneva Agreements, but they were included under SEATO's protection.

At the same time, the U.S. believed it had found its Vietnamese anti-Communist leader in Ngo Dinh Diem, Bao Dai's premiere. With U.S. support, Diem would consolidate his control over South Vietnam. Bao Dai would fade from the scene, and Diem would become President of the Republic of Vietnam (RVN), bolstered by U.S. economic and military aid. Except for North Vietnam, Southeast Asia remained outside the Communist orbit. The Chiefs' worst fears did not materialize—yet. [60]

## NATO

Meanwhile, a major U.S. buildup had taken place in Europe. Concerned that the Soviet Union might yet launch an offensive on the continent, the U.S. had increased its forces there from one to five divisions and strengthened NATO's ground, air, and naval forces. In response, the alliance had adopted a "forward defense" strategy that contemplated a defense of West Germany as far east of the Rhine as possible. [61]

The conclusion of the Korean War, the death of Stalin, and the launch of a Soviet peace initiative a short while later led to an easing of international tensions and a slowing of the NATO buildup. This allowed the U.S. and its Allies to shift their attention toward improving communications and the construction of roads, airfields, and logistical depots. As those efforts proceeded, the U.S. began to press for German rearmament. Despite strong opposition from the Communist Bloc, the Western Allies agreed to the idea in 1954, approving the formation of a twelve-division German army.

The U.S. also moved to remedy a growing imbalance between Communist and NATO ground forces by fitting tactical nuclear warheads to artillery shells and missiles. As the weapons came online, the alliance based its planning on an assumption that they would form the foundation of its response to a Soviet attack. Cracks appeared in NATO's common front, however, when the U.S. declined to share its exclusive control of the devices through consultation with its Allies. In the end, the British and French decided to lessen their dependence upon the U.S. by developing nuclear weapons of their own. [62]

## Naples

In mid-June, Wheeler was ordered to Trieste after General McFadden suffered a heart attack. Betty explained:

> As Trieste is a separate command, General Gruenther couldn't send him without consulting [General] Ridgway. But he cabled Washington and said that Wheeler was immediately

available to be the stop gap until a replacement was found. No one knew how seriously Gen. McFadden was and it left Trieste without a general. They [ended up sending] a Major General in from Germany, who will assume command permanently. However, it made Bus feel very good that General Gruenther thought of him immediately, and it certainly had all circles buzzing, and caused considerable excitement as you can imagine. [63]

On 10 July, a series of moves occurred among the general officers of Admiral William M. Fechteler's Allied Forces Southern Europe headquarters. Brigadier General Frank Roberts, Assistant Chief of Staff for Plans and Operations, succeeded Major General Clovis E. Byers as Chief of Staff. Wheeler replaced Roberts as Assistant Chief of Staff for Plans and Operations. Brigadier General Mike Michaelis replaced Wheeler as Readiness Officer. [64] This was a big move upward for Bus, as Betty explained to her parents:

> We went to a tremendous cocktail party for an Italian general last night. I was interested in the group gathering around "the new boss" (Bus)! It's the plans and operations section and a considerably larger job. So that leads us to this. We will undoubtedly be here another full year. Bus come Sept. is due for reassignment. He's delighted with the job, delighted to work with Frank [Roberts]. He and Frank have talked it over. Bus has made all this clear, but has told Frank that he will not ask to stay. So Admiral Fechteler will ask. As Bus says, it's one thing to stay at the admiral's request, and quite another on his own. This opens the question of whether there are other plans for Wheeler. By another month or six weeks maybe sooner, we should know exactly where we stand. … Time will tell, but whatever, I'm quite sure it can only work out for the good of all concerned. [65]

"I have taken over a new job here," Bus informed Betty's father later that month. "I imagine I will be staying on for another year. At least the Boss has asked to retain my services and will probably receive an affirmative." [66]

Oftentimes, Wheeler helped entertain dignitaries visiting the command. The usual protocol included taking them on the admiral's barge to Capri.

The scenario is always the same: we go from Naples to the large harbor on Capri, go up on the funicular to the village, have a beer in the town square and then walk down the other side of the mountain to Gracie Fields' place. There the barge meets us, and we usually have a swim before starting back to Naples. Of course, after the swim we have a couple of martinis and then eat. All in all it makes for a good day in the open. [67]

Bus described the visit of Mr. Bob Stevens, a VIP friend of Betty's father:

A squall came up just before we got back on the barge and stirred the sea up to the point where I was not about to go swimming, because as you know I am not too good a swimmer anyway. Frank Roberts did not go in either and I noticed that the Admiral and Mr. Stevens were in barely long enough to get damp. At any rate, we violated the Admiral's rule that if you don't go swimming you are not entitled to a drink before lunch. On this occasion, he turned the matter over to Mr. Stevens since the rule had been violated by two generals. Mr. Stevens stated that he would take the matter under consideration. Since I saw the messboy coming up the ladder with a tray of drinks, I told Mr. Stevens that I hoped he was a man of quick decisions because he was faced with one at that moment. To this he replied that he was reasonably fast in making decisions and made them himself; that, for instance, no one had had to urge him, and it hadn't taken him very long to tell Senator McCarthy to go to hell. At this he turned to the Admiral, 'Of course, some of my decisions are wrong but at least they are decisions.' [68]

As with all U.S. Army officer families, money was tight with the Wheelers, and had been especially so during their two Italian tours. Betty was "the member of the family who manages the money," which was severely stretched in the summer of 1954.

First of all, they needed a new car to replace their ailing Austin. Bus selected a Morris Oxford station wagon, a woody with grey paint and red leather interior. (They would later ship it back to the States, and Bim would continue drive it through most of high school.) They kept the brand-new Morris in a very narrow stall in their building's parking garage. Bim, now fourteen years-old, decided to test his driving skills and attempted to pull it out of the garage. He scraped up the exterior pretty badly, which prompted another "Come over here and sit down, son" experience. [69]

The Wheelers bore the expense of frequent official entertaining out of their own pocket. Betty explained:

> We are faced with a big party. I could almost cry, which is ridiculous because certain things have to be done. Payment for success, but at such moments [I] wish for higher pay or an expense account! Since Bus took over [the Plans & Operations Division] we've been going round and round as to how to meet the problem. After all you don't entertain at home for nothing. Bus now has forty some officers under him and of all the NATO nationalities. If we entertained at home, it meant dividing the group, and I'll admit, I was the one who was dead set against it. So, I went to the club to make arrangements for a party on the 20th [of August]. Being involved with [Plans & Operations] and the Readiness office, we were [faced with] a hundred [guests] before we turned around. Anyway, once having started, we're getting all the foreign [senior officers] and [our senior officers], and doing the works. From all the invitations we'll send, we'll probably have a hundred and fifty accept. ... I am in high hopes that Bim will consent to receive with us, or at least come. [70]

That month, Wheeler's former West Point roommate and best man was selected for promotion to Brigadier General. Betty reported:

> We have been very happy to learn Jim Woolnough is on the list to be made BG. The three boys – Bus, Chuck [Churchill], and Jim – were so close, and I don't think the 'wives' [cadet slang for roommates] could break the bond they formed the three years they lived together at West Point. In fact, I'm sure it must be a record that they should be [selected for promotion] within two years of one another (as roommates, not classmates). It's funny. We were talking about it the other

night, and I said I hoped he got [selected] soon. It would be an awful thing to live with because, whatever the reason, we'd all blame Aggie [Woolnough]! Also, maybe this will bring out the best in her instead of the worst. God help the aide and his wife. On the other hand, the Army is full of 'queens' – [I] may even be one myself someday – so she won't be the first. I'll admit it must be a hard pill for some of the lovelier class-mates' wives to take. Aggie doesn't know it, but I'm probably the best friend she's got! To the Pascals, Davidsons, you and Bus, I've had quite a few remarks on the subject, but never a crack 'out of the family' as it were. Anyway, I hope to be pleasantly surprised when our paths cross again. [71]

*Betty with her parents Walter & Becca Howell on the patio of their house on Via Aniello Falcone overlooking Naples, Italy, 1954. (Wheeler Family Records).*

The Wheelers greatly enjoyed their terrace, and until late November would spend a lot of time relaxing, entertaining, and dining on it. They had always grilled frequently, mostly steaks, which Bus adeptly grilled to perfection. According to Betty:

We cooked steak last night. …We've [had] the same tonight. We've lived on meat and salads this summer. Bus is dieting. I think he needs to cut down on beer and wine. However, no sandwiches, and after a fashion we count calories. He has lost a little, and around the middle, which seems to be the only place he's put it. Bim has had a wonderful time [teasing] him. [72]

Overseas tours for military dependents, even those of senior officers such as Wheeler, could be challenging. Like many teenage "Army brats", Bim was nostalgic to return to the States. He informed his grandmother Becca that he had been in Italy so long that he was eligible for citizenship!

> My trip to Germany was great fun, especially since I got to get away from Italy for two weeks. Pop as you may know has been more or less extended for another year. … Pop says that even if he and mom have to stay over even beyond my freshman year in high school I will get to go home. At least that's some consolation. [73]

A month later, Bim added:

> I can't wait to get home to the gold old USA!!! But it looks as if I won't make it soon. Pop & I constantly have arguments over what I am going to take back with me & so on. I am telling you I've got enough stuff to start a pawn shop. [Since the family's tour in Germany, Bim had enjoyed collecting military antiques and weapons.] I aim to get it all back home though it seems as if I will have a hard time sneaking it in so Pop won't know I packed it. [74]

In late August, the Wheelers received word that Mumsie's former boss at the Veterans Bureau, a Dr. Schneider, would soon arrive in Naples and wished to visit with them. They dreaded the idea, as she had apparently left her job under tense circumstances. The visit that transpired illustrates the Wheelers' uncommon proclivity for making new friends across social and ethnic lines, a talent they would later employ constantly when he wore four stars.

The doctor and his wife were due to arrive on a Saturday. That Friday evening, Bus said, "I can't bear the thought."

Betty replied, "If you feel that way, nothing says you must, and we'll send flowers to the hotel and so sorry, not in town."

"No," Bus said. "We must as long as [we're] not honestly off elsewhere do something [with them]." He felt Dr. Schneider had gone through a lot himself and been understanding [of Mumsie's alcoholism].

"Saturday morning, we left a note at the [Schneiders'] hotel," Betty reported. "We would pick them up at seven, come here for drinks and D'Angelo's for dinner. As Bus said a change of scene, and then dump them at the hotel. [As it turned out], Bus and I were crazy about them."

Mumsie had badly tainted their preconceptions with derogatory remarks about Schneider. He was "a Russian, [who] made his way in the world. In a whisper, a Jew." [75]

After a delightful evening, Betty concluded:

> Well, if either he or his wife are Jewish, it's nothing to be held against them! … She is also a doctor. He in addition to his Veterans Bureau job is a professor at Georgetown. And what is more, they are both actively engaged as physicians. Bus and I enjoyed our evening thoroughly. And except for five or ten minutes, no talk of 'family'. He did say that if Mumsie would come back to work tomorrow, he'd be delighted! And he meant it. [76]

Three weeks later, the Wheelers were visited by Brigadier General (Retired) and Mrs. Camp. He had been Bus's Battalion Commander in the 29th Infantry Regiment at Fort Benning. Betty recorded:

> Grant (one of Bus's drivers) picked us up, and then we went to the Excelsior. [Despite not having seen the Camps since 1936,] I would have known them any place. We had a perfectly wonderful evening with them. They couldn't have been more fun. And whatever we thought was hard to take, I realize they and we have aged beautifully, and may the Wheelers continue to mellow! [77]

Betty's letters to her mother often included detailed descriptions of the latest dresses she was sewing. For twenty-two years now, she had sewn all her own clothing.

"The last [women's clothing] I bought in a store was [eight years earlier] in Natchez [in] May 1946, my ideas but not my work [in] 1948, and the three-piece suit in the wholesale house [in] Jan. of '49. I have moments when I long for a 'store bought' dress, and a shopping spree." [78] (She would continue to sew all her formal gowns during Bus's last eight years in uniform when she was in constant need of new ones.)

Meanwhile, Bim was growing up. "Our wonder boy is shaving," Betty wrote. "I don't know whether to laugh or cry. His mustache got so black, Bus suggested he use his electric razor."

Bim was embarrassed. "Gee, Pop, I'm only a fourteen year old!"

"Nothing further was said," wrote Betty, "but after a bit the upper lip disappeared. Yesterday or Saturday, Bus was after him again, much conversation, all in the light vein, and the fourteen year old boy [comment] came up again."

Bus said, "Son, you may be a fourteen year old boy, but you sure got a lot of peach fuzz!"

Bim drew himself up and said, "But, *pah, ah lahkes ma* peach fuzz!"

"I thought I'd collapse!" Betty laughed. [79]

Wheeler always put in long hours at the office. As a treat one Sunday in August, Fechteler invited him and Betty and other senior couples aboard his barge for a cruise to the Blue Grotto, which Bus hadn't seen yet. The following day was a holiday, but Bus worked in the morning. He did the same during the next "headquarters holiday" a few weeks later. [80]

Betty lamented the impact of his extended work hours:

> I'm dying to get back to the Venice area … and do Florence and Rome … by car, of course. Bus is going to be more confined than ever and I don't think there's a prayer of getting away. Possibly over Christmas, which is slow, and as he says, if he has to retire to do it, we're going to Sicily in the spring! So anything else I do, it would or will have to be on my own. [81]

## Ravello

In early November, NATO granted a five-day holiday in conjunction with All Saints Day. Bus "work[ed on] Saturday and Sunday mornings, and five hours on Thursday. … [He] worked for an hour or two Monday also." [82]

He took leave over the next five days to spend with Betty on her forty-first birthday. They drove to Ravello, a favorite weekend destination where they had always enjoyed the breathtaking views of the mountainous coastline from the Hotel Palumbo. Their trip was marred by tragedy.

You saw in the paper of the disaster from Salerno to Amalfi. … It was way overcast, not a bit pretty. … It sprinkled a little and then stopped. We could see across to Naples and there was spotty sun. When we started across the mountain the rain began. And it rained harder and harder and harder. Bus crawled along but with good windshield wipers … and the demisters. We had enough vision that we didn't stop. We were the only people on the road anyway. All along water pouring in gushes down the mountainside. All stairs were waterfalls. A truck driver, halted, in one of the tunnels waved us down, advised us to watch for rocks, better still stop, but in any event, be careful. As we approached Amalfi the rain had slackened, that is compared to what we'd been through. We reached Ravello about four, almost dark and a drizzle.

We walked into a beautiful snug room. … The fire was laid and in a matter of minutes blazing. More than made up for the rain! We sat in front of the fire, had a drink, read, and dozed. We couldn't have been more contented. The rain was coming down in buckets again, but it just added to the plea-sure of the fire.

About six-thirty we dressed and went downstairs. Had a drink in front of the fireplace. The owner joined us. … We went into the dining room about eight, and there sat a British Navy Captain from Naples and his wife. … The four of us had the [run of the] hotel. After dinner we had coffee and liquors together in front of the fire.

We went to sleep by the light of our own fire. Woke up many times during the night, as there was some thunder and light-ning. Also, I've never known it to rain so hard for so long, and it seemed to be getting worse. But as there was no wind, just a steady lulling downpour.

When I awoke at eight-thirty the sun was out. It was warm, and clouds were rising up out of the sea. We were able to have breakfast on the balcony (of our room). It appeared a beautiful world after the rain. Bus was in the tub when the boy came to get the tray. I don't know how he kept the news. Anyway, he couldn't contain it any longer and in little English and much Italian he told me of the disaster. At that time twenty dead. In fact … the concern was so great for the two little towns nearest us, that we had no idea how much worse it was at Salerno and Vietre. Ravello was buzzing. I don't believe anyone went to work. Everywhere groups were gathering. You could feel the concern and tragedy in the air.

After lunch, we drove down to Minore. It was a shambles. Mud and filth, cars crushed. Obviously the force of the water had rolled them. The town was crowded. The fire truck brought water while we were there, and naturally everyone was out. They pulled a body out of the sea, but fortunately we weren't close enough for a good view. The sea was filled with timber, and all around the beaches where the wind had churned the water, had turned blood red. [83]

The Wheelers spent another night at the hotel. "The food was wonderful, and the whole stay a treat," Betty wrote. "We regret the horrible misfortune of the others, and needless to say have had every reason to thank God that it was not the Ravello hillside that went into the sea." [84]

They stopped in Sorrento for lunch on their way back to Naples. "It was a heavenly day and has stayed that way all week. Bus and I have gotten on the terrace by eleven and stayed until the sun left around two-thirty. I've enjoyed his leave every bit as much as he did. In fact, it's been a weeklong birthday celebration. … How could anyone mind being forty-one when each year proves fuller and richer and one has so many, many blessings?" [85]

We'd barely gotten back from Ravello when the telephone started (ringing) … partly to be sure we were alright, and after Bus to come to the office. I gather that there was considerable concern for our welfare! Very flattering I suppose, but hardly restful. … The whole week slipped by all too fast. Bus got a much needed rest, and in the long run relaxed more at home than if we'd had a long trip. He didn't get home last night until 6:30. I think he had moments where he wondered if it was worth it. [86]

## *Drudgery*

"Three years ago today we landed in Trieste," Betty recalled on 7 November. "How fortunate we were to have the experience of a year there. Also, as of today, Bus, two years ago, was promoted [to Brigadier General]. What a full and unexpected time we've put in, in this tour overseas." [87]

But life as a general's lady wasn't all travel and parties. There was obligatory volunteer work to be performed. Betty did her part, but detested being told what she *must* do.

At a dinner party she attended solo due to Bus's short-notice departure for Paris earlier that day, she approached Mary Michaelis about taking over her duties with the USO.

"There's nothing to do but go to a board meeting once every two months," Betty explained.

Admiral Leaf McLean, who was Chairman of the USO board, interrupted. "Oh, we've changed all that. You're Chairman of the Hostess Committee."

"I am not!" Betty retorted. "And what's more, I won't be. And what's more, I'll send in my resignation, and you can get someone else."

McLean attempted to soothe her. "You don't mean that, and anyway you're the brightest spot on the board, and I couldn't get along without you. You know you don't mind being Chairman. You don't have to work."

"I do mind!" Betty shot back. It's a good thing I found out about this now, she thought, because the shock at the meeting would have been embarrassing.

"All right," McLean said. "Come to the meeting a few minutes early, and we'll talk about it."

"I'll be there," Betty replied, "but there's nothing to talk about, and Admiral, if you're trying to get a rise out of me, brother, you've succeeded!"

When she arrived, another spouse greeted her cheerfully. "Betty, you're the Chairman of the Hostess Committee!"

"I am not!" Betty exclaimed.

"Oh. You don't have to do anything," the woman suggested helpfully.

"Hmmm. I'm sorry, but I will not be on a committee," Betty reiterated. Looking at the agenda, she was furious to read "Our new Chairman, Mrs. Wheeler."

McLean came in, looked at the agenda, didn't say a word, and drew a line through Betty's name. He looked at her and said, "Just stay on the board. I know when I'm licked!"

*Amen*, Betty thought smugly. Bus would have handled the matter more delicately had he not been away. [88]

A month later, Betty vented to her mother again:

> Tuesday, I got roped into the damn Ladies Luncheon. As so often happens a tempest came up. I don't know the details, never going to the luncheon, but sparks were flying. Yesterday's meeting was very important. They planned to vote on a new program. ... After all the stew and all the fuss, it was voted to keep everything as it was! ... I arrived at 12:30 and didn't get away until four. Bored to tears! ... Well the duty is done and I hope they can get along without me from now on! [89]

## *Fall*

Between his usual long hours at the office, including some weekends, business trips, and a full social calendar, Wheeler sustained a blistering pace through the fall of 1954. Betty reported:

> He's been working awfully hard, and has been burdened with a lot of things that aren't actually his job. ... Thursday was a holiday (Armistice Day), and Bus stayed home. ... Yesterday (Saturday) ... Bus had a conference with the Admiral, but came home around ten. I took Bim and [his friend] to the football field around eleven. When I got home, Bus was in the sun. He said he felt too lazy to move, so we just sat and rested and soaked up the sun. We decided it was too beautiful to do anything so we went out for lunch. ... We listened to a ball game, but Bus felt steadily worse. He seemed to be up

and down all night. He was asleep when I went off to church, but typing when I got home. [90]

"Bus worked Thanksgiving morning," Betty reported. "I was supposed to take candy to the USO. I'd bought it, but forgot to take it in. It was a beautiful day. … When we came home we had beer and sandwiches outside." [91]

"Mike [Michaelis] is a very funny guy," she informed her mother. "[He] has his 2nd star much on his mind, is very rank conscious, and he's two years senior to Bus, and the fact that he took Bus's job seems to rankle. There have been constant undercurrents and as long as we're together it's better to keep the relationship friendly." [92]

As the crush of the holiday entertaining season approached, the Wheelers converted a room in their cramped house into a dining room.

"It is such a relief to have a dining room," Betty wrote. "This summer, it didn't matter, but we really need it."

They didn't have a dining room table, so Bus constructed one out of saw horses and plywood.

> Poor Bim is aching. He said he never heard of a General eating off of ply board. Well, neither the General nor his lady care. The dining room is by itself, and when we have guests [the table] will have a cloth on it. … At least we have a table that seats eight comfortably and that is what I'm after at the moment. [93]

The table took shape after Betty finished tacking on plastic and painting the saw horses. Bim exclaimed, "Mom, I oughta know when you get an idea about the house it's usually a good one!" Betty thought, *what greater compliment could one have?*

They hosted their first dinner guests on 12 December.

> The three couples we had were in Bus's division. One, an Italian Colonel and his wife. She didn't speak a word of English. I felt so pleased. I groped for words, at times, and my grammar was probably terrible, but, I got through the evening with ease, and none of the exhaustion that previously followed my efforts in Italian for any length of time. [94]

The Wheelers hoped to get away over the holidays, but "[General] Frank Roberts is leaving for Garmisch. He has told Bus that he will have to stay in Naples, so we wouldn't be able to take off even for a little while. Well, maybe this time next year we'll be in the States," Betty mused. [95]

On 19 December, Betty reported that they had tackled the large and perfect Christmas tree that Lena picked out.

> It seems a little early to be setting it up, but Bus may have to fly to Paris tomorrow for two or three days. ... Bim put the lights on with my holding them. ... We've been on a social tear, and the holidays are filling up. I refused all the ones at the club, and we're trying to go to people's homes, and for each refused, another invitation comes in. [96]

Bus's West Point roommate and best man Jim Churchill—a lifelong bachelor—arrived on 23 December to spend Christmas with the Wheelers. Betty explained:

> He will stay at the Vesuvio but will be with us most of his time. We plan to do as we always do at home, and have our dinner Christmas Eve. We think there will be a church service at ten. If there is we will go. At midnight, we'll have champagne and open the presents. [97]

# 1955

## *Massive Retaliation*

Meanwhile, the Soviet Union had not been idle. Responding to NATO's buildup, it strengthened its defenses by arming its ground forces with tactical nuclear weapons, developed hydrogen bombs and an intercontinental jet bomber to deliver them, and pushed ahead with the production of long-range missiles.

By 1955, as a result, the race between the two sides had produced such huge nuclear arsenals that both became concerned. Meeting at a conference in Geneva, U.S. and Soviet representatives agreed that a full-scale nuclear war could only lead to mutual suicide. From then on, an understanding between the sides developed that neither would use nuclear weapons unless its own survival was at stake. [98]

As the U.S. role in South Vietnam grew, U.S. defense policy underwent review. Officials in the Eisenhower Administration believed that wars like those in Korea and Vietnam were too costly and should be avoided in the future. "Never again" was the rallying cry of those who opposed sending U.S. ground forces to fight a conventional war in Asia. Instead, the Administration relied on the threat or use of massive nuclear retaliation to deter or, if necessary, to defeat the armies of the Soviet Union and Communist China. Ground forces were relegated to a minor role, and mobilization was regarded as an unnecessary luxury. In consequence, the Army's share of the defense budget declined, the modernization of its forces was delayed, and its strength was reduced by 40% from 1,404,598 in 1954 to 861,964 in 1956. [99]

Ridgway and his successor Taylor opposed the Administration's new strategy. Both advocated balanced forces to enable the U.S. to cope realistically with a variety of military contingencies. Events of the late 1950s would later appear to support their demand for flexibility, when contingencies in Lebanon and the Straits of Taiwan underlined the importance of avoiding any fixed concept of war.

Advocates of the "Flexible Response" doctrine foresaw a meaningful role for the Army as part of a more credible deterrent and as a means of intervening, when necessary, in limited, small wars. They wished to strengthen both conventional and unconventional forces, to improve strategic and tactical mobility, and to maintain troops and equipment at forward bases close to likely areas of conflict. They placed a premium on highly responsive command and control to allow a close meshing of military actions with political goals.

The same reformers were deeply interested in the conduct of brush-fire wars, especially among the underdeveloped nations. In the so-called Third World, competing Cold War ideologies and festering nationalistic, religious, and social conflicts interacted with the disruptive forces of modernization to create the preconditions for open hostilities. Southeast Asia was one of several such areas. There, the central concern of the U.S. was the threat of North Vietnamese and perhaps Chinese aggression against South Vietnam and other non-Communist states.

The U.S. had taken the lead in forming a regional defense pact, the Southeast Asia Treaty Organization (SEATO), signaling its commitment to contain Communist encroachment in the region. Meanwhile, the 342 American advisors of the Military Advice & Assistance Group (MAAG), Vietnam (which replaced MAAG, Indochina, in 1955), trained and organized Diem's fledgling army to resist an invasion from the North.

For the most part, the Viet Minh in the South avoided armed action and subscribed to a political action program in anticipation of Vietnam-wide elections in 1956, as stipulated by the Geneva Agreements. But Diem, supported by the United States, refused to hold elections, claiming that undemocratic conditions in the North precluded a fair contest. Following his own election as President in 1955 and by the adulation of his U.S. supporters, Diem's political strength would rise to its apex. [100]

## *Bim*

Meanwhile, Naples was wide open to anything one could pay for. For most U.S. military teenagers, that meant drinking and smoking. The Wheelers left Bim alone on smoking since Bus had begun smoking at a very young age. Bim usually smoked a pipe in his room with a friend while listening to jazz music. Sometimes, the smoke was so dense that it completely socked-in the room.

During his Freshman year in Naples, Bim took algebra, a subject that his old man, the former mathematics professor, knew cold. Whenever Bim had trouble with algebra, he went to Bus for help. Bim learned very quickly not to show up without pencil and paper. When Bim showed Bus a problem that he had attempted to solve, Bus would read his partial answer and the problem itself. He often gave the paper back with a big "RTP" on it – standard procedure for the West Point Math Department meaning "read the problem." Bim soon inculcated RTP into his logic and seldom received that rebuke again. (Years later, while working toward his PhD in mathematics, Bim explained an advanced math problem to Bus, who conceded that it was way over his head. The son had finally surpassed his father, Bim thought, very pleased with himself.) [101]

The Wheelers entrusted their teenage son to go out on weekday evenings. Bim did not have to declare his destination, associates, or planned activities. They insisted that he earn good grades and never embarrass his father. Acceptable grades meant having to look Bus in the eye and declare that he had done the best that he could. This resulted in straight A's.

The issue of not embarrassing his father was another matter, however. A military dependent could be shipped back to the States for transgressing too often or too egregiously. Bim's shenanigans sometimes stretched the limits of his parents' tolerance, but he was not shipped home in disgrace. "It was a near run thing, though," Bim recalled. The U.S. military police cut him some extra slack as "the General's boy" and often did not inform his parents whenever they caught him doing something inappropriate. [102]

In the winter of Bim's Freshman year, his high school arranged a ski trip to Roccaraso, about fifty miles east of Rome in the spectacular Abruzzo region. With tall, craggy mountains, Abruzzo was the least populated region of Italy. The Wheelers agreed to serve as chaperones for the group. They, Bim, and his friend drove in their Morris while the remainder of the students rode a U.S. Navy bus.

Bim and his fellow students who weren't skiers spent most of their time hanging out in the hotel bar, dancing, gambling, and drinking. They got smashed one afternoon with a bottle of Ballantine scotch that Bim had "borrowed" from his father's stock. That evening, they ran into Bus and Betty as they emerged from an elevator. The boys were a little nonplussed. They thought they hadn't been caught until Bim ran into his father again the next morning. Bus asked him how he was feeling.

"Pretty good," Bim answered.

"You were feeling pretty good last night, too," Bus replied.

This was one of many times that Bus had "broken the code" with his son, who was convinced that his old man knew him better than Bim knew himself. [103]

On the drive home to Naples, the Wheelers' car passed the bus carrying the rest of the group. Bim and his friend rolled down their windows and gave their friends a "high sign" above the roof of the car. Bus looked back at them and asked, "Who are giving the finger to, boys?" [104]

## *Second DC Tour*

The Wheelers concluded their tour in Naples in September 1955. Prior to their departure, their restaurant owner friends in Posilipo threw them a farewell dinner. As their Morris had already been shipped home, they took a taxi to the restaurant. Afterwards, the owners insisted on driving them home. [105]

*Betty Wheeler and Chief of Staff of the Army General Maxwell D. Taylor (right) promote Wheeler to Major General in the Pentagon, Washington, DC, 21 December 1955. (Wheeler Family Records).*

In October, the family returned to Washington, DC. Wheeler joined the Army Staff in the Pentagon as the Director of Plans in the Office of the Deputy Chief of Staff for Military Operations. General Maxwell D. Taylor, the Chief of Staff of the Army, had appointed Wheeler to this position, pinned a second star on him on 21 December, and would exert considerable influence over much of the rest of Wheeler's career. [106]

Pursuant to his assignment to the Army Staff, Wheeler was again the subject of an FBI background investigation. His former commander in Naples described Wheeler as a highly competent officer whose character, loyalty, and associates were completely above reproach. A colleague who had known Wheeler for the past fifteen years both professionally and socially and had served with him in Naples concurred, adding that Wheeler's reputation and integrity were also completely above reproach. Two other officers interviewed had each known Wheeler for 23 years and made similar laudatory comments. [107]

The Wheelers lived in the Presidential Gardens apartment complex in Alexandria, Virginia, for one month before renting an eighteenth-century house at 103 Prince Street in picturesque, cobble-stoned Old Town Alexandria. [108]

The FBI interviewed someone from the real estate company from which the Wheelers rented the house in Old Town. This person said it was her impression that Wheeler would be departing soon for military quarters at Fort Myer. Special agents also interviewed one of the Wheeler's new neighbors, who stated that Wheeler, his wife, and son appeared to be "high type" individuals who were quiet and orderly neighbors. [109]

A former neighbor in Fairfax during their previous tour in Washington, DC described them as fine neighbors of excellent character, personal habits, and conduct. He described Wheeler as reserved and military in his manner, but well-behaved and a real gentleman. Everything the neighbor knew about Wheeler and his wife was of a favorable nature, and he would not question the loyalty or associates of either of them. Two other acquaintances interviewed by the FBI substantially provided the same information. [110]

*Bim as a high school senior at St. Stephens School, Alexandria, Virginia, 1957. (Wheeler Family Records).*

The Wheelers enrolled Bim at St. Stephen's, an Episcopal boys' school in Alexandria. During his Junior and Senior years, he would letter in football, soccer, and baseball. Bus was unable to attend any of Bim's games or other school activities. Bim was not embittered by his father's absence. Bim always knew that Bus loved him, although it was never stated. He innately understood his dad's commitment to the demands of his job, and he admired him for it.

## 1956

Bus realized his lifetime dream and bought a used Lincoln convertible around the same time that Bim got his driver's license. It was baby blue with a white top and white leather seats. Bus didn't want Bim to drive it and convinced him that there was no insurance on the car. With their Morris in the shop one day, there was no other choice but for Bim to drive the Lincoln to school. Bus admonished him to be very careful.

On the way home, Bim was hit by another car. The damage was minimal. Bim told his father that he had grabbed a pamphlet from the glove box and waved it around like it was an insurance policy at the other driver. Bus laughed when he heard that the pamphlet turned out to be a guide to the best restaurants in Washington, DC. [111]

## *Vietnam*

While international tensions eased on the strategic level, competition would continue unabated on every other. The Soviet Union would continue its struggle with Capitalist imperialism through "wars of national liberation" and by other means less destructive than full-scale war. [112]

Diem, a Roman Catholic of mandarin background, sought to assert his authority over the chaotic conditions in South Vietnam in hopes of establishing an anti-Communist state. An expatriate for over 20 years, Diem had returned to Saigon in the summer of 1954 as Premier with no political following except his family and a few Americans. His authority was challenged by the religious sects, organized crime, and even his own army. Weathering the threat of an Army coup, Diem dispelled U.S. doubts about his ability to survive a jungle of Vietnamese politics.

For the next two years, the U.S. commitment to defend South Vietnam's independence would be synonymous with support for Diem. Americans were now providing advice and support to the Army of the Republic of Vietnam (ARVN). At Diem's request, they replaced French advisors throughout his nation's military establishment. [113]

By the early 1960s, the North Vietnamese would actively seek to complete the task of unifying Vietnam under Communist rule. As the threat to South Vietnam grew, the U.S. would engage ever more deeply in the struggle, initially by expanding its program of military advice and support and ultimately with direct commitment of ground, air, and naval forces. American military leaders would have the chance to apply the lessons the French had supposedly failed to learn. [114]

## 1957

### *Cold War*

Throughout the period, the U.S. had keyed its nuclear deterrence efforts to the strategic bomber; but to be on the safe side, it had also pushed development of offensive missiles. A jurisdictional dispute between the Army and Air Force, which shared responsibility for the development of ballistic missiles, led the Secretary of Defense in 1957 to assign the Air Force responsibility for all land-based ballistic missiles. Although the Army retained control over development and testing of its Jupiter intermediate-range ballistic missile, tensions with the Soviet Union soon eased, lessening the sense of urgency that had propelled the program to that point.

The lull lasted only until October, when the Soviet Union launched Sputnik, the first Earth satellite. The accomplishment came as a shock to the United States, which lacked the sort of high thrust rocket the Soviets had used. Considerable time would elapse before the U.S. would produce a rocket engine equal to that of the Soviets.

The nuclear threat overshadowed developments in other areas during the 1950s. For example, although the U.S. sought to avoid involvement in limited war, challenges arose continually that required it to supply military or economic aid or to dispatch combat forces. American commitments to provide advisory groups and military missions around the world thus multiplied throughout the period, despite attempts in Congress and the Eisenhower Administration to cut costs.

The nation did, nevertheless, have its limits. It had little choice but to maintain two U.S. Army divisions south of the demilitarized zone (DMZ) in Korea and to provide substantial military assistance to South Korea's armed forces. It had drawn the line, however, when France sought U.S. support to reclaim its empire in Indochina. Confronted by French threats of noncooperation with NATO, the U.S. had compromised by providing military supplies, equipment, and economic aid. Lacking support from its other Allies, however, it declined to commit U.S. troops or bombers.

Although the U.S. had clearly been reluctant to become embroiled in Asia so soon after the Korean War, it had sponsored SEATO, which called for mutual help and consultation to resist overt aggression or other threats to internal security. [115]

## *Little Rock*

In June, Wheeler assumed duties as Assistant Deputy Chief of Staff for Military Operations, a position he would hold until September 1958. In this capacity, he would once again find himself on the frontline, this time on important issues facing society, the Department of Defense, and the Army. With the new job came a change of address for the family to Quarters 30-A on Fort Myer. [116]

*As a Major General, Wheeler was designated as President Eisenhower's personal representative during the Little Rock Crisis of 1957. (Wheeler Family Records).*

Tensions had grown out of efforts by African Americans to achieve equal rights that forced the Federal government to intervene in civil disturbances on a scale not seen since the 19th century. The first and most dramatic instance occurred in Little Rock, Arkansas that September. Wheeler was designated as Eisenhower's personal representative on the scene. [117]

Despite the Supreme Court's 1954 ruling in *Brown vs. Board of Education*, resistance to integration was strong across the South. In early 1957, the District Court required that the ruling be implemented by admitting nine African-American students to the city's Central High School. Rioting followed, and Arkansas Governor Orval Faubus called up the National Guard to enforce segregation.

Eisenhower federalized the Arkansas National Guard instead and deployed a battle group of the 101st Airborne Division from Fort Campbell, Kentucky. This was one of only a few times in U.S. history that a President used either Regular Army or National Guard forces over the opposition of a state's Governor. Wheeler was already there when the paratroopers arrived. [118]

Major General Edwin Walker, The Adjutant General of the Arkansas National Guard (who would later be shot by Lee Harvey Oswald in an assassination attempt), summoned the local School Board President, Wayne Upton, to his office. Walker introduced Upton to a tall man in civilian clothes, but of obvious military bearing—Wheeler.

Wheeler laid out the facts for Upton. A detachment of the 101st Airborne Division was moving in under orders from the President. "They have already started landing at Little Rock Air Force Base," said Wheeler, "and they will soon be coming here." He pointed out the window to the Broadway Bridge and a glimmering streak of lights in the growing darkness.

Upton asked whether their arrival couldn't be postponed until the atmosphere had calmed down a little.

"No," replied Wheeler, "the orders from the President are to open the school for Negro students tomorrow, and we will do it tomorrow. It's too late to get anything changed now."

Wheeler informed Upton that more troops had been brought in than was necessary. Hopefully, the opposition would realize that they held a losing hand. If force was needed, he assured Upton that civilian casualties would be held to a minimum. He also stated, "We don't want to hurt anybody, but those Negro students are going into that school." [119]

The paratroopers had arrived with live ammunition. Wheeler ordered it all to be collected up. Any trooper retaining even one live round would be court martialed. He also told the unit commander that if his paratroopers couldn't handle civilians with rifle butts and bayonets alone then something was wrong.

Wheeler met with the Governor and informed him of the way things stood.

"Come, come General, surely we can reach some kind of compromise?" Faubus suggested.

"Governor," Wheeler replied, "you can have any kind of compromise you want as long as those Negro children go to your white school." [120]

The paratroopers ended up escorting the children into the school and dispersing a mob that gathered. This stabilized the situation, but resistance in Arkansas was not over. Faubus would later close Central High School for the 1958-59 school year. A variety of other tricks and obfuscations were attempted, but ultimately failed to thwart the inevitability of integration. [121]

# 1958

## *Bim Graduates*

Although Bus had missed all his son's high school activities, he did attend Bim's graduation in June 1958. Bus's presence was a complete surprise to everyone, as he arrived unannounced and sat in the general seating area with Betty.

Bim received top honors in Spanish and Math. His favorite teacher, Thomas Gale, a retired Marine Corps Colonel, presented him the math award. (Gale was severely stricken with debilitating rheumatoid arthritis. When he passed away in 1962, Bus again showed up unannounced to honor this educator who had meant so much to his son. Bim considered this one of the most touching examples of his father's love.) [122]

Bus had never held out any expectations that his son should also serve in the military, but Bim had always wanted to attend West Point. This did not surprise Bus, but he had reservations. He knew that Bim was immature and would rebel against the system at some point. Bus encouraged his son to emulate his experience by instead enlisting in the Army first to gain valuable experience and maturity that would serve him well as a cadet. He advised Bim not to confuse how things worked at West Point with the way things were in the real Army. Bus also cautioned that life at the academy was akin to joining the priesthood.

"I really believe that he meant every word of it," Bim later wrote, "and that it was the basis for his view of many of the issues that he later had to deal with." [123]

Despite his father's advice, Bim was determined to go to the academy that summer. Eisenhower had awarded him a Presidential appointment, selection for which was based on merit, not political connections. Bus had him decline the appointment because "someone else would be cut out if [he] took it." Instead, Bim sought out and received a congressional appointment from Congressman Gerald Ford of Michigan. At that time, it was not uncommon for unused appointments to be awarded to applicants from outside the member's district or state. [124]

Not long after Bim's high school graduation, Betty drove him up to West Point. After spending the night in the Hotel Thayer, she dropped him off the next morning to begin "Beast Barracks." Because Bim wouldn't turn eighteen until the following month, Bus had signed a release for him to enter the academy. [125]

## *Brushfires*

Meanwhile, troubles had proliferated in both Asia and Southeast Asia throughout the 1950s. A prime point of contention stood in the Strait of Taiwan, where Chinese Communist forces were bombarding Nationalist Chinese positions on two tiny offshore islands, Quemoy and Matsu. Since loss of the islands might open the way for an invasion of Taiwan, Congress issued a joint resolution back in 1955 empowering the President to act immediately if the Communists moved to seize either. Shelling tapered off after that but resumed in the summer of 1958.

In response, the U.S. provided warships to convoy supply vessels and armed Nationalist Chinese aircraft with missiles. A U.S. composite Air Strike Force also took up station on Taiwan to strengthen Nationalist defenses against a Communist invasion. The Communists ended the crisis by reducing their fire shortly thereafter, but Quemoy and Matsu would remain a bone of contention between the U.S. and China for years to come.

While tensions in the Far East were products of Cold War competition, others arising in the Middle East were attributable to nationalism and Arab hostility to the Jewish state of Israel. Although the U.S. took a standoff approach to the region's intermittent crises, Eisenhower understood that the U.S. had deep interests in the area. As a result, he requested and obtained a joint resolution from Congress back in January 1957 that pledged U.S. military assistance to Middle Eastern nations subject to Communist aggression. Empowering the President to use the Armed Forces if necessary, the legislation became known as the Eisenhower Doctrine.

The U.S. acted in 1958, when factions favoring Egyptian leader Gamal Abdel Nasser became active in Lebanon, Jordan, and Iraq. When rebellion followed in Lebanon and the King of Iraq was assassinated to establish a republic under pro-Nasser leadership, the President of Lebanon and the King of

Jordan requested American assistance. Within 24 hours, naval units from the U.S. 6th Fleet took up station off Lebanon, and a battalion of Marines landed near Beirut. Additional Marines arrived two days later, and the Army began to move airborne, tank, and combat engineer troops into the country to stabilize the situation. By early August, U.S. forces in Lebanon would total more than 5,800 Marines and 8,500 soldiers. A U.S. composite Air Strike Force backed them from Turkey, and a British airborne contingent was positioned in Jordan.

By October, tensions had subsided enough for the U.S. to withdraw its forces. In their place, the U.S. gave Lebanon and Jordan special assistance to build up their defenses and to prevent additional outbreaks of political unrest. Shortly afterward, the U.S. concluded separate defense treaties with Turkey, Iran, and Pakistan. When those three countries and Great Britain formed the Central Treaty Organization (CENTO) along NATO lines the following year, the U.S. declined membership. It would, however, participate in the association's economic, military, and anti-subversion committees and send representatives to CENTO meetings.

Closer to home, the U.S. chose not to intervene in a revolution in Cuba in 1958, but kept careful tabs on the movement's leader, Fidel Castro, and his followers. When they succeeded in overthrowing the Cuban government, the U.S. initially recognized the new regime, but Cuban-American relations deteriorated quickly when Castro aligned his nation with the Communist Bloc. American military and economic assistance to Cuba would cease in 1960, but Castro replaced it with arms and other aid from the Soviet Union and Communist China. The U.S. would respond by cutting off diplomatic relations with Cuba in January 1961. [126]

## *Defense Budgets*

With U.S. forces and assistance either on-call or committed around the world, it appeared that the U.S. was more likely to become involved in local wars than in a general conflagration. American military budgets, however, had emphasized deterrence of nuclear conflict over preparations for lower-level contingencies and limited conventional wars.

It was hardly surprising that Eisenhower would seek to cut defense spending following the high cost of the Korean War. His decision to rely more heavily upon strategic air power than on ground units, however, created imbalances both in the military budget and in the distribution of forces. In 1953, for example, the Army had more than 1. 5 million men: 20 combat divisions (eight in the Far East, five in Europe, and seven in the United States). The Army's budget came to nearly $13 billion, 38% of the total allocated to the Armed Services for Fiscal Year 1954.

Over the next four years, the Department of Defense trimmed more than 600,000 men from the Services. Although the Air Force and Navy experienced reductions, most of the cuts came from the ground forces. As a result, by 1958, the Army had shrunk to 15 divisions and fewer than 900,000 men. Two reduced-strength divisions remained in Korea and one in Hawaii. The totals in Europe and the continental U.S. remained the same, but several stateside divisions were operating at reduced strength. Funds obligated to the Army for Fiscal Year 1959 would fall to about $9 billion, some 22% of the total military budget.

Despite these economies, the defense budget would climb from $34 billion in 1954 to more than $41 billion in 1959. Much of the expense went toward high-tech air and missile systems necessary to deter and defend against nuclear attack. Not only were these weapons costly to obtain, they sometimes became obsolete overnight as newer, better models came online. In addition, the personnel necessary to maintain them came not only at high cost but they also required expensive, on-the-job training to keep abreast of trends. [127]

## *Defense Reorganization*

Interservice competition for scarce resources had impinged upon the Chiefs' ability to cooperate in the interest of national security. Differences among the Chiefs had centered on the definition of "roles and missions" of the Services. How the Chiefs defined roles and missions determined force size and structure, as well as the research, development, and procurement of new weapons systems. Conflicts between the Services had led to inefficiency and redundancy. During his second term as President, Eisenhower grew increasingly concerned that, if the Chiefs did not cooperate and transcend their narrow Service views, civilians less familiar with the complexities of warfare, such as the Secretary of Defense, would assume the Chiefs' responsibilities. [128]

Eisenhower sought a structural solution to the problems of Service parochialism and inefficiency. The Defense Reorganization Act, approved by Congress in August 1958, was intended to centralize control over the Services, remove redundancies, streamline command channels, and provide for tighter civilian control at the Pentagon. Although Congress expected the act to affirm Joint Chiefs of Staff responsibility to provide military advice and plan operations within unified commands, the law permitted the Office of the Secretary of Defense to share the Chiefs' advisory role, and it removed the Chiefs from the chain of command that ran from the President to the commanders in the field. The Secretary of Defense would direct the unified commands while the Chiefs performed executive functions, such as translating guidance from the Secretary of Defense into military orders and directives. Although the Chiefs retained their charter as "principal military advisors," the wide latitude given to the Secretary of Defense to provide for more effective and efficient administration would permit a strong-willed Secretary to concentrate power in his hands. The erosion of the Chiefs' power and influence, which Eisenhower had predicted, was closer to becoming a reality. Centralization in the Department of Defense did nothing to attenuate interservice rivalry. In fact, Eisenhower's defense policies intensified competition between the Services. [129]

Sweeping changes followed. The new arrangement abolished the system that made the military departments executive agents for operations in the field. Instead, most of the nation's active combat forces came under unified commands that answered to the President and the Secretary of Defense through the Joint Chiefs of Staff. As part of his enlarged role, the Secretary of Defense received greater freedom to transfer functions within the Services. In doing so, he would be assisted by a new Directorate of Research and Development that would oversee all military research and development programs. [130]

General Andrew Goodpaster recalled:

> Some of the changes introduced by the Act of 1958 clearly reflected dissatisfaction at the higher levels of the government with the form and degree of Service rivalry then manifest. The Act took steps to eliminate such sterile rivalry and emphasized corporate responsibility. It gave the Chairman of the Joint Chiefs of Staff statutory powers for increased

influence in JCS deliberations and greater control over the Joint Staff.

It strengthened the role of the Vice Chief in each Service, to enable him to shoulder a larger part of the burden of Service operations, thus clearing the agenda of the Chief and allowing him to spend more time on his corporate responsibility. [131]

Meanwhile, the Joint Chiefs of Staff received authorization to make interservice planning and decision making more effective. Wheeler headed a joint committee that studied methods for improving techniques and procedures. His committee recommended, and the Chiefs approved, that they shift many of their routine duties to subordinates by delegating more authority to their Vice Chiefs. As a result, the Joint Staff that answered to them grew from about 180 officers. Because of Service sensitivities, however, it received specific instructions to avoid organizing or operating as an overall general staff. [132]

Goodpaster described in retrospect the law's intended and unintended consequences:

The Act of 1958, in clarifying the authority of the Secretary of Defense, has had a result not anticipated or consciously intended by those who participated in its formulation. With regard to operational planning and the military and tactical advice that is offered to decision makers, the intent of the legislation was to concentrate responsibility in the Joint Chiefs of Staff, thus ending the situation in which the individual Services, acting separately, extended operational influence over field commands. The Secretary of Defense and his immediate office would exert policy direction and control.

But in the application of the Act, a further shift has occurred, resulting in a more detailed treatment of a wider range of matters at the civilian level of the Office of the Secretary of Defense than was then foreseen. ... Where the Act visualized fixing the responsibility for military operational matters in the Joint Chiefs of Staff and assigning the conduct of combat operations to the unified commands, there has evolved in practice a sharing of the Joint Chiefs of Staff roll and the retention of operational decisions on a more centralized basis at the Secretary of Defense level of control than was anticipated in 1958. [133]

## Army Reorganization

The U.S. Armed Forces, for their part, had already reorganized internally to improve efficiency and adjust to the changes required by the threat of nuclear war. By 1955, for example, the Army had replaced its Army Field Forces Command with a new Continental Army Command (CONARC) to reduce the number of commands reporting directly to the Chief of Staff. The new organization assumed responsibility for the six U.S. armies and the Military District of Washington, along with certain other units, activities, and installations. CONARC had charge of training the Active Army and Reserves, preparing the future Army and its equipment, and planning and conducting the ground defenses of the United States.

Those functions continued under the new system. The Army and the other Services retained their roles in training, equipping, and organizing combat forces. The difference was that the units transferred to unified commands when war threatened. Answering to the Secretary of Defense, the Services also developed the weapons and equipment the troops would need. If the unified commands had control of the units assigned to them, moreover, the Services retained command of everyone else and provided logistical support to all their personnel, whether attached to unified commands or not.

The need to adjust to the nuclear threat had a deep impact on the Army. Old ways of organizing for combat seemed inadequate to meet a nuclear attack, yet historical precedents were lacking when it came to devising new ones. The vast destructive power of nuclear weapons argued that armies could no longer mass to launch offensives or to hold along a solid front. An enemy could sweep aside all opposition with atomic bombs. [134]

In consequence of declining manpower levels, intense competition for limited funds, and the threats of brushfire conflicts in remote theaters and general war on the nuclear battlefield, the Army replaced its old triangular infantry and airborne divisions with units composed of five self-contained battle groups capable of independent action. Wheeler helped Taylor implement this reorganization.

Manned by 13,500 soldiers rather than the usual 17,000, these "pentomic" divisions theoretically increased survivability and responsiveness while reducing overhead. The new division also integrated new technology, particularly tactical nuclear weapons, for greater combat power and strategic mobility.

Seven divisions stationed in the continental U.S. would back these forces as a strategic reserve. In 1957, four of these reserve units (two airborne and two infantry) had become the Strategic Army Corps (STRAC), which stood in high readiness for quick deployment in case of an emergency. The other three served both as reinforcements and as a training base for an Army expansion should a prolonged crisis or a large-scale war develop.

The Army's regular divisions completed the changeover by 1958. National Guard and Reserve units followed by 1960. [135]

## *Army Rearmament*

Wheeler also helped oversee the fielding of a steady stream of new weapons and equipment by the nuclear Army. From improved rifles and mortars at the company-level to powerful rockets and artillery in the support commands, the firepower of Army combat forces grew. The families of surface-to-surface and surface-to-air missiles also emerged, as did larger and heavier weapons designed to be air transportable. The M113 armored personnel carrier and the M60 battle tank would become operational in 1960. [136]

The most dramatic efforts to increase the Army's mobility occurred in the field of aviation. To secure both firepower and maneuverability, the Army pushed development of helicopters and low-speed fixed-wing aircraft. The helicopter had already proven itself in Korea by moving troops and supplies and evacuating casualties. Some of the new fixed-wing planes were designed for short takeoffs and landings that would increase the Army's ability to deliver heavy payloads to forward areas.

As the Army's mobility and firepower increased, so did the need for more effective communications. With rapidly moving pentomic units operating independently over large areas, light but reliable radio equipment was essential. Dramatic technological breakthroughs in the miniaturization of component parts spurred by the space program provided the solutions the Army needed.

The improvement of tactical communications was only one benefit of the technological revolution that commenced during Wheeler's tenure on the Army Staff. Ponderous early computers would begin to give way to smaller versions that could process, store, and recall more information more swiftly than ever before. From the coordination of weapons fire to the storage and retrieval of personnel and logistical information, these computers would assume many functions at all levels of the Army. They became particularly valuable where the storage and retrieval of intelligence were concerned. Indeed, the need to secure the data necessary to feed the machines required the development of new families of surveillance equipment. More sophisticated radar and sonar sets emerged. So too did infrared, acoustic, and seismic devices to aid ground and air surveillance; highly accurate cameras; and side-looking radar that could detect enemy concentrations by day and night under all weather conditions.

Once combat operations commenced, the Army would have to supply the troops on the battlefield. Since nuclear wars would probably be short, planners expected to rely upon stockpiled munitions rather than wait for U.S. industry to gear up. This meant that they would have to establish depots both at home and abroad. The effort to move supplies from those facilities to the troops would pose problems, but modern technology seemed to hold the answers. Processing requisitions on computers, logisticians would use fast naval vessels, air transport, and cross-country vehicles to deliver at least the minimum essential requirements to the point where they were needed most. [137]

## *Army Manpower*

As with the logisticians, the Army's personnel planners soon realized that forces in being would have to fight future conflicts. In earlier wars, the Army had used the draft to mobilize and train civilians for up to two years before committing them to war. This would no longer be possible. The war would be over before anyone would arrive to fight it. Well-trained forces on-hand or in the Individual Ready Reserve would have to do the fighting.

Fortunately for the Army, the advantages of a military career were many. The 20-year retirement option was a strong inducement for soldiers who had already served 10 years or more learning their specialty. Free family medical care, post exchange and commissary privileges, and the Army's extensive recreational and educational facilities also figured in. It also mattered that military service had gained prestige because of the many civilians who had served in World War II and Korea. The Army was no longer as isolated from American society as it had been.

In one respect, however, a military career had become less inviting. Military pay had not kept pace with civilian salaries. In response, Congress voted in 1958 to increase service members' salaries, to improve retirement benefits, and to authorize proficiency pay for highly skilled personnel.

Although the Army made significant gains in retaining key personnel, it could not depend upon voluntary enlistments to fill its need for manpower. In an emergency, it could fall back upon its Individual Ready Reserve and Standby Reserve, but neither force was available on a day-to-day basis. The Individual Ready Reserve became available only when the President declared an emergency and only in numbers authorized by Congress. The Standby Reserve became liable for service only in a war or emergency declared by Congress itself. For all other needs, the Army had to rely upon the draft, which Congress had enacted during the Korean War. It obligated all physically and mentally qualified males between the ages of 18 and 26 to eight years of combined active and reserve military service.

Under legislation passed in 1955, Congress reduced the term of obligatory service for reserve enlistees to six years. It also authorized voluntary enlistment in the reserve of up to 250,000 young men. Under the new law, the President could call up to 1 million Individual Ready Reservists to active duty in an emergency that he alone proclaimed. He could also recall selected members of the Standby Reserve in case of a congressionally declared national emergency.

Whatever the efforts of Congress, in a period of restricted funding and irregular enlistments, many reserve units fell below authorized strength. Although budget cuts forced the active Army to lower its manpower ceiling, the Army continued its efforts to strengthen its Reserve Components. [138]

# CHAPTER 5

## RISING STAR
## (SEPTEMBER 1958 - SEPTEMBER 1962)

### *Fort Hood*

In late September 1958, Wheeler relinquished his duties as Assistant Deputy Chief of Staff for Military Operations. He had been selected to command the 2nd Armored Division at Fort Hood, Texas. [1]

After several weeks of well-deserved leave, the Wheelers arrived there on 30 October. Betty wrote:

> We have had a royal welcome, and I do mean it. General Brown met us at the gate on the 30th a little after two. Sergt. Keyes [their enlisted orderly from Fort Myer who had relocated with them] was here to greet us, and Sergt. Lee, a little black boy with a wonderful smile. He and Sergt. Keyes seem to get along fine and I think (hope and pray) we have the makings of a good staff. The honeymoon was over. Bus was snatched off immediately to interview aides! I felt like a caged lion, and paced! [2]

She also recorded the events of Bus's assumption of command day:

> At eight [AM] there was an honor guard for Bus. The troops were on the field. He arrived to the ruffles and the salute boomed forth. It was quickly over. … There was a lovely dinner party at the club [that] night. The Div. sent me a white orchid. We received. Dinner was good. Champagne and toasts, and short speeches! The color guard arrived after dinner, and that's a colorful ceremony. [3]

The next morning, the division passed in review for its new commander. Betty was mightily impressed.

> The day was perfect, a snap to the air, blue skies and enough breeze to make the flags stand out. It was a thrilling sight to see six thousand strong pass in review. The band always plays

in front of the reviewing stand and is the last to go off. As they turned to leave, about a dozen helicopters came over, followed by six or so light planes with colored smoke trailing. When all this is for yours it's overwhelming. … As the planes came in, under them, I swear not fifteen feet off the ground, in single file came three helicopters. When the middle one was even with the reviewing stand, they turned as one toward it and dipped in unison in a salute! Then again with precision made a left turn. The first helicopter dropped a banner that said 'Welcome', the second 'General & Mrs.', and the third 'Wheeler'. … There was a reception immediately following. All of the field grade officers and the townspeople of note. [4]

That evening, the Wheelers attended a dinner at the division Chief of Staff's house. The following morning, they resumed their previous practice when in command of attending unit chapel services. That afternoon, it warmed up enough for Betty to "change into a pair of shorts, spread a blanket just off of the terrace, and enjoy a beautiful, private lunch and drinks with Bus in our completely private back yard." Thus, Wheeler's tour as a division commander began. [5]

After their spacious 19th century quarters on Fort Myer, the Wheelers were startled by the tiny dimensions of their new quarters at 6794 Patton Park (named Patton Spur today). They would later occupy another set of quarters at 799 Ranch House when Bus became III Corps commander. As Betty reported, she set to work immediately to bring the Patton Park quarters up to their standards.

The house was a shock! Don't remember being so depressed about anything since the first sight of Block 23 (in Naples)! I assure you there is no comparison, but it is so small. It's a nice living room, and I can't imagine why anyone complained about the dining room. It and the kitchen are the only rooms that seem good sized to me. The bedrooms are boxes, smaller than the house in Fairfax. The yard is lovely, and while the planting is new, and the trees little, it's well done. The patio off the living room is a great addition, and I'm delighted with it. … Between the living rooms were accordion pleated doors, and also into the dining room. Bus agreed with me if we had to buy four rollers and paint, something had to be done! [6]

Colonel Young, the Post Engineer, soon visited Betty. In no time, painters repainted the entire house, removed the "dutch door" from the kitchen into the living room and blocked over the folding pleats, installed a new wall, and repositioned some built-in book cases that the previous family had had installed. Most of the Wheelers' household goods went into storage after Betty sorted out the things they needed for this small set of quarters. [7]

During the renovations, Betty and Bus ate lunch most days at the Officers Club. She shared highlights of her exploratory trips around their new environs.

> I spend a couple of hours each day in Killeen. I'm getting oriented. I can see that I will have to go elsewhere for a good many things, but there is quite a bit here. I'm sure, too, that there is a lot that I haven't found yet. ... [We] have wide streets. Somehow, I rather like it. It's such a rough little diamond with such friendly people. It has its charm. How living in so many places broadens one! This is my home, and I'm looking at it, expecting it to give me something, and already there is warmth and friendliness. [8]

About a week after assuming command, the Wheelers attended "a big reception at the club ... for field grade officers only. Hearkening back to their company grade years at Fort Benning, Betty had an idea.

> I really felt badly about not meeting a Capt. or Lt. and [their] wives ... I had a chance to ask Bill Harvey the division [Chief of Staff] about it. Before I approached Bus on the subject, I wanted to know how many and how much [it would cost]. With the idea of course that we [would] pay the bill. I told Bill that it seemed sad not to meet the junior officers, explaining why I wanted to know how many and how much. I wanted to be able to give Bus all the facts and prices, or know in my own mind that it couldn't be done! (This passage is insightful into Wheeler's expectations when issues were brought to him for decision.) He said that including wives there would be

between 700 and 800 [guests]! But for coffee, pastries, sherry, and port, the club charged 25 cents a person. I imagine at Fort Myer coffee and a doughnut was $1 a person. I could certainly very much better put $200 into the house and/or [to put new clothing] on my back and it would have meant waiting for a bit. But it could be done. [9]

"No one has given the junior officers a thought," Harvey said. "I am sure that we can do this and certainly it is not for you and General Wheeler to pay the bill. When do you want it?"

"Next Saturday morning," Betty replied.

Of course, Monday [Harvey] talked it over with Bus and Bus with the staff. Bus naturally felt that they knew the pulse of the junior officers and he did not want a reception if they felt that the junior officers couldn't care less about it or felt 'soireed' into something. (It had nothing to do with cost!) All agreed that it was a fine idea. It was a beautiful party. ... I am so glad that it was done. I certainly know when we were younger it meant something to at least feel that you had met the top people. In fact, I still feel that way! [10]

While on a business trip to Washington, DC later that fall, Bus visited Bim up at West Point. Bim found it odd saluting his old man for the first time. Bus related stories of his cadet experience as they spent the afternoon visiting various sites around the grounds. Bus's old M Company barracks happened to be next to the ones that Bim had occupied during Beast (basic cadet training). Their enjoyable visit was abruptly ended by the call for dinner formation. [11]

This was the Wheelers' first Christmas without Bim, who as a Plebe was stuck at the academy for the holidays. Betty informed her mother that "all my 'maternal glands' have been functioning like mad! I've been so blue. I've missed him, and all the youthful activity more than I can say." [12]

On "a gloomy day after Christmas" while Bus was at a range shooting his pistol or the shotgun he hunted birds with, Betty wrote to her mother.

Each year we say that we have never had such a beautiful tree and we repeat it again this year. It's a big, full cedar. Sgts. Lee & Keyes went out in the woods last Saturday and cut it down. We didn't put it up until Christmas Eve morning. The boys put the lights on and Bus did all the decorating. I hadn't even gotten the wreath on the front door, so I worked on the house decorations while Bus did the tree. By five o'clock, the house was beautiful and we were dressed and ready for cocktails. We have been having dinner at six. [Since the holiday leave period had begun] Bus is rarely later than a quarter of five coming in. By the time he changes it makes it cocktail time. How we are enjoying these long evenings! … The tree is filled with lots of memories of Christmas past. One red bell light is still left from [Fort] Lewis [1938-40]. There are the little Santa Clauses from Paris [1946-47], the cute ornaments from Italy, the little Christmas trees that were on the train table in the library [in Trieste] the night that Santa Claus came, and last but not least, the whole room is a reminder of the last, beautiful Christmas in Connecticut.

"[On Christmas Day], we were busy," Betty continued. "We went to a lovely church service (at the 37th Street East Chapel) at ten. The official car met us at the chapel at eleven. Bus went to see six mess halls. I was so pleased to be invited to accompany him." They went to yet another mess hall for dinner. "We have kept tonight free but from tomorrow until the Monday after New Years Day we will be on the go almost constantly." [13]

## 1959

On several occasions during his command of the 2nd Armored Division, Wheeler assumed concurrent duties as Commanding General, III Corps. The longest of these periods would run from 25 March 1959 through 10 March 1960 when his tour at Fort Hood ended. [14]

### Southeast Asia

Meanwhile in Laos, a Communist movement, the Pathet Lao, had taken control of several provinces bordering North Vietnam and China. The non-Communist Laotian government signed a peaceful coexistence agreement with the group in 1956, but open warfare broke out again in 1959. Neither side gained the upper hand in the fighting that followed, despite U.S. assistance to the government's 25,000-man army and substantial military aid to the Pathet Lao from the Communist Bloc. With concern growing that the struggle might lead to a direct East-West confrontation, suggestions arose that the Great Powers should convene a conference to neutralize the country. By then, however, the Eisenhower Administration was turning over to a new government headed by President-Elect John F. Kennedy. The likelihood of an agreement seemed remote until his new Administration could establish itself. [15]

In Vietnam, the insurgents, now called the Viet Cong (VC), launched more frequent attacks against government paramilitary forces, and occasionally against the South Vietnamese Army (ARVN). In 1959, after assessing conditions in the South, Ho Chi Minh and his inner circle of Communist leaders in Hanoi sanctioned the use of armed force in pursuit of national liberation and unification, giving it equal weight with political efforts to undermine Diem and reunify Vietnam. They also determined to return a small number of Viet Minh who had regrouped to the North after Geneva. [16]

## *Mexico*

In early November, Bus and Betty spent eight days of leave on a road trip through Mexico from Laredo to Monterrey. Their car had no air conditioning, and it got progressively hotter the farther south they drove. Each evening, they cooled down in the hotel swimming pool.

Betty recounted coming around a curve in rain and fog along a treacherous, high mountain road to Zimipan.

> Mexicans were all over the road, and a woman was frantically waving us down. We stopped. She spoke English. Four of them in a car had gone over a cliff. Three were unhurt but one quite badly. Would we try to get a doctor? A car had gone the way we'd come but an old Mexican kept saying a doctor was thirty-three kilometers ahead. About that time, a very bloody man was brought up. He was leaning heavily on two people, but he was on his feet. For once the back seat wasn't loaded, so we got him into the car and one girl came along. I have never ridden a tenser or longer 20 miles. There

was no telling what state the man was in. Also the fog and the curves didn't help. The girl said that they were not going fast, and she didn't know what happened, except she was sure the car turned over three times. When it stopped, the other three had been thrown out, but she was still in it, unhurt. In fact, it's nothing short of a miracle that any of them were alive. When we got to the first little town of any size, Jacala, where the old Mexican said that we would find a doctor, we stopped at the first gas station. The *padrone* sent a young boy with us. Believe it or not there was a new hospital. The doctor was young, spotless in his white coat, and we couldn't help but feel good that at least we were leaving the man where he would undoubtedly get good care. [17]

She continued.

We have spent considerable time wondering about the foursome. I did ask where they were from. One, a redheaded man, attractive with his red beard, [was from] Scotland. David, our wounded, and the only name we learned, [was] from England. David's friend [was] from New Zealand, and the other girl [was] from Australia! How do you suppose they got together? It might seem simple to ask now, but at the time ... it seemed like prying. Not only that, in the thick fog, and curves, and with a man bleeding all over your back seat, somehow it was no time for conversation. ... Through the years, we shall wonder from time to time what became of the four of them, and David's blood, I am sure, will be visible on the back seat until the seat wears out. [18]

From Zimipan, they travelled on to Mexico City where they visited friends and toured the sites, including some Aztec pyramids. From there, they ventured on to Taxco. They intended to take a quicker and more direct route back to Fort Hood but decided instead to retrace the scenic route they had driven down. [19]

# 1960

## *Bim*

Meanwhile, Bim was now in his Yearling [Sophomore] year at West Point. He had gotten himself into serious trouble while on leave, made a poor decision about it, and was subsequently dismissed from the academy. Bim realized that he had disappointed and embarrassed his parents, and he was deeply disappointed in himself. He had no intention of returning home in disgrace to Fort Hood. Instead, he decided to enlist in the Army, but acquiesced when Bus insisted that he come home straightaway.

Woolnough gave Bus more of a hard time over Bim's dismissal than Bus gave Bim over it. Bus was certainly disappointed, but he did not come down hard. Rather, he handled it like all disappointments, whether personal or professional. He made his point succinctly and did not belabor it. In his sole conversation with Bim about his separation from the academy, Bus simply remarked, "What I cannot understand is that you can sleep with the Commandant's wife, but you cannot lie, cheat, or steal."

Bim replied, "Well, Pop, there's nothing I can do about it now, except get on with my life." [20]

Bim took a job at a bank in Killeen. He also joined a local Army Reserve unit and served inconspicuously as a mechanic. Understandably, he kept it under wraps that his father was the senior commander on Fort Hood. [21]

## *Third DC Tour*

*Chief of Staff of the Army General Lyman Lemnitzer promotes Wheeler to Lieutenant General, Washington, DC, 21 April 1960. (Office of the Chief of Staff of the Army).*

Wheeler became the Director of the Joint Staff in April 1960. This plum assignment was a "workhorse" job, a highly visible position that would propel Wheeler's career to the highest levels. Wheeler would come to personify "the new breed of military men who grew up since unification and made their mark on a united service approach." He was promoted to temporary Lieutenant General on 21 April and became a permanent Brigadier General the following month. On 30 June 1961, he would be promoted to permanent Major General. [22]

During the presidential election of 1960, Wheeler was designated to provide the Democratic candidate, John F. Kennedy, with weekly briefings on the military situation. Kennedy was impressed with Wheeler's intelligence, charm, and easy manner and would remember him two years later when it came time to select a new Chief of Staff of the Army. [23]

Wheeler recalled:

> I came away from meeting candidate Kennedy with the impression that I was dealing with a very intelligent man; a man who probably didn't know too much as to the details of National Defense; in fact, a man who probably didn't have

many other areas in governmental affairs with which he was intimately familiar. But he certainly had a shrewd intelligence, he asked intelligent questions, and he tried to bore in and get at the bottom of things rather than being content to accept the surface explanation. ... I must say I came away from this first meeting with Mr. Kennedy with a most favorable impression of him. [24]

# 1961

## *New Frontiersmen*

In January 1961, Kennedy entered the White House with a new vigor toward U.S. responsibilities for global leadership. In Western Europe, NATO Allies would be introduced to a new defense strategy. In the Far East, a similar move away from "massive retaliation" toward more "flexible response" would introduce a new set of ideas stressing the need to raise the nuclear threshold but lower the point at which the U.S. would use conventional forces in limited wars. [25]

A series of world events added impetus to this new strategic view. From Soviet Premier Nikita Khrushchev's speech in December 1960, Kennedy perceived a direct challenge in the new Soviet preference for protracted conflict fought with neither nuclear weapons nor conventional forces but through wars of national liberation using proxy armies. While Kennedy may have discounted the notion of monolithic Communism, the flow of events after Khrushchev's prophetic speech added to Soviet prestige as the recognized leader of the Communist world. A pragmatic politician, Kennedy realized that he must arrest this trend. [26]

By the end of the Eisenhower years, it had become evident that the "New Look" doctrine of massive retaliation was neither credible nor had it achieved its purpose. A campaign issue that Kennedy had taken up with some vigor was that of the need for reform in national defense strategy and the management of the Department of Defense. To lead this reform, the President-elect selected Robert S. McNamara as his Secretary of Defense. An advocate of the application of statistical analysis to management problems and highly self-assured, McNamara quickly earned Kennedy's high regard as the perfect man for the job. [27]

For his Secretary of State, Kennedy selected Dean D. Rusk. Unprepossessing and introspective, Rusk had built a solid reputation for loyalty and trustworthiness during his years of government service. [28]

Despite their collegiality, McNamara had little positive to say about Rusk in retrospect. "Dean ... failed utterly to manage the State Department and to supervise (U. S. Ambassador to South Vietnam Henry Cabot) Lodge. Nor did he participate forcefully in presidential meetings. ... It was not a secret that President Kennedy was deeply dissatisfied with Dean Rusk's administration of the State Department." [29]

Kennedy selected McGeorge Bundy as his National Security Advisor. Abrupt and imperious with those he considered his intellectual inferiors, Bundy met Kennedy's premium on academic qualifications and superior intellect, as did McNamara and Rusk. [30]

Recalling "Mac Bundy," McNamara said, "his personality was so forceful and so influential during the years we worked together for Presidents Kennedy and Johnson. ... A Harvard junior fellow at age 22, biographer of Henry Stimson at 29, and Dean of Harvard's Arts and Sciences Faculty at 34, he possesses one of the keenest intellects I have ever encountered. And he was by far the ablest National Security Advisor I have observed over the last 40 years." [31]

Kennedy also wanted men who shared his broad interests and could engage in wide-ranging, informal discussions. Perhaps the most important determining factor of each man's relative influence would be his ability to establish a close, personal rapport with the President. McNamara and Bundy would prove more adept than Rusk at securing Kennedy's confidence and affection.

Kennedy's personal style influenced the way he structured the White House staff to handle national security decision making. Lacking executive experience, Kennedy was unaccustomed to operating at the head of a large staff organization. Regarding Eisenhower's National Security Council (NSC) structure as cumbersome and unnecessary, Kennedy resolved not to use the NSC except for the pro forma consultation required by the National Security

Act of 1947. In place of the formal Eisenhower system, Kennedy would rely on an ad hoc, collegial style of decision-making in national security and foreign affairs. He formed task forces to analyze particular problems and met regularly with an "inner club" of his most trusted advisors to discuss problems informally and weigh the advantages and disadvantages of potential courses of action.

Kennedy's elimination of the NSC apparatus would diminish the voice of the Joint Chiefs of Staff (JCS) in national security matters. Under Eisenhower, military officers connected with the JCS had been assigned to the NSC's Planning Board and its Operations Coordinating Board. Through these representatives, the Chiefs placed items important to the military on the NSC agenda. During NSC meetings, Eisenhower considered different opinions and made decisions with all the Chiefs in attendance. Kennedy's structural changes, his practice of consulting frankly with only his closest advisors, and his use of larger forums to validate decisions already made would transcend his own Administration and continue as a prominent feature of Vietnam decision-making under President Lyndon Johnson. Under the Kennedy-Johnson system, the Chiefs would lose their direct access to the President, and thus their real influence on decision making, that the Eisenhower NSC structure had provided.

The Chiefs' diminished access to the President reflected Kennedy's opinion of his senior military advisors. Kennedy and the young New Frontiersmen of his Administration viewed Eisenhower's Chiefs with suspicion. Against the backdrop of Kennedy's efforts to reform the Department of Defense, and under the strain of foreign-policy crises, a relationship of mutual distrust between senior military and civilian officials would develop. Two months after Kennedy assumed the presidency, tension between the New Frontiersmen and the Old Guard would escalate over a foreign policy blunder—the Bay of Pigs incident in mid-April 1961. The Old Guard in the Pentagon would soon be relegated to a position of little influence. [32]

"The Kennedy Administration came in and right from the start we got the back of the hand," General Curtis E. LeMay, Chief of Staff of the Air Force, recalled. "We don't like you people. We have no respect for you. Don't bother us." The disdainful attitude was held not only by the Whiz Kids, but by

McNamara himself. "We [the Chiefs] started off trying to talk to him. It was like talking to a brick wall. We got nowhere. Finally, it was just a waste of time and effort. We could state opinions when we had a chance. That was all." [33]

## *Cold War*

When Kennedy assumed office in January 1961, the prospects for peace were hardly encouraging. The Soviets had been cool to the U.S. since the spring of 1960, when a Soviet missile shot down an American U-2 intelligence aircraft in Soviet airspace. Although the possibility of a general nuclear war had receded by the time Kennedy took office, Soviet support for wars of national liberation had increased. [34]

Kennedy was willing to renew the quest for peace but understood the effort might be long and success elusive. In that light, he was determined to give the Armed Services the sort of flexibility that would back the nation's diplomacy with a credible military threat. Kennedy's de-emphasis of massive retaliation and his stress on the need for ready, nonnuclear forces as a deterrent to limited war came just in time.

By 1961, the tight, bipolar system that had developed between the U.S. and the Soviet Union following World War II was breaking down. The Soviet Union's Ally in the East, Communist China, had become impatient with Soviet conservatism and strongly opposed to peaceful coexistence. From Cuba, Castro was pursuing his own program of intrigue and subversion in Latin America. Complicating matters further, groups favoring the Soviet, Chinese, or the Cuban brand of Communism were emerging in many countries.

Disunion was also mounting within the Western alliance. With the success of the Marshall Plan and the return of economic prosperity to Western Europe during the 1950s, France, West Germany, and other nations had become creditor countries less and less dependent on the United States. The efforts of French President Charles de Gaulle to rekindle his nation's former glory by playing an increasingly independent role in international affairs had meanwhile produced growing discord within NATO.

Outside of Soviet and U.S. circles, the presence of a third force in the world had also become apparent. Most of Europe's former colonial possessions in the Middle East, Asia, and Africa had received their independence during the fifteen years after World War II. Since these new nations contained about one third of the world's population and a large portion of its raw materials, particularly oil, both sides courted them. Many suffered, however, from basic political and economic failings that made them apt candidates for Communist subversion and wars of national liberation. As revolts to end injustice, tyranny, and exploitation broke out, Kennedy observed, the Communists would inevitably supply arms, agitators, and technicians to capture the rebel movements. The U.S. could hardly stand by passively and allow them free rein. [35]

## *Bay of Pigs*

With half the world still in the balance; insurgent movements blooming in areas as diverse as Laos, Vietnam, the Congo, and Algeria; and the threat of revolutionary outbreaks hanging over other countries in South America, Africa, and Asia, it was ironic that Kennedy's first brush with the Communists would result from U.S. support for an insurgent group. [36]

The U.S. had severed diplomatic relations with Cuba during the closing days of the Eisenhower Administration, but the presence of a Communist satellite so close to the U.S. mainland remained a constant source of irritation. In April 1961, a band of American-sponsored Cuban exiles attempted to remedy that problem by launching an invasion of the island at the Bay of Pigs. When the Cuban people failed to rally in support of the attack, the operation collapsed, damaging U.S. prestige, emboldening the Soviets, and seeming to indicate that the U.S. could not support a successful insurgency against a Communist regime. Khrushchev seized the moment to drop dark hints that he was ready to employ Russian missiles in support of his Communist Allies if that became necessary. [37]

Although the President publicly assumed responsibility for the Bay of Pigs failure, he placed a large measure of blame for the disaster on poor military advice from the Joint Chiefs of Staff. He thought his senior military advisors should have been more assertive about their doubts over the operation's chances of success.

For their part, the Chiefs believed that the President's ire was misdirected. He had consulted them only after making his decision to launch the invasion. The Armed Services had provided personnel on special assignment to the CIA but remained unaware of their activities. The Chiefs were skeptical about the operation's chances of success and stated that the landing could only succeed if the landing force controlled the airspace. They blamed the President for not consulting them earlier and considered reprehensible his disapproval of their requests to provide direct U.S. support to the besieged invaders stranded on the beach. "There was too much of a tendency within the government," Wheeler recalled, "to go right around the military in dealing with this particular problem, which was regarded as being far more a political problem then it was a military problem." The debacle exacerbated mutual distrust between the President and his senior military advisors. [38]

### *Laos*

Meanwhile, another foreign policy challenge had developed in Laos. At the time Kennedy assumed office in January 1961, the Pathet Lao had seized key objectives on the strategically vital Plain of Jars and threatened the fragile American-supported government. By late April, the President was considering U.S. military intervention.

Smarting from what they believed had been unfair criticism after the Bay of Pigs, the Chiefs were determined that any commitment of U.S. military force not suffer from the indecision and lack of firepower that had been evident in the abortive Cuban invasion. They informed Kennedy unambiguously that military action in Laos could involve the U.S. in a large-scale land war in Southeast Asia and might escalate into a confrontation with China. They recommended that if any troops were deployed, they should arrive in a strength of at least 60,000 men. Army General Lyman Lemnitzer, the Chairman of the Joint Chiefs of Staff, and General George H. Decker, the Chief of Staff of the Army, warned Kennedy not to act unless he was prepared to use nuclear weapons to "guarantee victory." A military commitment in Laos reminded Lemnitzer and Decker of the same sort of limited, costly, protracted commitment that the generals had experienced in Korea. [39]

"There is no question of resisting civilian authority," Admiral George W. Anderson, Jr., the Chief of Naval Operations, stated. "However, it is very proper for the military commander to point out to civilian authorities the military risks of military decisions." [40]

During the Laotian Crisis, Kennedy was again dissatisfied with the advice he received from the Chiefs, whose thinking he regarded as outmoded and unimaginative. He found their estimate of the number of troops required excessive and ordered only 10,000 Marines stationed in Japan to prepare for deployment to Laos. He believed that strategic options in military affairs should give him more flexibility than a stark choice between inaction and large-scale commitment. [41]

In May 1961, an international conference on Laos assembled in Geneva. Not until July 1962 would a diplomatic settlement finally be reached. It would leave the Pathet Lao in control of the eastern half of Laos, a region that North Vietnam was using to supply and reinforce the Viet Cong insurgents in their fight against the American-backed South Vietnamese government. The unfavorable Laotian settlement, combined with the apparent connection between U.S. threats of Marine deployment and Soviet willingness to negotiate, reinforced Kennedy's opinion that the Chiefs' advice was of limited value and further heightened the distrust between the President and his senior military advisors. [42]

## Taylor

Because the front line against Communism had not been drawn in Laos, South Vietnam would become the principal focus of U.S. policy in Southeast Asia. [43]

Kennedy wanted someone to advise him "to see that I am not making a dumb mistake as Commander-in-Chief." Taylor seemed the model of the soldier-statesman, and it was, in part, his reputation as both a warrior and a scholar that made him particularly attractive to Kennedy. [44]

"General Taylor had an influence with President Kennedy that extended far beyond military matters," Wheeler recalled, "rightly, he regarded him as a man of broad knowledge, quick intelligence, and sound judgment." [45]

Taylor had been a successful combat commander during World War II and the Korean War. In 1955, he replaced Ridgway as Chief of Staff of the

Army. Like Ridgway, Taylor soon became frustrated by his inability to persuade Eisenhower or his indecisive Secretary of Defense that a larger and more capable Army was vital to U.S. national security. Taylor's frustration stemmed in part from Eisenhower's subordination of military policy to domestic economic priorities, as well as his "New Look" national defense strategy, which rejected Ridgway's and Taylor's arguments that U.S. military forces must remain "balanced" in size or configuration with those of the Soviet Union and relied instead upon the military doctrine of "massive retaliation." [46]

As Taylor's "Operations Deputy" at that time, Wheeler had been entrusted with the Army's strategic planning. He and Taylor were "very much on the same wavelength," a fellow officer observed. [47]

Unlike Eisenhower, Kennedy was sympathetic to Taylor's argument that massive retaliation be supplanted with the military doctrine of "flexible response." In his book *The Uncertain Trumpet*, Taylor proposed a military doctrine of flexible response that would "give multiple choices to our political leaders" and allow them to "cope with threats of many gradations, extending from subversive insurgency ... to limited war -- conventional or nuclear -- and finally to unlimited nuclear war." To rebuild its ability to fight conventional wars, Taylor argued that the U.S. had to expand and reinforce its ground forces overseas and create a robust strategic reserve of ground and air forces on U.S. soil. [48]

Wheeler was an advocate for flexible response and later articulated its premise: "We cannot deter intercontinental missiles with muskets, but neither can we resist guerrillas with hydrogen bombs." [49]

Taylor's argument convinced Kennedy that "we have not brought our conventional war capabilities into line with the necessities." In June 1961, the President brought Taylor back on active military duty to assume an unprecedented White House position as Military Representative of the President. In this capacity, Taylor would help Kennedy affect a doctrinal shift that influenced deepening U.S. involvement in Vietnam, as well as redress the balance of the President's troubled relationship with the Chiefs. [50]

Kennedy outlined Taylor's duties in a memorandum designed to avoid criticism from the Chiefs and members of Congress who might view the unprecedented position as an infringement upon the statutory responsibilities of the Joint Chiefs of Staff (JCS).

The Chiefs had reason to believe that Taylor would assert himself in areas that had been their sole responsibility. His experience as Chief of Staff of the Army had led him to recommend radical reform in the JCS organization. He had retired exhausted from "continuous conflict" with civilian leaders in the Eisenhower Administration and his fellow Chiefs. [51]

Taylor's difficult experience stemmed, in part, from the institutional conflict endemic in U.S. democratic government. After World War II, questions of defense policy figured prominently in the continuing power struggle between the Executive Branch and Congress. Dissent from members of the JCS could weaken the President's position with the legislature and undermine the Administration's policy decisions. Although Eisenhower had described the Chiefs' statutory right to appeal to Congress as "legalized insubordination," Taylor disapproved of the President's expectation that military officers mold their advice to the views and feelings of superiors and accept public responsibility for policy decisions that they opposed. Taylor thought that Eisenhower was obsessed with "loyalty and team play," and castigated him for creating an environment in which members of the Administration pressured the Chiefs to accept a "preconceived politico-military line." In Taylor's view, the military's "ultimate loyalty" to the Constitution and the people, as embodied by their congressional representatives, outweighed personal fealty to the Commander-in-Chief. He believed that Congress and the public should be aware of the dissenting views of the nation's top military leaders. Taylor would, however, revise his opinions on the proper relationship between the military and the Commander-in-Chief after he returned to active duty under Kennedy. [52]

In *The Uncertain Trumpet*, Taylor advocated even greater centralization of JCS advisory responsibility than provided for in the Defense Reorganization Act of 1958. Deeply affected by conflict among the Chiefs, Taylor argued for the dissolution of the organization and its replacement with a single Defense Chief of Staff, who, as the senior military officer of the U.S. government, would report directly to the Secretary of Defense and the President. Taylor recognized that pressures from within the Armed Services colored the Chiefs' advice. If a Chief was thought to have abandoned his Service's interests, he risked losing all credibility and respect. Taylor urged the formation of a Supreme Military Council, an advisory body independent of the Armed Services, which would consist of senior officers from each of the Services who were either retired or on their last tour of duty. [53]

Aware of Taylor's views, Lemnitzer, as Chairman, had been less than enthusiastic about Taylor's appointment as Military Representative of the President. Kennedy moved to defuse potential criticism from the Pentagon, Congress, and the press sympathetic to the Chiefs that Taylor was usurping their advisory responsibilities.

Privately, Kennedy acknowledged that Taylor's responsibilities could easily have been performed by the Pentagon's senior military officers. However, the President was not only dissatisfied with the Chiefs' advice but also frustrated by his inability to establish with them the kind of friendly rapport that he enjoyed with the rest of his staff and with many of his Cabinet officials. To Kennedy, generals and admirals were too formal, traditional, and unimaginative.

According to Bundy, the President "would never feel really secure" about the military until "young generals of his own generation in whom he has confidence" filled the top uniformed positions of the defense establishment. Bundy new that it was important to Kennedy that the top military men be able to "conduct a conversation" with the President to give him a "feeling of confidence and reassurance." Taylor would strive to satisfy the President's need, both in his own actions and his later nomination of Wheeler to replace Decker as Chief of Staff of the Army. [54]

Realizing that the Chiefs and the Secretary of Defense viewed him as a competing voice in national security issues, Taylor moved to head-off potential animosities and assured his old friend Lemnitzer that he would be more of an ally than a source of competition. He told Lemnitzer that his "close personal relations with the President and his entourage" would help to ensure that the Chiefs' advice reached Kennedy. [55]

Yet, Taylor's first responsibility to investigate the Bay of Pigs invasion did nothing to foster his new relationship with the Chiefs. While he concluded that they were "not directly responsible" for the misadventure, he criticized them for not warning the President more urgently of the dangers. When the Administration sought military advice on narrow questions about the operation, the Chiefs had given competent answers but offered no overall assessment because "they hadn't been asked." Taylor concluded that relations between the Commander-in-Chief and the Chiefs had reached the "crisis" level. [56]

To address the problem, Taylor urged the President to specify his expectations of military advice from the Chiefs. In June, Kennedy signed National Security Action Memorandum (NSAM) 55, which directed the Chiefs to initiate advice, as well as respond to specific requests. Moreover, the Chiefs should fit "military requirements into the overall context of any situation, recognizing that the most difficult problem in government is to combine all assets in a unified, effective pattern." [57]

Taylor's recommendations revealed how much his few weeks' association with the Kennedy Administration had evolved his thinking about the advisory role of the Joint Chiefs of Staff. When he departed the Eisenhower Administration, Taylor believed that the Chiefs should provide narrowly focused military advice with "limited, if any, attention to political or economic factors, since these components of national strategy had qualified spokesman elsewhere in the governmental structure." After witnessing the "crisis" that grew out of mutual dislike and distrust between the President and the Chiefs, Taylor abandoned his previous view that the Chiefs should not "take into account the views and feelings of superiors," and supplanted it with an acknowledgment of the "importance of an intimate, easy relationship, born of friendship and mutual regard between the President and the Chiefs." He revised his conviction that he had held as Chief of Staff of the Army that the Chiefs should remain a "nonpolitical body" whose loyalty to the Constitution and the people superseded allegiance to any particular administration. [58]

## Quantitative Analysis

McNamara managed the Department of Defense through a central staff office known as the Office of the Secretary of Defense (OSD). It had sections to manage everything from the minutia of weapons development to monitoring the readiness of the Armed Services. McNamara even had a small office known as International Security Affairs (ISA), which tracked national security policy, a sort of counterpart to the NSC staff or the State Department. [59]

Wheeler recalled:

> I've heard Mr. McNamara say that when … he agreed to take office as Secretary of Defense that President Kennedy gave him only one directive which he never changed, and that is for him to determine the forces that were needed for the defense of the United States and American security interests, to create those forces, and to manage them without regard to what it might cost. Now, he added that President Kennedy had said to him, 'Now, as it regard the operating of the forces, I want you to do it as economically as you can.' Which I think is a very fair directive to give to a senior executive of a government. [60]

In June, the Chiefs scrambled to keep up with the new Secretary's demands for information and quantitative justifications for existing policies and programs. Kennedy had given McNamara thirty days to accomplish a complete review of defense policy and the organization of the Pentagon. He instructed McNamara to develop a program to eliminate waste and inefficiency. Eager to provide "active, imaginative, and decisive leadership" in the Department of Defense and abandon "the passive practice of simply refereeing the disputes of traditional and partisan factions" that had characterized the efforts of Eisenhower's Secretaries of Defense, McNamara undertook a comprehensive analysis of his department. [61]

The Chiefs were unable to respond to McNamara's demands fast enough, and their cumbersome administrative system exacerbated the Administration's unfavorable opinion of them. Interservice rivalry complicated an already cumbersome administrative system. McNamara quickly lost patience with the Chiefs' unresponsiveness and squabbling. [62]

"I never hesitated to disagree with the Joint Chiefs [of Staff] when I thought them parochial in vision or wrong in judgment," McNamara recalled, "but I never forgot that they – and the soldiers, sailors, and airmen of all ranks they commanded – were motivated by deep and noble desire to serve their country, and a willingness to sacrifice their lives if necessary to achieve that end." [63]

As Director of the Joint Staff, Wheeler played a crucial, central role in the frantic effort to provide McNamara the information he demanded. Wheeler recalled:

> It became apparent almost from the outset, that there was going to be a vast change in the pattern of operations within the Department of Defense. ... Secretary McNamara wished to explore very meticulously, very minutely the various planning actions, contingency plans, programs within the Department of Defense . . . My people were working sixteen, in some cases eighteen hours a day, seven days a week in order to turn out this information. I must say that many of the studies were not satisfactory to me or to anyone else . . . namely [for] a lack of information, very short deadlines. I regarded many of them as being only rough cuts or approximations of the studies that really were required in order to get ahead with the job. [64]

Remarkably, Wheeler escaped McNamara's ire and emerged from this crucible with his reputation enhanced. Wheeler recalled:

> Under my tenure as Director, we made a lot of changes in the internal structure of the Joint Staff as to functions, as to the creation of additional posts. ... Also, we had started and implemented a series of administrative improvements having to do with how you prepare and handle papers. All of this was for the purpose of speeding up the handling of problems; In other words, making the Joint Staff more responsive to the needs of the Chiefs, the Secretary of the Chiefs, the Secretary of Defense, and in the long term the President. ... It was obvious that the Joint Staff and the JCS machinery was simply not fast enough to cope with problems of this kind. Therefore, we had to do something to shorten the response time and to provide a better product. [65]

McNamara's answer to the mutually reinforcing problems of parochialism and administrative inefficiency was to increase centralization within

OSD. Kennedy had given his new Secretary of Defense carte blanche, and McNamara took full advantage of it. Drawing upon his experience with analytical methods and statistics, he forced new management techniques upon a reluctant department. He brought in several bright young analysts to assist him, and employed the wide latitude given to the Secretary of Defense in the Defense Reorganization Act of 1958 to create a staff structure that mirrored military staff functions. Independent from the Joint Chiefs of Staff for analysis, McNamara would exert civilian control over what had previously been almost exclusively military prerogatives. [66]

## Whiz Kids

McNamara's principal staff included intelligent young men like John T. McNaughton, who would replace Paul H. Nitze as Assistant Secretary of Defense for International Security Affairs in 1963, and Alain C. Enthoven, for whom McNamara created a new Office of Systems Analysis.

"My associates in the Kennedy and Johnson Administrations were an exceptional group: young, vigorous, intelligent, well-meaning, patriotic servants of the United States," McNamara recalled. With his "full backing," the young civilians soon dubbed the "Whiz Kids" would vigorously discharge their responsibilities and exert their authority. [67]

The Whiz Kids were like-minded men who shared McNamara's penchant for qualitative analysis and suspicion of proposals based solely upon "military experience." Many of them had worked in think tanks and research corporations and were eager to apply their techniques to the issues of the Department of Defense.

Enthoven quickly became McNamara's point man in establishing firm civilian control over the Pentagon. His flair for quantitative analysis was exceeded only by his arrogance. Enthoven held military experience in low regard and considered military men intellectually inferior. He was convinced that "there was little in the typical officer's early career that qualifies him to be a better strategic planner than . . . a graduate of the Harvard Business School." He used statistics to analyze defense programs and issues and then provided the Secretary of Defense and the President information they needed to make decisions. Enthoven saw no limits to the applicability of his methods. [68]

The military's mutual distaste for McNamara and his ilk lingered for decades. General Barry R. McCaffrey, a division commander during Operation DESERT STORM, had served as a young officer in Vietnam. He recalled, "To many of us, McNamara exemplified a brilliant mind that knew the price of everything and the value of nothing." [69]

McNamara's autocratic style and the condescending attitude of his young civilian assistants deeply disturbed the Chiefs and other senior military officers. They resented the youthful Whiz Kids' lack of respect for military experience and viewed Enthoven and the rest of McNamara's staff as adversaries. "They didn't know what they didn't know," Goodpaster recalled charitably. [70]

General Michael S. Davison recalled, "Most of my colleagues and I saw the 'whiz kids' as very smart and energetic but lacking in basic knowledge of the Armed Services and matters affecting operational and tactical doctrine and training. On occasion, their decisions were inappropriate or disruptive. As a consequence, it got to be pretty damn difficult." Differences arose between the JCS and OSD over new management techniques, the military budget, and weapons procurement. Diplomatically, Wheeler skated a fine line through the dilemma. [71]

Although united in their frustration with McNamara and his staff, the Chiefs remained divided on substantive defense issues. This enabled McNamara, who had promised to act "decisively and effectively to accomplish . . . solutions," to intervene to resolve issues of contention between the Chiefs. Neglected during the Eisenhower years, the Army benefited from McNamara's belief in strong conventional forces to fight limited wars.

In less than eighteen months, McNamara would add more than 300,000 troops to the Army. Differences over defense allocations and structure diminished the Chiefs' influence relative to McNamara's civilian analysts. [72]

## Sidelined

Officers on Taylor's personal staff warned him that the Kennedy Administration was making a deliberate effort to minimize the military's influence over defense policy. Part of the responsibility rested with the Chiefs' inability to abandon their preoccupation with Service interests. Unless they began to project their advice "outward and upward" and address policy concerns rather than narrow Service interests, the prospect for harmonious civil-military relations would remain dim. [73]

Taylor discovered that McNamara often suppressed the Chiefs' advice in favor of the views of his civilian analysts. On several defense issues, McNamara either failed to consult the Chiefs or did not forward their views to the White House. Taylor's staff reported that, in addition to McNamara's strict control over the Chiefs, greater centralization in the Kennedy Administration prevented military advice from reaching the President. Kennedy had increased his reliance upon ad hoc gatherings of "principals" that usually included Bundy and McNamara. Informal committees with responsibility for particular issues conducted closed deliberations and often sent papers directly to the President. Loose associations of second-level officials in the White House and the Defense and State Departments furthered their own defense agendas by working "across channels by personal contact" and calling upon their associates who were "members of the club, and whom they [could] count on to agree with them." The members of Kennedy's inner circle protected their ideas with ideological fervor. [74]

### *Berlin Crisis*

The timing of the Bay of Pigs fiasco was particularly unfortunate. Kennedy was scheduled to meet with Khrushchev in Vienna during June to discuss Berlin, where the growing prosperity of the Western zone contrasted sharply with the poverty and drabness of the Soviet sector. In that sense, West Berlin had become as great an irritation to the Communists as Cuba was to the United States. In 1958, Khrushchev had threatened to conclude a separate treaty with East Germany unless Western forces withdrew from the city within six months. This would have given the Germans sovereignty over the transportation corridors into the area and would have allowed the Soviets to abandon the obligation they had assumed in 1945 to guarantee Western access to the city. Although Khrushchev later backed off from his threat and even showed signs of a conciliatory attitude, he returned to the issue at the Vienna summit. Unless the West accepted the Soviet position, he informed Kennedy, he would move on his own to resolve the Berlin impasse.

If Khrushchev hoped to intimidate the new President in the wake of the Cuban setback, his threat had the opposite effect. Rather than concede another victory to the Communists, Kennedy requested and received additional defense funding from Congress and the authority to call as many as 250,000 members of the Individual Ready Reserve to active duty. Kennedy refrained from declaring a national emergency but was determined to strengthen U.S. conventional forces in case Soviet pressure on Berlin required some sort of armed response.

Tensions mounted during August, when thousands of refugees crossed from East to West Berlin, and the Communists responded by constructing a high wall around their sector to block further departures. With pressure rising, Kennedy decided in September to increase the size of the Armed Forces by adding ground, air, and naval units. He also called many reservists and reserve units to active duty to strengthen continental U.S. forces. As a result, by October, the Army's regular troop strength had grown by more than 80,000, while almost 120,000 troops, including two National Guard divisions, had returned to active duty.

When the Soviets realized that the U.S. might call their bluff, they pulled back. The wall remained, but the threats and other pressures diminished. In the same way, Kennedy's reserve call-up would end by mid-1962, but the increase in the regular force would remain. [75]

## *Flexible Response*

Soon after Kennedy became President in 1961, he significantly increased military and economic aid to South Vietnam to help Diem defeat the growing insurgency. For Kennedy, insurgency challenged international security every bit as seriously as nuclear war. The Administration's approach to both extremes of conflict rested upon the precepts of the flexible response. Regarded as a form of "sub-limited," or small war, insurgency was treated largely as a military problem—conventional war writ small—and hence susceptible to resolution by timely and appropriate military action. Kennedy's success in applying calculated military pressures to compel the Soviet Union to remove its missiles from Cuba in 1962 would reinforce the Administration's disposition to deal with other international crises, including the conflict in Vietnam, in a similar manner.

Kennedy's policy, though commendable in its degree of flexibility, also had its limitations. Long-term strategic planning would yield to short-term crisis management. Planners would tend to assume that all belligerents were rational and that the adversary subscribed as they did to the seductive logic of the flexible response. Hoping to give the South Vietnamese a margin for success, Kennedy would periodically authorize additional military aid and support between 1961 and November 1963, when he was assassinated. But the absence of a coherent operational strategy for the conduct of counterinsurgency and chronic military and political shortcomings on the part of the South Vietnamese would nullify potential benefits. [76]

## *Army Build-Up*

The primacy of the manned bomber as the nation's main nuclear deterrent was coming to an end. Following trends already begun during the Eisenhower Administration, Kennedy and McNamara replaced some of the big aircraft with nuclear missiles. As for the U.S. Army, the growth of the war in Vietnam brought a reaffirmation that ground forces remained supreme. In 1961, as a result, the Army's decline that had begun during the Eisenhower Administration ceased. The Army began to grow in size and its share of the defense budget. [77]

The U.S. Army would play a major role in Kennedy's buildup of the U.S. advisory and support efforts in South Vietnam. In turn, that role would be possible in large measure by Kennedy's determination to increase the strength and capabilities of U.S. Army forces for both conventional and unconventional operations. Between 1961 in 1964, the Army would grow from 860,000 troops to more than 1.06 million men, and the number of combat divisions would grow from 11 to 16. Navy and Air Force conventional units also made modest gains. These increases were accompanied by an ambitious program to modernize Army equipment and, by stockpiling supplies and equipment for bases, to increase the deployability and readiness of Army combat forces. The buildup, however, did not prevent the call up of 120,000 reservists to active duty in the summer of 1961, a few months after Kennedy assumed office.

Facing renewed Soviet threats to force the Western Powers out of Berlin, Kennedy mobilized the Army to reinforce NATO, if necessary. But the mobilization revealed serious shortcomings in reserve readiness and produced a swell of criticism and complaints from Congress and reservists alike. Although Kennedy sought to remedy the exposed deficiencies and set in motion plans to reorganize the reserves, the unhappy experience of the Berlin Crisis would remain fresh in the minds of national leaders when they faced the prospect of war in Vietnam a few years later. [78]

## Vietnam

By the time the Kennedy Administration assumed office, what had been a "problem" for Eisenhower was becoming a crisis. Vietnam quickly became one of the most important issues because of its perceived impact upon the superpower confrontation and its potentially damaging effect on Kennedy's political future. Consequently, as the insurgency grew more aggressive, Kennedy would intervene more dramatically, waging what the Communists called a "special war" —a U.S.-sponsored war fought primarily by the Army of South Vietnam (ARVN) without direct large-scale U.S. combat involvement. Kennedy would increase the number of advisors from fewer than 1,000 to 16,000, some of whom would undertake limited combat roles. The ARVN would receive new weapons, including napalm, helicopters, fixed-wing aircraft, and armored personnel carriers. [79]

In early April 1961, there was no debate on the efficacy of providing more military assistance to South Vietnam. The only suitable question asked was, "What kind and how much?" [80]

Early the following month, Kennedy sent Vice President Lyndon B. Johnson to South Vietnam to reassure the South Vietnamese that despite his decision to accept a neutral Laos, the U.S. could be counted on for support. In a report submitted immediately after his return on 15 May, Johnson argued for prompt U.S. actions to show support for friendly governments in Southeast Asia, including increased military and economic aid. Johnson concluded that U.S. troops were neither desired by Asian leaders nor immediately required.

The report also reflected Johnson's realization that a "fundamental decision" must soon be made whether or not the U.S. should commit itself to a "major effort" in Southeast Asia. This decision, Johnson wrote prophetically, "must be made with the knowledge that at some point we may be faced with the further decision of whether we commit major United States forces to the area or cut our losses and withdraw should our efforts fail. We must remain masters of this decision." [81]

The Chiefs believed that the fall of Vietnam was inevitable unless substantial numbers of U.S. troops were introduced. They also believed that given the stakes, the U.S. government had to think long and hard before becoming directly involved. Was the nation ready to pay the potentially high price of direct involvement? Most importantly, the Chiefs believed that the U.S. should avoid a policy of gradualism, in which the number of troops and amount of force deployed would slowly increase. If the U.S. decided to use force in Vietnam, then the undertaking should be carried out on an all-or-nothing basis. The last of these three reservations would haunt the U.S. government and lead to numerous clashes between the Chiefs and senior politicians for years to come. [82]

Facing trouble spots in Latin America and Africa in addition to Southeast Asia, Kennedy would take a keen interest in the U.S. Army Special Forces, formed in 1952 to prepare to lead guerrilla wars against the Soviet Union in Eastern Europe. He believed their skills in unconventional warfare also made them well-suited to countering insurgency. During his first year in office, he would increase the Special Forces from about 1,500 to 9,000 men, and he would greatly enlarge their role in South Vietnam. [83]

Besides the Special Forces, the Army's most important contribution to the conflict would be the helicopter. Neither Kennedy nor the Army anticipated the rapid growth of aviation in South Vietnam when the first helicopter transportation companies arrived in December 1961. In South Vietnam, the helicopter's effect on organization and operations would be as sweeping as the influence of mechanized forces in World War II.

In addition to the Special Forces and helicopters, Kennedy would greatly expand the entire U.S. advisory effort. With the expansion of the advisory and support efforts would come demands for better communications, intelligence, and medical, logistical, and administrative support, all of which the Army sourced from its active forces, drawing upon skilled men and units from forces based in the continental United States. The result would be a slow, steady erosion of its capacity to meet worldwide contingency obligations. But if Vietnam was depleting the Army, it would also provide certain advantages. The war was a laboratory in which to test and evaluate new equipment and techniques applicable to counterinsurgency. As the activities of all the Armed Services expanded, U.S. military strength in South Vietnam would increase from under 700 at the start of 1960 to almost 24,000 by the end of 1964. [84]

## DOD Consolidation

McNamara quickly began to make heavy use of the extensive authority his office had received under the Defense Reorganization Act of 1958. The guidelines he received from Kennedy were simple: while operating the nation's Armed Services at the lowest possible cost, he was to develop a force structure necessary to meet U.S. military requirements without regard to arbitrary or predetermined budget ceilings.

In accordance with McNamara's idea of centralized planning, the Chiefs, assisted by the Services, continued to develop military plans and force requirements they deemed necessary to support U.S. national security interests. In a new process that Wheeler, as Director of the Joint Staff, was centrally involved in implementing, the forces were now separated according to function—strategic retaliation, general purpose, reserves, etc.—with each going into what planners call program packages. When McNamara received these packages, he weighed each against the goal it sought to achieve, correlated the cost-effectiveness of weapon systems involved, and inserted the approved packages in the annual budget that he sent to the President and Congress. To improve long-range planning, he also compiled and annually reviewed a five-year projection of all forces, weapons systems, and activities that fell within the scope of his authority.

Initially, the Kennedy Administration had three basic defense goals: to strengthen U.S. strategic forces; to build up conventional forces so they could respond flexibly to lesser challenges; and to improve the overall effectiveness and efficiency of the nation's defenses. To attain the first objective, McNamara supported a nuclear triad that included strategic bombers, intercontinental ballistic missiles in steel-reinforced concrete silos, and Polaris nuclear submarines. If one of the three systems went down in a Soviet attack, the other two could retaliate.

McNamara gradually centralized many activities in each Service formerly administered separately. Seeking greater efficiency and reduced costs, he also instituted changes in organization and procedures that made use of the latest management techniques and computer systems. In that way, he directed the centralization and coordination of the Defense Department's intelligence operations into one office, which would prepare his intelligence estimates. Thus, the Defense Intelligence Agency was established in 1961.

The effects of the 1958 reorganization were most noticeable in the decision-making process. By maintaining close watch over budgets and finances, manpower, logistics, research, and engineering, McNamara tightened civilian control over the Services and carried unification much further than had any of his predecessors. His creation of the U.S. Strike Command in 1961 was a case in point. By combining the Army's Strategic Army Corps with the Air Force's Tactical Air Command, the new organization possessed combat-ready air and ground forces that could deploy quickly to meet contingencies. The Army and Air Force components of the new command remained under their own Services until an emergency arose. Then, they passed to the operational control of the command itself. [85]

## *Quarters 16-A*

Twenty-year old Bim had accompanied his parents in their move from Fort Hood to Quarters 16-A on Fort Myer. He enrolled at George Washington University and majored in mathematics. Gale, his former math teacher, helped him get a job teaching math at St. Stephen's during the 1961-62 school year. (Bim would eventually earn a Bachelor of Science in 1963, a Master of Arts in 1966, and a Ph. D in 1970.) [86]

One time when Bus was out of town for more than a week on an inspection trip, Bim took advantage of his absence and grew a moustache. When Bus returned home, he greeted Bim and proceeded up the stairs.

About half way up, Bus stopped, turned, and said, "You or the moustache. Do you understand?"

"Yes, sir," Bim replied, then promptly shaved it off. [87]

In early 1961, Bim's cousin Doneld Howell had informed Bus of his plans to attend Washington and Jefferson College in Washington, Pennsylvania. Bus inquired whether the college had a Reserve Officers Training Corps (ROTC) program. It did. Bus recommended that he join since, otherwise, he would almost certainly be drafted after graduation. Far better to be an officer than a private! Doneld took his recommendation. (Bus would speak at his graduation ceremony in 1965.) [88]

(Wheeler would later oversee a revision of the ROTC program to improve the flow of qualified officers into both the Active Army and Army Reserve. Beginning in 1964, the Army would strengthen the four-year program at colleges and universities by providing for scholarships. Although most newly commissioned National Guard officers were products of state-run officer candidate schools, ROTC would be the primary source of new officers for both the Regular Army and Army Reserve between 1965 and 1970.) [89]

That fall, Bus bought a new Sunbeam Alpine sports car for Bim. Over the Thanksgiving weekend, Bim fell asleep at the wheel and wrecked it. The car was drivable, but really banged up. Bim was lucky not to have been injured. When he got home, he informed Betty about the accident. She told him to leave the matter alone until morning. Meanwhile, she informed Bus. At about 6:00 A. M., Bim sensed a presence at the foot of his bed. It was Bus, who said, "I was mad as hell when your mother told me about the car. However, I am relieved not to be attending your funeral." He departed, and nothing more was ever said between them about the accident. [90]

One December evening, Bus and Betty authorized Bim to host a small Christmas party for some of his friends from George Washington University and Montgomery Junior College while they were out at a function. Like a typical college party, the number of attendees swelled, many of them unknown to Bim. At one point, the long metal table in the Wheelers' kitchen had a pyramid of beer bottles and cans stacked all the way to the fifteen-foot ceiling. Before his parents were due home, Bim announced clean up time. Incredibly, by the time they returned, the house was spotless. Bim introduced his parents to his friends, whom he had allowed to remain after kicking everyone else out. They found Bus somewhat formal and reserved, yet approachable. Betty later discovered a single broken glass, the only casualty from Bim's soiree. [91]

Another evening when Bus and Betty were out, Bim and his lifelong friend Gordon Peyton were having a couple "toots" from Bus's private stash. The only scotch Bim could find was Black and White. When he went to refill Gordon's glass, Gordon referred to it as, "that goddamn Black and White!" The next time Gordon came over, Bus said, "Gordon, what can I fix you to drink? A martini, a manhattan, or how about some of that goddamn Black and White?" One of the orderlies must have overheard and relayed Gordon's remark. [92]

## 1962

### *Fourth European Tour*

Wheeler's tenure as Director of the Joint Staff concluded on 23 February 1962. The following day, he was reassigned as the Deputy Commander-in-Chief, United States European Command (EUCOM) at Camp de Loges, in Paris. On 1 March, he was promoted to four-star rank. [93]

The Wheelers assumed this would be Bus's final tour and that he would eventually replace retiring U.S. Air Force General Lauris Norstad in his dual-hatted roles as the Commander-in-Chief, EUCOM (his national role) and NATO's Supreme Allied Commander, Europe (SACEUR) (his multinational role). *A fine capstone to Bus's career,* Betty thought. They both looked forward to another European tour (his fourth and her third) and to the spectacular Parisian lifestyle that awaited them. [94]

SACEUR was the highest international military command position, and in terms of influence and prestige, no other assignment during the Cold War was more coveted. As Eisenhower had first discovered, virtually nothing in NATO was "nonpolitical," and no SACEUR could avoid the political and economic aspects of international collective defense. According to Goodpaster, who would later replace Lemnitzer as SACEUR in 1969, "consultations with Europe are neither simple in execution nor a panacea for our deeper differences: the process is fraught with as many complexities as are the issues." [95]

Wheeler would have made a great SACEUR, the effectiveness of which Goodpaster ascribed to adroit political skills as much as military expertise. Wheeler was humble, innovative, solid, reliable, cautious, persuasive, and possessed almost limitless patience. He was even-tempered and business-like, yet approachable and had a witty sense of humor. He was neither reserved nor effusive. A future aide-de-camp would dub him 'the quiet general" since he never raised his voice. Wheeler had certain expectations of people and responded accordingly to their performance. These skills and attributes, coupled with his experience in international political and military arenas, would enable Wheeler's success as Chief of Staff of the Army and later as Chairman of the Joint Chiefs of Staff, and they would also have served him well as SACEUR or, for that matter, as a U.S. Ambassador in Europe. [96]

## *Paris*

Betty set to work to make their designated quarters more habitable, although they expected to occupy the SACEUR's house in a matter of months. From a Parisian hotel, she wrote her mother:

> Had lunch there yesterday and went over it, but this morn-
> ing … will go with pencil and paper and try to figure out
> what is best to do. Would love to do it all over! Gen. Norstad
> (and this is confidential) advises that we do the minimum
> as we will move to other quarters in the fall, not later than
> November. So-o. [97]

She would take some getting used to the social obligations incumbent upon NATO's senior military leadership and their spouses:

> [At] the luncheon Monday, at Mrs. [Isabelle] Norstad's, there
> were about twenty-four screaming women. I have never
> heard such a din. NATO was represented somewhat. French
> was largely spoken although most of the women could speak
> English. Between the noise, and a foreign language, I came
> home exhausted! I was pleased to learn that such a large lun-
> cheon is not usual. [98]

"I also learned something," Betty added, about Wheeler's predecessor as Deputy Commander-in-Chief, EUCOM. "The Palmers were not in this particular circle. Except for a few, they didn't know Gen. Palmer. Between you and me the 'heir apparent' is already in evidence. Nothing may come of it, as Bus says, but it [is] obviously in the making." [99]

The Wheelers continued their association with Major General Berton "Bert" E. Spivy and his wife Frances "Frannie". Bus and Bert had both just departed the Joint Staff and previously had been hunting and fishing buddies in Germany after the war. (Spivy's career had and would continue to benefit tremendously from his personal and professional association with Wheeler, who would appoint him to his old job as Director of the Joint Staff in 1967.) They got along much better than their wives. [100]

"I can't take Frannie," confided Betty, relating their most recent conversation.

Frannie said, "When did you stop smoking? You smoked the last time I saw you."

"Oh no," Bus replied. "Betty hasn't smoked since she came back from Germany."

Betty continued, explaining that Frannie "started to say something and stopped. The last time we met, remember, she called me 'a god-damned liar!'" [101]

In Bus's new four-star job, the Wheelers would have several enlisted orderlies to help run their household. In early March, Betty gave her mother an initial assessment:

> We're going to have to make some changes with the help. One of the men went back to the States with Gen. Palmer. Felix the cook, we're saddled with until he retires in the fall. Bus agreed with Gen. Palmer to keep him on. He cooks, doesn't do one other thing, and he keeps a dirty stove! Keyes knows he's with us, so [I] hope it all works out. Sgt. Gill, a colored man, I think will prove a jewel. God knows he's the only one who has done anything this week. Then there is Sgt. Stevens, who Jean told me runs the house. It's quite evident that this is not so, and he drives. He arrives at eight, leaves at five, but helps when there is a party. He stood behind Jean's chair to tell the help when the plates were empty! Well, this is a body

that we can do without! Sgt. Dawson drove for Marie Byers when they were in Paris. There will be a job for a driver about the middle of April (in the motor pool), so in the meantime Sgt. Stevens can be showing Hillard the ropes. I am going to have to run a more efficient house, but Bob Guthrie, Bus's junior aide can take over when things don't do. Sgt. Gill can cook, so as soon as Felix leaves, he will go into the no-cook slot. [102]

The services of the official help were not all that Betty looked forward to. "I've hired a French maid!" she added. "There is little excuse for things not to be done right. She will do laundry, mend, press for me and guests, make beds, take care of me, and <u>lovely,</u> turn down the beds! It will be a fine house." [103]

A week later, Betty reported, "Keyes, Hillard, and Dawson arrived at the house. … Did they ever look good to me!" Gill was already there. Together, they helped Betty get the house in order. The Wheelers had been particularly distressed about the original condition of their new living room, but once Betty and her crew had redone it, Bus exclaimed in appreciation, "I never would have believed that I would walk into this room without shuddering." [104]

"The [enlisted orderlies'] rooms are pleasant, but small," she explained. "I put Lilliane [her pretty but snaggle-toothed French maid] in the largest because it has its own wash basin and toilet. Three rooms are on the 2nd floor, two in the basement. We do have a full house!" Lilliane would only last a couple weeks, however. She and the enlisted orderlies just could not get along. [105]

Betty decided "to have Monday morning sessions with Keyes in the hopes that we can keep this house going a little better. I think he's going to love it! I have a little room with a desk. He sits on one side and we discuss things! He's a regular old lady." [106]

With the domestic help in place, Betty now had time to pamper herself. She discovered a French hairdresser, Claude Ryf, whose skill she adored. (Later, when Bus was Chairman, she would continue to patronize Claude's salon whenever she accompanied Bus on business trips to Paris.)

> It's [been] years since my hair looked like this. … Claude cut off some more, and when I left he said, 'Now you are beginning to look Parisian, very chic' (in French!) I had [my hair]

streaked before I left Washington. Bus kept complaining
about my dark hair. This is very pretty, and becoming, as it
lightens my hair and yet doesn't make me blonde. [107]

Looking chic and classy certainly facilitated Betty's success as a senior
general officer's wife, but much more significantly, like Bus, she was a gracious
host with an affinity for European culture, a friendly, diplomatic demeanor,
and an ability to communicate in several other languages. Soon after arriving
in Paris, she resumed taking French lessons "two hours three times a week." [108]

No sooner had the Wheelers occupied their new house on 23 March,
then they went "house hunting" a few days later for one they would relocate
into once Bus became SACEUR:

Not really house hunting, but we did look at a beautiful, beautiful, enormous house. I doubt we will get it, but such fun to
see. Sept. 30th is the deadline, and it may take awhile to locate
an adequate place, and one that can be afforded. Between
you and me, I don't like the Norstad's house, and can't help
but wonder what the appeal was for Mamie. Should by any
odd chance we move into the other house, it would kill me
to move. Bus said as the French gov't has something to do
with Norstads' house, should he get the job we'd be obliged
to move [in]. [109]

Betty added that she had counted up "the number of places I had actually moved into and set up housekeeping. The number came to 31 … and four
extended visits home … in 30 years! Wouldn't change it for the world." [110]

## *Margie*

Bim had remained behind in Washington, DC to continue his studies
at George Washington University. Bus rented a small apartment for him outside of Fort Myer. Bim had been dating Margaret "Margie" Ann Long, and
their relationship had become serious. Although they had discussed getting
married with Betty and Bus before their departure for France, Bim and Margie
couldn't wait, and they soon eloped. [111]

Betty wrote to her parents:

I am in hopes that Bim by now has told you that he and Margie were married on the 16ᵗʰ [of March]. We got the word [five days ago]. Margie is a lovely girl, pretty, blonde, blue eyes, and Protestant! … Bim brought her home when he knew we were leaving [for Paris]. … When we left there was to be a large wedding when we came home for the commanders' conference in November. … Bus and I have complete confidence that they will make a go of it, if for the next year they can get along without added financial aid. We can manage without it hurting! Ah me, c'est la vie! [112]

On 9 April, Betty's parents received from Margie's father, Air Force Colonel William M. Long, a wedding announcement and invitation to a reception at the Bolling Air Force Base Officers Open Mess on 22 April. [113]

In a letter of congratulations and best wishes, Betty's father advised Bim, "In marriage it is teamwork that counts and learning to give and take. A wife can pull a man down or help him rise to great heights. I think Betty and Bus are prime examples of good teamwork in marriage." [114]

"This has been a very busy time for me," Bus advised Bim in early June:

We have had an unending stream of visitors, [Betty & I] have done some traveling, and I have done more, and the social schedule has been awful. We leave Tuesday morning for Scandinavia (Denmark and Norway). We have never visited there, and we are looking forward to the trip. Apropos of trips, my trip back to the States seems to have fallen through; maybe I'll come but probably not. I really don't care; I have much to do here and Omaha in June is no place to be. … [We expect to] travel back to the U.S. – hopefully in November (for the commanders' conference). [115]

## Vietnam

Back in February, changes made to command arrangements attested to the growing American commitment to South Vietnam. The Chiefs established the U.S. Military Assistance Command, Vietnam (MACV) in Saigon as the senior U.S. military headquarters. McNamara appointed General

Paul D. Harkins as commander (COMUSMACV). Harkins reported to the Commander-In-Chief, Pacific, (CINCPAC) in Hawaii, but because of high-level interest in South Vietnam also enjoyed special access to military and civilian leaders in Washington. Overseeing all military activities in Vietnam, MACV soon moved into the advisory effort that had been directed by the existing Military Assistance and Advisory Group (MAAG). To simplify the advisory chain of command, the latter would be disestablished in May 1964 when MACV assumed direct control. [116]

The U.S. Air Force commenced Operation RANCH HAND, an aerial herbicide spraying program, while various CIA counterinsurgency initiatives were nurtured, including helping the Special Forces organize the Montagnards into Civilian Irregular Defense Groups to help defend South Vietnam's western border in the Central Highlands.

Equally important, the U.S. supported South Vietnam's Strategic Hamlet Program, a "pacification" plan launched in late 1961. Pacification entailed winning the peasants' "hearts and minds" by separating them from the guerrillas, providing security from VC attacks, and improving living conditions through social, economic, and political reforms. Accomplishing all three tasks well would prove a challenge throughout the war.

The infusion of advisors and new weapons, combined with the success of some strategic hamlets, stopped the hemorrhaging that characterized Diem's war effort from 1960 through mid-1962. Neither side foresaw imminent victory. [117]

By October, there was interagency consensus that the military situation was critical, and direct military intervention must be seriously considered.

On 11 November, McNamara and Rusk submitted a joint memorandum to the President urging economic aid, military equipment, and training, but no U.S. combat troops. The resulting policy program, "First Phase of Vietnam Program," was an example of policy incrementalism derived from a complex set of factors, including, but not limited to, reports on conditions in South Vietnam, expectations of Congressional and public approval, and President Kennedy's perception of the problem and potential solutions.

Kennedy's policy on Vietnam was to raise the U.S. commitment, yet keep it limited. He would neither permit the war's escalation into a general war, nor bargain away South Vietnam's security at the conference table, despite being pressed along both lines by advisors impatient to win or withdraw. In essence, Kennedy's strategy was to avoid escalation, retreat, or a choice limited to those two options, all the while seeking time to make policies and programs of both the U.S. and South Vietnamese governments more appealing to the peasantry; time to build an anti-guerilla capability sufficient to convince the Communists that they could not seize the country by military force; and time to put the Vietnamese themselves in a position to achieve a settlement that only they could achieve by bringing terrorism under control.

In retrospect, Kennedy's Vietnam policy could be called an interlude between the inattentive assistance of the Eisenhower Administration and the massive involvement that would follow under President Johnson. [118]

While the U.S. strengthened its position in South Vietnam and Thailand, the Communists tightened their grip in Laos. The U.S. had supported the nation's pro-Western military leaders with aid and advice, but all efforts to unify the country by force had failed, and three different factions now controlled segments of the country. With conditions growing worse, Kennedy sought to avoid a Communist takeover by pushing for a neutralized Laos. Agreements signed in Geneva in July confirmed the independence and neutrality of the country, which was be ruled by a coalition government. In turn, Laos pledged to refrain from military alliances, and all foreign military forces were required to leave the country. More than 600 U.S. advisors and technicians officially left by the end of the year, although covert advisors remained. North Vietnam did not honor the agreements. Its army, together with Laotian Communist forces, consolidated its hold on areas adjacent to both North and South Vietnam through which passed the Ho Chi Minh Trail. As a result, it became easier to move supplies south to support the Viet Cong in the face of the new dangers embodied by U.S. advisors, weapons, and tactics. [119]

## *Army Reorganization*

In mid-1962, the Administration released the National Guard units that it had called up for the Berlin Crisis, but it authorized the Army to reactivate two regular divisions, bringing the total to sixteen. The Army also received authorization to maintain a permanent strength of 970,000. The addition of new troops allowed many Army units to fill out their ranks. The Army's budget also rose from $10.1 billion to $12.4 billion in Fiscal Years 1961 and 1962. Almost half of that increase went for the purchase of new weapons and equipment, such as vehicles, aircraft, and missiles.

In view of the changes occurring in the Department of Defense, it was hardly surprising that in 1961 McNamara had also directed a thorough review of the Army's makeup and procedures. A broad reorganization plan resulted, which Wheeler would later implement during his tenure as Chief of Staff of the Army. Approved by Kennedy in early 1962, it called for major shifts in the tasks performed by the Army Staff and the agency's technical services. The Army Staff gained primary responsibility for planning and policy, while the execution of decisions fell squarely upon field commands. In effort to centralize personnel, training, and research and development while integrating supply operations, the new system abolished most of the technical services.

Most of the operating functions released by the Army Staff and the technical services went to the U.S. Army Continental Army Command and to two new commands: the U.S. Army Matériel Command and the U.S. Army Combat Development Command. The Continental Army Command became responsible for almost all the Army's schools and for the training of all individuals and units in the United States. It relinquished control over the development, testing, production, procurement, storage, maintenance, and distribution of supplies and equipment to the Army Materiel Command, which established subordinate commands to handle those functions. Meanwhile, the Combat Development Command assumed responsibility for answering questions on the Army's organization and equipment and how it was to fight in the field. It developed organizational and operational doctrine, produced material objectives and qualitative requirements, conducted wargames and field experiments, and ran cost-effectiveness studies. [120]

## *ROAD*

A major overhaul of the Army's tactical organization accompanied the reorganization of the Army Staff. Experience had demonstrated that the pentomic division lacked staying power and that it needed more troops to conduct sustained combat operations. The Army had addressed those issues in 1961 by revising its divisional structure to ensure greater flexibility and better balance between mobility and firepower. Under the Reorganization Objective Army Division (ROAD) concept it developed, the Army formed four types of divisions: infantry, armor, airborne, and mechanized. [121]

The Army tested the ROAD concept in 1962 by reactivating its 1st Armored and 5th Infantry (Mechanized) Divisions. Wheeler would later devote long hours as Chief of Staff of the Army overseeing the conversion of the Army's remaining 14 divisions and reorganization of the National Guard and Army Reserve. This transformation process, begun in 1963, would be completed by the end of Wheeler's tenure in mid-1964. [122]

## Civil Rights

Several instances of civil disturbance related to the equal rights movement had and would continue to occur during the Kennedy and Johnson Administrations. In late September, the Governor of Mississippi attempted to block the court-ordered registration of an African-American, James H. Meredith, at the University of Mississippi in Oxford. Kennedy sought at first to enforce the law by calling in Federal marshals, but when they proved incapable of restoring order, he deployed troops: eventually some 20,000 regulars and 10,000 federalized Mississippi National Guardsmen. Most stood in reserve, but 12,000 took up station near the university. With the military in firm control, the tension eased. Most of the troops returned home within a short while; nevertheless, Federal forces would maintain a presence in the area throughout the remainder of the school year. [123]

## You Don't Say No to the President

Meanwhile, the Cold War crises during Kennedy's first months as President had shaped advisory relationships within his Administration and influenced his foreign policy decisions. Already predisposed to distrust the senior military officers he had inherited from the Eisenhower Administration, the Bay of Pigs incident and Laotian crisis prompted Kennedy to seek a "changing of the guard" in the Pentagon by replacing the "holdover" Chiefs with his own men who would be less likely to resist his defense policies. Lemnitzer, the Chairman, had been unequivocal on Laos. His belief that the U.S. should be prepared to employ its full power before deciding to intervene anywhere may have been appropriate under Eisenhower's policy of massive retaliation, but it was anathema to Kennedy's and Taylor's concept of flexible response. In September, Kennedy appointed Lemnitzer to replace Norstad as SACEUR in order to create a vacancy in the chairmanship, which he filled with Taylor in a break from the traditional rotation among the Services. [124]

Simultaneously, Kennedy and McNamara forced Decker, who had told McNamara in April 1961 that "we cannot win a conventional war in Southeast Asia," to retire after only two years as Chief of Staff of the Army. Convinced that Wheeler could be counted upon for his loyalty and support, Taylor recommended that he replace Decker. The handsome Wheeler had favorably impressed Kennedy during the 1960 presidential election with his intellect and gentlemanly, affable demeanor. Kennedy was drawn instinctively to men who, like himself, were sharp-witted and prepossessing in appearance. [125]

This could have been considered good news by Wheeler, as the two most coveted assignments before retirement for the most senior Army officers were Chief of Staff of the Army and SACEUR. The former job was certainly no step down from the latter. But Wheeler was disappointed and protested to Lemnitzer. He was only seven months into his new assignment, and he wanted to stay on with NATO. He argued that there were many general officers who were worthy candidates for the Army's top job. He, on the other hand, possessed unique and extensive experience in dealing with NATO Allies. He and Betty integrated easily with other cultures and enjoyed the exposure. They had always treated foreign dignitaries as equals and with great respect. Bus's argument was for naught, and he knew it. "You don't say no to the President of the United States," he told Betty. [126]

French President Charles De Gaulle personally liked Wheeler and expected him to replace Norstad. When Kennedy summoned Wheeler to Washington instead, De Gaulle was incensed that Kennedy had not bothered to consult him about it beforehand. This perceived slight may have been a contributing factor in France's withdrawal from NATO later that year. [127]

Wheeler's aides took him and Betty out for a farewell dinner. "We had a wonderful time," recorded Betty. "They found an old, old restaurant, a plaque on the door, say [year] 15-something. It was small, all the cooking was done over a fire in our midst. The meats were hanging over the cutting table. A large tray was brought and you picked what you wanted cooked." [128]

On 12 September, the EUCOM headquarters held a cocktail party reception for the Wheelers. Betty wrote:

> Saturday [was] free, and an absolutely perfect summer day. I worked at packing all morning, and when Bus came in we decided to enjoy our beautiful garden. We had lunch, and then sat ... in the upper garden until the sun left it. ... It rained off and on all day but cleared when we went to the airport ... to meet the McConnell's. [Wheeler's USMA '32 classmate, U.S. Air Force General John P. McConnell, had been appointed to replace Wheeler as Deputy Commander-in-Chief, EUCOM.] We went out in the little helicopter. Loved it, had never gone to the airport, and never had it been so clear. And how the clouds fell away for just that short time I don't know. We could see all of Paris, even Sacre Coeur with the sun shining on it. It was absolutely magnificent. What a picture to take away. Coming back, it clouded over and rained, but just over Versailles came a beautiful rainbow. I wondered if it was for us or the McConnell's, but later, I looked out of my bedroom window, and there was another beautiful rainbow. No question, this was for me! [129]

"Mrs. [Sally] McConnell is young, nice looking," Betty noted. "[She] hadn't been off the plane two minutes before she had the aides running! The honeymoon is over! He, well, he's no Bus." [130]

Betty never liked the disruption of moving their household, but their enlisted orderlies attempted to ease the transition as much as possible.

> The packers packed [on 13 and 14 September], and were out of the house by a little after five on [the second day]. I stayed upstairs ... didn't go downstairs all day. Truly, couldn't bear the thought or the sight of the house all torn up. ... Bus said let's play some gin and have a drink. When I went downstairs,

I couldn't believe my eyes. (It was bingo night and Sgt. Gill was there). Sgt. Gill had the lights lit. He'd made the packers stack boxes in the corner of the living room, so that as I came down the stairs, there was no evidence of packers (the furniture had not yet been moved out). He had redone the flowers using glass bowls and goblets. The niches in the dining room had decanters filled with flowers. I could have cried, I was so touched. I wouldn't have believed it possible. [131]

Wheeler's tour with EUCOM concluded on 22 September. He and Betty travelled through Lisbon and the Azores enroute to the States. They spent their first few days back visiting with Bim and Margie. [132]

# CHAPTER 6

## CHIEF OF STAFF OF THE ARMY
## (OCTOBER 1962 – NOVEMBER 1963)

The Service Chief is the senior military officer of his respective Service. Having spent his entire adult life in the military, he represents his Service in a manner in which no political appointee possibly could. He is the essence of the military professional and in this role usually considers himself apolitical. He is also the father of his Service and there to protect it and its budget as best he can.

—Brigadier General Douglas Kinnard, U.S. Army Retired [1]

### *Mississippi*

During the week prior to Wheeler becoming Chief of Staff of the Army, Decker encouraged him to become well-acquainted with the civil rights situation heating up in Mississippi and the Army's plans for assisting the Department of Justice there. [2]

The Army was surprised when the Justice Department moved Meredith onto the University of Mississippi campus on Sunday, 30 September. The Army understood the move would not occur until the following day, but initially all was quiet. That evening, the Army War Room kept Wheeler apprised of the situation. At around midnight, Wheeler was informed that there was a mob forming and that the decision had been made to get ready to move some troops in. The situation did not require him to come in. At about 2:00 AM, Secretary of the Army Cyrus R. Vance called Wheeler. He said that "all hell had broken loose and asked me to join him in the War Room, and this I did. And I found that things were in a pretty mess. We were really having a hell of a time." [3]

The U.S. marshals were being attacked by the mob and were running low on tear gas. The President and his brother the Attorney General Robert F.

Kennedy were on the phone continuously with the Pentagon wondering where the troops were.

The troops, as a matter of fact, had been at the Memphis Naval Air Station, and there was a problem of just getting them there. There was time and space. No one knew the routes. Attempting to move these people by helicopter after dark just plain took time. There had been instructions issued to change the armament of the troops. Initially, they had been directed to use only MP (military police) equipment dash—billy clubs, tear gas—and this was with good reason and I think justifiably changed at the last moment, and the troops took their usual weapons: rifles, bayonets, etc.

> At any rate, this was a very tumultuous night, and I recall leaving the War Room on the morning of October 1st about 9:00 o'clock, going back to the BOQ at Fort Myer, bathing, shaving, and putting on a uniform, and coming back to be sworn in as Chief of Staff of the Army at 10:00 AM on October 1st. I may not be the best Chief of Staff that was ever sworn in, but I was the sleepiest. There's no question of that. [4]

*Wheeler takes the oath of office during his swearing-in ceremony to become Chief of Staff of the Army, Washington, DC, 1 October 1962. (Office of the Chief of Staff of the Army).*

Bim attributes his father's elevation to the Army's top spot, in part, because of his tremendous work ethic. Bus was not an ambitious climber; rather, "he took his jobs very seriously; he worked very long hours; and he performed very well. … He abided by the principles of 'Duty, Honor, Country. … He was very smart, both analytical and creative, but not overtly ambitious. The patronage he received from General Taylor certainly helped, too." [5]

## Quarters 1

Betty, meanwhile, set to work establishing their new household. "[The curtailed assignment in Paris] already seems a dream," she wrote, "but maybe when we get out of here it will seem a dream too. I feel weighted down already." [6]

> We moved into Quarters One [on 2 October]. That is our clothes, etc. I'm waiting for the furniture from storage at the moment. I suppose now that we're in the house I can get myself organized. I doubt it. The task of settling seems immeasurable. The house is very dark. … However, as the Deckers did not move in until April everything is in beautiful condition. So I'll work around it the best I can. The dining room is lovely, but looks like an ad for furniture. Maybe, I can do something. At the moment I'm more or less devoid of ideas. [7]

The following evening, Betty wrote, "It's now 6:30. Perhaps Bus will be home before eight. Last night we had a fire. I had been sent flowers, so there was a bouquet in the library. All warm and friendly, first night home." [8]

*Former President Dwight D. Eisenhower greets Wheeler during the General George C. Marshall Memorial Dinner at the Sheraton Park Hotel, Washington, DC, 10 October 1962. (Office of the Chief of Staff of the Army).*

Wheeler soon selected Major Louis W. Odom as his Personal Aide or Aide-de-Camp. Odom, an Infantry officer, had served in the Army Air Corps during World War II and as an Infantry company commander during the Korean War.

One of Odom's myriad duties was to ensure the smooth functioning of the Quarters 1 household staff. Ten enlisted men work there under the immediate supervision of Staff Sergeant Fofi, the head chef. One soldier, who was Mrs. Wheeler's driver in addition to his other duties, slept in a room in the basement. The household staff was responsible for everything needed to support the Wheelers in their quarters. This included housecleaning every day, laundry as needed, receiving telephone messages, cooking and serving private meals, cooking and serving at official receptions and dinners, purchasing food products, greeting guests, buying alcoholic beverages for the Chief's official and personal stocks, packing and unpacking bags, making beds and changing linens, submitting repair orders to the Post Engineer, submitting telephone repair requests to Post Communications, passive security during the daytime, securing and checking the house at night, and other duties as required.

Odom recalled:

> While I, as Aide, was responsible to ensure that the orderlies and cooks did their jobs well, I found that Mrs. Wheeler

preferred that I get involved only when things seemed not to go right. Sometimes General Wheeler, on our way to work, would say, 'Lou, I think you need to see Betty today and straighten out those yeahoos.' I would do so, and generally find out that nothing was ever very serious. [9]

During the ride home one evening early in Wheeler's tenure as Chief, he asked his Aide, "When are our communications going to get beyond the wig wag stage?" Wheeler said the President had called him the previous night, and that he had had to race downstairs to answer the phone since his bedroom phone didn't work. Odom promptly contacted the Fort Myer Post Commander and gave him a deadline of 24 hours to install an up-to-date communications system in Quarters 1. [10]

Odom found that Betty wanted to run Quarters 1 on her own and that she wanted to put it "on the map" for its beauty and comfort. This was not unusual, in that new occupants were given an allowance for floor coverings, painting, wallpaper, draperies, etc.

It was obvious that Mrs. Wheeler saw herself as somewhat in competition with Mrs. Jacqueline Kennedy – in other words, she could make Quarters 1 as fine as the White House; and she [Betty] was 'First Lady' of the Army.

I do believe that if she had been more accepting of my help, we would have been able to reduce her workload, and increase my involvement, particularly with regard to the cooks and house boys. These enlisted personnel would tend to play her against me, though cagily, until it became necessary for her to either call on me to rescue her or when General Wheeler saw that she needed my help. [11]

## *Taylor*

Simultaneous with Wheeler becoming the Chief of Staff of the Army, Taylor became the Chairman of the Joint Chiefs of Staff. The other Chiefs, still embittered over what they regarded as Kennedy's unfair criticism in the wake of the Bay of Pigs episode, viewed Taylor's selection as the imposition of a Kennedy man on an organization designed by law to give impartial military advice to the Commander-In-Chief. [12]

Taylor quickly cultivated a warm relationship with McNamara whom many military officers in the Pentagon deeply resented. Taylor and McNamara found common ground in their belief in the need for administrative reform in the Pentagon, faith in the flexible response strategy, and utter devotion to the President. Like McNamara, Taylor concluded that the answer to problems of Service rivalry and administrative inefficiency was increased centralization of power in the chairmanship and the Office of the Secretary of Defense (OSD). The bond of respect between the two men was mutual. McNamara considered Taylor "one of the wisest, most intelligent military men ever to serve [and] the wisest uniformed geopolitician and security advisor I ever met." Much to the other Chiefs' chagrin, Taylor and McNamara formed a partnership. Taylor's overwhelming influence with the Secretary of Defense and the President made opposition to his views an exercise in futility. [13]

## *Southeast Asia*

The U.S. policy of containment met its most serious challenge in Southeast Asia, where Communist efforts to take control of Laos and South Vietnam had gained momentum. Using the political instability of those countries to advantage, the Communists had gradually brought large segments of both under control. Efforts by local governments to regain control by military operations had proven unsuccessful despite the presence of both U.S. advisors and arms. The U.S. soon discovered that the effort to keep Laos and South Vietnam from falling into the Communist camp was even more complicated than it seemed. By the early 1960s, following decades of French rule, many Indochinese leaders were willing to accept U.S. assistance but were clearly unenthusiastic about launching political and economic reforms that might diminish their own power.

By late 1962, with Communist troops maneuvering in Laos near the Thai border, the U.S. was also becoming concerned about Thailand, which was part of SEATO. To deter Communist expansion into the country, the U.S. established a joint task force at the request of the Thai government, dispatched a reinforced battalion of Marines to Thailand, and followed up with a battle group from the 25th Infantry Division. Army signal, engineer, transportation, and service troops provided support for those forces and training and advice to the Thais. The quick response strengthened the Thai government's position, and the Communist threat abated, enabling first the Marines and then the Army troops to withdraw. Service support forces stayed on, however, in order to maintain training and support programs. When the war in Vietnam intensified, the roads, airfields, depots, and communications they built would become extremely important to the evolving American effort in that country. [14]

## *Cuban Missile Crisis*

The Soviets' next move after their Berlin threat was less direct but more dangerous. After the Bay of Pigs invasion, Khrushchev had dispatched military advisors and equipment to Cuba to bolster the Castro government and repel future attacks. [15]

On 1 October—the day Wheeler and Taylor were sworn-in to their new positions—the Joint Chiefs of Staff (JCS) received an intelligence briefing about the possibility of Soviet ballistic missiles in Cuba. Two weeks later when the President authorized aerial reconnaissance to confirm the missiles' presence, the Chiefs recommended mobilization of the 150,000 reserves that Congress had authorized several weeks earlier. They believed that military action against Cuba was a certainty and recommended a powerful airstrike to destroy all significant military targets, a naval blockade to isolate Castro's regime from external support, and an invasion to ensure the eradication of the missile threat and the removal of Castro from power. The Chiefs had been planning a full-scale invasion of the island since November 1961. [16]

Odom recalled:

> Every day we arrived early at the Army War Room, where [Wheeler] was briefed – then he faced a day and late evening schedule of meetings, trips to and sessions with the Joint Chiefs of Staff, the Secretary of Defense, and the President. Further, there were trips to South Carolina and Florida to observe and to evaluate the readiness of our forces. [17]

When the missiles' presence in Cuba was confirmed in mid-October, Kennedy took quick steps to have the weapons removed. Warning Khrushchev that the U.S. would mount a nuclear response if Cuban missiles struck U.S. soil, he put the Strategic Air Command's heavy bombers on 15-minute alert. Meanwhile, fighter squadrons and antiaircraft missile batteries were deployed to Florida and other states near Cuba. Submarines armed with Polaris missiles also took up station at sea within range of the Soviet Union. [18]

Wheeler recalled the President asking him to come over one day to talk to him about the Army's participation in a possible invasion of Cuba.

> After I went over the troop list explaining from maps exactly the concept of how we were going to do it, the troop units involved, [the President] said that he was concerned that we might be trying to do this with too few people. He placed this on the basis, one, we had to have a quick decision because of political pressures that would inevitably arise and, secondly, he was afraid that if we went in with too little that this would increase American casualties because the Cubans would be able to fight that much longer. In other words, he talked of putting enough in to overwhelm the Cubans. As a result of this, I came back [to the Pentagon] and revised the Army plan and increased the strength by about one additional division. So that in the final plan, we had ready to go on the Army side about five and a half divisions from the strategic reserve in the United States. [19]

On 15 October, Kennedy convened the Executive Committee (EXCOM) of the National Security Council to analyze the situation and formulate a response to this national security threat. McNamara, Nitze, and Deputy Secretary of Defense Roswell L. Gilpatric represented the Pentagon along with Taylor, the only professional military officer present.

The following day, McNamara offered an alternative to the Chiefs' recommendations for a full-scale air strike, blockade, and invasion. He suggested that the U.S. blockade Cuba to search approaching ships and remove offensive weapons, as well as "overt military action of varying degrees of intensity" including a naval "quarantine," aerial overflights of Cuba, and the mobilization of a large military force. Confident, articulate, and providing what seemed reasoned judgment and cogent analysis, McNamara set the agenda for the discussions. Although the President's advisors had initially favored offensive military action against Cuba, a consensus soon formed around McNamara's proposal. On 18 October, Kennedy decided to reject a first strike option in favor of the blockade. [20]

The Chiefs resented being excluded from the EXCOM meetings. Every evening during the crisis, they anxiously awaited Taylor's return from the White House and grilled him to ensure that he had accurately represented their recommendation to bomb the missile sites and follow the airstrike quickly with a ground invasion of Cuba. Having absorbed much of the blame for the Bay of Pigs, the Chiefs wanted to make unambiguous their position on the level of force required.

At Taylor's request, the President invited the Chiefs to the White House on 19 October to allay their concerns over not being consulted directly. Kennedy had already decided upon a naval quarantine of Cuba, however, so his meeting with the Chiefs was designed to keep them from opposing his decision rather than to solicit their advice. [21]

The Chiefs suggested that failure to act decisively in Cuba would embolden the Soviets in Berlin and elsewhere. LeMay argued that the blockade option would encourage further Soviet aggression and result in the U.S. gradually drifting into war under unfavorable conditions. General Bruce Palmer, Jr., who later served as Vice Chief of Staff of the Army, described LeMay as a "big, cigar chewing Midwesterner from Ohio, [who] was often arrogant and rude and manner, talking loudly (partly no doubt because of hearing difficulties) with an abrasive voice that could whine like a turbine engine." If the President took strong action, LeMay declared, the Soviets would be forced to back down and would not respond in Berlin or elsewhere. The other Chiefs reinforced LeMay's argument, describing a surprise airstrike, blockade, and invasion as the "lowest risk course of action." Taylor seemed to support his colleagues, but the Chiefs suspected that he did not really share their views and doubted that he was faithfully representing their position during EXCOM deliberations. Their concerns were well founded, as Taylor had, in fact, distanced himself from the Chiefs' position. [22]

On 22 October, Kennedy announced that he would seek the endorsement of the Organization of American States (OAS) for a quarantine on all offensive military equipment in transit to Cuba. He added that he would tighten surveillance of the island and reinforce the U.S. naval base at Guantánamo on the island's western tip. With OAS approval, the quarantine went into effect two days later. Meanwhile, the Armed Forces removed all U.S. military dependents from Guantánamo, and Marines arrived by air and sea to defend the base. As those steps continued, the Army began to move some 30,000 troops, including the 1st Armored Division, and more than 100,000 tons of supplies and equipment into the southeastern States to meet the emergency. The Navy's 2nd Fleet commenced enforcement of the quarantine on 25 October. Hundreds of Air Force and Navy planes also spread out over the Atlantic and Caribbean to locate and track ships that might be carrying offensive weapons to Cuba. With construction continuing at the Soviet missile sites in Cuba, the world seemed on the brink of nuclear war.

As the crisis mounted, negotiations proceeded between Kennedy and Khrushchev. On 28 October, the Soviet Union agreed to remove its offensive weapons from Cuba. Over the next three weeks, it gradually did so, dismantling the missile sites and loading both missile systems and technicians on ships. Negotiations for the removal of the Soviet bombers ended in November. They shipped out for home in early December. In turn, the U.S. ended the quarantine on 20 November. Deployed Army troops would all return to base by Christmas, but many U.S. air units remained behind to ensure that the missile sites remained inactive. [23]

Wheeler believed that the Cuban Missile Crisis marked a turning point in Kennedy's attitude toward the military.

> After seeing the troops, the celerity with which they moved into position, the first class shape that the troops were in, the obvious sharpness of the commanders, everything ready to the last detail—planning and otherwise—President Kennedy, perhaps for the first time, realized the tremendous asset, the very powerful tool that he had at his command in dealing with matters of foreign policy where military force was necessary.
>
> I also thought that I detected in later meetings with him perhaps a friendlier, a more appreciative attitude toward the

military than ever before—not that I mean to say that he had ever been disagreeable or curt or ungracious, but I believe that the Bay of Pigs business had, I don't like to use the term poisoned his mind against the military, but I think that he had some very grave doubts as to the role of the military and their capability to carry out the things that he wanted done. I think that after the Cuban Crisis, all of these doubts were dispelled or at least he recognized more clearly than ever before that the military were perhaps the one element that he could depend upon under any circumstances that might face this country.

I feel that having come back from his meeting with Khrushchev in '61 rather a shaken man wondering where to turn and how to accomplish what he felt should be done, that the Cuban affair bolstered his confidence that he could deal with these very serious foreign policy matters from strength, and that he was not dealing from weakness, that he too had a lot of cards to play, that Khrushchev didn't have all the aces, that he had his fair share and perhaps more than Khrushchev. As a matter of fact, he did have more than Khrushchev, and I think he probably recognized this. [24]

Later that month, Bus and Bim planned to attend a Washington Redskins football game. This was the first and only father-son outing they would take since Bus had become a general officer eleven years earlier. Their departure was delayed by an unscheduled and "interminably long hand-wringing session" of the National Security Council. The Attorney General's endless second-guessing of decisions made during the crisis galled Wheeler to no end. Wheeler "absolutely loathed" Robert Kennedy, who "would look you in the eye and lie straight to your face." [25]

The Cuban Missile Crisis emboldened McNamara in the realm of strategic planning and enhanced his reputation as a level-headed advisor. Subsequently, he became more assertive in the area of military strategy and operations. Having gained confidence in these areas, McNamara no longer felt as though he needed military advice in developing strategic options. [26]

McNamara was determined to remove obstacles that might prevent him from assuming the role of chief strategist in the Pentagon. During the Cuban Missile Crisis, McNamara kept tight control over the ships, submarines, and aircraft enforcing the quarantine around Cuba to ensure that the demonstration of U.S. resolve sent the proper message to the Soviets. To control military operations in times of crisis, he and the President would require officers on the Joint Chiefs of Staff who would permit civilian oversight in areas that had been previously regarded as sacrosanct and free from civilian "interference." Kennedy had already brought Taylor and Wheeler onboard, and he was ready to sack LeMay, but McNamara advised him to hold off. (In May 1963, Kennedy would announce Admiral George W. Anderson's replacement as the Chief of Naval Operations with Admiral David L. McDonald.) The desire to control military operations more closely at the civilian level in the OSD and in the White House coincided with advances in communications technology that made possible the detailed monitoring of military activities in faraway theaters. [27]

### Front Office

As Chief of Staff of the Army, Wheeler had three Aides. Odom, Wheeler's "Aide-de-Camp," had a private office that adjoined Wheeler's. On the other side of Odom's office was the Social Secretary who assisted Odom in matters of protocol at social events hosted by the Wheelers, such as table seating arrangements, guest lists, setting up and mailing invitations, and recording responses.

Odom's duties were "a grab bag." He traveled with Wheeler wherever he went. He picked up Wheeler at Quarters 1 every morning except Sunday (and sometimes Sunday) at about 7:30 AM and delivered him back to his quarters any time between 5:30 PM and midnight depending on Wheeler's workload and the situation around the world. Odom generally briefed Wheeler enroute to Quarters 1, left notes in his "take-home bag," and talked on the way back to the Pentagon the next morning. [28]

Odom planned for and accompanied Wheeler on all official trips. This entailed clarifying dates, times, and purpose of trips; arranging for transportation; publishing schedules; collecting data books, classified information, and other materials Wheeler needed to take; coordinating a "uniform to be worn list" with the house orderly who packed Wheeler's luggage; ensuring Betty had all necessary information if she were to accompany; sending information forward to individuals at the points of destination; and drawing treasurer's checks from the Finance Office to pay for official aspects of the trip.

Wheeler had a Senior (Operations) Aide, a full Colonel, who served as an overall coordinator for the Chief on policy matters. According to Odom, the Senior Aide was the "wheel horse" for the Chief on contacts with the Army Staff and actually served as a sounding board concerning significant decisions that were to be made within the Joint Chiefs of Staff arena, as well as policies, studies, and decisions which affected the Army and/or the Army's roles and responsibilities at the national level. While the Chief did rely upon the experience, wisdom, and advice of the Vice Chief of Staff of the Army and the Army Staff itself, his Senior Aide served as something of a Chief of Staff to the Chief of Staff of the Army. He would also "get the word out" to the Army's generals, as directed and permitted by Wheeler.

Colonel George I. Forsythe, a combat infantryman of World War II and Korea served as Wheeler's Senior Aide for about fourteen months after Odom arrived. Odom described Forsythe as "very practical, non-militaristic," and a "lovable gentleman … highly respected by generals and by all of lesser rank." Forsythe was replaced by Colonel Marvin J. "B'wig" Berensweig, who had served as an Aide to Wheeler in the U.S. European Command. Odom recalls "B'wig" as one of the sharpest looking officers he had ever met, but "he was no Forsythe." "B'wig's" informality with Betty and his apparent crush on her also did not endear him to Odom. [29]

The Administrative Aide was a Lieutenant Colonel. His responsibilities dealt mainly with compiling and scheduling the Chief's calendar. "No one, but no one planned anything for the Chief without checking first with this Aide," recalled Odom. This position was not a mechanically driven job, as much judgment and decision-making were required. The Administrative Aide had to have insight into the Chief's desires, priorities, who and what he wanted to see or do, and, in such cases as possible, juggle the Chief's schedule without having to consult the Chief. Also, he had to have the common sense to check with the Chief in case of doubt. The officer who filled this position was

Lieutenant Colonel Robert "Bob" Guthrie, a Korean War combat infantryman. Odom recalled several occasions when Wheeler "lashed out" because Guthrie let someone in to see him whom he did not want to see. [30]

The top enlisted position in the Chief's office was an Army Sergeant Major, but not the Sergeant Major of the Army, a position established later. Sergeant Major Loikow was the Chief's stenographer who took dictation and prepared correspondence for the Chief's signature. Wheeler never once complained about Loikow's work. Loikow had a separate office, and when the Chief wanted him, he would "buzz" him.

Rounding out Wheeler's office staff was a Women's Army Corps (WAC) Sergeant who served as the Administrative Aide's Secretary. "Tiny, blonde, pretty, and very businesslike," her job was to answer phones, receive visitors in the outer office, and type.

Wheeler traveled in a Cadillac "stretch" limousine and was assigned two drivers. Master Sergeants Steinweinder and Cook were "well-versed" ahead of time on where they were to take the Wheelers, and knew the Virginia, Maryland, and Washington, DC areas "like the back of their hands." [31]

## *Thanksgiving*

While Bus was "off with the President" the day after Thanksgiving, Betty informed her mother how they had spent the abbreviated holiday (their 30th as a couple):

> Wednesday night we had Thanksgiving dinner. Bim and Margie were with us. ... Thursday, Bus stayed home. ... We let all the help go. The telephone only rang once. Bus did work a little, but it was so peaceful. The first such day since we left Paris. I had meant to go to church but the weather was awful. So as I had no transportation stayed home. There was a service in the concourse at the Pentagon on Wednesday, and I had gone to that. [32]

"I've been going to the post chapel on Sunday," she added. "I feel that if I go to church anywhere I should support it. I have to admit, I'm not too fond of the chaplain." [33]

## *Army-Navy Game*

*Bus and Betty Wheeler watch the Army-Navy football game with President John F. Kennedy, Philadelphia, Pennsylvania, 1 December 1962. (Office of the Chief of Staff of the Army).*

On 1 December, the President attended the annual Army-Navy football game in Philadelphia. Wheeler recalled that Kennedy was "a little shocked by the fact that Army was getting beat so badly, and secondly, he had been impressed by the fact that when the Corps of Cadets and the Brigade of Midshipmen marched on at the beginning of the game … that the Corps of Cadets was only about half the size of the Brigade of Midshipmen." Kennedy had the impression that both academies were the same size. Not true, Wheeler informed him. Due to various laws, West Point had a total enrollment of about 2,600 cadets while the Naval Academy had more than 4,600 midshipmen. "Well," Kennedy replied, "you better do something about this." The eventual outcome of this exchange was legislation that would expand the Military Academy and the Air Force Academy to the size of the Naval Academy. "Luck could have it I might be still President another four years," Wheeler recalled Kennedy saying. "I want to sit here when the two academies are the same size." [34]

## *Army Reserves*

The Army's new major subordinate commands had become operational in the summer of 1962. Over the next year, Wheeler would oversee other major changes affecting staff responsibilities. In January 1963, an Office of Reserve Components was established to exercise general supervision over all plans, policies, and programs concerning National Guard and Reserve forces. The responsibility of the Chief, National Guard Bureau, to advise the Chief of Staff of the Army on National Guard affairs and to serve as the link between the Army and the States' Adjutant Generals remained unchanged. However, the Chief of the Army Reserve lost control over the Reserve Officers Training Corps (ROTC) program, which was transferred to the Office of Reserve Components in February and would later be moved to the Deputy Chief of Staff for Personnel in 1966.

Concerned over the expenditure of defense funds for Reserves that were long on numbers but short on readiness, McNamara had announced in 1962 a plan to reorganize the Army National Guard and to lower the paid drill strength of the Army Reserves. However, opposition from Congress and many State officials led him to delay the move until 1963. When he finally acted, he not only realigned reserve forces, but also eliminated four National Guard divisions, four Army Reserve divisions, and hundreds of smaller units.

In September, Congress would revise the Reserve Forces Act of 1955 to obtain the troops necessary to fill out the Reserve. The new law would provide for direct enlistment—an optional feature of the 1955 act—and would reduce the term of obligated service from eight to six years. [35]

## 1963

### *Vietnam is the Place*

Khrushchev's threat in 1961 to support Communist insurgents fighting wars of national liberation in countries of the developing world, the Bay of Pigs debacle, the Berlin Crisis, and the Cuban Missile Crisis convinced Kennedy that the U.S. needed to make its "power credible." [36]

After Kennedy was forced to accept an unsatisfactory compromise settlement in Laos, his interest grew in a strategy to counter Communist insurgencies in Southeast Asia and elsewhere. South Vietnam had become a U.S. laboratory for counterinsurgency programs and techniques, and the Kennedy Administration had dramatically increased economic and military aid to the American-backed government in Saigon. By the summer of 1963, 16,500 military advisors were in South Vietnam. Although Vietnam remained a national security concern of tertiary interest until 1963, the U.S. imperative to contain Communism impelled U.S. involvement in what would otherwise have been considered an insignificant place, unworthy of even the most cursory policy deliberations. [37]

At first, the enhanced mobility and firepower the U.S. had provided the South Vietnamese Army (ARVN) in the form of helicopters, armored personnel carriers, and close air support had surprised and overwhelmed the Viet Cong. By early 1963, however, the Viet Cong had learned to cope with the ARVN's new weapons and more aggressive tactics and had begun a campaign to eliminate the strategic hamlets. The much-publicized defeat of ARVN forces at village of Ap Bac in the Mekong Delta in January 1963 demonstrated both the Viet Cong's skill in countering the ARVN's new capabilities and the latter's inherent weaknesses. The defeat was a portent of things to come. Now able to challenge regular army units of equal strength in quasi-conventional battles, the Viet Cong were moving into a more intense stage of revolutionary warfare.

As the Viet Cong became stronger and bolder, the ARVN became more cautious and less offensive-minded. The Viet Cong's campaign profited from Saigon's failures. The government had built too many hamlets to defend and scattered them around the countryside, often outside of mutual supporting range. [38]

Amid these developments, Wheeler made his first trip to Vietnam as the Chief of Staff of the Army on 16-25 January 1963. His itinerary typified the scope and focus of his numerous, subsequent trips there.

Upon arriving at the Pentagon at 8 AM on Monday, 10 January, Wheeler learned that the President had decided to send an assessment team to Vietnam the next day. Wheeler would lead the team as the President's representative. Air Force Lieutenant General David A. Burchinal, the Director of the Joint Staff, would represent that group and the Air Force. Major General Victor H. Krulak, the Joint Staff's Special Operations Chief and an Assistant to the Commandant of the Marine Corps, would also accompany Wheeler. Forsythe would go too since during a previous tour in Vietnam he had served as an advisor to the Vietnamese Army and had become good friends with General Duong Van "Big" Minh. Odom recalled, "After our round of the necessary immunizations at the Pentagon dispensary, the planning began." [39]

Wheeler's party flew on a Boeing C-135B jet, the cargo version of the Boeing 707, which was equipped with a "McNamara Kit" of double-decker bunks used by the Secretary of Defense for sleeping during long trips across the Pacific. In one of his first actions after becoming Secretary of State, McNamara had canceled orders for a third Air Force One and several small but expensive Lockheed jets for use by Department of Defense executives. He did authorize, however, $20,000 to design a few seats that could be temporarily affixed into an Air Force cargo plane when senior personnel needed to travel on special missions. Outfitted with wing fuel tanks, the "Poor Man's 707" possessed nearly enough range to fly from Washington to Saigon with only one stop. The aircraft lacked soundproofing, which made conversation difficult, but McNamara refused to spend the money to install it. Eventually, he relaxed the expenditure limits enough to add a few bunks and a secretary's desk, which allowed reports to be typed enroute back to Washington. [40]

Wheeler's party flew nonstop from Andrews Air Force Base to Hickam Field, Hawaii. Upon arrival, they were taken to their quarters at Fort Shafter, some distance away. They spent the night there and were briefed by the Commander-In-Chief, Pacific (CINCPAC) and the Commander-In-Chief, U.S. Army, Pacific (CINCUSARPAC) and their staffs before proceeding on to South Vietnam.

Odom recalled:

> Somewhere between Hawaii and Saigon, we were discussing the stresses of the Cuban Missile Crisis, the Bay of Pigs debacle, the Vietnam mess, and Pentagon interservice problems.
>
> General Wheeler made a statement that I should remember to my dying day. He said, 'George [Forsythe], I don't know what's wrong with me. I actually like people; but sometimes when so many of them are hanging on me, telling me different things, and pulling on me from all directions, I just lose my patience and blow up.' And he really did this too!! Not at us, but others on the Army Staff – and even to Bob Guthrie, who was his administrative and appointments aide. All of us got to work in the Pentagon before 8 AM and many times didn't leave before 7:30 or 8 PM. Forsythe replied, 'General,

I think you're too generous with your time. You just need to say no to some of those placing demands on your schedule and time.' [41]

Odom reflected:

I suppose that this encounter, high above the blue waters of the Pacific, was the one that triggered my growing admiration and great respect for this great American general who, like all of us, was willing to give us a peek into a part of his being that showed he was a real person with feelings, not at all related to just being a person with four stars whom we perceived as being all-powerful, invulnerable, and without a flaw.

As we were approaching Saigon, General Wheeler said he needed to shave. I told him my Norelco Electric was ready so he need not dig into his bag. He smiled, looked at me approvingly and said, 'Thanks Lou!' I felt like a small puppy that had just been patted on the head by his master. He then completed shaving what was an above average heavy beard. [42]

"We could feel the humid, almost oppressive sweat-producing air as the doors opened and we trod down the portable stairs" at Tan Son Nhut Airbase, Odom recalled. Harkins and Lodge greeted Wheeler's party. [43]

*Wheeler and General Paul D. Harkins, Commander of the Military Assistance Command, Vietnam, greet the commander of the South Vietnamese Armed Forces, Saigon, Republic of Vietnam, 18 January 1963. (Office of the Chief of Staff of the Army).*

Wheeler and Odom went to Harkins's compound, which contained a beautiful stucco mansion, and nearby servant/guest quarters. The compound was protected by a white stucco wall and guards manning the gates. The other members of Wheeler's party checked into a downtown hotel. That evening, Wheeler, Harkins, and Lodge met with President Diem. Forsythe had a secret rendezvous with General "Big" Minh.

Over the first three days, Wheeler received multiple briefings from MACV, visited the Republic of Vietnam Armed Forces (RVNAF) headquarters with Harkins, and attended a formal dinner party in white mess dress with senior MACV and RVNAF officers and their wives.

Wheeler's party met up at Harkins' compound on the morning of 19 January before moving to the airport to begin an extensive series of tours of the major cities of South Vietnam.

"The purpose of our trip[s]," Odom recalled, "was to determine just what the state of readiness the South Vietnamese Armed Forces were in; what was the capability of the enemy; and what, at this time, the U.S. must do to make Ho Chi Minh's North Vietnam leave South Vietnam alone." [44]

Wheeler's party boarded Harkins' four-engine C-54 and headed north. Odom soon noticed two South Vietnamese Air Force T-6 Texan single-engine fighters accompanying their aircraft.

> Obviously, this was a sign that we definitely were in a some-what hostile environment. My main worry was that the pilots seemed to be 'cowboys' – flying ever so close that they seemed almost to touch our aircraft's wings. I thought what a tragedy to be killed by an accident while in South Vietnam. [45]

That day, Wheeler visited the Cu Chi strategic hamlet and some U.S. aircrews at Bien Hoa Airbase before visiting other U.S. Navy and Air Force aircrews of the 2nd Air Division at Tan Son Nhut Airbase.

The following day, he inspected camp facilities at Plei Mong, then met with ARVN Lieutenant General Nguyen Khanh, the Commanding General of II Corps. Continuing north, Wheeler visited I Corps, where he met with ARVN Rangers of the 10th Special Battalion at Hoa Cum. He then observed a training demonstration at the Civil Guard Training Center at Da Nang. [46]

Odom recorded:

> During these visits we met with U.S. Special Forces troops whose mission was to equip South Vietnamese soldiers and civilians as Self-Defense Forces – to fight off Viet Cong guer-rillas who had been recruited from the South Vietnamese populace to harass, terrorize, rob, and kill South Vietnamese. Most interesting among the Self-Defense Forces were the mountain people (Montagnards).
>
> We also visited [Lieutenant General Nguyen Khahn's II Corps headquarters] near Dalat. [Khanh] was a medium height, blocky build, impressive soldier. He carried a swagger stick and wore a French style TAM (hat) like those later adopted by our Special Forces. We had lunch at his headquarters – fish, shrimp, rice, potatoes, and, of course, wine.
>
> All of the above trips took about six days – realizing that we had to return to Saigon by the end of each day. So it was to get up in the morning – head north again with those T-6s close by – and back to Saigon for the evening. [47]

Odom added:

> After two days, it became obvious that Forsythe and I would
> best be housed at the MACV compound with General
> Wheeler. So we each had a private bedroom and bath in the
> guest quarters with General Harkins' aide. What a life – ceil-
> ing fans, servants bringing eggs and bacon for breakfast, etc.

> We did get to see a great deal of Saigon – especially at night.
> Once we took rickshaws to a fine restaurant where we had
> genuine French onion soup and steak. We were warned,
> though, to beware of the fact that we could be subject to
> attack by Viet Cong – even in the streets of Saigon, although
> inner-city incidents were rare at this time due to heavy pres-
> ence of ARVN soldiers – they were in sight almost all the
> time. One had to especially be alert to children, some of
> whom had hidden grenades in a loaf of bread, and dropped
> it where it could do damage. [48]

Odom had noticed large ceramic elephants guarding the steps of
Harkins' residence and was determined not to leave Saigon without some. On
the suggestion of Harkins' aide and supplied with South Vietnamese currency,
he got a taxi to the Chinese District of Cholon.

> It was a holiday, so we had to knock on many doors. It was
> also spooky, being there in that doubtful area, not knowing
> Viet Cong from locals. Finally, we reached the place where
> elephants were made – we accompanied the owner, picked
> up four – paid, and scooted back to the compound. ... I
> gave Mrs. Wheeler her choice of two – she expressed sincere
> appreciation. [49]

Wheeler spent the last day of his trip in III Corps, where he watched
a training demonstration by ARVN Rangers at the Ranger Training Center at

Duc My and visited the Montagnard strategic hamlet at Ban Me Thout and the 8th Field Hospital at Nha Trang.

*Wheeler with "Tuffy," the 8-month old tiger mascot of the 93rd Transportation Company, Soc Trang, Republic of Vietnam, 25 January 1963. (Office of the Chief of Staff of the Army).*

Wheeler also visited Soc Trang, where he had his picture taken with "Tuffy", the Tiger cub mascot of the 99rd Transportation Company (Light Helicopter CH-21). "One of the trip highlights was our petting this large Bengal tiger (on a leash, of course), and General Wheeler [being] photographed kneeling down with his arm around 'Tuffy's' neck," Odom recorded. Wheeler would display this photo in his Pentagon office. He also visited the 57th Transportation Company, another helicopter outfit, as he was particularly interested in the combat development of Army aviation units like these. [50]

Wheeler's party departed Saigon on the thirteenth day, headed for Okinawa. They remained there overnight in preparation for the next leg to Honolulu. Odom recalled:

> We went directly to Fort De Russey on Waikiki Beach from the airport. There, General Wheeler, all other party members, a battery of secretaries and typists began discussions that would result in the report to the Joint Chiefs of Staff.

Colonel Forsythe, being General Wheeler's Operations Aide, had responsibility for the actual administrative aspects.

The next day we left Honolulu for Washington. Seven hours and 15 minutes later we landed at Andrews Air Force Base. We were informed by the pilot that we had set an unofficial Honolulu to Andrews AFB speed record. I think it was 720 mph ground speed – caused by strong jetstream. [51]

Wheeler submitted a "relatively favorable" report on the ability of the U.S. to bring the insurgency under control by 1965. "We are winning slowly on the present thrust," Wheeler reported. Concluding that there was "no compelling reason to change" the current policy, Wheeler's report echoed Harkins's similarly optimistic periodic reports on the situation in South Vietnam. Wheeler merely recommended augmenting U.S. support troops and advisors to help the Saigon government deal more effectively with the Viet Cong insurgency. [52]

According to U. S. presidential historian Robert Dallek, "Wheeler frustrated and irritated Kennedy with a report [national security aide Michael V.] Forrestal described as 'rosy euphoria' and a 'complete waste of … time.'" The picture Wheeler painted, however, also illustrated some "disquieting" factors, including the South Vietnamese Army's shortage of noncommissioned officers and junior officers and "the continuous build-up of the Viet Cong in strength and quality of their weapons." [53]

## Air Mobility

Seeking to improve mobility in 1962, an Army board had compared the cost and efficiency of air and ground vehicles. Concluding that air transportation had much to commend it, the group recommended that the Army consider forming new air combat and transport units. The idea that an "air assault division" employing air-transportable weapons and aircraft-mounted rockets might replace artillery raised delicate questions about the Air Force and Army missions, but McNamara approved a thorough test of the concept.

Organized in February 1963, the 11th Air Assault Division would undergo two years of testing as part of a long-term effort by the Army to improve its aviation capabilities. Although Army-Air Force agreements and decisions at the Department of Defense-level during the 1950s had restricted the size and weight of Army aircraft and had limited the areas in which they could operate, the Army had more than 5,500 aircraft in its inventory by 1960. Close to half of them were helicopters. The versatility of the rotary-wing aircraft made them ideal for observation and reconnaissance, medical evacuation, and command-and-control missions. Under the Army's agreements with the Air Force, all these activities were permissible on the battlefield. When the Army moved to provide itself with armed helicopters, however, it inevitably raised questions with the Air Force, which considered the provision of aerial fire support its own function.

The two Services would later reassess and reapportion their roles and mission assignments in 1966. The Army would cede its larger transport aircraft to the Air Force but would maintain control of its helicopters because of their demonstrated value to ground combat operations. [54]

## *Early Spring*

*Wheeler observes artillery fire at Fort Hood, Texas, March 1963. (Office of the Chief of Staff of the Army).*

In addition to his normal office workload, Bus and Betty were kept busy by a continuous string of social obligations and official trips. Their schedule over the first half of 1963 well-illustrates the blistering pace they would maintain for the next seven years and provides an appreciation for the myriad other issues and obligations Wheeler dealt with besides Vietnam.

Betty reported on 10 March that "from the 13th of February until this afternoon, Bus and I haven't been alone in the house. That's a long time." [55]

> The Chief of Staff of the Argentine Army and his wife were in town on the 26th. We gave a beautiful reception at the [Fort] Myer [Officers] Club. ... Bus was presented with a gun. What he'll do with it, I wouldn't know. It's a soldier's gun, the newest NATO weapon. I now possess the most beautiful alligator bag. [56]

A weapons aficionado, Wheeler hung the plaque mounted Spanish CETME rifle in his Pentagon office. He had a large partner desk set at a 45-degree angle to a rear wall corner. The desk, upon which sat a small gargoyle statue—probably a souvenir from Notre Dame Cathedral in Paris—was flanked by the U.S. flag and the colors of the Chief of Staff of the Army. Behind Wheeler's desk was a credenza, above which he customarily displayed photographs of the President, the Secretary of Defense, the Deputy Secretary of Defense, and the Joint Chiefs of Staff. He hung the rifle next to the photos and would later add other weapons as they were presented to him. [57]

In late March, Betty updated her mother on their latest news. "Believe it or not the Wheelers are in the lower garden. Bus and I are in shorts. It's heavenly. It's been a long winter!"

"Kitsy [Westmoreland] was here," she continued. "We had lunch together and then I put her on the train for New York. She is a dear, but really a bore. A little goes a long way." [58]

> Bim has signed a contract to teach at St. Stephens next year. He is so happy. ... He has nothing to lose financially and everything to gain. Now, he'll know whether he wants to teach. And I know if he goes back to business he won't always wish he'd taught. It is certainly a better atmosphere in which to study for his Masters. [59]

A privilege the Wheelers had previously enjoyed during their abbreviated assignment in Paris, they were provided first-run movies for their private viewing. They played the reel-to-reel films on a projector and a pull-up screen in their family room. Bim, Margie, and Mums often joined them for dinner and movie nights. [60]

In March, Odom's wife Charlotte underwent cancer surgery at Walter Reed Army Medical Center. Betty sewed a quilt for her. "Dear Charlotte, Bus and I have had you in our thoughts and prayers a great deal these past days," Betty wrote on 23 March. "By the grapevine I hear that your room is a tower of flowers, so maybe you'll enjoy a change of 'bed dress'. Bus joins me in get well wishes. With affection, Betty." [61]

"The helicopter trip (to Carlisle) was marvelous," Betty informed her mother in early April. "Saw so much. It was a heavenly day up. It was a well managed visit, the first I've been as the wife of (someone so important.) I really didn't enjoy the stay, and unless there is a change in command there, I'll stay home another time." [62]

## Puerto Rico

Betty also informed her mother that Bus would have surgery for a hiatal hernia at Walter Reed Army Medical Center on 28 March.

> [His doctor] General Heaton seems to feel the old appendix scar tissue has something to do with it. He'll be in the hospital about a week, and then we're going to Puerto Rico. ... The hospital there has become a recuperative haven for the ailing, and because of the facilities we can get out of Washington. [63]

A few days after the surgery, she added:

> Bus is doing beautifully. I go out [to Walter Reed] around five-thirty. ... The hospital, except for the first night has been like a club. ... We play gin, have two drinks, eat at seven ... very good food. ... Until [the] night before last, I ate on a tremendous tray presented by Pres. & Mrs. Eisenhower, complete with brass plaque. ... All lovely! If one must be in the hospital. [64]

Betty provided another update on 7 April:

Bus came home this morning. In his clothes, he looks very thin. However, he is progressing normally. We leave [on 10 April], which cuts a day off our stay in Puerto Rico. However, it certainly is wise to be sure that he is ready for the flight." For the next three days, Bus worked several hours each morning. [65]

Betty described their 7-day trip to Puerto Rico:

We had an easy flight down. It took about five hours. ... We were met at the plane by the C. O. here and the C. O. of the Caribbean (Antilles) Command plus wives. ... They brought us to the quarters, and thank God, left shortly.

One of the sets of quarters has been made into a VIP residence. It's a nice house, high ceilings, tiled floors. There are lots of palms and banana trees, hibiscus, the usual tropical shrubs. There is an orderly (Rodriguez) and he gets the meals, cleans, etc. Out back, overlooking the Bay of San Juan is a terrace, really an outside room. It covers the top of five garages. About ¾ is covered. The rest for sunning.

I was disappointed at first that we are not accessible to the water or a beach to walk upon. However, I have almost forgotten that there is such a thing as a long, lazy day. We have all our meals out here, starting with breakfast at eight or a little after. Lunch at noon, dinner at seven. The first night we were in bed around nine. Read, of course, no radio, no television, just plain lazy.

[We went] to a dinner [at some friends' house] that Ponce de Leon built! It is magnificent and the location marvelous. There were quite a few Puerto Ricans there, so it was an interesting evening. Since then we've been on our own. Yesterday, we had lunch at the club. Last night, we had a wonderful dinner in the oldest restaurant in San Juan. ... Afterwards, we went to 'El Convento', a hotel which once been a convent. The bar and dining room were in what was once the chapel. I didn't like the feeling! There was a show, some excellent dancers, but after that a singer that seemed to be going on and on. He drove us away!

We made a short visit to El Morro and have visited the 2nd oldest church in the new world, and ridden around old San Juan. Bus finds it still difficult to move with ease, so we do just little things. He is gathering momentum each day. I just hope this leave will be long enough.

As it is Easter, we have let Rodriguez go. After breakfast, that is. … Have been doing lots of reading, … knitting a little, sunning, so it goes. Bus works some in the morning. Someone brings the cables, and a secretary comes when needed. Still, it's quiet. The days are long, and very restful. [66]

A few days after their return home, Betty added:

It was a good vacation and I'm sorry that it's over. Bus is much improved. I imagine he will have to go slowly for awhile. Wish that he could have had a couple more weeks. … On [16 April], we flew to St. Thomas. We walked (and shopped), had a car and drove up a mountain for lunch. As the drive didn't bother Bus, we took a drive in Puerto Rico the next day. Had lunch up in the mountains, drove through the rain forest and came on home. All things considered we did more than I thought we would and certainly got quite a feel for the island. [67]

## *Back to Work*

*Wheeler always enjoyed talking with junior enlisted soldiers while observing their field train-ing, April 1963. (Office of the Chief of Staff of the Army).*

Bus and Betty went straight to work after their vacation. The follow-ing excerpts are illustrative but by no means all-inclusive of their busy, var-ied schedule.

On 25 April, Wheeler received his British counterpart, General Sir Richard A. Hull, Chief of the Imperial General Staff, in his office and in a review ceremony at Fort Myer. [68]

Betty, meanwhile, bemoaned, "Last week was full to overflowing and I can hardly bear the thoughts of this one. In fact the calendar for May is stag-gering." [69]

A few days after their return from Puerto Rico, Betty drove over to Fort Meade for a tea, which "was a fund raising project for the Distaff Hall and the Soldiers, Sailors, Marines, and Airmen Club. The latter, I'm vitally interested in. The former, I can't afford to be completely detached about, although I've managed to stay off the board." [70]

On 30 April, she hosted a luncheon for the wives of the senior officers gathered for the Army Commanders Conference.

> [I] hosted a luncheon for 40, including the 21 commanders'
> wives who accompanied their husbands. Mrs. [Diddy] Taylor
> [and I were] very pleased as all the top civilian wives in the

Defense Department came – Mrs. [Margie] McNamara, Mrs. Gilpatrick, Mrs. Pratt, Mrs. Ignatius, Mrs. Pierpont, and Mrs. Larsen. Everyone seemed to have an awfully good time. … That night the Vances and ourselves gave a reception at the club. About 600 (guests). It was a full day. … Everybody is so glad to see everybody. [71]

That evening, the Wheelers attended a formal dinner party at the Fort Myer Officers Club as part of the conference. While the event itself was unremarkable, what is noteworthy is that Wheeler wore upon his mess dress jacket both the Army Staff Identification Badge and the new Office of the Joint Chiefs of Staff Identification Badge, perhaps for the first time. Before the latter badge's institution in February 1963, Wheeler had worn the Office of the Secretary of Defense Identification Badge while serving as a member of the Joint Chiefs of Staff. Going forward, he would alternate between wearing the latter two badges. [72]

## *Alabama*

Meanwhile, civil disturbances related to the equal rights movement continued. Bombings and other racially motivated incidents in Birmingham had forced Kennedy to send regular troops into the city during May. Wheeler oversaw this effort. Later in the year, integration crises in the public schools of several Alabama cities and at the University of Alabama would lead the President to federalize the Alabama National Guard. [73]

As Odom recalled, "Blacks were forming marches all over [Birmingham], confronting anyone who got in their way. The city was quickly degenerating into anarchy. Yet the governor would not take steps to establish law and order." [74]

The Army established an operations center in the Pentagon and planned for "an invasion" of Birmingham if the situation became totally unmanageable by local officials. The President was on the phone frequently with Alabama Governor George C. Wallace and the Mayor of Birmingham as isolated riots broke out all over the city.

Kennedy sent Nicholas Katzenbach, the Deputy U.S. Attorney General, to Birmingham along with a team to assess the situation and make recommendations.

In coordination with Katzenbach, Wheeler and the Army Staff made plans to bring enough military force to bear to create a safe and peaceful situation in the city. Wheeler frequented the "war room", where he was kept up to date on the current situation and briefed on the status of plans for troop movements. When it became clear that the Army should have a presence in Birmingham, Wheeler dispatched Brigadier General Creighton W. Abrams, Jr. there.

At the peak of the crisis, some 10,000 paratroopers from the 82nd Airborne Division were moved from Fort Bragg, North Carolina to Fort McClellan, Alabama. Eventually, a decision was made to load the paratroopers on the aircraft, takeoff, and orbit in the vicinity of Birmingham. The first wave of aircraft orbited for quite some time. Then, after much negotiation by Abrams, Katzenbach, and calls by the President, Birmingham officials relented. As a result, public accommodations were open to blacks, and a plan was initiated to integrate the public schools. [75]

## *Washington*

On 2 May, the Wheelers attended a White House reception for recipients of the Medal of Honor.

> We stood on the porch and faced the Medal of Honor winners. Afterwards went into the Cabinet Room for juice, and out through the Pres. office to the big party. The Pres. made no effort to greet those of us who were so honored. And later only people with determination could have shaken his hand. Needless to say, our paths did not cross! This may be informality, but to me it's more, 'I'm supposed to have the military, and now I've done it.' The only reason it can possibly matter whether you go to the White House is because you've been received. We weren't! Did have a tour of the White House given by Ted Clifton the Pres. military aide. Getting critical in my old age. I was disappointed. [76]

Two days later, Betty wrote, "Bus took off at three for Hawaii. Imagine he'll be at work here on Tuesday. Damn Mr. McNamara!" [77]

Later that month, Wheeler visited his former command, the 2nd Armored Division, at Fort Hood, Texas. There, he was honored during a formal dinner party and by an impressive mounted division review with armored vehicles. [78]

Odom recalled a nearly fatal trip to New York City with Wheeler who had accepted an invitation to speak to a group of ROTC cadets at Fordham University followed by dinner with a group of Wall Street officials. At Andrews Air Force Base, Wheeler and Odom boarded a Martin 202, a plush, twin-engine, 26-passenger aircraft and took off for LaGuardia. About halfway there, the weather changed and got progressively worse.

"We were completely surrounded by clouds," Odom recalled. "Rain was enveloping us, and the plane began shaking as if it would be spat out of the sky. Lightning and thunder were just outside, and for the first time, I saw 'Saint Elmo's light' dancing around inside the plane."

Wheeler turned around and asked, "Lou, what's going on?"

Odom made his way to the cockpit and saw the pilot struggling with the controls. "What's going on?" Odom asked.

"We ran unexpectedly into a severe thunderstorm," the pilot replied. "Air traffic control gave me the choice of going on or turning back. I told them it can't possibly be any worse ahead, so I decided to continue on." [79]

After what seemed like an eternity, the plane finally broke into the clear. It landed at LaGuardia about ten minutes later and was met by the head of the Fordham ROTC program.

As the pilot came down the steps, he directed the party's attention to the skies and said, "That's what we just came through." It was a very dark and red billowing thunderhead with a large anvil top, probably up to 60,000 feet and reaching almost to LaGuardia. The pilot told the party that the weather service was taken by surprise by the severe storm front that had formed. He further advised that they probably would not be able to fly back that night. [80]

Halfway through Wheeler's Wall Street dinner, the host informed him that the pilot had called to say that flying back to Washington, DC that evening would be impossible. The pilot had even requested that an executive jet be dispatched to pick up Wheeler but had been told that no aircraft were flying between New York and Washington.

The only other option was to take the train. At Pennsylvania Station, Wheeler and Odom boarded the train and discovered that there were no more seats available. "It was standing room only," recalled Odom.

> Now, here was the Chief of Staff of the Army with his four stars, and his Aide-de-Camp with his gold aiguilette, standing and shaking all the way – about 3 ½ to 4 hours. And, as luck would have it, one of America's raunchiest looking bums sidled up to us, and asked General Wheeler if he was in the Army. The general very politely replied,' Yes', to which the bum replied – 'I was in the Army too – years ago – but got out on a medical discharge.' To our luck, he disappeared soon. [81]

Clifton, the Senior Military Aide to the President, had told Betty that "anytime I wanted to bring people through [the White House] … to feel free to make an appointment." As she was entertaining old friends visiting Washington, she took him up on his offer on 23 May. [82]

> We were there at 8:30. We were … met by Hower Grunther. … It was about nine [when we] started through but we had a front row seat, very few in the party, and the guide told us about things as we went along. I still don't like what's been done [with First Lady Jacqueline Kennedy's White House renovations], but it's all point of view. I thought that after the surprise of my first visit, I might be able to look at it differently. I find that I like it less! Many people rave though, so guess it's me.
>
> Ted Clifton met us at the end of the tour. We were so lucky. On the mornings of a press conference the Pres. gives a breakfast so he didn't or doesn't come to the [Oval] office until late. Ted took us in to the office wing. We met the Pres. secretary. When she found out that I was Mrs. Wheeler, she was so pleased! Made me realize how much time Bus spends in the White House. We must have been in the Pres. office a

good ten minutes. We looked at pictures and trophies and things. Margie was invited to sit in the Pres. rocker but I think it embarrassed her, so she won't be able to tell that one! We saw the Cabinet Room and the Press Room, a big conference room and then word came that the Pres. was on the way down and we had to move on. We went downstairs and had coffee in the mess. ... Then on out. It was quite a morning. [83]

Betty took her visitors to the Pentagon the following morning.

One asked Bus if she could see his office. Except for the fireplace, the Pres. has very little on him! Bus was in Norfolk so we were free to poke [around]. Even I saw things that I'd never seen before. Afterwards we went down to the concourse so they had a good look. [84]

That evening, the Wheelers went to the French Embassy for an awards ceremony in honor of Wheeler's recent tour as Deputy SACEUR.

Madame Alphard and the Ambassador greeted us. Ambassador [Herve] Alphard presented Bus with a medal. It was a short but moving ceremony. The Ambassador gave a short but fine talk. Bus responded magnificently. Afterwards we went into the dining room for champagne, and left shortly thereafter. Madame Alphard said to me as we went into the dining room, 'I always find this a moving ceremony, but today there was something special about it.' I think we all felt that way. 1) Ambassador Alphard had to have been briefed from France as to his remarks, and we know that Bus left more than a passing impression during our short stay in Paris, 2) Bus's words were so right, 3) Of course, he looked magnificent! [85]

Bus spent the Saturday of Memorial Day weekend "going through stacks and stacks of paper." That evening, he and Betty hosted a party for Wheeler's office group.

We had about 200 to a buffet. The evening [was] perfect. The garden [was] lovely. We greeted everyone outside, had music, supper outside, but had coffee, cake, crackers & cheese, and fruit in the dining room. The house was open, and all who wanted to could look. There were a lot of Majors, many Lt. Colonels, so it was a young group, and I think and hope that they loved it. [86]

### *Summer*

Betty had received a letter in late April from artist Frank Herring and his wife Frances, whom they had befriended during Bus's one-year tour of duty as an instructor at the Military College of Georgia in Milledgeville. Now that Bus had become Chief of Staff of the Army, the Herrings requested that he visit, suggesting that he deliver the college's commencement address on 27 May. They wrote, "Your last visit to us together was in 1936 and then you, Betty, brought Bim by during the war when he was less than two years old." The Wheelers thought it was a fine idea. [87]

Odom recalled, "It turned out that they were both artists and writers, and had settled into their retirement in Milledgeville. They had grown old and the house had almost fallen down around them. The visit to the college, which included a barbecue on campus, was a lot of fun, even though it was hot and the flies and gnats were much of a problem." [88]

*Wheeler delivered the graduation address at the Georgia Military College, where had had served as a tactical officer in 1935-36, Milledgeville, Georgia, 27 May 1963. (Office of the Chief of Staff of the Army).*

"[We] landed in Macon [Georgia], and took a little Army plane into Milledgeville," Betty reported. "The band was out, a company of cadets, [and] friends to meet us." They attended a barbeque lunch with the college faculty and afterwards a review by the Corps of Cadets. That evening, they had an outdoor supper and a barge ride on the nearby lake. The next morning, they attended a breakfast for about 30 guests before the graduation ceremony. "Bus's talk [was] terrific," wrote Betty. They viewed Herring's mural in the local post office before lunch and then departed for Fort Benning, where they were greeted by "a beautiful honor guard." [89]

After briefings and demonstrations by the 11th Air Assault Division in the Sand Hill and Harmony Church areas, Wheeler and Odom were loaded into a UH-1 Huey helicopter to experience the "helicopter confidence course," which was designed to give helicopter pilots practice, expertise, and confidence in flying at variable speeds using "nap of the earth" techniques close to the ground. "Had I known in advance what we were in for, I'm not sure that I would have told General Wheeler, 'It's just too risky for the Chief of Staff of the Army. (And for me to, of course.)'" [90]

> We took off, headed south and then west along Upatoi Creek. We soon experienced true nap of the earth flying. Upatoi Creek was a very narrow, zigzagging body of water whose banks were lined with everything from bushes to medium height and very tall trees. We literally flew near creek bank level – never in a straight line. To avoid trees on the bank, the pilot would bank – lifting his rotors to the right or left, and quickly change speed and direction. General Wheeler was very quiet – so was I.
>
> After what seemed to be an eternity, we 'scooted' to a safe altitude and gave a sigh of relief. But there was more confidence to come. The pilot began a quick descent toward a dirt road and we headed down it at about 4 feet above the ground. Straight ahead were two long telephone poles with a rope between the two and across the road. Yes, we were on a course that would take us under that rope or to 'kingdom come'. It was about as if they had set us up for a suicide mission. I couldn't believe it would all end here now. We went

under that rope as if we were on a high-speed train, stirring up clouds of dust and dirt behind us from the roadbed.

Finally, we put down on a grassy meadow, almost fell out of the chopper, and after bragging on the pilot, went to another Huey with one star on it. What do you know, flying this one was the Assistant Commandant of the Infantry School. My first thought was that I didn't want to fly with a general who probably got out of flight school because of rank. But he did a good job, taking us back to the main post where we then loaded into our plane at Lawson Field and headed back to Washington. [91]

While Bus viewed the airmobile demonstrations by the 11th Air Assault Division, Betty was provided her own itinerary. Her escort was none other than Betty Rich, who along with her husband Brigadier General Charlie Rich, had shared the large house in Vaucresson with the Wheelers in 1946-47. "Betty [Rich] and I have never had anything in common," Betty wrote. Furthermore, she had never shown the slightest kindness to the much younger Betty. Yet, here she was now, all smiles as she escorted the visiting wife of the Chief of Staff of the Army. [92]

"The main post of [Fort] Benning [was] little changed [since we lived there in 1932-37]," Betty noted, "and [we] never had time to see anything else." [93]

The Wheelers then visited the Air War College at Maxwell Field in Montgomery. Certainly, the ongoing civil rights disturbances in Alabama were a topic of discussion on this last day of their trip. [94]

The first half of June was typically busy for them. Besides an overnight trip on 3-4 June to attend the West Point graduation ceremony, the Wheelers also had a reception at the Spanish Embassy on their schedule. "This will be the first embassy invitation we've accepted," Betty wrote. "Diplomatically [we] feel they can't be ignored. We really have a 'position'!" Despite their eagerness to attend, they later declined. They simply had too much going on. [95]

"Bus, bless him, was in El Paso with Mr. Kennedy the night of Bim's graduation [from his Masters program at George Washington University on 5 June.]" Because diplomas were not handed out at that time, Bim didn't even want to attend, but ended up inviting Betty, Mums, and Margie's parents. After the long, hot ceremony, they returned to Quarters 1 where chilled champagne awaited them. "Thus ended a chapter [in Bim's life]," Betty concluded. [96]

Another chapter was just beginning. The other big news was that Margie was pregnant. Bus and Betty were going to be grandparents. [97]

They found time the following Sunday to get out to the countryside. "We've been talking about going out to Antietam and Harpers Ferry. Had a lunch packed and off we went. Had a lovely day. … We got back about 4:30. … Bus can't drive yet, so I'd driven." This trip sowed the seeds of an idea that they could use a place in the country as a weekend retreat. [98]

The following weekend, Wheeler spoke at the Army War College graduation. Betty, as promised, did not accompany him on this trip to Carlisle. [99]

In late June, Wheeler accompanied the President on a visit to Berlin and the 3rd Armored Division. Kennedy inspected the division's static displays of vehicles and equipment while riding in the open-top Lincoln Continental convertible limousine in which he would be assassinated five months later. [100]

In July, the Wheelers took overnight trips to Panama to meet with his South American counterparts during a Conference of American Armies; to Fort Hood where Betty "had a lovely day seeing old friends;" and to their former duty station in Naples to visit NATO's Southern European Task Force (SETAF). Bus also visited Camp Grayling, Michigan, where he observed training conducted by the 38th Infantry Division of the Indiana National Guard. [101]

For Wheeler's trip to Camp Grayling, Odom and Master Sergeant Steinweinder picked up Wheeler at Quarters 1 at about 7 AM. Upon arrival at the ramp at Andrews Air Force Base, they were told that Vice President Johnson "outranked" them and would use the Jet-Star that they had been scheduled to take. Wheeler was assigned a twin-engine T-29 jet from the Air Force Tactical Air Command instead.

Both pilots were Air Force Second Lieutenants. Odom recalled thinking that he did not like the setup, but they proceeded with the flight anyway.

Later, Odom noticed the aircraft began losing altitude and entered a circling pattern. The pilot attracted Odom's attention and motioned him forward. He pointed earthward and asked, "Does that look like it?" Odom was flabbergasted. "Here we were, high above the earth, with our lives in the hands of what now appears to be a 'green' Second Lieutenant, who, by all rights, should have known where he was to land before he left Andrews, asking me the passenger, if that looks like we were supposed to land."

Odom replied, "I've never been here before." Scanning the ground, he noticed several trucks and jeeps and troops along the airstrip. He added, "That must be it."

The pilot replied, "We're going in." [102]

Odom recalled:

> I knew we were on final approach, and that we were coming in fast. But I was not prepared for what happened as we touched down. It was if an explosion occurred under the cabin, then the aircraft shuddered and shook as we rattled down the runway. I loosened my seatbelt, look through the windshield between the pilot and copilot and yelled to General Wheeler, 'It looks like we're running out of runway.' At that moment the pilot yelled, 'No brakes!' At that, the plane spun to the left, off the runway, and came to a sudden jolting stop in the grass. [103]

The pilot left his seat, came back to the passenger cabin and said, "I'm really sorry, general, but we had a real emergency on our hands." He opened the outside door and lowered the steps for Wheeler to deplane.

> There to meet us was the Adjutant General of the [Indiana] National Guard, a fire truck, several jeeps, and ambulance and about 100 or so officers and soldiers. All, of course, joined us, in our almost state of shock – especially as we viewed the crippled jet. There it was, its left wheel ground down to a ball of metal about the size of basketball. The tire had completely disappeared! The underside of the left wing was riddled with holes that had been caused by metal shearing from the wheel. It was that metal that severed hydraulic lines that caused brake and even controls loss. That the plane did not overturn and burn was, without a doubt, a miracle and a testimony to the durability of the aircraft and skill of the two pilots. [104]

As Wheeler visited Camp Grayling, Odom telephoned Andrews Air Force Base to request another aircraft. When told that another T-29 would be dispatched, Odom replied, "We will not accept it! Get us something else." What arrived the next morning was a large, four-engine Lockheed Constellation named "Columbine", which had famously served as Air Force One during the Eisenhower Administration. [105]

In early August, Wheeler visited III Corps at Fort Hood for Exercise SWIFT STRIKE III. In a ceremony in his office a few days later, he received an Ecuadoran decoration from Dr. Neffali Ponce Miranda, the Foreign Minister of Ecuador, as Vance, the Secretary of the Army, and General "Ham" Hamlett, the Vice Chief of Staff of the Army (VCSA), looked on. [106]

Later that month, Wheeler visited the 77th Infantry Division at Camp Drum, New York to observe its annual training. He was greeted by guard of honor at the airfield before donning a field jacket over his khaki uniform and boarding a helicopter to begin his inspections. With his trousers bloused into highly shined tanker boots, Wheeler rode in a jeep with the Division Commander between training sites. He talked to individual soldiers—something he had always enjoyed; ate at a field mess in the woods; watched up-close as engineers practiced river crossing operations; and finally presided over a division review at the airfield. [107]

As the day approached for Martin Luther King Jr.'s march on Washington, all law enforcement and military forces were revving up once again. The Military District of Washington, Fort Belvoir, and the 1st Army headquarters at Fort Meade, Maryland were on alert. Odom recalled:

> General Wheeler and I came to work early. Everyone was watching TV or listening to radio. Believe it or not – the Chief didn't even have a TV in his office. As the day progressed, General Wheeler expressed a desire to fly over the masses to get a feel for what was going on. I ordered a helicopter – we want to the Pentagon 'chopper pad', and got in – side-by-side behind the pilot.
>
> We lifted off, headed for the Lincoln Memorial. What a sight! A sea of blacks from there – to the Washington Monument – to the U.S. capital – it was estimated at well over 1 million. It

seemed almost as if we are looking at people of another country. General Wheeler was speechless. However, he seemed 'at
ease', because there was no sign (or reports) of violence. We
went back to our 'safe place' on the Pentagon E Ring – Office
of the Chief. And all this time, King was giving his 'I have a
dream' speech. [108]

*Wheeler greets an officer of Company A, 5th Special Forces Group outside the American
Legion Convention, Miami, Florida, 11 September 1963. (Office of the Chief of Staff of the
Army).*

September 1963 was another busy, varied month for Wheeler, but
a happy one, too. Margie delivered a baby boy whom she and Bim named
William "Billy" or "Bill" Gilmore Wheeler. On the 11th, Wheeler spoke at an
American Legion convention in Miami Beach, Florida. While there, he took
time to talk with the soldiers and NCOs providing static displays for the
event. The Special Forces exhibit drew a lot of conference attendees. Ten days
after Miami, Wheeler found himself in Iceland during a layover enroute to
Finland. [109]

## *Finland*

In September, Wheeler accepted an invitation from General Jaakko
Sakari Simelius, the Commander-In-Chief of the Finnish Armed Forces,
to spend seven days in Finland on "business and pleasure." Accompanying
Wheeler on the Chairman of the Joint Chiefs of Staff's loaned, four-engine,

specially equipped DC-7 were Betty, Odom, and Berensweig. Their flight took them to Goose Bay, Labrador, and Reykjavík, Iceland, for refueling stops, then onto Helsinki. Odom recalled seeing the Great Northern Lights over Iceland.

The Wheelers first had lunch with Finland's President Juho K. Kekkonen. As guests of the Neste Oil Company, they then traveled to western Finland where they stayed at the company's lakeside resort. The ladies in the party went off on their own itinerary while the men departed in a powerboat to fish for Great Northern Pike in the rough waters of the Gulf of Finland.

Afterwards, the men were escorted to a large sauna, the first that Wheeler, "B'Wig", or Odom had ever taken. They were instructed to dip tree branches in the water and slap one another on the back, which according to the Finns, caused the pores to open more and hence, more perspiration.

> Here we were 'nekkid as jay birds,' trading blows – even with the Chief of Staff of the Army, and having fun. But there was more to come. We then went out of the sauna – still naked, and ran into a cold lake. This was supposed to be the best part. What a sight to see General Wheeler, about 6 feet, 2 or 3 inches tall, running naked to the water, and B'Wig and I following. And what a shock when we entered the ice-cold water. Anyway, we survived it, took our towels from soldiers on the bank, and headed for our cabins to dress; and then have open roasted pike fish for supper.
>
> By the way, our hosts pointed out that the ladies were taking sauna across the lake and pointed them out as they were running for the lake. It was too far to identify anyone, but later, we shared with Mrs. Wheeler that we did see some women running around, to which she replied that they saw us too. This was truly far away from the formalities and even restraints of the Pentagon and Washington life. [110]

*Wheeler fires a Finnish submachinegun during a tour of Finland, September 1963. (Office of the Chief of Staff of the Army).*

The Wheelers' party then flew to Rovaniemi just above the Arctic Circle. While ladies of the Army Post entertained Betty, the officers journeyed farther north to visit a Finnish Army unit conducting field maneuvers. Odom recalled the Finnish soldiers as professional, well-trained, and highly enthusiastic. A highlight was their burning of very large logs, having supper there by campfire, and being entertained by Finnish troops singing several of their native songs.

"Waking up in a hotel that far north, with snow on the ground, was like being in a fairyland," Odom recalled. "After making a short trip to the Arctic Circle, and taking pictures of us standing north of the Arctic Circle, we boarded our plane and headed for a visit to an army unit on Finland's border with the Soviet Union." [111]

> The commander of the local Finnish forces briefed Wheeler on the situation. Essentially, they still did not trust the Soviets after World War II, and had battle plans to resist an invasion should it occur. All along and a comfortable distance from the border, they had erected storage buildings housing vehicles, skis, tanks, artillery, ammunition, and supplies. On the appropriate signal, every able-bodied man (all were trained reservists) from every community would rush to his particular assembly area, and join up with his equipment and defend the border, or counterattack as the need should demand. There was no fondness nor trust for the Soviets.

That evening, the Finns hosted a "very strange" dinner, mainly of crayfish and beer. Odom recalled:

> They donned us with bibs (with a sketch of crayfish on the front) and began to 'flood' us with the crayfish and beer. The supper got louder and louder every minute. The host said that you cannot eat crayfish without beer, and that the purpose of eating crayfish is to drink beer. Many stories were told – one of which teased one of their officers who they pointed out was not really a Finn because all Finns have blue eyes. He really was the only one there with brown eyes. It was at this supper I learned that toasting in Scandinavia is an almost endless exercise. You must catch the eye of each present, raise your glass and say, 'SKOL!', to which the other person raises his glass and says, 'SKOL.' [112]

During the Wheelers' trip to Finland, Betty began a hobby of collecting historical maps of the places they visited. "They were cheap," she reasoned, and gave her something to focus on during the ample shopping time usually allocated to her travel schedules. [113]

The following month, Wheeler made a similar visit to Sweden to observe Swedish Army field training. Betty accompanied him once more. [114]

## *Cold War*

The aftermath of the crises in Berlin and Cuba produced several unexpected developments. Apparently convinced that further confrontations might be unwise, the Soviet Union had adopted a more conciliatory attitude in its propaganda and suggested that at long last it might be willing to conclude a nuclear test ban treaty. Under the provisions of the accord that followed in the fall of 1963, the Soviet Union, the United Kingdom, and the U.S. agreed to refrain from conducting nuclear test explosions underwater, in the atmosphere, or in space. Only underground explosions would be permissible, but no radioactive material from such tests was ever to reach the surface. Although France weakened the treaty by declining to either ratify or adhere to it, the pact still marked a major breakthrough in what had been a long history of fruitless negotiations over nuclear weapons.

A possible explanation for the Soviets' willingness to cooperate with the West in the 1960s may have been the growing independence of Communist China. The Chinese had never embraced the idea of peaceful coexistence with Capitalist countries and criticized Moscow for being too soft on the West. As the Sino-Soviet rift had widened, the Soviet Union seemed to adopt a less threatening stance in Europe, although no direct correlation could be proven.

The shift had far-reaching effects on the system of alliances the U.S. had designed to guard Western Europe against Soviet aggression. NATO had centered its defenses upon the U.S. strategic deterrent. With the growth of the Soviet Union's ability to devastate the U.S. with nuclear weapons, the credibility of U.S. determination to defend Western Europe came into serious question. The reinforcement of U.S. conventional forces in Europe at the time of the Berlin Crisis served to demonstrate U.S. good faith. [115]

## *Turning Point*

Meanwhile in South Vietnam, if the decline in rural security across the country was not readily apparent to some Americans, the lack of enlightened political leadership on Diem's part was all too obvious. He habitually interfered in military matters by bypassing the chain of command to order operations, had forbidden commanders take casualties, and had appointed military leaders based on political loyalty rather than competence. Many military and civilian appointees, especially province and district chiefs, were dishonest and put their own aggrandizement above the national interest.

Many U.S. leaders feared Diem would ultimately fail because they believed political and economic reforms were more important than winning battles. The U.S. Army's *Operations Against Irregular Forces* field manual maintained that an insurgency was the "outward manifestation" of popular discontent with social and political conditions. An important corollary was that repression alone would not suffice; the only permanent solution was to rectify the underlying conditions that produced the insurgency. From the perspective of many Americans, Diem relied too heavily on repression and too little on reform. [116]

When Buddhist opposition to certain policies erupted into violent anti-government demonstrations in 1963, Diem's uncompromising stance and use of military force to suppress the demonstrators caused some ARVN generals to decide that he was a liability in the fight against the Viet Cong. [117]

For several weeks that summer, Kennedy and his advisors debated options concerning the future of the Diem government. The Chiefs agreed with former Ambassador Frederick Nolting that there was no viable alternative to Diem, and they were unified in their position that the U.S. should do nothing to engineer a change in government in South Vietnam. Members of Kennedy's inner circle, however, thought that getting rid of Diem was the only alternative. True to a well-established pattern among members of the Administration, these men worked surreptitiously to advance their own solution to the problem. Ultimately convinced that authoritarianism foreclosed success, Kennedy sanctioned a coup by a group of reform-minded generals on 1 November that resulted in the murders of Diem and his brother. [118]

Kennedy's top civilian advisors, including McNamara and Rusk, were guardedly optimistic that with the major impediment of Diem and his regime out of the way, progress could be made in Vietnam, that new leadership would heed U.S. guidance about democratic reforms and inspire more vigorous efforts on the battlefield and in pacification.

Their optimism was cut short by several developments. Pacification, a program to win the hearts and minds of the Vietnamese people, was not proceeding satisfactorily. The year-end report submitted by MACV substantiated the lack of progress and indicated downward trends in most performance measures.

In Washington, the idea emerged that military victories would give the South Vietnamese confidence in their government and end the "revolving door" of military coups. McNamara and Assistant Secretary of State Roger S. Hilsman stressed the need for military success and physical security as prerequisites to political stability. Conversely, MACV concluded that the military effort was dependent on political stability and could not succeed without effective political leadership in Saigon.

Neither such leadership nor military victories were forthcoming, however, with political turmoil the result. "In the first [part] of November '63, things went to hell in a handbasket," Wheeler recalled. "We have never been able to recover the same degree of military success that we were having a year earlier. The political situation insofar as the South Vietnamese government is concerned has steadily gotten worse; the government has gotten weaker." Seven more coups would rack South Vietnam over the following year. From 1963 until 1966, Saigon's political machinations would virtually paralyze the ARVN, severely hindering the war effort. [119]

Sensing the demise of America's "special war," North Vietnam's Ninth Party Plenum not only stepped up the political struggle in December 1963 but also ordered the insurgency to go on the offensive, aiming to demoralize the ARVN and further undermine political authority in the South, hoping to win a swift victory and thereby preempt a protracted war involving the United States. Emboldened by instability in the South, the insurgents stepped up operations and increased their control over many rural areas. As Viet Cong military activity quickened, regular North Vietnamese Army (NVA) units began to train for possible intervention in the war. Men and equipment continued to flow down the Ho Chi Minh Trail, with North Vietnamese conscripts replacing the dwindling pool of Southerners who had belonged to the Viet Minh. [120]

A turning point had been reached. The U.S. role in fomenting a change in the South Vietnamese government saddled the U.S. with responsibility for its successor. The deteriorating situation would force the U.S. to consider deepening its involvement in what had become a new war. Kennedy's assassination later that month would leave those decisions to his Vice President, Lyndon Johnson. [121]

## *Kennedy's Assassination*

The President had a great deal of confidence in Wheeler and asked him many times for his advice and counsel on subjects that were not even in the Army's domain. The high regard was mutual, Wheeler recalled.

> One of the things I liked about him particularly was the fact that he had an extremely fine sense of humor. ... It isn't very often that you find a man who was as quick witted as he was in the ad lib area and the way even when things were looking pretty bleak was able to turn a joke. In fact, on one occasion during the Cuban affair, why he turned a joke by quoting a

passage from Shakespeare, which is a rather unusual attribute these days. [122]

In the early part of the week in which he was killed, the President spent 45 minutes with Wheeler going over the records and capabilities of the senior officers of the Army. "He had asked for some such briefing because he was concerned about the future of the high command of the Army, who were the people that were coming along, who were the men to keep your eye on, who did I think might be my successor, and so on," Wheeler recalled. "I might add that was the last time I saw him." [123]

Odom recalled that he and Wheeler arrived at the Pentagon at the regular time on 22 November. They were already aware of the President's visit to Dallas, Texas.

> I was in my office next to the Chief's when I heard an unusual 'hustle and bustle' in the hall outside my door. Word immediately spread that, 'The President has been shot!' General Wheeler was told – and he immediately turned on his radio. Without any hesitation, all three of us Aides went in to listen. All barriers broke down. Rank did not matter. It was a four-star general and his Aides, plus Master Sergeant Loikow, bending ears to hear every word coming from that small radio. The announcer – Walter Cronkite – gave a running summary of the situation; including the pursuit of the killer, and his capture at the theater. Then, finally, came the shocking and unbelievable announcement: 'The President is dead; the president is dead.' There was deafening silence among us – there was total disbelief. Our thoughts then turned to the task ahead in planning for and participating in President Kennedy's funeral. [124]

"Mums and I were having lunch here," Betty recorded. "Larry broke the news. It was all over shortly. Bus called and said that he didn't feel as though he could stand going out to dinner. I shouldn't wonder." [125]

The Military District of Washington (MDW) was responsible for planning and conducting a presidential funeral. "We stayed in the Pentagon late into the night," Odom recorded, "knowing that MDW would be contacting the Kennedy family to get their (particularly Mrs. Kennedy's) input on exactly what she wanted. She had arrived in late afternoon; and, as the MDW representative told me, it was not easy, considering that the President had died only a few hours earlier." [126]

> Since the plan called for the Chiefs of the Army, Navy, and Air Force, and the Chairman of the Joint Chiefs of Staff to march behind Mrs. Kennedy as honorary pallbearers, they put up a howl. Here, four middle-aged men, in their uniforms and street shoes, were called on to walk about 6+ miles on hard surfaced streets. General Taylor may have been able to do it, but I know General Wheeler never exercised, General LeMay was overweight, and Admiral McDonald was not the picture of a man in good physical shape. Somehow, reality set in, and Mrs. Kennedy settled for the plan to walk only on the second day from the White House to the church. [127]

At around nine o'clock the following morning, the Wheelers went to the White House to pay their official respects in the East Room. "[At home later], we sat absolutely mesmerized by the television. We looked at the same things (over and over). We heard the same things but we couldn't turn the darn thing off." [128]

*The Joint Chiefs of Staff process through Washington, DC during President Kennedy's funeral honors, 25 November 1963. (Office of the Chief of Staff of the Army).*

Betty continued, "The Joint Chiefs marched to the Capitol [accompanying the horse-drawn caisson carrying Kennedy's flag-draped coffin] on Sunday. I went to the mass with Helen LeMay [on Monday, 25 November]. The Chiefs walked from the Capitol to the White House, thence to the church [again accompanying Kennedy's coffin]. Quite a hike for the boys! As Bus had to leave the church ahead of me, I didn't go to the cemetery. Back home to the television." [129]

The church service went on through the lunch hour, and practically every commercial establishment was closed out of respect. "Still," Odom recalled, "I felt a bit hungry; and thought General Wheeler and Admiral McDonald might want a snack enroute to Arlington Cemetery. So I scouted around and found a drugstore, knocked on the door, and they let me in. I bought some cheese crackers and three half-pints of milk and put them in the limo." [130]

Odom recalled:

> As the church began to empty, all to be in the cortège to the cemetery were formed up. First was the casket-bearing artillery caisson, then 'Black Jack', then Mrs. Kennedy and family in the presidential limousine, then the [remainder of the] Kennedy family in limousines, then General Taylor and General LeMay in a limousine; and following them in our limousine were General Wheeler, Admiral McDonald, and me. Streets were lined with masses of people, standing respectfully on both sides. Some could be seen weeping – wiping their eyes. [131]

The Chiefs were accustomed to being constantly busy, and they were restless during the long, slow car ride. Odom recalled:

> As we proceeded, I told General Wheeler and Admiral McDonald I had some snacks. They eagerly took them. They (and I) realized they had a problem. How can they be seen by people as they ate crackers and drank milk? I suggested they bend over below window level. Like little boys getting away with something, they did just that! [132]

As the cortège proceeded, Wheeler noticed smoke coming from the window of the limousine carrying LeMay and Taylor. Wheeler chuckled. "Look, Curt's smoking his cigar. I'll bet Max is mad as hell!"

Further on, McDonald pulled up his pants leg and said, "Hey, Bus, do you ever have leg dandruff?"

Wheeler looked and said, "Yeah, I get that flaking skin sometimes. I use Jergens lotion." [133]

Business resumed immediately after Kennedy's funeral, albeit not as usual. On 26 November, Wheeler received Lieutenant General Sean McKeown, the Chief of Staff of the Irish Defense Forces, in a protocol visit.

Betty, meanwhile, wrote, "The events of the past few days have certainly been staggering. Feel exhausted and spent today." [134]

Bus recorded his own thoughts on the assassination in a letter to Betty's father on 29 November.

> I am sorry that I was sort of drowsy when you called yesterday afternoon. As I told you, I was watching the Texas—Texas A&M football game and my mind, if not my eyes, was at least half shut. Of course, I had been working on my papers most of the day until that time, and I was pretty bored with the whole affair.
>
> The murder of President Kennedy really threw the whole government into a turmoil. In fact, we have not yet gotten back to the normal tempo of events; everything is on sort of a crash basis because of the need for President Johnson to take hold in many areas where heretofore he has had no responsibility, although he may have been informed as to problems and programs.
>
> I must admit that, although my feet were sore from the marches of last Sunday and Monday, my legs reminded me that I am a middle-aged gentleman of sedentary habits. It has been a long time since I have marched on city streets 3 or 4 miles and my leg muscles told me so!
>
> One thing about the funeral on Monday impressed me more than any other. The Washington police estimated that the

funeral cortège was witnessed by at least 1 million people. I have been in many processions in my time, and I have witnessed many others—some of them in Europe of a rather solemn religious nature. However, this is the only procession that I have ever attended at which the onlookers were absolutely silent and without a smile. When you consider the number of people, many of them children, it made a profound impression on me to march through absolutely silent streets with the only sounds being the beat of the drums, the sound of marching troops, the rattle of the caisson and the noise of horses' hooves on the asphalt.

Other than that the murder of the President was a most traumatic blow to the American people. I cannot fix what conclusions, if any, can be drawn. Certainly, many of the onlookers at the President's funeral would not agree, and in some cases would violently disagree, with his policies and programs. Even so, I would hope that only a fanatic fringe would do other than deplore the event. [135]

Bus added as a footnote:

Marge and Bim have gone off to Williamsburg. Betty was very busy yesterday with young Bill and, although I know she enjoyed herself with him, I think she is rather glad that we did not have a late family. In fact, she said to me last night that she simply could not imagine what anyone with twins did. Hope you had a nice Thanksgiving. Ours was quiet and very pleasant. [136]

# CHAPTER 7

## New Administration
## (November 1963 – July 1964)

At the Secretary of Defense/Joint Chiefs of Staff level … military-civilian
relationships must be balanced and effective. Otherwise, either the professional
military voice will not be heard enough or else it will be heard too much.
– General Earle G. Wheeler, 26 October 1967 [1]

The first order of business for Johnson's new Administration was to
provide continuity in the relationship between the U.S. and South Vietnam
and to demonstrate confidence in the new government in Saigon. Toward this
end, only three days after assuming the presidency, Johnson announced his
support for the Kennedy policy and allayed concerns of any radical departures
from previous policy initiatives. [2]

Along with the question of what to do about Vietnam, Johnson inherited Kennedy's closest advisors and the relationships that had developed among
them. The relationship between the Chiefs and those to whom they provided
military advice had become one of deep distrust. The Chairman, selected for
his personal loyalty to the President, had forged a closer relationship with the
Secretary of Defense than the one he enjoyed with his military colleagues.
McNamara, emboldened in the realm of strategic planning, was poised to
become the President's dominant advisor on military affairs. Convinced that
military advice based on the objective of achieving victory was outmoded,
even dangerous, he would use his talent for analysis and the experience of
the Cuban Missile Crisis to develop a new concept for the use of U.S. military
power. Kennedy bequeathed to Johnson an advisory system that limited real
influence to his inner circle and treated others, particularly the Chiefs, more
like a source of potential opposition than of useful advice. [3]

Kennedy's relations with the Chiefs were never good, largely due to a culture clash. He failed to understand the Chiefs and how they operated, and the Chiefs could not adapt to a very different kind of President with a leadership style at odds with their own culture. From their perspective, Kennedy constantly violated military culture, especially during the Bay of Pigs and the Cuban Missile Crises: he would not let the Chiefs do their job; he criticized them when they tried to provide advice; and he confused them with his seminar-like decision-making process.

The military, particularly the Navy, was appalled at the Administration's efforts to micromanage military operations. To senior officers, the overzealous meddling in their prerogatives stemmed from the Ivy League brain trust's naïveté about military affairs, rather than the Administration's concern over the political implications of military decisions. The idea of politicians telling senior military officers not only how to handle operational matters but when and how to drive ships completely countered naval tradition.

From the President's perspective, the military had failed to provide him with valuable counsel. When the Chiefs tried to become the kind of political-military advisors the President wanted, it became painfully obvious that their past isolation from such spheres precluded them from knowing what kind of advice to provide. Too often, they came across as "political Neanderthals" unequipped to function in the world of politics and diplomacy. [4]

## *Disharmony in the Tank*

Taylor had a mixed relationship with the Chiefs. He had spent a great deal of time trying to reconcile his differences of opinion with LeMay, whom he had antagonized with forceful attacks on the Air Force in *The Uncertain Trumpet*. Taylor was not the only one who disagreed with LeMay's opinions, however. The Air Force general's impassioned recommendations for bombing as the definitive solution to military problems had earned him a reputation as a "loose cannon." His outstanding combat and command records would have made removing him from the Joint Chiefs of Staff (JCS) controversial. When LeMay's first two-year term came to an end, Kennedy, rather than risk opposition from the general's supporters in Congress, extended his appointment for only one year, sending LeMay a clear message. (Ultimately, LeMay would remain in office until 1 February 1965.) [5]

LeMay was unable to conceal his animosity for Taylor. The bad feelings were mutual. Taylor regarded LeMay as politically naïve and believed that his appointment as Chief of Staff of the Air Force had been a "big mistake." Seating protocol in "the tank," the Joint Chiefs of Staff secure conference room, placed LeMay at Taylor's immediate right. Aware of Taylor's aversion to tobacco smoke, he intentionally puffed the thick smoke from his ever-present cigar toward Taylor. Both men were hard of hearing, and the seating arrangement only exacerbated their misunderstandings, which worsened the tension between them. [6]

During the Chiefs' tank sessions when issues directly affected the Marine Corps, General David M. Shoup, Commandant of the Marine Corps, sat on LeMay's right. The last remaining holdover from the Eisenhower Administration, Shoup had grown frustrated with Taylor's predecessor, Lemnitzer, because he never directly questioned McNamara's controversial methods. [7]

Disagreements among the Chiefs often reflected differences in their philosophies of war. LeMay felt that the U.S. should respond to security threats with massive retaliation from the air, whereas Shoup was against using military force at all unless vital U.S. interests were at stake. To Shoup, the "lesson" of the Korean War was that the U.S. was not adept at fighting protracted, limited wars. In contrast, Taylor believed that the U.S. could take military action in Southeast Asia short of committing to war, and that fighting limited wars was essential to a strategy of flexible response, which would avoid the extremes of either buckling to Communist aggression or resorting to nuclear war. Accordingly, Taylor was frustrated with those like Shoup and LeMay who refused to support the shift in national security strategy to Taylor's concept of flexible response.

The Navy stayed out of the debate because its outcome was less consequential for the Navy than for the Air Force or the Army. McDonald, like the Chiefs of Naval Operations before him, was interested primarily in maintaining U.S. global dominance at sea. [8]

McDonald had fared better during the Kennedy Administration than his predecessor, Anderson. A "quiet, gentlemanly" Nebraskan, "grizzled from years of sea duty," McDonald was "a thoughtful, serious man who spoke sparingly but with authority." More politically adept than Anderson, he was well-suited to maintain the Navy's bargaining power within the government. Perfectly willing to make compromises to further the Navy's interest, McDonald's tact and political sensitivity contrasted sharply with LeMay's stubbornness.

In the tank, Wheeler sat next to McDonald and across from Taylor. Like McDonald, Wheeler was particularly adept at working within the Washington bureaucratic maze and would prove uniquely talented at forging compromises between parties otherwise disinclined to reconcile their differences. [9]

### *New Old Team*

Consistent with his decision to stress continuity during his sudden elevation to the presidency and recognizing his own foreign-policy inexperience, Johnson asked Kennedy's team to remain with him. This was not surprising, for he already held McNamara and Rusk in high regard. They and National Security Advisor McGeorge Bundy had all played prominent roles in shaping Kennedy's Vietnam policy. [10]

Johnson and his key advisors considered Vietnam vital to U.S. foreign policy goals. By 1964, policy makers would begin to perceive the extent to which major changes in world politics were challenging long-standing Cold War assumptions. Open squabbling between the Soviet Union and China particularly undermined the most basic assumption that in Vietnam, as in elsewhere, the U.S. confronted a monolithic Communism united in its drive for world domination.

However, most foreign policy experts still believed that it was essential to hold the line in Vietnam. The ethos of the Cold War, which was deeply engrained by this point, placed a premium on toughness and viewed compromise as a sign of weakness, retreat as a sign of cowardice. The U.S. was obliged to continue demonstrating to the major Communist powers its certainty of purpose and strength of will. A firm stance in Vietnam would discourage Soviet adventurism and encourage the emerging trend toward détente with the United States. It was especially important to continue to contain the presumably more aggressive Communist Chinese. Policy makers believed that the manner in which the U.S. responded to Communist provocations in Vietnam would engender profound consequences everywhere. Turbulence in Southeast Asia and elsewhere in the Third World appeared to pose considerable dangers to U.S. credibility and world order. Firmness in Vietnam would help ensure stability throughout the world by demonstrating that the U.S. would resist any violent changes to the status quo. [11]

"Like most Americans, I saw Communism as monolithic," McNamara recalled. "I believed the Soviets and Chinese were cooperating in trying to extend their hegemony. ... Communism still seemed on the march. ... And now Castro had transformed Cuba into a Communist beachhead in our hemisphere. We felt beset and at risk." [12]

## *Johnson*

While Johnson would retain Kennedy's informal, ad hoc style of consultation with his advisors, Johnson felt comfortable with different people and favored their views.

Johnson's first meeting with the Joint Chiefs of Staff occurred on 29 November. Taylor suggested to the President that military advice should transcend "purely military considerations" and recommended that Johnson adopt Kennedy's instructions to the Chiefs to place military advice in a broader political and economic context. Johnson agreed to retain those guidelines. He also indicated that he expected the Chiefs' unqualified support. [13]

The new President was an extraordinarily complex individual, a physically imposing man with an ego and ambitions the size of his native Texas. A remarkably adroit politician, brilliant legislator, and highly successful Senate majority leader, he was a driven man, prodigiously energetic, single-minded, manipulative, and often overbearing. At the same time, he could be generous, warm, and compassionate toward other people, and he was fiercely loyal to those who stood by him. [14]

McNamara recalled:

Lyndon Baines Johnson was one of the most complex, intelligent, and hard-working individuals I have ever known. He possessed a kaleidoscopic personality: by turns open and devious, loving and mean, compassionate and tough, gentle and cruel. He was a towering, powerful, paradoxical figure. … Johnson was a very rough individual, rough on his friends as well as his enemies. He took every person's measure. He sought to find a person's weakness, and once he found it, he tried to play on it. He could be a bully, though he was never that way with me. He learned that I would deal straight with him, telling him what I believed rather than what I thought he wanted to hear, but also that once he, as the President, made a decision, I would do all in my power to carry it out. [15]

Despite his considerable accomplishments, Johnson remained profoundly insecure, especially regarding foreign policy. He viewed the emerging crisis in Vietnam as a crucial test of strength for his personal prestige, his authority as President of the United States and leader of the Free World, and indeed for his manhood. [16]

According to McMaster, Johnson's insecurity made him crave and demand affirmation. His lack of self-confidence manifested itself in a reluctance to trust those around him. His preoccupation with consensus and unity derived from his insecurity and his consequent distrust of his advisors. At times, Johnson would seem almost paranoid about dissent. His quest for reassurance and support, rather than wide-ranging debate on policy issues, would taint Johnson's relationship with the Chiefs and his other advisors and determine who exerted influence over U.S. policy toward Vietnam. Johnson was especially distrustful of his military advisors. His self-doubt and his willingness to forgo the truth would color his relationship with his principal military advisors and shape the process by which the U.S. would become more deeply involved in the Vietnam War. [17]

Johnson was a strong believer in the efficacy of military force as an instrument of foreign policy, but he had little confidence in the nation's top military leaders. Having sat on a series of congressional committees as a self-appointed "watchdog" over the military establishment, Johnson had grown disillusioned with the policy expertise of admirals or generals who seemed to him uninspired, disorganized, and ill-informed. "We must get rid of the indecisive, stupid, selfish, and incompetent among our generals, admirals, and others in high military positions," Johnson once exclaimed. Few uniformed leaders beyond Eisenhower had the new President's respect, and none could claim his friendship. [18]

The more Johnson learned about the workings of the Pentagon, the less he admired the workings of the so-called military mind. As Vice President, Johnson had particularly disdained LeMay. Johnson would later boast as President of having told the Chiefs, "You've done a good job of protecting my two girls for seventeen years, but you're the biggest wasters and spenders in the country." Initially, Johnson expected his senior military leaders to simply execute his orders. He did not trust them with any part in policy making beyond being implementers or obedient uniformed servants of a policy formulated by his civilian national security advisors. (Johnson's perspectives and expectations would evolve over time. He would come to trust Wheeler's counsel and eventually consider "Buzz" one of his closest friends in Washington.) [19]

Johnson also brought with him to the White House a long history of taking positions on military issues to enhance his political fortunes. Fully aware of how an ambitious politician might use military issues to attack his Administration, he would take great care to maintain the appearance, if not the reality, of close consultation with his military advisors. [20]

Johnson had the worst relationship with the American military of all 20th-century Presidents. Indeed, post-World War II civil-military relations would reach their nadir under his Administration. Against a background of organizational chaos, Johnson would ignore the Chiefs (and most other senior military officers), fail to provide them with clear policy guidance, personally insult them on more than one occasion, and patronize them on others. McNamara, too, would mislead and occasionally lie to the Chiefs—all the while expecting them to win a war in Vietnam, a war on which their counsel counted for little. [21]

## *Taylor*

Taylor had enjoyed close personal ties with Kennedy and his family, but Johnson may have considered that a liability. The status of their relationship was unclear at first. Nevertheless, Taylor required the new President's help to consolidate his power in the chairmanship and expand that position's prerogatives. In order to centralize authority, he assigned unprecedented responsibilities and latitude to Goodpaster, who became a de facto Deputy Chairman. In Taylor's absence, Goodpaster would attend White House and other high-level policy and planning sessions instead of another Chief. This allowed Taylor to retain more control over the advice that the JCS gave, and thus, the other Chiefs had less access to and influence with the President. Taylor wanted to formalize Goodpaster's position as the Assistant Chairman, Joint Chiefs of Staff, a maneuver that required considerable political support. The Chiefs, however, recognized Taylor's bid to expand his power, and they resisted it.

On 11 December, Johnson voiced his support for Taylor's consolidation of advisory influence at the chairman-level since it would help satisfy his penchant for unity and consensus. Taylor would help keep the Chiefs from voicing dissent over Administration policies while limiting their access to deliberations on sensitive issues. Johnson also pledged his unqualified backing for McNamara and the civilians who worked for him. In turn, Taylor would demonstrate the same loyalty to Johnson that he had shown to Kennedy. As Johnson confronted instability in Vietnam, Taylor's and McNamara's dominance over the Chiefs would grow. [22]

## *1964*

## *Official Functions*

Aboard a military aircraft bound for Colorado, Betty penned a letter to her mother on 14 January 1964.

> I had planned a session with all the help yesterday morning. It took them so long to get in they weren't all there early. Saw the cooks. Laid the plans for the dinner next Tuesday (have really worked over this one.) We've such a heavy schedule the next two weeks, we planned meals through the 27th. By then

everyone was in. What a session! Such a bunch of 'little boys'. Sgt. Short about the worst. By the time we were through, I think they sounded silly to themselves and also realized that I valued Sgt. Short as my cook, but he is not a personal friend, and that no one of them was a fair-haired boy. What a life! It's wonderful! [23]

The Wheelers had recently attended a dinner party at the White House.

Mrs. Johnson really did look extremely pretty. Bus and I sipped champagne in the Red Room while the dancers danced. A little after twelve Ted Clifton came along and said that it was all right to leave before the President did. On the way out met Happy Hubert Humphrey, and he asked me to dance. Most pleasant, and not as silly as some of his pictures make him look. That over, we went. [24]

The Wheelers had also attended the Neighbors Club tea at the Trinidad & Tobago Embassy. Betty was the Assistant Treasurer of the group. "I have the meeting next month," she wrote. "Will take them to the Pentagon. Bus is going to take them to 'the Tank' and give them a short briefing on the Joint Chiefs, then back to the house for lunch." [25]

*Wheeler speaks with members of the 5th Infantry Division while observing field training at Fort Carson, Colorado, January 1964. (Office of the Chief of Staff of the Army).*

In Colorado, Wheeler attended a convention of the Association of the United States Army (AUSA), visited the Air Force Academy and the North American Aerospace Defense Command (NORAD) headquarters, and observed field training conducted by the 5th Infantry Division (Mechanized) at Fort Carson.

He and Betty stayed in a new wing of the old Broadmoor Hotel, site of the AUSA convention. "What a suite we had", Betty wrote, "to include two little dressing rooms and two baths, a magnificent view. How blessed we are in the wonderful experiences that we're being given. ... The AUSA dinner was the usual banquet. ... I had a delightful time. Bus's talk good, not too long." [26]

Three days later, Betty reported that "Kitsy [Westmoreland] arrived this morning ... for breakfast. She is already moving into the quarters [at Fort] Wainwright [in Manila] ... and it is miserable there. Westy goes to Vietnam. They pull out in the next few weeks. She's such a dear but she wears me out." [27]

In a ceremony in the Pentagon on 20 January, Vance presented the Distinguished Service Medal to Wheeler as Vice Chief of Staff of the Army General "Ham" Hamlett read the citation. The following day, Wheeler and other senior Army commanders met with the President in the Cabinet Room. [28]

## Frustrated and Misled

Former Chief of Staff of the Army Ridgway cautioned that the Secretary of Defense's and the President's decisions, "on which the fate of this nation depends, *must be made only after full consideration has been given to the views of all the Joint Chiefs.* Certainly they should never be made on the advice of one member only, no matter how closely his views may accord with their wishes, whether he be the Chairman or any other." [29]

Johnson's deep distrust of his senior military officers manifested itself in exclusive advisory forums that limited the Chiefs' access to him. Taylor deliberately misrepresented the Chiefs' opinions in those forums and helped McNamara forge a consensus behind a fundamentally flawed strategic concept that would enable deepening American involvement in Vietnam without consideration of its long-term costs and consequences. [30]

General Wallace "Wally" M. Greene, Jr. replaced Shoup as the Commandant of the Marine Corps on 1 January 1964. General Bruce Palmer, Jr. described Greene as "courteous, poker-faced ... sometimes quite professorial in his approach, which had earned him the nickname of 'schoolboy Greene'." [31]

*General Maxwell D. Taylor, Admiral David L. McDonald, General Curtis E. Lemay, and Wheeler during the Forrestal Memorial Dinner, Washington, DC, March 1964. (Office of the Chief of Staff of the Army).*

On 6 March, the Chiefs visited the headquarters of the Atlantic Command in Norfolk, Virginia and toured several naval vessels the U.S. Atlantic Fleet. [32]

## *Quarters 1*

Meanwhile back at Fort Myer, the Wheelers had decided they needed to replace the noncommissioned officer-in-charge of their nine-man household staff. Betty recorded:

> Sgt. Paul is clearing 'his' office and he will be out of the house before today is over. He and I had a calm talk and we parted friends, certainly on the surface. Bus has gotten him a good job here, so that he won't have to give up his quarters or make a drastic change. Bus, by the way, did the firing, but naturally I couldn't let him go without talking to him. Sgt. Cavello takes over. One thing [is] sure, he will run the house. I wouldn't be surprised if Hillard and Dunston [their drivers] are short

timers. Bus has a session with everyone in the morning. I've talked to Sgts. Short and Gill. They will take over the marketing. The flowers may become my department. However, I have always loved doing them and I will have to be a little less free with my time on party days. One thing I know, if absolutely necessary, Gill can do a beautiful job. [33]

Sergeant First Class Hank Covello, a former World War II paratrooper, proved just the man for the job and would supervise the Wheelers' household staff in both Quarters 1 and Quarters 6 until his retirement in 1965. [34]

Covello made purchases for the official dinners and cocktail parties that Betty often hosted. He also prepared Bus's uniforms and gave his shoes and boots an "Airborne spit-shine." On trips away from Washington, Covello often carried Bus's briefcase. During the Wheelers' trip to Finland, Bus looked out the window as their aircraft taxied up to a large welcoming party. "Sergeant Covello," he said, "your honor guard awaits you!" [35]

Covello also helped Betty with the family's personal purchases, including clothing, cigarettes, and alcohol "for the general's private stock." He recalled Bus had no favorite brand of cigarette and smoked Lucky Strikes, Pall Malls, or whatever Covello brought home that was on sale. Bus would switch to milder cigarettes and pipes after his heart attack in July 1967, but never attempted to quit altogether. [36]

Master Sergeant Bill Stewart, who would join the Wheeler's household staff later that year, distinctly remembers, "Betty drank vermouth with a lemon or lime twist over crushed ice. Bus liked scotch and soda, and both always had wine with dinner." Bim added, "Bus [also] liked a very dry martini before dinner. I had many of them with him. He was a heavy drinker, but in my mind controlled." [37]

Betty had been right about Hillard being a short timer. Covello suspected him and two other orderlies of "stealing some of the booze from the general's own stock." He started marking the bottles, and when he had enough evidence of their guilt informed Betty of the situation. Bus relieved them. One black orderly made Betty nervous, so she asked Bus to get rid of him, too. Bus always supported Betty's decisions, since the household was her domain. [38]

Stewart recalls the Wheelers as very kind and generous in gift giving to their household staff. Covello agreed, saying that Bus and Betty were both very gracious and appreciative of their enlisted help. Covello said that he could do no wrong by them, and he found them both very easy to work with. He described Bus as "a Southern gentleman" who "never raised his voice" and always complimented the work of his household staff. Covello particularly appreciated Bus's gratitude when severe weather forced the relocation of a 400-seat garden party indoors on short notice. [39]

"[He was] a general of generals," Covello said. "A wonderful man to work for ... thoughtful, gracious, and affectionate with his family." [40]

According to Stewart, the Wheelers were more diplomatic than many of the other senior general officers and their wives whom he worked for. The Wheelers, he said, "seemed destined to be in those high positions." [41]

Covello remembers Betty as "a beautiful, nice lady who was fussy and always knew what she wanted." She showed him how make the flower arrangements look just so. Her "persnickety" attention to detail and high standards were appropriate, he thought, considering they often entertained such illustrious guests as former President Eisenhower, retired General of the Army Omar Bradley, and World War I hero Sergeant Alvin York. [42]

Covello recalled that Bus's breakfast routine never varied. It always included cigarettes, bacon, eggs, grits, and more cigarettes. "He would read the papers and smoke. And then he'd eat, have another cigarette, and eat some more. All the while, he was looking at the newspapers." [43]

"John Fischer.... was my first boss," Bim recalled. "He and his wife Jenny were the only ones of my friends who were allowed to call my father Bus." Fischer recalled that Drew Pearson, a syndicated columnist, had written an article in which he criticized General Wheeler by name. "I asked [Bus] whether he was going to reply. He looked at me and said, 'My friend, you never get into a pissing contest with a skunk.'" [44]

Bus never skipped the sports page. He had always loved baseball and followed the major league closely. His recollection of statistics and players was phenomenal. His all-time favorite player was Walter Johnson, who famously pitched for the Washington Senators from 1907-1927. [45]

Bus's mother, Mums, frequently spent the night with the Wheelers in their quarters. She had lived in northern Virginia with Bus's stepsister Betty Jean for several years. Betty Jean and her husband both worked, so it had been agreed that Mums would watch over their young children during workdays. This arrangement would have been fine, but for Mums's often-incapacitating drinking binges. Several mornings, Betty Jean was compelled to beg Betty to come over from Fort Myer to watch the kids because Mums was plastered. This was quite an inconvenience, given the busy schedule Betty kept with all the official functions she was obligated to attend or host in her quarters. Nevertheless, she always picked up the slack. She was none too happy about it, though. Bus was also exasperated with his mother, often referring to her as "that stupid little woman." [46]

Despite her frequent incapacitation, Mums was very intelligent and had a sharp memory. She was a formidable bridge player who kept track of every card in play. Stewart had no knowledge of her alcohol related incidents and remembered Mums as very nice and sweet. "Now Bus," Stewart recalls her saying on more than one occasion, "you be good to my boys (the household orderlies)." Whenever she stayed at Quarters 6, "she always had four slices of crispy bacon, one slice of toast, a Coca-Cola, and a cigarette for breakfast." [47]

Betty's parents also stayed with them several times. Whenever they did, Covello picked up brand-new five-dollar bills from the bank for Betty's dad to hand out as tips for the staff. [48]

## Army Matters

Hamlett suffered a heart attack on 26 March. "As a result, the Argentina trip has been cancelled," Betty reported. "The plans for us were wonderful, and I've been looking forward to it. [But,] it's time Bus had a break again. ... Even Italy is questionable but at the moment we'll probably get to Paris & England ... for the Queen's birthday party and Ascot." [49]

On the Saturday before Easter, the telephone in Quarters 1 rang at 5:30 A. M., summoning Wheeler to the Pentagon. There had been a devastating earthquake in Anchorage, Alaska.

"What an awful thing," Betty commented. "I let the help go after I had my lunch. It seemed good to have a completely empty house. We need it once in awhile." Bus returned home later that afternoon. "We played gin. Bus grilled Cornish hens. Afterwards we looked at a movie." On Easter Sunday, the Wheelers attended a service at the Fort Myer Chapel. That evening, "more gin, steaks … early to bed." [50]

## Tuesday Luncheons

Meanwhile, Johnson drew his advisory circle even tighter as the election approached. He met with his closest advisors every Tuesday for lunch. The principal participants in this advisory and decision-making forum were Rusk, McGeorge Bundy, and McNamara. Begun on 4 February, just eleven weeks after Johnson became President, these Tuesday luncheons became councils in which Johnson discussed both foreign and domestic policy. Twenty more would be held in the spring and summer of 1964. According to Johnson's later National Security Advisor, Walt W. Rostow, the Tuesday luncheons were the "heart" of the national security process, and "the only men present were those whose advice the President most wanted to hear." The agenda often included both Vietnam and the election campaign. No military officer, not even Taylor, was a regular member of the select group. [51]

The luncheon forum was designed to achieve consensus on major policy issues and, by its exclusivity, to prevent leaks of those discussions to Congress or the press. The advisors' desire to demonstrate unity inspired them to coordinate their positions before discussing them with Johnson. Rusk and McNamara "almost never went to the President with a divided opinion." They encouraged close contact between their departments at all levels. According to Rostow, Bundy, McNamara, and Rusk "regarded themselves as kind of a family." Because McNamara was the most assertive of the President's personal advisors, his opinions on the war dominated the discussions. [52]

The Tuesday luncheons further isolated the Chiefs from the planning and decision-making process. Because the advice that Johnson received represented a coordinated position between the Secretaries of State and Defense, it was unlikely that the President or the other civilian advisors would question it. The President would remain ignorant of the Chiefs' opinions, and the Chiefs would remain ill-informed of the direction in which the Administration's Vietnam policy was headed (at least until Wheeler as Chairman finally demanded and was granted a seat in April 1966.) [53]

## *Far East*

On 18 April, Wheeler, Rusk, and Assistant Secretary of State for Far Eastern Affairs William P. Bundy departed for Saigon with their wives. The Wheelers would then take an extended, twelve-day trip through the Far East. [54]

Betty wrote about the party's layover in Anchorage, where they viewed the destruction from the recent earthquake and the ongoing recovery efforts.

> We were met at the plane, taken to coffee and then we had a forty minute ride around Anchorage. It really is a shambles. Like the bombings, one must see [it] to really believe. The miracle is that so few lives were lost. Also, that it didn't come when school was in session. Both the high school and grade school were destroyed. All plans seem to be to build on the same spot. To me it looks hopeless as there are so many deep crevices. [55]

Upon their arrival in South Vietnam, they were met planeside by "Kitsy and Westy ... along with Betty and Paul Harkins. It was well after dark so we saw little of Saigon on the way in. [The change in time zones] was strange. Had no feeling of the loss of the day. We came in, Paul and Bus went to work almost immediately for an hour. Betty showed me the house."

The Wheelers stayed overnight in the Harkins's ample quarters.

> It is magnificent. An entrance hall, a huge living room, the ceilings are at least twenty feet high, four ceiling fans, a large dining room, a serving pantry, the kitchen out of the house as are old plantation homes. There is a covered walk. There is a beautiful porch off the dining room. Off the living room, a small room, air conditioned, and another small room with a bar in it, air conditioned. For all this house, I think only two bedrooms and two baths, the bedrooms [are] air conditioned. [56]

While Wheeler, Rusk, and Bundy met with Lodge, Harkins, and Westmoreland, Betty accompanied the other wives on tours around Saigon. She reported:

> As would be expected Saigon is very French. Lots of balconies and wrought iron. Interestingly there seem to be no bugs. It's hot, hot, hot. There has been no rain since October and yet everything is green. The bougainvillea [is] heavenly. The rain will come in May I am told.
>
> Kitsy, Betty [Harkins], and I started out at 8:30 Thursday morning. The Americans are confined to the city. It is hard to realize that a serious war is going on not fifty miles away. We drove around, and then went to the market. It is filled with everything under heaven. The fruits and vegetables [are] beautiful. There is stall after stall of brass. We've been to lunch and dinner every day. Last night the Lodges gave a dinner for the Rusks. Everyone most affable. [57]

Their evenings were filled, as well. "Betty and Paul had a dinner for us the night after we got in," Betty continued. "Tonight, the men go to a stag dinner given by General Khanh. Kitsy is having us, the ladies, tonight." [58]

> I unfortunately woke up with a bug this morning. I managed to attend a morning coffee but gave up on a trip to hospitals and lunch. Betty [Harkins] said she was glad I hadn't tried to go [to] the Vietnam Hospital with my stomach in the state it was. She said the hospital was jammed. They were bringing in wounded and dead while they were there, and she said they were spared nothing. I think she was slightly ill when she came in. [59]

On 27-28 April, the Wheelers visited Singapore and Kuala Lumpur, Malaysia, where Bus met with his counterpart, Lieutenant General Tenguku Osman, the Chief of Malaysian Armed Forces. The following afternoon, they departed for Hawaii. They left Hawaii the next night and arrived in Washington on the morning of 30 April. [60]

## *Germany*

Over the weekend of 9-10 May, the Wheelers accompanied the McNamaras on an official trip to Germany and Austria. Their itinerary, as recorded by Betty, was typical of the numerous European trips the Wheelers would subsequently take over the next six years.

> In Bonn, Margie McNamara and I were greeted with huge bouquets of pink carnations. After the official greeting and McNamara's press conference we took off for the American Embassy residence. It's a lovely house with a large garden. It's on the Rhine. [61]

After lunch at the embassy, they went to the airport for a flight to Munich where "Bus had to pay a call on the Minister-President of Bavaria." That evening, they attended the opera and then had a late dinner.

At "ten-thirty ... the next morning ... they took us by helicopter to the Linderhof for a tour of the palace and grotto." Next, they flew on to Garmisch, where they boarded a cable car for lunch on the summit of the Zugspitze. (Remarkably, during none of the many times the Wheelers had stayed in Garmisch since 1947, had they never been to the summit!) "We were back in Bonn ... by seven."

The next morning, while Bus attended meetings, Betty and the other ladies took a two-hour drive through the vineyards planted along the steep slopes of the region, followed by an hour-long river cruise from Linz to Bonn. "Bus met the boat, we bid goodbye and went to the airport. ... It was a marvelous trip!" [62]

## *Entertaining*

In mid-May, Betty invited Washington social columnist Betty Beale to their quarters to write an article about one of their official dinner parties. "Have dreaded having [her]," she informed her mother. "She's old Washington family, and very acceptable. However, her column can be acid, and hated to expose us to it. Considering all [Sgt.] Short has to do is cook, he should cook better than any General! We just didn't mention that we have two cooks." [63]

Betty had always enjoyed her role as a hostess, and she entertained to impress. Every Monday morning, she met with the staff to review the week's social requirements. Each month, she required new dishes to be introduced. Betty and Bus nominated some, the staff others. The Wheelers approved all new recipes before they were served to guests. [64]

Betty was a stickler for impeccable table service. It was the major domo's responsibility to observe the meal and direct the waiters when to clear a course, when to begin serving the next, and when to freshen guests' glasses. Timing was everything, and whenever it was off, Betty became most anxious and told the staff about it afterwards. For less formal dinners when it was inappropriate to have a major domo in the dining room, Betty had a buzzer installed under the table at her place so she could prompt the wait staff herself. [65]

The waiters served dinners in the Russian style, which meant the meat, starch, vegetables, and sauce were served together from a single platter. This differed from the French style in which the components were served from separate platters. [66]

After a particularly wonderful dinner party at the Wheelers', Beale proclaimed Quarters 1 the "best restaurant in town." It was a tremendous honor that made the Wheelers and their household staff very proud. [67]

As a special reward to the staff during particularly successful formal dinners, Betty would summon them into the dining room at the end of the meal and introduce them to their distinguished guests. Stewart recalls that other general officers later emulated this practice that the Wheelers had initiated. [68]

Bus worked very long hours as the Chief of Staff of the Army and continued to do so later as the Chairman, frequently as late as 10:30 PM. On the nights he was able to get home at a decent hour, it was most often to host or attend an official function. Regardless of the time that Bus got home, Betty always waited to have dinner with him. If it was particularly late, the kitchen staff would leave whatever dinner they had prepared for the family on a hotplate. [69]

Throughout the final eight years of Bus's career, the Wheelers usually dined formally, even if it was just the two of them. This kept the wait staff in top form, Betty insisted. They always dressed for dinner, Betty into a long gown, Bus replacing his uniform coat with a sports jacket. They often requested lamb chops for dinner, Stewart recalls. They always had cocktail hour, too, during which they recounted the highlights of their day, discussed plans for upcoming events and functions, played cards, or did a crossword puzzle. [70]

Wearing the summer dress white uniforms of their respective Services, the Chiefs and their wives joined the McNamaras, Vances, the new Secretary of the Army Stephen Ailes and his wife, plus other senior DOD civilians and their wives at the White House on 19 May for a garden party.

"President and Mrs. Johnson gave the Military Reception," Betty explained. "We were received in the Blue Room. The 'we' being … not more than 15 or 20. It was very nice. She, as can be imagined, is easy to talk to and I certainly feel now that we have met socially." [71]

Betty also informed her mother that she and Bus were going "to England on the 11th [of June]. … Can't you just see Bus in a morning coat with a grey-gray ascot and pearl-gray top hat? He wears the same on three separate occasions." [72]

## Fort Monroe

On 28 May, the Wheelers visited Fort Monroe, Virginia with Lieutenant General Harold K. "Johnny" Johnson and his wife Dorothy. As the Assistant Deputy Chief of Staff for Military Operations (Operations and Plans), or "Ops Deputy", Johnson was one of Wheeler's right-hand men and often attended the Chiefs' tank sessions with him.

In retrospect, one may suppose that the trip was an opportunity for Wheeler to vet Johnson — a 52-year-old native of Bowesmont, North Dakota and a survivor of the Bataan Death March -- as a potential candidate to replace him as Chief of Staff of the Army, but it wasn't. [73] Wheeler would not discover until 22 June — the day before the President announced it — that he had been selected to replace Taylor as the Chairman of the Joint Chiefs of Staff. It seems, rather, that a curious coincidence of duty took them to Fort Monroe.

Betty recorded:

> We had a good time [there]. ... I'd rather hoped [to spend] the morning with ... [Dorothy] Johnson, but of course, that didn't work. However, she and Johnny were at the honor guard for Bus. Johnny was a Capt. – Company Commander when we went to [Fort] Benning. Saw them last about ten years ago. [74]

The Wheelers' hosts took them out on the Chesapeake Bay to fish and have lunch. "While on the boat, Gen. Taylor called Bus, no JCS meeting the next day, so Bus decided to stay over in the morning." They attended a reception that evening, to which the Johnsons had also been invited. [75]

The next day, the Johnsons joined them on a second fishing trip. "So, we had a good chance to catch up. Such fun to see them happy and fun to be with. Some of these folks can be pretty depressing," opined Betty. "We were home [at Fort Myer] about five. Let the help go. We had Cornish hens on the spit." [76]

*Bus and Betty Wheeler after he received an honorary Doctor of Laws degree from the University of Akron, 2 June 1964. (Office of the Chief of Staff of the Army).*

On the afternoon of 1 June, the Wheelers departed Washington for a trip to Ohio. Bus had been invited by the University of Akron to deliver the graduation address, help award diplomas, and to receive an honorary Doctor of Laws degree. "Very nice of them," Betty remarked. [77]

An undercover security guard provided by the university for Wheeler gave Odom a copy of the Akron newspaper with an article concerning Wheeler's visit. A smaller article next to it was entitled "How to Become a General," written by a local nine-year-old boy. The gist of the article was that to become a general, one has to crawl through the mud, under barbed wire, through sewer pipes, and be able to shinny up trees. Then he becomes a general. After returning to the Pentagon, Odom sent the article in to Wheeler, who replied red ink, "I'm not sure I can do any of these, at least not now." [78]

## Aides

Meanwhile, Wheeler had recently selected two new Aides-de-Camp. Odom had been selected to command an Infantry battalion in Vietnam and was scheduled to deploy in mid-July.

The Wheelers hosted "an 'Aides' party for Lou and [his wife] Charlotte" on 9 June. "I haven't met the new Aides yet, or their wives," Betty added. "Charlotte will go home [to Mississippi on the] 15th of June. Lou leaves middle of July [for Vietnam. Colonel] Bob Guthrie in August." [79]

(Thirty-nine years later, Odom would write to Bim, "If such were possible, I would 'cast out' a nationwide challenge for any previous or current Aide-de-Camp to any Army Chief of Staff and Chairman, JCS; who benefited by and enjoyed that position more than me. I still 'pinch myself' when my thoughts harken back to my service to your father (and your mother)." ) [80]

## England

Betty had continued sewing her own dresses, even after Bus became Chief of Staff of the Army. Her letters to her mother are replete with descriptions of whatever dress she was currently sewing to wear whatever upcoming social to event. For their upcoming trip to England, however, Betty splurged. "I went to Garfinkles and spent a fortune. My outfit for Ascot is very lovely. … It's a smashing outfit! I can parade with my handsome man in his gray top hat!" [81]

The Wheelers departed Washington for England at 6:00 P. M. on 11 June. "We had dinner on the plane," Betty recorded. "After [a layover for refueling in] Newfoundland we went to bed." [82]

They landed at Northholt, the Royal Air Force Base at 2:00 P. M. London time. "We were greeted by General and Lady Baker, and our military attaché and his wife, the Dyers. The Bakers had been in Paris while we were there. ... There was an honor guard and then we drove into town. ... It took about 45 minutes to get to the Grosvenor House." [83]

On the drive, Lady Baker asked Betty, "Do you go on to Paris from here?"

Betty replied, "Oh no. We have to go right home. We missed the Paris part of the trip."

"I don't mean that," said Lady Baker. "When do you take Lemnitzer's place?"

"I didn't know we were," replied Betty.

Lady Baker said cheerily, "Well then if you really don't know, I suppose you couldn't say. I'm telling you, you are. Everyone here knows it!" (The rumors would persist even after Wheeler was sworn in as Chairman. "Observers say there is a distinct possibility that he will eventually succeed Gen. Lyman Lemnitzer as the Supreme Allied Commander (in Europe)," the *New York News* would report in July.) [84]

The Wheelers had tea that afternoon at their hotel. That evening, "Bus [went] to a stag dinner and I [left] at 6:45 for the ballet 'Sleeping Beauty' at the theater ... and supper ... at a very gay little restaurant ... with Lady Hull and Mrs. Dyer." [85]

They attended the Trooping of the Colour the next day. Betty wrote:

> You should have seen Bus. He looked absolutely divine, and surely had been wearing a 'topper' all his life! ... Needless to say, we had marvelous seats. ... It was a magnificent sight. The Queen Mother arrived in her coach. The trooping of the colour [is] a tremendous thing to see. The whole ceremony takes a little over an hour. There was a reception in the Old War Office (just across the street from the ceremony) afterwards. [86]

After lunch on their own in the hotel, the Wheelers changed clothes and packed to go to the country for the weekend. "We [went] to Bovington, the British Armoured Center near Dorset," Betty explained. "We stopped to see the cathedral at Salisbury. ... Our hosts at Bovington were Gen. and Mrs. Armitage. ... We got in ... with barely time to change for an eight o'clock black tie dinner." [87]

The following morning, Bus and General Armitage went fishing. "No luck," Betty reported. She and Mrs. Armitage joined their husbands for a picnic lunch. Afterward, the men resumed their fishing while their wives visited an ancient church near Steeple. "An ancestor of George Washington had attended there and on the wall his coat of arms – stars & bars. [Some] British feel this may be why Washington chose stars & bars for the [American] flag." They had a small dinner that night with their hosts and Odom. [88]

The next day, the Wheelers returned by helicopter to London. "What a thrill it was, the last little bit we came down the Thames. ... Bus gave a speech." That afternoon, "Bus donned his finery again and off we went to Windsor Castle" to attend the Order of the Garter investiture ceremony. [89] Betty continued:

> We had absolutely perfect seats on the aisle. The Queen Mother, the Queen and Phillip all smiled at me when they went by. I suppose that I should have been 'bobbing'. Lady Hull was as excited as I about the whole thing. The Hulls by the way were our hosts. He's the British Chief of Staff. She said the likes of them would never get invited to such a ceremony. She was grateful for our influential friends! Our friend by the way was Lord Louis [Mountbatten who had had remained in contact with Bus ever since their first encounter in Trieste.]! Lady Hull was sure that he had told the Queen where we'd be. Otherwise, why should all three of them be turning toward us as they went by? A nice thought. It was a most impressive ceremony. Some of the members of the order were so old it was a tug at the heart. [90]

Later, they returned to London, changed clothes, then attended a cocktail party at "Dickie" Mountbatten's residence. "[We] saw the upstairs this time," Betty wrote. "Such a beautiful house. It was a very fine party." The Wheelers encountered more speculation that Bus would soon return to Paris to replace Lemnitzer as SACEUR. "Lord Louis had Ambassadors to London at his party, and Bus says something is afoot," Betty continued. "However, I'm afraid it's because they were so sure when he came home [to become Chief of Staff of the Army] that he'll be back. Something will have to break soon." The Wheelers discussed the matter over dinner alone that evening. [91]

The following morning, they drove out to the Royal Military Academy at Sandhurst where Bus and Betty were taken on separate tours. Afterward, they changed into formal outfits in the Commandant's house, then departed for lunch and the races at the Royal Ascot. They departed England that evening and returned home to Washington on the morning of 17 June. [92]

## *New Country Team*

Meanwhile the previous day, Johnson had announced his decision to replace the U.S. leadership team in South Vietnam. Taylor would retire from the U.S. Army for the second time and replace Lodge as U.S. Ambassador. U. Alexis Johnson, a highly esteemed career diplomat, was appointed as Taylor's deputy. Westmoreland would replace Harkins as MACV Commander. These changes had a cascading effect, as an acceptable replacement would have to be found for Taylor as Chairman, which, in turn, would create a vacancy in one of the Service Chiefs' positions. [93]

*Wheeler during General Harkins's retirement ceremony, Fort Myer, Virginia, 22 June 1964.*
*(Office of the Chief of Staff of the Army).*

On 22 June, Betty reported that "Paul and Betty Harkins arrived today. Bus met them. They had no date for dinner, so they had dinner with us. ... Feel like they should be staying with us. I'm not much in the mood but it doesn't matter. ... They don't seem to know what they'll do [in retirement]. They'll be here [in Washington] about six weeks." [94]

"I talked to Helen LeMay this morning," she added.

Helen had asked her, "When do you leave for Paris?"

"I'm not that I know of," replied Betty.

"That's funny," Helen said. "That's all anyone talks about over there [in Europe]."

*So, what goes on?*, Betty wondered. They found out later that day, but the news was not what they had anticipated, nor what they had hoped for. [95]

## Wheeler's Selection

"I have come to understand the importance of an intimate, easy relationship, born of friendship and mutual regard, between the President and the Chiefs," Taylor wrote. "It is particularly important in the case of the Chairman.

... The Chairman should be a true believer in the foreign policy and military strategy of the Administration which he serves." [96]

How the Chiefs would respond to the President's expectations going forward would largely depend upon the character of the man who replaced Taylor as Chairman. Accepting Taylor's recommendation, Johnson announced on 23 June his appointment of Wheeler for the job. [97]

Wheeler's selection was largely by default. LeMay was *persona non grata* with the Administration and was scheduled to retire in eight months. Greene and McDonald, who were outspoken critics of the Administration's foreign policy in Southeast Asia, could not be counted upon as "team players." McDonald had also been on the job for only ten months, *Time* magazine noted, and "[he] is still learning the ropes." This left only Wheeler. [98]

Initially, LeMay was suspicious of Wheeler and, in reference to his relationship with Taylor, once referred to him as "Polly Parrot." A Marine Colonel on Greene's staff regarded Wheeler as "the Army's highest-ranking sycophant." Deference to Taylor's views was not surprising, however, given that he had arranged Wheeler's promotions. Certainly, Wheeler and Westmoreland both recognized Taylor's preponderant influence with the President. Taylor later described relations between the three of them as "harmonious." [99]

Wheeler would be the third Army officer in a row to serve as Chairman. "The Pentagon high command change announced yesterday shatters the precedent of rotating the Chairman of the Joint Chiefs of Staff among the Services and continues the Army-dominated thinking at the top defense level," reported the *Washington Post*. McMaster suggests, therefore, that Wheeler's appointment was "immensely unpopular," particularly among Navy and Air Force officers. [100]

The *Washington Post* praised Wheeler's appointment, however, noting that "for the first time it puts into the nation's top ranking military post [an] officer who is better known for his joint service attitude than his service partisanship. Gen. Earle G. Wheeler ... is one of the new breed of military men who grew up since unification and made their mark working on joint planning staffs with emphasis on a united Service approach." [101]

Cautiously and non-parochially, Wheeler had deferred committing himself in the ongoing Army-Air Force dispute over aviation roles and missions until studies could be completed. [102]

The *Washington Post* explained:

> Most previous Chairmen have been rather partisan minded and, while they tried to be fair in their unofficial role as chief military advisor to the President and the Secretary [of Defense], their Service usually fared better than its rivals during their regime. … While Wheeler certainly is less parochial than past Chairmen, his basic thinking is Army oriented. He is something of a protégé of Taylor, a strong man who has strongly influenced U.S. military policy since 1961, along land warfare concepts rather than seapower and airpower lines. [103]

The *New York Times* predicted that Wheeler:

> … will in presiding over the most important military body in the government, be a mediator and an advocate, rather than a 'boss,' or a representative for the Secretary of Defense. He will do no violence to the point of view of those who believe that our strategic concepts must be the product of group thought, not that of one man. But his skill as a conciliator will probably help preserve the harmonious relationships between the White House and the Pentagon that distinguished the chairmanship of Gen. Maxwell D. Taylor. [104]

Goodpaster may well have had Wheeler in mind when he observed, "The elements that go into inspiring trust are a style that is not offensive to the majority, a transcending honesty, a high-level of intelligence, a willingness to deal with problems that immediately touch people's lives, a sense of patriotism, and public confidence in those to whom Presidents lend their prestige and authority." [105]

Wheeler and Goodpaster were prime examples of what historian Arthur M. Schlesinger Jr., describes as an emerging "new class of professional warriors." They were quite similar, both in personality and leadership style, which may explain their professional and personal affinity for one another. According to Bim, "Dad really liked Andy." [106] (Wheeler would appoint Goodpaster to his old job as Director of the Joint Staff in 1966.)

Both were unassuming, understated, quietly self-confident, and focused. They were serious, yet approachable in a no-nonsense way. They dressed neatly, but not stylishly. They smiled readily, and were courteous, but not obsequious. Both led by quiet persuasion, rational discourse, and by unfailing courtesy and consideration for others. Bellicosity was not their style. Both succeeded in playing by the rules at each level of their careers, yet neither was a "yes-man." They did not seek the limelight, nor did they shirk from it, either. Wheeler and Goodpaster reflected Marshall's professional values by keeping their political views to themselves. Both fit in well in whatever professional situations they found themselves, which is why both were so highly regarded in all quarters. Not coincidentally, both attracted the support of superiors influential in furthering their interests at every stage of their military careers. [107]

Furthermore, Wheeler and Goodpaster were among the best generals of their generation to successfully balance "the sometimes abstract nature of diplomacy as practiced by the professional diplomat with the practicality of the professional soldier." Few achieved this blend better. [108]

Wheeler's selection as Chairman was a shift away from appointing combat commanders toward officers more experienced in staff work and managing information. The Chairmen who preceded Wheeler had distinguished combat records, while "he [had] not had the personal experience of intimate leadership of men in combat" and was relatively little known to the American public. Bradley commanded a corps, an army, and an army group in World War II. Radford commanded a carrier division during the war. Twining commanded air forces in the Pacific and Europe. Lemnitzer commanded air defense brigades during World War II and an infantry division in the Korean War. Wheeler's background contrasted sharply with those officers' and that of his immediate predecessor, Taylor, who commanded an airborne division during World War II and UN forces during the last months of the Korean War. According to McMaster, some officers in the Pentagon, LeMay included, felt that without combat command experience, Wheeler lacked credibility for the job. [109]

The *New York Times* reported:

Some officers have greeted General Wheeler's promotion with mixed emotions. For his experience and his reputation have been chiefly those of a staff officer; he has had very little combat experience. His personality helps to offset this lack. And two new appointments to top commands in the Army are also counterweights. [110]

On the positive side, the *Washington Post* also reported that Wheeler "might be called the beau ideal of the modern U.S. military commander. He fits like a glove the exacting specifications laid down by President Kennedy and Defense Secretary Robert S. McNamara." The article reported that Wheeler had been "McNamara's choice for the post, ever since he served as Director of the Pentagon Joint Staff in the early days of the New Frontier." *Time* magazine reported, "Wheeler is McNamara's kind of general – a skilled staff officer who specializes in analytical answers to complex problems." [111]

Wheeler had established a good relationship with the similarly analytical-minded McNamara, who wanted "team players," not opinionated, irascible military heroes. Wheeler implemented McNamara's reforms without complaint and supported him when McNamara needed it most, during congressional hearings on the Nuclear Test Ban Treaty with the Soviet Union and Pentagon budget reforms. Wheeler rebutted, point by point before the Congress, LeMay's concerns about proposed limitations on nuclear testing and told the Senate Appropriations Committee that McNamara's budgetary methods represented a "great step forward." [112]

As Chief of Staff of the Army, Wheeler had displayed "no dramatic gift, but a notably analytical sense and a gift for clear and concise expression." The *New York News* described him as a "hard-nosed Army man … a no-nonsense officer." Wheeler had impressed McNamara and his civilian colleagues as a military officer with a feeling for facts, as well as for tradition. Wheeler had gotten along well with both the other Services and McNamara's "whiz kid" advisors. He was especially close with Vance, who on 21 January 1964 had been promoted from Secretary of the Army to Deputy Secretary of Defense. Wheeler was also mutually fond of Ailes, a native of Romney, West Virginia, who had served as Undersecretary of the Army since 1961 before replacing Vance as Secretary of the Army. [113]

"Essentially, what won Wheeler his new post was his capacity to subordinate the Army's parochial causes to 'the big picture,' plus his congeniality to such concepts as cost-effectiveness evaluation, civilian control, and flexible response," *Newsweek* reported. [114]

"Gen. Earle Wheeler won't rock the Pentagon boat," the *Wall Street Journal* estimated. "Administration men have long watched the new Joint Chiefs of Staff Chairman. They made sure his views jibed closely with the Johnson-McNamara line. Wheeler leans to stronger action in Vietnam, but the difference is only a matter of degree." [115]

Unlike a high-ranking officer coming to Washington for the first time, Wheeler was sensitive to and familiar with the political machinations of the Pentagon, the White House, and Capitol Hill. A "suave and personable Washingtonian," Wheeler's sensitivity to the politics of executive-legislative relations made him an attractive choice for Johnson. [116]

On 28 June, the *Washington Star* printed an interview with Wheeler that highlighted his unique skill at diplomatic communication:

(Wheeler), the new Chairman of the Joint Chiefs of Staff, can be expected to give high priority to the job of explaining the military to civilians and the civilians to the military. As Chief of Staff of the Army for the past two years, he has been conscious of poor communications between military men and the civilian bosses and has tried to be a bridge between the two. Gen. Wheeler has indicated in the past that he does not believe there is a serious military-civilian conflict in the Pentagon – it's just a problem of two different kinds of people talking different languages, he feels. He tries to translate. Military men become exasperated when civilians fail to see the merits of some proposal. Gen. Wheeler's solution is to present the proposals in terms acceptable to Secretary of Defense McNamara and his 'Whiz Kid' analysts. The result is that the Army now uses more thorough, open arguments based on cost-effectiveness studies and accompanied by alternative proposals for the attainment of a given objective. As a result, civilian analysts under Mr. McNamara say the Army gradually is regaining the status it lost when

Mr. McNamara set out to put Pentagon decisions on a more logical basis. Gen. Wheeler believes that all of the Services have learned the lesson and will gain more by speaking the McNamara language. [117]

The *Washington Post* noted that "there is some criticism in the Pentagon that the Joint Chiefs system is cumbersome and will not work in time of war." [118]

There is little likelihood that [Wheeler] will press for broad changes in the Joint Chiefs organization. He will try to improve procedure within the present structure. The other side of the argument – which Gen. Wheeler can be expected to make – is that a similar system worked during World War II and that present minor frictions will easily be mooted out in the great common effort that war would bring. [119]

Reportedly, Wheeler was "not worried by the efforts of civilian officials to take tight control of military operations during past crises – the Cuban blockade, for instance." Wheeler explained:

World War II gives precedent. Civilians, like President Roosevelt and Prime Minister Churchill, took personal charge of broad strategy and sometimes dipped deep into the tactics of particular operations. In a future crisis the civilians rightly will insist on supervising the details. In a war, the details would be so vast that the military commander on the scene would almost always have to run his own show – as he normally wants to do. [120]

"In general," the *Washington Post* concluded, "the new Chairman of the Joint Chiefs of Staff will seek no basic change in the role of the military." [121]

In time, Wheeler would develop a close association with the President. Johnson would eventually count Wheeler among his ten best friends in Washington. According to Goodpaster, Johnson had a way of "befriending" people and then using that friendship to exact acquiescence on controversial issues. Wheeler "did not like direct confrontation" and thus was susceptible to the President's patronage. Loyalty was the criterion Johnson and McNamara thought essential for their appointees, and they believed they could count on Wheeler to be a "team player." [122]

Wheeler would eventually prove, however, more independent-minded than anyone anticipated. Not a mere loyal pushover as Taylor, LeMay, the President, certain members of his Administration, some fellow officers, or the press may have initially mistaken him for, Wheeler would demonstrate, over the duration of his six-year tenure as Chairman, that he was "no shrinking violet." [123]

Wheeler was a man of principle, as well. "I will tell you," said Bim, "that Dad was the epitome of the West Point honor code." Once, when a noncommissioned officer who had been awarded the Medal of Honor for gallantry in Korea was charged with domestic assault, Wheeler was adamant that he be court martialed and not given a pass. [124]

By all accounts, Wheeler had rendered a highly successful performance during his two-year tenure as the Chief of Staff of the Army. Immediately, he had found himself thrust into overseeing Army support of civil authorities in response to civil rights disturbances associated with the integration of universities in Mississippi and Alabama. Wheeler had also found himself immediately providing counsel to the President and deploying thousands of troops in a nuclear showdown with the Soviet Union over Cuba. He improved the overseas reinforcement system and helped persuade the other Chiefs to support the Limited Nuclear Test Ban Treaty. Wheeler had "worked long and hard" to revitalize the Army along the lines of Taylor's "flexible response" doctrine rather than overwhelming reliance on massive nuclear retaliation. He had overseen the Army's expansion from 11 to 16 combat-ready divisions (an end-strength increase from 870,000 to 976,000 soldiers), as well as the Army's substantial modernization, reorganization, and the realignment of its Reserve Components. Wheeler had improved the Army's mobility in the field, increased the efficiency of its greatly reorganized supply forces, and resourced increased troop deployments to Vietnam. [125]

"There has been excitement the last few days," Betty reported on 25 June. "Telegrams and letters are pouring in. The only bad thing is the move [from Quarters 1 to Quarters 6]. It will all work out but I dread it. Diddy [Taylor] is going to take her own sweet time leaving. I suppose it's alright. But once I know I have to move I'd like to get started. Oh well." [126]

## *Wheeler's Replacement*

Wheeler's selection to replace Taylor as Chairman of the Joint Chiefs of Staff created a "short fuse" to find Wheeler's replacement as Chief of Staff of the Army. "The problem was," Odom explained, "that there was no seasoned Vice Chief to replace him, in that General Hamlett was convalescing from his heart attack. Obviously he would not become Chief of Staff." [127]

Odom recalled observing through the peephole in Wheeler's office door Wheeler's conversation over lunch with Lieutenant General Hugh Harris, the Commanding General of Continental Army Command at Fort Monroe, Virginia. Odom could tell the moment Wheeler asked him to become Chief of Staff because Harris's face turned "blood red".

Wheeler later related Harris's response with Odom. "Bus, during my whole career I have somehow avoided service in the Pentagon. I don't plan to break my record now." [128]

Instead, Wheeler nominated "Johnny" Johnson, a mere, junior-in-grade Lieutenant General, whom, according to Odom, "was the one individual who would not require 'breaking in', because he was in charge of all plans and operations for the Army. Further, he had always accompanied the Chief to the Joint Chiefs of Staff meetings in 'the tank' during this time of several national crises – the Vietnam War, the Civil Rights and Cuban Missile Crises. [129]

When Wheeler informed "Johnny" of his nomination, Johnson exclaimed, "Bus, you can't do this!"

"What are you trying to tell me, Johnny?" Wheeler replied. "That you don't want the job, or you don't think I have the authority to make you Chief of Staff?" [130]

McNamara and the President approved of Johnson's nomination. According to the *Baltimore Sun*, the appointee was rather a surprise.

> The Pentagon brass has had a series of shocks, but none from which recovery is unlikely. More sensational [than Wheeler's selection as Chairman], was the selection of Lt. Gen. Harold K. Johnson as Army Chief of Staff. ... The White House passed over 43 senior generals, twelve of them a rank higher, to make the appointment. In both cases Secretary McNamara

is the key. He has watched the two men at work and found them acceptable in both skills and temperament. They can be expected to stand up for their views, but not to the point of defiance of civilian authority. It is an attitude on which Mr. McNamara places a premium. [131]

"Chosen was sandy-hair, mild-looking Harold K. (for Keith) Johnson, who has been a three-star general for less than a year," reported the *New York News*. "Little-known outside the military, he nevertheless has impressive credentials."

> Johnson [was] a survivor of the Bataan Death March. He was serving with the Philippine Scouts when the Japanese attacked, and was captured with the Bataan garrison. He was held prisoner until the war ended. [132]

> Five years later, he was in Korea with the 1st Cavalry Division during the desperate defense of the Pusan perimeter. He fought in the United Nations sweep north, met the Red Chinese hordes and retreated with the other American troops during those critical days.

> A 1933 West Pointer, he has over the years held a variety of other assignments, in Washington and with NATO forces in Europe. Four years ago he was Commandant of the Army Command and Staff School at Fort Leavenworth, and went from there to staff posts in the Pentagon.

> As the Deputy Chief (of Staff for) Operations, he held one of the pivotal jobs in handling the 981,000-man Army spread around the globe. He also has been the 'backup' or the 'first Indian' for the Army Chief of Staff in preparations for meetings of the Joint Chiefs.

> The slightly built Johnson is of the scholarly soldier type which has come into favor since the first days of the Kennedy Administration. [133]

## *Taylor's Legacy*

McMaster argues that Taylor liked to weaken any post he left to guarantee that he had no rival to undermine his influence in his new position. Although Taylor could not modify the Chiefs' legal responsibilities, before leaving for Vietnam he drafted and had the President sign a letter that, in addition to his duties as the President's diplomatic representative, gave him complete control over the military effort in South Vietnam.

Meeting with the Joint Staff for the last time on 2 July, Taylor encouraged the assembled officers to provide military advice in the broadest context—not just the military. He counseled them to view the problems of national security through the "eyes of the President." Taylor offered similar advice to his colleagues on the Joint Chiefs of Staff (JCS), encouraging them to be "more than military men." [134]

Taylor had helped Kennedy replace recalcitrant JCS members with men who would prove more sensitive to domestic political concerns. He had been instrumental in appointing Harkins and Westmoreland and had helped to shape the American effort in Vietnam.

Taylor's most significant legacy was his shaping of the relationship between the Chiefs and the President that had affected the decision-making on Vietnam in 1963 and 1964. Long an advocate of the centralization of responsibility in the position of Chairman of the Joint Chiefs of Staff, Taylor possessed the dominant military voice in connection with U.S. policy toward Vietnam. Although he had lamented divisions among the Chiefs during the Eisenhower Administration, he used those divisions to his advantage during the Johnson Administration. When he found it expedient to do so, he misled the Chiefs, the press, and the NSC. He deliberately relegated his fellow senior military officers to a position of little influence and assisted McNamara in suppressing the Chiefs' objections to the concept of graduated pressure, reinforcing McNamara's confidence in his ability to develop strategic options for Vietnam independent of the Chiefs' advice. Ever loyal to the President, and sensing Johnson's election-year desire for unity and consensus, Taylor had shielded him from the views of his less politically sensitive colleagues while telling the Chiefs that their recommendations had been given full consideration. To keep

the Chiefs from expressing dissenting views, he had helped to craft a relationship based on distrust and deceit in which the President obscured the finality
of decisions and made false promises that the Chiefs' conception of the war
might one day be realized.

Neither the insidious relationship between the leading civilian and
military officials in the Johnson Administration nor the planning efforts in
the spring of 1964 pre-destined the Johnson Administration to escalate U.S.
military involvement in Vietnam, McMaster asserts. Nevertheless, they firmly
established in the minds of key decision-makers a flawed strategy for fighting
what seemed to them a war without precedent. [135]

### *Farewell*

Upon his departure for the Joint Chiefs of Staff, Wheeler disseminated
the following message to the Army:

> I leave the position of Chief of Staff of the Army with min-
> gled emotions of pride, respect, and regret: pride in the
> Army which has defended our nation throughout its history;
> respect for the men and women of the Army who have sup-
> ported me so loyally and unstintingly; regret that after 36
> years I am, in a sense, leaving home.
>
> I leave with the knowledge that the Army has grown and is
> continuing to grow in firepower, mobility, and in all other
> material means of accomplishing our mission. Even more
> important, I leave with the conviction that the Army con-
> tinues to hold true to the moral, spiritual and professional
> values which have guided us through the 189 years of our
> history. I see these values demonstrated in the integrity, in
> the sense of duty, and in the determination and resourceful-
> ness of all ranks, at all stations. My association with the Army
> – both personal and professional – has been the high reward
> of my career. This association I will always cherish.
>
> I know that under the capable guidance of Secretary Ailes
> and the able direction of General Johnson, the Chief of Staff

of the Army, you will continue to press forward in the service of our country. God bless you all. [136]

# CHAPTER 8

## CHAIRMAN OF THE JOINT CHIEFS OF STAFF
## (JULY 1964 – DECEMBER 1966)

At the apex of the military pyramid whose base is the multitudes of men and
women in uniform is the Chairman of the Joint Chiefs of Staff, usually the
most respected military member of the inner circle of presidential advisors.
The strength of this link between the broader political process and the military
depends to a great extent upon the relationship between the Chairman and his
two civilian superiors, the Secretary of Defense and the President.
—Charles R. Scribner, 1980. [1]


### *Swearing-In*

During his confirmation hearing before the Senate Armed Services
Committee on 2 July 1964, Chief of Staff of the Army nominee "Johnny"
Johnson stated, "I hold the view that my first obligation is to the defense of
my country, and when I appear before this committee or any committee of the
Congress, it is incumbent upon me to be completely honest with the Congress
and to respond to any questions that I am competent to answer." Johnson testified that he had discussed this very matter with McNamara who had given his
assurances that Johnson had complete freedom to do so. [2]

Meanwhile that day, Betty accompanied Bus to the White House. "Max
Taylor took the oath to become an Ambassador. Tonight the McNamara's are
giving a reception for the Taylors." [3] Betty added afterwards:

> [It was] a very lovely party. We got there at seven and were
> leaving at 8:15 when they said, 'Don't go. The President and
> Mrs. Johnson are on their way.' So we stayed and greeted
> them. I know now why her mouth is so crooked. She bites
> her inside lower lip. I'll be, she hasn't a sweet disposition! [4]

"Bus may have a holiday [over the Fourth of July weekend]," Betty continued. "He will be sworn in tomorrow so there will be no gap. But the big to-do will be [on 6 July]. We move all day long from one thing to the next. A review and reception." [5]

Wearing his khaki service dress uniform adorned with only the Army Staff Identification Badge and seven ribbons, Wheeler was sworn in as Chairman of the Joint Chiefs of Staff in a private ceremony in McNamara's office on the morning of 3 July 1964.

"The wedding will be on Monday," quipped Deputy Secretary of Defense Cyrus R. "Cy" Vance, referring to the public ceremony to follow in three days. [6]

The Army did not want to be without a Chief of Staff during the brief interval between Wheeler's ceremony and Johnson's, and so oaths were administered to both officers that Friday. [7]

Thirty minutes after Wheeler's private ceremony, "Johnny" Johnson received his fourth star and was sworn-in as Chief of Staff of the Army in a similarly low-key ceremony in Secretary of the Army Stephen "Steve" Ailes's office. LeMay, McDonald, and Greene attended both ceremonies. [8]

After Johnson was sworn in by The Judge Advocate General of the Army, he was asked to make remarks, which he concluded, saying, "I have found that, throughout my Army career, most of my strength comes from spiritual sources; and with that, would you join me in a word of prayer?"

Odom recalled there was "deafening silence." Peeking at the others present, Odom could tell that everyone other than he and Johnson were most uncomfortable. "General Johnson prayed like a Baptist deacon. At the amen – there was a quiet and respectful handshaking and congratulations."

After returning to his office, Odom described the ceremony to Wheeler's Social Secretary, Mona Nason, a devout Christian Scientist. She said, "You know, if they had known he was going to do that they would never have selected him." [9]

On the morning of 6 July, Betty, Bim, and Margie arrived at the Pentagon around 10 o'clock. They met Bus in his office, then went upstairs to McNamara's office for a "quiet" reenactment of the swearing-in ceremony. McNamara paid tribute to Wheeler's "dedication." Wheeler vowed to strive for harmony among the Armed Services. "I know we will continue to work harmoniously in the future," he said. [10]

"The photographers and press took more time than the ceremony," Betty reported. "Have had several [people] say they saw us on TV. I never had time to look. We were back at the house a little after eleven." Betty got her hair done, then "it was time to get ready for the review." [11]

Johnson was also re-sworn-in by Ailes. Johnson's remarks reflected a message to the Army that he would release three days later.

> First and foremost, our every effort must be pointed toward a high state of preparedness for the Army which, in cooperation with our sister Services and our Allies, will ensure the defense of freedom throughout the world. To accomplish this task, we must continue the intensified effort initiated by General Wheeler to develop the doctrine [referring to air mobility, which lends to *maneuver* and *offensive*] and material necessary to sustain our Army forces in the land battle. [12]

After their official swearing-in ceremonies, Wheeler and Johnson were honored at a military review at Fort Myer. "It was absolutely marvelous," Betty Wheeler reported. [13]

> For the first time the whole regiment was turned out. The outfit is so perfect, it was a beautiful show. Steve Ailes gave a short but wonderful talk about Bus. ... He said something about his spot being hard to fill. Then, 'the Army hates to have him leave, (it never occurred to me, he was leaving the Army!) but it is with great pride to all of us that he has become our country's number one military man'. [14]

*The Johnsons, Wheelers, and Ailes during a reception in honor of both generals, Patton Hall, Fort Myer, Virginia, 6 July 1964. (Office of the Chairman of the Joint Chiefs of Staff)]*

Afterward, the honorees and their multitude of guests thronged into the air-conditioned Patton Hall, the Fort Myer Officers Club, for a reception. "The reception … was for about 550," Betty wrote. "The Ailes, we, and Johnsons were in the receiving line." (Photos from that day's events show that Wheeler had replaced the Army Staff Identification Badge on his khaki service dress coat with the Joint Chiefs of Staff Identification Badge. In most photos of him as Chairman, however, he wore the former badge, which he seemed to favor.) [15]

After the reception, the Wheelers rushed back to Quarters 1 for a black-tie dinner they had previously scheduled for their long-time friends, Army Lieutenant General and Mrs. Robert W. Colglazier, who were soon departing for his assumption of command of the 6th Army at Fort Sam Houston. [16]

"What a week this has been!" Betty exclaimed. [17]

"We've certainly come a long way in the last four years," Bus said. [18]

## *Straight to Work*

The tremendous accomplishments that Wheeler had scored over the last two years as Chief of Staff of the Army had come at great personal cost. The combined effects of his relentlessly long, hard work, frequent consumption of alcohol and rich party food, his lack of exercise, and constant smoking had left him with a heart problem, high blood pressure, and a paunch around his waistline. Medically speaking, he probably should have retired from the Army in July 1964. He was spent.

Army General Bernard W. Rogers, who had served as an Executive Assistant to both Wheeler and Taylor, recalled that, although Wheeler was the youngest officer to serve as Chairman, the 56-year-old seemed "tired out" when he took over. Greene's Operations Deputy, Marine Lieutenant General Henry W. Buse, mistook Wheeler's exhaustion and physical afflictions for apathy. [19]

Odom, Wheeler's Aide-de-Camp, remained with him for a month in the Chairman's office before departing for the Armed Forces Staff College. He recalled:

> It was quite amazing how much less the pressure of events and work was in that office. Of course, [Wheeler] had been Director of the Joint Staff as a Brigadier General; so he knew many of the 'ins and outs' there. Our hours of work also diminished. The pressure of work was much less in the Chairman's office than in the office of the Chief of Staff of the Army. In this new position, his orientation and contacts were mainly with the Secretary of Defense and the President. [20]

Before Odom departed, the Wheelers hosted a dinner for him and his wife Charlotte in Quarters 1. He recalled:

> What an honor! As we finished eating, I was prompted to rise and to say how much I appreciated all [Wheeler] had done for me; and how much I had enjoyed being his aide. He then responded, 'Well, Lou, since you made a speech, I guess I had better make one too.' He then thanked me for my service and presented me with a departing gift. [21]

In addition to writing a glowing evaluation report on Odom, Wheeler also sent him the following letter dated 15 July 1964:

> Throughout your assignment, you have been a trusted and valued assistant in handling a wide variety of matters in connection with my official commitments in the operations of

my quarters staff and drivers, and I have relied heavily on your judgment and advice concerning my official and social responsibilities. I have been particularly impressed with your businesslike but cheerful manner, your mature judgment and dependability, and your ability to anticipate and follow through on even the smallest matters without losing sight of the larger issues. Your warm personality, strength of character, and helpful attitude have been a source of pride to me and have reflected most favorably upon the Office of the Chief of Staff and the Army. You may be sure that you carry with you my personal thanks for a job well done and my best wishes for continued success and happiness in your Army career. [22]

Years later, Odom would recall Wheeler as "a great American, a devoted husband and father, a diplomat, a listener, a quick decision-maker, highly intelligent, mild-mannered, kind, and compassionate. … If I had a three-word moniker for General Earle G. (Bus) Wheeler, it would be 'the quiet general.'" [23]

## Room 2E878

The office of the Chairman of the Joint Chiefs of Staff is in Room 2E878 on the wedge of the Pentagon that faces Washington, DC across the Potomac River. Across the hall is the Chairman's Dining Room, and a few doors down is "The Tank", the conference room used since 1957 that Wheeler described as "a modern black hole of Calcutta wherein the [Chiefs] meet at least three times a week." [24]

Wheeler's modest desk occupied the right side of Room 2E878 as one entered it. Squarely facing the center of the room, the desk was uncluttered but for several telephones and Wheeler's small gargoyle statue. On a credenza behind his desk were a binder with his daily calendar and a phone roster. The credenza was flanked by the U.S. flag and the flag of the Chairman of the Joint Chiefs of Staff. To the left of Wheeler's desk, paisley drapes adorned the two windows flanking a bookcase. Square columns outside partially obscured his view of Washington. In the corner between the bookcase and the credenza was a large globe. To the right of Wheeler's desk was a recliner chair, and next to it, closest to the door, was a table with five chairs. Wheeler did not have a television in his office but did monitor the news on a transistor radio. On the opposite side of the room from Wheeler's desk was a seating area with upholstered chairs and side tables. [25]

Above Wheeler's credenza, he initially hung a photograph of the President. (In mid-1965, he would move Johnson's portrait to another wall to make room for a huge, 6-foot tall relief map of Southeast Asia.) He also displayed portraits of McNamara and the Chiefs, as well as signed portraits of Mountbatten and Norstad. Over the course of Wheeler's six-year tenure as Chairman, he would also adorn the walls of his office with several weapons. These included an early prototype M16 rifle, an AK-47 presented to him by Yitzhak Rabin of Israel, and the CETME rifle he had received from the Chief of Staff of the Argentinian Army. Also displayed were an engraved, gold-plated Belgian High Power 9mm pistol presented by the Chief of Staff of the Belgian Army and a French Model 1873 revolver given to him by his French counterpart. [26]

The Wheelers attended a dinner at the State Department on 17 July. "We sat at the table with the Harrimans," Betty recorded. "I [sat] on his right. I like him so much. This time I had an opportunity to talk to her after dinner. I like her too." [27]

"Bus is working late these nights when we're not going out [to official functions]," Betty reported. He made an exception on 20 July to celebrate Bim's birthday.

Betty reminisced:

> This was certainly a memorable day in our lives twenty-four years ago. How we have travelled and progressed in Bim's lifetime. Seems almost incredible that Bus should have gone from the grade of First Lieutenant to become the senior or the number one military man in the country. We celebrated Bim's birthday last night. ... We had snails and steak, followed by coffee and birthday cake in the garden. [28]

Betty informed her mother that "it came out in an article here that if [Republican Senator Barry M.] Goldwater is elected [President] he will or can be expected to make LeMay the Chairman of the Joint Chiefs! Needless to say, I don't think he's very bright!" [29]

"Betty didn't have the full story of the newspaper article," Bus clarified in an attached note to her father. "It said in effect: If Goldwater wins, LeMay will become Chairman, JCS, in fact if not in name. I debated (not seriously) writing the gentleman that if LeMay became Chairman in <u>fact</u>, but not in <u>name</u>, one thing was damn sure, the 'name' won't be Wheeler!" [30]

## *Quarters 6*

The following day, the Post Engineer visited Betty. "I feel much encouraged about the new house [Quarters 6]," she wrote. "I can't bear the thoughts of the move, but a couple of things I asked about at this distance can be done. By Christmas we may be settled again." [31]

"A very nice thing has happened," Betty had written a few days earlier.

Diddy [Taylor] put up a pair of crystal chandeliers in the living room. They add so much. They're hers. Last night, I asked her if she would have one of her men measure the width and length, in the hopes that I might be able to get some. So, said she, 'I'm so glad you like them and it would be so much better if they stayed where they are. I would love to leave them with you.' So, I'm thrilled. ... They do add so much. [32]

"Dorothy Johnson is going through the house [Quarters 1] this afternoon," Betty wrote on 9 July. "It is a wrench. It's agony, in a way, to be waiting, for once we move [after Diddy Taylor finally moves out of Quarters 6] I'll be too busy coping to think too much and I'm sure by the time all's in place there will be no looking back." [33]

"I still get ridiculously tired," Betty complained eleven days later. "However, I let the damn house get me when I woke up in the night, and also whenever I think of it I get tired! I still have no idea when the Taylors are moving out. Diddy is certainly packing. I think she probably doesn't know herself yet. She says August, with no time. ... Also, no matter what, Bus is taking leave the 21st-27th [of August]." [34]

The Wheeler's move to Quarters 6 was still in limbo at the end of July. "I'm trying to know that God's plan for us didn't put us or Bus in this elevated spot to be a complete letdown," Betty wrote. "Giving up the house [Quarters 1] grows harder daily, and I know these are thoughts to be conquered." [35]

It wouldn't be until 15 October that Betty finally reported, "We cleared Quarters 1 today, so that stage of our lives is behind us." She wouldn't return for seven months until Dorothy Johnson hosted a tea. "It looks lovely, and I had no feeling that I'd ever lived there," Betty then wrote. [36]

The Taylors had been having issues with their household staff. Betty would have none of it. Since the Chairman's quarters were an international showcase of American hospitality, only the best service would do. Bus empowered Covello, who would move with the family from Quarters 1, to assemble the finest staff he could muster. Covello appropriated Master Sergeant Bill Stewart from Major General Benjamin F. Taylor's quarters to replace Sergeant Short as Chief Cook. (Stewart would prove a gem and remain with the family until Bus's retirement six years later.) Sergeant Jim Harrington also joined the Quarters 6 staff from elsewhere on Fort Myer. [37]

Betty was well-pleased with the efficiency of their household staff during the hectic transition between quarters. It was the one bright spot of the drawn-out move. "Sgt. Covello is … doing a fine job," she reported. [38]

Stewart was honored to join the household staff and recalled years later the Wheelers' kindness and generosity. Betty was a very good manager, and she taught him well. "They gave you your head to do things," Stewart said. [39]

### Harkins Retires

On the steamy morning of 28 July, Wheeler donned his dress white uniform to preside over Harkins's retirement ceremony at Fort Myer.

"It's hotter than Hades," Betty wrote. "[I] dread the hour in the sun." Still, she managed to arrive early to the parade field. [40]

The *Washington Post* reported that Wheeler "spoke with feeling of Gen. Harkins's establishment of a determined spirit among the Army, Navy, Air Force and Marines, under his command in Vietnam, his last command, and probably the most difficult one of his 35 years of service since his graduation from West Point in 1929." [41]

"The retirement ceremony … [was] one of the most beautiful I have ever seen," Betty recounted. "Bus and I left the reception [we hosted at the Officers Club] afterwards about six. We had a beautiful dinner [at home in Quarters 1]. The Harkins made up the guest list. … We had twenty-four. Mrs. Taylor came. Still no news as to when she will finally get out. I've pretty much been able to stop thinking about it." [42]

Two days later, the Wheelers attended a ceremony "in the garden at the White House."

An excited Betty wrote on 1 August. "[In three days] Bus and I go to New York for the night. Bus [is] attending a luncheon. I am going to walk Fifth Avenue. We're staying over to have dinner by ourselves on the town. It's been so long." [43]

## Gulf of Tonkin

Meanwhile, as each side in the Vietnam conflict undertook more provocative military actions, the likelihood of a direct military confrontation between North Vietnam and the U.S. increased. [44]

On 2 August, an incident occurred between a U.S. Navy destroyer and North Vietnamese gunboats in international waters of the Gulf of Tonkin. Two days later, two U.S. warships reported being similarly attacked. [45]

Wheeler kept his luncheon engagement in Manhattan on the day of the first incident, but then hurried back to Washington. Betty wrote:

> I met him at 2:30, and now we're homeward bound. What a life, but I'm praying [the incident] is not too serious. We had a lovely suite overlooking Central Park in the Essex House. I certainly would have liked to stay to enjoy it. By the way, this is the first trip we have taken in Bus's plane (tail number 229)! [46]

"I guess all the news was in the papers this morning!" Betty wrote late that evening. "Bus [came] home around ten P. M. to eat. I haven't seen him since." [47]

## Tiger by the Jowls

A *New York Herald-Tribune* reporter observed a photograph in Wheeler's office of him holding a Vietnamese tiger cub by the jowls. "That really is not a smile on my face," Wheeler was quoted. "That is a look of apprehension." The reporter commented, "For a man now confronted by a world full of tigers that would seem a reasonable attitude, especially toward those which have to be held by the tail." [48]

> The lean, 6-foot-3-inch general gives the impression of a man possessing enormous competence, who will keep the 'big picture' clearly in focus, who will stay in the background if possible and who will refrain from over-optimism – or pessimism. People who have worked with Gen. Wheeler speak of him as 'quick and brilliant ... unruffled and self-assured ... articulate but not glib.' A one-time mathematics instructor at West Point, the general can be expected to analyze before he acts. [49]

Asked whether large nations involved in small wars should assess the long-range effect of that victory on the world balance of power, Wheeler responded:

> I think this has always been true. No war can be fought with any degree of purpose without a definite political objective. Most military plans today are drawn to support some national objective; otherwise, they are useless. If you undertake to fight a war, you must take a long look down the road and see where you will be afterwards. You could win a war and lose the peace. [50]

In a ceremony in Ailes's office on 4 September, "Johnny" Johnson received new help with managing the Army's internal affairs when Ailes and Wheeler promoted Lieutenant General Creighton W. Abrams to General, and Abrams became the Vice Chief of Staff of the Army. [51]

## Math Tutor

Meanwhile that September, Betty's niece, eighteen-year-old Linda Howell, began her freshman year at George Mason College, a new branch of the University of Virginia in Fairfax. Because dormitories had not yet been built, Linda became a full-time member of the Wheeler household. She was fortunate to have her "Uncle Bus" to help her with mathematics. After obtaining the most recent college math books from West Point, Bus tutored Linda after he finished his own "homework" around 9:30 – 10:00 PM. His assistance helped her pass Freshman math and gain admission as a Sophomore at Mary Washington College in Fredericksburg. (Since Linda's parents had moved to Florida, she would continue to spend considerable time in the Wheelers' house over the next three years.) [52]

## 1965

On 13 January 1965, Bus's staff threw him a birthday party in the Chairman's Dining Room. President Johnson's inaugural festivities were coming up later that month, but Betty didn't feel up to them.

> I seem to be plagued off and on [with recurring illnesses] ever since [the trip to] Saigon. I get up a couple hours in the morning, get to bed right after lunch and struggle out just in time to make myself presentable for Bus. Fortunately, the calendar has been free so I haven't had to go out or bow out in the evenings. … Bus says I need to be packed off to sunshine. However, just too much is going on, so I'll get my sun in late February or March. [53]

> Next week we start and don't stop until February. This year we seem to be "in" on everything. … We've been invited to the Governors' luncheon at the Capitol following the [Presidential] swearing-in ceremony. I don't particularly want to go to the [inaugural ball at the] Armory, but Bus has been given two boxes for the ball. At least we'll have a place to sit! Ted Clifton says the big doings will be at the Armory. We'll see. [54]

On a trip to West Point later that month, the Wheelers attended a service in the neo-gothic Cadet Chapel.

> The organ in the chapel is so beautiful. The service was mostly music, and a few passages read from the Bible. Bus has said

that he wants to be buried at West Point. I hope that I'm not around, but if I am, I'll be eternally grateful that we didn't walk that long, long aisle together on our wedding day. [55]

Bus would later change his mind, deciding instead to be buried in Arlington National Cemetery. "I don't want to soiree the Corps," he explained. [56]

Sometime during his tenure as Chairman, Bus was asked which academy he hoped would win the upcoming football game between Navy and Air Force. Like a good West Pointer, he quipped, "I hope they both lose!" [57]

According to Betty, the last day of January was "LeMay Day". LeMay's 34-year military career would conclude the following day.

We went to the ceremony at the White House at noon. After all the glowing words one wonders why he is being retired at 58 without being given his fourth year as Chief [of Staff of the Air Force]. ... In the afternoon we went to Bolling Field for the retirement review and a reception afterwards. Bus had a meeting at 6:30. It was almost 8:30 before he got home. [58]

"Bus testifies before Congress tomorrow," Betty wrote on 1 February. "As McNamara is in the hospital, he'll go it alone. Says his head may roll next. (So sad when he's such a comfort to the President.)" [59]

That evening, the Wheelers "went to the McCones's for dinner in honor of the new Senator Murphy from California. All Republicans except Senator & Mrs. Symington and the non-partisan Wheelers. We had a pleasant time." [60]

## McConnell

On 1 February, McConnell was sworn in as Chief of Staff of the Air Force in a ceremony officiated by Vance. The President and his top advisors, long anticipating LeMay's retirement, had selected McConnell ten months earlier and installed him, meanwhile, as Vice Chief of Staff of the Air Force. [61]

The contrast between McConnell and LeMay was dramatic. *Newsweek* magazine opined that McConnell's "brains and thrust" had replaced LeMay's "dedication and crust." Unlike LeMay's gruff manner and appearance, McConnell's countenance was kind and thoughtful. *Time* magazine announced that McConnell's appointment "marked the end of an era in military leadership." By appointing McConnell, the President completed the shift of the Joint Chiefs of Staff away from "heroes" to military men who were McNamara-style "planners and thinkers." [62]

McConnell and Wheeler were similar in many ways, from their career paths, hobbies, and high intelligence, to their personalities and manner of communicating. Whereas LeMay had been one of the architects of heavy bombing strategy and tactics and had led men in combat, McConnell, like Wheeler, had made a name for himself as a staff officer expert in plans, training, and logistics. McConnell also shared Wheeler's love of hunting and fishing.

Little-known outside the Air Force when he was appointed Chief of Staff, McConnell was sometimes called "the brain" within it. He had a "steel trap mind" with a gift for staff work and organizational leadership. [63]

Pentagon analysts predicted that with the "new breed" of officers like McConnell and Wheeler, interservice rivalry would diminish, and relations between civilian and military officials would "flourish." While McConnell would, in fact, enjoy a friendlier relationship with McNamara and other civilian officials in the Pentagon than did LeMay, he would later clash in frustration with McNamara and Johnson over their direction of the Vietnam War. Tempered by his belief in civilian control of the military, McConnell would make his thoughts known. If he disagreed with higher authorities, he could at least speak their language and would be reappointed twice as Chief of Staff. His personality could be disarming and charming as any polished staff officer, or as earthy and blunt as his native Ozarks. McConnell could disagree with his critics without seeming abrasive. [64]

McConnell had a rocky relationship with "Johnny" Johnson. Not only did they differ in their institutional perspectives concerning the use of military force, but they had also had a difficult relationship as West Point cadets. Wheeler would have to mediate between them. [65]

"Bus worked all day Saturday [the day of the Pleiku attack] and slept in the Pentagon," Betty reported. Two days later, he was sick and had to bow out of a dinner that he and Betty hosted in Quarters 6. [66]

Bus seemed to have a lifelong propensity to catch colds frequently. During one of his many trips to Vietnam, he was prescribed antibiotics so he could function. The long hours he spent travelling back and forth across the Pacific Ocean and the continental U.S. in poorly heated military aircraft did nothing for his health. [67]

When another Viet Cong attack occurred at Qui Nhon on 10 February, "Bus went to the office at ten." He gave the fifty-two ladies [attending Betty's ladies group luncheon] a marvelous briefing (before going home to bed)." The President ordered another series of airstrikes against North Vietnam, but with one significant change. This was part of a plan for "continuing action against North Vietnam," as Johnson informed Taylor in a cable, "with modifications up and down in tempo and scale in the light of our recommendations … and our own continuing review of the situation." The air war against North Vietnam had commenced. [68]

By 13 February, a Saturday, all the crucial decisions instituting the airstrikes against North Vietnam had been made. (Naturally, Wheeler had spent the day in the office. He was feeling better, as if that had mattered one bit.) Within the span of a week, the U.S. had significantly escalated the war and deepened its involvement. [69]

With the President's approval of retaliatory airstrikes against North Vietnam, the evacuation of U.S. military dependents from Saigon was also ordered. On 13 February, Betty received "a note from Diddy Taylor. She is sending two suitcases here to hold until she arrives. Only too pleased. I just pray that she leaves the chests and chandeliers! She says she's going to rent a little apartment so I imagine I'm safe for awhile. Kitsy [Westmoreland] is going to Hawaii. So grateful I'm where I am!" [70]

Johnson's decision to wage the bombing program against North Vietnam provided the pretext for the introduction of U.S. ground combat forces into South Vietnam. [71]

On 1 March, the President indicated that he was willing to look with favor upon a recommendation for the deployment of more U.S. ground combat forces to boost the counterinsurgency effort, but without drawing public attention to the escalation of the war. [72]

"Seven o'clock, no Bus," Betty informed her mother that evening. "He has put [in] long hours the last little bit, or is it always? Our trip to [Fort]

Benning was cancelled on Saturday. Bus worked all day [instead]. He hadn't gotten home until ten-thirty the night before." Post-scripting her letter, Betty added, "Still no word from Bus." [73]

Despite the Joint Staff's intensive and time-consuming preparations to commence the air war against North Vietnam, Wheeler's other commitments as Chairman continued. Vietnam was a hot topic when Wheeler addressed Naval War College students in Newport, Rhode Island on 2 March. Air operations against North Vietnam were commencing as the situation in South Vietnam continued to deteriorate. Wheeler and the Chiefs no longer viewed a stand-alone air campaign as sufficient and recommended the commitment of U.S. ground forces. [74]

Fast-moving decisions on Vietnam necessarily pushed other matters requiring Wheeler's attention to the back burner. At least one of his out of town trips in mid-month was cancelled. He did, however, venture across the Potomac on 23 March to address the Inter-American Defense Council at Fort McNair.

"I'm working on Bus in the hopes that he will take a long weekend," Betty wrote. "God knows he needs it more than I do." [75]

When Bus informed Betty on 5 April that "he has got to go to Hawaii the end of this month", she was hopeful they "can have a weekend on the beach". They were both in need of a break, and Betty had just stubbed her little toe and sprained her foot. Bus took time out of his busy schedule to take her to the dispensary. "No bones broken, but a bad sprain. ... I've an elastic on it, but can remove it for dress." [76]

*Bus and Betty Wheeler greet the Brazilian Minister of War at a dinner hosted byBrazilian Ambassador Magalhaea, Washington, DC, 9 April 1965. (Office of the Chairman of the Joint Chiefs of Staff).*

## *Honolulu*

The Wheelers boarded Bus's plane for Hawaii after a dinner party on 17 April, Betty wrote.

> After take off went to bed. We arrived in Hawaii 8 A. M. their time, an easy flight. The Sharps met us with leis. … I could have cried, the promised Sunday alone just didn't material-ize. Rain didn't help either. We had Oley and Pat [Sharp] with us every minute. [77]

"Bus says the conference was a good one," Betty wrote after their return to Washington, "and I guess that's most important." She added:

> I'm glad to have seen the island but as I'll always have to be taken care of every minute, I don't think that I'll go next time. Did manage to escape a luncheon and Pat was quite unhappy about it. Had a harbor trip on a Navy barge with guide. Most interesting. We left [on 20 April] after a big reception and small dinner at [the] Sharp's. [78]

On 28 April, an exasperated Betty wrote, "It's now seven-thirty. Bus just called and said that he didn't know when he'd get home. If it's not one thing it's another." [79]

Mums had been admitted to the hospital two days earlier with pneumonia. "She's had a cold for two weeks," Betty explained, "and I've tried to get her to call her doctor." While an inpatient, Mums would also undergo eye surgery. [80]

The following Sunday, "Bus ate and went to the office at the usual time. You can imagine what these days have been." The Chiefs and the Joint Staff were exceptionally busy implementing recent presidential decisions on Vietnam by identifying and preparing units for movement overseas and refining mobilization plans for Selected Reserve forces, as well as monitoring the deteriorating situation in the Dominican Republic. The frenetic pace was such that "Johnny" Johnson complained, "There just isn't enough thinking time in this job." [81]

Three days earlier, Bus had to bow out of a dinner at the Sulgrave Club given by "the Omar Bradley's." Betty went alone.

> The place was jammed. [Bus's aide] Bob Hunter picked me up. Bus was still at the White House. He finally got home at one [AM]. He just cancelled out on a dinner … on [this coming] Friday. He was dead tired. He finally got in around 7:45. We had a quiet dinner and then to bed. [82]

## *After Hours*

On 18 May, Bus informed Betty that he had "arranged for four days leave" that they would spend by continuing to scout around the region for a weekend retreat.

> Bus and I came [back home in time for] supper Sunday. I was exhausted! But, Bus was relaxed and rested. I'm sure we drove practically to California! The main thing was that Bus relaxed and enjoyed the days without a telephone.

> We looked at property from Pennsylvania to the northern neck of Virginia. … I got most interested in 80 acres out of Fredericksburg, two houses, endless possibilities, much restoration, beautiful, beautiful, beautiful farm land, but except for a few apple trees to the back almost treeless. … We went back to see a place on the water that we were crazy about, but it seemed too far. But, what's at the end of the drive is worth

considering. Whether Bus will even commit himself to anything, I'm doubtful. He does love the outings. I no longer read the ads. He makes the appointments and usually I don't have any idea what's at the end of the road. ... This was the kind of four days we had. We are learning property values, and I love to look at houses! Since we've been doing this, Bus doesn't work Sunday mornings and off we go, so it is good. I feel if we could come up with something he would gradually work it out to be away on Saturday too. ... We spent about forty-five minutes at Harpers Ferry. More restoration has been done since we were there last and we enjoyed walking around. The weather was glorious, not too hot. So while I found it tiring physically to drive around so much, it was lovely. [83]

While they were away, Margie had taken care of getting Mums discharged from the hospital. "[She] is coming along nicely. She will spend two weeks [recuperating in Quarters 6]. She has her eye dressed every other day." [84]

"The Bill Bundy's gave a dinner on [19 May]," Betty recorded. "He is McGeorge's brother, she Dean Acheson's daughter. The Achesons were at dinner. I enjoyed meeting him, so very distinguished looking." [85]

The following night, "the McNamara's had a dinner for the new Ambassador from New Zealand. Almost the same group. Bob didn't arrive until dessert. I personally can't believe that he couldn't be spared, particularly as he was entertaining a foreign guest. It makes us look like we're in a tizzy. Bus says, 'We're not!'" [86]

Two days later, the Wheelers travelled to Washington and Jefferson College in Washington, PA, where Betty's nephew Doneld Howell was graduating and receiving his commission as an Army officer. In addition to presenting the commissions, Bus received an honorary Doctor of Laws degree and pinned-on Don's "butter bars." After the graduation ceremony, the school gave a lunch in the Wheelers' honor. Don informed them later that the Colonel in charge of the college's ROTC program exclaimed to him, "I am mentally and physically exhausted by all of this. I need to get home and have a couple martinis." The Wheelers' visit was the biggest event ever to hit the school and Washington, PA. [87]

On 24 May, the Wheelers "had a party for Lord Louis [Mountbatten]. A smashing success! Dinner was superb and everyone had a good time. ... Today ... the new British Ambassador had a luncheon. The President has his military reception tomorrow for Dickie as Bus calls him but I haven't quite come to it! It was most pleasant." [88]

Considering Bus's long work hours and the continuous string of social events that the Wheelers were obligated to attend or host, they got no respite, even within their own quarters. As such, they decided to move their bedroom up to the third floor of Quarters 6. "We do need privacy. I love having everyone [stay over as guests], but sometimes it's nice to have a quiet spot and our bedroom isn't!" [89]

By early June, the Administration had reached an appropriate juncture for a thorough review of Vietnam policy and new initiatives. Although time was available for a thorough, in-depth formulation process, major decisions would be made in a crisis management atmosphere that severely limited meaningful deliberations or a reassessment of options. The Administration, therefore, would consider only short-range options or remedies. [90]

"One reason the Kennedy and Johnson Administrations failed to take an orderly, rational approach to the basic questions underlying Vietnam was the staggering variety and complexity of other issues we faced," McNamara recalled. "Simply put, we faced a blizzard of problems, there were only 24 hours in a day, and we often did not have time to think straight." He elaborated:

> Our failure was partially the result of having many more com-
> mitments than just Vietnam. Instability in Latin America,
> Africa, and the Middle East, and the continued Soviet threat
> in Europe all took up time and attention. We had no senior
> group working exclusively on Vietnam, so the crisis there
> became just one of many items on each person's plate. When
> combined with the inflexibility of our objectives, and the
> fact that we had not truly investigated what was essentially
> at stake and important to us, we were left harried, overbur-
> dened, and holding a map with only one road on it. Eager to

get moving, we never stopped to explore fully whether there were other routes to our destination. [91]

## *Europe*

Besides Vietnam, Wheeler had other matters to attend and other parts of globe with which to concern himself. Enroute to Europe, he and Betty visited Brown University in Providence, Rhode Island on 13 June, where he addressed newly commissioned Second Lieutenants from the university's ROTC program and received an honorary Doctor of Laws degree. [92]

On 14-17 June, Wheeler attended the Supreme Headquarters Allied Powers Europe Exercise (SHAPEX), the annual conference of senior officers from NATO's member nations in Paris. Meanwhile, Betty visited "Mr. Claude," her favorite hair stylist in Paris.

She explained:

> The Lemnitzer's gave a large dinner last night. Saw lots of old friends. ... [One] sent a clipping from a newspaper the other day. [It] said in effect that De Gaulle would press for a European to take over NATO unless the U.S. sent the Chairman, Bus, by name [to replace Army General Lyman L. Lemnitzer as Supreme Allied Commander, Europe (SACEUR)]. I myself feel that the time has passed. I'm sure I can do what I must, but I'd just as soon not must. Too many houses maybe. Bus says he doesn't think there is a chance that we will leave Washington, so I don't think that I need to worry. [93]

While Bus and Betty were away in Paris, Bim and Margie stayed at Quarters 6. "The help is not supposed to help," Betty explained, "but [I] suppose they will get some benefits."

The Department of Defense had policies for what duties enlisted orderlies could and could not perform for a general officer's family. "The Wheelers did not take from the Army," Stewart explained. "They were very scrupulous about abiding by the rules." Betty upheld very clear standards of performance and conduct in her relationship with the house staff. "She made it very clear that we worked *with* her *for* Bus," Stewart recalled. "We did not work *for* her." [94]

Whenever the Wheelers entertained, Bim and Margie often sat in as "fillers." Among the many high-level foreign military leaders with whom Bim enjoyed meeting and talking, his favorites were Yitzhak Rabin and Dickie Mountbatten. "Not only did they have a great and personal relationship with my father, but I was actually able to talk to them 'mano a mano' about things related to military history and their involvement." [95]

## *Off Duty*

Four days after returning from Paris, Wheeler attended the Central Treaty Organization (CENTO) conference. In between his frequent trips, he and Betty were now enjoying the above-ground pool they had recently installed behind Quarters 6.

"The pool is a joy," Betty wrote. "It really has already had a relaxing effect on us. It was fun to have the first week when the moon was full. We go in before bed. Billy [their five-year old grandson] loves it. We now have a fence, so we have a sense of privacy too." [96]

"Bus worked until late" on Saturday, 26 June. The following day, he and Betty returned to Sharpsburg, Maryland. They had recently looked at an old house adjacent to the Antietam battlefield, and were following up with the National Park Service on an easement issue.

"Bus seems to love it, an easy 1 ½ hours door to door. One thing sure, there is no hurry and it will work out if it's for us." For a few years it and a Florida house would be ideal and the 'old things' would be so happy! We shall see. [97]

Bus had always been greatly interested in the American Civil War. He wanted to write a book about it, but his work schedule as Chairman prevented the project from progressing beyond an outline and notes. [98]

## *Ailes Departs*

Ailes relinquished his duties as the Secretary of the Army on 1 July. Three days earlier, he and his wife Helen, "gave a large party for all the Army Generals as their swan song. Glad they will at least be in town," Betty wrote. "We're so fond of them." [99]

McNamara, Vance, Wheeler, and "Johnny" Johnson attended Ailes's retirement ceremony at Fort Myer on 2 July. Since Ailes had become Secretary of the Army on 28 January 1964, the Army had dealt with riots in the Panama Canal Zone; provided disaster assistance following earthquakes in Skopje, Yugoslavia, and Anchorage, Alaska; forged an agreement with the Federal Republic of Germany to jointly develop a new main battle tank; assumed responsibility for the nation's Civil Defense function; provided troops to protect American personnel and bring an end to the civil war in the Dominican Republic; and dispatched the first combat units to Vietnam. [100]

## *Saigon Trip*

"Bus (departs with McNamara for Vietnam) tonight," Betty wrote on 14 July. "[I] think he dreads it. ... Says he, 'If I had my way we'd go to Hong Kong, I'd leave you there, and we'd have a few days after Saigon.' Wishful thinking, because I'm sure when they return they will go from plane to White House, so he couldn't have planned differently had he gone alone." [101]

Wearing stiff, new jungle boots with his standard Army fatigues, Wheeler attended meetings and briefings with McNamara's party and also took time to speak with wounded servicemen in a combat hospital and to visit Navy flight crews. [102]

## *Washington*

Johnson had decided to commit massive U.S. ground forces to war without mobilization. The reserves would not be called up. The draft, which would be doubled from 17,000 to 35,000 each month, rather than a call-up of the Army Reserves, was a non-mobilization that could provide the manpower without declaring a national emergency. Voluntary enlistment programs would also be intensified. [103]

Shortly after Johnson's momentous decisions on Vietnam policy, Wheeler replaced the President's photo on the wall behind his desk with a giant relief map of Southeast Asia. Clearly, Vietnam was now front and center on Wheeler's mind. [104]

The workload was wearing on Wheeler. "Hopefully, Bus is going on a week's leave starting the sixteenth," Betty informed her mother on 9 August. "I don't know yet where we'll go or what we'll do. Bus needs rest and quiet. I wish that we could stay right here but he seems to feel that he wouldn't be let alone." The pool makes such a difference." [105]

Ten months into Bus's term as Chairman, Betty was already looking forward to it being over. "Hopefully, [we'll] be through in a year. Don't know what makes me think so."

"I may talk to you later tonight if Bus ever gets home," she added. "He's been at the White House almost all day briefing Senators on Vietnam." [106]

The Wheelers decided to remain in the local area during Bus's leave. "The first day of leave went alright," Betty reported. That night, they watched a pre-recorded ABC News "Issues & Answers" ] program on which Bus was a guest.

> Bus worked yesterday morning. That is, last night's television show was taped. It was almost two (P. M.) before he got home. We had a drink and lunch, then a swim. Then a nap. I slept about two and half hours, Bus three. We played gin, cooked a steak. By the time we finished dinner it was almost time for the ABC News 'Issues & Answers' program. I thought it quite good. Margie was afraid that Max [Taylor] wouldn't let Bus say a word. However, it seemed to me that he had more than his share of the time. [107]

The Wheelers had a long swim after the show. "The moon was rising, so lovely," Betty recorded. "Then to bed."

The following morning, they went fishing on the reservoir at Quantico.

> We have a boat and an outboard. It's hot, but there is a slight breeze. … We have lunch with us.

> If the telephone will leave Bus alone, I think this will be the perfect vacation. The house and yard are so lovely and Bus has little time to really enjoy them. Help comes for break-fast and keeps order. Lunch is packed, or will be left for us. The grill set up and trays left. The telephones switched. No amount of money could give us such service plus a private

pool. Guess an amount of money could, but would take an awful amount. [108]

"She definitely enjoyed the life," recalled Bim about his mother. The Wheelers enjoyed such great service from their household staff due to Covello's management. After Covello retired in 1965, Sergeant Major Don Taggett took over and would remain with the family until Bus's retirement in 1970. [109]

Betty reported on a close call she had experienced during rush hour:

I had a strange thing happen last Friday. It could have been awful. I certainly feel that I was taken care of (by Providence). After shopping with Mums in Northern Virginia, it was a little after five when I started home. Came by way of Wilson Boulevard. The traffic [coming] out of the city was quite hairy. I was going slowly along, in the right lane of a four-lane highway, when suddenly a car crosses into my side of the highway. I moved still further right then to the curb thinking surely this won't go on. Then the driver slumped over the wheel and he hit me. He was completely at an angle across the second lane. Do you know, he hit the bumper and there wasn't a scratch on my car and he only bent his license plate? A Navy man was behind me. The driver of the other car was drunk. The Navy man called the police. Traffic was all tied up and so there was nothing to do. My car was checked and not a mark, so the police straightened out the traffic, put the drunk in a patrol car, took over his car, and moved me on without ever having to ask my name. I was certainly fortunate. Even barring being hurt we could have had a badly messed up car. [110]

On 16 September, Wheeler was presented the Philippine Legion of Honor Medal in a ceremony at the Philippine Embassy. Betty helped place the red, white, and blue ribbon around his neck. "Johnny" Johnson received the award, as well.

On 24 September, the Wheelers departed Washington on another ten-day trip to Europe. [111]

In October, the 1st Cavalry Division received its baptism of fire in the Battle of the Ia Drang. Despite terrific U.S. casualties, the battle was lauded as the first major U.S. triumph of the Vietnam War. The airmobile division had relentlessly pursued the enemy over difficult terrain and defeated crack North Vietnamese Army units.

In part, the division's achievements underlined the flexibility that Army divisions had gained in the early 1960s under the Reorganization Objective Army Divisions (ROAD) concept that Wheeler had implemented while Chief of Staff of the Army. The ROAD division, organized around three brigades, facilitated the creation of brigade- and battalion-task forces tailored to respond and fight in a variety of military situations. The newly organized division reflected the Army's embrace of the concept of flexible response and proved eminently suitable for operations in Vietnam. The helicopter was given great credit, as well. [112]

## *November*

Meanwhile, illness, overseas trips, and social events filled the remainder of Wheeler's calendar. Betty reported:

> Bus had a relapse from the flu and has been running a fever [for three days]. Dr. Upton wanted him to go to the hospital last night, but Bus said he had one or two important things to take care of today and [then] he could clear his slate. He plans to go after dinner. Dr. Upton told me [two days ago] that [in two more days] he wanted him to leave town, get into the sunshine [for] at least [four days]. He's balking, but I think after today he'll be ready to go. [113]

A week later, she reported, "Bus [went] back to work this morning. I can't help but wish that he would take a few days to go sit in the sun some place. ... I feel miserable myself. [We're living in] a pest house. However, I have no fever. I'm staying quietly in my room and won't dress until dinner tonight. The virus seems to be going around. Certainly don't want to miss Princess Margaret tomorrow night. [114]

They didn't. "Quite a memorable evening," Betty wrote.

> We arrived at [British Admiral] Henderson's at eight. The
> Snowdons were fifteen minutes late. ... They were introduced
> as any couple would be arriving at a party. [Because] they
> didn't know [some of] the guests, Admiral Henderson went
> around the room with Princess Margaret. Lady Henderson
> with Lord Snowdon. She is as pretty as the lovely pictures.
> Very animated, very friendly, very natural. ... There were
> only twenty people. ... I sat next to Lord Snowdon, Bus at
> the other table next to Princess Margaret. He [is] a pleasant,
> affable young man, easy to talk to. I feel that of the official
> things, we really were 'in'.

Official social events occurred on top of Wheeler's already blistering workload. "Poor Bus worked all day [on a Saturday] and didn't get home until 8:15," Betty wrote. They both realized they needed to get away from the city as often as they could. [115]

> We did enjoy our day with the Ailles's [at their home in
> Martinsburg, West Virginia]. We thought we were just going
> for lunch, but they wanted us to stay on. Said they'd cook a
> steak and we'd eat at six so we wouldn't be late starting home.
> ... It made me realize that we could use a weekend spot, but
> more than that, we would love the country an hour & half
> to two hours from Washington later. That too will work out
> when the time is right. [116]

"Bus leaves Thanksgiving night for Paris with Bob McNamara," Betty wrote. "Hates to miss the Army-Navy game. Margie, Bim, [and another couple] will go up on the Cannonball Special. ... Bus can get good seats [for them]." [117]

Days after returning from France, Wheeler accompanied McNamara on another trip to Saigon. [118]

A week later, Wheeler was back in Europe to attend a NATO South conference in Naples. Lemnitzer and Admiral Thomas H. Moorer, (who would later succeed Wheeler as Chairman) also attended. [119]

In early December, the Wheelers found time to continue their house hunting, Betty explained.

Bus and I will take off on Sunday for the day. We have a couple houses to look at. One is in West Virginia that has been
advertised off and on for over a year. This is the first time
we've gotten around to it, because Bus forgets it in between
ads. It's such a beautiful drive and it will be good to just get
away. [120]

They had also long desired to build a retirement home on her parents'
choice property on Casey Key.

I've been thinking about the Florida land. ... I had a bright,
clear thought the other day. We've been approaching this
backwards. As we want something around here for a few
years, we should start with the guest house, building on
the end of the property toward the road. I came home yesterday afternoon and got out all the books of plans that we
have. I found exactly what I'd like. Bus had marked a plan
that appealed to him for the main house, way back, and suddenly there it all was. A little rearranging needed, but it all fit
together. I can see it, really see it! ... I really think I've something that Bus and I would enjoy living in until such time
as we came to stay permanently. Then we'd build our house
and have a place for Bim and Margie, all the grandchildren,
or nieces and nephews with their children should they care
to come, and friends. Well, 'tis fun to think about, especially
now that I know what to do. My thinking on the main house
has been much too large and getting bigger! It's all in propor-
tion now, even the swimming pool. [121]

In mid-December, the Wheelers spent a week in Paris for another NATO
conference. They stayed at their usual lodging, the Hotel Lotti. Bus's itinerary precluded him from attending the Supreme Headquarters Allied Powers
Europe (SHAPE) Ball, so his aide, Marine Colonel Bob Hunter, escorted Betty.

[It] was quite beautiful. It draws a large crowd and is held
in the beautiful, tremendous room where all the large can-
vasses of French victories are. [British] General Hull said it
was rather depressing to see so many Union Jacks in tatters!
Soldiers in all their most beautiful dress uniforms lined the

stairway. It was most impressive. ... At eleven-fifteen the Lemnitzer's had not arrived. In fact people were just starting to come [in]. Rather nice to see the ball room not so full. Not wanting to seat myself at the table before the Lemnitzer's, Bob and I decided to take a turn around the room. ... I told Bus [the next day] we seemed to create a bit of a stir as we paraded the room. 'Who was the handsome Marine and the middle aged lady?' ... When we got back to the table, the Lemnitzer's were there. ... Lem asked me to dance and then said we must tour the room. I didn't tell him that I'd already done it! ... I asked Bus what he supposed they thought when I was parading the room again on Gen. Lemnitzer's arm. Bus said, 'Why, that you were Mrs. Lemnitzer, of course!' [122]

Betty noted that with the upcoming French presidential election, "Bus is worried about NATO. How many things he has on his mind." [123]

## *Far East Trip*

The Wheelers wound down 1965 and rang in the New Year with a twenty-day trip throughout the Far East. After a stopover in Alaska, they arrived at Yokota Air Force Base in Japan on 19 December and were greeted by senior U.S. Air Force (USAF) and Japanese Navy officers. There, Betty had a separate itinerary and observed numerous aspects of Japanese culture. [124]

The Wheelers then flew to Thailand. Betty remained there and saw the sights while Bus visited Vietnam on 22-24 December. She reported:

The Air Chief Marshall (Thai) was giving a supper party aboard a large Navy barge for Bob Hope and troupe. All anyone talks about. He'd been here three days, given his fifth show at one that day. That's work in this heat. I had dinner with him, so now I can talk about Bob Hope too! ... Bus arrived safely [on Christmas Eve]. He hoped to rest, but Ambassador [Graham A.] Martin came, and they're still talking. ... We'll have dinner with the Martins tonight. [125]

Another morning after the Martin's huge reception in Bangkok for 900 and a smaller buffet for 50, Betty and Mrs. Alice Stilwell drove two hours to the coast, went out in a boat, found a beach, and swam in the Gulf of Siam. "The water was wonderful," Betty reported. They returned to Bangkok by air. The Thai government gave a dinner in the Wheelers' honor that evening. [126]

On 29 December, the Wheelers visited Taipei, which Betty considered the highlight of their trip.

> There was too little time, and my schedule was full, but it was a thrill. ... When we arrived (in the rain) we were greeted by quite a delegation. The wife of Bus's counterpart speaks excellent English. She greeted me with a beautiful orchid. After the greetings Bus took off for a press conference [at the airport]. I was taken to the ladies' lounge. There a tailor was waiting and I was asked to select material for a [traditional Chinese] dress. I did and was measured before I left the terminal. ... The President it seems likes for American women to wear Chinese dress when they dine with him. ... Bus's classmate D. B. Johnson is head of the MAAG [Military Assistance Advisory Group]. We're so fond of both of them. We stayed with them. They have a marvelous house furnished by the Chinese government. ... After luncheon we went shopping. ... Afterwards to a beautiful new museum [showcasing] treasures of old China that were brought from the mainland. ... My dress was awaiting me that evening when I got back to the house. [127]

The Wheelers were scheduled to attend a reception in their honor that evening.

> [But] the men never made it. Bus had a meeting with President Chiang Kai-shek. (In my old age, my spelling frustrates me, and as Bus says, I am now willing to recognize it as mental laziness.) The meeting lasted an hour and fifty minutes, unheard of, and Bus said he and the President (through an interpreter) did all the talking. From all sides, I heard what a magnificent job Bus did. [128]

"The President gave a dinner in our honor" later that evening. Betty had been cautioned by the State Department to expect Chiang to be reserved and not very friendly. On the contrary, she found him "delightful." Chiang was humorous and talkative. [129]

> Madame is still in the States. The residence is beautiful. ... At dinner, I could only think, 'I can't believe this is me.' I sat on the right hand of this very famous man. His oldest son [who had been educated in the States] was on my left. He interpreted for us. Through the son, I learned the President [was] most gratified that I looked so beautiful in Chinese dress. ... The President was most easy to talk with. I really got a thrill. [130]

Betty befriended Chang's daughter and would enjoy many lunches with her in later years. [131]

The next day, Bus attended to business while Betty toured an orphanage before they departed for Hong Kong. They spent New Year's Eve resting in the Hong Kong Hilton. [132]

> Bus did something or other and has pinched a nerve in his back. He made his briefings this morning, but feels miserable. He cancelled out our dinner tonight. ... Bus went back to bed. I've been looking at the magnificent view out of our window. ... I am so tired myself that it is a great relief to me that we have stayed home. In fact, I think it's good that Bus, himself, is forced to take time out. He has not paused a minute since we went to France. [133]

The Wheelers then visited Korea and did not return home to Washington until 7 January 1966. [134]

## 1966

### *Social Functions*

In early January, the Wheelers had taken another trip to Hawaii "as usual." Betty recorded that they rested indoors their first day there due to high winds and overcast skies. "Oley" and Pat Sharp hosted a dinner for the Wheelers that evening. The next day, Bus and Betty "had lunch on the beach with Kitsy" Westmoreland, whom Betty found "pleasanter." [135]

On Bus's birthday, 13 January, cake and cocktails were served in the Chairman's Dining Room for him, his personal staff, and numerous high-ranking colleagues. That evening, Bim's family joined Bus and Betty for a celebration in Quarters 6. [136]

Betty reported that they were still "swamped under the masses of Christmas cards" they had received. "There must have been close to a thousand this year, many from people we'd never heard of before." Betty had one of Bus's aides "open them as they came in so they were listed and those with notes separated." Betty replied to "a long list" of them. [137]

Betty had always been social and fashion conscious and had become a *grande dame*. In private, she was often critical of other women and had limited tolerance for their company, as evidenced by her impatient remarks about Kitsy Westmoreland over the years.

The cattiest remarks that Betty ever wrote regarded the wife of U.S. Attorney General Nicholas Katzenbach. Recounting a luncheon for "Mrs. Healy, wife of the British Defense Minister" hosted by Margie McNamara, Betty wrote:

> Mrs. Katzenbach was there. This is the first I've met her face to face. Saw her first at a distance in another room, a great beehive of black hair, lovely eyes, and fairly young. Close to, not so young, hard as nails. A pinstripe suit, too tight skirt above the knees and fancy black stockings. She looked like one might expect the lady of the street to appear! One can only wonder (and many did) why in the world she was the Snowdons' hostess. Interesting anyway. [138]

Wheeler's long and often unpredictable office hours occasionally conflicted with the official functions that were an integral component of his duties as Chairman:

> Poor Bus didn't get out of the White House until 8:20 and dinner [hosted by] Gen. & Mrs. Hussay … for Ambassador and Madame Lucet … was at 8:15. He finally made it at nine. I went on ahead. Dinner was held up a little but they finally went ahead. Bus arrived in proper sequence to get his first course as it was served. [139]

## *Honolulu*

On 7 February, a three-day conference between President Johnson and South Vietnamese Premier Nguyen C. Ky was underway in Honolulu when Betty wrote, "Bus came in last night and said he was leaving for Hawaii today." [140]

Wheeler arrived on the final day of the conference when Johnson and Ky issued a joint declaration that emphasized winning the war through a combination of military action and expanded civic reforms. [141]

## *Armchair Generals*

It seemed that everyone had ideas on how to fight the Vietnam War better. The problem was that owing to the President's intentional misleading of Congress, the military, the media, and the American public, considerable confusion existed over just what combat operations were supposed to accomplish. Was it classical victory as in World War II, or was it something less?

Wheeler and his fellow senior military leaders understood the Administration was intent upon the doctrinal definition of victory. Wheeler defended the feasibility of that objective in secret testimony before a subcommittee of the Senate Armed Services Committee. "I myself have no doubt that, in the long term, we can achieve military victory." [142]

On 8 February, Wheeler's long-time friend and former fellow West Point instructor, Lieutenant General (Retired) James M. Gavin, gave testimony to the Senate Foreign Relations Committee critical of the way the war was being fought. Gavin's testimony stirred up a controversy in the press. He was sensitive to the fact that his comments were critical of Wheeler's advice and support to the President.

"[Bus] had a letter from Jim Gavin," Betty wrote. "Jim said he hoped that he hadn't caused him any discomfort and that he never dreamed that he would stir up so much. Bus said he wrote [back] and told him the only discomfort caused was to have disagreement with a good friend and a fine soldier, publicly." [143]

Public emotions were already running high. "Bus is being swamped with mail, some for him, some violently opposed," Betty wrote. "One so violent, she is being investigated by the FBI. She says he should be assassinated! Bus thinks 'the doves' are more evil and violent than 'the hawks'!" [144]

The Wheelers were exhausted. "Bus and me slept until a quarter of ten this morning," Betty wrote on Sunday, 13 February. "Can hardly believe it. I think if he had slept on I would have. Our light was out by eleven so it was a good night. Bus is working now." [145]

## *Weekends*

Meanwhile, after dinner one Sunday night, Betty wrote to her mother while "Bus is doing some last minute work." Betty had just completed hosting a series of high-profile coffees. "They seemed successful, and I feel that if they continue to do this every year, it will grow into quite a thing. I believe that the congressional wives that came will spread the word. I personally, as I said before, am most impressed by the youth, and the caliber."

Betty was looking forward to visiting her parents. "Easter is about the worst time I could pick, but that is when Bus will be away. ... Bus will be away again at the end of the month and I can come then." [146]

The following weekend, the Wheelers stayed at the Tidewater Inn in Easton, Maryland:

> For a couple of weeks we've had reservations here for a long weekend. We planned to look at property and get away. ... Of all things to happen, the power steering went out on the new beautiful car [a Chevy Impala from Rosenthal's Chevrolet in Arlington that Bim bought as a surprise for his father.] It took us three hours to get here. ... The whole morning was a comedy of errors and maybe we should have stayed home. The car will be ready around three. We'll see the house we meant to see this morning this afternoon and the one this afternoon tomorrow morning. ... We may head to West Virginia on Sunday. [147]

The same letter gives an indication of the prominent guests whom the Wheelers often hosted at Quarters 6. "Our party was successful. We were sorry that Dean Rusk was down with the flu and didn't make it. ... Was pleased that the Auchincloss's came." [148]

Bim's friend Fischer recalled an occasion when, after dinner with the Wheelers, the party retired to the library for conversation and cordials. "The waitstaff cleaned up and the Sergeant-in-Charge appeared to tell Bus that the staff was finished, were preparing to leave for the evening, and *the phones had been switched*." Bus was always concerned that their enlisted orderlies should have adequate time to spend with their families, and so he usually dismissed them as soon as possible. Normally, while Quarters 6 was staffed during the day, telephone calls would come into the residence. After the staff left for the evening, however, incoming calls were routed to the Pentagon where they were screened for subject matter and the relative importance of the caller. On this evening, the phones had not been switched for some reason.

"While we were in the library, the phone rang at General Wheeler's elbow," Fischer recalled. "He picked it up and this is what we heard from his side of the conversation."

> General Wheeler. ... When did this happen? ... Calm down and tell me what happened.
>
> We listened to his one-sided conversation for several minutes, totally on tenterhooks, only to find out that a mother in Washington, DC had been notified that her son, based in Korea, had been involved in an accident (but not combat related), and all she knew was that her son was hurting.
>
> For some reason, the phones hadn't been switched and this mother, realizing she couldn't get through to the President, tried the next on her list, the Chairman of the Joint Chiefs of Staff. Her attempt paid off.
>
> General Wheeler spent perhaps twenty minutes assuring her that as soon as he could find out her son's location and, if he was capable of talking to her, she would be patched through to him. He treated her as though her son was the most important soldier in his Army. [149]

Linda Howell, the Wheeler's niece, had lived with them for almost two years. A student at George Mason University, Linda had started dating Captain Tony Lattore, a Marine officer stationed at Quantico, Virginia. An instructor,

Lattore trained newly commissioned Second Lieutenants for combat assignments in Vietnam. [150]

One evening, Tony called Quarters 6 to speak to Linda. He anticipated that one of the house orderlies would answer the phone. When Bus answered, "General Wheeler," Tony was tongue tied and chagrined.

Eventually, Tony was invited over to meet Uncle Bus and Aunt Betty. He had always picked up Linda at the back door, so that is where he went. One of the enlisted orderlies opened the door, let him in, and notified the Wheelers that he was in the kitchen. Betty was appalled that their guest, a young officer, had used the back door. Bus chuckled in amusement. [151]

Stewart recalled an occasion when Margie's dog Sammy was left unattended in the house. He got into the kitchen and ate the base of a cake under preparation. The dog also pooped all over the house. One of the orderlies offered to clean it up, but Bus declined. Saying that the dog had left it for him and his owner, Bus cleaned it up himself with a spatula and paper towels. [152]

## Reappointment

Wheeler's activities over the month of April illustrate how packed his calendar was with all the many other issues worldwide besides Vietnam. He spent the first week of the month in Iran. On 19-21 April, Wheeler hosted a visit to Washington by Lieutenant General Garcia Barragan, the Mexican Secretary of National Defense. Five days later, Wheeler was awarded the Order of Service Merit First Class in a ceremony at the residence of Dr. Hyun Chul Kim, the South Korean Ambassador to the United States. A photo from that ceremony captured Betty beaming with pride up at Bus. "She certainly knew how to play the role," says Bim, "especially around foreigners." Wheeler then spent three days in London. Upon his return to Washington, he went straight to the Pentagon and only returned to Quarters 6 late that afternoon. [153]

While Bus was in England, Betty sent a letter to "Mr. Jetton," their builder in the Florida Keys. Before Bus departed, he and Betty "finally had a chance to take more than a casual glance at the plans together" for building a main house and a guest house on their property on Casey Key. "We both feel that it is important to have the larger house plans before building. It is the only way we can be sure of the way the two houses 'mesh' and fit the land." [154]

In late April, the President, with McNamara's concurrence, reappointed Wheeler for a second two-year term as Chairman. "You don't get extended as Chairman unless you're doing something right and they like what you're doing," Casey observes. At the blistering pace Bus had maintained, it is understandable that Betty wrote, "The reappointment is viewed with mixed emotions. Certainly, to live in the manner in which we do for another two years, can't be hard to take. I just wish that there was some way for Bus to have more rest and also a real vacation." [155]

Wheeler leveraged Rostow's influence and now insisted upon a regular seat for himself at the President's Tuesday luncheons. Wheeler had long resented how these private forums among Johnson's closest civilian advisors had contributed to the Chiefs' isolation from the planning and decision-making process. Because the advice that Johnson received during these luncheons had been pre-coordinated between McNamara and Rusk, it was unlikely that the President or other civilian advisors present would question it. This arrangement had kept Johnson ignorant of the Chiefs' opinions, and the Chiefs had remained ill-informed of the true direction of the Administration's Vietnam policy. Not anymore. [156]

Wheeler recalled, "When Walt Rostow became the Special Assistant for National Security Affairs, President Johnson started the so-called Tuesday luncheons, which I always attended." [Wheeler meant to say that *he* started to attend these luncheons when Rostow became National Security Advisor in April 1966. Johnson had commenced the luncheons on 4 February 1964.] "I was one of the regular invitees," Wheeler recalled. "I would put forward the military point of view when it was necessary or comment on anything else as far as that goes. Mr. Johnson didn't confine me to commenting on military affairs at all."

Wheeler also explained:

> When I talked to the President or to the Secretary of Defense,
> I knew what the other Chiefs' views were. Not only that, if a
> particular problem was coming up, I always consulted with
> them if I had time. ... I always reported to them practically

verbatim what went on at the meetings, what I had said. And if we were talking about a problem where there was a divergency of view among the Chiefs, I would always express the divergent view. I made this a practice. So that he [President Johnson] was not receiving merely my advice, but he was receiving the corporate advice of the other Chiefs. [157]

## *Man of Martinsburg*

When in Washington, Wheeler had to be accessible to the President and McNamara on short-notice. Frequent changes in Wheeler's schedule played havoc with the couple's official social calendar.

"Bus and I were going out to dinner tonight," Betty wrote on 3 May. "He called around two and said he'd cancelled. It was one of those tremendous affairs at the Hilton. It started at six-thirty … and he couldn't get away. I don't know why he accepts the early ones, something usually happens." [158]

Wheeler had been successful in carving out at least some personal time on some weekends to look for a weekend house to which he and Betty could escape.

"Bus and I drove down to the Northern Neck on Sunday," Betty wrote. "We saw some beautiful property. None for us." The following weekend, she reported:

> Saturday, Bus took the day off and we drove into West Virginia. It was a glorious day. I think we've gone the full cycle now and are back to a weekend house. I think Bus has just about bought himself a half mile of fishing stream. Beautiful, beautiful country but a poor, pitifully ugly little house. I think it's been found at a time when it's badly needed. I feel sure that if we have a place, he will take a long weekend a couple times a month. Especially if he has a place to work part of the time, but can get out and fish and just walk through the woods discovering what he has. [159]

A week later, Betty wrote:

> Bus is so happy. His offer was accepted on the property in West Virginia. Already, he has booklets on trees, gardens,

shrubs, equipment, and restorations! ... The house at the moment is in excellent condition. It's small, but everything is there to do with. I'm glad that he will now have a destination. The drive is about an hour and three quarters, but an easy one. I know I mentioned the half mile of fishing creek, but did I mention the hundred and fifty plus acres? And at that, [it's] just six miles from downtown Martinsburg. It could well turn into an investment we (he) didn't know that he was making! (or does he?). [160]

The other big news in the Wheeler family in May was that Bim and Margie gave Bus and Betty their second grandson, John Robinson "Robbie" Wheeler. [161]

## NATO

On 5 June, Wheeler was presented an honorary Doctor of Science degree from Norwich University. Six days later, he joined the chiefs of nine other North Atlantic Treaty Organization (NATO) countries' Armed Forces for the seven-day Supreme Headquarters Allied Powers Europe Exercise (SHAPEX) conference hosted by Lemnitzer. [162]

Since 1963, the U.S. had assigned three Polaris submarines to the U.S. European Command and suggested that NATO consider the establishment of a multilateral naval force. The idea stood until 1965, when it became clear that de Gaulle intended to disengage France militarily from NATO. Conditions had changed in Europe since 1949, he explained. The threat to the West from the Soviet Union had diminished. The French had cut their ties gradually, participating less and less in NATO military exercises while increasing the size of their own nuclear strike force. De Gaulle served notice in 1966 that although France had no intention of abandoning the alliance, French forces would withdraw from NATO command during the year and all NATO troops would have to depart French territory. [163]

Bus returned home to Washington in time to celebrate "a beautiful and festive" wedding anniversary with Betty, their thirty-fourth. "All of my life such lovely things have been given to me and done for me," she wrote. "Then these last years, due to Bus's job, there have been so many things coming in.

But these last have made me really stop and count all my blessings and feel rather humble and really undeserving." [164]

## *Eye Surgery*

Meanwhile back in Washington, the Wheelers hosted a dinner for forty in their quarters on 5 July. "The Chiefs gave it for Dave Burchinal, Director of the [Joint Staff] who leaves for Europe. ... Bus hated the idea of [having the dinner in the officers] club." [165]

The following morning on 6 July, "Bus went out to the hospital" for a pre-op appointment, "but was home by noon." He had started having vision problems in his right eye in 1964, and a cataract had developed in 1965. [166]

Betty explained that he would undergo surgery for the cataract on 8 July:

> He has kept quiet about this and except for the President, Vance, McNamara, and me, no one knows. Just don't want you to read a press release. It doesn't seem too bad that he will be house bound for a couple weeks and his mother will be here. ... Bus and I are hard pressed for any time alone. Don't mean that the way it sounds. If he were working there would be activity anyway. Just seemed, though, as long as he would be here that it would be nice to be without company every meal. No matter, Mums will enjoy the opportunity to see more of him and he can always shut himself up [in his study]. [167]

Three days after the surgery, Betty reported:

> Bus is doing beautifully. This enforced rest may be a blessing. He slept most of the first two days. I believe the plans are to keep him at Walter Reed until the early part of next week. ... Bim drove out with me to see Bus Saturday afternoon. He was watching the ball game and the beer ads were too much. Sgt. McTeague went off and got some for us, and I would say Bus enjoyed it too. ... Bus is walking up and down the halls. He looks wonderfully. [168]

Following his release from the hospital, Bus took several days of leave to rest and recuperate at home. "With Bus home, we're up later than normally, and are usually at the pool around eleven-thirty," Betty wrote. "Bus comes in to nap around one, but I generally stay out a couple of hours more." [169]

## Ugly Duckling Manor

"This morning ... Bus has gone to Walter Reed expecting to be cleared to go to the country for two days," Betty reported on 25 July. "The house has been empty for almost three weeks. We need to check it out. Bus hopes to spend the first week in August there, so we need to get it ready to receive the furniture. ... The property ... is so exactly what Bus wants." [170]

During the following week, the Wheelers stopped by Cameron Station in Alexandria. "The [Post Exchange] is the largest in the area and I want him to see the hardware and household supplies," Betty explained. "With so much to get, every penny saved will be a help." That weekend, they cleaned, painted, moved beds inside, and had the chimney and a door frame inspected. [171]

On 8 August, Betty reported on the help they had received in getting the Martinsburg house in order.

> (In the country), we worked hard! However a great deal was accomplished. ... Two little boys (11 & 13 1/3) arrived on their bicycles. ... Bus asked if they thought their parents would let them work for us. They arrived promptly at eight the next three mornings. All the junk was gotten out of the attic, basement, and a room under the porch and piled in the barn. ... Well, the boys did a fine job. I'm sure they never saw so much money, and I can also see it is needed. The county road runs to our property. The house is about a half mile further in. The boys live in the last house and I know they will know every car that passes and whether it should go into the property or not. ... They were a big help, let me tell you.
>
> The property is beautiful. I asked Bus if he had any idea for a name for the house. He said he hadn't come up with one. What did I think? I said that I had a name but I was afraid that it would hurt his feelings! It now has a name – 'Ugly

Duckling Manor' – with the hopes that it will turn into a beautiful swan! [172]

The Wheelers still intended to build a retirement home and guest house on Betty's parents' property on Casey Key. A seawall had just been installed to retain a massive amount of dredged earth from the intercoastal waterway project that her father volunteered to have dumped at the back of his property. This was a shrewd decision, for it greatly increased his acreage. Betty suggested, "Maybe we should call the [planned] Florida house 'The Beautiful Swan'. 'Ugly Duckling Manor' will delay anything in Florida for awhile, I'm sure, at least until order is established." [173]

In fact, the Wheelers would never build their Florida dream home. After Bus passed away in 1975, Betty would remain in Martinsburg until her death in 2004. A few years earlier, Bim and his second wife Judy moved out there from Washington, DC to care for Betty, and they still live there. The house, incidentally, did achieve the dramatic transformation Betty envisioned, and it is now a showcase home under Judy Wheeler's care. [174]

"Bus and I left for the country about one on Saturday," Betty wrote on 15 August.

> It rained the better part of the weekend. Such a blessing for the fields. We slept under a blanket, windows wide open, so cool, so quiet. The Ailles' dropped by with the Abrams' (Vice Chief of Staff of the Army) Sunday afternoon. They just stayed about twenty minutes. ... Hopefully, we'll get down again this [coming] weekend. [175]

Two weeks later, Betty reported, "We started for the country about four-thirty."

> The dining room is small – the menu limited, the wine list terrible, the drinks good (Bus said his martinis were. Hard to go wrong on dry vermouth.) The food was well prepared, and I believe with prior planning an even better meal could be prepared. ... It was around nine when we got in. We opened up the house, had a night cap, and early to bed. The air was cool and fresh. ... In the morning, to work, to work. Bus started my bath – and I bit the bullet – and got under the sink – and

then I took the drawers out of the stove and yelped for Bus. It was so awful, I wanted him to poke around first! All is now beautifully clean and a days' work it was. I still have to paint the cupboard under the sink and remove the masking tape from the floor & windows – the latter a mean job.

We're going back again Thursday, no Friday morning and I think not come home until Tuesday morning. If we leave Monday, we'll come back in the early afternoon and come through Leesburg, staying off the beltway, which I'm sure will be jammed. [176]

## *Town and Country*

"It was beautiful in the country," Betty wrote on 6 September.

On Sunday we had a little much needed rain. Everything is so dry. We slept late. Worked hard. Stopped around six. … One evening, we rode to the swimming hole and then walked along the creek. Bus cast a few times but didn't get anything. It is peaceful. Every evening we saw the moon come up. The fields are so pretty in the moonlight. We have a herd of four-teen Black Angus cows! No, not ours. There must be a break in the fence across they way and they came up the streambed. Look mighty pastoral. Hopefully they won't get up near the house.

We won't get back there this weekend. Bus has to go to West Point on Saturday (me too). … I don't know whether we're off to Italy the following week or not. [177]

Three days later, Betty wrote:

Yesterday I went with Bus to the arrival ceremony for General Ne Win of Burma. … In the evening we went back to the White House to a reception. Mrs. Johnson was wearing a most beautiful dress. She really looks lovely. Lynda [Johnson] was there. It's the first I've seen her since her 'new look.' She's really got it and she's stunning. Whatever the makeup man in Hollywood taught her to do was worth every penny. She really has emerged quite a 'swan!' [178]

A couple weeks later, Betty reported that she and Bus had had another "pleasant weekend in the country."

> It was almost five before we got to the house as we stopped at the Post Office and the shopping center. ... It was a beautiful evening. We went up the creek. Didn't stay long as Bus snagged his line and lost his lure. Hadn't brought replacements. ... Our stove is in. It was pleasant enough to sit out for drinks. I love the lights over the meadows as the sun sets. We moved in for supper and had our first fire. It couldn't be cuter. The room is tiny, but cozy and quaint. [179]

Word got around town quickly about the new celebrity residents. "Have mailed the Martinsburg paper," Betty wrote. "Read editorial page. One might not think to look there to find Bus. Can say we feel welcome." [180]

The Wheelers were looking forward to visiting Betty's parents in the Keys. "If we're lucky, we will be down over my birthday. We plan to have a car waiting in Tampa and will drive down." [181]

## *Frequent Flyer*

Between 29 September and 4 October, Wheeler toured Canada and the U.S. with Lemnitzer and the Chiefs of Staff from other NATO countries. Their tour, hosted by U.S. Air Force General R. J. Reeves, the Commander-in-Chief, North American Aerospace Defense Command (CINCNORAD), included a visit to the NORAD regional headquarters in North Bay, Ontario. Wheeler accompanied the delegation on their return trip to Europe. [182]

Wheeler would state in a speech six months later:

> I believe that the enduring strength of our free society, fully protected by military power, permits us safely to explore new avenues of understanding with friend and foe alike. Indeed, a society such as ours is obligated to seek new ways to lessen tension and promote peace. I favor, then, such hopeful ventures toward understanding as a limited nuclear test ban, the consular treaty, the space treaty, cultural exchanges, and the US-USSR negotiations on deployment of anti-ballistic missile systems. Peace is the ultimate aspiration of all Americans.

But I would emphasize that only the strong and secure are free to venture with assurance. The record of our adversaries makes it clear that the American Eagle must continue to clutch the arrows as well as the olive branch.

Wheeler continued:

I see the world as an arena where we are properly and unavoidably committed to support the high principles we cherish. I see no obstacles we cannot surmount if we keep our eyes on the forest and not on the trees. ... Above all, we must be constant in principle and purpose. As General Omar Bradley said long ago, 'The United States has matured to world leadership—it is time we steered by the stars, and not by the lights of each passing ship.' We cannot recant either power or conscience to buy ease or peace at any price. I see our NATO policy as a continued test of this. Vietnam is another test in another place. I am convinced that we are right in the course we pursue, and I am convinced that right will prevail. [183]

Betty reported Bus's quick turnaround in Washington before he was off again.

[Almost immediately after returning from Europe], Bus got off last night for Vietnam. It was a short one night stand [at home]. He's been living that way the last ten days. He has been sort of depressed about NATO, but came home encouraged and felt that there was renewed determination. Let us pray so. I gather as always the food was superb. Bus kept me posted on the roast beef diet. ... Bus felt [the dinner on the final evening] a perfect ending to what appeared to be a highly successful trip.

"Bus gets back [from Vietnam] on Friday [14 October]," Betty added. "He'll have to go to the office Saturday morning, but we hope to go down [to the country] next weekend. It will be a shame if he doesn't get there, because the color will be on the wane by the following week." His travel and work requirements impinged upon their plans to visit Betty's parents. "Bus and I will only be in Florida with you three nights at most." [184]

On 19 October, Betty wrote, "We started for the country about six o'clock Saturday evening. It was well worth it. ... We had a lovely evening to drive. ... We unloaded, lit the open and grill fires, listened to a repeat of the West Point game, and were in bed shortly after eleven. The foliage is so lovely. ... Bus (fingers crossed) and I are going [back] to the country Friday after work." [185]

## Worldwide Commitments

Meanwhile back in Washington, Wheeler's schedule was often filled with ceremonial duties. On 1 November, he presided over a joint honors ceremony at the River Entrance to the Pentagon for Iranian General Aryana, Chief of the Supreme Commander's Staff. In a similar ceremony at the end of the month, Wheeler presented Republic of China Admiral Ni Yue-Si, Chief of the General Staff, Ministry of National Defense, with the Legion of Merit. [186]

Betty recorded how extremely busy Bus was throughout the holiday period.

> On Thanksgiving day, we had the house to ourselves for the first time in so long. I went to the Thanksgiving service at ten. ... Bus was with the Joint Staff most of the day. However, he gave up at five-thirty. We had our first gin game in months. ... As Bus had to work Saturday morning, we didn't go to the country until after the Army-Navy game. [187]

A few days later, she wrote, "Bus is fighting the battle of the budget and we won't get to the country this weekend after all. I am sorry. It does us both so much good." [188]

Betty happily accompanied Bus on another business trip to Paris on 10 December.

> We stayed at the Hotel Lotti as usual. It's exciting to be back in Paris. ... The welcome mat is always out here and it makes one feel so good. ... There were flowers from the management, a basket of fruit from the Burchinal's, [and] flowers from [former colleagues]. ... The Lemnitzer's gave a reception last night. ... He is on the search for a house in Belgium. He really lives a charmed life, but it would be nice

if someone with a little 'know how' could do the selecting. Everyone got all excited over the article in Newsweek that Lem was retiring, Bus replacing him, and Dave McDonald taking over from Bus. Bus asked Cy Vance about it and Cy laughed and said never had he seen three big errors in one short sentence. [189]

"As always, we had a good trip," Betty reported. Not so much for Bus's new Aide de Camp, Marine Major George Christ.

"Tuesday morning was chaotic!" Betty recalled. "The first thing I remember is waking up with the lights on, Bus partly dressed and wild eyed. I mean it."

"What's the matter?" Betty asked him.

"It's nine-thirty," Bus replied. "I've overslept. I didn't wake up until nine-twenty, and I have a ten o'clock appointment!"

> Well, you can imagine. He made the appointment, no breakfast, furious with Maj. Christ and Sgt. Harrington for not checking, as he had ordered the car for 8:15. They just decided he wanted to sleep. They're learned. I'm sure the wrath would have been less great, if any, had he been wakened when he wanted to sleep if he hadn't said so. Things were popping.

That evening, "Bus worked until almost seven-thirty. We had a quiet dinner in the hotel. A fitting ending after the hectic morning." [190]

As usual during Bus's business trips to Paris, Betty shopped, went to several museums, visited old friends, had her hair done, and toured the city, which was decorated for the holidays. Bus had no official duties on the last day of their visit, so they were able to meet some old friends for lunch.

"Bus and I walked to the Louvre, took a last look at the Winged Victory, strolled through the Greek and Egyptian and Roman periods to the Venus de Milo. Then [we] walked slowly home past the shops on the Rue de Rivoli. By the time we were back to the hotel, it was time to depart.

Their free day in Paris was a brief respite. "It is unlikely that we [will] go to Germany [to visit some old friends] unless Bus takes a few days [of leave],"

Betty explained. "But Washington gets worse instead of better and he always feels that the minute business is over, he must get back." [191]

Wheeler received a letter from Odom, his former Aide-de-Camp, in Vietnam informing him that his family home had burned completely to the ground. Wheeler replied in a letter dated 28 December.

> I received only yesterday your letter written on Christmas Eve. It has been a long time since we heard from Charlotte and you. Needless to say, I am extremely sorry to learn of the loss of your house. That is really a blow both financially and psychologically. I do hope that Charlotte has rebounded [from cancer], and sees life a bit more happily despite your absence and the loss of your personal belongings.
>
> The surgery on my eye was a great success. I am now able to wear a contact lens and, while I would not attempt to fool you that I am as good as ever, I at least can see again from my right eye. This is satisfactory to me for it is something I have not been able to do for about the past two years.
>
> At any rate, you shall see for yourself that, barring the wear and tear of the years, I am doing all right. I say this because I will be visiting Vietnam for about a week commencing 8 January. While I am there, I hope to visit the 199th [Infantry] Brigade and see you.
>
> In the meantime, my very best wishes to you for the New Year. Take care of yourself; we've got plenty of heroes! [192]

## Christmas

"[On 23 December], I had tea with Madame Chiang Kai Shek," Betty wrote. "I must say that I enjoyed it. She is a beautiful woman (70?), so gentle to have such an iron hand. It was an interesting half hour." [193]

On Christmas Eve, the extended Wheeler family enjoyed themselves in the well-decorated Quarters 6. "It was a happy evening," Betty reported. "The table beautiful with fresh holly that I'm sure Sgt. Wiggam stole from the [Arlington National] cemetery, and then interlaced with artificial poinsettias." [194]

"The staff gave us an ice crusher for the country. I always have my vermouth here on crushed ice, and Bus has taken to having scotch over it. They were so pleased with themselves, and we were touched that they would chip in and get it for us." Betty used some of the money her parents had given them to buy a fancy outfit. "Bus bought some shoes for the country and some rubber boots. He has some [money] left, but he says he'll happily put it in my 'suit pot.'" [195]

The Wheeler's nephew, Doneld Howell, was now a Captain at Fort Bliss, Texas. Due for reassignment, Don informed Bus that he would like to become a courier and "see the world." Bus declined to pull any strings for him but advised Don that if he applied for the program, he would probably be sent to Asia. Don's acceptance led to an 18-month tour in Okinawa with a small joint courier station distributing cryptologic codes. During this tour, Don would see Japan, Korea, the Philippines, Thailand, and Vietnam. [196]

Meanwhile, "deep in the budget," Wheeler spent much of the holidays in the office, albeit with somewhat abbreviated hours. "About four-thirty [on the day after Christmas] we looked at a movie, played some gin later, then ate and to bed," Betty wrote. [197]

The following day, she added:

Bus stayed home today, although he is out now to a meeting with Dean Rusk. Usually, when he goes downstairs, he wakes me up. He didn't this morning and I slept until 10:30. … If Bus isn't too late we plan to look at a movie. He may be out of the mood by the time he gets back. I know if we had left this morning [for the country] 'they' would have gotten along without him. [198]

# CHAPTER 9

## PINNACLE
## (JANUARY 1967 – JULY 1970)

### 1967

### *Martinsburg*

The Wheelers rang in 1967 at their "new" old place in West Virginia. Betty wrote:

> The country was absolutely beautiful driving down on Friday. We had no trouble getting in. We hadn't been in the house five minutes before a truck drove in. The man introduced himself as Max Brown, our neighbor who owns the dairy up the road. Imagine a true 'Farmer Brown.' He said that he'd seen us go by and he wanted to be sure that we had gotten in alright. Anytime we need help just call him. That's right neighborly, I'm thinking. [1]

"Good, honest, hard-working country folk," as Bim describes them, Max and Retha Brown would become close friends of the Wheelers. Max would lease Bus's pastures for his French Charolais cattle. Years later, after Bus and Retha had both died, Max and Betty would often have dinner together in town. (Bim and Judy Wheeler are still close to the Brown family today.) [2]

The Wheelers hadn't gone to the country simply to relax. There was still much work to be done to bring the old farmhouse up to Betty's exacting standards.

> I painted my way through the days. The dining room that I thought would give no trouble and I was sure would take only one coat on the ceiling, took two, the walls three, and the new dining room door <u>five</u>. So – there's still woodwork to be done. ... I am so anxious by spring to have the interior finished. The little fireplace room is tiny but comfortable. It

is ready for curtains and a rug. I'm going to try to go down while Bus is in Saigon. It's slow going but we are loving it. … Bus [returns to Quarters Six] relaxed and refreshed, but I'm usually tired! A nice satisfied tired, but I'll be glad to get the manual labor over with. Four rooms down – three to go and a little bath. [3]

Now that they had gotten to know their neighbors, Bus was fine with leaving Betty in the country while he returned to DC. [4]

While Bus was away, Betty attended the Presbyterian Church in Martinsburg for the first time. She liked the service and intended to return. [5]

### *Growing Unpopularity*

*Wheeler appears on the TV news show Meet the Press, 1967. (Office of the Chairman of the Joint Chiefs of Staff).*

Wheeler's optimism for how things were shaping up in Vietnam was contrasted by the growing unpopularity of the war at home. Draft calls had risen dramatically and were increasing. Selective Service began to eliminate deferments that had shielded graduate students, as well as families with members already serving in the military. Public opinion polls remained stable but fragile, with slight gains for the antiwar side and fewer respondents who expressed no opinion. Protesters were marching in greater numbers. At Stanford University on 20 February, the Secret Service had to physically extricate the Vice President from his limousine when protesters swarmed and pummeled it. [6]

An issue of *Life* magazine carried a full-page, close-up picture of Wheeler and McNamara aboard an aircraft carrier watching aircraft being launched. Both had their arms folded and wore "Mickey Mouse" ear protectors. Bim's friend Fischer cut out the picture. His wife gave it to Bim, who in turn passed it to Bus. Bus carried it into his next meeting with McNamara and said, "I have a picture I would like you to autograph for a friend of mine." McNamara pulled out his pen, eager to sign, until he saw the picture in question.

"Why should I sign *that* picture?" McNamara asked.

Bus replied, "Listen, this young man is an admirer of yours, and right now, you need all the admirers you can get!"

McNamara said, "You're right," and promptly signed it. The following Christmas, Bim gave the framed picture to Fischer, who removed it from the frame for Bus to add his signature. [7]

## Quarters 6

Meanwhile, Betty kept grandsons Billy and Robbie while their parents enjoyed a five-day getaway in Martinsburg. She wrote:

> Billy usually got to the kitchen for breakfast before Bus, and then joined Bus while he was having breakfast. As you know, Bus always goes through the kitchen and passes the time with whoever is in. Billy announced that he had had a good breakfast. He was stuffed, and couldn't eat another thing. He followed Bus to the table. There, Bus said, was a big bowl of beautiful strawberries. [Five-year old] Billy immediately wanted some.
>
> Bus said, 'Billy, you said you were stuffed. I don't think you should eat any more. You might get sick.'
>
> Bus said Billy, as quick as a flash, said, 'Oh Babu, I just want to taste them to be sure they're good and won't make you sick!'
>
> Needless to say he had some berries.

Betty also informed her mother that:

> Bus brought home a translation of a piece in a paper or magazine in Russia giving much information about the six American war criminals McNamara, Taylor, Wheeler, Sharp, Westmoreland, and Stillwell. To everyone else's four or less typewritten pages, Bus's covered eight. It's unbelievable how awful he is, what an opportunist he is and how he's gotten ahead, starting at 16 years old when he joined the National Guard. He's been at a desk all his career, shuffles papers (with brilliance). Only five months in combat whether by accident or his plan. Good God! [8]

Betty had gone "to Alice Haislip's for lunch yesterday. Ham has re-re-tired after 15 years [as] head of the 'Soldiers' Home.'" Betty had hoped Bus could take that job after he retired from the Army, but, "Ham didn't hold out quite long enough!" [9]

### Guam & Home

Wheeler departed for the Far East on the evening of 15 March after working a full day in the office. After a stopover and coordinations with Sharp in Hawaii, Wheeler and Sharp travelled together to Vietnam enroute to Guam. Their visit included a meet-and-greet on 18 March with Marine flight crews in the II Field Force area of operations. [10]

While Bus was in Vietnam, Betty woke up from an afternoon nap to discover an antiwar protest being staged in front of their quarters:

> I could hardly believe my eyes. There were at least thirty pickets going round and round on the sidewalk taking in the area of the house. The signs were mostly 'Peace', 'Get out of Vietnam', nothing personal, but I must say not a very pretty sight. ... I could never be a politician's wife! The press and photographers were out and NBC was making television. I saw the six o'clock news and saw that a letter had been left in the box! The [enlisted orderly] men were off so there was no one to answer the door. Perhaps just as well. Anyway – the MPs [Military Police] blocked all traffic on the front line and it was a sight to see. I will say, from the third floor the actual

picketers were not a bad looking lot. There were two women in the group – however, on the side lines were a few grubby, longhaired, bearded characters. It couldn't have been fun. It was bitterly cold and the wind was whipping. As snow flurries arrived they departed. I have no idea how long they were actually there, but I watched for about a half hour. Believe the purpose was for Bus to mend his ways and at Guam recommend getting out of Vietnam. They should have arrived a few days sooner. [11]

While Bus was at the Guam conference between senior U.S. and South Vietnamese officials, Betty updated her mother on their upcoming schedule, which typifies the myriad other matters that occupied Bus besides the war in Vietnam.

We leave the first [of April] for London getting home on the sixth. Bus gives a stag dinner that night. ... The thirteenth and fourteenth are taken up with a SEATO [Southeast Asia Treaty Organization] conference and we entertain forty on the fourteenth. ... [We have] a dinner every week. ... We go to Paris on the sixth of May for ten days. ...We go to West Point for Bus's 35th reunion on the 2nd and third of June. The 25th, 35th, and 50th [reunions] are the big ones and we have had reservations since last summer. [12]

While in Asia, Bus missed the party that Betty hosted for Bim and Margie's fifth anniversary. Betty's description illustrates how they entertained at Quarters 6.

The dining room was a picture. The table its usual size was placed across the room. There were two round tables to the front and two to the rear with the buffet in the center. Used the long blue skirts with the white organdy clothes. The epergnes had daffodils, flags, a few small yellow chrysanthemums, and sprigs of forsythia. I used two skirts on the buffet and used [her mother's] beautiful lace cloth over it. In the center, was the cake. It was a work of art. ... The food was delicious and everything was a picture. ... The tables of course, were set and we had red wine and champagne. Tables properly cleared and the finger bowls brought. Margie & Bim cut the first piece of cake – then Sgts. Stuart and Harrington took over – put the slices on glass platters and then the cake was passed. There were toasts and I'm sure it was a truly memorable fifth anniversary. ... It's sad. Bus once again missed a landmark in Bim's life. [13]

Bus had put in long hours for many days and finally got some time off on Saturday, 25 March. "We got off for the country at nine. We had two glorious days. We really worked but the windows were open and the birds were singing. It was lovely. Bus took Monday off and then had to come back for a four-thirty meeting. That meant we had to leave by one-thirty."

"For quite awhile now, Bus has been coming in [from work] between six-thirty and seven," Betty wrote on 25 March. "I do hope he can keep it up." [14] (Little did she know that in four months Bus would suffer a heart attack.)

## NATO Departs France

Meanwhile, the North Atlantic Treaty Organization (NATO) alliance had also been under strain. On 30 March, the Supreme Headquarters Allied Powers Europe (SHAPE) closed its headquarters in Rocquencourt, France. The split between France and NATO's military structure had developed over several years, despite Wheeler's repeated efforts to help maintain the alliance. Successive French governments had become increasingly dissatisfied with what they perceived as Anglo-American domination of the command structure and insufficient French influence throughout the command.

After his reelection in December 1965, De Gaulle had sought a more independent role for France to maximize its global influence and status. Increasingly critical of developments in NATO, he described the military integration practiced at SHAPE as obsolete and designed to ensure French subordination to U.S. policy.

In February 1966, De Gaulle declared that the evolving world situation had "stripped of justification" NATO's military integration and that France was, therefore, reestablishing its sovereignty over French territory. As such, all Allied forces within French borders would have to fall under French control by April 1969. Soon afterward, France announced that it was withdrawing from the headquarters of Allied Command Europe and that SHAPE and its subordinate headquarters Allied Forces Central Europe (AFCENT) must depart French territory by 1 April 1967. [15]

The Allies and Wheeler, who enjoyed a close personal relationship with De Gaulle, attempted unsuccessfully to persuade the French government to reconsider. DeGaulle's decisions constituted a major setback for the alliance. Several lines of communication emanated from SHAPE headquarters in Paris to NATO forces throughout France. [16]

After France withdrew most of its military personnel from SHAPE in July 1966, the Allies decided to move NATO's political headquarters from French territory, as well. That September, NATO approved Belgium to host both the NATO and SHAPE headquarters and the Netherlands to host AFCENT.

On 1 April 1967, SHAPE opened its new headquarters facility at Casteau, Belgium. The United States European Command (EUCOM) shifted its headquarters to Germany, and the Allied Command Central Europe moved to the Netherlands. NATO supplies and equipment went to bases in the United Kingdom, Belgium, Germany, and the Netherlands. [17]

Wheeler articulated his views on NATO in a speech before the Washington Institute of Foreign Affairs on 11 April.

> NATO, with the military forces deployed to support it, can be likened to a levee which was erected when a Communist tide unquestionably threatened to flood Europe. The levee held, and still holds. The alliance, with its unity of determination and visible strength, balanced the power between East and West, permitted both political and economic resurgence, and preserved both peace and freedom in Europe.
>
> There are some who would now take down the levee, or at least allow it to erode, because it is costly, troublesome to maintain, because the flood threat seems to have receded. I do not agree with them.
>
> It may be that the intentions of the Warsaw Pact nations have changed. I hope so, and it seems happily clear that they are a less monolithic force than once was the case. For the moment, too, their tactics are less aggressive. But I am quite

certain that the determined presence of NATO has had much to do with the improved climate. I have no evidence of a shift in fundamental Soviet objectives. And I bear in mind that intentions can change overnight.

On our part, NATO forces, standing together, can discourage aggressive adventures, defeat incursions, and deter major war. In my view, they contribute directly to the stability of Europe. These forces also contribute to the political unity of the West and to the balance of power throughout the world.

… NATO has been a magnificent success and the need for it continues today. I fully understand that many, important, nonmilitary factors are involved in determining the future course of the alliance. [18]

## *London*

On 1 April, before departing on a 5-day trip to London, Wheeler, actress Martha Rae, and two dignitaries presented trophies during the AMVETS 1967 Silver Helmet Awards Luncheon in the Sheraton Park Hotel in Washington. [19]

"Around four" that afternoon, the Wheelers departed Washington. When flying overseas, they changed into their pajamas to sleep enroute. "Time for a drink before dinner," Betty recorded. "We ate at 6:30 and I'm sure were in bed by nine-thirty. ... The trips to London and Paris are easy on us. When we get on[board] we're always ready for 'early to bed'. We get off [the plane] shortly after a light breakfast."

On the night of 3 April, General and Mrs. Hull gave a "black tie" reception and buffet. "He is Bus's opposite number," Betty reminded her mother. "Bus made it, but by the time we got away you could see that he felt more than a little badly. Except for Bus's misery, it was a lovely party."

Bus attended meetings the following morning and "stayed through a luncheon, but by that time the strep throat showed up so he was home to bed and cancelled out of his dinner. ... Poor Bus arrived with a cold and by Tuesday morning the doctor realized he had a strep throat. Needless to say, he was pretty miserable."

While Bus worked, Betty shopped, saw some museums, and watched a play. On the final day of their visit, "Bus and I took a short walk, had tea, and then on our way."

Bus was feeling somewhat better during the flight back to Washington. "I'm just sorry that he has to plunge right into meetings all day," Betty wrote. "He hosts a luncheon, and then faces the stag dinner at the house tonight." [20]

Two days later, Bus was "not completely over everything yet," Betty wrote. "Bus has an unexpected three days on the hill next week. Glorious weather and we'll have to stay in town as he has to study." [21]

## Westmoreland Returns to Washington

Meanwhile, Westmoreland had cabled a request for another 200,000 troops. He was summoned back to Washington for consultations on Vietnam policy at the White House. [22]

The Wheelers would host a dinner for the Westmorelands, but Betty was having a fit with the planning.

> What a to-do, the last few days. Kitsy and Westy are not coming in until tomorrow. In time for dinner? No, yes, no, yes, no, and now it's yes! The dinner for tonight had to be changed until Thursday [27 April]. That meant quite a few [guests] had other engagements. The whole week has been a series of juggling acts. ... Monday, a complete rearranging of plans for the week. ... I suppose by the time the Westmorelands get here, all will be running smoothly. I'm exhausted with them before they arrive! [23]

The Wheelers always kept a packed schedule, and any changes to Bus's official duties often frustrated their plans to get away on weekends. "Bus had a meeting [last Saturday] so we were late starting [for the country]," Betty wrote. "It was a glorious evening. The blossoms, dogwood and redbud [were] much fuller this week. There was a beautiful sunset and the moon was full. I should tell you! ... The woods were filled with wild flowers." [24]

On 25 April, the Wheelers attended a farewell ceremony for "Abe" Abrams, whom the White House had announced nineteen days earlier would become Westmoreland's deputy. "Bus and I went and later spent a little time at the reception," Betty reported. "Bus went back to work and it's now almost six-thirty. I do hope that he won't be tied up too long." [25]

Rumors abounded about Wheeler moving to another job, as well. "On all sides, 'When are you leaving?'" Betty wrote. "Much talk about the great turnover in the spring. We seem to be included in the plans. One thing sure, to date, no one has approached Bus!" [26]

Among the guests at the Wheelers' dinner party for the Westmorelands were Secretary and Mrs. Vance, Secretary and Mrs. Katzenbach, Mr. and Mrs. Komer, McConnell, Palmer, several other generals and their wives, as well as Kitsy's brother and his wife. [27]

On 6 May, the Wheelers departed on a ten-day trip to Paris. Wheeler was needed to help Lemnitzer smooth the aftereffects of NATO's recent relocation to Belgium.

"This time everyone was sad to see us leave [Paris]," Betty noted afterward. "I think until the troops actually left they didn't believe it – and of course, this is our third 'last time.'" While Bus worked, Betty enjoyed herself around Paris and had her hair done. "That Claude ... he always takes my poor head and makes it look beautiful." [28]

## Other Matters

On 22 May, Wheeler addressed students and faculty of the Air War College at Maxwell Air Force Base in Montgomery, Alabama. The following day, he addressed the Industrial College of the Armed Forces and the National War College at Fort McNair in Washington, DC. [29]

The preceding weekend, the Wheelers had gone "to the country on Saturday. Unfortunately, [Bus] couldn't get away until almost four o'clock." After lunch with Bim and Margie on Sunday, at "about four o'clock Bus and Bim returned to Washington."

On 24 May, they returned to Martinsburg by helicopter, this time for an official duty.

A gorgeous day and a beautiful trip. Bus gave a talk to the Rotary Club. I was included. It was announced in last night's paper that today was Gen. Earle Wheeler's day! The school band was playing in front of the hotel, much fanfare. The Mayor gave Bus a key to the county, much to do. He is now an honorary member of the Rotary Club, and we are honorary members of the Golf and Country Club. That is really nice as I understand that it has a nice little club and there is a dining room. We may be very glad to use it from time to time. We were certainly warmly welcomed. [30]

That evening, back in Washington, the Wheelers attended "a delightful dinner" at the Australian Embassy ... for Lord and Lady Casey.

He was the first Australian minister to the United States and purchased the residence in 1940. Except for [us] all the guests were close friends. Averell Harriman's, Dean Acheson's, Allan Dulles', to mention a few. Keith Waller [our] host and the currently serving Australian Ambassador said they all made him feel like a mere boy so I should feel like a little girl. It's wonderful to see, in their seventies, still actively serving their country. However, I don't wish [the] same for Bus and I hope that he will [be] out of it before too long. [31]

*West Point Cadets Jack Wood (center) and Jeffrey Madsen present a copy of the Howitzer yearbook to Wheeler, Washington, DC, 1 June 1967. (Office of the Chairman of the Joint Chiefs of Staff).*

During a hearing on Capitol Hill, Wheeler was asked whether he foresaw an impending war between Israel and its Arab neighbors, and if so, how he thought such a conflict would play out. There would be war, he asserted. Israel would win, and it would be over in a week. The congressmen were startled by his certainty. [32]

On 5 June, war erupted between the Arabs and Israelis. Intensive diplomatic activity at the United Nations by the U.S. heavily engaged the President's attention, dominated all other problems, and eventually lead to a summit meeting with Soviet Premier Alexei N. Kosygin in Glassboro, New Jersey later in the month. [33]

In later congressional testimony after the Six-Day War concluded, Wheeler began by apologizing to the committee for having been wrong in his predictions. He had stated that the war would be over in a week, and it had only taken Israel six days to win! [34]

In his memoirs, McNamara posed the rhetorical question of "how presumably intelligent, hard-working, and experienced officials – both military and civilian – failed to address systematically and thoroughly questions [about Vietnam policy] whose answers so deeply affected the lives of our citizens and the welfare of our nation." He asserted, "Simply put, such an orderly, rational approach was precluded by the 'crowding out' which resulted from the fact that Vietnam was but one of a multitude of problems we confronted." [35]

"The crush of events that summer and fall made it increasingly hard for the President and the senior officials in State, Defense, and the National Security Council to focus sharply on Vietnam," McNamara recalled. "We were confronted with a deluge of other crises and problems: a Middle East war that led to the first use of the hotline between Moscow and Washington; a Soviet anti-ballistic missile program that threatened to upset the nuclear balance between East and West; a looming conflict between Greece and Turkey over Cyprus that endangered NATO's eastern flank; race riots in our major cities; and, of course, rising protests against the war, which included a massive attempt to shut down the Pentagon." [36]

With NATO, Vietnam, and now another Arab-Israeli war competing for his time, Wheeler was keeping long hours. "It's now eight-thirty (P. M.) and still no Bus," Betty wrote on 7 June. "Bus cancelled out on the West Point trip. We did have a beautiful weekend in the country. … Bus needless to say, is up to his ears. What a muddle." [37]

Wheeler had accepted an invitation to deliver the commencement address at the Virginia Military Institute. He and Betty planned to spend the day prior at Natural Bridge, Virginia, where they'd celebrate their 35th wedding anniversary:

> Bus called about ten and said that it couldn't be done. The help had packed the picnic basket with champagne, glasses, and the sweetest, prettiest little cake. It was a shame that it all had to be unpacked. Bus got home around five. We had a swim. (Much better your own than a hotel, *n'est pas*!) We let the help go and grilled and had a pleasant evening.

> Sunday, we flew down to Lexington, leaving our own parade ground here and landing on theirs. I think the 'chopper' caused the most excitement of the day. Pinkie Burress was there to greet us. He was head of Constabulary after Ernie Harmon. Bus was always fond of him. We only were able to have a few minutes with him, but it seemed to mean so much.

After lunch at the Commandant's house, "Bus gave a fine talk" at the graduation ceremony, "which was well received", despite the day being "hotter than Hades." After "a soothing gin and tonic" at the Superintendent's house, they reboarded the helicopter for the trip home." [38]

## *Social Functions*

Besides the extra-long hours that Bus was keeping at work, his evenings continued to be filled with numerous social functions. "This has been a full week, but seemingly endless!" Betty exclaimed. "I miss it when we don't get to the country." [39]

Some functions had been scheduled long in advance, such as the wedding of the Wheelers' niece, Linda Howell, to Marine Captain Tony Lattore. After the couple's ceremony in the Fort Myer Chapel, Betty and Bus hosted their reception. Tony's Marine officer groomsmen were awestruck by the opportunity to talk with the nation's highest-ranking military officer. Bus was just as excited to speak with them. [40]

Other official functions were short-notice or spontaneous, such as on 20 June.

> Bus called about six [P. M.] and asked if I'd like to have a boat ride on the Potomac. Needless to say, I would so the car picked me up at 6:45. We met in the Diplomatic Room at the White House. The ladies arriving first and not too long after seven the men joined us, coming over from the President's office. He invited Bus and me to ride with him to the dock. Needless to say, he was in high spirits over the birth of his grandson. It proved quite an evening. We had drinks and dinner onboard the 'Honey Fitz'. There were probably thirty. It was a hot, hot night, but the moon rose, full and red. It was glorious. It was almost 11:45 by the time we got back to the White House. Said goodnight at the door and came on home. It was an experience, but I wonder how those that are at 'beck and call' constantly stand it. [41]

Vance was departing as Deputy Secretary of Defense. On 28 June, "the McNamara's gave a reception for the Vance's. How Bus is going to miss Cy," Betty wrote. "I do think, Paul Nitze wants the relationship to be as good and that will help." [42]

Two days later, McNamara and Wheeler presided over a Joint Honors Ceremony outside the River Entrance of the Pentagon for Vance. That evening, the Wheelers hosted a dinner for thirty-two for the Vances. Betty reported:

> It was quite a group. Vance, McNamara, Katzenbach, Nitze, Resor, MacDonald, McNaughton, Walt Rostow, Ignatius, Goulding, Ailes, Brown, Warnke. ... The food was out of this world. Almost a whole new menu. A sole mousse with a caviar sauce. Squab stuffed with mixture rices [sic] and water chestnuts. The squab boned except for backbone and bone in legs to hold shape. [43]

## Saigon Trip

McNamara, Wheeler, and Katzenbach visited Vietnam on 5-12 July for an update on recent developments. Arriving at Tan Son Nhut Air Base on the morning of 7 July, McNamara's party immediately began ten hours of meetings in the U. S. Military Assistance Command, Vietnam (MACV) headquarters' "High Noon Conference Room." Two days of intensive briefings were followed by visits to combat zones, a tour of pacification programs in the Mekong Delta, and private meetings with Thieu and Ky. [44]

While climbing a steep hill near Pleiku in the heat and humidity, Wheeler became acutely short of breath and was also noticeably nauseated. He sensed there was something not right with his heart but attributed it to the heat and being out of shape. He felt better the next day, so he discounted the matter. He did, however, experience more fatigue during and immediately after the trip than he usually experienced. [45]

Bim's friends, the Fischers, joined the Wheelers for dinner on the day Wheeler returned from Vietnam. "My wife, Jenny, was seated next to General Wheeler," Fischer recalled. "My wife asked him if he was exhausted from his trip."

Bus replied, "Oh, yes, totally exhausted."

"And, with that response, feigning exhaustion, he leaned forward and his nose dipped into his wine glass." This elicited laughs all around. [46]

Jokes aside, Wheeler was exhausted and had, in fact, suffered a heart attack during the trip. It would go undiagnosed for several weeks.

## Moorer

Conflict was also raging in American streets. Racial violence had increased sharply, and more than 50 cities would report disorders during the first nine months of 1967. These ranged from minor disturbances to extremely serious outbreaks in Newark and Detroit.

The disorder in Detroit on 23-27 July was so destructive that the Governor of Michigan not only employed the National Guard, but also requested and obtained federal troops. In the end, the task force commander at Detroit had more than 10,000 guardsmen and 5,000 Regular Army soldiers under his authority. He deployed nearly 10,000 of them before the crisis ended.

On 28 July, the President appointed a National Advisory Commission on Civil Disorders to determine the underlying causes and seek possible remedies. Concluding that more riots were inevitable and that the National Guard was itself racially imbalanced, the Army strengthened its troop training programs and began advance planning to control possible future disturbances. [47]

Meanwhile, the senior leadership of the U.S. Navy was in transition. McNaughton, a key architect of the Vietnam engagement strategy, had been nominated to become Secretary of the Navy. Before he assumed the position, however, he was killed in an aircraft accident on 19 July. McNamara's doubts about the war were exacerbated by the personal loss he felt at the tragic death of his close collaborator. [48]

On 1 August, Admiral Thomas H. Moorer replaced McDonald as the Chief of Naval Operations. [49]

A week prior, the Wheelers attended a dinner in McDonald's honor hosted by the Joint Chiefs of Staff and Ladies at Bolling Air Force Base. McNaughton's death cast a somber tone over the occasion. [50]

### Heart Attack

"Strong differences of judgment did divide us," McNamara recalled, "and the frictions they caused created stress, which took its toll." [51]

More than a month after his Pleiku incident, Wheeler still wasn't feeling completely well and went to Walter Reed for a check-up. The cardiologist determined Wheeler had "a distinct abnormal change in his lecture cardiograms, reflecting an anteroseptal myocardial infarction with residual anterior peri-infarction block". In other words, he had suffered a heart attack. He was admitted immediately. Further tests indicated the myocardial infarction was not immediate and that his condition was stable. After several weeks of rest, during which "Johnny" Johnson served as Acting Chairman, Wheeler would return to duty.

On 5 September, Wheeler replied to a get-well note from the President:

I appreciate greatly your thoughtfulness in sending me the two autographed books which I shall treasure. Even more, I appreciate the letter which you wrote to me. Knowing as I do the tremendous domestic and international burdens which you must shoulder, I also note the extra exertion needed to add even one more letter to the stack of work which you must do.

Also, your reminder that you too have gone through this experience is a heartening and sustaining thought as to my own future.

No doubt Bob McNamara has told you that the doctors believe that I am doing quite well. Apparently, this attack occurred in early July with Bob and I were visiting Vietnam and, therefore, much of the recuperation period is behind me. This is not to say that I don't have an additional convalescent period ahead because I do. The doctors told me this morning that they are engaged in reviewing all of the tests and will give me within the next couple of days a schedule for me to follow. As soon as I know where I stand, Mr. President, I shall report the facts to you. [52]

"I am distressed to learn that you have suffered a heart attack," Sharp cabled Wheeler two days later. "Glad it was only a minor one and that your progress is good and you'll return to duty soon. Having been with you each day during the July Vietnam visit I must say you were a healthy looking and vigorous patient." [53]

*Wheeler candidly discusses his recent heart attack with the President in the White House Oval Office, Washington, DC, 13 September 1967. (LBJ Library).*

Discharged from Walter Reed after resting for two weeks, Wheeler still required additional rest time. Worried that he physically might not be able to continue the job, Wheeler offered to resign. He recalled:

> When I got out on convalescent leave, I went to see President Johnson. I told him what my physical condition was and the what the prognosis was and so on, and the fact that I was going to be out of action for at least another six weeks, and it could be considerably more than that. I suggested to him that I should retire and that he should appoint somebody else as Chairman of the Joint Chiefs of Staff.
>
> Well, he talked to me about 45 minutes. Finally, he said to me, 'Now, Buzz,' he said – Buzz was what he always called me – 'You just go along and do what the doctors tell you to do to improve your health. I don't want anybody else as Chairman of the Joint Chiefs of Staff,' he said, 'but, on the other hand, I don't want you to kill yourself in that job. After you've had another checkup in about six weeks or so, if the doctors say you can do the job,' he said, 'then I want you to stay on.' Then

– we were in his office, this was about 7:30 or so at night – he got up, and walked to the door with me, and put his arm around my shoulder, and said, 'I can't afford to lose you. You have never given me a bad piece of advice.' [54]

The cardiologist prescribed exercise, which Bus endeavored to fit into his schedule, at least on weekends in the country. "Bus never stopped smoking," says Bim, "although after his heart attack he did switch to a pipe and milder cigarettes." [55]

On 13 September, Wheeler sent a note of thanks to Lieutenant General Leonard D. Heaton, the Surgeon General of the Army.

I wish to express my thanks to you and through you to the many members of the staff at Walter Reed Army Medical Center who contributed to my care and well-being during my recent hospitalization. As always, the medical care was of the highest order of professional competence. For this care I am, of course, most grateful to the staff members.

I am particularly grateful also to those personnel on Ward #3 and Ward #8 who devoted so much time and effort to my comfort and well-being. Since the list of those I wish particularly to thank is long, I am attaching it as an enclosure to this letter. I would appreciate you transmitting my thanks to these fine people in any way you consider appropriate. [56]

Two weeks later, Bus wrote a letter to Betty Hodgson, an old family friend.

I read your nice newsy letter last night when Betty and I got back from a stay on the farm. I had to come back for a session with the doctors today. You'll be interested to know that they assured me I am doing very well indeed.

We go back to the farm tomorrow for another couple of weeks. I really think that this is the best time of the year up there with the leaves changing and the weather crisp and cool at night and pleasantly warm in the daytime. [57]

"He had really worn himself out," Spivy recalled. "Doc Upton, who was in the Pentagon or JCS dispensary, was a heart specialist. He [henceforth] traveled with Wheeler all the time." Stewart recalls that the Wheelers' household staff took lessons in cardiopulmonary resuscitation and practiced it semi-annually as a precautionary measure. [58]

Tony Lattore, the Marine officer who had recently married the Wheelers' niece, was departing for Vietnam. At a family farewell dinner in Quarters 6, Bus took him aside and said that Tony's mother had written to him, asking Bus to give her son some words of advice. Bus told him, "The best advice I can possibly give you is that you should go and do your duty as best as you can, but do not try to be a hero." [59]

October began on a peaceful note for the Wheelers but would end in an environment of discord. Meanwhile, Bus's heart attack had forced him to slow down somewhat.

During an extended leave in the country, Betty wrote:

> It's [a] heavenly afternoon. I'm sitting in a deck chair, in my bathing suit. Bus is running his tractor up and down the slope. I love the smell of the new cut grass. ... The days are going by unbelievably fast. I was a quarter of nine getting up this morning. Bus is usually well ahead and has walked to the gate and back (a distance of one mile) by the time I'm down. [Ordered by his cardiologist, such walks were Bus's first real exercise in over five years]. ... We grill at night, but I'm getting my hand back in with omelets and scrambled eggs with mushrooms for lunch yesterday. I did the fettuccini and it was good. Bus isn't supposed to eat too much bread, so we're off of the sandwich routine. ... We go home on the tenth, and will come back after lunch on the twelfth, staying then until Sunday the fifteenth. [60]

Wheeler returned from convalescent leave to a full slate of activities. "He looked terrible," one aide remembered, "as if he would rather have been anywhere else." [61]

"Under doctor's orders, I divorced myself from the daily 'flaps', the constantly ringing phones, buzzing buzzers, rushing action officers, not too brief briefers, and reports on reports on reports," Wheeler would state in a speech before the Armed Forces Staff College on 26 October. "I then found I had time to think—to reflect on several of the key issues confronting us these days. I think you'll agree that, in our governmental process, our senior civilian and military policy makers apparently have too little time to think. The top posts within our government are administered on the dead run while short deadlines pry policies and programs off the stove before they're done." [62]

## Antiwar Sentiment

"We're off to the country in the morning," Betty wrote on 20 October.

> Everyone is pretty uneasy about the [antiwar] march [on the Pentagon] tomorrow. As Bus's office is on the ground floor and so close to the entrance, he was advised to stay away. Gates have been put on [Fort] Myer. Tomorrow only govt. stickers or 'good reasons' let you in. ... MPs [Military Police] are already covering this area and one is posted outside of the house. Isn't it terrible that this is a 'peace march?' I guess we better pray that it will be, but there are so many elements involved. [63]

As the culmination of the Stop the Draft Week, the protest began at the Lincoln Memorial where almost 100,000 protesters, including radicals, liberals, black nationalists, hippies, professors, women's groups, and war veterans, converged. After the rally, nearly 35,000 protesters marched across the Potomac River toward the Pentagon. Violence erupted when the more radical element clashed with soldiers and 236 federal marshals. [64]

## Reorganizing the Reserves

Although the President had steadfastly refused to authorize mobilization to reconstitute the strategic reserve, at least the reserves could be better organized to achieve McNamara's objective of bringing them into balance with contingency planning. Wheeler facilitated a compromise plan between the Department of Defense (DOD) and Congress under which the Army Reserve would retain all of its training and support units, but only three combat brigades. Its paid drill strength would drop from 300,000 to 260,000. The Army National Guard would maintain its endstrength at 400,000. While the number of separate brigades in the Guard would rise from 7 to 18, the total of its divisions would decline from 23 to 8. All units in the National Guard and Army Reserve would be manned at 93% or better of their wartime strength, and each was to have a full supply of whatever equipment, spare parts, and technical support it required. [65]

## *Westmoreland Returns to DC*

Westmoreland returned to the States and expressed exuberant optimism in several highly publicized appearances. "I have never been more encouraged in my four years in Vietnam," he said on 15 November. [66]

The Westmoreland family would stay with the Wheelers in Quarters 6, or maybe not. Exasperated, Betty wrote:

> I met the plane [on 15 November] at 10:45. Kitsy, Margaret (II), and I came back to the house. ... A little later Westy joined us. I forgot to tell you, Bus called about 9:30. Hold everything. No house guests. The Pres. and Mrs. Johnson wanted them at the White House. After coffee, Westy went to see Bus. ... Westy came in later and had lunch on a tray. Then all the Westmoreland's went to bed.

Betty went out to visit an ailing relative in the hospital. When she returned home, she found:

> Kitsy still at the house and Westy at the Pentagon. He and Bus arrived shortly thereafter. They had a drink with us and left for the White House at 7:15. Really, it was ridiculous. Pres. and Mrs. Johnson were out to dinner, but please feel 'at home' and ask anyone they wanted to [join them for] dinner in the 'family' dining room. As both of Kitsy's brothers and wives are here, they decided on a family party of six. We were all in hysterics as to how to notify the President's cook that one would like to dine at 8:45! Haven't heard from Kitsy since. By grapevine the news is they will arrive at Qtrs. Six tomorrow to stay through Tuesday. We shall see! ... [Later, she added.] Word tonight is that the Westmoreland's will stay with the Johnson's. I could almost cry, I am so relieved. [67]

"The Westmoreland's have gone to Camp David for the weekend," Betty updated two days later. "Bus says they may yet come tomorrow. It really has been a godsend to me that they haven't been here this week. We go out to dinner tomorrow, so I hope that they continue to accept the President's hospitality." [68]

Bus had too full a plate at work to also be entertaining house guests. "[He] is working on the budget, so he's awfully busy" Betty wrote. "I think the hope is to get the budget to the President early this year so that there won't be the usual rat race during the holidays. ... Congressional hearings are starting, so add it all up with the additional meetings because Westy is here." [69]

Wheeler wrote on 18 November to General S. M. Wang of the Chinese delegation to the United Nations Military Staff Committee:

> I think that I am doing quite well physically. This is not to say that I have not been forced to reduce the scope of my activity somewhat because I have. Still, the doctors are very much pleased with my progress, and I hope by taking due care that I will be as good as new in the not-too-distant future.
>
> You are very kind indeed to state that my health is important to others than myself. Perhaps you overstated the case just a bit – something to be expected from a friend – but I value your kind words most highly. Betty joins me in all the best to your wife and to you. [70]

The Westmorelands did not return to Quarters 6, but Betty was still obligated to entertain Kitsy. "[She] and I had lunch at the Rive Gauche. What a strenuous girl she is. ... We are so completely different. And she is so much 'THE Mrs. Westmoreland'. God knows it can't have been an easy life these last years." [71]

"Bus picked up a little cold," Betty reported. "He felt miserable, and he looked so terribly tired. After [dinner] he went straight to bed. ... [Later, she added.] The cold is gone and he looked much, much better this morning." [72]

During Westmoreland's visit to Washington, Wheeler raised the possibility of his reassignment. Under the provisions of a bill recently passed by Congress, the Chiefs' tour length was limited to four years except in times of declared national emergency. Although "Johnny" Johnson had been appointed under another law, it was still likely that he would retire after having served four years as Chief of Staff of the Army, in July 1968. [73]

"You know, I love Kitsy [Westmoreland] dearly," Betty admitted, "but every time she comes here I get the feeling that, in her mind, she is redecorating the place." [74]

The Wheelers were already looking forward to Bus's tenure as Chairman being over. "It's anybody's guess what we'll do. Bus says he hopes after his birthday in January, he can bring things to a head." [75]

In October, Wheeler explained to Armed Forces Staff College students the dual nature of his responsibility to the President and to the Congress.

> This characteristic involves the seeming impossibility of obeying two masters who may agree on the requirement for military strength, but who are likely to disagree as to what constitutes that strength and as to how it should be attained.
>
> The military leader regularly is summoned before the Congress as it examines the President's national security policies or requests for authority and funds to implement these policies. Here, the established procedure is for the military representatives to present prepared statements after which they are open to detailed questioning—and very searching questions, I might add. In answer to direct questions, the military leader has no moral alternative to giving the Congress the same candid professional judgments that he has previously stated within the JCS or to the Secretary of Defense and the President. This does not compromise his acceptance of the President's basic decision. It does, on the other hand, provide Congress with information to which it is legally entitled in fulfilling its responsibilities and national security affairs. [76]

"Bus didn't get in until 9 (P. M.)," Betty reported on 9 December. She had gone to a luncheon at Fort McNair that day.

> Picked up Dorothy Johnson. Saw more of her than I've seen in a long time. She has started house hunting. I know she'll be glad when these four years are up. Unless it's [an] official [social function] and a must, they never go out. ... And

Johnny always has his dinner in the Pentagon. Pretty awful life I would think. [77]

## 1968

In mid-February 1968, the nightly news reported that the siege of Khe Sanh was heating up again. Linda Lattore, the Wheelers' niece, was distressed by the media's continual hyping of the deadly comparison between Khe Sanh and Dien Bien Phu. Her husband Tony was fighting with the 26th Marines at Khe Sanh. During the height of the siege in March, Uncle Bus quietly reassured her that "the United States will never allow the defeat of our Americans at Khe Sanh." Tony would soon be wounded by friendly fire from U.S. Army gunships while leading a patrol to "clear the wire." He survived and had his shoulder reconstructed with a titanium joint. [78]

On 28 February, McNamara left the Administration and was replaced as Secretary of Defense by the hawk Clark M. Clifford. That day, Wheeler and the Chiefs were among hundreds of spectators standing in the rain outside the Pentagon's River Entrance as the President presided over a "cold, wet, and miserable" Joint Honors Ceremony for the departing McNamara. "Rain marred the honor ceremony and forced cancellation of the flyover," McNamara recalled. Presenting McNamara with the Medal of Freedom, Johnson said, "For seven years ... you have brought a new dimension to defense planning and decision-making." [79]

Vietnam policy had reached a critical juncture at which a monumental presidential decision would have to made, one way or the other. Wheeler had labored diligently to muster support for the military's recommendations, but other matters competed for his attention amid the crisis atmosphere.

On Sunday, 19 March, he hosted a visit by his South Korean counterpart, General Im Chung Sik. Betty was presented an ornate, pale blue, traditional Korean gown. The Wheelers were obliged to attend a reception for Sik at the South Korean Embassy. [80] Betty wrote:

> Under these circumstances, of course we had to go. Bus was mobbed, as we never go to these things, all the foreign officers, plus the American officers, plus the press, all wanted a few words with him. We stayed almost two hours, and that

again we never do, but there was no breaking away. I must say, Bus looked so completely relaxed at the reception. It was hard to imagine the strain that he's been under these last weeks. (We won't even mention the Kennedy's!) [81]

That same day, Wheeler took time to respond to an elementary school-age girl, Monica Rosa Lara of Topeka, Kansas, who had written to him about his health condition.

"I usually am much too busy to answer personally all the letters I receive daily," Wheeler wrote. "However, in this instance I'm replying to your letter to let you know that I'm feeling very well in spite of a very demanding schedule."

Ms. Lara had written to Wheeler that she had heart issues herself and was afraid of her doctors. He advised, "The most important thing in over-coming heart problems is to obey the doctors. I do not look upon them as my enemies, but as very good friends who are doing their very best to keep me in good health. It is wonderful that we have such dedicated men and that there are hospital facilities where we can go for the best possible care."

In response to Ms. Lara's admission that as a self-described tomboy she was restless in constraining her physical activities, Wheeler replied:

> I do not understand your being such a tomboy if you must take care of your heart at this period in your life. Fighting and rushing about is hard on the heart, and it does not seem to me to be appropriate conduct for a young lady. Perhaps if you would settle down to a quiet life and cooperate with your doctors, you would find that in time your heart would mend. Now that you must rest, you have a wonderful opportunity to know the joy of quiet periods, of learning to read well and to appreciate good books, and of learning to write and spell with exactness. These are all important to one's future hap-piness and success. You are very fortunate to have a private tutor so you will not fall behind in your studies. But it is up to you, and you alone, to learn. No one else can make you do that; they can only provide the opportunities.
>
> … In the meantime, let us both place our faith in God that He will take good care of us and keep us well. Again, I say, do

not fear your doctors, but believe that they are truly striving to make you well. As you requested, I am sending you my photograph. [82]

"We were going to England," Betty wrote on 20 March. "We're not. I'm so disappointed. It would have been good to get away." Instead, Bus made a quick, unannounced trip to the Philippines to review the dire situation with Westmoreland and Abrams and to craft their arguments for an upcoming meeting with the President. With Clifford having turned dove and Johnson's rejection of Westmoreland's troop request, Wheeler knew this would probably be the military's final shot to convince Johnson to stay the course and not to de-escalate. [83]

"Bus got back with Abe Abrams around seven [on 25 March]," Betty reported. "As nearly as I can tell, no one picked up the fact that Bus had been out of town, or has yet." [84]

In "emotionally charged" meetings with the President and Rusk the following day, Wheeler and Abrams gave it everything they had. The embattled Johnson sought to deflect the military's criticism of his peace moves. [85]

"Abe stayed with us, and supposedly left at seven tonight," Betty wrote on 27 March. "It's seven-thirty and still no Bus." [86]

## *Turmoil at Home*

The assassination of Dr. Martin Luther King, Jr., in Memphis, Tennessee, on 4 April provoked waves of rioting, looting, and arson in cities across the country. In most instances, the States were able to employ their National Guard units to subdue the rioters. However, the Federal Government deployed some 40,000 federalized National Guardsmen and regular troops to Washington, Baltimore, and Chicago.

"My wife and I happened to be invited to Quarters 6 for dinner the day after Martin Luther King was killed," Fischer recalled. "Through a very circuitous route, because of all the turmoil, we were able to get there in time for dinner." A large plate glass window in the residence's living room provided a view of Washington in the distance. "As we were having dinner (and later into the evening, as well) we observe plumes of smoke arising from the city. We felt as Nero must have felt, except that no fiddles were to be heard." [87]

On 12 April, Margie McNamara sent a thank you letter to the Wheelers, Johnsons, McConnells, Moorers, and Chapmans.

> Bob and I wish to express to you our thanks and appreciation for the wonderful 'family' defense dinner and that beautiful coffee table. We would specially like to tell you how much it has meant to both of us but to Bob even more to have had your support and understanding of his difficult position of making decisions that sometimes were difficult for you and sometimes more so for him.
>
> The word that comes to mind in your working together as military and civilians under the most emotional conditions is the 'dignity' with which everyone accepted these decisions. No one has really had the time to look or speak of this and I look at it as an amazing display of restraint and mutual respect.
>
> Our best wishes to all of you and your families – most sincerely and with affection. [88]

In the wake of the riots, on 22 April, the Army established the Directorate for Civil Disturbance Planning and Operations in the Office of the Chief of Staff. This organization provided command facilities for the Army when it operated as lead agent for the Department of Defense in civil disturbances. It would later evolve into the Directorate of Military Support in September 1970.

Although the years immediately following 1968 produced no great racial outpourings, they did see several antiwar demonstrations that required the commitment of both Federal and National Guard troops. [89]

In a *Reader's Digest* article that month, Eisenhower lamented the growing defeatism within the government and society:

> In a long life of service to my country, I have never encountered a situation more depressing than the present spectacle of an America deeply divided over a war. ... What has become of our courage? ... patriotism? ... One large defeatist group proclaims loudly and positively that 'we can never win

the Vietnam war.' Others insist, contrary to the best military judgment and to clear evidence, that our air strikes 'do no good.' ... It is unthinkable that the voices of defeat should triumph in our land. [90]

## *Good for the Soul*

Meanwhile back in Washington, the Wheelers had hosted a successful dinner for the Cliffords. Betty reported:

> I think that she or they enjoyed the evening with an all military group. Certainly our people were pleased to have the opportunity to meet the Cliffords. Once again, the [household staff] did themselves proud. She said that she had never sat down to a more beautiful table, never one so perfectly superb, and dinner a joy. High praise indeed. [91]

The Wheelers spent 5-12 May in Belgium, where Bus attended the annual Supreme Headquarters Allied Powers Europe Exercise (SHAPEX) and Military Chief/Chief of Staff meetings in Brussels with his counterparts from the other NATO nations. [92]

With everything going on in Vietnam, it was a challenge for the Wheelers to depart Washington. "Within minutes of leaving [Quarters 6] yesterday," Betty wrote, "The President called and off Bus went to the White House. We were two hours late in leaving but made up an hour en route. Bus had a meeting scheduled at three at NATO headquarters. He went straight there and I came here [to the Hotel Amigo in Brussels]."

From the hotel, she added later, "It's almost six. I can't imagine where Bus is as he was sure his meeting would not be more than an hour. Washington is trying to get [a hold of] him and if he's between the two places, he's overdue."

"This is a busier trip than last time because we spend two nights here, move to Casteau (stay with the Parkers) for two nights, then back here for two nights. Except for dinner tonight and Friday, [we have] a dinner every night, [and] a lunch tomorrow." [93]

Betty wrote another letter to her mother on the flight home:

This has proved quite a trip. ... A week out of Washington is good for the soul. It's long enough to feel that we have been away, and I know that while Bus has been busy, the pace and pressures [were] not nearly so great. We had a busy social life, but the free day yesterday and eleven hours sleep last night has started the week off well rested.

At NATO headquarters, it was widely assumed that Wheeler was the heir-apparent to Lemnitzer, who would retire in a year.

"Mrs. Lemnitzer had called and wanted me to see her house," Betty wrote. "It is quite evident that everyone expects Bus [to replace Lemnitzer as SACEUR]."

Thrilled that they were invited to a garden party hosted by the King and Queen of Belgium, Betty had "dashed out Saturday morning and bought a hat" for the occasion.

We had to dress and be at the SHAPE headquarters to take the helicopter with the Lemnitzers to Brussels (about an hour and forty-five minutes by auto.)It was a fascinating ride. ... The garden party was in the Green House. ... I can't begin to describe it. I have never seen a more fabulous sight in my life. It was glorious. The King and Queen entered with no fanfare, and just walked slowly, shaking hands as they went. ... We had been told that the King had asked that he meet Bus. ... We were brought forward and introduced. The King looks marvelous now that he is wearing contact lenses instead of glasses. She seemed very frail ... [and] has gone through a series of operations. ... How awful it must be to have your marriage and your children so vital to the country. It was all very beautiful and very exciting. [94]

### MACV Changes Command

On 11 June, after nearly four and a half years in Vietnam, Westmoreland relinquished command of MACV to Abrams. Westmoreland would serve as Chief of Staff of the Army until his retirement from the Army on 30 June 1972. [95]

Betty accompanied Bus to Saigon for the change of command ceremony. Her nephew, Captain Doneld Howell, was now serving at Bien Hoa, about sixteen miles away. A member of Bus's staff phoned Don's unit to relay the message that Don was invited to Sunday lunch at MACV headquarters and that they would send a helicopter for him. Don's chain of command had no idea that his uncle was the Chairman of the Joint Chiefs of Staff, so the message came as quite a shock. Don had lunch with Betty, Bus, "Abe" Abrams, and his wife Julia at Abrams's quarters. Afterward, he accompanied the wives on a tour of Saigon. An atypical Sunday for a lowly Army Captain, and one that certainly led to many questions. [96]

## Storms in Washington

"Heavy showers this afternoon," Betty wrote on 24 June. "Such interesting lights. Green, green grass and leaves. A gray river. The Lincoln Memorial stark white. Gray clouds. Just a few buildings [visible], all else lost in mist." [97] Her weather report was metaphoric for the political storms raging in Washington.

Divisions within the U.S. government became even more pronounced during this new phase of the war. The split between the President's civilian and military advisors was deepening, with a growing doubt that the war, even assuming it could still be won, would be worth the expenditure, not only in troops and matériel, but also in national honor. [98]

## Military Leader Transitions

July brought more changes to the top military positions. The month began with Wheeler swearing-in Westmoreland as Chief of Staff of the Army on 3 July. [99]

Wheeler was reappointed for what would be the first of two consecutive one-year terms following enactment of a Joint Resolution of Congress, which provided exceptions to the law that the Chairman of the Joint Chiefs of Staff could be appointed for only two two-year terms except in time of war declared by Congress. [100]

Later that month, Clifford and Wheeler visited Vietnam and were scheduled to visit Dong Ha, to which the 26th Marines had relocated following the closure of Khe Sanh. Wheeler's aide sent a message to the regimental command post to inform Captain Lattore that "Sharpshooter" (Wheeler's call sign) would be arriving at the Dong Ha airfield and that security would be alerted to allow him through. Upon Lattore's arrival at the airstrip, the official party was just being welcomed by the senior U.S. officers present. When Wheeler noticed Lattore, he immediately interrupted the welcoming officials to warmly greet Tony. Wheeler then called out to Clifford, "Clark, Clark, come and meet my niece's husband who served at Khe Sanh." An astounded Major General Rathvon M. Thompkins, the Commanding General of the 3rd Marine Division, marveled at the scruffy Captain receiving all the attention from the Secretary and the Chairman. [101]

On 31 July, Wheeler presided over the U.S. Pacific Command's change of command ceremony in which Sharp was replaced as Commander-in-Chief by Admiral John S. McCain, Jr.. Sharp had served in that capacity since 30 June 1964. [102]

On 31 August, the President sent Wheeler a personal note. "Your reassurance of friendship and support on my sixtieth birthday strengthens me in the challenges we face. Your confidence and counsel have always helped to lighten the load we bear. And the memory of your friendship will brighten all the years ahead. Thank you – and God bless you for your thoughts." [103]

## *NATO*

On 13 October, Wheeler and Clifford joined Lemnitzer and Burchinal for a round of NATO meetings in Bonn, Berlin, and Stuttgart, West Germany. [104]

Wheeler had made his views on NATO known publicly in a speech to his fellow veterans of the 36th Infantry Division in August.

> We need the [NATO] alliance and the alliance needs us, now more than ever. Some might have truly believed that the Soviets are so concerned with meeting the consumer needs of their people that the brave new world is on us. Tragically, as we have seen, this is not the case. The facts are (1) An increase of the Soviet ICBM force; (2) The appearance of a Soviet ABM [anti-ballistic missile] system; (3) The continuing modernization of Russia's land power; (4) The

projection of Soviet seapower into the Mediterranean and Indian Ocean; and (5) The demonstrated capacity and will of the Soviet Union to employ force with power and precision even against one of their own allies. This brutal and cynical maneuver gives special meaning to the old saying 'With friends like these who needs enemies.'

There are those who argue that the Communist camp is in ferment, citing the recent dramatic events in Eastern Europe. I am not in the business of gauging changes in 'atmospherics,' and neither are my colleagues on the Joint Chiefs of Staff. Whether Communist power is now 'polycentric' as opposed to being 'monolithic,' I find little strategic difference. I don't want the United States to be squeezed to death by one octopus or several octopi. [105]

Wheeler, like many senior military officers, was relieved when Nixon won the close election, primarily because they believed that a change in national leadership was at least better than continuing along the same path charted by Johnson. But when Nixon appointed Wisconsin Congressman Melvin R. Laird as his Secretary of Defense, the Chiefs were dubious. They had long experience in dealing with Laird, who had served nearly all his sixteen years in the House as a member of the Subcommittee on Military Preparedness, and they knew he wanted to get the U.S. out of Vietnam as quickly as possible.

Serving as an initial bridge between the military and the new Administration, Goodpaster would inform Wheeler that Nixon was more willing to listen to the Chiefs than Johnson, that he admired the military and Wheeler, and that he hoped that Wheeler would stay on as Chairman.

Wheeler remained skeptical. While he desired good relations between the Chiefs and the new Administration, he was physically worn out by his service during the previous five years and wanted to retire. The inauguration of a new President, he thought, would be an appropriate juncture to initiate a change, a point of view that he communicated to the incoming Administration but was ignored. Wheeler was adamant, but he did not have a chance to broach the subject until after Nixon had been inaugurated. [106]

## *Force Restructuring*

Meanwhile, the phase-down of U.S. military operations in Vietnam and accompanying cutbacks in active-force levels caused the nation to place renewed reliance on its reserve forces. In November, Congress passed the reserve forces "Bill of Rights." The act gave the Service Secretaries responsibility for developing reserve forces capable of attaining peacetime training goals and of meeting mobilization readiness objectives. The act also established positions for Assistant Secretaries for Manpower and Reserve Affairs within each of the military departments and gave statutory status to the position of Chief of the Army Reserve.

Since the President had declined to call up the reserve forces in the early stages of the war, the main burden of meeting the Army's need for manpower in Vietnam had fallen upon the Selective Service. The increased draft calls and voluntary enlistments that followed had swelled the Army from 970,000 troops in mid-1965 to over 1. 5 million in 1968.

Even as the Vietnam War raged, the Department of Defense had begun tentative planning to transition to an all-volunteer force. With the election of Nixon, the prospect of ending the draft became a real possibility. In November, a study project entitled "Project Volunteer" was initiated to determine the feasibility of recruiting an all-volunteer force while still maintaining military effectiveness. Many key issues quickly surfaced: how to recruit enough high-quality soldiers, how to retain them, how to pay for them, and what management and leadership practices would create an effective military force out of this voluntary manpower. [107]

## *Transition*

*Wheeler (right), his Aide-de-Camp Lieutenant Colonel Schreiner (left), and an unidentified fellow fisherman with their catch, Key West Naval Station, Florida, 2 January 1969. (Wheeler Family Records).*

With the Johnson Administration in its final days, the Wheelers were able to escape Washington and spent the holidays in the Florida Keys. Besides visiting Betty's parents on Casey Key, Bus went deep sea fishing from the U.S. Navy base in Key West. The pace would ratchet right back up after Nixon's inauguration on 20 January 1969, so it was a timely and well-deserved respite for the Wheelers. [108]

## 1969

*President Johnson presents the Distinguished Service Medal with Oak Leaf Cluster to Wheeler in the East Room of the White House, Washington, DC, 10 January 1969. (Office of the Chairman of the Joint Chiefs of Staff).*

On 10 January, President Johnson presented Wheeler the Army Distinguished Service Medal with 1st Oak Leaf Cluster in an award ceremony in the East Room of the White House. While Johnson had begun his Administration mistrustful of his military advisors and had frequently discounted their recommendations, he had come to consider "Buzz" a true and loyal friend. [109]

Wheeler's remarks were characteristically succinct:

> Thank you, Mr. President. I am, of course, honored as any soldier would be, to receive this generous award from my Commander-in-Chief. In all honesty, I am touched as I see in this historic room so many old friends, associates and mentors. My words will be few. I have been proud all my life to have been permitted to serve as a soldier of my country. I have never been prouder of my calling than over the past few years when, as always in our history, our Armed Forces have met and succeeded in the unforgiving test of combat. It is

with the thoughts of our fighting men foremost in my mind that I view this award to me as being custodial in nature.

… Mr. President, I shall always treasure my association with you. You have provided an unforgettable example of leadership and grace under pressure. Mrs. Wheeler and I join in every good wish for you and Mrs. Johnson for the productive years that lie ahead for you both. Again, sir, thanks. [110]

The following week, Wheeler sent a thank you note to George A. Carver, Jr., the Special Assistant for Vietnamese Affairs in the Office of the Director, Central Intelligence Agency.

Thank you for your kind note of congratulations on my receiving the Distinguished Service Medal from the President. I am most grateful for this honor and for the warm response I have received from my friends and associates. It all adds up to something to be remembered with pride. Certainly one of the finest benefits to flow from my present assignment has been the opportunity to work with so many dedicated and outstanding individuals in the service of their Government. [111]

Wheeler and the Chiefs visited the office of Deputy Secretary of Defense Paul Nitze to present him a gift upon his retirement.

At lunch that day, Wheeler promoted one of his mess stewards, Chief Petty Officer Juan Mangosing, in front of all the Chiefs. Wheeler had always been gracious and grateful to his staff, especially the enlisted men. [112]

## Resignation

Before the Nixon Administration's first National Security Council meeting on 21 January, Wheeler tendered his resignation in a private meeting with Nixon in the Oval Office. After exchanging pleasantries, including the traditional pledge of cooperation from the Chiefs, Wheeler said that he wanted to retire, that Nixon deserved a Chairman of his own choosing. Wheeler recited his role in the Johnson Administration to make certain that Nixon understood his position.

Wheeler told Nixon that he had served the nation for five full years, well beyond the usual four-year term for a Chairman of the Joint Chiefs of Staff, only because Johnson had insisted that he serve until the official end of his Administration. Now, Wheeler said, it was time for him to retire; he had served his country well past the time most Army officers retired. He expected Nixon's thanks for a job well done and agreement that it was time for a new man. But Nixon shook his head and disagreement and surprise. Hadn't Wheeler already been confirmed by Congress? Why would he want to resign? How could he be replaced?

Wheeler later admitted to colleagues that he did not know whether to be complemented or suspicious. Apparently, it had never occurred to Nixon that Wheeler would want to leave, that he would choose retirement over power. It was a notion so foreign to Nixon as to be beyond belief. Wheeler had his reasons, which he repeated in increasingly insistent tones: not only had he served well past the time of other Chairmen, he had actually served longer than any other individual, including Bradley and Radford. To serve any longer, he told Nixon, would set a bad precedent. Again, Nixon disagreed, saying that he not only liked Wheeler personally, he admired the position he had taken on the war in Vietnam. Wheeler was one military man who had wanted to win the war, Nixon said, adding that he understood just how difficult it had been for him over the last several years. As for precedent, Congress had already settled that matter by extending Wheeler's term another year. They could do so again. [113]

It was not so much that Wheeler did not want to set a precedent; actually, he was exhausted. "He had suffered a heart attack in 1967 and could not be sure that he was medically fit for the job," Bim explains. Wheeler needed a change, rest, a chance to recover his health. Then, perhaps, he could continue to serve the nation in some other capacity. He had been looking forward to retirement. Nixon would not listen. He dismissed Wheeler's arguments with a wave of his hand, ready to change the subject. Only when Wheeler continued to press his point, leaning impolitely over the President's desk, did Nixon finally comprehend that Wheeler was serious. Surprised by Wheeler's continued argument, Nixon appealed to Wheeler's patriotism, telling him the nation had not passed its "moment of decision" in Vietnam and that his invaluable experience was desperately needed. He promised Wheeler his full cooperation and tantalizingly stated his Administration intended to take the military's advice on the war more seriously than the previous one had. [114]

Wheeler may have been intrigued by Nixon's offer and implicit promise that the war could and would be, won; that it would end with a military victory, or at the very least Nixon and his appointees intended to see the war through to its conclusion. Undeterred, Wheeler admitted to Nixon that he was dying and had served long enough. "Of course, sir, if you make it a direct order, I will do as you wish." Otherwise, he was leaving. After a short pause, Nixon gave the order. [115]

"He didn't hear a goddamn thing I said!" Bus later exclaimed to Bim. [116]

In requesting Wheeler's reappointment for a sixth year as Chairman, Laird wrote that he and Nixon believed that retaining Wheeler would be in the best interests of the nation. "General Wheeler's intimate knowledge of our overall military posture and requirements, including operations in Southeast Asia, acquired during his tenure as Chairman of the Joint Chiefs of Staff, makes it prudent and wise to retain his invaluable experience and counsel during the current and impending period of operations and negotiations affecting Southeast Asia." [117]

"Wheeler's integrity and experience proved so indispensable that Nixon extended his term by yet another year," Dr. Henry A. Kissinger recalled. "Tall, elegant, calm, Wheeler by that time was deeply disillusioned. He looked like a wary beagle, his soft dark eyes watchful for the origin of the next blow." [118]

"Wheeler had participated in a series of decisions any one of which he was able to defend, but the cumulative impact of which he could not really justify to himself," Kissinger recalled. "He was a gentleman to the core, a fine officer who helped his country through tragic times and was himself inwardly eaten up by them." [119]

## *Laird, Nixon, and the Chiefs*

A former leader of the House of Representatives, Laird was a smart, shrewd, and consummate politician. One senior military officer called Laird "a political animal to the marrow of his bones. … He could use one line on the

[Chiefs], a somewhat different one with the Service Secretaries, and a third version in dealing with key members of Congress, many of whom were close personal friends." As far as the Chiefs were concerned, Laird hit a home run in his first meeting with them by clearly stating that he would work with them as a team and would welcome their advice and counsel.

Like everything else in the Nixon Administration, the relationship between Laird and the Chiefs was unorthodox. Laird had difficulty accepting the Chiefs' belief that they were apolitical. Indeed, there were times when he believed some of them were playing politics to get into good graces with the White House. Any problems in his relationship with them stemmed less from any political behavior on their part than from his views on the situation in Vietnam. He was strongly opposed to any widening of the war and in fact wanted the U.S. to withdraw as quickly as possible.

The Vietnam War would dominate the Chiefs' relationship with Nixon. Relieved to be free of Johnson's micromanagement, they were happy to greet Nixon, but soon learned that his unscrupulous actions and his secretive behavior put them in a very difficult situation. He would violate one canon of military culture after another. Nixon and Kissinger would ignore the chain of command whenever it suited them. The Chiefs were appalled by their efforts to bypass Laird regardless of the reason. Wheeler refused to comply with Kissinger's efforts to get him to work directly with him.

The Chiefs appreciated Nixon's willingness to do what they had advocated ever since the U.S. had gone to war in Vietnam: bomb extensively. They appreciated his massive attacks on Cambodia, Laos, and then North Vietnam, the operational details of which he left to the military.

Ultimately, however, the Chiefs would grow to distrust and dislike Nixon. Frustrated with his Vietnam War policy, they also could not get over Nixon's lies, his deceitful ways, and his many efforts to get them to commit open violations of the chain of command. [120]

### *All-Volunteer Force*

Meanwhile, the process of ending the draft had accelerated when Nixon requested that the Department of Defense act to eliminate the draft and create an all-volunteer force. The Gates Commission was formed to develop a complete plan on how to implement the new force.

The Army began its own study on how it could implement such an idea. The "Project Volunteer in Defense of the Nation (PROVIDE)" addressed such topics as cost, standards of quality, personnel management, numbers needed to recruit, and even the possible socioeconomic impact of an all-volunteer force. Perhaps the biggest single hurdle in creating an all-volunteer force was funding. The government would have to provide sufficient funds for monetary incentives—viable wages and even bonuses for some specialties—for new recruits. Without competitive pay, the military could not enlist or retain the best servicemen. Funding was also required for advertising if the military was to become an attractive career choice and bring in enough quality American youths. [121]

Meanwhile, Wheeler's health issues still plagued him. During his annual physical exam, an electrocardiogram detected an arterial blockage that subsequent electrocardiograms would also observe over the next twelve months. Wheeler told his doctor that he had not experienced any associated systems. [122]

### Eisenhower Passes

Over the nine years since his presidency, Eisenhower had gone through several "ups and downs" with his health. After recently experiencing another downturn, Eisenhower had been admitted to Walter Reed Army Medical Center again. [123]

On 26 March, Betty went out to the Soldiers Home to cut the ribbon opening the new women's wing. "It was most interesting and I enjoyed it," she said. She then went up to Walter Reed to call upon Mamie. The following day, she wrote about their visit.

> I was sitting with Mrs. Eisenhower, and had a lovely time. She had planned to come to [a Wives Club] lunch [that Betty attended] today. I talked to her [again] last night. Naturally she's not stirring from Walter Reed. She was a little choked up, but very dear. She told me the doctors said that there was nothing more that they could do. [A friend of the Wheelers had talked to another doctor last night who] said it had not

seemed impossible that he could live until morning, yet morning found him chatting and alert. However, he went down again yesterday, and I gather his heart is very tired, so it would seem any moment now for an old soldier. [124]

Eisenhower died the following day, 28 March. Two days later, he was given a state funeral in the rotunda of the U.S. Capitol building. "Bus came in from the funeral, but is off to the White House reception," Betty reported. [125]

## SACEUR

In May, Wheeler attended the 17th Annual Supreme Headquarters Allied Powers Europe Exercise (SHAPEX) in Belgium. As always, Betty accompanied him. [126]

On 18 June, Wheeler received official notification from the President that his tenure as Chairman was being extended. "It was indeed a pleasure for me to reappoint you as Chairman of the Joint Chiefs of Staff for an additional year, and I would like to extend my personal congratulations to you," Nixon wrote. "In addition, I would like to express my gratitude to you for your past dedicated service in this most demanding of all military positions and for your willingness to continue to serve." [127]

This meant someone other than Wheeler would have to replace Lemnitzer as Supreme Allied Commander Europe (SACEUR). Wheeler had wanted the job since becoming Deputy SACEUR in 1962. After he was notified by Taylor that he would replace Decker as Chief of Staff of the Army, Wheeler tried to convince Taylor to argue that he should become SACEUR instead. Betty still would have liked for him to take the job now, as most Allied officers had presumed all along that he would. It was not to be, however, so Bus nominated his good friend and protégé "Andy" Goodpaster. [128]

With Wheeler's long history in Europe, the extensive list of international relationships he had formed there, as well as his unique perspective on how Vietnam had negatively impacted the U.S. contribution to the collective defense of Europe, it was unfortunate that he could not have become SACEUR instead of Goodpaster. Perhaps though, once Wheeler had retired from the military and taken some time to regain his health, he could still be of some similar service to the Administration in Europe.

Goodpaster assumed duties as SACEUR in a ceremony on 1 July. The political situation that he faced was an unenviable one. His greatest immediate challenge was to contend with strong antiwar sentiment fueled by the frustrations of the war in Vietnam, not only among the European Allies, but also in North America with the Canadians. He said later, "There was uncertainty about the future of Europe. The attitude to the common defense was a curious mixture of unwillingness to augment European efforts and fear of American withdrawal." Since taking office, the Nixon Administration had been searching for ways to balance increasing domestic discontent over war expenditures, brought on partly by the seemingly interminable conflict in Vietnam, with a need to convince the European Allies that the real battle front of the Cold War remained the division between East and West in Europe. In short, Goodpaster faced an alarming state of affairs.

> Because of both the demands of the war in Vietnam and the turbulent social conditions at home ... this resulted in units that were grossly understrength, racked by continual massive turnover in those who were assigned, plagued by widespread problems of drug abuse, racial disharmony, dissent, and indiscipline, and thus not only much reduced in operational capability but also poor examples for the NATO Allies that the U.S. was trying to [convince to] contribute more and better forces to the alliance. [129]

The U.S. had reduced its forces in Europe from 408,000 in 1963 to 300,000 by 1969. With Wheeler's help, Goodpaster would urge the Europeans to do more while the U.S. was doing less.

Goodpaster was also immediately concerned with attempting to counter strong sentiment both in the U.S. and in Europe favoring withdrawal, rather than a further build-up, of U.S. forces. The war in Vietnam would remain a constant drag on Goodpaster's efforts to increase the European member nations' contributions to NATO. [130]

*(From left) General John D. Ryan, Laird, Moorer, and Wheeler during a ceremony in Laird's office honoring Wheeler's extension as Chairman, The Pentagon, Washington, DC, 3 July 1969. (Office of the Chairman of the Joint Chiefs of Staff).*

On 3 July, Laird presided over a ceremony in his office that was attended by the Chiefs in which Wheeler's tour as Chairman was extended. Later that day, Wheeler hosted a luncheon in the wood paneled Chairman's Dining Room in honor of Lemnitzer's retirement. Several dignitaries attended, including McNamara, Admiral Arleigh A. Burke, Taylor, and the Chiefs. [131]

In early October, Betty accompanied Bus on another trip to the Far East. In South Korea, they were greeted at Kempo Air Base by General Mun, Bus's South Korean counterpart. [132]

"I judge that we are on the right track," Wheeler said in Saigon on 7 October. In a planeside news conference following his return to Washington two days later, he affirmed, "Vietnamization is on schedule and in some places ahead of schedule." [133]

## SALT

Meanwhile, the Administration continued to pursue the more important aspects of its foreign policy that Vietnam was detracting from. On 10-12 November, Wheeler, Laird, and others within the Administration attended a strategic planning retreat at Airlie House in rural Warrenton, Virginia. [134]

The U.S. and the Soviet Union opened Strategic Arms Limitation Talks (SALT) to explore ways to stop the nuclear arms race and to begin the task of disarmament. Progress would come slowly because of many technical points that had to be settled, but it was a start.

Meanwhile, despite considerable congressional and public opposition, the U.S. proceeded with plans to deploy a ballistic missile defense system. Known as SAFEGUARD, the program envisioned a phased installation of missiles, radars, and computers at key sites across the country by the mid-1970s. Although the proposed system provided at best a thin line of defense, the U.S. declined to halt construction until the SALT negotiations had produced an agreement. [135]

# 1970

## *At Long Last*

For the fifth and final time, the staff of the Chairman's Dining Room served cake and champagne to celebrate Wheeler's 62nd birthday on 13 January 1970. [136]

"I see that, at long last, they're going to let you retire," former President Johnson had written to Wheeler on 15 April.

> I know perhaps better than anyone else the quality of the service you rendered—the professional judgment, integrity, wisdom, discretion, and loyalty you brought to these difficult years.
>
> I was startled once when General Eisenhower told me he thought Westmoreland's task in Vietnam was more difficult than his in Europe. On reflection, I believe he was correct. And I would add, your task has been more difficult than George Marshall's during the Second World War.
>
> You faced all the complexities, abroad and at home, with extraordinary steadiness and grace. As President, no man gave me more strength and comfort. I shall always be grateful to you. [137]

One week later, Wheeler was briefly hospitalized at Walter Reed for a thorough pre-retirement physical exam. His physician recorded:

> Gen. Wheeler, in addition to being a heavy smoker for many years … has been diagnosed as having chronic bronchitis. General Wheeler states he does not consider himself short of breath with normal day-to-day activities, but I personally had the opportunity to climb one long flight of stairs with him and I can professionally vouch that he is more short of breath with the exertion and for a longer period after the exertion than expected for his age and the activity involved. [138]

The physician recommended that Wheeler be referred by the Medical Board to the Physical Evaluation Board as medically unfit due to his chronic obstructive pulmonary disease and chronic bronchitis and that he be medically retired. [139]

### USS Billfish

When the Navy christened a new nuclear attack submarine, the USS Billfish (Sturgeon class # 676), on 1 May, Betty broke the bottle over its bow before it slid into the water for the first time. Considering her dedicated service in support of Bus's thirty-eight military career, it was a fitting honor for Betty to be selected as the ship's "sponsor". [140] She was thrilled and described their trip to Connecticut at length.

> What a glorious and exciting day yesterday was. Never, never did I imagine that the christening would be such a thrill! … Bus let me ask both Charlie and Walt and Sarah and Mida [Bus's aides and their wives] to come with us [on] the trip on [Bus's plane, tail number] '229'. We were a little late starting due to the President being in the Pentagon for a briefing [about Cambodia].
>
> We arrived [in] Groton about twelve-thirty. … The day grew progressively more beautiful. … We were met at the plane by Mr. and Mrs. Lewis. He is the President of General Dynamics. … [The official party went to] the rehearsal. The area around the 'Billfish' was roped off … for guests. There was an aisle

going down to … two platforms, one slightly above the people, and a higher one at the keel. … After three tries and a
good hit every time [with] … a wooden champagne bottle,
it was decided there was no need to practice more. Bim and
Bus were looking at the underpinnings while this was going
on. … Then on to lunch.

As we left the launching site, Admiral Rose gave me a letter
from Tom Moorer. [It explained] that the ship christened is
considered to be the sponsor's ship. Isn't that marvelous, I
have a nuclear submarine for my very own, and Uncle Sam
will take care of her for me! … The fact that the 'Billfish' was
'my ship' was mentioned many times [in Moorer's letter], but
I was so glad that Tom told me first and in the beautiful manner in which he did.

After lunch, the Wheelers' party toured the seaport, then drove to
Admiral Perry's quarters on the submarine base. Betty changed into one of
her favorite dresses that she had made five seasons earlier and was proud of
her handiwork in updating it. "When I came downstairs I felt good, and felt I
could uphold the Army in the face of the Navy!" The party then moved to the
hospital next to the launching site.

Promptly at five, we started the walk to the platform. The
band was playing. The place was filled with people and you
could feel the excitement. … The invocation by a young Navy
chaplain was superb. … It was so perfect for my submarine. … There were some introductions. … Bus gave a talk,
about seven minutes. It was excellent. After he finished, my
moment had come. Up we went to the upper deck. Margie,
Bus, and Mr. Lewis with me. … There was a minute or so
allowing cameramen to take pictures and then the count-
down – ten, nine, eight, seven, six, five, four, three, two, one
– launch. On launch, wham, 'I christen thee U.S.S. Billfish.'
The timing was so perfect that I could have believed it was
my hit that started her down the greased ramp. What a sight.
About halfway down, her deck came into sight and there was
her crew standing at attention and saluting. … As she started

to go, her whistles blew, the band played. I have never seen anything like it. The sun was exactly right. ... When she hit the water and made her 'curtsy' the splash and she looked golden. ... It was a glorious sight.[141]

As far as Bim was concerned, the ceremony was not without incident. Although his wife Margie carried flowers for Betty as part of the official party, Bim had no role in it. He had been told by Perry's aide to stand at a corner of the General Dynamics building and that he would be picked up by the official party as it moved to the ceremony location. That way, Bim would be seated in the front group of viewers, which included all the shipbuilders and their families. [142]

As it happened, the official party passed by on the other side of the building, and Bim was forgotten. He rushed down to the christening site and was denied entry into the viewing area. After the ceremony, the dignitaries departed while Bim and his fellow spectators were required to stay put. Bim had been left behind again with no idea where the official party had gone. He learned where they had gone, called a cab, and then could not locate the reception. The panicked Admiral's aide finally appeared and exclaimed, "Where have you been?" Bim told him his story, and the young officer offered to pay for his cab. An annoyed Bim told him, "Not on your life! You're not going to ruin this story, and I intend to tell it!" [143]

The ceremony participants had gone to the library of the Mystic Marine Historical Association for a small reception, then on to the main reception at the Morgan Inn.

> During the gift presentation, Mr. Lewis said with tears in his eyes, 'In all the launchings I have been to, I have never seen a ship go into the sunlight as this one did. It was so beautiful, I will never forget it. I'm sure this ship is something special, and I feel all of us here feel that this has been a special day thanks to her lovely and charming sponsor.' Wasn't that nice? ... Admiral Rickover sent a telegram and had Mr. Lewis give me a model of the 'Billfish' for him. Then he gave me a paperweight made from the first keel block. It has the submarine insignia on it.

The Wheelers then joined the larger party and enjoyed seeing many old friends during dinner.

> [We were invited back to the launching] on March 4th '71 and to stay a few days, because usually, two days after the launching the men invite their families aboard for a ride, and we are invited too. ... We'll all go back ... in the fall, when the leaves are perfection. ... It almost gives me goose pimples to realize that when the color is at its peak, we can just go! Great day!

Betty concluded, in her letter about the Billfish christening with the observation, "Do you realize we'll only be home 36 days before July 1$^{st}$ and packing to do! Probably this will be the last real letter until 'down on the farm.'" [144]

Betty would earn a reputation as the best sponsor the Navy ever had because she stayed with the USS Billfish all the way to its decommissioning. She attended every change of command ceremony and always hosted a dinner for the incoming and outgoing commanding officers. Bim claims he "almost got a hernia every Christmas carrying a box of books, which were a gift to the ship's library!" [145]

## Turkey

Betty reported on their trip to Turkey in mid-May.

> We stayed in the palace guest house for foreign visitors ... in Ankara. A lovely two nights. We had the place to our-selves. It was across from the palace. Set high, it overlooked the city. ... On 19th May, we left ... at 7:30 ... up bright and early on to Istanbul. ... We were in Istanbul at 8:45. Headed straight for the Blue Mosque. I really wasn't prepared for its beauty. It was a magnificent sight. Following that we visited St. Sophia mosque which is now a museum of sorts. Then to the Topkapi museum. Most interesting. As it was a holiday it was closed to the public. The curator took us through. ... We finally got to the Istanbul Hilton at twelve-thirty. We had a beautiful suite overlooking the Bosporus. [After a luncheon given in the Wheelers' honor] a beautiful boat was waiting at

a dock next door. … We had a beautiful tour of the Bosporus, saw some beautiful houses. The yacht left us at Dolmabache Palace. Bus went back to the hotel, but I wasn't about to miss anything, tired though I was. … It must have been six before I got back to the Hilton, and we had a seven-thirty dinner to attend. It was a beautiful dinner party. … After dinner, there was a performance of Turkish folk dances. Home after midnight, a long but rather wonderful day. … We left the hotel at eight the next morning and were in Ismir a little after nine. Bus went to meetings while I went to the bazaar with [an old friend] stationed there. … We left by helicopter at ten-thirty for a place called Kusadasi for lunch. … Luncheon was at a small inn [with] a beautiful terrace dining room overlooking the Aegean Sea. We returned by helicopter to the city. [146]

At the end of the month, the Wheelers received the itinerary for Bus's farewell tour of Europe, which would include Venice, Brussels, and Paris.

Meanwhile, the Army's Physical Review Council had considered Bus's medical record and recommended his disability rating be raised to 70%. [147]

### Last Month in Uniform

With less than thirty days remaining before his retirement, Wheeler attended to numerous recurring duties for the final time. On 3 June, he addressed the Industrial College of the Armed Forces.

Betty's preparations for their upcoming move from Quarters 6 to Ugly Duckling Manor were punctuated by several events, including her receipt of "a beautiful Steuben bowl from the Chiefs' wives," for which she felt "most undeserving. … I'm trying not to panic", she added, "but Lord the stuff still piled up around that I don't know what to do with!" [148]

### Paris

On 15 June, the Wheelers arrived in Paris. The Associated Press noted that Wheeler's visit was the first by the Chairman of the Joint Chiefs of Staff since de Gaulle loosened ties with the North Atlantic Treaty Organization in 1967.

U.S. sources [in Paris] say they interpret Wheeler's visit as a sign of the improvement of relations between France and the United States. The decision to push French-American cooperation was taken last February when President Georges Pompidou visited Washington, the sources said. Mr. Pompidou is said to have told President Nixon that he thought the time was ripe for it.

Gen. Wheeler also met with French Defense Minister Michel Debre, but officials made no report about their talks. The sources said they believed Gen. Wheeler might discuss with the French the conditions for providing U.S. tactical nuclear support for French forces in Germany until France's own tactical nuclear weapon is operational in 1972. They also speculated that Gen. Wheeler may also begin preliminary talks with the French on coordinating the targeting of U.S. and French strategic weapons. [149]

The American public was unaware that Nixon was considering Wheeler to replace R. Sargent Shriver as the next U.S. Ambassador to France. The French government knew and literally gave Wheeler its seal of approval by conferring upon him the medal of a Grand Officer of the Legion of Honor, one of France's highest decorations. Ultimately, Wheeler's poor health would preclude his immediate selection in favor of Arthur K. Watson, the Chief Executive Officer of the IBM World Trade Corporation, although he would remain a candidate to replace Ambassador Watson later. [150]

## *May It Be Said, "Well Done"*

On 26 June, the Wheelers attended a reception and dinner in their honor at the Bolling Air Force Base Officers Club. On the White Mess Dress jacket in which he would be buried just five years later, Bus uncharacteristically wore both the Army Staff and Joint Staff Identification Badges. As always, though, he did wear his non-regulation infantry-blue cummerbund. Betty wore a beautiful dress that she had sewn herself.

Seated at the head table with the Wheelers were the Chiefs and their wives. The menu was spectacular and befit the level to which Betty had entertained for eight years. It featured Harvey's Bristol crème sherry, chilled vichyssoise, Graves Cruse, deviled crab au gratin, Mateus Rose, broiled filet mignon bordelaise, asparagus hollandaise, broiled stuffed tomatoes, hearts of romaine vinaigrette, Bollinger Special Cuvee, crepe suzette, and demitasse liqueurs.

While dining, the attendees were entertained by the White House Ensemble of the U.S. Marine Corps Band, the United States Army Combo, the Strolling Strings, and the Sea Chanters. Moorer, as Wheeler's replacement as Chairman, delivered the farewell address and presented Bus with a coffee table inscribed, "To General Earle G. Wheeler, Chairman, Joint Chiefs of Staff, with great affection and highest esteem from his colleagues The Joint Chiefs of Staff, 26 June 1970." [151]

Wheeler retired on 2 July 1970 in a ceremony inside a packed hanger building at Bolling Air Force Base. Wheeler wore his Dress White uniform more fully adorned than ever before with the Army and Joint Staff Identification Badges and ribbon bars for the 20 medals and decorations he had earned. Significantly, of the many foreign award breast stars he had been awarded, Wheeler only wore the French Legion of Honor.

The ceremony commenced with music by the U.S. Army Band, which played "Liberty Bell" by John Philip Sousa and "Spirit of Independence" by Abe Holtzmann. At 11:00 AM, the reviewing party of Wheeler, Laird, and Deputy Secretary of Defense David Packard assumed its position. Honors were then rendered and consisted of a nineteen-gun salute, four ruffles and flourishes, and the "General's March." Wheeler then inspected the troops from all four Services while the "The Official West Point March" was played. After presentation of the colors by the Joint Color Party and "The National Anthem", Wheeler was awarded the Army, Navy, and Air Force Distinguished Service Medals. Laird praised Wheeler as "a great soldier-statesman" who has "forever his country's respect, its confidence, and its gratitude." After the retirement order was read, the Old Guard Fife and Drum Corps led the reviewing party to an outdoor reviewing platform, followed by guests directed by ushers. A flyover of twenty-six military jets then occurred, followed by a pass in review by a Joint Honor Guard. The final salute to Wheeler was performed by the U.S. Army Band playing "Army Blue" and "The Army Goes Rolling Along."

*Bus and Betty Wheeler with grandsons Robbie and Billy after Bus's retirement ceremony, Bolling Air Force Base, Washington, DC, 2 July 1970. (Office of the Chairman of the Joint Chiefs of Staff).*

After the retirement ceremony present the concluded, senior dignitaries congratulated Wheeler as his black Cadillac limousine pulled into the hanger. Bus and Betty shared their ride to the reception with their young grandsons, Robbie and Billy. At the Officers Club, the Lairds, Wheelers, and Packards greeted guests in the receiving line. Taylor and Clifford were among the many notable attendees. Meanwhile, Robbie and Billy helped themselves to heaping platefuls of cookies and found a sofa on which to eat them. Laird sat down and joined them. [152]

"Gen. Earle G. Wheeler retired today, stepping out of a 38-year military career that began as a teen-age National Guardsman and ended with a record six-year term as the nation's No. 1 soldier," a newspaper article reported that day. "Although his military service officially dates from his graduation from West Point, it is 46 years since Gen. Wheeler at the age of 16, joined the National Guard in Washington, D.C."

The article reported that Wheeler had made no retirement plans and would rest at his farm in West Virginia before deciding what he will do. He would also maintain his home in Alexandria.

"There are too many people these days who think the Joint Chiefs of Staff are fire breathing monsters trying to control government policy, foreign and domestic," the article stated. "Anyone who has met Gen. Wheeler should know this is not the case."

Wheeler was credited as epitomizing what the architects of Federal government had in mind when they established a system of military advice under civilian control. "Gen. Wheeler presented and defended the military view in the highest councils of government. But he was willing to break with the other Chiefs when he disagreed – as in supporting the nuclear test ban treaty in 1963. And when he was overruled by a President or defense secretary – as occurred when Mr. Johnson and former Secretary McNamara spurned the Chiefs' advice to take tougher measures against North Vietnam early in the war – Gen. Wheeler took his orders and followed them to the letter."

"Gen. Wheeler has served – and served well," the article concluded, "through a period that included an unpopular war and saw the public image of the military battered by its critics. This troubled the general but never interfered with his loyal devotion to duty." [153]

On his official retirement date of 3 July 1970, Wheeler had completed 38 years and 28 days of active service. He was credited with having served 3 years, 10 months, and 27 days in the DC National Guard, and his career included 8 years, 4 months, and 26 days of foreign service. [154]

*The Wheeler family with President Nixon in the White House rose garden following the President's first-ever presentation of the Defense Distinguished Service Medal to Wheeler. Margie Wheeler is at left, 9 July 1970. (Office of the Chairman of the Joint Chiefs of Staff).*

On the morning of 9 July, the President honored Wheeler in an awards ceremony in the White House Rose Garden. Beforehand, Bus, Betty, Bim, Margie, Robbie, and Billy had assembled in the Oval Office. Bus informed Nixon that Bim had just earned his Ph. D. a couple weeks earlier, and that it was in a "practical discipline" like Dr. Kissinger's.

During the ceremony, Nixon awarded Wheeler a new decoration, the first Defense Distinguished Service Medal ever presented. Laird read the citation before Nixon pinned the medal to Wheeler's Service Dress Green uniform coat, which was now adorned with 25 ribbon bars and the breast star of the French Legion of Honor. [155]

Wheeler's award citation perfectly summarized the exceptional nature of his most recent military service. He had assumed the Chairmanship at a critical point in the nation's history and served for six years as its senior military officer. During these years, he carried a heavy responsibility of providing military advice to the President, the Secretary of Defense, and the National Security Council. This advice had invariably been both wise and clear. His judicious understanding of the complex problems of national security had provided the basis for the strongest confidence placed in him by the nation.

In addition, the quality of Wheeler's professional consultation with government and military leaders of other nations had promoted credence in as well as respect for the interests of the U.S. and the security of its Allies.

Wheeler's disciplined judgment and breadth of vision were key factors in assuring the wisdom of the military counsel of the Joint Chiefs of Staff. His administration of the Chairman's responsibilities, including the operation of the Organization of the Joint Chiefs of Staff, was particularly noteworthy. During his tenure, the voice of each Service was clearly heard in the forum of the Chiefs, with the assurance that all viewpoints were fully considered. Under his leadership, the role of the Joint Chiefs of Staff was expanded to make that body's considered advice more readily available in the development of military programs for the future.

As Chairman of the Joint Chiefs of Staff, Wheeler provided military advice to two Presidents of the United States and three Secretaries of Defense. He agreed to serve unprecedented additional terms as Chairman at the personal request of two Presidents. These presidential initiatives were themselves the soundest measures of his leadership, the wisdom of his counsel, and the great value placed on his services.

"Throughout his long and distinguished career, culminating with duty as Chairman, Joint Chiefs of Staff, General Wheeler has devoted his efforts to maintaining and improving security and well-being of his country," the citation concluded. "He has given unstintingly of himself. This distinguished soldier has truly earned his place in the front rank of those American patriots who guided the destinies of the United States of America." [156]

Nixon wrote a personal note to Wheeler.

As you end your long and distinguished career of dedicated service, I would like to join with your many other friends in expressing my personal congratulations for your great contribution to the defense of our country.

During the months that we have worked together, I have been grateful for your advice, your support and your loyal friendship. In particular, I appreciate your willingness to serve well above and beyond the call of duty by accepting reappointment as Chairman of the Joint Chiefs of Staff for an additional year. Your ready sacrifice of your personal interests on behalf of the nation are typical of your spirit and devotion to the cause of peace which has inspired those who served with you in the military forces. [157]

# CHAPTER 10

## THE LEAST POMPOUS GREAT MAN
## (JULY 1970 – DECEMBER 1975)

### 1970

### *Taking Stock*

For Wheeler, the last eight years of relentless, hard work, frequent consumption of rich party food and alcohol, lack of exercise, and constant smoking had all exacted a devastating toll on his health. "I think [the job] killed him," Spivy said. Wheeler received a 60% disability rating but elected not to receive the Veterans Administration disability compensation. [1]

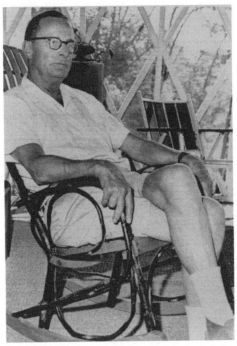

*Wheeler relaxes in the rocking chair he received as a retirement gift from President Johnson, on the screen porch of Ugly Duckling Manor, outside Martinsburg, West Virginia, 12 July 1970. (UPI Telephoto CWP071201).*

Letters from world leaders streamed in. The President of South Vietnam, Nguyen V. Thieu wrote on 14 July 1970:

> I regret very much that you are relinquishing your responsibilities as Chairman of the Joint Chiefs of Staff, upon your retirement from active service.
>
> You can certainly look back with pride on your outstanding achievements throughout the many decades you have devoted to the service of your country, and of the Free World. It is however with melancholy that I see such a great soldier as you leaving the scene.
>
> You have, in spite of your modesty and discretion, played a significant role in the recent years in which the Free World was confronted with so many challenging problems. For my part, I shall always remember with deeper appreciation for the great contribution you have made in the common efforts of our two countries for the defense of freedom in the move toward a just and lasting peace.
>
> I do not believe that 'old soldiers just fade away', and earnestly hope that you can sometimes come again to Viet-Nam, if not any longer as Chairman of the United States Joint Chiefs of Staff, at least as a long-standing friend who has secured a warm affection in the hearts of all the Vietnamese who have come to know you. [2]

The same day, Yitzhak Rabin of Israel wrote, "Please accept, sir my personal salute and my expressions of goodwill for the success of all your future endeavors." [3]

Wheeler was adjusting to life without his personal staff of aides, executive officers, and secretaries. It was not until three weeks later that he replied to Rabin.

> I deeply appreciate your kind and very generous letter. Coming from a soldier of your attainments, I value [it] all the more. ... Among the few things I regret in retiring from active service is the loss of my frequent contacts with those men at the center of world events. I enjoyed my conversations

with you, Mr. Ambassador, and I profited by them. Our discussions broadened and sharpened my understanding of the issues in the Middle East, the forces at work there, and—I think—helped me to do my job a bit better. [4]

## *Appalling State*

The U.S. Army that Wheeler retired from was in an appalling state due to the deleterious effects of the Vietnam War. The U.S. Army War College produced a report on the general state of the officer corps that:

> ... surprised and, in some cases, shocked many of the Army's senior leaders. ... In general, it discovered that the majority of the officer corps perceived a stark dichotomy between the appearance and reality of the appearance of senior officers to the traditional standards of professionalism, which the words duty, honor, and country sum up. Instead, these officers saw a system that rewarded selfishness, incompetence, and dishonesty. [5]

In August, Wheeler joined the Board of Directors of the Monsanto Company. His earnings would eventually enable him to pay off the mortgage on their farm for Betty. [6]

On 16 September, South Vietnamese Ambassador Bui Diem presented Wheeler the National Order Second Class and the Gallantry Cross with Palm in a ceremony at the South Vietnamese embassy that was attended by Westmoreland and Moorer. [7]

## *Modern Volunteer Army*

As the war still raged in Southeast Asia, the Nixon Administration reiterated its commitment to ending the draft, and the Army moved to implement a new concept. In October, Westmoreland initiated the Modern Volunteer Army (MVA) Program to lay out a blueprint for what would amount to a major cultural change while the Army was still at war. [8]

In an interview, Wheeler did not rule out the practicality of an All-Volunteer Army, but he was not optimistic, either.

A purely volunteer Army, in today's times, hasn't been proven yet. As of June, I believe, there were 815,000 in the Army. From what I read in the papers, they're short of what they hope to have – so much each month. It appears – again, on today's standards – the higher education of the men you have, the less disciplinary problems you have. Now, that wasn't true back in '32, when I became a regular officer. As I recall, we had 130,000 in the entire Army and Air Corps, all volunteer. Many of those at that time hadn't even finished grade school. But they were damned good soldiers. It was no disciplinary problem with most of them. So I really can't say about an all-volunteer Army today. [9]

## USS *Billfish*

On 14 December, Betty received a status report on "her" submarine from Rickover.

As the sponsor of our 50th attack type nuclear submarine, the USS BILLFISH, I thought you'd be interested to know that we are returning from the ship's first sea trials. The ship completed all tests including full power operation, both sur-face and submerged. The BILLFISH is the second United States submarine and to bear this name.

The first BILLFISH was commissioned in April 1943 for her service during World War II, and received seven battle stars.

The new BILLFISH is equipped with the latest navigation and electronic systems and a computer-controlled weapons system, which enable her to detect and attack targets at con-siderable distances. These characteristics, combined with the ability to operate at high speeds for long periods of time and the environmental independence provided by nuclear pro-pulsion, make for a powerful weapon against surface ships and submarines alike.

In addition to the 50th attack type nuclear submarines, we also have 41 Polaris submarines and a deep submergence ocean engineering submarine, making a total of 92 nuclear submarines in operation. When all nuclear submarines presently authorized by Congress are completed, the United States will have 65 attack and 41 Polaris submarines. [10]

## 1971

### *Groton*

Betty described the Wheeler's return to Connecticut in March 1971 to visit the USS Billfish.

> Tom Moorer authorized [aircraft tail number] 229 for Bus's use. It was exciting to have another ride on her. … It was cold, but a sunny, crisp, cold [day] and of course, I was dressed warmly. … After the ceremony, we had a tour of the boat. She looks small above the water, but she goes below four or five decks. It was an unbelievable experience and one the boys [grandsons Billy and Robbie Wheeler] will never forget. … The Governor of Connecticut gave a short, absolutely marvelous talk. We were most impressed. [11]

### *Martinsburg*

Meanwhile back in Martinsburg, the Wheelers had become regular members of the community. Bus continued to perform civic duties, albeit at the local level. Betty wrote:

> Bus and I went to a funeral service yesterday afternoon. Bus visited quite awhile with a young man the day we were in the veterans' hospital. I've talked to his mother on the telephone, but wouldn't know her if I saw her. She called yesterday morning. Fortunately, Bus answered the telephone. Would we please come to the services? We went. Bus signed the book. It was a short, very sweet service, so guess it was little enough to do, if it meant something to the family. [12]

Wheeler often accepted public speaking invitations. He did not, however, accept any honoraria, asking only that his travel expenses be covered. In his mind, the only reason why an organization would want to hear him speak was because of his former position as Chairman of the Joint Chiefs of Staff. As such, he felt it would be improper for him to benefit financially from the performance of his official duties. [13]

Bus happily attended the occasional civic functions to which he was invited as an honored guest. "Last night, Bus was guest speaker at the American Legion," Betty reported. "We were back home before nine-thirty so it wasn't too bad." [14]

Bus looked forward to frequent visits with his two grandsons. He also enjoyed chatting with the locals at the post office or store. Whenever the Seventh Day Adventists came around proselytizing, he usually spent a couple hours talking with them on the front porch. When Betty questioned him about spending so much time with them, he simply replied that they were just nice, friendly people. [15]

Stewart, the former head of the Wheeler's household staff at Quarters 6, visited them in Martinsburg at least every year and continued to visit Betty after Bus died. Stewart recalls an occasion when Bus, working in a pair of cut-off fatigue pants, told him he could stop calling him "Sir" and to call him "Bus" instead. Stewart never could bring himself to that, but four or five years after Bus's death he did begin to address Betty by her name. [16]

A massive, secure communications system had been installed in Wheeler's farmhouse soon after retirement to keep him in contact with authorities in Washington. "He was always up to date," Bim recalls, "and he ulcerated about Vietnam." On 16 March, the President signed Wheeler's appointment to the President's Commission on White House Fellowships. [17]

During the Wheeler's occasional trips to Casey Key to visit Betty's parents, Bus's West Point roommate, best man, and lifelong friend, Colonel (Retired) Jim Churchill, often stayed at their farm in Martinsburg. Churchill was a widower and enjoyed looking after the place while the Wheelers were away. On 9 April, they returned home to discover that he had died in their absence. [18]

---

## FBI Investigation

Meanwhile, preparations continued for Wheeler's nomination to become U.S. Ambassador to France. In July, the State Department requested the Federal Bureau of Investigation (FBI) investigate Wheeler, stating that he was "under consideration for a Presidential appointment requiring Senate confirmation." Wheeler's case file noted:

> [He] is being considered for Presidential appointment, position not stated with the Department of State. ... An investigation was conducted on Wheeler a few months ago by the Civil Service Commission concerning his appointment to the Board of Directors of the Monsanto Chemical Company, whose headquarters is in St. Louis, Missouri. He has no credit or arrest record. [19]

On 29 July, the FBI reported its findings back to the Secretary of State and to the Deputy Assistant to the President, Alexander P. Butterfield. The FBI's 156-page report summarizes 41 interviews with Wheeler's fellow general and flag officers, senior federal government officials, and other members of the Monsanto board of directors. None of the respondents were named, but some were identifiable by the nature and dates of their association with Wheeler. The report is replete with accolades of the highest magnitude and contains only three mildly critical comments from Wheeler's anonymous peers.

An unidentified retired Army General who had been acquainted with Wheeler since 1930 and had known him intimately since 1960 described Wheeler as possessing "impeccable integrity with deep devotion to his country and [possessing] the highest intellectual and moral character." He also described Wheeler as "very diplomatic, well-regarded by all associates, completely trustworthy, and of outstanding reputation and ability." He stated that Wheeler "is a devoted family man whose wife and son are of excellent character, associations, reputation, and loyalty." He described Betty Wheeler as being "very gracious, shy, and totally devoted to her husband." Furthermore, he described Bim Wheeler as "very stable" and that Bim "enjoys an excellent relationship with his family." This General stated that he "knows of absolutely no derogatory information concerning General Wheeler or members of his family" and that he "would unhesitatingly recommend" Wheeler for any position.

Norstad described Wheeler as "an extremely capable person of unquestioned loyalty, a person of excellent character, reputation, and associations", and that he "would recommend him, without question, for any position".

LeMay described Wheeler as "an extremely competent individual … well-qualified for any administrative position". [Author's emphasis. Even now, LeMay may still have faulted Wheeler's lack of combat command experience.] He considered Wheeler "a dependable, proficient, diligent, conscientious, and efficient individual of high scruples whose honesty, integrity, and ability are above question."

Westmoreland described Wheeler as "a highly intelligent man whose character, reputation, loyalty, and associates are above reproach as there is no finer man of high caliber and unfaltering patriotism."

McConnell described Wheeler as "an outstanding individual and a very patriotic, loyal American … [whose] character, reputation, morals and integrity are impeccable. He is not the type of individual who will accept any position he does not feel he can handle." [20]

True to McConnell's statement, Bus's worsening medical conditions would eventually compel him to withdraw his name from consideration to become an Ambassador. [21]

"Johnny" Johnson said Wheeler "has great natural abilities, unlike those of his predecessors. He has a great understanding of the national scene. He has a good ability to handle people and get a job done. Wheeler has great mental abilities and managerial skills." Johnson supposed that "other persons who knew and had worked with Wheeler would speak highly of him, also."

An unidentified retired Air Force General who had known Wheeler from 1955 until 1960 during their service together on the Joint Staff stated that "if Wheeler has any faults, it is only that he often works too hard".

The Lieutenant Colonel who became Wheeler's Aide-de-Camp in May 1969 described him as "the greatest man I've ever met."

The FBI interviewed several senior government civilian officials who had served with Wheeler.

McNamara described Wheeler as "a person of the highest integrity, intelligent, skillful, and diplomatic, and the most capable United States Army

General". He pointed out that Wheeler "is skillful and tactful in dealing with others and is well-able to judge a situation in which he is involved". McNamara had been "impressed with Wheeler's deep sense of patriotism, his industry, and his expertise and ability", and he felt "the United States would indeed be fortunate to have Wheeler serving in any regard". He remarked that Wheeler's wife had also impressed him as "a very wonderful person".

The FBI gleaned from Wheeler's most recent efficiency reports that he "is an outstanding officer. He has demonstrated dynamic leadership, initiative, good judgment, and common sense. He brings to any assignment a breadth of vision, a devotion to duty, and a mental alertness that is refreshing and challenging."

The FBI also interviewed Wheeler's fellow directors on the Board of the Monsanto Company. Each advised that "to their knowledge, Wheeler had neither character defects nor moral problems and partakes of intoxicants only moderately."

One director stated that it soon became evident to him after Wheeler joined the board "why he had achieved the highest position in the military sense by his manner and action. ... [Wheeler] inspires trust, confidence and respect, and in addition, is a concerned, people-oriented person."

Another director who had only known Wheeler about a year stated that he did not know him too well but considered him extremely honest and introverted. Although unable to comment on Wheeler's abilities, he felt that Wheeler was "miscast as a corporate officer". He stated that Wheeler was "not overly intelligent" and that he "would not hire him to run his business". That said, he would recommend Wheeler for a position of trust [in the government].

Another director who had been acquainted with Wheeler for approximately ten years described him as "an exceptionally capable and fine person ... with a fine reputation among his peers", and that "he has ... exceptional ability in everything he attempts to do". He stated that Wheeler "is extremely honest and always attempts to do as good a job as he possibly can". He added that Wheeler "is soft-spoken and attempts to stay out of the public eye". [22]

## 1972

Upon his retirement, Wheeler had instructed his personal and household staff to let him know if they ever needed his help in any professional matter. He added, "Let me know soon because my influence around here will wane considerably after about five years." True to his word, Wheeler helped place Stewart as the head of Abrams's household staff when Abrams became Chief of Staff of the Army in 1972. [23]

In April, Wheeler wrote a letter to The Adjutant General of the Army on behalf of Mrs. Helen Paschal, who wished to replace her late husband's military decorations. In 1941, Betty and Bim stayed with the Paschals in their quarters on Fort Sam Houston while Bus was away at Camp Bowie with the 36th Infantry Division. Helen's husband Paul had retired as a Brigadier General. [24]

### Declining Health

Wheeler's work on the Monsanto board of directors continued. He had joined the local Rotary Club, and both he and Betty kept active in numerous community programs. On occasion, they joined friends at the horse races in Charlestown, West Virginia, about thirty minutes away. Bus handicapped the races himself beforehand and always arrived with his bets predetermined. [25]

Asked in an interview whether it would be safe and practical for the U.S. to reduce its forces in Europe, Wheeler replied, "If we could achieve a balanced reduction in U.S. forces as between Warsaw Pact powers and NATO powers, the situation would not be untenable." [26]

As Wheeler kept abreast of developments in Paris and Vietnam, Bim continued to press his father to finish his memoirs. Two years had passed since Bus's retirement, and he had completed a draft of several hundred pages. In truth, he was disgusted by the unfolding Vietnam debacle.

"If you believe that as a professional soldier I am in any way proud of my association with the Vietnam War, you are damn wrong!" Bus finally exploded. "I don't want to hear another goddamned word about that war! Do you understand?"

"Yes, sir!", Bim replied, and he never again brought up the subject.

Wheeler had been given an office in the Pentagon for documenting his tenure as Chairman. To his secretary Mary Feeley's great surprise, he entered the office one day and told her to shred his manuscript. Feeley told Stewart that Wheeler said he was at peace with himself and with his God with what he done. [27]

As Bim explains, Bus didn't need "some tweed-wearing, pot-smoking, young college professor who had never served a day in the military second-guessing his actions in situations and circumstances that he would know nothing about. He always said that he had all the proof [back channel messages, etc.] to eviscerate the opposition." [28]

Bim also recalls his father saying he "didn't want to hurt the families of those with whom he'd worked and admired." Although filled with personal bitterness, Wheeler kept his own counsel, refusing to engage in recriminations against those who had decided a policy that he vehemently opposed. [29]

A further rationale was that Wheeler was exhausted and angered by the war and thinking about it exhausted and angered him even more. In consequence, Wheeler would remain an enigma among the major characters of the Vietnam Era for over 46 years.

## 1973

Wheeler made his views known on how the war had been bungled and by whom in his congressional testimony about Cambodia in July 1973.

"This war in Vietnam—there is no question about it—went on and on and on," Wheeler testified. "It should have been wound up within a few months. If we had bombed earlier in the very beginning as President Nixon has done in the last year, the war wouldn't have lasted in my judgment but a few months." [30]

An article in the local Martinsburg paper reported:

One of the nation's top military commanders through the war-torn, tension-taut 1960s has shifted his focus from Sabre jets to hummingbirds. … It's a quiet, peaceful life for him now. His farm produces only an abundance of birds and deer and assorted other wildlife 'but that's the way we like it,' he explained. He likes to assist his wife with her main hobby

– birdwatching.' We have several hummingbird feeders near the porch, where we normally have breakfast and dinner,' he said.' It's a treat to watch them. They're fascinating.' Quail and other game birds abound in his fields, but he hasn't hunted them for years. As for deer, Wheeler said he hasn't killed one since 1949 in Europe and that was 'for the pot' because meat was scarce at that time.' I guess I'm too fond of watching them,' he admitted with a grin. The wear and tear of a career soldier's life is beginning to show around the edges, but the firm, ramrod discipline of a professional military man is readily evident in Wheeler's walk and in his talk. But he has a ready chuckle that punctuates [his] articulate speech. [31]

Bus's intention of returning to public service faded with the realization that his health had not improved, but in fact had deteriorated. Bus never discussed his health issues with Bim, whose first inkling that his father was not well came in 1973 when Bus made sure he knew where his will and other important papers were kept. [32]

Sometime later, the two went to lunch in Georgetown. Having parked about 300 yards from the restaurant, Bus was acutely out of breath from the exertion of walking and had to stop and rest. After lunch, Bim insisted that Bus wait in the restaurant while he went and got the car. [33]

"Bus was a very sick man, not well," Bim recalls. "He knew he was dying. He had horrible emphysema. He couldn't walk half a block without stopping to catch his breath. Testifying (in July) must have been terribly draining on him." [34]

## Cambodia Bombing Hearings

After newspaper accounts of the secret bombing campaign in Cambodia were published in July, the Senate Armed Services Committee convened a hearing into the matter of falsification of reports associated with this operation. [35]

Summoned to testify, Wheeler revealed that he had, on Nixon's personal orders, directed secret and, when made public, highly controversial, bombing missions over Cambodia in 1969-70. [36]

Commenting on "the spirit of Watergate" in an editorial on 5 August, the *New York Times,* reported that Wheeler "saw nothing wrong with these actions because nobody 'with a need to know' had been deceived." [37]

At the end of Wheeler's eight-hour testimony, South Carolina Senator James Strom Thurmond, Sr. said, "I want to thank you, General Wheeler, for coming here and testifying on this occasion. We appreciate your presence, and we hope you will enjoy good health and happiness in the future." [38]

In August, Betty received a letter from Mamie Eisenhower.

> I am terribly sorry you and Billy did not call me when you were here in Gettysburg for I would have loved to have seen you both and could probably have given Billy pointers on how not to waste his time on useless tourist traps up here.

> You know our farm has been made a national historic site and as it was here during the Civil War and our property goes to the Confederate line, Billy would have been interested in some of the things on the farm like the old pump and windmill and some of the trees that have been sent to us by all the different states of the union. I could really have given him a fifty-dollar tour of the house and grounds. Please come back again.

Betty had informed her that Bus had recently undergone some surgical procedure. Mamie replied, "Tell your husband I saw him on television down on the Hill. Sorry he had to have this operation but glad it is not serious. I often think how he used to come in and visit me when I was sitting out there at Walter Reed with Ike." [39]

In late October, the Wheelers took an overnight trip to Washington, their former hometown of so many years, to attend a friend's funeral and a dinner. Betty marveled:

> Do you know, this is the first time I've ever stayed in a hotel in D.C.? We have a beautiful bed-sitting room on the 5th floor overlooking Lafayette Park and the White House. The first night was bedlam! Demonstrators on the Elipse, chanting and singing – noise, noise, noise – until 2:30 AM. If that isn't disturbing the peace!

[On their second night] Dear God the noise. There were demonstrators in front of the White House this time, and the honking of horns was constant. We learned on the way home from dinner when we passed the White House that the demonstrators were carrying signs 'If you think [Nixon is] guilty, honk your horn.' It was evident that there was a group or groups of cars going round and round the White House, as there would be short lulls, an occasional horn and then bedlam again – awful. ... We went to the Museum of Natural History. Bus had never been before.

[We had lunch in Old Town Alexandria] just around the corner from our [old] house on Prince Street. ... Afterwards, Bus went to the car and napped, while [Betty and their friends] investigated the shops along King St. [40]

## 1974

For the policymakers in Washington who had directed the U.S. involvement in Vietnam and for their families, memories of the long nightmare were already being subsumed by warmer thoughts of comradery and friendships formed under the stress of managing that unpopular war. The Wheelers stayed in frequent touch with their contemporaries. "I think of you often and hope life is full and happy for you both—and that our paths will cross in '75," wrote Lady Bird Johnson to Betty in a Christmas card. [41]

## 1975

### *Wheeler Passes*

At home on 18 December 1975, Wheeler suffered what doctors at the King's Daughter's Hospital in Martinsburg believed was "a mild stroke." Assuming he was well enough to get to Walter Reed Army Hospital by ambulance within ninety minutes, Army doctors did not dispatch a medevac helicopter, although a landing pad had been constructed on Wheeler's farm after his retirement. [42]

Enroute to Walter Reed, Bus's condition suddenly worsened, and he was diverted to the Frederick Hospital emergency room where he died shortly thereafter from cardiac arrest. The coroner identified the cause of death as arteriosclerotic cardiovascular disease. [43]

Bim was in Martinsburg that day but did not learn of his father's passing until his girlfriend [later his second wife], Judy, told him that she had heard the news on the radio. [44]

Bim had never known the severity of Bus's heart attack in 1967 and did not discover the extent of his father's medical issues until after Bus died. [45]

"News of the death of General Wheeler has been received with deep regret in the Department of Defense," Secretary of Defense Donald H. Rumsfeld announced. "He leaves behind fond memories of a dedicated and stalwart professional who served his country long, well, and faithfully. The entire Department of Defense joins me in extending condolences to the Wheeler family." [46]

In an enduring tradition of announcing the deaths of its most senior general officers, the Army published General Orders Number 26 on 19 December 1975. [47]

> In the performance of his duties at the highest levels of responsibility, Gen. Wheeler displayed outstanding judgment, great energy, and the nobility of high order, which proved to be invaluable to the United States. With his passing, the country has lost a prominent citizen and the Army a very distinguished leader.
>
> As a mark of respect to the memory of Gen. Wheeler, the national flag will be displayed at half-staff on all installations under control of the Department of the Army from the day of death, 18 December 1975 until retreat on day of burial, 22 December 1975. [48]

The Wheeler family asked that any remembrances be in the form of donations to the Berkeley County Red Cross memorial fund for a chapter house or to the Soldiers, Sailors, Marines, and Airmens Club in Washington, DC. [49]

Arlington National Cemetery officials showed Betty the proposed location for Bus's gravesite, a nondescript spot adjacent to a trash pile. She said, "If that's what you think of a Chairman who served three Presidents, I'll take him home to Martinsburg." Very quickly, the cemetery officials determined that General Bradley did not require the eight plots that had been reserved for his family. [50]

## *Funeral*

On a sunny but near-freezing day on 22 December, Wheeler was laid to rest in Section 30 of Arlington National Cemetery. [51]

Inside the Fort Myer Memorial Chapel, Bus's longtime friend and former colleague Stephen Ailes delivered the eulogy to a constellation of currently serving and retired general and flag officers and many current and former senior civilians from three administrations and the Department of Defense. Ailes's remarks are insightful and are quoted in their entirety.

> We are here today to pay our respects to one of the United States Army's most distinguished sons, an officer who rendered outstanding service at all levels of command, including the nation's top-most military assignment.

> General Wheeler's military credentials are impeccable. He was highly respected as a professional soldier by his associates in uniform, regardless of the service in which they served. He was greatly admired by his civilian colleagues, without exception.

> This is neither the time nor the place to dwell on the details of his remarkable career or to assess his professional accomplishments, the decisions he made, the causes he espoused, or the positions he advocated. The record of his career is duly entered in the nation's annals, the analyses we leave to history, totally confident of the verdict.

> Each Chairman of the Joint Chiefs of Staff, including the present one, has had an arduous assignment and has served the nation well during a difficult period. But almost everyone here would agree that the unprecedented six-year term

served by General Wheeler placed extraordinary demands on the Chairman, demands which he was uniquely qualified to meet.

The wisdom and judgment which he brought to the task, based on a lifelong study of world affairs, a lifelong habit of critical appraisal of all policies as they developed, and a determination to bring about sound practical results were important in this regard.

So also was the total support of the Army, earned by his performance over the years.

He had a rare ability to bring about consensus, an ability based upon patience, fairness, good humor, his own intellectual contribution to the solution of the problems, and respect in which he was held by his colleagues on the Joint Chiefs.

He made a unique, personal contribution to the relationship between the military establishment and the civilian leadership of the nation. His thorough comprehension of military needs and capabilities was important in this role, but his sensitivity to the forces at work in the larger society, and his ability to see the whole problem were more important still.

And finally, at a time when civilian-military stresses were growing, no better man could have served in the role of Chairman. Congressional leaders, the press, and the public at large had confidence in General Wheeler as a person. This was so, in no little part, because, in Secretary Laird's appropriate phrase (at the retirement review in 1970) he viewed all issues 'through a wide-angle lens.'

Sadly, these years took their toll, and the price of being the indispensable man was high. The officer who was honored at that review that July day in 1970 had worked himself to exhaustion and had, knowingly, sacrificed his health to do his job, as later events clearly proved.

In the years when I worked closely with him, I marveled at his ability to function so effectively with so little fanfare, and to read books and see people, and reflect about the broader national issues at the same time. I knew that he was well-organized and that he was in the habit of making a highly concentrated personal effort; but he was a most effective leader, clearly in charge, without making a great to-do about getting things done.

In later years, I asked him how this could be. Quite typically, he said something about the importance of having able people and of relying on them.

Of course, this is only the beginning. As Cy Vance puts it: 'In Bus, there was a rare combination, a coupling of strength, firmness, and decisiveness on the one hand, with gentleness, kindness, and compassion on the other. I've never heard of him being harsh or cruel or unkind with a subordinate.'

A senior officer who served directly under him for a long time said, 'His approach was always low key. He didn't trip over any of the little things. He respected people. He had complete trust and confidence in his subordinates. Everybody wanted to justify his confidence.'

Similarly, his civilian colleagues were aware of his consideration for and loyalty to them. The close and effective relationships that resulted, so essential to the proper functioning of our system, were never more needed than in that period of time.

During the last five years, Bus and Betty found peace and quiet and a great deal of happiness on their farm in Berkeley County, West Virginia—an idyllic existence—a richly earned a rest—interrupted only occasionally by a reporter seeking to reopen some old issue. All were treated courteously, but for a few the record was set straight in no uncertain fashion.

Those of us who were so privileged will always treasure the recollection of evenings in that comfortable home, sitting in front of the fire, or better yet, sitting out on that porch looking out across the fields at the big sycamores along the creek, talking about old times, laughing about amusing things that happened long ago, settling the affairs of the world.

This nation owes General Wheeler a debt of gratitude beyond measure. All of us who worked with him are the better for it and will never forget him. He was a superb human being. [52]

The following day, Clifford wrote to Ailes. "I want to thank you for the comforting and inspiring remarks you made at the Bus Wheeler funeral. I worked very closely with him and had the greatest affection and respect for him as a man and as a public servant." Ailes forwarded a copy of Clifford's note along with the text of his eulogy to Betty the following week. [53]

## *Public Accolades*

The Washington Post noted that former President Johnson had referred to Wheeler in his memoirs as a "level-headed and experienced soldier." The article credited Wheeler with understanding the need to subordinate the individual and competing demands of the Army, Navy, Air Force, and Marine Corps to the nation's overall military strategy and requirements. "(As Chief of Staff of the Army), he was highly praised for his implementation of plans for expanding and modernizing the service. ... Gen. Wheeler has also been credited with a key role in the eventual passage of the Kennedy administration's nuclear test ban treaty." [54]

The Martinsburg Journal reported:

The entire nation and this community in particular lost a fine American and a fine citizen in the death the other day of Gen. Earle G. Wheeler, retired chairman of the U.S. Joint Chiefs of Staff, the number one military position in the country.

Not only did he hold this position for longer than anyone else in history, six years, but he also held it at a time of national agony, most of the period of the unpopular Vietnam War. When he was first appointed, in 1964, the big build-up of troops was getting underway and he stayed on until 1970 when the winding-down process of American withdrawal had been developed.

He was a perfect example of the true soldier serving his country to the fullest extent of his ability. He believed it was a soldier's duty to carry out the orders of his commanding officer, in this case the Commander-in-Chief, the President of the United States.

Gen. Wheeler's entire life was devoted to the military service, from the time he enlisted in the National Guard in Washington, through his four years of training at West Point and then up the ladder to the rank of a four-star general.

With all of this military background, however, and even with the great success he attained, Gen. Wheeler remained a quiet, modest and unassuming man in his social contacts, although anyone who knew him could see he had the ability to command and to be forceful in his opinions under the proper circumstances.

How he stood up under the unbelievable pressures of six years of directing the nation's military machinery in an unpopular war is difficult to comprehend. Particularly in the latter years of that war, he was subjected to all sorts of indignities, especially from posturing congressional and other leaders who found it easy to be critical even though when things were going [well] they had supported the war.

It was also remarkable how he was able to retire and also completely walk away from his awesome duties to come to his rural home near Martinsburg. It was after he had come here in retirement in 1970 that this writer had the privilege of getting to personally know Gen. and Mrs. Wheeler and found them to be friendly, gracious and interesting individuals who had no desire but to fit well into their newly-adopted community of Martinsburg, a place they took pride in calling their home.

His unexpected death came all too early in life, a life that was devoted to following ordinary pursuits in which he and Mrs. Wheeler found such obvious happiness. [55]

## *Personal Condolences*

For months, Betty received numerous letters of condolence from friends and colleagues from throughout Bus's long years of military service. From these letters emerges a clear picture of the professional respect and admiration and personal fondness for Bus and Betty that was shared by those who knew them best.

Paul R. Ignatius, who had served as Under Secretary of the Army and later Secretary of the Navy, wrote to Betty:

> Steve spoke for all of us yesterday when he recalled in simple, human terms what Bus had accomplished and what he had meant to his friends. I could not help but notice your fine young grandson during the solemn ceremony, and the beautiful moment when you handed him the flag. It was a gesture, it seemed to me, with great personal meaning for the boy, but it symbolized also that Bus' achievements went far beyond himself and would represent a high standard for others to emulate. [56]

> Bus was a friend – a good friend – and a person we greatly admired. Having worked closely with him over so long a period, I knew at first-hand what a great leader he was and how tremendously effective he could be in composing differences of views and bringing about resolution of difficult issues. It was a rare talent and one that we greatly need today as we confront the many difficult and divisive issues that face us. [57]

Retired Brigadier General Alfred "Ham" Hamblen wrote:

> I was privileged to attend Bus's funeral. Never have I seen such a senior, multi-service group so in total agreement on one subject – how blessed our country has been to have had one such as Bus among us. As one general said, 'Wherever Bus went, it was better because he was there.'

> [My wife] Rundy and I often recall with pleasure the wonderful evening we spent at your Ft. Myer home at a dinner party. ... All my life I've been a camera buff. What fun it was

to see Bus enjoying himself taking pictures of his guests. And to top it off, instead of the usual request to say 'cheers' to get smiling faces, he doubled us up with laughter by saying the French 'fromage'!

It was so apparent from my first meeting with him that Bus was a very happily married man. He loved his family so, and spoke endearingly of them. Your love undoubtedly played a major role in his tremendous success. [58]

Vance wrote:

He was a superb man whose friendship I treasure. The leadership that he gave to the Army and to our military forces in one of the most difficult times in our history is shared by only a handful of men in our two hundred years.

I know the strength of will and courage it took for him to continue in office and the toll it took upon him. He was a true patriot.

I shall always treasure knowing him and the enjoyment I had in working with him. His wisdom blended with compassion was an inspiration to all who had the privilege of knowing him. [59]

Retired Air Force General William F. McKee wrote:

Over the years I have held Bus in the highest regard. I spent many hours in the tank when he was Chief of Staff of the Army, and I was sitting in for Curt LeMay. After I retired, I watched his performance as Chairman with admiration. Having known all the Chairmen since the beginning of the Office of Secretary of Defense, I rate Bus at the top in being objective, non-parochial, eminently fair and most of all a really great American. [60]

"I simply want to tell you first-hand how much I admired Bus over the years," Moorer wrote. "He was a tower of strength during some very turbulent times and his wise counsel and broad knowledge combined with great compassion makes him in my view one of America's greatest. He was particularly helpful to me during some rides down very rocky roads." [61]

"Wally" Greene wrote:

> It was a privilege to get to know Bus and you so well as we did when he was Chairman of the Joint Chiefs of Staff. Having served in various staff assignments under all of the Chairmen prior to Bus, I often told him that, in my opinion, he was the best and the greatest of them all – a tremendous worker, wise and even-handed in his decisions, calm and unruffled under great and continuous pressures, the epitome of West Point's Duty, Honor, Country. He served the United States well and his passing is a great loss to his family, his country and his many friends. [62]

"He was a remarkable and able man," Norstad wrote. "My greatest regret is that we did not have an opportunity to serve together longer." [63]

General Bruce Palmer, Jr. wrote:

> Bus truly gave his life to our country. The President, more than once, called on him time and again and Bus never failed them, but always came through. For me, he was my Beau Ideal – a man I instinctively trusted and greatly admired – someone we all tried to emulate. He set an example for our country which cannot be equaled. You should be immensely proud of him. [64]

In his 1984 book on the Vietnam War, Palmer described Wheeler as "a fine Chairman, who literally gave his life for his country. The great responsibilities and pressures of the job broke his health. … He was highly respected and had the ear of the President, but he was overshadowed by such men as … Kissinger." [65]

Condolences from numerous still-serving senior officers point toward the enduring legacy of Wheeler's leadership that would influence his successors at the highest levels of the Armed Forces for many years.

General Louis H. Wilson, Jr., Commandant of the Marine Corps, wrote, "General Wheeler had a long and distinguished career as a citizen and a soldier. His record of service, both in peace and war, have set an example of devotion to the ideals of our nation that all Americans might admire and emulate." [66]

General Frederick C. Weyend, Chief of Staff of the Army, wrote, "Bus's strength of character, his courage and vision, and his magnificent service are legend, and his loss will be deeply felt by the Army and the Nation to whom he gave his full measure of devotion." [67]

General David C. Jones, Chief of Staff of the Air Force, wrote, "The Chairman has earned a reputation within the Air Force as a leader of men, a manager of resources and a servant to his nation in peace and war granted few others." [68]

General Alexander M. Haig, Jr., then serving as Supreme Allied Commander Europe, wrote:

> We cherish our memory of [Bus] as a man of unusual ability and integrity with a deeply imbued personal sense of duty. His magnificent contributions to his country and its armed forces throughout his career and especially during the very trying period as Chairman are remembered vividly by those of us privileged to know him. [69]

General Bernard W. Rogers, then serving as Commanding General of Forces Command, wrote, "Even though he was retired from active duty, his influence was felt throughout the Army and he will be sorely missed by all the Armed Services. You have every right to be proud of sharing in his accomplishments." [70]

Betty also received numerous personal letters of condolence from fellow spouses of senior officials.

Darsy Goodpaster wrote, "As Secretary Ailes said, Bus was one of the great men of our generation and we feel privileged to have known him. His example will be a shining light for the younger officers to follow." [71]

"You and our country have lost a fine soldier, patriot, and citizen," Diddy Taylor wrote. "I thought Steve Ailes' remarks especially deserved and appropriate, and I'm sure were a comfort." [72]

Margie Clifford wrote, "Clark and I are so very saddened by Bus' death. It's still hard for us both to believe for he seemed indestructible to us. He was such a loving friend and he had every quality that I admired the most. I always loved to be with you and Bus for the wonderful love between you warmed my heart." [73]

Dorothy Johnson wrote, "You both have been such great examples– your devotion to country and to each other and your marriage." Her sentiment was echoed by Isabelle Norstad, who observed, "You were such a devoted pair." [74]

Julie Abrams wrote, "When Abe died, Bus wrote me a letter that I will forever cherish. Steve Ailes's impression of love and admiration sums up for all of us our heartfelt thanks for having known you both and having shared in your service to our country." [75]

## Epilogue

Not long after Bus's funeral, Betty received a call from a Major in the Women's Army Corps who wanted to deliver some photos from the funeral service to her at the farm. Betty insisted that the officer did not need to make a special, four-hour round trip for that purpose, and that she should just put the photos in the mail. The Major had apparently been given a short deadline to complete the task and said that she would come right out in a helicopter! This seemed rather ironic to Bim, considering that the Army had not provided an aircraft to take his stricken father to the hospital, yet now one was available to drop off his funeral pictures. [76]

Five years later, Bim and "Johnny" Johnson had an emotional lunch in the Army-Navy Country Club. Bim told him that he was aware of the tremendous stress the Chiefs were under during the Johnson Administration and that Bus had informed him and his mother that the Chiefs had considered resigning en masse after McNamara's testimony during the Stennis hearings in August 1967. That was true, Johnson admitted, despite the vow the Chiefs had sworn never to reveal the incident. "Your father died for his country as surely as any GI who was shot between the eyes in Vietnam," Johnson told Bim. [77]

The Wheelers had been married for 43 years when Bus died. Five years later, Betty married another four-star general, Frank S. Besson Jr., one of Bus's West Point classmates from the class of 1932. Besson was the first Commanding General of the Army Materiel Command. He and Betty lived in

Alexandria until his death in 1985. Three years later, Betty christened her second warship, the Army logistical support vessel *General Frank S. Besson, Jr.* [78]

*Betty Wheeler visits the Beltzhoover family with whom she and Bim lived for three years during World War II, Natchez, Mississippi, early 1980s. (Wheeler Family Records).*

After Besson's death, Betty resumed using Bus's last name and moved back to their farm in Martinsburg. As she got older and needed assistance, Bim and his second wife Judy moved out to the farm and still reside there to this day.

*Three generations of the Wheeler family celebrate Bim's 60th birthday, July 2000. Bim is seated right. Betty is seated second from left. Judy is standing second from right. Rob and Bill are standing at left. (Wheeler Family Records).*

Over time, arthritis prevented Betty from continuing the sewing she had always loved and taken so much pride in. A Christian Scientist like her mother, Betty "avoided visits to the doctor like the plague unless something appeared life threatening." She had gone to the hospital to give birth to Bim and again when she had her hysterectomy, but it was not until the end of her life when she developed cancer that she ever went back. "Preventive medicine was something she simply did not believe in", Bim explains. Toward the end, Betty adamantly refused to go to a nursing home, so Bim and Judy converted their first floor living room into a hospital room for her. At age 90, Betty died from melanoma on 1 July 2004 and was buried next to Bus in Arlington National Cemetery. [79]

Besides their son Bim, Bus and Betty Wheeler are survived by their two grandsons, William Gilmore Wheeler and John Robinson Wheeler, and two great-grandchildren, Chelsey Anne and William Gilmore, Jr. [80]

### *Conclusion*

"Wheeler set the standard for professional excellence in the postwar era," writes journalist and author Mark Perry.

> No JCS Chairman who followed has been able to equal the great respect his name has engendered, nor would any JCS member so glibly threaten resignation, knowing that he refused the act under more serious circumstances. But if Wheeler set the precedent for military loyalty to civilian control in his refusal to resign, his actions also became the test of military silence in the face of civilian incompetence. Since Wheeler's tenure, it has been impossible for a JCS member to assent silently to policies with which he strongly disagreed. [81]

Bus Wheeler was an eminently decent, hard-working, self-sacrificing, diplomatic, humorous, family man and patriotic American. There is no wonder that such a fine person rose to the pinnacle of the military profession. He displayed a degree of personal integrity that is exceptional by today's comparisons. In retirement, he never accepted a dime in honoraria for his speeches. During his periodic trips to South Vietnam, Wheeler was often near the fighting. On one occasion, he came under a rocket attack in Saigon. A member of his entourage pointed out that this exposure made him eligible to receive hostile fire pay. Wheeler would hear nothing of it. It was simply out of the question because he was a mere visitor there, not assigned to the theater of combat. [82]

Betty Wheeler was a *grande dame* in a poor man's Army. Her social skills and hospitality certainly facilitated the success of her husband's long military career. They made a great team and were a lovely, loving couple. [83]

The collective, collaborative efforts of historians to understand as completely and accurately as possible the important figures, events, or periods of our past is akin to building a puzzle in which the complete image is obscured. It is a lengthy process over decades wherein individual historians locate missing pieces of the puzzle and fit them together. Without benefit of crystal balls or time machines, historians can never see the puzzle in its entirety or with 100% accuracy. Disparate interpretations result. Over time and through the contributions of many, a more perfect and accurate shared understanding is formed.

I am honored to contribute to the puzzle that is our collective understanding of the Vietnam experience by offering several pieces pertaining to one of its major players – an exceptional man who deserves the better judgment of history, and his equally exceptional wife.

# APPENDIX

## *General Earle G. Wheeler's Military Awards and Badges*

### United States Awards:

Defense Distinguished Service Medal

Distinguished Service Medal (Army) with two oak leaf clusters

Distinguished Service Medal (Navy)

Distinguished Service Medal (Air Force)

Legion of Merit

Bronze Star Medal with oak leaf cluster

Joint Service Commendation Medal

Army Commendation Medal with oak leaf cluster

American Campaign Medal

European and African Middle Eastern Campaign Medal

World War II Victory Medal

Army of Occupation Medal (Germany)

National Defense Service Medal

### Foreign Awards:

Brazil: Order of Military Merit, Degree of Grand Officer, 1967.

Ecuador: Order of Abdon Calderon, First Class with Certificate, 1963.

Finland: Order of White Rose with Certificate, 1963.

France: Legion of Honor, Degree of Grand Commander, 1970; Legion of Honor, Degree of Commander, 1963; Legion of Honor, Degree of Officer, 1947; Croix de Guerre with Palm, 1945.

Federal Republic of Germany: Grand Cross of the Order of Merit, 1964.

Republic of Korea: Order of Service Merit, First Class, 1966.

Mexico: Decoration of Military Merit, First Class, 1959.

The Philippines: Legion of Honor, Degree of Commander, 1965.

Sweden: Knighthood; Loyal Order of the Sword, Grand Cross, 1964.

Thailand: Exalted Order of the White Elephant, First Class, 1965.

Republic of Vietnam: Grand Officer of the National Order; Gallantry Cross with Palm, 1970.

## Badges:

Army Staff Identification Badge

Department of Defense Identification Badge

Joint Staff Identification Badge [1]

# CHAPTER NOTES

## Introduction

1. Casey, George W. Conversation with Mark A. Viney. 25 Apr. 2018.

2. Ibid.

3. Wheeler, Gilmore. Interview with Mark Viney. 9 Oct. 2013.

4. Wheeler, Gilmore. Interview with Mark Viney. 24 Apr. 2013.

## Chapter 1

1. Wheeler, Gilmore. Interviews with Mark Viney. 25 Feb. and 9 Oct. 2013. The spelling of "Earl" versus "Earle" is not a typographical error, as explained later in the text. President Johnson's secretary asked him why he addressed General Wheeler as "Buzz" when his nickname was actually "Bus." Johnson replied, "Little lady, I call him 'Buzz.'" Johnson addressed Wheeler in writing with this moniker, as well.

2. Department of the Army. *DA Form 66.* 15 Feb. 1969; United States Army. *Standard Form 88, Report of Medical Examination.* 23 Oct. 1953; Wheeler, Gilmore. Interviews with Mark Viney. 10 Mar., 14 May, and 9 Oct. 2013. Wheeler's medical report indicates instead that his father died of pneumonia at age 38. It does not indicate that he had tuberculosis. The spelling of "Gillmore" versus "Gilmore" is not a typographical error but reflects the original spelling of the name.

3. Wheeler, Gilmore. Interview with Mark Viney. 25 Feb. 2013; KidsHealth. Downloaded from the internet on 16 Jan. 2016 at http://kidshealth. org/teen/your_mind/families/cop-ing_alcoholic. html#.

4. Supreme Court of the District of Columbia. *Decree From Adoption Case No. 534, In Re: Adoption of Earl Gilmore Stone and Helen Friedrich Stone,* 14 Sep. 1923; Wheeler, Gilmore. Interviews with Mark Viney. 25 Feb., 10 Mar., and 9 Oct. 2013. Clifton Wheeler died around 1944.

5. United States Army. Office, Chief of Information. *Biography: Gen. Earle G. Wheeler.* No date; Wheeler, Gilmore S. *Unpublished Monograph.* 1 Oct. 2010.

6. Wheeler, Gilmore S. *George Deuhring.* Monograph. 25 Apr. 2014; Wheeler, Gilmore. Interviews with Mark Viney. 25 Feb., 10 Mar., and 9 Oct. 2013.

7. War Department. *Historical Record of Officer, Statement of Officer upon Original Appointment and Regular Army.* June 1932; New York Times. *'Staff Man' in Chief.* 24 Jun.

1964: page unknown; Wheeler, Gilmore S. *Unpublished Monograph*; Wheeler, Gilmore. Interview with Mark Viney. 25 Feb. 2013.

8. United States Atomic Energy Commission. *Personnel Security Questionnaire*. 11 Jul. 1950.

9. War Department. *Historical Record of Officer, Statement of Officer upon Original Appointment and Regular Army*. June 1932; New York Times. *'Staff Man' in Chief*. 24 Jun. 1964: page unknown; National Observer. *General Wheeler's Rising Stars, It's 3-for-3 for the Army As Taylor 'Protégé" Gets Top Job*. 29 Jun. 1964: 2; Wheeler, Gilmore S. *Unpublished Monograph*.

10. United States Army. United States Military Academy. *Cadet Service Record*. 1932.

11. War Department. *AGO Form No. 63, Report of Physical Examination*. 12 Feb. 1946; United States Army. *Standard Form 88, Report of Medical Examination*. 23 Oct. 1953; Wheeler, Gilmore. Interviews with Mark Viney. 10 and 14 Mar. 2013; The Forgotten General. Downloaded from the internet on 13 Feb. 2013 from http://theforgottengeneral. com/wp-content/uploads/2010/12/JCS-Biography. pdf.

12. Wheeler, Gilmore. Interview with Mark Viney. 25 Feb. 2013.

13. United States Army. United States Military Academy. *Cadet Service Record*. 1932; Wheeler, Gilmore S. *Untitled Monograph*.

14. Deuhring, George. *Letter to Inez Douglas*. 15 Sep. 1928.

15. Deuhring, George. *Letter to Inez Douglas*. 14 Oct. 1928.

16. Wheeler, Gilmore. Interview with Mark Viney. 25 Feb. 2013.

17. United States Army. United States Military Academy. *Cadet Service Record*. 1932; War Department. *AGO Form No. 63, Report of Physical Examination*. 26 Aug. 1935; United States Army. Walter Reed General Hospital. *Clinical Record*. 22 Apr. 1970.

18. Wheeler, Gilmore. Interview with Mark Viney. 25 Feb. 2013.

19. Ibid.

20. United States Army. United States Military Academy. *Cadet Service Record*. 1932.

21. War Department. *Report of Physical Examination*. 15 Jul. 1929.

22. United States Army. United States Military Academy. *Cadet Service Record*. 1932.

23. War Department. *AGO Form 66-2*. 23 Apr. 1954; United States Army. Office, Chief of Information. *Biography: Gen. Earle G. Wheeler*. No date; Wheeler, Gilmore. Interview with Mark Viney. 25 Feb. 2013.

24. United States Army. United States Military Academy. *Cadet Service Record.* 1932; Wheeler, Gilmore S. *Untitled Monograph.*

25. Wheeler, Gilmore. Interview with Mark Viney. 9 Oct. 2013.

26. Wheeler, Gilmore S. *Untitled Monograph.*

27. Wheeler, Gilmore. Interviews with Mark Viney. 25 Feb. and 10 Mar. 2013.

28. United States Army. United States Military Academy. *Cadet Service Record.* 1932; New York Times. *Gen. Earle Wheeler Dies; Ex-Head of Joint Chiefs.* 19 Dec. 1975; Wheeler, Gilmore. Interview with Mark Viney. 25 Feb. 2013. Wheeler's son states that his father finished at the top of his class in every professional military school he attended. Documentary evidence has not been located to fully corroborate his claim, but McMaster states that Wheeler graduated first in his class from both the Infantry Officer Advanced Course and the U.S. Army Command and General Staff College.

29. Howell, Walter R. Wedding Invitation. No date; Frances R. Wheeler. Interview with Gilmore S. Wheeler, Disc 6, 2003; Wheeler, Gilmore. Interview with Mark Viney. 25 Feb. 2013; Army Historical Foundation. Downloaded from the internet on 13 Feb. 2013 from https://armyhistory. org/09/general-earle-g-wheeler/. Betty recalled that Bus originally wanted to wait a year to get married to first pay back Colonel Millard for his tuition loan.

30. War Department. *Officer's and Warrant Officer's Qualification Card.* 4 August 1947; Wheeler, Gilmore. Interviews with Mark Viney. 25 Feb. and 9 Oct. 2013.

31. Frances R. Wheeler. Interviews with Gilmore S. Wheeler, 2003-2004; Wheeler, Gilmore. Interviews with Mark Viney. 25 Feb. and 9 Oct. 2013.

32. Wheeler, Gilmore. Interview with Mark Viney. 25 Feb. 2013.

33. Ibid.

34. Wheeler, Gilmore. *Untitled Monograph.* 5; Wheeler, Gilmore. Interview with Mark Viney. 9 Oct. 2013.

35. Wheeler, Gilmore. Interviews with Mark Viney. 25 Feb. and 10 Mar. 2013.

36. War Department. *AGO Form No. 0485-2.* 11 Jun. 1940.

37. Wheeler, Frances R. Letter to Rebecca Howell. 23 Sep. 1954.

38. Frances R. Wheeler. Interviews with Gilmore S. Wheeler, 2004.

39. Frances R. Wheeler. Interviews with Gilmore S. Wheeler, 2004; Wheeler, Gilmore. Interviews with Mark Viney. 25 Feb. and 10 Mar. 2013.

40. Wheeler, Gilmore S. *Untitled Monograph.*

41. United States Army. *Memorandum, Subject: Change of Name.* 1 May 1936; Wheeler, Gilmore. Interview with Mark Viney. 25 Feb. 2013; Army Historical Foundation. Downloaded from the internet on 13 Feb. 2013 from https://armyhistory. org/09/general-earle-g-wheeler/; Arlington National Cemetery. Downloaded from the internet on 13 Feb. 2013 from http://www. arlingtoncemetery. net/ewheeler. htm.

42. War Department. *AGO Form No. 0485-2.* 11 Jun. 1940; Wheeler, Gilmore. Interviews with Mark Viney. 24 Apr. and 9 Oct. 2013.

43. Deuhring, George. Letter to Inez Douglas. 11 Sep. 1928.

44. Deuhring, George. Letter to Inez Douglas. 14 Oct. 1928.

45. Stewart, 65-66, 69.

46. Wheeler, Gilmore. Interviews with Mark Viney. 10 Mar. and 9 Oct. 2013.

47. War Department. *AGO Form No. 0485-2.* 11 Jun. 1940; United States Army. *General Orders Number 26.* 19 Dec. 1975; Department of the Army. *DA Form 66.* 15 Feb. 1969; United States Army. Walter Reed General Hospital. *Clinical Record.* 22 Apr. 1970.

48. War Department. *AGO Form No. 0485-2.* 11 Jun. 1940; Group photo, I Company, 15th Infantry Regiment, Fort Lewis, WA, 1939. The 15th Infantry Regiment of the 1930s was akin in prestige to today's 75th Ranger Regiment in that it attracted the best and most ambitious infantry officers who gained instant credibility for their service there.

49. Wheeler, Gilmore. Interview with Mark Viney. 25 Feb. 2013.

50. War Department. *Memorandum.* 30 Apr. 1937; Wheeler, Gilmore. Interviews with Mark Viney. 10 Mar. and 9 Oct. 2013.

51. War Department. *AGO Form No. 0485-2.* 11 Jun. 1940; Wheeler, Gilmore. *Untitled Monograph.*

52. New York Times. *'Staff Man' in Chief.* 24 Jun. 1964.

53. Wheeler, Gilmore. *Untitled Monograph*; Arlington National Cemetery. Downloaded from the internet on 13 Feb. 2013 from http://www. arlingtoncemetery. net/ewheeler. htm.

54. 15th Infantry Regiment Association. Downloaded from the internet on 7 Jun. 2018 at http://www. 15thinfantry. org/documents/issues/October2010. pdf.

55. Frances R. Wheeler. Interviews with Gilmore S. Wheeler, 2004; Army. *Eisenhower and MacArthur: Toil, Trouble and Turbulence in the Philippines.* Feb. 2015; *15th Infantry Regiment Association.* Downloaded from the internet on 7 Jun. 2018 at http://www. 15thinfantry. org/documents/issues/October2010. pdf.

56. Frances R. Wheeler. Interviews with Gilmore S. Wheeler, 2004.

57. War Department. *AGO Form No. 0622.* 7 Mar. 1940; 182. Wheeler, Gilmore. Interview with Mark Viney. 24 Apr. 2013; Army Historical Foundation. Downloaded from the internet on 13 Feb. 2013 from https://armyhistory. org/09/general-earle-g-wheeler/.

58. Wheeler, Gilmore. *Untitled Monograph.* 4.

59. Frances R. Wheeler. Interviews with Gilmore S. Wheeler, 2004; Army Historical Foundation. Downloaded from the internet on 13 Feb. 2013 from https://armyhistory. org/09/general-earle-g-wheeler/.

60. Stewart, 71.

61. Wheeler, Gilmore. Interview with Mark Viney. 9 Oct. 2013; New York Times. Downloaded from the internet on 7 Jan. 2014 from http://www. nytimes. com/1990/02/25/ obituaries/lieut-gen-james-gavin-82-dies-champion-and-critic-of-military. html.

## *Chapter 2*

1. United States Army. *General Orders Number 26.* 19 Dec. 1975; Walker, Fred L. *From Texas to Rome, A General's Journal.* Dallas, TX: Taylor Publishing Company, 1969: 3; Wheeler, Gilmore. *Unpublished Monograph*; Texas State Historical Association. Downloaded from the internet on 11 Nov. 2014 at http://www. tshaonline. org/handbook/ online/articles/fwa17.

2. Frances R. Wheeler. Interviews with Gilmore S. Wheeler, 2004; New York Times. Downloaded from the internet on 7 Jan. 2014 from http://www. nytimes. com/1990/02/25/ obituaries/lieut-gen-james-gavin-82-dies-champion-and-critic-of-military. html.

3. Wheeler, Frances R. Letter to Rebecca Howell. 7 Oct. 1941.

4. Ibid; Walker, 15.

5. Walker, 28.

6. Wheeler, Gilmore. Interview with Mark Viney. 9 Oct. 2013.

7. Wheeler, Frances R. Letter to Rebecca Howell. 13 Oct. 1941.

8. Wheeler, Frances R. Letter to Rebecca Howell. 21 Oct. 1941.

9. Ibid.

10. Wheeler, Frances R. Letter to Rebecca Howell. 12 Nov. 1941.

11. Wheeler, Frances R. Letter to Rebecca Howell. 16 Dec. 1941.

12. Wheeler, Frances R. Letter to Rebecca Howell. 22 Dec. 1941.

13. Wheeler, Frances R. Letter to Rebecca Howell. 26 Dec. 1941.

14. Department of the Army. *DA Form 66*. 15 Feb. 1969; United States Army. *General Orders Number 26*. 19 Dec. 1975; Department of Defense. *DD Form 214*. 3 Jul. 1970; Walker, 104; Wheeler, Gilmore. *Untitled Monograph*. 1; Army Historical Foundation. Downloaded from the internet on 13 Feb. 2013 from https://armyhistory. org/09/ general-earle-g-wheeler/.

15. Army Historical Foundation. Downloaded from the internet on 13 Feb. 2013 from https://armyhistory. org/09/general-earle-g-wheeler/; Arlington National Cemetery. Downloaded from the internet on 13 Feb. 2013 from http://www. arlingtoncemetery. net/ ewheeler. htm.

16. McMaster, Herbert R. *Dereliction of Duty*. New York: HarperCollins Publishers, 1997: 13.

17. United States Army. *General Orders Number 26*. 19 Dec. 1975; United States Army. Headquarters, 141st Infantry Regiment. *Memorandum, Subject: Commendation*. 20 Jun. 1942; Walker, 58, 65; Wheeler, Gilmore. Email to Mark Viney. 22 Mar. 2013.

18. United States Army. *General Orders Number 26*. 19 Dec. 1975; Wheeler, Gilmore. *Untitled Monograph*.

19. Walker, 104.

20. Walker, vii.

21. United States Army. *General Orders Number 26*. 19 Dec. 1975; Wheeler, Gilmore. *Untitled Monograph*. 1 Oct. 2010: 1; Wheeler, Gilmore. Interview with Mark Viney. 9 Oct. 2013; Army Historical Foundation. Downloaded from the internet on 13 Feb. 2013 from https://armyhistory. org/09/general-earle-g-wheeler/; History of the 63rd Infantry Division. Downloaded from the internet on 17 Jul. 2015 at http://www. 63rdinfdiv. com.

22. Stewart, 118-119.

23. Wheeler, Frances R. Letter to Rebecca Howell. 8 Sep. 1942; The Generals of WWII. Downloaded from the internet on 7 Jun. 2018 at http://www. generals. dk/general/ Lawrence/Thompson/USA. html.

24. Wheeler, Frances R. Letter to Rebecca Howell. 8 Sep. 1942; Wheeler, Gilmore. *Untitled Monograph*.

25. Wheeler, Gilmore. *Untitled Monograph*. 2; Wheeler, Gilmore. Email to Mark Viney. 1 Nov. 2013.

26. Wheeler, Gilmore. *Untitled Monograph*. 2.

27. Department of the Army. *DA Form 66*. 15 Feb. 1969; Department of Defense. *DD Form 214*. 3 Jul. 1970; Wheeler, Gilmore. *Untitled Monograph*.

28. Wheeler, Frances R. Letter to Rebecca Howell. 12 Jan. 1943.

29. Wheeler, Frances R. Letter to Rebecca Howell. 15 Jan. 1943; Wheeler, Gilmore. *Untitled Monograph*; Army Historical Foundation. Downloaded from the internet on 13 Feb. 2013 from https://armyhistory. org/09/general-earle-g-wheeler/.

30. United States Army. *Memorandum, "63d Infantry Division (Army of the United States)."* No date; Walker, 162; Wheeler, Gilmore. Email to Mark Viney. 9 Jun. 2013; Albert Lea Tribune. Downloaded from the internet on 11 Nov. 2014 at http://www. albertleatribune. com/2002/11/he-led-the-hot-shots-of-the-blood-and-fire-division/; Army Historical Foundation. Downloaded from the internet on 13 Feb. 2013 from https://armyhistory. org/09/general-earle-g-wheeler/.

31. United States Army. *General Orders Number 26.* 19 Dec. 1975; United States Army. *Memorandum, "63d Infantry Division (Army of the United States)."* No date; Wheeler, Gilmore. *Untitled Monograph.* 1-2, 33.

32. Wheeler, Frances R. Letter to Rebecca Howell. 7 May 1943.

33. United States Army. *Memorandum, "63d Infantry Division (Army of the United States)."* No date; Wheeler, Gilmore. *Untitled Monograph.* 1-2, 33; Wheeler, Gilmore. Interview with Mark Viney. 10 Mar. 2013; Wheeler, Gilmore. Email to Mark Viney. 9 Jun. 2013; Army Historical Foundation. Downloaded from the internet on 13 Feb. 2013 from https:// armyhistory. org/09/general-earle-g-wheeler/. The 99th Infantry Division would later play a prominent role in the Battle of the Bulge.

34. Wheeler, Gilmore. *Untitled Monograph.* 2.

35. Ibid.

36. Ibid.

37. Frances R. Wheeler. Interviews with Gilmore S. Wheeler, 2004; Wheeler, Gilmore. Interviews with Mark Viney. 25 Feb. and 10 Mar. 2013.

38. Stewart, 119.

39. Stewart, 142; Texas State Historical Association. Downloaded from the internet on 11 Nov. 2014 at http://www. tshaonline. org/handbook/online/articles/fwa17. The 36th Infantry Division would later fight in the battles of the Rapido River, Cassino, and Mt. Artemisio on the drive north through Rome and beyond.

40. Wheeler, Frances R. Letter to Rebecca Howell. Mid-Sep. 1943. (Exact date unspecified); Wheeler, Gilmore. Email to Mark Viney. 21 Nov. 2013.

41. Ibid.

42. History of the 63rd Infantry Division. Downloaded from the internet on 17 Jul. 2015 at http://www. 63rdinfdiv. com.

43. United States Army. *Standard Form 88, Report of Medical Examination.* 23 Oct. 1953; United States Army. Walter Reed General Hospital. *Clinical Record.* 22 Apr. 1970; History of the 63rd Infantry Division. Downloaded from the internet on 17 Jul. 2015 at http://www. 63rdinfdiv. com.

44. Wheeler, Gilmore. *Untitled Monograph.* 4.

45. United States Army. *Memorandum, "63d Infantry Division (Army of the United States)."* No date; United States Army. 63rd Infantry Division. *Blood and Fire, Victory in Europe.* No date.

46. Wheeler, Earle G. Letter to Frances R. Wheeler. 5 Jan. 1945; United States Army. *General Orders Number 26.* 19 Dec. 1975; Wheeler, Gilmore. Interview with Mark Viney. 9 Oct. 2013.

47. Wheeler, Earle G. Letter to Frances R. Wheeler. 5 Jan. 1945.

48. Wheeler, Earle G. Letter to Frances R. Wheeler. 8 Jan. 1945.

49. Wheeler, Earle G. Letter to Frances R. Wheeler. 15 Jan. 1945.

50. Wheeler, Earle G. Letters to Frances R. Wheeler. 17 and 24 Jan. 1945.

51. Wheeler, Earle G. Letters to Frances R. Wheeler. 17 Jan. and 7 Feb. 1945.

52. Wheeler, Earle G. Letters to Frances R. Wheeler. 19 Jan. and 22 Jul. 1945.

53. Wheeler, Earle G. Letter to Frances R. Wheeler. 15 Jan. 1945.

54. Wheeler, Earle G. Letter to Frances R. Wheeler. 1 Feb. 1945.

55. Wheeler, Earle G. Letter to Frances R. Wheeler. 7 Feb. 1945.

56. United States Army. *Memorandum, "63d Infantry Division (Army of the United States)."* No date.

57. Wheeler, Earle G. Letter to Frances R. Wheeler. 7 Feb. 1945.

58. Wheeler, Earle G. Letters to Frances R. Wheeler. 15 Jan. and 11 Mar. 1945.

59. Wheeler, Earle G. Letter to Frances R. Wheeler. 8 Feb. 1945.

60. Wheeler, Earle G. Letter to Frances R. Wheeler. 7 Feb. 1945.

61. Ibid.

62. Wheeler, Earle G. Letter to Frances R. Wheeler. 9 Feb. 1945.

63. Ibid.

64. Wheeler, Earle G. Letter to Frances R. Wheeler. 11 Feb. 1945.

65. Wheeler, Earle G. Letter to Frances R. Wheeler. 7 Feb. 1945.

66. Wheeler, Earle G. Letter to Frances R. Wheeler. 11 Feb. 1945.

67. Wheeler, Earle G. Letter to Frances R. Wheeler. 14 Feb. 1945.

68. Ibid.

69. Wheeler, Earle G. Letter to Frances R. Wheeler. 11 Feb. 1945.

70. Ibid.

71. Wheeler, Earle G. Letter to Frances R. Wheeler. 13 Feb. 1945.

72. Wheeler, Earle G. Letter to Frances R. Wheeler. 14 Feb. 1945.

73. Wheeler, Earle G. Letter to Frances R. Wheeler. 13 Feb. 1945.

74. Wheeler, Earle G. Letter to Frances R. Wheeler. 14 Feb. 1945.

75. United States Army. *Memorandum, "63d Infantry Division (Army of the United States)."* No date; United States Army. 63rd Infantry Division. *Blood and Fire, Victory in Europe.* No date.

76. Wheeler, Earle G. Letter to Frances R. Wheeler. 22 Feb. 1945.

77. Ibid.

78. Wheeler, Earle G. Letter to Frances R. Wheeler. 23 Feb. 1945.

79. Ibid.

80. Wheeler, Earle G. Letter to Frances R. Wheeler. 25 Feb. 1945.

81. Wheeler, Earle G. Letter to Frances R. Wheeler. 23 Feb. 1945.

82. Wheeler, Earle G. Letter to Frances R. Wheeler. 25 Feb. 1945.

83. Wheeler, Earle G. Letter to Frances R. Wheeler. 1 Mar. 1945.

84. Ibid.

85. Ibid.

86. Wheeler, Earle G. Letters to Frances R. Wheeler. 3 and 7 Mar. 1945.

87. Wheeler, Earle G. Letter to Frances R. Wheeler. 9 Mar. 1945.

88. Wheeler, Earle G. Letter to Frances R. Wheeler. 3 Mar. 1945.

89. Wheeler, Earle G. Letter to Frances R. Wheeler. 7 Mar. 1945; United States Army. *Memorandum, "63d Infantry Division (Army of the United States)."* No date.

90. Wheeler, Earle G. Letter to Frances R. Wheeler. 7 Mar. 1945.

91. Ibid.

92. Wheeler, Earle G. Letter to Frances R. Wheeler. 11 Mar. 1945.

93. Wheeler, Earle G. Letter to Frances R. Wheeler. 9 Mar. 1945.

94. Wheeler, Earle G. Letter to Frances R. Wheeler. 11 Mar. 1945.

95. Ibid.

96. Ibid.

97. Ibid.

98. United States Army. 63rd Infantry Division. *Blood and Fire, Victory in Europe.* No date.

99. Ibid; United States Army. *Memorandum, "63d Infantry Division (Army of the United States)."* No date.

100. United States Army. *Memorandum, "63d Infantry Division (Army of the United States)."* No date.

101. Wheeler, Earle G. Letters to Frances R. Wheeler. 11 and 23 Mar. 1945.

102. Wheeler, Earle G. Letter to Frances R. Wheeler. 23 Mar. 1945.

103. Ibid.

104. Ibid.

105. Ibid.

106. Ibid.

107. United States Army. Headquarters, 63rd Infantry Division. *General Orders Number 58.* 24 Mar. 1945; Wheeler, Earle G. Letter to Frances R. Wheeler. 3 Apr. 1945.

108. United States Army. 63rd Infantry Division. *Blood and Fire, Victory in Europe.* No date; United States Army. *Memorandum, "63d Infantry Division (Army of the United States)."* No date.

109. Wheeler, Earle G. Letter to Frances R. Wheeler. 3 Apr. 1945.

110. United States Army. *Memorandum, "63d Infantry Division (Army of the United States)."* No date.

111. United States Army. 63rd Infantry Division. *Blood and Fire, Victory in Europe.* No date.

112. Wheeler, Earle G. Letter to Frances R. Wheeler. 12 Jun. 1945.

113. United States Army. *Memorandum, "63d Infantry Division (Army of the United States)."* No date.

114. Wheeler, Earle G. Letter to Frances R. Wheeler. 12 Apr. 1945.

115. Ibid.

116. Wheeler, Earle G. Letter to Frances R. Wheeler. 16 Apr. 1945.

117. United States Army. 63rd Infantry Division. *Blood and Fire, Victory in Europe.* No date; United States Army. *Memorandum, "63d Infantry Division (Army of the United States)."* No date; History of the 63rd Infantry Division. Downloaded from the internet on 17 Jul. 2015 at http://www. 63rdinfdiv. com; Albert Lea Tribune. Downloaded from the internet on 11 Nov. 2014 at http://www. albertleatribune. com/2002/11/he-led-the-hot-shots-of-the-blood-and-fire-division/.

118. United States Army. 63rd Infantry Division. *Blood and Fire, Victory in Europe.* No date.

119. Ibid.

120. United States Army. Headquarters, 63rd Infantry Division. *Memorandum, subject: Special Rating of Officers Recommended for Promotion to the Grade of Brigadier General (Temporary).* 17 May 1945; Wheeler, Gilmore. *Untitled Monograph.* 1-2; Wheeler, Gilmore. Email to Mark Viney. 22 Mar. 2013.

121. Wheeler, Earle G. Letter to Frances R. Wheeler. 6 May 1945; Wheeler, Gilmore. *Untitled Monograph.*

122. Shirer, William L. *The Rise and Fall of the Third Reich, a History of Nazi Germany.* New York: Simon and Schuster, 1960: 1105-1106.

123. Wheeler, Earle G. Letter to Frances R. Wheeler. 4 May 1945.

124. Ibid.

125. Ibid.

126. Wheeler, Earle G. Letter to Frances R. Wheeler. 5 May 1945.

127. Wheeler, Earle G. Letter to Frances R. Wheeler. 6 May 1945.

128. Ibid.

129. Wheeler, Earle G. Letter to Frances R. Wheeler. 6 Jul. 1945.

130. Wheeler, Earle G. Letter to Frances R. Wheeler. 6 May 1945.

131. Wheeler, Earle G. Letter to Frances R. Wheeler. 10 May 1945.

132. Wheeler, Earle G. Letter to Frances R. Wheeler. 8 Jul. 1945.

133. Wheeler, Earle G. Letter to Frances R. Wheeler. 10 May 1945.

134. Ibid.

135. Wheeler, Earle G. Letter to Frances R. Wheeler. 6 May 1945.

136. Wheeler, Earle G. Letter to Frances R. Wheeler. 10 May 1945.

137. Ibid.

138. Wheeler, Earle G. Letter to Frances R. Wheeler. 12 May 1945.

139. Ibid.

140. Wheeler, Earle G. Letters to Frances R. Wheeler. 12 and 20 May 1945.

141. Headquarters, 63rd Infantry Division. *General Orders Number 58*. 21 May 1945; Wheeler, Earle G. Letter to Frances R. Wheeler. 20 May 1945; United States Army.

142. Wheeler, Earle G. Letter to Frances R. Wheeler. 20 May 1945.

143. United States Army. Headquarters, 63rd Infantry Division. *Memorandum, subject: Special Rating of Officers Recommended for Promotion to the Grade of Brigadier General (Temporary)*. 17 May 1945.

144. Wheeler, Earle G. Letter to Frances R. Wheeler. 20 May 1945.

145. United States Army. 63rd Infantry Division. *Blood and Fire, Victory in Europe*. No date.

146. Wheeler, Earle G. Letter to Frances R. Wheeler. 12 May 1945.

147. Wheeler, Earle G. Letter to Frances R. Wheeler. 20 May 1945.

148. Ibid.

149. Ibid.

150. Wheeler, Earle G. Letter to Frances R. Wheeler. 25 May 1945.

151. Wheeler, Earle G. Letter to Frances R. Wheeler. 12 May 1945.

152. Wheeler, Earle G. Letter to Frances R. Wheeler. 25 May 1945.

153. Wheeler, Earle G. Letters to Frances R. Wheeler. 25 May and 13 Jul. 1945.

154. Wheeler, Earle G. Letter to Frances R. Wheeler. 27 May 1945.

155. Wheeler, Earle G. Letter to Frances R. Wheeler. 28 May 1945.

156. Ibid.

157. Ibid.

158. Ibid.

159. Ibid.

160. Wheeler, Earle G. Letter to Frances R. Wheeler. 31 May 1945.

161. Ibid.

162. Ibid.

163. Wheeler, Earle G. Letter to Frances R. Wheeler. 5 Jun. 1945.

164. Wheeler, Earle G. Letter to Frances R. Wheeler. 7 Jun. 1945.

165. Wheeler, Earle G. Letter to Frances R. Wheeler. 10 Jun. 1945.

166. Ibid.

167. Ibid.

168. Wheeler, Earle G. Letter to Frances R. Wheeler. 17 Jun. 1945.

169. Wheeler, Earle G. Letters to Frances R. Wheeler. 31 May and 17 Jun. 1945.

170. Wheeler, Earle G. Letter to Frances R. Wheeler. 17 Jun. 1945.

171. Wheeler, Earle G. Letters to Frances R. Wheeler. 17 and 19 Jun. 1945.

172. Wheeler, Earle G. Letter to Frances R. Wheeler. 23 Jun. 1945.

173. Wheeler, Earle G. Letters to Frances R. Wheeler. 23 and 28 Jun. 1945.

174. Wheeler, Earle G. Letters to Frances R. Wheeler. 3 and 4 Jul. 1945.

175. Wheeler, Earle G. Letter to Frances R. Wheeler. 3 Jul. 1945.

176. Wheeler, Earle G. Letter to Frances R. Wheeler. 4 Jul. 1945.

177. Ibid.

178. Ibid.

179. Ibid.

180. Wheeler, Earle G. Letters to Frances R. Wheeler. 6 and 8 Jul. 1945.

181. United States Army. Headquarters, European Theater of Operations. *General Orders Number 140*. 30 Jun. 1945.

182. Wheeler, Earle G. Letters to Frances R. Wheeler. 6 and 8 Jul. 1945.

183. Wheeler, Earle G. Letter to Frances R. Wheeler. 8 Jul. 1945.

184. Wheeler, Earle G. Letter to Frances R. Wheeler. 13 Jul. 1945.

185. Ibid.

186. Ibid.

187. Ibid.

188. Wheeler, Earle G. Letter to Frances R. Wheeler. 18 Jul. 1945.

189. Ibid.

190. Ibid; Wheeler, Gilmore. Email to Mark Viney. 22 Mar. 2013.

191. Wheeler, Earle G. Letter to Frances R. Wheeler. 20 Jul. 1945; Albert Lea Tribune. Downloaded from the internet on 11 Nov. 2014 at http://www. albertleatribune. com/2002/11/he-led-the-hot-shots-of-the-blood-and-fire-division/.

192. Wheeler, Earle G. Letter to Frances R. Wheeler. 22 Jul. 1945.

193. United States Army. Headquarters, 63rd Infantry Division. *General Orders Number 412.* 22 Jul. 1945; War Department. *AGO Form 66-2.* 23 Apr. 1954; Wheeler, Earle G. Letter to Frances R. Wheeler. 22 Jul. 1945.

194. Wheeler, Earle G. Letter to Frances R. Wheeler. 22 Jul. 1945.

195. Wheeler, Earle G. Letter to Frances R. Wheeler. 24 Jul. 1945.

196. Wheeler, Gilmore. Interviews with Mark Viney. 25 Feb., 10 Mar., and 9 Oct. 2013.

197. Wheeler, Earle G. Letter to Frances R. Wheeler. 30 Jul. 1945.

198. Wheeler, Earle G. Letter to Frances R. Wheeler. 22 and 30 Jul. 1945.

199. Wheeler, Gilmore. Interviews with Mark Viney. 25 Feb., 10 Mar., and 9 Oct. 2013.

200. Wheeler, Earle G. Letter to Frances R. Wheeler. 8 Jul. 1945.

201. Wheeler, Earle G. Letters to Frances R. Wheeler. 31 Jul. and 2 Aug. 1945.

202. Ibid.

203. Wheeler, Earle G. Letter to Gilmore S. Wheeler. 31 Jul. 1945. The Wheelers encouraged their son from an early age to address them by their first names. They never discussed their medical issues with Bim, even in his adulthood. He only learned about his mother's hysterectomy and the extent of his father's heart condition after their deaths.

204. Wheeler, Gilmore. *Untitled Monograph.* 4.

205. Wheeler, Earle G. Letter to Frances R. Wheeler. 30 Jul. 1945.

206. Wheeler, Gilmore. Interview with Mark Viney. 25 Feb. 2013; Arlington National Cemetery. Downloaded from the internet on 20 Oct. 2013 from http://www. arlington-cemetery. net/bespivy. htm.

207. Wheeler, Earle G. Letter to Frances R. Wheeler. 2 Aug. 1945.

208. Ibid; Baymor, Michael, ed. *The 63rd Infantry Division Chronicles, June 1943 to September 1945.* Publisher Unknown:63rd Infantry Division Association, 1991: 222.

209. Wheeler, Earle G. Letter to Frances R. Wheeler. 31 Jul. and 2 Aug. 1945.

210. Wheeler, Earle G. Letter to Frances R. Wheeler. 2 Aug. 1945.

211. United States Army. *Memorandum, "63d Infantry Division (Army of the United States)."* No date; Albert Lea Tribune. Downloaded from the

internet on 11 Nov. 2014 at http://www. albertleatribune. com/2002/11/
he-led-the-hot-shots-of-the-blood-and-fire-division/.

212. United States Army. *Memorandum, "63d Infantry Division (Army of the United States)."* No date; Department of the Army. *DA Form 66.* 15 Feb. 1969.

213. Wheeler, Gilmore. *Untitled Monograph*; The New York Times. *Gen. Earle Wheeler Dies; Ex-Head of Joint Chiefs.* 19 Dec. 1975.

214. Hamblen, Arch. Letter to Betty Wheeler. 17 Jul. 1976.

215. War Department. *AGO Form 66-2.* 23 Apr. 1954; United States Army. *General Orders Number 26.* 19 Dec. 1975; United States Army. *Memorandum, "63d Infantry Division (Army of the United States)."* No date.

## *Chapter 3*

1. Stewart, 204.

2. United States Army. Field Artillery School. *Memorandum, Subject: Award of Army Commendation Ribbon.* 8 May 1946; United States Army. *General Orders Number 26.* 19 Dec. 1975; Wheeler, Earle G. *Professional Resume.* 1971.

3. United States Army. Field Artillery School. *Memorandum, Subject: Award of Army Commendation Ribbon.* 25 Apr. 1946.

4. National Observer. *General Wheeler's Rising Stars, It's 3-for-3 for the Army As Taylor 'Protégé" Gets Top Job.* 29 Jun. 1964: 2.

5. United States Army. Field Artillery School. *Memorandum, Subject: Award of Army Commendation Ribbon.* 8 May 1946; War Department. *AGO Form 66-2.* 23 Apr. 1954.

6. War Department. *AGO Form 66-2.* 23 Apr. 1954; United States Army. *General Orders Number 26.* 19 Dec. 1975; United States Army. Walter Reed General Hospital. *Clinical Record.* 22 Apr. 1970.

7. Wheeler, Gilmore. *Untitled Monograph.* 5; Wheeler, Gilmore. Interview with Mark Viney. 9 Oct. 2013; Army Historical Foundation. Downloaded from the internet on 13 Feb. 2013 from https://armyhistory. org/09/general-earle-g-wheeler/.

8. Wheeler, Gilmore. *Untitled Monograph.* 5.

9. Frances R. Wheeler. Interviews with Gilmore S. Wheeler, Disc 3. 2004; Wheeler, Gilmore. *Untitled Monograph.* 5; Wheeler, Gilmore. Interview with Mark Viney. 9 Oct. 2013.

10. Wheeler, Gilmore. *Untitled Monograph.* 5-6.

11. Wheeler, Gilmore. Interview with Mark Viney. 25 Feb. 2013.

12. Wheeler, Gilmore. *Untitled Monograph*. 16; Wheeler, Gilmore. Interview with Mark Viney. 9 Oct. 2013.

13. War Department. *AGO Form 66-2*. 23 Apr. 1954; Department of Defense. Headquarters, United States Forces, European Theater, Mission to France. *Memorandum, subject: French Award to United States Officer*. 22 Jan. 1947; Wheeler, Gilmore. *Untitled Monograph*. 6.

14. Stewart, 202; McMaster, 13-14.

15. Stewart, 204-205.

16. Gott, Kendall D. *Mobility, Vigilance, and Justice: The US Army Constabulary in Germany, 1946-1953*. Fort Leavenworth, Kansas: Combat Studies Institute Press, 2005: 6-7, 10.

17. Ibid, 10-12.

18. Ibid, 15.

19. Ibid, 26.

20. War Department. *AGO Form 66-2*. 23 Apr. 1954; Gott, 26; Wheeler, Gilmore. *Untitled Monograph*. 6; Washington Post. *Gen. Withers A. Burress, Head of First Army During 1950s*. 14 Jun. 1977: C6.

21. Wheeler, Gilmore. *Untitled Monograph*. 6.

22. Ibid. Heidel's grave marker is located at the Wheelers' farm in Martinsburg, WV.

23. Wheeler, Gilmore. *Unpublished Monograph*. 6-7; Wheeler, Gilmore. Interview with Mark Viney. 10 Mar. 2013.

24. Department of Defense. *DD Form 214*. 3 Jul. 1970; Department of the Army. *DA Form 66*. 15 Feb. 1969; Stewart, 203.

25. Wheeler, Gilmore. *Untitled Monograph*. 6-7; Army Historical Foundation. Downloaded from the internet on 13 Feb. 2013 from https://armyhistory. org/09/general-earle-g-wheeler/.

26. Wheeler, Gilmore. *Untitled Monograph*. 7, 11; Wheeler, Gilmore. Interview with Mark Viney. 10 Mar. 2013.

27. Ibid.

28. Wheeler, Gilmore. *Untitled Monograph*. 7-8.

29. Ibid.

30. Frances R. Wheeler. Interviews with Gilmore S. Wheeler. Disc 3. 2004; Wheeler, Gilmore. *Untitled Monograph*. 8-9.

31. Wheeler, Gilmore. *Untitled Monograph*. 8. Howell, Rebecca. Letter to Frances R. Wheeler. 23 Jun. 1948.

32. Wheeler, Gilmore. *Untitled Monograph*. 8.

33. Wheeler, Gilmore. Interview with Mark Viney. 25 Feb. 2013; Wheeler, Gilmore. *Untitled Monograph*. 9.

34. Wheeler, Gilmore. *Untitled Monograph*. 9.

35. Stewart, 206-207.

36. Armstrong, David A. Editor. *The Joint Chiefs of Staff and the First Indochina War, 1947-1954*. Washington, DC: Office of Joint History, 2004: 19-20.

37. Ibid.

38. Stewart, 207-210.

39. Gott, 26-28.

40. Stewart, 213-214.

41. Howell, Rebecca. Letter to Frances R. Wheeler. 23 Jun. 1948.

42. Ibid; Wheeler, Gilmore. *Untitled Monograph*. 9; Wheeler, Gilmore. Interview with Mark Viney. 9 Oct. 2013.

43. Gott, 26-27; Army Historical Foundation. Downloaded from the internet on 13 Feb. 2013 from https://armyhistory. org/09/general-earle-g-wheeler/.

44. New York Herald Tribune. *Clay Sees a Long Siege at Berlin But No War 'Around the Corner'*. 14 Sep. 1948:1.

45. Ibid.

46. Howell, Rebecca. Letter to Frances R. Wheeler. 14 Sep. 1948.

47. Ibid.

48. New York Herald Tribune. *Marshall Concedes Relations With Russia Are Deteriorating*. 15 Sep. 1948:1.

49. Howell, Rebecca. Letter to Frances R. Wheeler. 15 Sep. 1948.

50. Ibid.

51. Ibid.

52. Howell, Rebecca. Letter to Frances R. Wheeler. 17 Sep. 1948.

53. Howell, Rebecca. Letter to Frances R. Wheeler. 20 Oct. 1948.

54. Ibid; Wheeler, Gilmore. Email to Mark Viney. 21 Nov. 2013.

55. United States Army. Headquarters, United States Constabulary. *Memorandum, Subject: Commendation.* 25 Jan. 1949.

56. Stewart, 214.

57. War Department. *AGO Form 66-2.* 23 Apr. 1954;

58. Wheeler, Gilmore. *Untitled Monograph.* 9.

59. Wheeler, Frances R. Letter to Rebecca Howell. 15 Jan. 1943; Wheeler, Gilmore. *Untitled Monograph.* 10.

60. Wheeler, Gilmore. *Untitled Monograph.* 10-11; Army Historical Foundation. Downloaded from the internet on 13 Feb. 2013 from https://armyhistory. org/09/general-earle-g-wheeler/.

61. United States Army. *Standard Form 88, Report of Medical Examination.* 6 Dec. 1956; United States Army. Walter Reed General Hospital. *Clinical Record.* 22 Apr. 1970; Wheeler, Gilmore. *Untitled Monograph.* 11; Wheeler, Gilmore. Interview with Mark Viney. 9 Oct. 2013.

62. Ibid.

63. War Department. *AGO Form 66-2.* 23 Apr. 1954; United States Army. *General Orders Number 26.* 19 Dec. 1975.

64. Jordan, Robert S. *An Unsung Soldier, The Life of General Andrew J. Goodpaster.* Annapolis: Naval Institute Press, 2013: ix.

65. Stewart, 214.

66. Stewart, 211.

67. Stewart, 203; McMaster, 13.

68. Ibid.

69. Armstrong, 19.

70. Armstrong, vii, 13, 15.

71. Armstrong, vii.

72. Armstrong, 19-20.

73. Armstrong, 20.

74. Armstrong, 214-215.

75. Armstrong, 36.

76. Armstrong, 214.

77. Armstrong, 40-42.

78. Ibid.

79. Armstrong, 35-36.

80. Ibid.

81. Armstrong, 33, 35.

82. Armstrong, 41, 43.

83. Armstrong, 50.

84. Wheeler, Gilmore. *Untitled Monograph*. 11.

85. Stewart, 217.

86. Stewart, 215.

87. Jordan, 34.

88. Armstrong, 53.

89. Stewart, 215.

90. Stewart, 215; Millet, Allan R., Maslowski, Peter, and Feis, William B. *For the Common Defense, A Military History of the United States from 1607 to 2012*. New York: Free Press, 2012: 453.

91. Stewart, 217.

92. United States Department of Justice. Federal Bureau of Investigation. *Memorandum Re: Earl Gilmore Wheeler – WA - 19028, Atomic Energy Act - Applicant*. 26 Jul. 1950; War Department. *AGO Form 66-2*. 23 Apr. 1954; United States Army. *General Orders Number 26*. 19 Dec. 1975.

93. Department of Defense. *Certificate for Award of the Department of Defense Identification Badge*. 1 Jan. 1951; Arlington National Cemetery. Downloaded from the internet on 13 Feb. 2013 from http://www. arlingtoncemetery. net/ ewheeler. htm; The Forgotten General. Downloaded from the internet on 13 Feb. 2013 from http://theforgottengeneral. com/wp-content/uploads/2010/12/ JCS-Biography. pdf; United States Army. Office of the Administrative Assistant to the Secretary of the Army. The Institute of Heraldry. Downloaded from the internet on 16 Dec. 2017 at http://www. tioh. hqda. pentagon. mil/Catalog/Heraldry. aspx?HeraldryId=15493&CategoryId=9148&grp=2&menu=Uniformed%20 Services&ps=24&p=0.

94. War Department. *AGO Form 66-2*. 23 Apr. 1954; United States Army. *General Orders Number 26*. 19 Dec. 1975; Wheeler, Gilmore. Interview with Mark Viney. 25 Feb. 2013.

95. Wheeler, Gilmore. *Untitled Monograph*. 11.

96. Wheeler, Frances R. Letter to Rebecca Howell. 31 Jul. 1950.

97. Ibid.

98. Armstrong, 53.

99. Armstrong, 67.

100. Jordan, 23-24.

101. Ibid; Armstrong, 67.

102. Armstrong, 69.

103. Armstrong, 69-70, 76-77.

104. Armstrong, 70, 79.

105. Daddis, Gregory A. *Westmoreland's War: Reassessing American Strategy in Vietnam.* Oxford: Oxford University Press, 2014: 44-45.

106. Armstrong, 79-80.

107. Sebree, E. B. Letter to Earle G. Wheeler. 30 Aug. 1951; Waddington, David. *TRUST, A Picture Story of the United States Forces in the Free Territory of Trieste.* Trieste: David Waddington Publications, 1952; Wheeler, Gilmore. *Untitled Monograph.* 12. Given command of one of the most elite units of the U.S. Army - akin in prestige to today's 75th Ranger Regiment - Wheeler was marked for stars.

108. Waddington; Wheeler, Gilmore. *Untitled Monograph.* 12. Trieste is part of Italy today. Opicina is now a resort town connected to Trieste by a twenty-minute ride on a funicular railway.

109. Sebree, E. B. Letter to Earle G. Wheeler. 7 Sep. 1951.

110. Muir, James I. Letter to Earle G. Wheeler. 13 Sep. 1951.

111. Sebree, E. B. Letter to Earle G. Wheeler. 17 Sep. 1951.

112. War Department. *AGO Form 66-2.* 23 Apr. 1954; Wheeler, Gilmore. *Untitled Monograph.* 14.

113. Wheeler, Frances R. Letter to Rebecca Howell. 11 Nov. 1951; Wheeler, Gilmore. Email to Mark Viney. 21 Nov. 2013.

114. War Department. *AGO Form 66-2.* 23 Apr. 1954; United States Army. *General Orders Number 26.* 19 Dec. 1975.

115. Waddington; Wheeler, Gilmore. *Untitled Monograph.* 12. Miramare Castle is now a museum.

116. Wheeler, Frances R. Letter to Rebecca Howell. 11 Nov. 1951.

117. Ibid.

118. Ibid.

119. Ibid.

120. Wheeler, Frances R. Letters to Rebecca Howell. 22 Nov. 1951 and 9 Apr. 1952; Wheeler, Gilmore. Email to Mark Viney. 21 Nov. 2013.

121. Wheeler, Frances R. Letter to Rebecca Howell. 11 Nov. 1951.

122. Wheeler, Frances R. Letter to Rebecca Howell. 27 Nov. 1951.

123. Wheeler, Frances R. Letter to Rebecca Howell. 21 Feb. 1952.

124. Wheeler, Frances R. Letter to Rebecca Howell. 27 Nov. 1951.

125. Wheeler, Frances R. Letter to Rebecca Howell. 29 Nov. 1951.

126. Ibid.

127. Wheeler, Frances R. Letters to Rebecca Howell. 13 Mar. 1952 and 8 Oct. 1953; Wheeler, Gilmore. Email to Mark Viney. 21 Nov. 2013.

128. Wheeler, Frances R. Letter to Rebecca Howell. 4 Dec. 1951.

129. Ibid.

130. Ibid.

131. Wheeler, Frances R. Letter to Rebecca Howell. 6 Dec. 1951.

132. Wheeler, Earle G. Letter to Walter R. Howell. 9 Dec. 1951.

133. Wheeler, Frances R. Letter to Rebecca Howell. 20 Dec. 1951.

134. Wheeler, Gilmore. *Untitled Monograph*. 14.

135. Wheeler, Frances R. Letter to Rebecca Howell. 20 Dec. 1951; Wheeler, Gilmore. *Untitled Monograph*. 22-23; Wheeler, Gilmore. Interviews with Mark Viney. 25 Feb., 14 Mar., and 9 Oct. 2013.

136. Wheeler, Frances R. Letter to Rebecca Howell. 22 Jan. 1952; Wheeler, Gilmore. *Untitled Monograph*. 13.

137. Wheeler, Gilmore. *Untitled Monograph*. 12.

138. Hackworth, David H. *About Face*. New York: Simon and Schuster, 1989.

139. Wheeler, Gilmore. *Untitled Monograph*. 13.

140. Wheeler, Frances R. Letter to Rebecca Howell. 27 Dec. 1951.

141. Ibid.

142. Ibid.

143. Wheeler, Frances R. Letter to Rebecca Howell. 14 Jan. 1952.

144. Wheeler, Frances R. Letters to Rebecca Howell. 17 and 22 Jan. 1952.

145. Wheeler, Frances R. Letters to Rebecca Howell. 22 Jan. and 5 Jun. 1952.

146. Wheeler, Frances R. Letter to Rebecca Howell. 14 Feb. 1952.

147. Wheeler, Frances R. Letter to Rebecca Howell. 18 Feb. 1952.

148. Ibid.

149. Wheeler, Frances R. Letter to Rebecca Howell. 24 Mar. 1952.

150. Wheeler, Earle G. Letter to Walter R. Howell. 1 Apr. 1952.

151. Wheeler, Frances R. Letter to Rebecca Howell. 1 Apr. 1952.

152. Ibid.

153. Stewart, 243-244.

154. Stewart, 204, 244.

155. Wheeler, Frances R. Letter to Rebecca Howell. 9 Apr. 1952.

156. U.S. Army in Germany. Downloaded from the internet on 23 Jul. 2018 at https:// www. usarmygermany. com/Sont. htm?https&&&www. usarmygermany. com/Units/ TRUST/TRUST_main. htm.

157. Wheeler, Gilmore. Interview with Mark Viney. 9 Oct. 2013; Anderson, Karen. *Little Rock: Race and Resistance at Central High School.* Princeton, NJ: Princeton University Press, 2013; Meredith, James. *Mississippi: A Volume of Eleven Books.* Jackson, MS: Meredith Publishing: 1995.

158. Armstrong, 83.

159. McMaster, 34.

160. Armstrong, 89.

161. United States Army. Headquarters, Trieste United States Troops. *Memorandum, Subject Commendation.* 17 Jun. 1952.

162. Waddington.

163. Wheeler, Frances R. Letter to Rebecca Howell. 12 Jun. 1952.

164. Wheeler, Frances R. Letter to Rebecca Howell. 1 Jul. 1952.

165. Ziegler, Philip. *Mountbatten: The Official Biography.* London: HarperCollins, 1985.

166. Wheeler, Frances R. Letter to Rebecca Howell. 1 Jul. 1952; Ziegler.

167. Wheeler, Frances R. Letter to Rebecca Howell. 12 Jun. 1952; Wheeler, Gilmore. *Untitled Monograph*. 12.

168. Wheeler, Frances R. Letter to Rebecca Howell. 1 Jul. 1952.

169. Wheeler, Frances R. Letter to Rebecca Howell. 6 Aug. 1952.

170. Wheeler, Frances R. Letter to Rebecca Howell. 11 Aug. 1952.

171. Ibid.

172. Wheeler, Frances R. Letter to Rebecca Howell. 17 Aug. 1952.

173. Wheeler, Frances R. Letter to Rebecca Howell. 3 Sep. 1952.

174. Collins, J. Lawton. *Lightning Joe: An Autobiography*. Baton Rouge, LA: Louisiana State University Press, 1979.

175. Wheeler, Frances R. Letter to Rebecca Howell. 11 Sep. 1952; Wheeler, Gilmore. Email to Mark Viney. 21 Nov. 2013.

176. Wheeler, Frances R. Letters to Rebecca Howell. 17 Aug. and 25 Sep. 1952; Frances R. Wheeler. Interviews with Gilmore S. Wheeler. Disc 6. 2003.

177. Wheeler, Frances R. Letter to Rebecca Howell. 13 Oct. 1952.

178. Ibid.

179. United States Army Signal Corps. Photograph. 8 Nov. 1952; War Department. *AGO Form 66-2*. 23 Apr. 1954; United States Army. *General Orders Number 26*. 19 Dec. 1975; The Forgotten General. Downloaded from the internet on 13 Feb. 2013 from http://the-forgottengeneral. com/wp-content/uploads/2010/12/JCS-Biography. pdf; Army Historical Foundation. Downloaded from the internet on 13 Feb. 2013 from https://armyhistory. org/09/general-earle-g-wheeler/.

## *Chapter 4*

1. Armstrong, 91-93, 100.

2. Armstrong, 97-98.

3. War Department. *AGO Form 66-2*. 23 Apr. 1954.

4. Wheeler, Gilmore. *Untitled Monograph*. 14.

5. Wheeler, 17; Wheeler, Gilmore. Interview with Mark Viney. 9 Oct. 2013.

6. Wheeler, Gilmore. *Untitled Monograph*. 14.

7. Wheeler, 16-17; Wheeler, Gilmore. Interviews with Mark Viney. 24 Apr. and 9 Oct. 2013.

8. Ibid.

9. Wheeler, Gilmore. *Untitled Monograph.* 14, 17.

10. Ibid.

11. Wheeler, Frances R. Letters to Rebecca Howell. 2 and 9 Aug. 1953.

12. Wheeler, Gilmore. Interview with Mark Viney. 9 Oct. 2013.

13. Armstrong, 135-136.

14. Stewart, 248-249.

15. Millet, Maslowski, and Feis, 474, 453.

16. Armstrong, 137, 140.

17. Ibid.

18. Armstrong, 115-116.

19. Daddis, 19.

20. Jordan, 78.

21. Wheeler, Frances R. Letter to Rebecca Howell. 16 Aug. 1953.

22. Wheeler, Frances R. Letter to Rebecca Howell. 8 Oct. 1953; Wheeler, Gilmore. Email to Mark Viney. 21 Nov. 2013.

23. Wheeler, Frances R. Letter to Rebecca Howell. 5 Aug. 1953; Wheeler, Gilmore. *Untitled Monograph.* 15.

24. Wheeler, Gilmore. *Untitled Monograph.* 17.

25. Wheeler, Frances R. Letter to Rebecca Howell. 9 Aug. 1953.

26. Wheeler, Frances R. Letter to Rebecca Howell. 25 Aug. 1953.

27. Wheeler, Frances R. Letter to Rebecca Howell. 29 Aug. 1953.

28. Ibid.

29. Wheeler, Frances R. Letter to Rebecca Howell. 11 Sep. 1953.

30. Ibid.

31. Ibid.

32. Ibid.

33. Ibid.

34. Wheeler, Frances R. Letter to Rebecca Howell. 22 Sep. 1953; Army Historical Foundation. Downloaded from the internet on 13 Feb. 2013 from https://armyhistory.org/09/general-earle-g-wheeler/.

35. Wheeler, Frances R. Letter to Rebecca Howell. 1 Oct. 1953.

36. Wheeler, Frances R. Letters to Rebecca Howell. 22 Sep. and 13 Oct. 1953; Wheeler, Gilmore. Email to Mark Viney. 21 Nov. 2013; Army Historical Foundation. Downloaded from the internet on 13 Feb. 2013 from https://armyhistory. org/09/ general-earle-g-wheeler/.

37. Wheeler, Frances R. Letter to Rebecca Howell. 13 Oct. 1953.

38. Wheeler, Gilmore. *Untitled Monograph*. 15-16.

39. Ibid.

40. Wheeler, 15; Wheeler, Gilmore. Interview with Mark Viney. 9 Oct. 2013.

41. Ibid.

42. Jordan, 86-87.

43. Ibid.

44. Armstrong, 251; Jordan, 43-44.

45. Jordan, 43-44.

46. Armstrong, 252.

47. Jordan, 85, 89.

48. Armstrong, 252.

49. Wheeler, Frances R. Letters to Rebecca Howell. 12 Dec. and 5 Jan. 1954; Wheeler, Gilmore. *Untitled Monograph*. 15; Wheeler, Gilmore. Email to Mark Viney. 21 Nov. 2013.

50. Wheeler, Gilmore. *Untitled Monograph*. 16.

51. Ibid.

52. Wheeler, Frances R. Letters to Rebecca Howell. 5 and 12 Jan. 1954; Wheeler, Gilmore. Email to Mark Viney. 21 Nov. 2013.

53. Wheeler, Gilmore. *Untitled Monograph*. 18.

54. Wheeler, Frances R. Letters to Rebecca Howell. 10 and 19 Jan. 1954.

55. Wheeler, Frances R. Letter to Rebecca Howell. 19 Jan. 1954.

56. Wheeler, Frances R. Letter to Rebecca Howell. 26 Jan. 1954.

57. Armstrong, 213-214; Jordan, 50.

58. Armstrong, 214.

59. Summers, Harry. *On Strategy: A Critical Analysis of the Vietnam War*. Novato, CA: Presidio Press, 1982: 98-99.

60. Armstrong, 214-215.

61. Stewart, 252.

62. Stewart, 252-253.

63. Wheeler, Frances R. Letter to Rebecca Howell. 20 Jun. 1954.

64. War Department. *AGO Form 66-2*. 23 Apr. 1954; Wheeler, Frances R. Letters to Rebecca Howell. 29 Jun. and 29 Nov 1954.

65. Wheeler, Frances R. Letter to Rebecca Howell. 29 Jun. 1954.

66. Wheeler, Earle G. Letter to Walter R. Howell. 20 Jul. 1954.

67. Ibid.

68. Ibid.

69. Wheeler, Gilmore. *Untitled Monograph*. 18.

70. Wheeler, Frances R. Letter to Rebecca Howell. 5 Aug. 1954.

71. Wheeler, Frances R. Letter to Rebecca Howell. Month and day unspecified (probably late July) 1954; Wheeler, Gilmore. Email to Mark Viney. 21 Nov. 2013.

72. Wheeler, Frances R. Letter to Rebecca Howell. 16 Aug. 1954.

73. Wheeler, Gilmore S. Letter to Rebecca Howell. 17 Aug. 1954; Wheeler, Gilmore. Email to Mark Viney. 21 Nov. 2013.

74. Wheeler, Gilmore S. Letter to Rebecca Howell. 12 Sep. 1954; Wheeler, Frances R. Letter to Rebecca Howell. 7 Nov. 1954.

75. Wheeler, Frances R. Letter to Rebecca Howell. 6 Sep. 1954.

76. Ibid.

77. Wheeler, Frances R. Letter to Rebecca Howell. 23 Sep. 1954.

78. Ibid.

79. Ibid.

80. Wheeler, Frances R. Letters to Rebecca Howell. 16 Aug. and 6 Sep. 1954.

81. Wheeler, Frances R. Letter to Rebecca Howell. 19 Sep. 1954.

82. Wheeler, Frances R. Letters to Rebecca Howell. 28 Oct. and 1 Nov. 1954.

83. Wheeler, Frances R. Letter to Rebecca Howell. 1 Nov. 1954.

84. Ibid.

85. Ibid.

86. Ibid.

87. Wheeler, Frances R. Letter to Rebecca Howell. 7 Nov. 1954.

88. Ibid.

89. Wheeler, Frances R. Letter to Rebecca Howell. 8 Dec. 1954.

90. Wheeler, Frances R. Letter to Rebecca Howell. 14 Nov. 1954.

91. Wheeler, Frances R. Letter to Rebecca Howell. 29 Nov. 1954.

92. Ibid.

93. Wheeler, Frances R. Letters to Rebecca Howell. 14 Nov., 8 and 12 Dec. 1954.

94. Wheeler, Frances R. Letter to Rebecca Howell. 19 Dec. 1954.

95. Wheeler, Frances R. Letter to Rebecca Howell. 14 Nov. 1954.

96. Wheeler, Frances R. Letter to Rebecca Howell. 19 Dec. 1954.

97. Wheeler, Frances R. Letter to Rebecca Howell. 15 Dec. 1954; West Point Association of Graduates. Downloaded from the internet on 15 Dec. 2017 at http://apps. westpointaog. org/Memorials/Article/9579/.

98. Stewart, 253.

99. Ibid.

100. Stewart, 280, 288-289.

101. Wheeler, Gilmore. *Untitled Monograph*. 20.

102. Ibid; Wheeler, Gilmore. Interview with Mark Viney. 9 Oct. 2013.

103. Wheeler, Gilmore. *Untitled Monograph*. 21.

104. Ibid.

105. United States Army. *General Orders Number 26*. 19 Dec. 1975; Wheeler, Gilmore. *Untitled Monograph*. 15; Wheeler, Gilmore. Interview with Mark Viney. 9 Oct. 2013.

106. United States Army. *General Orders Number 26*. 19 Dec. 1975; Wheeler, Gilmore. *Untitled Monograph*. 22; Army Historical Foundation. Downloaded from the internet on 13 Feb. 2013 from https://armyhistory. org/09/general-earle-g-wheeler/; Arlington National Cemetery. Downloaded from the internet on 13 Feb. 2013 from http://www. arlingtoncemetery. net/ewheeler. htm; The Forgotten General. Downloaded from the internet on 13 Feb. 2013 from http://theforgottengeneral. com/wp-content/uploads/2010/12/JCS-Biography. pdf.

107. United States Army. *Standard Form 88, Report of Medical Examination*. 6 Dec. 1956; Wheeler, Gilmore. *Untitled Monograph*. 22; United States Army. Walter Reed General Hospital. *Clinical Record*. 22 Apr. 1970.

108. Ibid.

109. United States Department of Justice. Federal Bureau of Investigation. *Memorandum Re: Earl Gilmore Wheeler – WA - 19028, Atomic Energy Act - Applicant.* 13 Dec. 1955.

110. Ibid.

111. Wheeler, Gilmore. *Untitled Monograph.* 23; Wheeler, Gilmore. Interview with Mark Viney. 9 Oct. 2013.

112. Stewart, 253.

113. Stewart, 286-288.

114. Armstrong, 215.

115. Stewart, 254-255.

116. United States Army. *General Orders Number 26.* 19 Dec. 1975.

117. Stewart, 270; Baltimore Sun. *A Military Man is Chosen and Chief Knows Him Well.* 24 Jun. 1964; Wheeler, Gilmore. *Untitled Monograph.* 24.

118. Stewart, 270; Wheeler, Gilmore. *Untitled Monograph.* 25.

119. Wheeler, Gilmore. *Untitled Monograph.* 26; Wheeler, Gilmore. Interview with Mark Viney. 9 Oct. 2013.

120. Ibid.

121. Ibid.

122. Wheeler, Gilmore. *Untitled Monograph.* 24; Wheeler, Gilmore. Interview with Mark Viney. 10 Mar. 2013.

123. Wheeler, Gilmore. Interviews with Mark Viney. 10 Mar. and 9 Oct. 2013; Wheeler, Gilmore. Email to Mark Viney. 26 Apr. 2014.

124. Wheeler, Gilmore S. Email to Mark Viney. 23 Sep. 2015.

125. Wheeler, Gilmore. Interview with Mark Viney. 9 Oct. 2013.

126. Stewart, 256-258.

127. Ibid.

128. McMaster, 4.

129. Stewart, 258; McMaster, 14.

130. Stewart, 258; Jordan, 77-78.

131. Jordan, 77-78, 86.

132. The New York Times. *Gen. Earle Wheeler Dies; Ex-Head of Joint Chiefs*. 19 Dec. 1975; Stewart, 258; Wheeler, Gilmore. *Untitled Monograph*. 24.

133. Jordan, 77-78.

134. Stewart, 258-259.

135. Stewart, 259-260; Wheeler, Gilmore. *Untitled Monograph*. 24.

136. Stewart, 260.

137. Stewart, 260-263.

138. Ibid.

## Chapter 5

1. United States Army. *General Orders Number 26*. 19 Dec. 1975; Wheeler, Earle G. *Professional Resume*. 1971.

2. Ibid.

3. Ibid.

4. Wheeler, Frances R. Letter to Rebecca Howell. 3 Nov. 1958.

5. Ibid.

6. Wheeler, Frances R. Letter to Rebecca Howell. 3 Nov. 1958; United States Army. *Standard Form 88, Report of Medical Examination*. 12 Jan. 1960.

7. Wheeler, Frances R. Letter to Rebecca Howell. 3 Nov. 1958.

8. Wheeler, Frances R. Letter to Rebecca Howell. 10 Nov. 1958; Wheeler, Gilmore. Email to Mark Viney. 21 Nov. 2013.

9. Wheeler, Frances R. Letter to Rebecca Howell. 10 Nov. 1958.

10. Ibid.

11. Wheeler, Gilmore. Interview with Mark Viney. 9 Oct. 2013.

12. Wheeler, Frances R. Letter to Rebecca Howell. 26 Dec. 1958; Wheeler, Gilmore. Email to Mark Viney. 21 Nov. 2013.

13. Wheeler, Frances R. Letter to Rebecca Howell. 26 Dec. 1958.

14. Department of the Army. *DA Form 66*. 15 Feb. 1969; United States Army. *General Orders Number 26*. 19 Dec. 1975; Wheeler, Earle G. *Professional Resume*. 1971; Wheeler, Gilmore. Interview with Mark Viney. 10 Mar. 2013; Arlington National Cemetery. Downloaded from the internet on 13 Feb. 2013 from http://www. arlingtoncemetery. net/ ewheeler. htm.

15. Stewart, 256.

16. Stewart, 290.

17. Wheeler, Frances R. Letter to Rebecca Howell. 9 Nov. 1959.

18. Ibid.

19. Ibid.

20. Wheeler, Gilmore. Interview with Mark Viney. 9 Oct. 2013.

21. Ibid.

22. Lawton Constitution. *Land Warfare Emphasis.* 2 Jul. 1964: page unknown; Army Historical Foundation. Downloaded from the internet on 13 Feb. 2013 from https://army-history. org/09/general-earle-g-wheeler/; Arlington National Cemetery. Downloaded from the internet on 13 Feb. 2013 from http://www. arlingtoncemetery. net/ewheeler. htm.

23. The New York Times. *Gen. Earle Wheeler Dies; Ex-Head of Joint Chiefs.* 19 Dec. 1975; Philadelphia Inquirer. *Change of Guard Over S. Vietnam.* 24 Jun. 1964.

24. Wheeler, Earle G. *Interview with Chester Clifton.* 1964: 6.

25. Stewart, 290-291.

26. Ibid.

27. Scribner, Charles R. *The Eisenhower and Johnson Administrations' Decisionmaking on Vietnamese Intervention: A Study of Contrasts.* Ph. D. diss., University of California Santa Barbara, 1980: 59-60.

28. McMaster, 3.

29. McNamara, Robert S. *In Retrospect: The Tragedy and Lessons of Vietnam.* New York: Times Books, 1995: 70, 94.

30. McMaster, 3-4.

31. McNamara, 95.

32. McMaster, 4-5.

33. Herspring, Dale R. *The Pentagon and the Presidency, Civil-Military Relations from FDR to George W. Bush.* Lawrence, KS: University Press of Kansas, 2005: 123.

34. Stewart, 263.

35. Stewart, 263-264.

36. Ibid.

37. Stewart, 264; Scribner, 60.

38. Ibid; Wheeler, Earle G. *Interview with Chester Clifton.* 1964: 23.

39. McMaster, 6-7.

40. Herspring, 118.

41. McMaster, 8.

42. Ibid.

43. Ibid; Scribner, 59-60.

44. McMaster, 8-10.

45. Wheeler, Earle G. *Interview with Chester Clifton.* 1964: 67.

46. McMaster, 8-10.

47. Washington Post. *Taylor Marked Wheeler Early for High Military Responsibility.* 24 Jun. 1964: A14; United States Army. Walter Reed General Hospital. *Clinical Record.* 22 Apr. 1970.

48. McMaster, 10.

49. Joint Chiefs of Staff. *Wheeler Addresses.* 145.

50. McMaster, 10-13.

51. Ibid.

52. Ibid.

53. McMaster, 14-15; Jordan, 71

54. McMaster, 15-17.

55. Ibid.

56. Ibid.

57. Ibid.

58. Ibid.

59. Prados, John. *Vietnam, The History of an Unwinnable War, 1945-1975.* Lawrence, KS: University Press of Kansas, 2009: 97-98.

60. Wheeler, Earle G. *Interview with Chester Clifton.* 1964: 68.

61. McMaster, 17-18.

62. Ibid.

63. McNamara, 176.

64. Wheeler, Earle G. *Interview with Chester Clifton.* 1964: 3-4.

65. Wheeler, Earle G. *Interview with Chester Clifton.* 1964: 31; McMaster, 17-18; Journal Register. *New JCS Chairman.* 27 Jun. 1964: page unknown.

66. McMaster, 17-18.

67. McNamara, xv; McMaster, 18-19.

68. McMaster, 19.

69. Dorland, Gilbert N. *Legacy of Discord: Voices of the Vietnam Era*. Washington, DC:Brassey's, 2001: 161.

70. Dorland, 18.

71. Dorland, 185.

72. McMaster, 20-21.

73. Ibid.

74. Ibid.

75. McMaster, 265-266.

76. McMaster, 293-294.

77. Stewart, 273.

78. McMaster, 294; Stewart, 294.

79. Millet, Maslowski, and Feis, 514; Scribner, 61-62.

80. Scribner, 61-62, 63-64.

81. Ibid.

82. Herspring, 142-143.

83. Stewart, 294-295.

84. Stewart, 278-279.

85. McMaster, 273-274.

86. Wheeler, Frances R. Letter to Rebecca Howell. 29 Dec. 1961; Wheeler, Gilmore. Emails to Mark Viney. 29 Jul. and 21 Nov. 2013; Wheeler, Gilmore. Interview with Mark Viney. 9 Oct. 2013.

87. Wheeler, Gilmore. Interview with Mark Viney. 24 Apr. 2013.

88. Wheeler, Gilmore S. *Doneld Howell*. Monograph. 25 Apr. 2014.

89. Stewart, 280.

90. Wheeler, Gilmore. Interview with Mark Viney. 24 Apr. 2013.

91. Ibid.

92. Wheeler, Gilmore. Email to Mark Viney. 30 Dec. 2013.

93. United States Army. *General Orders Number 26*. 19 Dec. 1975; Department of the Army. *DA Form 66*. 15 Feb. 1969; Wheeler, Gilmore. Interview with Mark Viney. 25 Feb. 2013.

94. Wheeler, Gilmore. Interviews with Mark Viney. 25 Feb., 10 Mar., and 9 Oct. 2013; Army Historical Foundation. Downloaded from the internet on 13 Feb. 2013 from https://armyhistory. org/09/general-earle-g-wheeler/; Arlington National Cemetery. Downloaded from the internet on 13 Feb. 2013 from http://www. arlingtoncemetery. net/ewheeler. htm; The Forgotten General. Downloaded from the internet on 13 Feb. 2013 from http://theforgottengeneral. com/wp-content/uploads/2010/12/JCS-Biography. pdf.

95. Jordan, XII, 124, 125, 129, 131, 133.

96. Jordan, 124-125, 133; Wheeler, Gilmore. Interviews with Mark Viney. 25 Feb. and 10 Mar. 2013.

97. Wheeler, Frances R. Letter to Rebecca Howell. 27 Feb. 1962.

98. Wheeler, Frances R. Letter to Rebecca Howell. 11 Mar. 1962; Wheeler, Gilmore. Email to Mark Viney. 21 Nov. 2013.

99. Wheeler, Frances R. Letter to Rebecca Howell. 11 Mar. 1962.

100. Arlington National Cemetery. Downloaded from the internet on 22 Oct. 2015 at http://www. arlingtoncemetery. net/bespivy. htm.

101. Wheeler, Frances R. Letter to Rebecca Howell. 11 Mar. 1962.

102. Ibid.

103. Ibid.

104. Wheeler, Frances R. Letter to Rebecca Howell. 18 Mar. 1962.

105. Ibid; Frances R. Wheeler. Interviews with Gilmore S. Wheeler, 2004. Disc 5.

106. Wheeler, Frances R. Letter to Rebecca Howell. 26 Mar. 1962.

107. Wheeler, Frances R. Letter to Rebecca Howell. 18 Mar. 1962.

108. Wheeler, Frances R. Letter to Rebecca Howell. 26 Mar. 1962.

109. Ibid.

110. Ibid.

111. Wheeler, Gilmore. Interview with Mark Viney. 9 Oct. 2013.

112. Wheeler, Frances R. Letter to Rebecca Howell. 26 Mar. 1962.

113. Long, William M. Letter to Walter R. Howell. 9 Apr. 1962.

114. Howell, Walter R. Letter to Gilmore S. Wheeler. 16 Apr. 1962.

115. Wheeler, Earle G. Letter to Gilmore S. Wheeler. 3 Jun. 1962.

116. Stewart, 297-298.

117. Millet, Maslowski, and Feis, 514.

118. Scribner, 65-68.

119. Stewart, 269, 298.

120. Stewart, 273-276.

121. Ibid.

122. The New York Times. *Gen. Earle Wheeler Dies; Ex-Head of Joint Chiefs*. 19 Dec. 1975; Stewart, 276.

123. Stewart, 270-271; 247. Baltimore Sun. *A Military Man is Chosen and Chief Knows Him Well*. 24 Jun. 1964; Journal of Mississippi History. *"The Fight for Men's Minds': The Aftermath of the Ole Miss Riot of 1962*. Spring 2009: 1-53; Wheeler, Gilmore. Interview with Mark Viney. 9 Oct. 2013.

124. McMaster, 22-23, 45, 109; Bell, William G. *Commanding Generals and Chiefs of Staff, 1775-1991, Portraits & Biographical Sketches of the United States Army's Senior Officer*. Washington DC: United States Army Center of Military History, 1992. Hereafter cited as Bell. *Commanding Generals*. The New York Times. *Gen. Earle Wheeler Dies; Ex-Head of Joint Chiefs*. 19 Dec. 1975; Philadelphia Inquirer. *Change of Guard Over S. Vietnam*. 24 Jun. 1964: 3; Source unknown. *Chiefs Chairman Gen. Wheeler Retires Today*. 2 Jul. 1970.

125. Ibid.

126. Wheeler, Gilmore. Interviews with Mark Viney. 25 Feb. and 10 Mar. 2013; Baltimore Sun. *A Military Man is Chosen and Chief Knows Him Well*. 24 Jun 1964: 1; Army Historical Foundation. Downloaded from the internet on 13 Feb. 2013 from https://armyhistory. org/09/general-earle-g-wheeler/; Arlington National Cemetery. Downloaded from the internet on 13 Feb. 2013 from http://www. arlingtoncemetery. net/ewheeler. htm; The Forgotten General. Downloaded from the internet on 13 Feb. 2013 from http://theforgot-tengeneral. com/wp-content/uploads/2010/12/JCS-Biography. pdf.

127. Wheeler, Gilmore. Email to Mark Viney. 3 Jul. 2014.

128. Wheeler, Frances R. Letter to Rebecca Howell. 17 Sep. 1962.

129. Ibid; United States Air Force. Downloaded from the internet on 4 Jul. 2018 at http:www. af. mil/About-Us/Biographies/Display/Article/106325/general-john-paul-mcconnell/.

130. Wheeler, Frances R. Letter to Rebecca Howell. 17 Sep. 1962.

131. Ibid.

132. Department of the Army. *DA Form 66.* 15 Feb. 1969; Wheeler, Frances R. Letter to Rebecca Howell. 26 Sep. 1962.

## Chapter 6

1. Scribner, 93.

2. Wheeler, Earle G. *Interview with Chester Clifton.* 1964: 58.

3. Ibid.

4. Ibid.

5. Wheeler, Gilmore. Interviews with Mark Viney. 25 Feb. and 10 Mar. 2013.

6. Wheeler, Frances R. Letter to Rebecca Howell. 26 Sep. 1962.

7. Ibid.

8. Wheeler, Frances R. Letter to Rebecca Howell. 3 Oct. 1962.

9. Odom, Louie W. *Challenging Journey: An Autobiography.* Publisher Unknown, 2008, 168.

10. Ibid.

11. Ibid.

12. McMaster, 22.

13. McNamara, 54; McMaster, 22-23.

14. Stewart, 266, 268-269.

15. Ibid.

16. McMaster, 24-26.

17. Odom, 192.

18. Stewart, 266.

19. Wheeler, Earle G. *Interview with Chester Clifton.* 1964: 59-60.

20. McMaster, 26-27.

21. Ibid

22. Palmer, Bruce Jr. *The 25-Year War, America's Role on Vietnam.* New York: Da Capo Press, 1984: 20; McMaster, 27-28.

23. Stewart, 266-267.

24. Wheeler, Earle G. *Interview with Chester Clifton.* 1964: 60-61.

25. Wheeler, Gilmore. Interviews with Mark Viney. 10 Mar. 2013 and 20 April 2016.

26. McMaster, 29-30.

27. Ibid, 30-31, 44; Watson, George M. *Secretaries and Chiefs of Staff of the United States Air Force.* Washington, DC: Air Force History and Museums Program, 2001. Hereafter cited as Watson. *Secretaries.* New York Times. *David Lamar McDonald, 91, Former Senior Naval Officer.* 23 Dec. 1997.

28. Odom, 167, 169-170.

29. Ibid.

30. Ibid.

31. Ibid.

32. Wheeler, Frances R. Letter to Rebecca Howell. 26 Nov. 1962.

33. Ibid.

34. Wheeler, Earle G. *Interview with Chester Clifton.* 1964: 68-69.

35. Stewart, 275-276, 279-280.

36. McMaster, 30-32.

37. Ibid.

38. Stewart, 298-300.

39. Odom, 182-183.

40. McNamara, 44-45; Odom, 183.

41. Odom, 182-184.

42. Ibid.

43. Ibid.

44. Ibid.

45. Ibid.

46. Department of the Army. Office of the Chief of Staff of the Army. Photo Album. *General Earle G. Wheeler.* Jun. 1964. Covers period 1 October 1962 – 28 February 1963; Department of the Army. Office of the Chief of Staff of the Army. Photo Album. *General Earle G. Wheeler.* Jun. 1964. Covers period January - May 1963; Department of the Army. Office of the Chief of Staff of the Army. Photo Album. *General Earle G. Wheeler.* Jun. 1964. Covers Wheeler's trip to Vietnam, 16-21 January 1963.

47. Odom, 185-186.

48. Ibid.

49. Ibid.

50. Department of the Army. Office of the Chief of Staff of the Army. Photo Album. *General Earle G. Wheeler*. Jun. 1964. Covers period 1 October 1962 – 28 February 1963; Department of the Army. Office of the Chief of Staff of the Army. Photo Album. *General Earle G. Wheeler*. Jun. 1964. Covers period January - May 1963; Department of the Army. Office of the Chief of Staff of the Army. Photo Album. *General Earle G. Wheeler*. Jun. 1964. Covers Wheeler's trip to Vietnam, 16-21 January 1963; Odom, 185.

51. Odom, 185-186.

52. McMaster, 38; Herspring, 144-145; The Forgotten General. Downloaded from the internet on 13 Feb. 2013 from http://theforgottengeneral. com/wp-content/uploads/2010/12/JCS-Biography. pdf.

53. Herspring, 144-145.

54. Stewart, 270, 277.

55. Wheeler, Frances R. Letter to Rebecca Howell. 10 Mar. 1963.

56. Ibid.

57. Department of the Army. Office of the Chief of Staff of the Army. Photo Album. *General Earle G. Wheeler*. Jun. 1964. Covers period 1 October 1962 – 28 February 1963.

58. Wheeler, Frances R. Letter to Rebecca Howell. 24 Mar. 1963.

59. Ibid.

60. Wheeler, Frances R. Letter to Rebecca Howell. 7 Apr. 1963.

61. Odom, 219.

62. Wheeler, Frances R. Letter to Rebecca Howell. 3 Apr. 1963.

63. United States Army. Walter Reed General Hospital. *Clinical Record*. 22 Apr. 1970; Wheeler, Frances R. Letter to Rebecca Howell. 24 Mar. 1963.

64. Wheeler, Frances R. Letters to Rebecca Howell. 3 and 7 Apr. 1963.

65. Wheeler, Frances R. Letters to Rebecca Howell. 7 and 9 Apr. 1963.

66. Wheeler, Frances R. Letter to Rebecca Howell. 14 Apr. 1963.

67. Wheeler, Frances R. Letter to Rebecca Howell. 20 Apr. 1963.

68. Department of the Army. Office of the Chief of Staff of the Army. Photo Album. *General Earle G. Wheeler*. Jun. 1964. Covers period January - May 1963.

69. Wheeler, Frances R. Letter to Rebecca Howell. 29 Apr. 1963; Wheeler, Gilmore. Email to Mark Viney. 21 Nov. 2013.

70. Wheeler, Frances R. Letter to Rebecca Howell. 29 Apr. 1963.

71. Wheeler, Frances R. Letter to Rebecca Howell. 8 Jun. 1963.

72. Department of the Army. Office of the Chief of Staff of the Army. Photo Album. *General Earle G. Wheeler*. Jun. 1964. Covers period January - May 1963; Department of the Army. Office of the Chief of Staff of the Army. Photo Album. *General Earle G. Wheeler*. Jun. 1964. Covers period 16 January – 22 June 1964; United States Army. Office of the Administrative Assistant to the Secretary of the Army. The Institute of Heraldry. Downloaded from the internet on 16 Dec. 2017 at http://www. tioh. hqda. pentagon. mil/Catalog/Heraldry. aspx?HeraldryId=15493&CategoryId=9148&grp=2&menu=Uniformed%20 Services&ps=24&p=0.

73. Stewart, 271.

74. Odom, 197-198.

75. Ibid.

76. Wheeler, Frances R. Letter to Rebecca Howell. 8 Jun. 1963.

77. Ibid.

78. Department of the Army. Office of the Chief of Staff of the Army. Photo Album. *General Earle G. Wheeler*. Jun. 1964. Covers period January - May 1963.

79. Odom, 171.

80. Ibid.

81. Ibid.

82. Wheeler, Frances R. Letter to Rebecca Howell. 26 May 1963.

83. Ibid.

84. Ibid.

85. Ibid.

86. Ibid; Wheeler, Frances R. Letter to Rebecca Howell. 27 May 1963.

87. Wheeler, Frances R. Letter to Rebecca Howell. 29 Apr. 1963.

88. Odom, 173-174.

89. Ibid.

90. Ibid.

91. Ibid.

92. Department of the Army. Office of the Chief of Staff of the Army. Photo Album. *General Earle G. Wheeler*. Jun. 1964. Covers period January - May 1963; Wheeler, Frances

R. Letters to Rebecca Howell. 27 and 29 May 1963; Wheeler, Gilmore. Email to Mark Viney. 21 Nov. 2013.

93. Ibid.

94. Ibid.

95. Wheeler, Frances R. Letters to Rebecca Howell. 29 May and 10 Jun. 1963.

96. Department of the Army. Office of the Chief of Staff of the Army. Photo Album. *General Earle G. Wheeler.* Jun. 1964. Covers period January - May 1963; Wheeler, Frances R. Letter to Rebecca Howell. 10 Jun. 1963.

97. Ibid.

98. Wheeler, Frances R. Letter to Rebecca Howell. 10 Jun. 1963; Wheeler, Gilmore. Email to Mark Viney. 21 Nov. 2013.

99. Department of the Army. Office of the Chief of Staff of the Army. Photo Album. *General Earle G. Wheeler.* Jun. 1964. Covers period 1 June – 28 July 1963; Wheeler, Frances R. Letter to Rebecca Howell. 10 Jun. 1963.

100. Department of the Army. Office of the Chief of Staff of the Army. Photo Album. *General Earle G. Wheeler.* Jun. 1964. Covers period 1 June – 28 July 1963.

101. Ibid; Department of the Army. Office of the Chief of Staff of the Army. Photo Album. *General Earle G. Wheeler.* Jun. 1964. Covers period 1 June – 28 July 1963; Wheeler, Frances R. Letter to Rebecca Howell. 4 May 1963.

102. Odom, 172-173.

103. Ibid.

104. Ibid.

105. Ibid.

106. Department of the Army. Office of the Chief of Staff of the Army. Photo Album. *General Earle G. Wheeler.* Jun. 1964. Covers period 5 August – 20 December 1963.

107. Ibid.

108. Odom, 198.

109. Department of the Army. Office of the Chief of Staff of the Army. Photo Album. *General Earle G. Wheeler.* Jun. 1964. Covers period 5 August – 20 December 1963; Wheeler, Gilmore. *Untitled Monograph.* 28.

110. Odom, 179-181.

111. Ibid.

112. Ibid.

113. Frances R. Wheeler. Interviews with Gilmore S. Wheeler, 2004. Disk 5.

114. Department of the Army. Office of the Chief of Staff of the Army. Photo Album. *General Earle G. Wheeler.* Jun. 1964. Covers period 5 August – 20 December 1963.

115. Stewart, 267-268, 300.

116. Millet, Maslowski, and Feis, 515.

117. Stewart, 300; Millet, Maslowski, and Feis, 515.

118. McMaster, 38-39.

119. Wheeler, Earle G. *Interview with Chester Clifton.* 1964: 66; Stewart, 300; Millet, Maslowski, and Feis, 515; Scribner, 68, 70-71.

120. Stewart, 300; Millet, Maslowski, and Feis, 515; Herring, George C. *America's Longest War, The United States and Vietnam, 1950-1975.* Fourth Edition. Boston: McGraw Hill, 2002: 132.

121. McMaster, 41.

122. Wheeler, Earle G. *Interview with Chester Clifton.* 1964: 66, 71.

123. Wheeler, Earle G. *Interview with Chester Clifton.* 1964: 66.

124. Odom, 194.

125. Wheeler, Frances R. Letter to Rebecca Howell. 26 Nov. 1963.

126. Odom, 194.

127. Ibid.

128. Wheeler, Frances R. Letter to Rebecca Howell. 26 Nov. 1963.

129. Ibid; Manchester, William. *The Death of a President.* New York: Harper & Row, 1967: 548.

130. Odom, 195.

131. Ibid.

132. Ibid.

133. Ibid.

134. Department of the Army. Office of the Chief of Staff of the Army. Photo Album. *General Earle G. Wheeler.* Jun. 1964. Covers period 5 August – 20 December 1963; Wheeler, Frances R. Letter to Rebecca Howell. 26 Nov. 1963; Wheeler, Earle G. *Letter to Walter R. Howell.* 29 Nov. 1963.

135. Wheeler, Earle G. *Letter to Walter R. Howell.* 29 Nov. 1963.

136. Ibid.

## Chapter 7

1. Joint Chiefs of Staff. *Wheeler Addresses.* 167.

2. McNamara, 147; Scribner, 68.

3. McMaster, 41.

4. Herspring, 148-149.

5. McMaster, 42-43; Watson. *Secretaries.*

6. McMaster, 43-44.

7. Ibid.

8. Ibid.

9. Palmer, Bruce. 20; McMaster, 44-45.

10. McMaster, 48; Herring, 135-136.

11. Herring, 136-137.

12. McNamara, 30.

13. McMaster, 48-49.

14. Herring, 135.

15. McNamara, 98-99.

16. Herring, 135.

17. McMaster, 50-51.

18. Scribner, 167-168.

19. Scribner, 168-169; Wheeler, Gilmore S. Interview with Mark A. Viney. 8 Nov. 2010.

20. McMaster, 51-53.

21. Herspring, 150.

22. McMaster, 51-53.

23. Wheeler, Frances R. Letter to Rebecca Howell. 14 Jan. 1964.

24. Ibid.

25. Ibid.

26. Department of the Army. Office of the Chief of Staff of the Army. Photo Album. *General Earle G. Wheeler.* Jun. 1964. Covers period 16 January – 22 June 1964; Wheeler, Frances R. Letter to Rebecca Howell. 16 Jan. 1964.

27. Wheeler, Frances R. Letter to Rebecca Howell. 17 Jan. 1964.

28. Department of the Army. Office of the Chief of Staff of the Army. Photo Album. *General Earle G. Wheeler*. Jun. 1964. Covers period 16 January – 22 June 1964; Department of the Army. Office of the Chief of Staff of the Army. Photo Album. *General Earle G. Wheeler*. Jun. 1964.

29. Scribner, 94.

30. McMaster, 63.

31. Palmer, Bruce. 20; Westmoreland, 144.

32. Department of the Army. Office of the Chief of Staff of the Army. Photo Album. *General Earle G. Wheeler*. Jun. 1964. Covers period 16 January – 22 June 1964.

33. Wheeler, Frances R. Letter to Rebecca Howell. 9 Mar. 1964; Wheeler, Gilmore. Email to Mark Viney. 21 Nov. 2013.

34. Covello, Hank. Interview with Mark Viney. 7 Jun. 2013.

35. Ibid; Wheeler, Gilmore. Interview with Mark Viney. 10 Mar. 2013.

36. Ibid.

37. Wheeler, Gilmore. Interview with Mark Viney. 25 Feb. 2013; Stewart, Bill. Interview with Mark A. Viney. 7 Nov. 2013.

38. Wheeler, Frances R. Letter to Rebecca Howell. 9 Mar. 1964; Covello, Hank. Interview with Mark Viney. 7 Jun. 2013.

39. Covello, Hank. Interview with Mark Viney. 7 Jun. 2013; Stewart, Bill. Interview with Mark A. Viney. 7 Nov. 2013.

40. Ibid.

41. Stewart, Bill. Interview with Mark A. Viney. 7 Nov. 2013.

42. Covello, Hank. Interview with Mark Viney. 7 Jun. 2013.

43. Ibid.

44. Wheeler, Gilmore S. Email to Mark Viney. 2 Feb. 2018.

45. Wheeler, Gilmore. Interview with Mark Viney. 25 Feb. 2013.

46. Wheeler, Gilmore. Interview with Mark Viney. 24 Apr. 2013.

47. Covello, Hank. Interview with Mark Viney. 7 Jun. 2013; Stewart, Bill. Interview with Mark A. Viney. 7 Nov. 2013.

48. Covello, Hank. Interview with Mark Viney. 7 Jun. 2013.

49. Wheeler, Frances R. Letters to Rebecca Howell. 27 and 30 Mar. 1964.

50. Wheeler, Frances R. Letter to Rebecca Howell. 30 Mar. 1964.

51. McMaster, 88; New York Times. *The Cold Warrior Who Never Apologized*. 8 Sep. 2017.

52. McMaster, 88-89.

53. Wheeler, Earle G. Interview with Dorothy P. McSweeny. Interview I, 21 Aug. 1969; McMaster, 89; Petitt, Clyde E. *The Experts*. Secaucus, NJ: Lyle Stuart, Inc., 1975: 212; Perry, x; New York Times. *The Cold Warrior Who Never Apologized*. 8 Sep. 2017. There is considerable disagreement among historians over when Johnson granted Wheeler a regular seat in his Tuesday luncheons. Petitt claims it did not happen until eighteen months into Johnson's term (June 1966). Perry says it occurred in October 1967. Wheeler himself stated in 1969 that he became a regular participant after Walt Rostow became National Security Advisor (April 1966).

54. Department of the Army. Office of the Chief of Staff of the Army. Photo Album. *General Earle G. Wheeler*. Jun. 1964. Covers period 16 January – 22 June 1964; McMaster, 94.

55. Wheeler, Frances R. Letter to Rebecca Howell. 18 Apr. 1964.

56. Ibid.

57. Ibid.

58. Ibid.

59. Ibid.

60. Department of the Army. Office of the Chief of Staff of the Army. Photo Album. *General Earle G. Wheeler*. Jun. 1964. Covers period 16 January – 22 June 1964;Wheeler, Frances R. Letter to Rebecca Howell. 18 Apr. 1964.

61. Wheeler, Frances R. Letter to Rebecca Howell. 15 May 1964.

62. Ibid; Wheeler, Gilmore. Email to Mark Viney. 21 Nov. 2013.

63. Wheeler, Frances R. Letter to Rebecca Howell. 15 May 1964; Wheeler, Gilmore. Interview with Mark Viney. 25 Feb. 2013; Wheeler, Gilmore. Email to Mark Viney. 21 Nov. 2013.

64. Stewart, Bill. Interview with Mark Viney. 20 Oct. 2013. Stewart retired in 1985 as a Sergeant Major after having served as a Senior Enlisted Aide to three Chiefs of Staff of the Army (Wheeler, Abrams, Rogers), two Chairmen of the Joint Chiefs of Staff (Wheeler, Vessey), one SACEUR (Rogers), as well as Generals Hollis and Crittenberger.

65. Stewart, Bill. Interview with Mark Viney. 20 Oct. 2013; Wheeler, Gilmore. Interview with Mark Viney. 10 Mar. 2013.

66. Stewart, Bill. Interview with Mark Viney. 20 Oct. 2013.

67. Ibid; Wheeler, Gilmore. Interview with Mark Viney. 10 Mar. 2013.

68. Stewart, Bill. Interview with Mark A. Viney. 7 Nov. 2013.

69. Stewart, Bill. Interview with Mark Viney. 20 Oct. 2013; Wheeler, Gilmore. Interview with Mark Viney. 10 Mar. 2013.

70. Stewart, Bill. Interview with Mark A. Viney. 7 Nov. 2013; Wheeler, Gilmore. Interview with Mark Viney. 25 Feb. 2013; Wheeler, Gilmore. *Untitled Monograph*. 27.

71. Department of the Army. Office of the Chief of Staff of the Army. Photo Album. *General Earle G. Wheeler*. Jun. 1964. Covers period 16 January – 22 June 1964; Wheeler, Frances R. Letter to Rebecca Howell. 22 May 1964.

72. Wheeler, Frances R. Letter to Rebecca Howell. 27 May 1964; Wheeler, Gilmore. Email to Mark Viney. 21 Nov. 2013.

73. Bell; Wheeler, Frances R. Letter to Rebecca Howell. 31 May 1964.

74. National Observer. *General Wheeler's Rising Stars, It's 3-for-3 for the Army As Taylor 'Protégé' Gets Top Job*. 29 Jun. 1964: 2; Wheeler, Frances R. Letter to Rebecca Howell. 31 May 1964.

75. Wheeler, Frances R. Letter to Rebecca Howell. 31 May 1964.

76. Ibid.

77. Department of the Army. Office of the Chief of Staff of the Army. Photo Album. *General Earle G. Wheeler*. Jun. 1964. Covers period 16 January – 22 June 1964; Monsanto Co. *Biographical Sketch of Gen. Earle G. Wheeler, U.S. Army (Retired)*. Sep. 1970; Wheeler, Frances R. Letter to Rebecca Howell. 31 May 1964; Odom, 175, 216.

78. Odom, 175, 216.

79. Wheeler, Frances R. Letter to Rebecca Howell. 9 Jun. 1964; Wheeler, Gilmore. Email to Mark Viney. 21 Nov. 2013.

80. Odom, Louie W. Letter to Gilmore S. Wheeler. 19 Mar. 2013.

81. Wheeler, Frances R. Letter to Rebecca Howell. 9 Jun. 1964; Wheeler, Gilmore. Email to Mark Viney. 21 Nov. 2013.

82. Wheeler, Frances R. Letter to Rebecca Howell. 22 Jun. 1964.

83. Ibid.

84. Wheeler, Frances R. Letter to Rebecca Howell. 22 Jun. 1964; New York News. *Staff Chief*. 9 Jul. 1964: page unknown.

85. Wheeler, Frances R. Letter to Rebecca Howell. 22 Jun. 1964.

86. Ibid.

87. Ibid.

88. Ibid.

89. Ibid.

90. Ibid.

91. Ibid.

92. Ibid.

93. Millet, Maslowski, and Feis, 516.

94. Wheeler, Frances R. Letters to Rebecca Howell. 22 and 25 Jun. 1964.

95. Wheeler, Frances R. Letter to Rebecca Howell. 22 Jun. 1964; Wheeler, Gilmore. Interview with Mark Viney. 25 Feb. 2013.

96. McMaster, 106.

97. McMaster, 108.

98. McMaster, 108; National Observer. *General Wheeler's Rising Stars, It's 3-for-3 for the Army As Taylor 'Protégé" Gets Top Job*. 29 Jun. 1964: 2; Time. *Three Top Soldiers*. 6 Jul. 1964.

99. McMaster, 110, 370.

100. McMaster, 110; The Washington Post. *Pentagon Shift Shatters JCS Rotation Precedent*. 24 Jun. 1964: A12; New York Times. *Rotation Ended For Joint Chiefs*. 24 Jun. 1964: 13; Time. *Three Top Soldiers*. 6 Jul. 1964.

101. The Washington Post. *Pentagon Shift Shatters JCS Rotation Precedent*. 24 Jun. 1964: A12; Wheeler, Gilmore. Interview with Mark Viney. 25 Feb. 2013.

102. Baltimore Sun. *A Military Man is Chosen and Chief Knows Him Well*. 24 Jun. 1964.

103. The Washington Post. *Pentagon Shift Shatters JCS Rotation Precedent*. 24 Jun. 1964: A12.

104. New York Times. *New Military Top Man*. 8 Jul. 1964: 32.

105. Jordan, 3, 147.

106. Schlesinger, Arthur M. Jr. *The Cycles of American History*. Boston: Houghton Mifflin Harcourt, 1999: 13; Wheeler, Gilmore S. Interview with Mark A. Viney. 28 Aug. 2014.

107. Jordan, 58, 141, 144.

108. Jordan, 125.

109. McMaster, 108; New York News. *Staff Chief*. 9 Jul. 1964: page unknown.

110. New York Times. *New Military Top Man*. 8 Jul. 1964: 32.

111. The Washington Post. *Pentagon Shift Shatters JCS Rotation Precedent*. 24 Jun. 1964: A12; Washington Post. *Taylor Marked Wheeler Early for High Military Responsibility*. 24 Jun. 1964: A14; Time. *Three Top Soldiers*. 6 Jul. 1964.

112. McMaster, 109; Bell. *Commanding Generals*; The Washington Post. *Pentagon Shift Shatters JCS Rotation Precedent*. 24 Jun. 1964: A12; Baltimore Sun. *A Military Man is Chosen and Chief Knows Him Well*. 24 Jun. 1964; Washington Post. *Taylor Marked Wheeler Early for High Military Responsibility*. 24 Jun. 1964: A14.

113. McMaster, 109; Bell. *Commanding Generals*.; The Washington Post. *Pentagon Shift Shatters JCS Rotation Precedent*. 24 Jun. 1964: A12; Baltimore Sun. *A Military Man is Chosen and Chief Knows Him Well*. 24 Jun. 1964; Washington Post. *Taylor Marked Wheeler Early for High Military Responsibility*. 24 Jun. 1964: A14; New York News. *Staff Chief*. 9 Jul. 1964: page unknown.

114. Newsweek. *Merit Will Be Rewarded*. 3 Jul. 1964.

115. Wall Street Journal. *Military Chieftain*. 26 Jun. 1964: page unknown.

116. McMaster, 109-110; Palmer, Bruce. 20.

117. Washington Star. *Wheeler Aims to Ease Civilian-Military Gap*. 28 Jun. 1964: 7.

118. Ibid.

119. Ibid.

120. Ibid.

121. Ibid.

122. McMaster, 110.

123. Wheeler, Gilmore S. Interview with Mark A. Viney. 10 Mar. 2013.

124. Wheeler, Gilmore. Interview with Mark Viney. 25 Feb. 2013.

125. Bell. *Commanding Generals*; Bell, William G. *Secretaries of War and Secretaries of the Army, Portraits & Biographical Sketches*. Washington DC: United States Army Center of Military History, 1982. Hereafter cited as Bell. *Secretaries*. Baltimore Sun. *A Military Man is Chosen and Chief Knows Him Well*. 24 Jun. 1964; Time. *Three Top Soldiers*. 6 Jul. 1964; New York Times. *Gen. Earle Wheeler Dies; Ex-Head of Joint Chiefs*. 19 Dec. 1975; Army Historical Foundation. Downloaded from the internet on 13 Feb. 2013 from https://armyhistory. org/09/general-earle-g-wheeler/; The Forgotten General. Downloaded from the internet on 13 Feb. 2013 from http://theforgottengeneral. com/wp-content/uploads/2010/12/JCS-Biography. pdf.

126. Wheeler, Frances R. Letter to Rebecca Howell. 25 Jun. 1964.

127. Odom, 199.

128. Ibid.

129. Ibid.

130. Wheeler, Gilmore. Email to Mark Viney. 4 Apr. 2011.

131. Baltimore Sun. *Two Generals*. 28 Jun. 1964: page unknown; New York News. *Staff Chief*. 9 Jul. 1964: page unknown.

132. New York News. *Staff Chief*. 9 Jul. 1964: page unknown.

133. Ibid.

134. McMaster, 104-106, 110-111.

135. Ibid.

136. Pentagram News. *Gens. Wheeler, Johnson Send Messages*. 9 Jul. 1964: page unknown.

## *Chapter 8*

1. Scribner, 92.

2. Sorley, Lewis B. *Honorable Warrior: General Harold K. Johnson and the Ethics of Command*. Lawrence, KS: University Press of Kansas, 1998: 175. Hereafter cited as Sorley. *Honorable Warrior*.

3. Wheeler, Frances R. Letter to Rebecca Howell. 2-3 Jul. 1964.

4. Ibid.

5. Ibid.

6. United States Army. *General Orders Number 26*. 19 Dec. 1975; Department of the Army. Office of the Chief of Staff of the Army. Photo Album. *General Earle G. Wheeler, Chief of Staff, United States Army, October 1962, Chairman of the Joint Chiefs of Staff, July 1964*. Jul. 1964; Wheeler, Frances R. Letter to Rebecca Howell. 2-3 Jul. 1964.

7. Los Angeles Times. *Wheeler, Johnson Take Up New Posts*. 7 Jul. 1964: B-7.

8. Odom, 199.

9. Ibid.

10. Los Angeles Times. *Wheeler, Johnson Take Up New Posts*. 7 Jul. 1964: B-7; New York Herald Tribune. *Gen. Wheeler Aims for Harmony*. 7 Jul. 1964: 3; Wheeler, Frances R. Letter to Rebecca Howell. 9 Jul. 1964.

11. Ibid.

12. Pentagram News. *Gens. Wheeler, Johnson Send Messages*. 9 Jul. 1964: page unknown.

13. Wheeler, Frances R. Letter to Rebecca Howell. 9 Jul. 1964.

14. Ibid.

15. Washington Star. *General Wheeler Honored.* 7 Jul. 1964: B-7; Joint Chiefs of Staff. Office of the Chairman of the Joint Chiefs of Staff. *Photo Album for General Earle G. Wheeler, Chairman, 1964-1965.* Jul. 1970; Wheeler, Frances R. Letter to Rebecca Howell. 9 Jul. 1964.

16. Washington Star. *General Wheeler Honored.* 7 Jul. 1964: B-7

17. Wheeler, Frances R. Letter to Rebecca Howell. 9 Jul. 1964.

18. Ibid.

19. McMaster, 360, 370; Washington Post. *Gen. Henry W. Buse, Official of Olympic Panel, Dies at 76.* 22 Oct. 1988; Wheeler, Gilmore. Interview with Mark Viney. 10 Mar. 2013.

20. Odom, 200.

21. Ibid.

22. Ibid.

23. Ibid.

24. Joint Chiefs of Staff. *Wheeler Addresses.* 145.

25. Joint Chiefs of Staff. Office of the Chairman of the Joint Chiefs of Staff. *Photo Album for General Earle G. Wheeler, Chairman, 1964-1965.* Jul. 1970; Odom. In 2012, the author and Wheeler's son were granted special access to Room 2E878 while its current occupant, General Martin Dempsey, was out of the office.

26. Wheeler, Gilmore. Interview with Mark Viney. 10 Mar. 2013.

27. Wheeler, Frances R. Letter to Rebecca Howell. 20 Jul. 1964.

28. Ibid.

29. Ibid.

30. Wheeler, Earle G. Letter to Walter R. Howell. 20 Jul. 1964.

31. Wheeler, Frances R. Letter to Rebecca Howell. 2-3 Jul. 1964.

32. Ibid.

33. Wheeler, Frances R. Letter to Rebecca Howell. 9 Jul. 1964.

34. Wheeler, Frances R. Letter to Rebecca Howell. 20 Jul. 1964.

35. Wheeler, Frances R. Letter to Rebecca Howell. 28 Jul. 1964.

36. Wheeler, Frances R. Letters to Rebecca Howell. 15 Oct. 1964 and 26 Apr. 1965.

37. Stewart, Bill. Interview with Mark Viney. 20 Oct. 2013

38. Wheeler, Frances R. Letter to Rebecca Howell. 2-3 Jul. 1964.

39. Stewart, Bill. Interview with Mark Viney. 20 Oct. 2013.

40. Joint Chiefs of Staff. Office of the Chairman of the Joint Chiefs of Staff. *Photo Album for General Earle G. Wheeler, Chairman, 1964-1965*. Jul. 1970; Wheeler, Frances R. Letter to Rebecca Howell. 28 Jul. 1964.

41. The Washington Post. *A Cavalryman Hangs Up His Boots*. 29 Jul. 1964: C3.

42. Wheeler, Frances R. Letter to Rebecca Howell. 1 Aug. 1964.

43. Ibid.

44. Stewart, 302.

45. Scribner, 74-76.

46. Wheeler, Frances R. Letter to Rebecca Howell. 4 Aug. 1964.

47. Ibid.

48. New York Herald-Tribune. *Gen. Wheeler, New U.S. Top Military Man*. 19 Aug. 1964: 22.

49. Ibid.

50. Ibid.

51. Joint Chiefs of Staff. Office of the Chairman of the Joint Chiefs of Staff. *Photo Album for General Earle G. Wheeler, Chairman, 1964-1965*. Jul. 1970.

52. Wheeler, Gilmore S. *Linda Howell and Tony Lattore*. Monograph. 25 Apr. 2014.

53. Joint Chiefs of Staff. Office of the Chairman of the Joint Chiefs of Staff. *Photo Album for General Earle G. Wheeler, Chairman, 1964-1965*. Jul. 1970; Wheeler, Frances R. Letter to Rebecca Howell. 14 Jan. 1965.

54. Wheeler, Frances R. Letter to Rebecca Howell. 14 Jan. 1965.

55. Wheeler, Frances R. Letter to Rebecca Howell. 1 Feb. 1965.

56. Wheeler, Gilmore. Email to Mark Viney. 21 Nov. 2013.

57. Wheeler, Gilmore. Interview with Mark Viney. 25 Feb. 2013.

58. Wheeler, Frances R. Letter to Rebecca Howell. 1 Feb. 1965; McMaster, 222-223.

59. Wheeler, Frances R. Letter to Rebecca Howell. 1 Feb. 1965.

60. Ibid.

61. Joint Chiefs of Staff. Office of the Chairman of the Joint Chiefs of Staff. *Photo Album for General Earle G. Wheeler, Chairman, 1964-1965*. Jul. 1970; McMaster, 222-223.

62. McMaster, 222-224.

63. Washington Post. *Ex-Air Force Gen. John McConnell Dies.* 22 Nov. 1986.

64. Ibid; McMaster, 222-223.

65. McMaster, 222-223.

66. Wheeler, Frances R. Letter to Rebecca Howell. 9 Feb. 1965.

67. Wheeler, Gilmore. Interview with Mark Viney. 14 Mar. 2013.

68. Wheeler, Frances R. Letter to Rebecca Howell. 9 Feb. 1965; Scribner, 81-82.

69. Wheeler, Frances R. Letter to Rebecca Howell. 13 Feb. 1965; Millet, Maslowski, and Feis, 517-518; Herring, 153; Scribner, 81-82.

70. Wheeler, Frances R. Letter to Rebecca Howell. 13 Feb. 1965.

71. Herring, 155; Scribner, 83-84.

72. McMaster, 244.

73. Wheeler, Frances R. Letter to Rebecca Howell. 1 Mar. 1965.

74. Joint Chiefs of Staff. Office of the Chairman of the Joint Chiefs of Staff. *Photo Album for General Earle G. Wheeler, Chairman, 1964-1965.* Jul. 1970; Webb, Willard J. and Cole, Ronald H. *The Chairmen of the Joint Chiefs of Staff.* Washington, DC: Historical Division, Joint Chiefs of Staff, 1989: 75.

75. Joint Chiefs of Staff. Office of the Chairman of the Joint Chiefs of Staff. *Photo Album for General Earle G. Wheeler, Chairman, 1964-1965.* Jul. 1970; Wheeler, Frances R. Letter to Rebecca Howell. 19 Mar. 1965.

76. Wheeler, Frances R. Letter to Rebecca Howell. 6 Apr. 1965.

77. Wheeler, Frances R. Letter to Rebecca Howell. 26 Apr. 1965.

78. Wheeler, Frances R. Letter to Rebecca Howell. 26 Apr. 1965.

79. Wheeler, Frances R. Letter to Rebecca Howell. 28 Apr. 1965.

80. Wheeler, Frances R. Letters to Rebecca Howell. 26 Apr. and 19 May.

81. Wheeler, Frances R. Letter to Rebecca Howell. 2 May 1965; Stewart, 304; Sorley, *Honorable Warrior.* 145.

82. Wheeler, Frances R. Letter to Rebecca Howell. 2 May 1965.

83. Wheeler, Frances R. Letter to Rebecca Howell. 19 May 1965.

84. Ibid.

85. Wheeler, Frances R. Letter to Rebecca Howell. 21 May 1965.

86. Ibid.

87. Monsanto Co. *Biographical Sketch of Gen. Earle G. Wheeler, U.S. Army (Retired)*. Sep. 1970; Wheeler, Gilmore S. *Doneld Howell*.

88. Wheeler, Frances R. Letter to Rebecca Howell. 25 May 1965.

89. Ibid.

90. Scribner, 86, 119.

91. McNamara, xvii, 108.

92. Wheeler, Frances R. Letter to Rebecca Howell. 15 Jun. 1965; Joint Chiefs of Staff. Office of the Chairman of the Joint Chiefs of Staff. *Photo Album for General Earle G. Wheeler, Chairman, 1964-1965*. Jul. 1970.

93. Wheeler, Frances R. Letter to Rebecca Howell. 15 Jun. 1965.

94. Wheeler, Frances R. Letter to Rebecca Howell. 15 Jun. 1965; Stewart, Bill. Interview with Mark A. Viney. 7 Nov. 2013.

95. Wheeler, Gilmore. Interview with Mark Viney. 25 Feb. 2013.

96. Wheeler, Frances R. Letter to Rebecca Howell. 15 Jun. 1965; Joint Chiefs of Staff. Office of the Chairman of the Joint Chiefs of Staff. *Photo Album for General Earle G. Wheeler, Chairman, 1964-1965*. Jul. 1970.

97. Wheeler, Frances R. Letter to Rebecca Howell. 28 Jun. 1965.

98. Wheeler, Gilmore. Interview with Mark Viney. 10 Mar. 2013.

99. Wheeler, Frances R. Letter to Rebecca Howell. 28 Jun. 1965; Wheeler, Gilmore. Email to Mark Viney. 21 Nov. 2013; Bell. *Secretaries*.

100. Joint Chiefs of Staff. Office of the Chairman of the Joint Chiefs of Staff. *Photo Album for General Earle G. Wheeler, Chairman, 1965-1966*. Jul. 1970; Bell. *Secretaries*.

101. Wheeler, Frances R. Letter to Rebecca Howell. 14 Jul. 1965.

102. Joint Chiefs of Staff. Office of the Chairman of the Joint Chiefs of Staff. *Photo Album for General Earle G. Wheeler, Chairman, 1965-1966*. Jul. 1970.

103. Sharp and Westmoreland, 109; Scribner, 180.

104. Joint Chiefs of Staff. Office of the Chairman of the Joint Chiefs of Staff. *Photo Album for General Earle G. Wheeler, Chairman, 1965-1966*. Jul. 1970.

105. Wheeler, Frances R. Letter to Rebecca Howell. 9 Aug. 1965.

106. Ibid.

107. Wheeler, Frances R. Letter to Rebecca Howell. 17 Aug. 1965.

108. Wheeler, Frances R. Letter to Rebecca Howell. 17 Aug. 1965.

109. Covello, Hank. Interview with Mark Viney. 7 Jun. 2013; Wheeler, Gilmore. Interviews with Mark Viney. 24 Apr. and 25 Feb. 2013.

110. Wheeler, Frances R. Letter to Rebecca Howell. 17 Aug. 1965.

111. Joint Chiefs of Staff. Office of the Chairman of the Joint Chiefs of Staff. *Photo Album for General Earle G. Wheeler, Chairman, 1965-1966.* Jul. 1970.

112. Stewart, 309-310.

113. Wheeler, Frances R. Letter to Rebecca Howell. 8 Nov. 1965.

114. Wheeler, Frances R. Letter to Rebecca Howell. 15 Nov. 1965.

115. Wheeler, Frances R. Letter to Rebecca Howell. 23 Nov. 1965.

116. Ibid.

117. Ibid.

118. Sharp and Westmoreland, 110-111.

119. Joint Chiefs of Staff. Office of the Chairman of the Joint Chiefs of Staff. *Photo Album for General Earle G. Wheeler, Chairman, 1965-1966.* Jul. 1970.

120. Wheeler, Frances R. Letter to Rebecca Howell. 3 Dec. 1965.

121. Ibid.

122. Wheeler, Frances R. Letters to Rebecca Howell. 3 and 12 Dec. 1965; Wheeler, Gilmore. Email to Mark Viney. 21 Nov. 2013.

123. Wheeler, Frances R. Letter to Rebecca Howell. 24 Dec. 1965; Joint Chiefs of Staff. Office of the Chairman of the Joint Chiefs of Staff. *Photo Album for General Earle G. Wheeler, Chairman, 1965-1966.* Jul. 1970.

124. Wheeler, Frances R. Letter to Rebecca Howell. 24 Dec. 1965.

125. Ibid; Joint Chiefs of Staff. Office of the Chairman of the Joint Chiefs of Staff. *Photo Album for General Earle G. Wheeler, Chairman, 1965-1966.* Jul. 1970.

126. Wheeler, Frances R. Letter to Rebecca Howell. 31 Dec. 1965.

127. Ibid; Joint Chiefs of Staff. Office of the Chairman of the Joint Chiefs of Staff. *Photo Album for General Earle G. Wheeler, Chairman, 1965-1966.* Jul. 1970.

128. Wheeler, Frances R. Letter to Rebecca Howell. 31 Dec. 1965.

129. Wheeler, Gilmore. Interview with Mark Viney. 25 Feb. 2013.

130. Wheeler, Frances R. Letter to Rebecca Howell. 31 Dec. 1965; Wheeler, Gilmore. Interview with Mark Viney. 25 Feb. 2013.

131. Wheeler, Gilmore. Interview with Mark Viney. 25 Feb. 2013.

132. Wheeler, Frances R. Letters to Rebecca Howell. 24 and 31 Dec. 1965.

133. Wheeler, Frances R. Letter to Rebecca Howell. 31 Dec. 1965.

134. Wheeler, Frances R. Letter to Rebecca Howell. 24 Dec. 1965.

135. Wheeler, Frances R. Letter to Rebecca Howell. 13 Jan. 1966.

136. Ibid; Joint Chiefs of Staff. Office of the Chairman of the Joint Chiefs of Staff. *Photo Album for General Earle G. Wheeler, Chairman, 1965-1966*. Jul. 1970.

137. Wheeler, Frances R. Letter to Rebecca Howell. 13 Jan. 1966.

138. Wheeler, Frances R. Letter to Rebecca Howell. 28 Jan. 1966; Los Angeles Times. *Nicholas Katzenbach Dies at 90; Attorney General Under Johnson*. 10 May 2012.

139. Wheeler, Frances R. Letter to Rebecca Howell. 28 Jan. 1966.

140. Wheeler, Frances R. Letter to Rebecca Howell. 7 Feb. 1966.

141. United States Marine Corps. 52.

142. Dorland.

143. Wheeler, Frances R. Letter to Rebecca Howell. 7 Feb. 1966; C-Span. Downloaded from the internet on 31 Jan. 2017 at https://www. c-span. org/video/?404455-1/ general-james-gavin-testimony-1966-fulbright-vietnam-hearings.

144. Wheeler, Frances R. Letter to Rebecca Howell. 7 Feb. 1966.

145. Wheeler, Frances R. Letter to Rebecca Howell. 13 Feb. 1966.

146. Wheeler, Frances R. Letter to Rebecca Howell. 13 Mar. 1966.

147. Wheeler, Frances R. Letter to Rebecca Howell. 18 Mar. 1966; Wheeler, Gilmore. Email to Mark Viney. 21 Nov. 2013.

148. Wheeler, Frances R. Letter to Rebecca Howell. 18 Mar. 1966.

149. Wheeler, Gilmore S. Email to Mark Viney. 2 Feb. 2018.

150. Wheeler, Gilmore S. *Linda Howell and Tony Lattore*. Monograph. 25 Apr. 2014.

151. Wheeler, Gilmore. Email to Mark Viney. 5 May. 2013.

152. Stewart, Bill. Interview with Mark A. Viney. 7 Nov. 2013.

153. Joint Chiefs of Staff. Office of the Chairman of the Joint Chiefs of Staff. *Photo Album for General Earle G. Wheeler, Chairman, 1965-1966*. Jul. 1970; Wheeler, Gilmore. Email to Mark Viney. 21 Nov. 2013.

154. Wheeler, Frances R. Letter to Rebecca Howell. 27 Apr. 1966.

155. Wheeler, Frances R. Letter to Rebecca Howell. 30 Apr. 1966; Casey, George W. Conversation with Mark A. Viney. 25 Apr. 2018.

156. Wheeler, Earle G. Interview with Dorothy P. McSweeny. Interview I, 21 Aug. 1969: 6-7; Petitt, 212; Perry, 169; McMaster, 89, 362; New York Times. *The Cold Warrior Who Never Apologized.* 8 Sep. 2017.

157. Wheeler, Earle G. Interview with Dorothy P. McSweeny. Interview I, 21 Aug. 1969: 6-7, 15.

158. Wheeler, Frances R. Letter to Rebecca Howell. 3 May 1966.

159. Ibid; Wheeler, Frances R. Letter to Rebecca Howell. 9 May 1966.

160. Wheeler, Frances R. Letter to Rebecca Howell. 13 May 1966.

161. Wheeler, Gilmore. Interview with Mark Viney. 9 Oct. 2013.

162. Joint Chiefs of Staff. Office of the Chairman of the Joint Chiefs of Staff. *Photo Album for General Earle G. Wheeler, Chairman, 1965-1966.* Jul. 1970; Monsanto Co. *Biographical Sketch of Gen. Earle G. Wheeler, U.S. Army (Retired).* Sep. 1970.

163. Stewart, 268.

164. Wheeler, Frances R. Letter to Rebecca Howell. 19 Jun. 1966.

165. Wheeler, Frances R. Letter to Rebecca Howell. 7 Jul. 1966.

166. United States Army. Walter Reed General Hospital. *Clinical Record.* 22 Apr. 1970; Wheeler, Frances R. Letter to Rebecca Howell. 7 Jul. 1966; Wheeler, Gilmore S. Interview with Mark A. Viney. 3 Jul. 2014.

167. Wheeler, Frances R. Letter to Rebecca Howell. 30 Jun. 1966.

168. Wheeler, Frances R. Letter to Rebecca Howell. 11 Jul. 1966.

169. Wheeler, Frances R. Letter to Rebecca Howell. 21 Jul. 1966.

170. Wheeler, Frances R. Letter to Rebecca Howell. 25 Jul. 1966.

171. Wheeler, Frances R. Letter to Rebecca Howell. 30 Jul. 1966.

172. Wheeler, Frances R. Letter to Rebecca Howell. 8 Aug. 1966.

173. Ibid; Wheeler, Gilmore S. Interview with Mark A. Viney. 3 Jul. 2014.

174. Wheeler, Gilmore S. Interview with Mark A. Viney. 3 Jul. 2014.

175. Wheeler, Frances R. Letter to Rebecca Howell. 15 Aug. 1966.

176. Wheeler, Frances R. Letter to Rebecca Howell. 29 Aug. 1966.

177. Wheeler, Frances R. Letter to Rebecca Howell. 6 Sep. 1966.

178. Wheeler, Frances R. Letter to Rebecca Howell. 9 Sep. 1966.

179. Wheeler, Frances R. Letter to Rebecca Howell. 20 Sep. 1966.

180. Wheeler, Frances R. Letter to Rebecca Howell. 27 Sep. 1966.

181. Wheeler, Frances R. Letter to Rebecca Howell. 20 Sep. 1966.

182. Joint Chiefs of Staff. Office of the Chairman of the Joint Chiefs of Staff. *Photo Album for General Earle G. Wheeler, Chairman, 1966-1967.* Jul. 1970.

183. Joint Chiefs of Staff. *Wheeler Addresses.* 146, 149.

184. Wheeler, Frances R. Letter to Rebecca Howell. 9 Oct. 1966.

185. Wheeler, Frances R. Letter to Rebecca Howell. 19 Oct. 1966.

186. Joint Chiefs of Staff. Office of the Chairman of the Joint Chiefs of Staff. *Photo Album for General Earle G. Wheeler, Chairman, 1966-1967.* Jul. 1970.

187. Wheeler, Frances R. Letter to Rebecca Howell. 29 Nov. 1966.

188. Wheeler, Frances R. Letter to Rebecca Howell. 3 Dec. 1966.

189. Wheeler, Frances R. Letter to Rebecca Howell. 12 Dec. 1966.

190. Wheeler, Frances R. Letter to Rebecca Howell. 17 Dec. 1966; Wheeler, Gilmore. Email to Mark Viney. 21 Nov. 2013; United States Central Command. Downloaded from the internet on 4 Aug. 2018 at http://www. centcom. mil/ABOUT-US/LEADERSHIP/Article/904768/george-b-crist/. Christ's career survived the incident, and he retired as a 4-star general in 1988.

191. Wheeler, Frances R. Letter to Rebecca Howell. 17 Dec. 1966.

192. Odom, 300.

193. Wheeler, Frances R. Letter to Rebecca Howell. 26 Dec. 1966; Wheeler, Gilmore. Email to Mark Viney. 21 Nov. 2013.

194. Wheeler, Frances R. Letter to Rebecca Howell. 26 Dec. 1966; Wheeler, Gilmore. Email to Mark Viney. 21 Nov. 2013. Bim recalled Wiggam as an African-American NCO who generously loaned him his car whenever he needed it for a date.

195. Wheeler, Frances R. Letter to Rebecca Howell. 27 Dec. 1966.

196. Wheeler, Gilmore S. *Doneld Howell.*

197. Wheeler, Frances R. Letter to Rebecca Howell. 26 Dec. 1966.

198. Wheeler, Frances R. Letter to Rebecca Howell. 27 Dec. 1966.

## Chapter 9

1. Wheeler, Frances R. Letter to Rebecca Howell. 3 Jan. 1967; Wheeler, Gilmore. Email to Mark Viney. 21 Nov. 2013.

2. Wheeler, Gilmore. Emails to Mark Viney. 21 Nov. 2013 and 10 Jul. 2017.

3. Wheeler, Frances R. Letter to Rebecca Howell. 3 Jan. 1967; Wheeler, Gilmore. Email to Mark Viney. 21 Nov. 2013.

4. Joint Chiefs of Staff. Office of the Chairman of the Joint Chiefs of Staff. *Photo Album for General Earle G. Wheeler, Chairman, 1966-1967*. Jul. 1970.

5. Wheeler, Frances R. Letter to Rebecca Howell. 13 Jan. 1967.

6. Prados. *Vietnam*. 181-182.

7. Wheeler, Gilmore S. Email to Mark Viney. 2 Feb. 2018.

8. Wheeler, Frances R. Letter to Rebecca Howell. 6 Mar. 1967.

9. Wheeler, Frances R. Letter to Rebecca Howell. 10 Mar. 1967.

10. Wheeler, Frances R. Letter to Rebecca Howell. 15 Mar. 1967; Joint Chiefs of Staff. Office of the Chairman of the Joint Chiefs of Staff. *Photo Album for General Earle G. Wheeler, Chairman, 1966-1967*. Jul. 1970.

11. Wheeler, Frances R. Letter to Rebecca Howell. 18 Mar. 1967.

12. Wheeler, Frances R. Letter to Rebecca Howell. 15 Mar. 1967.

13. Wheeler, Frances R. Letter to Rebecca Howell. 18 Mar. 1967.

14. Wheeler, Frances R. Letter to Rebecca Howell. 28 Mar. 1967.

15. Supreme Headquarters Allied Powers Europe. Downloaded from the internet on 2 Jul. 2017 at https://shape. nato. int/page1463252.

16. Stewart, 268; Supreme Headquarters Allied Powers Europe. Downloaded from the internet on 2 Jul. 2017 at https://shape. nato. int/page1463252.

17. Ibid.

18. Joint Chiefs of Staff. *Wheeler Addresses*. 146-147.

19. Joint Chiefs of Staff. Office of the Chairman of the Joint Chiefs of Staff. *Photo Album for General Earle G. Wheeler, Chairman, 1966-1967*. Jul. 1970.

20. Wheeler, Frances R. Letters to Rebecca Howell. 6 and 8 Apr. 1967.

21. Wheeler, Frances R. Letter to Rebecca Howell. 8 Apr. 1967.

22. United States Air Force. 13-14; *Gravel Pentagon Papers. Volume V*. 73-75.

23. Wheeler, Frances R. Letter to Rebecca Howell. 25 Apr. 1967.

24. Ibid.

25. Sharp and Westmoreland, 153; Wheeler, Frances R. Letter to Rebecca Howell. 25 Apr. 1967.

26. Wheeler, Frances R. Letter to Rebecca Howell. 25 Apr. 1967.

27. United States Military Assistance Command, Vietnam. *General Westmoreland's History Notes.* 10-30 Apr. 1967.

28. Wheeler, Frances R. Letter to Rebecca Howell. 11 May 1967.

29. Joint Chiefs of Staff. Office of the Chairman of the Joint Chiefs of Staff. *Photo Album for General Earle G. Wheeler, Chairman, 1966-1967.* Jul. 1970.

30. Wheeler, Frances R. Letter to Rebecca Howell. 24 May 1967.

31. Wheeler, Frances R. Letter to Rebecca Howell. 31 May 1967.

32. Department of Defense. *Pentagon Papers.* Volume IV. 187; Wheeler, Gilmore. Interview with Mark Viney. 9 Oct. 2013.

33. Department of Defense. *Pentagon Papers.* Volume IV. 187.

34. Wheeler, Gilmore. Interview with Mark Viney. 9 Oct. 2013.

35. McNamara, 277.

36. Ibid, 273.

37. Wheeler, Frances R. Letter to Rebecca Howell. 7 Jun. 1967.

38. Wheeler, Frances R. Letter to Rebecca Howell. 12 Jun. 1967.

39. Wheeler, Frances R. Letter to Rebecca Howell. 23 Jun. 1967.

40. Wheeler, Gilmore S. *Linda Howell and Tony Lattore.*

41. Wheeler, Frances R. Letter to Rebecca Howell. 23 Jun. 1967.

42. Wheeler, Frances R. Letter to Rebecca Howell. 1 Jul. 1967.

43. Joint Chiefs of Staff. Office of the Chairman of the Joint Chiefs of Staff. *Photo Album for General Earle G. Wheeler, Chairman, 1966-1967.* Jul. 1970; Wheeler, Frances R. Letter to Rebecca Howell. 1 Jul. 1967.

44. Joint Chiefs of Staff. Office of the Chairman of the Joint Chiefs of Staff. *Photo Album for General Earle G. Wheeler, Chairman, 1967-1968.* Jul. 1970; Berman, 54.

45. Joint Chiefs of Staff. Office of the Chairman of the Joint Chiefs of Staff. *Photo Album for General Earle G. Wheeler, Chairman, 1967-1968.* Jul. 1970; United States Army. Walter

Reed General Hospital. *Clinical Record*. 22 Apr. 1970; Wheeler, Gilmore. Email to Mark Viney. 10 Jul. 2017.

46. Wheeler, Gilmore S. Email to Mark Viney. 2 Feb. 2018.

47. Ibid, 272.

48. Prados. *Vietnam*. 207.

49. Spivy 737.

50. Joint Chiefs of Staff. Office of the Chairman of the Joint Chiefs of Staff. *Photo Album for General Earle G. Wheeler, Chairman, 1967-1968*. Jul. 1970; Washington Post. Downloaded from the internet on 4 Jul. 2017 at https://www. washingtonpost. com/ archive/local/1997/12/20/admiral-aviator-david-mcdonald-dies-at-91/344cf55b-13b1-4515-829e-9abab41dfd90/?utm_term=. 81a3a7bd548d.

51. McNamara, 291.

52. Wheeler, Earle G. Letter to Lyndon B. Johnson, 5 Sep. 1967.

53. United States Pacific Command. *Back Channel Message from Admiral Sharp, CINCPAC, Hawaii, to General Wheeler, CJCS, Washington*. 7 Sep. 1967.

54. United States Army. Walter Reed General Hospital. *Clinical Record*. 22 Apr. 1970; Wheeler, Earle G. Interview with Dorothy P. McSweeny. Interview II, 7 May 1970; Wheeler, Gilmore. Email to Mark Viney. 10 Jul. 2017.

55. Wheeler, Gilmore. Interview with Mark Viney. 25 Feb. 2013.

56. Wheeler, Earle G. Letter to Leonard D. Heaton, 13 September 1967.

57. Wheeler, Earle G. Letter to J. M. Hodgson, 26 September 1967.

58. Spivy, 744; Stewart, Bill. Interview with Mark A. Viney. 7 Nov. 2013.

59. Wheeler, Gilmore S. *Linda Howell and Tony Lattore*.

60. Wheeler, Frances R. Letter to Rebecca Howell. 2 Oct. 1967; Wheeler, Gilmore. Email to Mark Viney. 21 Nov. 2013.

61. Perry, 177.

62. Joint Chiefs of Staff. *Wheeler Addresses*. 165.

63. Wheeler, Frances R. Letter to Rebecca Howell. 20 Oct. 1967.

64. Sharp and Westmoreland, 51; Stewart, 272; History. com. Downloaded from the internet on 5 Jul. 2017 at http://www. history. com/ this-day-in-history/100000-people-march-on-the-pentagon.

65. Stewart, 279.

66. Millet, Maslowski, and Feis, 539; Petitt, 339.

67. Wheeler, Frances R. Letter to Rebecca Howell. 17 Nov. 1967.

68. Wheeler, Frances R. Letter to Rebecca Howell. 19 Nov. 1967.

69. Ibid; Wheeler, Frances R. Letter to Rebecca Howell. 23 Nov. 1967.

70. Wheeler, Earle G. Letter to S. M. Wang. 18 Nov. 1967.

71. Wheeler, Frances R. Letter to Rebecca Howell. 19 Nov. 1967.

72. Wheeler, Frances R. Letter to Rebecca Howell. 23 Nov. 1967.

73. Westmoreland, 361.

74. Wheeler, Gilmore S. Email to Mark Viney. 2 Feb. 2018.

75. Wheeler, Frances R. Letter to Rebecca Howell. 19 Nov. 1967.

76. Joint Chiefs of Staff. *Wheeler Addresses*. 167.

77. Wheeler, Frances R. Letter to Rebecca Howell. 9 Dec. 1967.

78. Wheeler, Gilmore S. *Linda Howell and Tony Lattore.*

79. Joint Chiefs of Staff. Office of the Chairman of the Joint Chiefs of Staff. *Photo Album for General Earle G. Wheeler, Chairman, 1967-1968.* Jul. 1970; Petitt, 354; Schandler, 118.

80. Joint Chiefs of Staff. Office of the Chairman of the Joint Chiefs of Staff. *Photo Album for General Earle G. Wheeler, Chairman, 1967-1968.* Jul. 1970.

81. Wheeler, Frances R. Letter to Rebecca Howell. 20 Mar. 1968.

82. Wheeler, Earle G. Letter to Monica Rosa Lara. 19 Mar. 68.

83. Wheeler, Frances R. Letter to Rebecca Howell. 20 Mar. 1968.

84. Wheeler, Frances R. Letters to Rebecca Howell. 20 and 27 Mar. 1968; Wheeler, Gilmore. Email to Mark Viney. 21 Nov. 2013.

85. Herring, 249; Barrett, 710.

86. Wheeler, Frances R. Letter to Rebecca Howell. 27 Mar. 1968.

87. Wheeler, Gilmore S. Email to Mark Viney. 2 Feb. 2018.

88. McNamara, Margy. Letter to the Wheelers, Johnsons, McConnells, Moorers, and Chapmans. 12 Apr. 1968.

89. Stewart, 64-66: 272.

90. Petitt, 358.

91. Wheeler, Frances R. Letter to Rebecca Howell. 5 May 1968.

92. Joint Chiefs of Staff. Office of the Chairman of the Joint Chiefs of Staff. *Photo Album for General Earle G. Wheeler, Chairman, 1967-1968*. Jul. 1970.

93. Wheeler, Frances R. Letter to Rebecca Howell. 5 May 1968.

94. Wheeler, Frances R. Letter to Rebecca Howell. 12 May 1968.

95. Sharp and Westmoreland, 188; Bell. *Commanding Generals.*

96. Wheeler, Gilmore S. *Doneld Howell.*

97. Wheeler, Frances R. Letter to Rebecca Howell. 24 Jun. 1968.

98. Herring, 252.

99. Bell. *Commanding Generals.*

100. Department of Defense. *Ceremony Program, In Honor of General Earle G. Wheeler, Chairman, Joint Chiefs of Staff, Andrews Air Force Base, Maryland.* 2 Jul. 1970.

101. Wheeler, Gilmore S. *Linda Howell and Tony Lattore.*

102. Joint Chiefs of Staff. Office of the Chairman of the Joint Chiefs of Staff. *Photo Album for General Earle G. Wheeler, Chairman, 1968-1969*. Jul. 1970; Sharp and Westmoreland, xv.

103. Johnson, Lyndon B. Note to Earle G. Wheeler. 31 Aug. 1968.

104. Joint Chiefs of Staff. Office of the Chairman of the Joint Chiefs of Staff. *Photo Album for General Earle G. Wheeler, Chairman, 1968-1969*. Jul. 1970; Joint Chiefs of Staff. Office of the Chairman of the Joint Chiefs of Staff. *Photo Album for General Earle G. Wheeler, Chairman, 1968-1969*. Jul. 1970; United States European Command. Downloaded from the internet on 23 Jul. 2017 at www. eucom. mil/media-library/article/20939/the-man-who-moved-eucom-gen-david-a-burchinal.

105. Joint Chiefs of Staff. *Wheeler Addresses.* 212.

106. Perry, 199-201.

107. Stewart, 281, 370.

108. Joint Chiefs of Staff. Office of the Chairman of the Joint Chiefs of Staff. *Photo Album for General Earle G. Wheeler, Chairman, 1968-1969*. Jul. 1970.

109. Ibid; Wheeler, Gilmore S. Interview with Mark A. Viney. 16 Feb. 2010.

110. Joint Chiefs of Staff. Office of the Chairman of the Joint Chiefs of Staff. *Memorandum for General Wheeler, Subject: Proposed Response by CJCS.* 7 Jan. 1969.

111. Wheeler, Earle G. Letter to George A. Carver, Jr. 17 Jan. 1969.

112. Joint Chiefs of Staff. Office of the Chairman of the Joint Chiefs of Staff. *Photo Album for General Earle G. Wheeler, Chairman, 1968-1969*. Jul. 1970; Wheeler, Gilmore S. Interview with Mark A. Viney. 10 Mar. 2013.

113. Perry, 201-202.

114. Wheeler, Gilmore S. Interview with Mark A. Viney. 14 Mar. 2013; Perry, 203.

115. Perry, 204.

116. Wheeler, Gilmore S. Interview with Mark A. Viney. 14 Mar. 2013.

117. Department of Defense. Brochure. *In Honor of General Earle G. Wheeler, Chairman, Joint Chiefs of Staff, Andrews Air Force Base, Maryland, 2 July 1970*: Jul. 70.

118. Kissinger, Henry A. *White House Years*. Boston: Little, Brown, 1979: 34.

119. Kissinger, 34-35.

120. Herspring, 188-189, 414- 415.

121. Stewart, 370.

122. United States Army. Walter Reed General Hospital. *Clinical Record*. 22 Apr. 1970.

123. Wheeler, Frances R. Letter to Rebecca Howell. 30 Mar. 1969.

124. Wheeler, Frances R. Letter to Rebecca Howell. 30 Mar. 1969; Eisenhower Presidential Library. Downloaded from the internet on 26 Jul. 2017 at http://www. dwightdeisenhower. com/156/Funeral-Ceremony.

125. Joint Chiefs of Staff. *Back Channel Message from General Wheeler, CJCS, Washington, to General Abrams, COMUSMACV, Saigon, and Admiral McCain, CINCPAC, Hawaii*. 27 Mar. 1969.

126. Joint Chiefs of Staff. Office of the Chairman of the Joint Chiefs of Staff. *Photo Album for General Earle G. Wheeler, Chairman, 1968-1969*. Jul. 1970.

127. Nixon, Richard M. Letter to Earle G. Wheeler. 18 Jun. 1969.

128. Wheeler, Gilmore S. Interviews with Mark A. Viney. 9 Jun. and 8 Nov. 2010.

129. Jordan, 125-128.

130. Ibid.

131. Joint Chiefs of Staff. Office of the Chairman of the Joint Chiefs of Staff. *Photo Album for General Earle G. Wheeler, Chairman, 1969-1970*. Jul. 1970.

132. Ibid.

133. Petitt, 380.

134. Joint Chiefs of Staff. Office of the Chairman of the Joint Chiefs of Staff. *Photo Album for General Earle G. Wheeler, Chairman, 1969-1970*. Jul. 1970.

135. Stewart, 268, 281-282, 349-350.

136. Joint Chiefs of Staff. Office of the Chairman of the Joint Chiefs of Staff. *Photo Album for General Earle G. Wheeler, Chairman, 1969-1970*. Jul. 1970.

137. Johnson, Lyndon B. Letter to Earle G. Wheeler. 15 Apr. 1970.

138. United States Army. Walter Reed General Hospital. *Clinical Record, Earle G. Wheeler*. 22 Apr. 1970.

139. Ibid.

140. Wheeler, Gilmore. Email to Mark Viney. 29 Mar. 2014.

141. Wheeler, Frances R. Letter to Rebecca Howell. 2 May. 1970.

142. Wheeler, Gilmore. Email to Mark Viney. 21 Nov. 2013.

143. Wheeler, Gilmore. Email to Mark Viney. 29 Mar. 2014.

144. Wheeler, Frances R. Letter to Rebecca Howell. 2 May. 1970.

145. Wheeler, Gilmore. Email to Mark Viney. 29 Mar. 2014.

146. Wheeler, Frances R. Letter to Rebecca Howell. 29 May. 1970.

147. Ibid; Department of the Army. U.S. Army Physical Review Council. *Memorandum, Subject: Review of Proceedings of the Physical Valuation Board*. 28 May 1970.

148. Joint Chiefs of Staff. Office of the Chairman of the Joint Chiefs of Staff. *Photo Album for General Earle G. Wheeler, Chairman, 1969-1970*. Jul. 1970; Wheeler, Frances R. Letter to Rebecca Howell. Date unspecified (early Jun. 1970).

149. Associated Press. *U.S. Military Chief in Paris; Given One of Highest Medals*. 15 Jun. 1970.

150. Ibid; New York Times. Downloaded from the internet on 22 Aug. 2017 at http://www. nytimes. com/1974/07/27/archives/arthur-watson-of-ibm-exenvoy-dies-on-international-role-known-as. html; John F. Kennedy Presidential Library and Museum. Downloaded from the internet on 22 Aug. 2017 at https://www. jfklibrary. org/JFK/The-Kennedy-Family/R-Sargent-Shriver. aspx.

151. Joint Chiefs of Staff. Office of the Chairman of the Joint Chiefs of Staff. *Photo Album for General Earle G. Wheeler, Chairman, 1970*. Jul. 1970.

152. Department of Defense. Brochure. *In Honor of General Earle G. Wheeler, Chairman, Joint Chiefs of Staff, Andrews Air Force Base, Maryland, 2 July 1970*: Jul. 70; Joint Chiefs of

Staff. Office of the Chairman of the Joint Chiefs of Staff. *Photo Album for General Earle G. Wheeler, Chairman, 1970.* Jul. 1970; Wheeler, Gilmore S. *Untitled Monograph.*

153. Source unknown. *Chiefs Chairman Gen. Wheeler Retires Today.* 2 Jul. 1970.

154. Department of Defense. *DD Form 214 for General Earle G. Wheeler.* 3 Jul. 1970.

155. Joint Chiefs of Staff. Office of the Chairman of the Joint Chiefs of Staff. *Photo Album for General Earle G. Wheeler, Chairman, 1970.* Jul. 1970; The White House. Brochure. *Presentation of the Defense Distinguished Service Medal to General Earle G. Wheeler, at The White House on Thursday, 9 July 1970 at 1000 Hours*; Wheeler, Gilmore. Email to Mark Viney. 29 Jul. 2013.

156. The White House. *Presentation of the Defense Distinguished Service Medal to General Earle G. Wheeler, at The White House on Thursday, 9 July 1970 at 1000 Hours.*

157. Nixon, Richard M. Letter to Earle G. Wheeler. 9 July 1970.

## *Chapter 10*

1. Wheeler, Earle G. Letter to Martin Brounstein, Adjudication Officer, Veterans Benefits Office, Veterans Administration. 15 Jul. 1970; Federal Bureau of Investigation. *Case File.* 15 Jul. 1971; Stewart, Bill. Interview with Mark A. Viney. 7 Nov. 2013; Wheeler, Gilmore S. Interview with Mark A. Viney. 3 Jul. 2014.

2. Thieu, Nguyen V. Letter to Earle G. Wheeler. 14 Jul. 1970.

3. Rabin, Yitzhak. Letter to Earle G. Wheeler. 14 Jul. 1970.

4. Wheeler, Earle G. Letter to Yitzhak Rabin. 4 Aug. 1970.

5. Jordan, 136.

6. Monsanto Co. *Biographical Sketch of Gen. Earle G. Wheeler, U.S. Army (Retired).* Sep. 1970; Wheeler, Gilmore. Interviews with Mark Viney. 25 Feb. and 10 Mar. 2013.

7. Joint Chiefs of Staff. Office of the Chairman of the Joint Chiefs of Staff. *Photo Album for General Earle G. Wheeler, Chairman, 1970.* Jul. 1970.

8. Stewart, 371.

9. Odom, 221.

10. Rickover, Hyman G. Letter to Betty Wheeler. 14 Dec. 1970.

11. Wheeler, Frances R. Letter to Rebecca Howell. 14 Mar. 1971.

12. Ibid.

13. Wheeler, Gilmore. Interview with Mark Viney. 24 Apr. 2013.

14. Wheeler, Frances R. Letter to Rebecca Howell. 14 Mar. 1971.

15. Wheeler, Gilmore. Interview with Mark Viney. 25 Feb. 2013; Wheeler, Gilmore. Interview with Mark Viney. 10 Mar. 2013.

16. Stewart, Bill. Interview with Mark A. Viney. 7 Nov. 2013.

17. Wheeler, Earle G. *Professional Resume*. 1971; Federal Bureau of Investigation. *Case File*. 15 Jul. 1971; Wheeler, Gilmore. Interviews with Mark Viney. 25 Feb. and 10 Mar. 2013.

18. West Point Association of Graduates. Downloaded from the internet on 15 Dec. 2017 at http://apps. westpointaog. org/Memorials/Article/9579/; Wheeler, Gilmore. Interview with Mark Viney. 24 Apr. 2013.

19. Ibid; Department of State. G. Marvin Gentile, Deputy Assistant Secretary for Security. Letter to the Honorable J. Edgar Hoover, Director, Federal Bureau of Investigation. 15 Jul. 1971; Federal Bureau of Investigation. *Case File*. 15 Jul. 1971. Wheeler's son obtained a redacted version of the FBI report under the Freedom of Information Act in 2009.

20. Federal Bureau of Investigation. *Case File*. 15 Jul. 1971.

21. Wheeler, Gilmore S. Interview with Mark A. Viney. 3 Jul. 2014.

22. Federal Bureau of Investigation. *Case File*. 15 Jul. 1971.

23. Stewart, Bill. Interview with Mark Viney. 20 Oct. 2013.

24. Bowers, Verne L. Letter to Earle G. Wheeler. 16 May 1972.

25. The Martinsburg Journal. *Gen. Wheeler Dies; County Resident Former JCS Head*. 19 Dec. 1975; Wheeler, Gilmore. *Untitled Monograph*. 16; Wheeler, Gilmore. Interview with Mark Viney. 9 Oct. 2013.

26. Odom, 221.

27. Stewart, Bill. Interviews with Mark A. Viney. 20 Oct. and 7 Nov. 2013; Wheeler, Gilmore S. Interview with Mark A. Viney. 9 Oct. 2013.

28. Wheeler, Gilmore. Email to Mark Viney. 4 Apr. 2011; Wheeler, Gilmore. Interviews with Mark Viney. 25 Feb. and 10 Mar. 2013; Perry, 211.

29. Ibid.

30. Congress. *Cambodia Hearings*. 157.

31. Martinsburg Journal. *Title Unknown*. 1973.

32. Wheeler, Gilmore. Interview with Mark Viney. 3 Jul. 2014.

33. Ibid; Wheeler, Gilmore. Interview with Mark Viney. 20 Apr. 2016.

34. Ibid.

35. Westmoreland, 389; Millet, Maslowski, and Feis, 551-552; Prados. *Vietnam*, 294.

36. Arlington National Cemetery. Downloaded from the internet on 13 Feb. 2013 from http://www. arlingtoncemetery. net/ewheeler. htm.

37. The New York Times. *Gen. Earle Wheeler Dies; Ex-Head of Joint Chiefs.* 19 Dec. 1975.

38. Congress. *Cambodia Hearings.* 137, 139-140, 160, 163-164, 180, 189.

39. Eisenhower, Mamie D. Letter to Betty Wheeler. 21 Aug. 1973.

40. Wheeler, Frances R. Letter to Rebecca Howell. 22 Oct. 1973.

41. Johnson, Lady B. Letter to Betty Wheeler. Dec. 1974.

42. Arlington National Cemetery. Downloaded from the internet on 13 Feb. 2013 from http://www. arlingtoncemetery. net/ewheeler. htm; Wheeler, Gilmore. Interview with Mark Viney. 10 Mar. 2013.

43. State of Maryland. Department of Health and Mental Hygiene. *Medical Examiner's Certificate of Death.* 30 Dec. 1975; Charleston Gazette. *Former Joint Chiefs Head, Wheeler, Dies.* 19 Dec. 1975; The Charlotte Observer. *Gen. Earle Wheeler, Ex-Military Chief.* 19 Dec. 1975; The Martinsburg Journal. *Gen. Wheeler Dies; County Resident Former JCS Head.* 19 Dec. 1975.

44. Wheeler, Gilmore. Interview with Mark Viney. 10 Mar. 2013.

45. Ibid.

46. Odom, 222.

47. United States Army. *General Orders Number 26.* 19 Dec. 1975.

48. Ibid.

49. The Martinsburg Journal. *Gen. Wheeler Dies; County Resident Former JCS Head.* 19 Dec. 1975.

50. Wheeler, Gilmore S. Email to Mark Viney. 2 Feb. 2018.

51. Arlington National Cemetery. Downloaded from the internet on 13 Feb. 2013 from http://www.arlingtoncemetery. net/ewheeler. htm; Wunderground. com. Downloaded from the internet on 30 Oct. 2017 at https://www. wunderground. com/history/airport/ KDCA/1975/12/22/DailyHistory. html?&reqdb. zip=&reqdb. magic=&reqdb. wmo=.

52. Ailes, Stephen. *Eulogy for General Earle Wheeler.* 22 Dec. 1975.

53. Ailes, Stephen. Letter to Betty Wheeler. 29 Dec. 1975; Clifford, Clark M. Letter to Stephen Ailes. 23 Dec. 1975.

54. The Washington Post. *Gen. Earle Wheeler Dies; Headed Joint Chiefs.* 19 Dec. 1975.

55. The Martinsburg Journal. *Editorial: Gen. Earle G. Wheeler.* 22 Dec. 1975.

56. Ignatius, Paul. Letter to Betty Wheeler. 23 Dec. 1975.

57. Ignatius, Paul. Letter to Betty Wheeler. 23 Dec. 1975.

58. Hamblen, Arch. Letter to Betty Wheeler. 17 Jul. 1976.

59. Vance, Cyrus. Letter to Betty Wheeler. 17 Feb. 1976.

60. McKee, William F. Letter to Betty Wheeler. 22 Dec. 1975.

61. Moorer, Thomas. Letter to Betty Wheeler. 9 Jan. 1976.

62. Greene, Wallace M. Letter to Betty Wheeler. 24 Dec. 1975.

63. Norstad, Lauris. Telegram to Betty Wheeler. 19 Dec. 1975.

64. Herspring, 202.

65. Palmer, Bruce. Letter to Betty Wheeler. 24 Dec. 1975.

66. Wilson, Louis H. Letter to Betty Wheeler. 24 Dec. 1975.

67. Weyend, Frederick C. Letter to Betty Wheeler. 19 Dec. 1975.

68. Jones, David C. Letter to Betty Wheeler. 20 Dec. 1975.

69. Haig, Alexander M. Telegram to Betty Wheeler. 19 Dec. 1975.

70. Rogers, Bernard W. Letter to Betty Wheeler. 19 Dec. 1975.

71. Goodpaster, Darsy. Letter to Betty Wheeler. 23 Dec. 1975.

72. Taylor, Diddy. Letter to Betty Wheeler. 25 Dec. 1975.

73. Clifford, Marny. Letter to Betty Wheeler. 22 Dec. 1975.

74. Johnson, Dorothy. Letter to Betty Wheeler. 19 Dec. 1975; Norstad, Isabelle. Letter to Betty Wheeler. 26 Dec. 1975.

75. Abrams, Julie. Letter to Betty Wheeler. 1 Jan. 1976.

76. Wheeler, Gilmore. Interview with Mark Viney. 10 Mar. 2013.

77. Wheeler, Gilmore. Email to Mark Viney. 4 Apr. 2011.

78. Arlington National Cemetery. Downloaded from the internet on 13 Feb. 2013 from http://www. arlingtoncemetery. net/ewheeler. htm; Wheeler, Gilmore. Interview with Mark Viney. 24 Apr. 2013.

79. Ibid.

80. Wheeler, Gilmore. Interview with Mark Viney. 25 Feb. 2013.

81. Perry, 167, 211.

82. Wheeler, Gilmore. Interview with Mark Viney. 24 Apr. 2013.

83. Ibid.

## *Appendix*

1. United States Army. *General Orders Number 26.* 19 Dec. 1975; Monsanto Co. *Biographical Sketch of Gen. Earle G. Wheeler, U.S. Army (Retired).* Sep. 1970.

# BIBLIOGRAPHY

## Books

Anderson, David L., ed. *Shadow on the White House: Presidents and the Vietnam War, 1945-1975*. Lawrence, KS: University Press of Kansas, 1993.

Anderson, Karen. *Little Rock: Race and Resistance at Central High School*. Princeton, NJ: Princeton University Press, 2013.

Armstrong, David A. Editor. *The Joint Chiefs of Staff and the First Indochina War, 1947-1954*. Washington, DC: Office of Joint History, 2004.

Barrett, David M. Gen. ed. *Lyndon B. Johnson's Vietnam Papers: A Documentary Collection*. College Station, TX: Texas A&M University Press, 1998.

Baymor, Michael, ed. *The 63rd Infantry Division Chronicles, June 1943 to September 1945*. Publisher Location Unknown: 63rd Infantry Division Association, 1991.

Bell, William G. *Commanding Generals and Chiefs of Staff, 1775-1991, Portraits & Biographical Sketches of the United States Army's Senior Officer*. Washington DC: United States Army Center of Military History, 1992.

Bell, William G. *Secretaries of War and Secretaries of the Army, Portraits & Biographical Sketches*. Washington DC: United States Army Center of Military History, 1982.

Berman, Larry. *Lyndon Johnson's War: The Road the Stalemate in Vietnam*. New York: Norton, 1989.

Bowman, John S. *The Vietnam War: An Almanac*. New York: World Almanac Publications, 1985.

Chomsky, Noam, ed. *The Pentagon Papers: The Defense Department History of United States Decisionmaking on Vietnam*. The Senator Gravel Edition. 5 vols. Boston: Beacon Press, 1971-1972.

Collins, J. Lawton. *War in Peacetime, The History and Lessons of Korea*. Boston: Houghton Miflin, 1969.

Collins, J. Lawton. *Lightning Joe: An Autobiography*. Baton Rouge, LA: Louisiana State University Press, 1979.

Daddis, Gregory A. *Westmoreland's War: Reassessing American Strategy in Vietnam*. Oxford: Oxford University Press, 2014.

Dorland, Gilbert N. *Legacy of Discord: Voices of the Vietnam Era*. Washington, DC: Brassey's, 2001.

Gardner, Lloyd C. *Pay Any Price: Lyndon Johnson and the Wars for Vietnam*. Chicago: Ivan R. Dee, Inc., 1995.

Gott, Kendall D. *Mobility, Vigilance, and Justice: The US Army Constabulary in Germany, 1946-1953*. Fort Leavenworth, Kansas: Combat Studies Institute Press, 2005.

Griess, Thomas E. Editor. *Definitions and Doctrine of the Military Art, Past and Present*. Wayne, New Jersey: Avery Publishing Group, Inc., 1985.

Johnson, Lady Bird. *A White House Diary*. Austin, TX: University of Texas Press, 2007.

Jordan, Robert S. *An Unsung Soldier, The Life of Gen. Andrew J. Goodpaster*. Annapolis: Naval Institute Press, 2013.

Hackworth, David H. *About Face*. New York: Simon and Schuster, 1989.

Herring, George C. *America's Longest War, The United States and Vietnam, 1950-1975*. Fourth Edition. Boston: McGraw Hill, 2002.

Herspring, Dale R. *The Pentagon and the Presidency, Civil-Military Relations from FDR to George W. Bush*. Lawrence, KS: University Press of Kansas, 2005.

Kissinger, Henry A. *White House Years*. Boston: Little, Brown, 1979.

Kozak, Warren. *The Life and Wars of General Curtis LeMay*. Washington, DC: Regnery Publishing, Inc., 2011.

LeMay, Curtis E. and Kantor, MacKinlay. *Mission With LeMay: My Story*. Garden City, NY: Doubleday & Company, Inc., 1965.

Manchester, William. *The Death of a President*. New York: Harper & Row, 1967.

McMaster, Herbert R. *Dereliction of Duty*. New York: HarperCollins Publishers, 1997.

McNamara, Robert S. *In Retrospect: The Tragedy and Lessons of Vietnam*. New York: Times Books, 1995.

Meredith, James. *Mississippi: A Volume of Eleven Books*. Jackson, MS: Meredith Publishing: 1995.

Millet, Allan R., Maslowski, Peter, and Feis, William B. *For the Common Defense, A Military History of the United States from 1607 to 2012*. New York: Free Press, 2012.

Odom, Louie W. *Challenging Journey: An Autobiography*. Publisher Unknown, 2008.

Palmer, Dave R. *Summons of the Trumpet: A History of the Vietnam War From a Military Man's Viewpoint*. New York: Ballantine Books, 1978.

Palmer, Bruce Jr. *The 25-Year War, America's Role on Vietnam*. New York: Da Capo Press, 1984.

Perry, Mark. *Four Stars*. Boston: Houghton Miflin, 1989.

Petitt, Clyde E. *The Experts*. Seacaucus, NJ: Lyle Stuart, Inc., 1975.

Porter, Gareth. *Vietnam: The Definitive Documentation of Human Decisions, Volume 2*. Stanfordville, NY: Earl M. Coleman Enterprises, Inc., 1979.

Prados, John. *Vietnam, The History of an Unwinnable War, 1945-1975*. Lawrence, KS: University Press of Kansas, 2009.

Rostow, Walt W. *The Diffusion of Power: An Essay in Recent History*. New York: The Macmillan Company, 1972.

Schandler, Herbert Y. *The Unmaking of a President: Lyndon Johnson and Vietnam*. Princeton: Princeton University Press, 1977.

Schlesinger, Arthur M. Jr. *The Cycles of American History*. Boston: Houghton Mifflin Harcourt, 1999.

Sharp, U.S. Grant and Westmoreland, William C. *Report on the War in Vietnam (As of 30 June 1968)*. Washington, DC: U.S. Government Printing Office, 1968.

Shirer, William L. *The Rise and Fall of the Third Reich, a History of Nazi Germany*. New York: Simon and Schuster, 1960.

Sorley, Lewis B. *Honorable Warrior: General Harold K. Johnson and the Ethics of Command*. Lawrence, KS: University Press of Kansas, 1998.

Stewart, Richard. Gen. ed. *American Military History, Vol. II, The United States Army in a Global Era, 1917-2003*. Washington, DC: United States Army, Center of Military History, 2005.

Summers, Harry. *On Strategy: A Critical Analysis of the Vietnam War*. Novato, CA: Presidio Press, 1982.

*The Senator Gravel Edition: The Pentagon Papers: The Defense Department History of United States Decisionmaking on Vietnam, Volumes III-V*. Boston: Beacon Press, 1971.

Tucker, Spencer C. *The Encyclopedia of the Vietnam War: A Political, Social, and Military History*. 2nd Edition. Santa Barbara, CA: ABC-CLIO, Inc., 2011.

Waddington, David. *TRUST, A Picture Story of the United States Forces in the Free Territory of Trieste*. Trieste: David Waddington Publications, 1952.

Walker, Fred L. *From Texas to Rome, A General's Journal*. Dallas, TX: Taylor Publishing Company, 1969.

Watson, George M. *Secretaries and Chiefs of Staff of the United States Air Force*. Washington, DC: Air Force History and Museums Program, 2001.

Webb, Willard J. and Cole, Ronald H. *The Chairmen of the Joint Chiefs of Staff*. Washington, DC: Historical Division, Joint Chiefs of Staff, 1989.

Westmoreland, William C. *A Soldier Reports*. Garden City, NY: Doubleday & Company, Inc., 1976.

Young, Kenneth T. *The 1954 Geneva Conference: Indo-China and Korea*. New York: Greenwood Press, 1968.

Ziegler, Philip. *Mountbatten: The Official Biography*. London: HarperCollins, 1985.

## Interviews, Speeches & Lectures

Casey, George W. *Speech to U.S. Army War College.* 23 Sep. 2008. Author's Records.

Casey, George W. *Conversation with Mark A. Viney.* 25 Apr. 2018. Author's Records.

Covello, Hank. *Interview with Mark A. Viney.* 7 Jun. 2013. Handwritten notes. Author's Records.

Johnson, Harold K. *Interview with Rupert F. Glover,* United States Army Military History Institute, Senior Officer Oral History Program, Volume III, 1978. Transcription.

Spivy, Berton E. *Interview with James Durham and Nelson Wood,* United States Army Military History Institute, Senior Officer Debriefing Program, Volume I, Section VI, 1 Dec. 1972. Transcription.

Stewart, Bill. *Interview with Mark A. Viney.* 20 Oct. 2013. Handwritten notes. Author's Records.

Stewart, Bill. *Interview with Mark A. Viney.* 7 Nov. 2013. Handwritten notes. Author's Records.

Viney, George C. *Interviews with Mark A. Viney.* 30 Apr. 2007 – 17 Dec. 2010. Transcription and handwritten notes. Author's Records.

Wheeler, Earle G. *Interview with Chester Clifton.* 1964. Transcription. Wheeler Family Records.

Wheeler, Earle G. *Interview with Dorothy P. McSweeny.* Interview I, 21 Aug. 1969. Transcription. Wheeler Family Records.

Wheeler, Earle G. *Interview with Dorothy P. McSweeny.* Interview II, 7 May 1970. Transcription. Wheeler Family Records.

Frances R. Wheeler. *Interviews with Gilmore S. Wheeler,* 2003-2004. Audio files on 9 disks. Wheeler Family Records.

Wheeler, Gilmore S. *Interview with Mark A. Viney.* 16 Feb. 2010. Handwritten notes. Author's Records.

Wheeler, Gilmore S. *Interview with Mark A. Viney.* 9 Jun. 2010. Handwritten notes. Author's Records.

Wheeler, Gilmore S. *Interview with Mark A. Viney.* 8 Nov. 2010. Handwritten notes. Author's Records.

Wheeler, Gilmore S. *Interview with Mark A. Viney.* 25 Feb. 2013. Handwritten notes. Author's Records.

Wheeler, Gilmore S. *Interview with Mark A. Viney.* 10 Mar. 2013. Handwritten notes. Author's Records.

Wheeler, Gilmore S. *Interview with Mark A. Viney.* 14 Mar. 2013. Handwritten notes. Author's Records.

Wheeler, Gilmore S. *Interview with Mark A. Viney*. 24 Apr. 2013. Handwritten notes. Author's Records.

Wheeler, Gilmore S. *Interview with Mark A. Viney*. 14 May 2013. Handwritten notes. Author's Records.

Wheeler, Gilmore S. *Interview with Mark A. Viney*. 9 Oct. 2013. Handwritten notes. Author's Records.

Wheeler, Gilmore S. *Interview with Mark A. Viney*. 3 Jul. 2014. Handwritten notes. Author's Records.

Wheeler, Gilmore S. *Interview with Mark A. Viney*. 28 Aug. 2014. Handwritten notes. Author's Records.

## *Official Documents*

Department of Defense. Brochure. *In Honor of General Earle G. Wheeler, Chairman, Joint Chiefs of Staff, Andrews Air Force Base, Maryland, 2 July 1970*: Jul. 70. Wheeler Family Records.

Department of Defense. *Certificate for Award of the Department of Defense Identification Badge*. 1 Jan. 1951. Wheeler Family Records.

Department of Defense. *DD Form 214, General Earle G. Wheeler*. 3 Jul. 1970. Wheeler Family Records.

Department of Defense. Headquarters, United States Forces, European Theater, Mission to France. *Memorandum, subject: French Award to United States Officer*. 22 Jan. 1947. Wheeler Family Records.

Department of Defense. *United States Vietnam Relations, 1945-1967 (aka The Pentagon Papers)* 12 books; Washington, DC: United States Government Printing Office, 1971.

Department of State. G. Marvin Gentile, Deputy Assistant Secretary for Security. *Letter to the Honorable J. Edgar Hoover, Director, Federal Bureau of Investigation*. 15 Jul. 1971. Wheeler Family Records.

Department of the Army. *Biography of Colonel George Catron Viney*. 20 Jun. 1974. Author's Records.

Department of the Army. *DA Form 66*. 15 Feb. 1969. Wheeler Family Records.

Department of the Army. Office of the Chief of Staff of the Army. Photo Album. *General Earle G. Wheeler, Chief of Staff, United States Army, October 1962, Chairman of the Joint Chiefs of Staff, July 1964*. Jul. 1964. Wheeler Family Records.

Department of the Army. Office of the Chief of Staff of the Army. Photo Album. *General Earle G. Wheeler*. Jun. 1964. Covers period 5 August – 20 December 1963. Wheeler Family Records.

Department of the Army. Office of the Chief of Staff of the Army. Photo Album. *General Earle G. Wheeler*. Jun. 1964. Covers period January - May 1963. Wheeler Family Records.

Department of the Army. Office of the Chief of Staff of the Army. Photo Album. *General Earle G. Wheeler*. Jun. 1964. Covers period 1 June – 28 July 1963. Wheeler Family Records.

Department of the Army. Office of the Chief of Staff of the Army. Photo Album. *General Earle G. Wheeler*. Jun. 1964. Covers period 1 October 1962 – 28 February 1963. Wheeler Family Records.

Department of the Army. Office of the Chief of Staff of the Army. Photo Album. *General Earle G. Wheeler*. Jun. 1964. Covers period 16 January – 22 June 1964. Wheeler Family Records.

Department of the Army. Office of the Chief of Staff of the Army. Photo Album. *General Earle G. Wheeler*. Jun. 1964. Covers Wheeler's trip to Vietnam, 16-21 January 1963. Wheeler Family Records.

Department of the Army. *Resume of Service Career of John Rutherford McGiffert II, Lieutenant General*. 1 April 1977. Author's Records.

Department of the Army. U.S. Army Physical Review Council. *Memorandum, Subject: Review of Proceedings of the Physical Valuation Board*. 28 May 1970. Wheeler Family Records.

Department of Defense. *Ceremony Program, In Honor of General Earle G. Wheeler, Chairman, Joint Chiefs of Staff, Andrews Air Force Base, Maryland*. 13 Feb. 1969. Wheeler Family Records.

Federal Bureau of Investigation. *Case File, Earle G. Wheeler*. Redacted. 15 Jul. 1971. Wheeler Family Records.

Joint Chiefs of Staff. *Addresses by General Earle G. Wheeler, Chairman, Joint Chiefs of Staff, Vol. II, 7 July 1964 to 2 July 1970*. Washington, DC: Joint Staff Historical Office, no date.

Joint Chiefs of Staff. *Earle G. Wheeler Papers, Chairman, Joint Chiefs of Staff, Calendar of Events, 1 Jan – 31 Dec 1967*. Wheeler NARA Records.

Joint Chiefs of Staff. Office of the Chairman of the Joint Chiefs of Staff. *Photo Album for General Earle G. Wheeler, Chairman, 1964-1965*. Jul. 1970. Wheeler Family Records.

Joint Chiefs of Staff. Office of the Chairman of the Joint Chiefs of Staff. *Photo Album for General Earle G. Wheeler, Chairman, 1965-1966*. Jul. 1970. Wheeler Family Records.

Joint Chiefs of Staff. Office of the Chairman of the Joint Chiefs of Staff. *Photo Album for General Earle G. Wheeler, Chairman, 1966-1967.* Jul. 1970. Wheeler Family Records.

Joint Chiefs of Staff. Office of the Chairman of the Joint Chiefs of Staff. *Photo Album for General Earle G. Wheeler, Chairman, 1967-1968.* Jul. 1970. Wheeler Family Records.

Joint Chiefs of Staff. Office of the Chairman of the Joint Chiefs of Staff. *Photo Album for General Earle G. Wheeler, Chairman, 1968-1969.* Jul. 1970. Wheeler Family Records.

Joint Chiefs of Staff. Office of the Chairman of the Joint Chiefs of Staff. *Photo Album for General Earle G. Wheeler, Chairman, 1969-1970.* Jul. 1970. Wheeler Family Records.

Joint Chiefs of Staff. Office of the Chairman of the Joint Chiefs of Staff. *Photo Album for General Earle G. Wheeler, Chairman, 1970.* Jul. 1970. Wheeler Family Records.

Monsanto Co. *Biographical Sketch of Gen. Earle G. Wheeler, U.S. Army (Retired).* Sep. 1970. Wheeler Family Records.

Office of Joint History. Office of the Chairman of the Joint Chiefs of Staff. *The Joint Chiefs of Staff and National Policy 1965–1968.* Washington, DC: 2012.

Office of Joint History. Office of the Chairman of the Joint Chiefs of Staff. *The Joint Chiefs of Staff and National Policy 1961–1964.* Washington, DC: 2011.

Office of Joint History. Office of the Chairman of the Joint Chiefs of Staff. *The Joint Chiefs of Staff and The First Indochina War 1947-1954.* Washington, DC: 2004.

State of Maryland. Department of Health and Mental Hygiene. *Medical Examiner's Certificate of Death, Earle G. Wheeler.* 30 Dec. 1975. Wheeler Family Records.

Supreme Court of the District of Columbia. *Decree From Adoption Case No. 534, In Re: Adoption of Earl Gilmore Stone and Helen Friedrich Stone.* 14 Sep. 1923. Wheeler Family Records.

The White House. *Presentation of the Defense Distinguished Service Medal to General Earle G. Wheeler, at The White House on Thursday, 9 July 1970 at 1000 Hours.* Wheeler Family Records.

United States Army. Field Artillery School. *Memorandum, Subject: Award of Army Commendation Ribbon.* 8 May 1946. Wheeler Family Records.

United States Army. Field Artillery School. *Memorandum, Subject: Award of Army Commendation Ribbon.* 25 Apr. 1946. Wheeler Family Records.

United States Army. *Field Manual 6-0 (Commander and Staff Organizations and Operations),* 5 May 2014. Army Publishing Directorate.

United States Army. *General Orders Number 26.* 19 Dec. 1975. Wheeler Family Records.

United States Army. Headquarters, European Theater of Operations. *General Orders Number 140.* 30 Jun. 1945. Wheeler Family Records.

United States Army. Headquarters, 141st Infantry Regiment. *Memorandum, Subject: Commendation.* 20 Jun. 1942. Wheeler Family Records.

United States Army. Headquarters, 63rd Infantry Division. *General Orders Number 58.* 24 Mar. 1945. Wheeler Family Records.

United States Army. Headquarters, 63rd Infantry Division. *General Orders Number 201.* 21 May 1945. Wheeler Family Records.

United States Army. Headquarters, 63rd Infantry Division. *General Orders Number 412.* 22 Jul. 1945. Wheeler Family Records.

United States Army. Headquarters, 63rd Infantry Division. *Memorandum, Subject: Special Rating of Officers Recommended for Promotion to the Grade of Brigadier General (Temporary).* 17 May 1945. Wheeler Family Records.

United States Army. Headquarters, Trieste United States Troops. *Memorandum, Subject Commendation.* 17 Jun. 1952. Wheeler Family Records.

United States Army. Headquarters, United States Constabulary. *Memorandum, Subject: Commendation.* 25 Jan. 1949. Wheeler Family Records.

United States Army. *Memorandum, "63d Infantry Division (Army of the United States)."* No date. Wheeler Family Records.

United States Army. *Memorandum, Subject: Change of Name.* 1 May 1936. Wheeler Family Records.

United States Army. Office, Chief of Information. *Biography: Gen. Berton E. Spivy, Jr.* Apr. 1965.

United States Army. Office, Chief of Information. *Biography: Gen. Earle G. Wheeler.* No date. Wheeler Family Records.

United States Army. 63rd Infantry Division. *Blood and Fire, Victory in Europe.* No date. Wheeler Family Records.

United States Army. *Standard Form 88, Report of Medical Examination.* 6 Dec. 1956. Wheeler Family Records.

United States Army. *Standard Form 88, Report of Medical Examination.* 12 Jan. 1960. Wheeler Family Records.

United States Army. *Standard Form 88, Report of Medical Examination.* 20 Jan. 1958. Wheeler Family Records.

United States Army. *Standard Form 88, Report of Medical Examination.* 27 Jan. 1959. Wheeler Family Records.

United States Army. *Standard Form 88, Report of Medical Examination.* 23 Oct. 1953. Wheeler Family Records.

United States Army. The Adjutant General. *Memorandum, Subject: Permanent Disability Retirement.* 4 Jul. 1970. Wheeler Family Records.

United States Army. United States Military Academy. *Cadet Service Record.* 1932. Wheeler Family Records.

United States Army. Walter Reed General Hospital. *Clinical Record, Earle G. Wheeler.* 22 Apr. 1970. Wheeler Family Records.

United States Army. War Department Message Center. *Telegram.* 26 Jul. 1932. Wheeler Family Records.

United States Atomic Energy Commission. *Personnel Security Questionnaire.* 11 Jul. 1950. Wheeler Family Records.

United States. Congress. House. Committee on Foreign Affairs. Subcommittee on Asian and Pacific Affairs. U.S. Policy and Programs in Cambodia: Hearings Before the Subcommittee on Asian and Pacific Affairs of the Committee on Foreign Affairs, House of Representatives, Ninety-third Congress, First Session. Washington, DC: U.S. Government Printing Office, 1973. Pentagon Library.

United States Department of Justice. Federal Bureau of Investigation. *Memorandum Re: Earl Gilmore Wheeler – WA - 19028, Atomic Energy Act - Applicant.* 26 Jul. 1950. Wheeler Family Records.

United States Department of Justice. Federal Bureau of Investigation. *Memorandum Re: Earl Gilmore Wheeler – WA - 19028, Atomic Energy Act - Applicant.* 13 Dec. 1955. Wheeler Family Records.

United States Pacific Command. *Back Channel Message from Admiral Sharp, CINCPAC, Hawaii, to General Wheeler, CJCS, Washington* (U). 7 Sep. 1967. Wheeler NARA Records.

Veterans Administration. Veterans Benefits Office. *Letter to Earle G. Wheeler.* 10 Jul. 1970. Wheeler Family Records.

War Department. *AGO Form No. 0485-2.* 11 Jun. 1940. Wheeler Family Records.

War Department. *Form No. 051-AGO.* 25 Feb. 1928. Wheeler Family Records.

War Department. *AGO Form No. 0622.* 7 Mar. 1940. Wheeler Family Records.

War Department. *AGO Form 66-2.* 23 Apr. 1954. Wheeler Family Records.

War Department. *AGO Form No. 63, Report of Physical Examination.* 5 Jun. 1939. Wheeler Family Records.

War Department. *AGO Form No. 63, Report of Physical Examination.* 14 Jun. 1940. Wheeler Family Records.

War Department. *AGO Form No. 63, Report of Physical Examination.* 18 Apr. 1935. Wheeler Family Records.

War Department. *AGO Form No. 63, Report of Physical Examination.* 13 Feb. 1934. Wheeler Family Records.

War Department. *AGO Form No. 63, Report of Physical Examination.* 6 Jul. 1943. Wheeler Family Records.

War Department. *AGO Form No. 63, Report of Physical Examination.* 16 Jun. 1938. Wheeler Family Records.

War Department. *AGO Form No. 63, Report of Physical Examination.* 12 Feb. 1946. Wheeler Family Records.

War Department. *AGO Form No. 63, Report of Physical Examination.* 27 Apr. 1948. Wheeler Family Records.

War Department. *AGO Form No. 63, Report of Physical Examination.* 26 Aug. 1935. Wheeler Family Records.

War Department. *AGO Form No. 63, Report of Physical Examination.* 22 Apr. 1947. Wheeler Family Records.

War Department. *AGO Form No. 63, Report of Physical Examination.* 2 Feb. 1937. Wheeler Family Records.

War Department. *AGO Form No. 63, Report of Physical Examination.* 2 Feb. 1933. Wheeler Family Records.

War Department. *Historical Record of Officer, Statement of Officer upon Original Appointment and Regular Army.* Jun. 1932. Wheeler Family Records.

War Department. *Officer's and Warrant Officer's Qualification Card.* 4 Aug. 1947. Wheeler Family Records.

War Department. *Report of Examining Board for Promotion of Officers.* 9 Aug. 1935. Wheeler Family Records.

War Department. *Report of Physical Examination.* 15 Jul. 1929. Wheeler Family Records.

War Department. *Memorandum, Subject: Authority to Travel by Automobile.* 27 Jul. 1932. Wheeler Family Records.

War Department. *Memorandum. 30 Apr. 1937; Wheeler, Gilmore.*

## Online Media

Albert Lea Tribune. Downloaded from the internet on 11 Nov. 2014 at http://www. albertleatribune. com/2002/11/ he-led-the-hot-shots-of-the-blood-and-fire-division/.

Arlington National Cemetery. Downloaded from the internet on 20 Oct. 2013 at http:// www. arlingtoncemetery. net/waburress. htm.

Arlington National Cemetery. Downloaded from the internet on 20 Oct. 2013 and 22 Oct. 2015 at http://www. arlingtoncemetery. net/bespivy. htm.

Arlington National Cemetery. Downloaded from the internet on 13 Feb. 2013 at http://www. arlingtoncemetery. net/ewheeler. htm.

Arlington National Cemetery. Downloaded from the internet on 19 Apr. 2018 at http://www. arlingtoncemetery. net/jehull. htm.

Army Historical Foundation. Downloaded from the internet on 13 Feb. 2013 at https://armyhistory. org/09/general-earle-g-wheeler/.

C-Span. Downloaded from the internet on 31 Jan. 2017 at https://www. c-span. org/video/?404455-1/general-james-gavin-testimony-1966-fulbright-vietnam-hearings.

Department of State. Office of the Historian. Downloaded from the internet on 17 Dec. 2017 at https://history. state. gov/historicaldocuments/frus1964-68v04/d216.

Ed Gallucci Photography. Downloaded from the internet on 22 Aug. 2017 at http://www. edgallucciphotography. com/march-washington-d-c-may-10-1970/.

Eisenhower Presidential Library. Downloaded from the internet on 26 Jul. 2017 at http://www. dwightdeisenhower. com/156/Funeral-Ceremony.

*15th Infantry Regiment Association.* Downloaded from the internet on 7 Jun. 2018 at http://www. 15thinfantry. org/documents/issues/October2010. pdf.

George Washington University. Downloaded from the internet on 4 Aug. 2018 at https://www2. gwu. edu/~erpapers/mep/displaydoc. cfm?docid+erpn-henlod.

History. com. Downloaded from the internet on 5 Jul. 2017 at http://www. history. com/this-day-in-history/100000-people-march-on-the-pentagon.

History. com. Downloaded from the internet on 2 Sep. 2010 at http://www. history. com/this-day-in-history. do?action=tdihArticleCategory&id=1967.

History of the 63rd Infantry Division. Downloaded from the internet on 17 Jul. 2015 at http://www. 63rdinfdiv. com.

John F. Kennedy Presidential Library and Museum. Downloaded from the internet on 22 Aug. 2017 at https://www. jfklibrary. org/JFK/The-Kennedy-Family/R-Sargent-Shriver. aspx.

KidsHealth. Downloaded from the internet on 16 Jan. 2016 at http://kidshealth. org/teen/your_mind/families/coping_alcoholic. html#.

Marines. Downloaded from the internet on 11 Jul. 2017 at http://marines. mil/News/Messages/Messages-Display/Article/886772/death-of-general-leonard-f-chapman-jr-former-commandant-of-the-marine-corps/.

New York Times. Downloaded from the internet on 7 Jan. 2014 at http://www. nytimes. com/1990/02/25/obituaries/lieut-gen-james-gavin-82-dies-champion-and-critic-of-military. html.

New York Times. Downloaded from the internet on 22 Aug. 2017 at http://www. nytimes. com/1974/07/27/archives/arthur-watson-of-ibm-exenvoy-dies-on-international-role-known-as. html.

New York Times. Downloaded from the internet on 2 May 2018 at https://www. nytimes. com/1989/03/12/books/the-age-of-brass. html.

New York Times. Downloaded from the internet on 19 Jul. 2017 at https://mobile. nytimes. com/2001/12/18/us/ulysses-s-grant-sharp-jr-vietnam-war-admiral-95. html.

Politico. Downloaded from the internet on 26 Jul. 2017 at http://www. politico. com/ story/2013/04/this-day-in-politics-089554.

Real Clear Defense. Downloaded from the internet on 11 Jul. 2015 at http://www. realcleardefense. com/articles/2015/07/11/chairman_of_the_joint_chiefs_is_a_commander_of_nothing_108209. html.

75th Ranger Regiment Association. Downloaded from the internet on 16 Dec. 2017 at http://www. 75thrra. com/history/n75_hx. html.

Supreme Headquarters Allied Powers Europe. Downloaded from the internet on 2 Jul. 2017 at https://shape. nato. int/page1463252.

Texas State Historical Association. Downloaded from the internet on 11 Nov. 2014 at http://www. tshaonline. org/handbook/online/articles/fwa17.

The Forgotten General. Downloaded from the internet on 13 Feb. 2013 at http://theforgottengeneral. com/wp-content/uploads/2010/12/JCS-Biography. pdf.

The Generals of WWII. Downloaded from the internet on 7 Jun. 2018 at http://www. generals. dk/general/Lawrence/Thompson/USA. html.

United States Air Force. Downloaded from the internet on 4 Aug. 2018 at http:www. af. mil/About-Us/Biographies/Display/Article/106325/general-john-paul-mcconnell/.

United States Army. Office of the Administrative Assistant to the Secretary of the Army. The institute of Heraldry. Downloaded from the internet on 16 Dec. 2017 at http://www. tioh. hqda. pentagon. mil/Catalog/Heraldry. aspx-?HeraldryId=15493&CategoryId=9148&grp=2&menu=Uniformed%20 Services&ps=24&p=0.

United States Central Command. Downloaded from the internet on 4 Aug. 2018 at http:// www. centcom. mil/ABOUT-US/LEADERSHIP/Article/904768/george-b-crist/.

United States European Command. Downloaded from the internet on 23 Jul. 2017 at www. eucom. mil/media-library/article/20939/ the-man-who-moved-eucom-gen-david-a-burchinal.

United States Pacific Command. Downloaded from the internet on 19 Jul. 2017 at http:www. pacom. mil/About-USPACOM/USPACOM-Previous-Commanders/.

U.S. Army in Germany. Downloaded from the internet on 23 Jul. 2018 at https://www. usarmygermany. com/Sont. htm?https&&&www. usarmygermany. com/Units/ TRUST/TRUST_main. htm.

Washington Post. Downloaded from the internet on 4 Jul. 2017 at https://www. washing-tonpost. com/archive/local/1997/12/20/admiral-aviator-david-mcdonald-dies-at-91/344cf55b-13b1-4515-829e-9abab41dfd90/?utm_term=. 81a3a7bd548d.

West Point Association of Graduates. Downloaded from the internet on 15 Dec. 2017 at http://apps. westpointaog. org/Memorials/Article/9579/.

## *Periodicals*

Army. *Eisenhower and MacArthur: Toil, Trouble and Turbulence in the Philippines.* Feb. 2015.

Army. *Historically Speaking, Earle G. Wheeler at 100.* Feb 2010.

Army History. Book review of *Westmoreland's War: Reassessing American Strategy in Vietnam.* Fall 2014.

Baltimore Sun. *A Military Man is Chosen and Chief Knows Him Well.* 24 Jun. 1964.

Baltimore Sun. *Two Generals.* 28 Jun. 1964.

Il Corriere Di Trieste. *Fascist Tactics.* 26-27 Mar. 1952.

Journal of Mississippi History. *'The Fight for Men's Minds': The Aftermath of the Ole Miss Riot of 1962.* Spring 2009.

Journal Register. *New JCS Chairman.* 27 Jun. 1964.

Lawton Constitution. *Land Warfare Emphasis.* 2 Jul. 1964.

Los Angeles Times. *Nicholas Katzenbach Dies at 90; Attorney General Under Johnson.* 10 May 2012.

Los Angeles Times. *Wheeler, Johnson Take Up New Posts.* 7 Jul. 1964.

Martinsburg Journal. *Editorial: Gen. Earle G. Wheeler.* 22 Dec. 1975.

Martinsburg Journal. *Title Unknown.* 1973. This newspaper clipping did not include the title of the article and date of publication.

National Observer. *General Wheeler's Rising Stars, It's 3-for-3 for the Army As Taylor 'Protégé' Gets Top Job.* 29 Jun. 1964.

Newsweek. *Merit Will Be Rewarded.* 3 Jul. 1964.

New York Herald Tribune. *Clay Sees a Long Siege at Berlin But No War 'Around the Corner'.* 14 Sep. 1948:1.

New York Herald Tribune. *Gen. Wheeler Aims for Harmony.* 7 Jul. 1964.

New York Herald Tribune. *Gen. Wheeler, New U.S. Top Military Man.* 19 Aug. 1964.

New York Herald Tribune. *Marshall Concedes Relations With Russia Are Deteriorating.* 15 Sep. 1948:1.

New York News. *Staff Chief.* 9 Jul. 1964.

New York Times. *David Lamar McDonald, 91, Former Senior Naval Officer.* 23 Dec. 1997.

New York Times. *Gen. Earle Wheeler Dies; Ex-Head of Joint Chiefs.* 19 Dec. 1975.

New York Times. *New Military Top Man.* 8 Jul. 1964.

New York Times. *Rotation Ended For Joint Chiefs.* 24 Jun. 1964.

New York Times. *'Staff Man' in Chief.* 24 Jun. 1964.

New York Times. *The Cold Warrior Who Never Apologized.* 8 Sep. 2017.

Observer-Reporter. *Retired General Dies at 76.* 21 Aug. 1990.

Pentagram News. *Gens. Wheeler, Johnson Send Messages.* 9 Jul. 1964.

Philadelphia Inquirer. *Change of Guard Over S. Vietnam.* 24 Jun. 1964.

Source unknown. *Chiefs Chairman Gen. Wheeler Retires Today.* 2 Jul. 1970.

Time. *Three Top Soldiers.* 6 Jul. 1964.

U.S. News & World Report. *Pentagon Shift – Generals Who Moved Up.* 6 Jul. 1964.

Washington Post. *A Cavalryman Hangs Up His Boots.* 29 Jul. 1964.

Washington Post. *Ex-Air Force Gen. John McConnell Dies.* 22 Nov. 1986.

Washington Post. *Gen. Earle Wheeler Dies; Headed Joint Chiefs.* 19 Dec. 1975.

Washington Post. *Gen. Henry W. Buse, Official of Olympic Panel, Dies at 76.* 22 Oct. 1988.

Washington Post. *Pentagon Shift Shatters JCS Rotation Precedent.* 24 Jun. 1964.

Washington Post. *Taylor Marked Wheeler Early for High Military Responsibility.* 24 Jun. 1964.

Washington Post. Gen. *Withers A. Burress, Head of First Army During 1950s.* 14 Jun. 1977: C6.

Washington Star. *General Wheeler Honored.* 7 Jul. 1964.

Washington Star. *Wheeler Aims to Ease Civilian-Military Gap.* 28 Jun. 1964.

Wall Street Journal. *Military Chieftain.* 26 Jun. 1964.

## *Records Collections*

Department of the Army, H. K. Johnson Papers, U.S. Army Military History Institute (USAMHI), Carlisle, PA.

Joint Chiefs of Staff, Chairman (GEN) Earle G. Wheeler, Official Records, Joint Chiefs of Staff, 3 July 64 – 2 July 70, National Archives, College Park, MD. This collection contains 219 boxes of mostly still-classified documents.

Wheeler Family Records, Martinsburg, WV. This unarchived collection contains Wheeler's official personnel records and vast family correspondence over the duration of Wheeler's military career.

## Theses

Scribner, Charles R. *The Eisenhower and Johnson Administrations' Decisionmaking on Vietnamese Intervention: A Study of Contrasts.* Ph. D. diss., University of California Santa Barbara, 1980.

## Unofficial Correspondence

(From Wheeler Family Records unless otherwise specified.)

Abrams, Julie. *Letter to Betty Wheeler.* 1 Jan. 1976.

Ailes, Stephen. *Letter to Betty Wheeler.* 29 Dec. 1975

Bowers, Verne L. *Letter to Earle G. Wheeler.* 16 May 1972.

Clifford, Clark M. *Letter to Stephen Ailes.* 23 Dec. 1975.

Clifford, Marny. *Letter to Betty Wheeler.* 22 Dec. 1975.

Crane, Conrad C. *Conversation with Mark Viney.* 5 Nov. 2010

Deuhring, George. *Letter to Inez Douglas.* 5 Sep. 1928.

Deuhring, George. *Letter to Inez Douglas.* 8 Sep. 1928.

Deuhring, George. *Letter to Inez Douglas.* 11 Sep. 1928.

Deuhring, George. *Letter to Inez Douglas.* 15 Sep. 1928.

Deuhring, George. *Letter to Inez Douglas.* 18 Sep. 1928.

Deuhring, George. *Letter to Inez Douglas.* 30 Sep. 1928.

Deuhring, George. *Letter to Inez Douglas.* 2 Oct. 1928.

Deuhring, George. *Letter to Inez Douglas.* 14 Oct. 1928.

Eisenhower, Mamie D. *Letter to Betty Wheeler.* 21 Aug. 1973.

Goodpaster, Darsy. *Letter to Betty Wheeler.* 23 Dec. 1975.

Greene, Wallace M. *Letter to Betty Wheeler.* 24 Dec. 1975.

Haig, Alexander M. *Telegram to Betty Wheeler.* 19 Dec. 1975.

Hamblen, Arch. *Letter to Betty Wheeler.* 17 Jul. 1976.

Howell, Rebecca. *Letter to Frances R. Wheeler.* 23 Jun. 1948.

Howell, Rebecca. *Letter to Frances R. Wheeler.* 14 Sep. 1948.

Howell, Rebecca. *Letter to Frances R. Wheeler.* 15 Sep. 1948.

Howell, Rebecca. *Letter to Frances R. Wheeler.* 17 Sep. 1948.

Howell, Rebecca. *Letter to Frances R. Wheeler*. 20 Oct. 1948.

Howell, Walter R. *Letter to Gilmore S. Wheeler*. 16 Apr. 1962.

Howell, Walter R. *Wedding Invitation*. No date.

Hull, John E. *Letter to Robert S. McNamara*. 14 Dec. 1966.

Ignatius, Paul. *Letter to Betty Wheeler*. 23 Dec. 1975.

Johnson, Dorothy. *Letter to Betty Wheeler*. 19 Dec. 1975.

Johnson, Lady B. *Letter to Betty Wheeler*. 21 Dec. 1974.

Johnson, Lyndon B. *Letter to Earle G. Wheeler*. 15 Apr. 1970.

Johnson, Lyndon B. *Note to Earle G. Wheeler*. 7 Feb. 1968.

Johnson, Lyndon B. *Note to Earle G. Wheeler*. 31 Aug. 1968.

Jones, David C. *Letter to Betty Wheeler*. 20 Dec. 1975.

Long, William M. *Letter to Walter R. Howell*. 9 Apr. 1962.

McKee, William F. *Letter to Betty Wheeler*. 22 Dec. 1975.

McNamara, Margy. *Letter to the Wheelers, Johnsons, McConnells, Moorers, and Chapmans*.
12 Apr. 1968.

Moorer, Thomas. *Letter to Betty Wheeler*. 9 Jan. 1976.

Muir, James I. *Letter to Earle G. Wheeler*. 13 Sep. 1951.

Nixon, Richard M. *Letter to Earle G. Wheeler*. 18 Jun. 1969.

Nixon, Richard M. *Letter to Earle G. Wheeler*. 9 Jul. 1970.

Norstad, Isabelle. *Letter to Betty Wheeler*. 26 Dec. 1975.

Norstad, Lauris. *Telegram to Betty Wheeler*. 19 Dec. 1975.

Odom, Louie W. *Letter to Gilmore S. Wheeler*. 19 Mar. 2013.

Palmer, Bruce. *Letter to Betty Wheeler*. 24 Dec. 1975.

Rabin, Yitzhak. *Letter to Earle G. Wheeler*. 14 Jul. 1970.

Rickover, Hyman G. *Letter to Betty Wheeler*. 14 Dec. 1970.

Rogers, Bernard W. *Letter to Betty Wheeler*. 19 Dec. 1975.

Sebree, E. B. *Letter to Earle G. Wheeler*. 30 Aug. 1951.

Sebree, E. B. *Letter to Earle G. Wheeler*. 7 Sep. 1951.

Sebree, E. B. *Letter to Earle G. Wheeler*. 17 Sep. 1951.

Taylor, Diddy. *Letter to Betty Wheeler*. 25 Dec. 1975.

Thieu, Nguyen V. *Letter to Earle G. Wheeler*. 14 Jul. 1970.

Vance, Cyrus. *Letter to Betty Wheeler*. 17 Feb. 1976.

Weyend, Frederick C. *Letter to Betty Wheeler*. 19 Dec. 1975.

Wheeler, Earle G. *Letter to Martin Brounstein, Adjudication Officer, Veterans Benefits Office, Veterans Administration*. 15 Jul. 1970.

Wheeler, Earle G. *Letter to Frances R. Wheeler*. 5 Jan. 1945.

Wheeler, Earle G. *Letter to Frances R. Wheeler*. 8 Jan. 1945.

Wheeler, Earle G. *Letter to Frances R. Wheeler*. 15 Jan. 1945.

Wheeler, Earle G. *Letter to Frances R. Wheeler*. 17 Jan. 1945.

Wheeler, Earle G. *Letter to Frances R. Wheeler*. 19 Jan. 1945.

Wheeler, Earle G. *Letter to Frances R. Wheeler*. 24 Jan. 1945.

Wheeler, Earle G. *Letter to Frances R. Wheeler*. 1 Feb. 1945.

Wheeler, Earle G. *Letter to Frances R. Wheeler*. 7 Feb. 1945.

Wheeler, Earle G. *Letter to Frances R. Wheeler*. 8 Feb. 1945.

Wheeler, Earle G. *Letter to Frances R. Wheeler*. 9 Feb. 1945.

Wheeler, Earle G. *Letter to Frances R. Wheeler*. 11 Feb. 1945.

Wheeler, Earle G. *Letter to Frances R. Wheeler*. 13 Feb. 1945.

Wheeler, Earle G. *Letter to Frances R. Wheeler*. 14 Feb. 1945.

Wheeler, Earle G. *Letter to Frances R. Wheeler*. 17 Feb. 1945.

Wheeler, Earle G. *Letter to Frances R. Wheeler*. 22 Feb. 1945.

Wheeler, Earle G. *Letter to Frances R. Wheeler*. 23 Feb. 1945.

Wheeler, Earle G. *Letter to Frances R. Wheeler*. 25 Feb. 1945.

Wheeler, Earle G. *Letter to Frances R. Wheeler*. 1 Mar. 1945.

Wheeler, Earle G. *Letter to Frances R. Wheeler*. 3 Mar. 1945.

Wheeler, Earle G. *Letter to Frances R. Wheeler*. 7 Mar. 1945.

Wheeler, Earle G. *Letter to Frances R. Wheeler*. 9 Mar. 1945.

Wheeler, Earle G. *Letter to Frances R. Wheeler*. 11 Mar. 1945.

Wheeler, Earle G. *Letter to Frances R. Wheeler*. 23 Mar. 1945.

Wheeler, Earle G. *Letter to Frances R. Wheeler*. 3 Apr. 1945.

Wheeler, Earle G. *Letter to Frances R. Wheeler*. 12 Apr. 1945.

Wheeler, Earle G. *Letter to Frances R. Wheeler*. 16 Apr. 1945.

Wheeler, Earle G. *Letter to Frances R. Wheeler*. 4 May 1945.

Wheeler, Earle G. *Letter to Frances R. Wheeler*. 5 May 1945.

Wheeler, Earle G. *Letter to Frances R. Wheeler*. 6 May 1945.

Wheeler, Earle G. *Letter to Frances R. Wheeler*. 10 May 1945.

Wheeler, Earle G. *Letter to Frances R. Wheeler*. 12 May 1945.

Wheeler, Earle G. *Letter to Frances R. Wheeler.* 20 May 1945.

Wheeler, Earle G. *Letter to Frances R. Wheeler.* 25 May 1945.

Wheeler, Earle G. *Letter to Frances R. Wheeler.* 27 May 1945.

Wheeler, Earle G. *Letter to Frances R. Wheeler.* 28 May 1945.

Wheeler, Earle G. *Letter to Frances R. Wheeler.* 31 May 1945.

Wheeler, Earle G. *Letter to Frances R. Wheeler.* 5 Jun. 1945.

Wheeler, Earle G. *Letter to Frances R. Wheeler.* 7 Jun. 1945.

Wheeler, Earle G. *Letter to Frances R. Wheeler.* 10 Jun. 1945.

Wheeler, Earle G. *Letter to Frances R. Wheeler.* 12 Jun. 1945.

Wheeler, Earle G. *Letter to Frances R. Wheeler.* 17 Jun. 1945.

Wheeler, Earle G. *Letter to Frances R. Wheeler.* 19 Jun. 1945.

Wheeler, Earle G. *Letter to Frances R. Wheeler.* 23 Jun. 1945.

Wheeler, Earle G. *Letter to Frances R. Wheeler.* 28 Jun. 1945.

Wheeler, Earle G. *Letter to Frances R. Wheeler.* 3 Jul. 1945.

Wheeler, Earle G. *Letter to Frances R. Wheeler.* 4 Jul. 1945.

Wheeler, Earle G. *Letter to Frances R. Wheeler.* 4 Jul. 1945.

Wheeler, Earle G. *Letter to Frances R. Wheeler.* 6 Jul. 1945.

Wheeler, Earle G. *Letter to Frances R. Wheeler.* 8 Jul. 1945.

Wheeler, Earle G. *Letter to Frances R. Wheeler.* 13 Jul. 1945.

Wheeler, Earle G. *Letter to Frances R. Wheeler.* 20 Jul. 1945.

Wheeler, Earle G. *Letter to Frances R. Wheeler.* 22 Jul. 1945.

Wheeler, Earle G. *Letter to Frances R. Wheeler.* 24 Jul. 1945.

Wheeler, Earle G. *Letter to Frances R. Wheeler.* 30 Jul. 1945.

Wheeler, Earle G. *Letter to Frances R. Wheeler.* 31 Jul. 1945.

Wheeler, Earle G. *Letter to Frances R. Wheeler.* 2 Aug. 1945.

Wheeler, Earle G. *Letter to George A. Carver, Jr.* 17 Jan. 1969.

Wheeler, Earle G. *Letter to Gilmore S. Wheeler.* 31 Jul. 1945.

Wheeler, Earle G. *Letter to Gilmore S. Wheeler.* 3 Jun. 1962.

Wheeler, Earle G. *Letter to Harold K. Johnson.* 6 May. 1967.

Wheeler, Earle G. *Letter to J. M. Hodgson,* 26 Sep. 1967.

Wheeler, Earle G. *Letter to Leonard D. Heaton,* 13 Sep. 1967.

Wheeler, Earle G. *Letter to Lyndon B. Johnson,* 5 Sep. 1967.

Wheeler, Earle G. *Letter to Monica Rosa Lara.* 19 Mar. 68.

Wheeler, Earle G. *Letter to S. M. Wang.* 18 Nov. 1967.

Wheeler, Earle G. *Letter to Walter R. Howell.* 9 Dec. 1951.

Wheeler, Earle G. *Letter to Walter R. Howell.* 1 Apr. 1952.

Wheeler, Earle G. *Letter to Walter R. Howell.* 20 Jul. 1954.

Wheeler, Earle G. *Letter to Walter R. Howell.* 29 Nov. 1963.

Wheeler, Earle G. *Letter to Walter R. Howell.* 20 Jul. 1964.

Wheeler, Earle G. *Letter to Yitzhak Rabin.* 4 Aug. 1970.

Wheeler, Frances R. *Letter to Rebecca Howell.* 4 Oct. 1941.

Wheeler, Frances R. *Letter to Rebecca Howell.* 7 Oct. 1941.

Wheeler, Frances R. *Letter to Rebecca Howell.* 13 Oct. 1941.

Wheeler, Frances R. *Letter to Rebecca Howell.* 21 Oct. 1941.

Wheeler, Frances R. *Letter to Rebecca Howell.* 31 Oct. 1941.

Wheeler, Frances R. *Letter to Rebecca Howell.* 12 Nov. 1941.

Wheeler, Frances R. *Letter to Rebecca Howell.* 1 Dec. 1941.

Wheeler, Frances R. *Letter to Rebecca Howell.* 16 Dec. 1941.

Wheeler, Frances R. *Letter to Rebecca Howell.* 22 Dec. 1941.

Wheeler, Frances R. *Letter to Rebecca Howell.* 26 Dec. 1941.

Wheeler, Frances R. *Letter to Rebecca Howell.* 8 Sep. 1942.

Wheeler, Frances R. *Letter to Rebecca Howell.* 12 Jan. 1943.

Wheeler, Frances R. *Letter to Rebecca Howell.* 15 Jan. 1943.

Wheeler, Frances R. *Letter to Rebecca Howell.* 7 May 1943.

Wheeler, Frances R. *Letter to Rebecca Howell.* Mid-Sep. 1943. (Exact date unspecified).

Wheeler, Frances R. *Letter to Rebecca Howell.* 31 Jul. 1950.

Wheeler, Frances R. *Letter to Rebecca Howell.* 11 Nov. 1951.

Wheeler, Frances R. *Letter to Rebecca Howell.* 22 Nov. 1951.

Wheeler, Frances R. *Letter to Rebecca Howell.* 27 Nov. 1951.

Wheeler, Frances R. *Letter to Rebecca Howell.* 29 Nov. 1951.

Wheeler, Frances R. *Letter to Rebecca Howell.* 4 Dec. 1951.

Wheeler, Frances R. *Letter to Rebecca Howell.* 6 Dec. 1951.

Wheeler, Frances R. *Letter to Rebecca Howell.* 20 Dec. 1951.

Wheeler, Frances R. *Letter to Rebecca Howell.* 27 Dec. 1951.

Wheeler, Frances R. *Letter to Rebecca Howell.* 14 Jan. 1952.

Wheeler, Frances R. *Letter to Rebecca Howell.* 17 Jan. 1952.

Wheeler, Frances R. *Letter to Rebecca Howell*. 22 Jan. 1952.

Wheeler, Frances R. *Letter to Rebecca Howell*. 14 Feb. 1952.

Wheeler, Frances R. *Letter to Rebecca Howell*. 18 Feb. 1952.

Wheeler, Frances R. *Letter to Rebecca Howell*. 21 Feb. 1952.

Wheeler, Frances R. *Letter to Rebecca Howell*. 13 Mar. 1952.

Wheeler, Frances R. *Letter to Rebecca Howell*. 24 Mar. 1952.

Wheeler, Frances R. *Letter to Rebecca Howell*. 1 Apr. 1952.

Wheeler, Frances R. *Letter to Rebecca Howell*. 9 Apr. 1952.

Wheeler, Frances R. *Letter to Rebecca Howell*. 5 Jun. 1952.

Wheeler, Frances R. *Letter to Rebecca Howell*. 1 Jul. 1952.

Wheeler, Frances R. *Letter to Rebecca Howell*. 6 Aug. 1952.

Wheeler, Frances R. *Letter to Rebecca Howell*. 11 Aug. 1952.

Wheeler, Frances R. *Letter to Rebecca Howell*. 17 Aug. 1952.

Wheeler, Frances R. *Letter to Rebecca Howell*. 3 Sep. 1952.

Wheeler, Frances R. *Letter to Rebecca Howell*. 11 Sep. 1952

Wheeler, Frances R. *Letter to Rebecca Howell*. 25 Sep. 1952.

Wheeler, Frances R. *Letter to Rebecca Howell*. 13 Oct. 1952.

Wheeler, Frances R. *Letter to Rebecca Howell*. 2 Aug. 1953.

Wheeler, Frances R. *Letter to Rebecca Howell*. 5 Aug. 1953.

Wheeler, Frances R. *Letter to Rebecca Howell*. 9 Aug. 1953.

Wheeler, Frances R. *Letter to Rebecca Howell*. 16 Aug. 1953.

Wheeler, Frances R. *Letter to Rebecca Howell*. 25 Aug. 1953.

Wheeler, Frances R. *Letter to Rebecca Howell*. 29 Aug. 1953.

Wheeler, Frances R. *Letter to Rebecca Howell*. 11 Sep. 1953.

Wheeler, Frances R. *Letter to Rebecca Howell*. 22 Sep. 1953.

Wheeler, Frances R. *Letter to Rebecca Howell*. 1 Oct. 1953.

Wheeler, Frances R. *Letter to Rebecca Howell*. 8 Oct. 1953.

Wheeler, Frances R. *Letter to Rebecca Howell*. 13 Oct. 1953.

Wheeler, Frances R. *Letter to Rebecca Howell*. 5 Jan. 1954.

Wheeler, Frances R. *Letter to Rebecca Howell*. 10 Jan. 1954.

Wheeler, Frances R. *Letter to Rebecca Howell*. 12 Jan. 1954.

Wheeler, Frances R. *Letter to Rebecca Howell*. 19 Jan. 1954.

Wheeler, Frances R. *Letter to Rebecca Howell*. 26 Jan. 1954.

Wheeler, Frances R. *Letter to Rebecca Howell.* 3 Jun. 1954.

Wheeler, Frances R. *Letter to Rebecca Howell.* 20 Jun. 1954.

Wheeler, Frances R. *Letter to Rebecca Howell.* 29 Jun. 1954.

Wheeler, Frances R. *Letter to Rebecca Howell.* 20 Jul. 1954.

Wheeler, Frances R. *Letter to Rebecca Howell.* Undated (probably late July) 1954.

Wheeler, Frances R. *Letter to Rebecca Howell.* 5 Aug. 1954.

Wheeler, Frances R. *Letter to Rebecca Howell.* 16 Aug. 1954.

Wheeler, Frances R. *Letter to Rebecca Howell.* 6 Sep. 1954.

Wheeler, Frances R. *Letter to Rebecca Howell.* 18 Sep. 1954.

Wheeler, Frances R. *Letter to Rebecca Howell.* 19 Sep. 1954.

Wheeler, Frances R. *Letter to Rebecca Howell.* 23 Sep. 1954.

Wheeler, Frances R. *Letter to Rebecca Howell.* 28 Oct. 1954.

Wheeler, Frances R. *Letter to Rebecca Howell.* 1 Nov. 1954.

Wheeler, Frances R. *Letter to Rebecca Howell.* 7 Nov. 1954.

Wheeler, Frances R. *Letter to Rebecca Howell.* 14 Nov. 1954.

Wheeler, Frances R. *Letter to Rebecca Howell.* 29 Nov. 1954.

Wheeler, Frances R. *Letter to Rebecca Howell.* 8 Dec. 1954.

Wheeler, Frances R. *Letter to Rebecca Howell.* 12 Dec. 1954.

Wheeler, Frances R. *Letter to Rebecca Howell.* 15 Dec. 1954.

Wheeler, Frances R. *Letter to Rebecca Howell.* 19 Dec. 1954.

Wheeler, Frances R. *Letter to Rebecca Howell.* 3 Nov. 1958.

Wheeler, Frances R. *Letter to Rebecca Howell.* 10 Nov. 1958.

Wheeler, Frances R. *Letter to Rebecca Howell.* 26 Dec. 1958.

Wheeler, Frances R. *Letter to Rebecca Howell.* 9 Nov. 1959.

Wheeler, Frances R. *Letter to Rebecca Howell.* 29 Dec. 1961.

Wheeler, Frances R. *Letter to Rebecca Howell.* 27 Feb. 1962.

Wheeler, Frances R. *Letter to Rebecca Howell.* 11 Mar. 1962.

Wheeler, Frances R. *Letter to Rebecca Howell.* 18 Mar. 1962.

Wheeler, Frances R. *Letter to Rebecca Howell.* 26 Mar. 1962.

Wheeler, Frances R. *Letter to Rebecca Howell.* 17 Sep. 1962.

Wheeler, Frances R. *Letter to Rebecca Howell.* 26 Sep. 1962.

Wheeler, Frances R. *Letter to Rebecca Howell.* 3 Oct. 1962.

Wheeler, Frances R. *Letter to Rebecca Howell.* 26 Nov. 1962.

Wheeler, Frances R. *Letter to Rebecca Howell.* 10 Mar. 1963.

Wheeler, Frances R. *Letter to Rebecca Howell.* 24 Mar. 1963.

Wheeler, Frances R. *Letter to Rebecca Howell.* 3 Apr. 1963.

Wheeler, Frances R. *Letter to Rebecca Howell.* 7 Apr. 1963.

Wheeler, Frances R. *Letter to Rebecca Howell.* 14 Apr. 1963.

Wheeler, Frances R. *Letter to Rebecca Howell.* 20 Apr. 1963.

Wheeler, Frances R. *Letter to Rebecca Howell.* 29 Apr. 1963.

Wheeler, Frances R. *Letter to Rebecca Howell.* 4 May 1963.

Wheeler, Frances R. *Letter to Rebecca Howell.* 26 May 1963.

Wheeler, Frances R. *Letter to Rebecca Howell.* 29 May 1963.

Wheeler, Frances R. *Letter to Rebecca Howell.* 8 Jun. 1963.

Wheeler, Frances R. *Letter to Rebecca Howell.* 10 Jun. 1963.

Wheeler, Frances R. *Letter to Rebecca Howell.* 26 Nov. 1963.

Wheeler, Frances R. *Letter to Rebecca Howell.* 14 Jan. 1964.

Wheeler, Frances R. *Letter to Rebecca Howell.* 16 Jan. 1964.

Wheeler, Frances R. *Letter to Rebecca Howell.* 17 Jan. 1964.

Wheeler, Frances R. *Letter to Rebecca Howell.* 9 Mar. 1964.

Wheeler, Frances R. *Letter to Rebecca Howell.* 27 Mar. 1964.

Wheeler, Frances R. *Letter to Rebecca Howell.* 30 Mar. 1964.

Wheeler, Frances R. *Letter to Rebecca Howell.* 18 Apr. 1964.

Wheeler, Frances R. *Letter to Rebecca Howell.* 15 May 1964.

Wheeler, Frances R. *Letter to Rebecca Howell.* 22 May 1964.

Wheeler, Frances R. *Letter to Rebecca Howell.* 27 May 1964.

Wheeler, Frances R. *Letter to Rebecca Howell.* 31 May 1964.

Wheeler, Frances R. *Letter to Rebecca Howell.* 9 Jun. 1964.

Wheeler, Frances R. *Letter to Rebecca Howell.* 22 Jun. 1964.

Wheeler, Frances R. *Letter to Rebecca Howell.* 25 Jun. 1964.

Wheeler, Frances R. *Letter to Rebecca Howell.* 2-3 Jul. 1964.

Wheeler, Frances R. *Letter to Rebecca Howell.* 9 Jul. 1964.

Wheeler, Frances R. *Letter to Rebecca Howell.* 20 Jul. 1964.

Wheeler, Frances R. *Letter to Rebecca Howell.* 28 Jul. 1964.

Wheeler, Frances R. *Letter to Rebecca Howell.* 1 Aug. 1964.

Wheeler, Frances R. *Letter to Rebecca Howell.* 4 Aug. 1964.

Wheeler, Frances R. *Letter to Rebecca Howell.* 15 Oct. 1964.

Wheeler, Frances R. *Letter to Rebecca Howell.* 1 Feb. 1965.

Wheeler, Frances R. *Letter to Rebecca Howell.* 9 Feb. 1965.

Wheeler, Frances R. *Letter to Rebecca Howell.* 13 Feb. 1965.

Wheeler, Frances R. *Letter to Rebecca Howell.* 1 Mar. 1965.

Wheeler, Frances R. *Letter to Rebecca Howell.* 19 Mar. 1965.

Wheeler, Frances R. *Letter to Rebecca Howell.* 6 Apr. 1965.

Wheeler, Frances R. *Letter to Rebecca Howell.* 26 Apr. 1965.

Wheeler, Frances R. *Letter to Rebecca Howell.* 28 Apr. 1965.

Wheeler, Frances R. *Letter to Rebecca Howell.* 2 May 1965.

Wheeler, Frances R. *Letter to Rebecca Howell.* 19 May 1965.

Wheeler, Frances R. *Letter to Rebecca Howell.* 21 May 1965.

Wheeler, Frances R. *Letter to Rebecca Howell.* 25 May 1965.

Wheeler, Frances R. *Letter to Rebecca Howell.* 15 Jun. 1965.

Wheeler, Frances R. *Letter to Rebecca Howell.* 28 Jun. 1965.

Wheeler, Frances R. *Letter to Rebecca Howell.* 14 Jul. 1965.

Wheeler, Frances R. *Letter to Rebecca Howell.* 9 Aug. 1965.

Wheeler, Frances R. *Letter to Rebecca Howell.* 17 Aug. 1965.

Wheeler, Frances R. *Letter to Rebecca Howell.* 8 Nov. 1965.

Wheeler, Frances R. *Letter to Rebecca Howell.* 15 Nov. 1965.

Wheeler, Frances R. *Letter to Rebecca Howell.* 23 Nov. 1965.

Wheeler, Frances R. *Letter to Rebecca Howell.* 3 Dec. 1965.

Wheeler, Frances R. *Letter to Rebecca Howell.* 12 Dec. 1965.

Wheeler, Frances R. *Letter to Rebecca Howell.* 24 Dec. 1965.

Wheeler, Frances R. *Letter to Rebecca Howell.* 31 Dec. 1965.

Wheeler, Frances R. *Letter to Rebecca Howell.* 13 Jan. 1966.

Wheeler, Frances R. *Letter to Rebecca Howell.* 28 Jan. 1966.

Wheeler, Frances R. *Letter to Rebecca Howell.* 7 Feb. 1966.

Wheeler, Frances R. *Letter to Rebecca Howell.* 13 Feb. 1966.

Wheeler, Frances R. *Letter to Rebecca Howell.* 13 Mar. 1966.

Wheeler, Frances R. *Letter to Rebecca Howell.* 18 Mar. 1966.

Wheeler, Frances R. *Letter to Rebecca Howell.* 27 Apr. 1966.

Wheeler, Frances R. *Letter to Rebecca Howell.* 30 Apr. 1966.

Wheeler, Frances R. *Letter to Rebecca Howell*. 3 May 1966.

Wheeler, Frances R. *Letter to Rebecca Howell*. 9 May 1966.

Wheeler, Frances R. *Letter to Rebecca Howell*. 13 May 1966.

Wheeler, Frances R. *Letter to Rebecca Howell*. 19 Jun. 1966.

Wheeler, Frances R. *Letter to Rebecca Howell*. 30 Jun. 1966.

Wheeler, Frances R. *Letter to Rebecca Howell*. 7 Jul. 1966.

Wheeler, Frances R. *Letter to Rebecca Howell*. 11 Jul. 1966.

Wheeler, Frances R. *Letter to Rebecca Howell*. 21 Jul. 1966.

Wheeler, Frances R. *Letter to Rebecca Howell*. 25 Jul. 1966.

Wheeler, Frances R. *Letter to Rebecca Howell*. 30 Jul. 1966.

Wheeler, Frances R. *Letter to Rebecca Howell*. 8 Aug. 1966.

Wheeler, Frances R. *Letter to Rebecca Howell*. 15 Aug. 1966.

Wheeler, Frances R. *Letter to Rebecca Howell*. 29 Aug. 1966.

Wheeler, Frances R. *Letter to Rebecca Howell*. 6 Sep. 1966.

Wheeler, Frances R. *Letter to Rebecca Howell*. 9 Sep. 1966.

Wheeler, Frances R. *Letter to Rebecca Howell*. 20 Sep. 1966.

Wheeler, Frances R. *Letter to Rebecca Howell*. 27 Sep. 1966.

Wheeler, Frances R. *Letter to Rebecca Howell*. 9 Oct. 1966.

Wheeler, Frances R. *Letter to Rebecca Howell*. 19 Oct. 1966.

Wheeler, Frances R. *Letter to Rebecca Howell*. 29 Nov. 1966.

Wheeler, Frances R. *Letter to Rebecca Howell*. 3 Dec. 1966.

Wheeler, Frances R. *Letter to Rebecca Howell*. 12 Dec. 1966.

Wheeler, Frances R. *Letter to Rebecca Howell*. 17 Dec. 1966.

Wheeler, Frances R. *Letter to Rebecca Howell*. 26 Dec. 1966.

Wheeler, Frances R. *Letter to Rebecca Howell*. 27 Dec. 1966.

Wheeler, Frances R. *Letter to Rebecca Howell*. 3 Jan. 1967.

Wheeler, Frances R. *Letter to Rebecca Howell*. 13 Jan. 1967.

Wheeler, Frances R. *Letter to Rebecca Howell*. 24 Jan. 1967.

Wheeler, Frances R. *Letter to Rebecca Howell*. 6 Mar. 1967.

Wheeler, Frances R. *Letter to Rebecca Howell*. 10 Mar. 1967.

Wheeler, Frances R. *Letter to Rebecca Howell*. 15 Mar. 1967

Wheeler, Frances R. *Letter to Rebecca Howell*. 18 Mar. 1967.

Wheeler, Frances R. *Letter to Rebecca Howell*. 28 Mar. 1967.

Wheeler, Frances R. *Letter to Rebecca Howell*. 6 Apr. 1967.

Wheeler, Frances R. *Letter to Rebecca Howell*. 8 Apr. 1967.

Wheeler, Frances R. *Letter to Rebecca Howell*. 25 Apr. 1967.

Wheeler, Frances R. *Letter to Rebecca Howell*. 11 May 1967.

Wheeler, Frances R. *Letter to Rebecca Howell*. 24 May 1967.

Wheeler, Frances R. *Letter to Rebecca Howell*. 31 May 1967.

Wheeler, Frances R. *Letter to Rebecca Howell*. 7 Jun. 1967.

Wheeler, Frances R. *Letter to Rebecca Howell*. 12 Jun. 1967.

Wheeler, Frances R. *Letter to Rebecca Howell*. 16 Jun. 1967.

Wheeler, Frances R. *Letter to Rebecca Howell*. 23 Jun. 1967.

Wheeler, Frances R. *Letter to Rebecca Howell*. 1 Jul. 1967.

Wheeler, Frances R. *Letter to Rebecca Howell*. 2 Oct. 1967.

Wheeler, Frances R. *Letter to Rebecca Howell*. 20 Oct. 1967.

Wheeler, Frances R. *Letter to Rebecca Howell*. 17 Nov. 1967.

Wheeler, Frances R. *Letter to Rebecca Howell*. 19 Nov. 1967.

Wheeler, Frances R. *Letter to Rebecca Howell*. 23 Nov. 1967.

Wheeler, Frances R. *Letter to Rebecca Howell*. 9 Dec. 1967.

Wheeler, Frances R. *Letter to Rebecca Howell*. 20 Mar. 1968.

Wheeler, Frances R. *Letter to Rebecca Howell*. 27 Mar. 1968.

Wheeler, Frances R. *Letter to Rebecca Howell*. 5 May 1968.

Wheeler, Frances R. *Letter to Rebecca Howell*. 12 May 1968.

Wheeler, Frances R. *Letter to Rebecca Howell*. 24 Jun. 1968.

Wheeler, Frances R. *Letter to Rebecca Howell*. 30 Mar. 1969.

Wheeler, Frances R. *Letter to Rebecca Howell*. 2 May. 1970.

Wheeler, Frances R. *Letter to Rebecca Howell*. 29 May. 1970.

Wheeler, Frances R. *Letter to Rebecca Howell*. Date unspecified (early Jun. 1970).

Wheeler, Frances R. *Letter to Rebecca Howell*. 14 Mar. 1971.

Wheeler, Gilmore S. *Email to Mark Viney*. 5 May. 2013. Author's Records.

Wheeler, Gilmore S. *Email to Mark Viney*. 1 Nov. 2013. Author's Records.

Wheeler, Gilmore S. *Email to Mark Viney*. 9 Jun. 2013. Author's Records.

Wheeler, Gilmore. *Email to Mark Viney*. 10 Jul. 2017. Author's Records.

Wheeler, Gilmore S. *Email to Mark Viney*. 3 Jul. 2014. Author's Records.

Wheeler, Gilmore S. *Email to Mark Viney*. 30 Dec. 2013. Author's Records.

Wheeler, Gilmore S. *Email to Mark Viney*. 31 Jan. 2014. Author's Records.

Wheeler, Gilmore S. *Email to Mark Viney*. 29 Jan. 2014. Author's Records.

Wheeler, Gilmore S. *Email to Mark Viney*. 29 Jul. 2013. Author's Records.

Wheeler, Gilmore S. *Email to Mark Viney*. 29 Mar. 2014. Author's Records.

Wheeler, Gilmore S. *Email to Mark Viney*. 21 Nov. 2013. Author's Records.

Wheeler, Gilmore S. *Email to Mark Viney*. 26 Apr. 2014. Author's Records.

Wheeler, Gilmore S. *Email to Mark Viney*. 23 Sep. 2015. Author's Records.

Wheeler, Gilmore S. *Email to Mark Viney*. 22 Mar. 2013. Author's Records.

Wheeler, Gilmore S. *Email to Mark Viney*. 2 Feb. 2018. Author's Records.

Wheeler, Gilmore S. *Letter to Rebecca Howell*. 17 Aug. 1954.

Wheeler, Gilmore S. *Letter to Rebecca Howell*. 12 Sep. 1954.

Wilson, Louis H. *Letter to Betty Wheeler*. 24 Dec. 1975.

### Unpublished Works

Ailes, Stephen. *Eulogy for General Earle Wheeler*. 22 Dec. 1975. Wheeler Family Records.

Viney, Mark A. *Determined to Persist*. Monograph. 29 Nov. 2012. Author's Records.

Wheeler, Earle G. *Professional Resume*. 1971. Wheeler Family Records.

Wheeler, Gilmore S. *Doneld Howell*. Monograph. 25 Apr. 2014. Wheeler Family Records.

Wheeler, Gilmore S. *George Deuhring*. Monograph. 25 Apr. 2014. Wheeler Family Records.

Wheeler, Gilmore S. *Linda Howell and Tony Lattore*. Monograph. 25 Apr. 2014. Wheeler Family Records.

Wheeler, Gilmore S. *Untitled Monograph*. 1 Oct. 2010. Wheeler Family Records.

# INDEX